The
Old Outboard
Book

Greetings of the Season To You 1919 is going to be a great year for the "Out-o'-doors". The "Boys" coming back from "Over there" and Camp like "over here" are going to be strong for going, hike, woods and water trails. Here's hoping you get your share, and then some, of this new business.

Yours
Dixie Carroll

The Old *Outboard* Book

Third Edition

Peter Hunn

International Marine /
McGraw-Hill
Camden, Maine • New York • Chicago •
San Francisco • Lisbon • London •
Madrid • Mexico City • Milan • New
Delhi • San Juan • Seoul • Singapore •
Sydney • Toronto

International Marine

A Division of *The* **McGraw·Hill** *Companies*

10 9 8 7 6 5 4 3

Library of Congress has cataloged the revised edition as follows:
Hunn, Peter
    The old outboard book / Peter Hunn.—Rev. and expanded.
      p.   cm.
    Includes index.
    ISBN 0-07-031281-8
    1. Outboard motors—Collectors and collecting. 2. Outboard motors—Conservation and restoration. I. Title.
VM771.H86   1994
623.8´7234´075–dc20   94-18675
                                                 CIP

Third edition ISBN 0-07-138309-3

Questions regarding the content of this book should be addressed to
International Marine
P.O. Box 220
Camden, ME 04843
www.internationalmarine.com

Questions regarding the ordering of this book should be addressed to
The McGraw-Hill Companies
Customer Service Department
P.O. Box 547
Blacklick, OH 43004
Retail customers: 1-800-262-4729
Bookstores: 1-800-722-4726

This book is printed on 60# Finch Opaque by Quebecor World
Design by Edith Allard
Production management by Janet Robbins
Edited by J.R. Babb, Heidi V.N. Brugger, Tom McCarthy

Contents

Dedication

Acknowledgments

For Carol, who tells people I write books about "outdoor" motors.

The Labor Day trip home to Connecticut from our family's Adirondack summer cottage was always bittersweet. But on one of those early September Mondays, my first copy of the *The Antique Outboarder* was there waiting amidst back-to-school sale flyers in a month-old pile of mail. With a flip of its cover, the magazine motored me past dozens of vintage engines I'd never before seen, and shared outboard industry histories that I could've never otherwise learned. Over the ensuing decades, scores of subsequent *The Antique Outboarder* issues have added to my repertoire. And wherever the publication left off on a particular topic, fellow members of the club that distributes it have kindly filled in the gaps. This is to say, I gratefully acknowledge that the ground covered by the editions of *The Old Outboard Book* has been plowed by hundreds of other buffs who've sent their discoveries to the aforementioned chronicle, and/or elaborated on the interesting information in a letter to me. So, for the record, I am simply a reporter, editor of correspondence, and teller of small boating/outboard motor tales.

While admittedly not nearly comprehensive enough, the following roster represents some of the Antique Outboard Motor Club membership who've either directly or indirectly helped me in preparing this work: Peter Allen, Rod Champkin, Art DeKalb, Dick Fuchs, Steve Green, Bob Grubb, Henry Johansson, Dick Hawie, Paul Huetter, Alan Jarvis, Tom Luce, Gary Mower, Doug Penn, Dave Reinhartsen, Bob Skinner, J. L. Smith, Riggs Smith, Ron Tackaberry, Bob Toffey, Sam Vance, Jim Webb, Angelo Vassena, Colin Wilson, Ole With, and Bob Zipps. A few have since passed from this life, with their motor collections now under the care of others. This leads me to acknowledge that I've long been drawn to fellowshipping with old outboard buffs because, whether by design or inadvertently, they model what God offers to do for those of us in need of restoration. In many cases, these folks have expended considerable effort finding, adopting, fixing, revitalizing, and then happily giving a home to some decades-old motor that other people had dismissed as junk. When these reborn engines are displayed or happily put into service on a rowboat, the old outboarding hobby is well positioned to make new friends and thus increase the enjoyment of buffs who love sharing their interest with others. I am most thankful for those who've influenced me in such a way.

The summer of 1958 saw my family's Rambler station wagon bouncing along the lengthy dirt driveway of an Adirondack resort. Near the end of that dusty thoroughfare, a woman motioned us to stop and apologized to all arrivals that the camp chef had just run off with Wanda, the waitress.

Rather than get a refund and point the Rambler back to New Jersey, or go broke eating in restaurants for a fortnight, my folks looked up some old friends who, coincidentally, had a vacation home a few miles away.

After dinner, our hosts treated us to a boat ride, and I got to sit right in front of the craft's bright blue, 35-horse Evinrude outboard. The big motor's throaty purr so impressed my five-year-old mind that it triggered an obsession with engines present, past, and future.

Since then, I've had the opportunity to amass lots of outboard literature and more than 100 vintage motors. This book is about some of those rigs and many other makes, one of which may be yours. It is written in a nontechnical style for anyone who has ever had an interest in outboard motors. Its pages should help you identify the year and history of your favorite motor, help you discover what kind of spark plugs and oil mixture it wants, and provide you with a look at dozens of classic outboards from the 1890s through the 1950s, both the recognizable and the unusual.

But be warned: Because old outboarding is relatively inexpensive and quite contagious, this book could lead you to enjoy "vintage iron" more than others feel is necessary. Even my immediate family can't help wondering what I could have written about if Wanda hadn't run off with the cook.

Preface to the **Third Edition**

In addition to a main ingredient of vintage American outboard coverage, the recipe for this third edition includes a large portion of old motor information from Australia and the United Kingdom. At least five dozen "newly discovered" U.S.-based outboard brands (from the 1910s to 1980) have been added to this volume, too. Both upgrades should make the third edition of *The Old Outboard Book* more international in scope and more useful to buffs everywhere.

Ironically, I revised the book on a kitchen tabletop computer. There, on several occasions, my wife sent word to pop something into the oven. Perhaps you could say I then had to quit writing about outboards in order to start cooking . . . quite unlike the Adirondack camp chef who indirectly turned me into an old motor nut.

Introduction

Sue Miller's husband, Jack, had retired recently, and his strange behavior had her worried. Jack's new conduct either kept him in the cellar or combing through back rooms of seedy outbuildings. And, he kept dragging home all kinds of weird items. . . . Sue just didn't understand. It all began when the couple was enjoying a leisurely drive to the grocery store. Suddenly, Jack hit the brakes, and, leaving the car door wide open, ran for a foul-smelling greasy thing leaning against a pine tree.

"I don't believe my eyes," Jack beamed. "This is a 1928 Elto Speedster outboard motor! When I was a kid, the guy next door had one. It was the hottest rig on the lake!"

Seconds later, the surprised yard-sale cashier folded away a pair of 10-dollar bills and watched as the joyful husband and his skeptical spouse loaded the vintage outboard into their car.

"What in the world are you going to do with that old thing?" Sue asked when they arrived at the grocery store. "You already have a nice new fishing motor the kids gave you."

"I'm gonna fix it up," Jack retorted happily while pushing the shopping cart a bit faster than normal.

"And revitalize that old Elto, he did," Sue later recounted to her friends. "Trouble is, then Jack found another obsolete outboard to fix up . . . and another . . . and another!"

The Girls cautiously looked down the basement stairs and consoled Sue. "What does he do with all of those?" they wondered aloud.

"Well, he works on them during the week and then putt-putts around the lake all weekend. Now other old motor people are calling here asking for Jack . . . wanting to buy or sell, or to stop over to see his outboard collection. And Jack, he's always happy—especially when his trunk is full of junk. However, I never expected retirement to be quite like this."

Dave Wyler was years from retirement and regretted not having enough free time to spend with his youngster. He was searching for some hobby or common interest around which father and son could relate. The solution came rather unexpectedly at a local sporting goods shop, where he and his boy had gone to see about picking up an economical aluminum rowboat and a little fishing gear. Without adequate funds for a current model motor, Dave asked about used outboards.

"Take a look on the racks in back," the proprietor said.

"We'll have to find something affordable," cautioned Dave as he and his son went to have a look-see. Near the end of the top row, Dave's son noticed a small red kicker with its starter cord dangling toward a pile of related parts. Nuts and screws in a grimy plastic bag were secured to the rubber steering handle via sticky electrical tape.

"Dad, how much do you think that one would be?"

"Don't know, but it looks really shot, son."

"Well, maybe we could fix it up together this winter."

"Yes, maybe we could do just that!"

"The old Sea King horse and a half?" queried the shop owner. "Kinda hate to see it go . . . been around so long. Oh, let's see. . . . How about five bucks? I'll even throw in the original parts booklet!"

Throughout the next six months, the Wylers took their little Sea King down to the last bolt, cleaned it up, and reassembled it. A new paint job highlighted the duo's endeavor. Everyone involved agreed that the motor looked and ran great. All for $5 plus a few parts.

Unlike retiree-turned-antique-outboard-collector Jack Miller, Dave Wyler and his boy never amassed a cellarful of vintage egg beaters, but they did receive a lot of pleasure running their Sea King. Every once in a while, however, they do talk about getting another, forgotten old outboard—maybe a bigger one—and enjoying another father-son collaboration.

Wally Jenkins never projected any historical value onto his 1956 Buccaneer outboard. As a commercial fisherman, he relied on the 25-horse twin as a partner; it was not an "antique motor" to him. When fellow saltwater anglers suggested he should upgrade, however, prices of the new kickers sent Walt into sticker shock. Soon, a deeper level of appreciation bonded him to his colorful "25." He became interested in locating replacement parts, and even curious about the Buccaneer's lineage. Spruced-up, the engine delighted Wally by prompting positive comments from peer and vacationer alike. Pride in ownership paced Mr. Jenkins' fishing rig a step ahead of more ordinarily powered outboard craft.

Throughout the years, millions of outboard motors have been manufactured in the United States. Although many no longer exist, scores of them reside everywhere from formal collections to rickety backyard sheds. It is difficult to imagine any area without a good share of still undiscovered motors. Contrasting with the numbers of available old iron, are the relatively few people wanting them. As a result, vintage outboard prices have not aproached (and probably never will match) those of classic cars or other antiques.

Anyone liking old outboard motors, especially if interested in garden variety (Evinrude, Johnson, Merc, Sears-Elgin, etc.) fishing rigs, is assured an adequate supply of inexpensive engines and parts. Sometimes they may have to search a little, but that's typically part of the fun.

Best of all, an old kicker collection, be it 2 or 200, can be put to use. Few folks have ever turned down a rowboat ride powered by some ancient putt-putt. The conversations, interest, and local newspaper articles these rigs generate are legendary.

Those using "space limitations" as an excuse not to enter antique outboarding have never seen a 1940, 9-pound, ½-hp Evinrude. One New York City motor buff stores his four-member Mercury collection in a hall closet. Lack of funds seldom stop old outboard nuts either. While some very rare racing models or pre-

World War I rigs bring big ($500-plus) bucks, Antique Outboard Motor Club swap meets, boat shops, and garage sales often feature common kickers with price tags between $5 and $50. By the way, unusual is the collector who hasn't been the beneficiary of at least one *free* motor, and sometimes 10!

Vintage outboard motors are simply the hot dogs and hamburgers of our technological world. People from all walks of life enjoy them. And just like a good summer cookout, there are many ways to savor such machines. While it's perfectly acceptable to cruise your favorite waterway with a vintage outboard, some folks use theirs to water-ski, troll, or race in sanctioned as well as informal events.

Whether you plan to take just a few hours per year working on a kicker alone, involve your family in the collecting and/or restoring of an old outboard, or join an Antique Outboard Motor Club chapter and really get involved, you will be surprised at how much satisfaction and discovery is waiting within that little motor. It's true; others will see just a bunch of dented aluminum, but you will recognize that old outboard as the key to a real adventure.

Keep your starter rope dry and enjoy *The Old Outboard Book*!

The Old Outboard Book

1
Outboard Motor Pioneers

Sometime in 1960, the Johnson Outboard Company ran a small advertisement picturing a pistol-toting, bikini-clad woman in bare feet and cowboy hat. A surrealistic "marshal's star" frivolously pinned to the top of her swimsuit centered attention on the fact that Johnson was seriously looking for old outboard motors. That ad, promoting "The Great Sea Horse Trackdown," has been an old outboard collector's nightmare ever since.

Although Johnson was indeed searching for some of its vintage products, many of the engines sought were extremely rare. Should one possess such a rig, one was supposed to cart the motor to the nearest Johnson Sea Horse dealer for model and serial number verification. A 25-or-fewer-word statement why Johnsons were the most dependable brand also had to be composed. Only then could the owner be registered for a chance to win a new Johnson outboard.

That exclusive contest quickly took its place in portable marine propulsion history as the "Free Outboard" story and spread through the country faster than a rumor of a bathroom tissue shortage.

Of course, that contest is long gone, and today many might consider those 1960 prize motors to be antiques. Nevertheless a few folks remain completely convinced that they can trade their "old," salt-scored, early-seventies fishin' engine for a new boat-motor-trailer-tackle-box combo if they simply "write the factory" to come pick up their classic outboard.

While these incidents prove aggravating for old outboard enthusiasts trying reasonably to pry a rusty kicker from some guy's damp basement, they do serve to raise a question pertinent to the beginning of this book: Specifically, just how old is an old outboard motor?

Many custom laws define *antique* as 100 years old or older. Since outboards were first invented a little over a century ago, few are truly antique, in that sense of the word. However, all the outboards in this book qualify as "objects of a period earlier than the present," and in this sense are antiques. Some kicker collectors make a distinction between *antique* and *old*, drawing the line at 1950, after which post-World War II technology rapidly

made itself evident in the outboard industry. No collector questions the antique status of the very first outboards.

The 1887 Harthan

In 1887 S. Emerson Harthan of Worcester, Massachusetts received a patent for "his self-contained steam motor (with 4-bladed propeller) that could be completely detached from the stern" of a small boat.[1]

Reportedly, though the plans looked interesting, the inventor eventually decided his steam outboard would fall into a category no more glorious than that of "confounded contraption" and elected to leave it on the drawing board. While this book focuses primarily on gasoline-powered outboards produced in the United States, Mr. Harthan's patent is mentioned because it "prevent[ed] anyone else from getting full protection" for any subsequent outboard motor.[2]

The 1896 American

The earliest documentation of an American gasoline-powered outboard motor describes a small 1896 line of detachable rowboat engines from the American Motor Company of Long Island City, New York.

A late-nineteenth-century book, *Gas, Gasoline and Oil Vapor Engines for Stationary, Marine, and Vehicle Motive Power*,[3] devoted four pages to the novel 4-cycle, air-cooled engines. The single-cylinder model featured a 3¼-inch bore, a 4-inch stroke, battery ignition, and 1 to 2 hp at 400 to 600 rpm.

Also mentioned was a twin-cylinder version of the American. This may have been a pair of single-cylinder power plants mated to a common flywheel and drive shaft. The twin boasted exactly twice the smaller unit's power. On both models a remote fuel tank was standard. A simple carburetor was attached to the gas tank, and fuel vapor reached the crankcase via a flexible tube. Although primitive, the 1896 American outboard's basic layout would not be unrecognizable to present-day boaters.

Folks in antique outboard circles often quote 25 as a production figure for the American outboard motor. I am not certain where such a number originated and really wonder if any at all were ever produced. Respected outboard historian W.J. "Jim" Webb, once a top executive with the Evinrude Company, tried to track down additional information on the American. He discovered that the firm's building had passed into the hands of a movie company. No traces of the motors, or anyone with firsthand knowledge of the early outboard venture, have ever been located.

It is possible the American Motor Company's outboards (if produced) were not labeled American. In the same fashion that no General Motors car is called a General, the American outboard may have sported some other model name. To add to the mystery, a Detroit company produced an early (1913 to 1918) detachable rowboat motor. It, too, was known as the American.

The 1898 Miller

The name Harry Armenius Miller is inseparably linked to the glory days of the American race car scene. His cars, his unique carburetors, and, most notably, his 91-cubic-inch engines claimed many prestigious victories. In addition to automotive speed records, the Miller 91- and 151-cubic-inch power plants, when mounted in a speedboat, "were nearly invincible on water."[4]

A Wisconsin native with a keen interest in machinery, Harry Miller traveled west, where he worked in a Los Angeles bicycle shop. A few years later he married and quickly took his wife to his hometown of Menomonie.

Shortly after his 1897 return to the Midwest, Harry built a special bicycle equipped with a single-cylinder motor. Some say this was America's first motorcycle. In any event no patents were ever requested.

Harry Miller usually stayed interested in a project only until a new one could be dreamed up.[5] He mentioned to a few close friends that his ideas came from someone (in another world) telling him what to do.[6]

In the summer of 1898 the spirit moved him and "he worked out a peculiar 4-cylinder [outboard] engine, clamped it to a rowboat, and showed his cronies how to enjoy their afternoons off."[7] Although the motor apparently did what it was designed to do, Miller lost interest in the outboard and sought no patents. It is not known what became of the pioneer rig.

Miller's wife longed to return west, so shortly after the outboard incident, they headed to California. The Golden State became home to other Miller projects including the manufacture of carbs, race engines, and cars, as well as what may have been the first aluminum pistons in the United States.[8]

While it's evident that Harry Miller's circa 1898 outboard never went into any kind of mass production, the possibility that the previously mentioned 1896 American may not have, in fact, gotten off the drawing board, places Miller's as the first U.S. gasoline-powered outboard with a written record of actual

operation. Interestingly, one eyewitness to the Miller outboard excursion could have been another young Wisconsin native who worked with Harry in the Menomonie shop. That fellow's name was Ole Evinrude.[9]

In the early 1930s a California company produced a very strange looking four-cylinder outboard motor. The firm belonged to Harry Miller.

The 1898 Savage

Nineteenth-century rowboats, no doubt, started Rochester, New York, resident Edward Savage thinking about a power source more swanky than oars. The inventor put together an aft-pointing, single-cylinder, 2-cycle outboard sporting an enclosed lower-unit gear case, a sight oiler, and variable-pitch prop. (This contraption's power head looked a bit like the 1896 American.) The rudder-steered Savage outboard made its debut on Lake Ontario in 1898. Although one neat-looking prototype was built, Ed Savage's other interests (in the toy design field) kept the motor from further production.

The 1900 Imperial

A family-owned Minneapolis machine shop advertised its detachable boat engine in 1900. This early outboard, called the Imperial, weighed 75 pounds and produced 2 hp. Its creators, Fred and Robert Valentine, claimed the water-cooled, rudder-steered outboard could be hooked to any boat within 15 minutes and provide speeds of 6 to 8 mph.[10]

As is the case with many long-expired firms, no one is certain what happened to the Valentine brothers' company. None of its vintage outboards has been discovered. In fact, had an Antique Outboard Motor Club member in 1982 not seen an old ad in a dusty city directory, the Imperial wouldn't have received its rightful place in this book.

The 1906 Submerged

Some six years after the introduction of its 1900 electric outboard, the Submerged Electric Motor Company added a "new portable gasoline submerged propeller" to the small-boat propulsion line. The one-cylinder engine on the Submerged appeared to be, indeed, under water (like the 1930s Clarke Troller), while its cylindrical fuel tank made up the unit's top. The tube joining top and bottom sections rode on an adjustable collar so the Submerged could be "raised and lowered to run in shallow water."

Although few competitors made up the day's outboard field, the Menomonie, Wisconsin, firm claimed the Submerged (being the "lightest, most practical, most powerful, and easiest applied") was the genre's front-runner. The early outboard company also promised its gas-powered rowboat motor was "sure to go." Unfortunately, the whole outfit went the way of the wind a few years later.

Waterman's "Coughing Sarahs"

A 1903 autumn evening in New Haven, Connecticut, set the stage for Yale law student Cameron B. Waterman to consider servicing his Regal motorcycle. The little power plant on that two-wheeler

"Vertical cylinder" Waterman outboard, 1908–9. After the motor starts, you have to quickly pull the starting crank from its fitting on top of the crankshaft, then gingerly adjust the carb, making sure water is exiting the cylinder water jacket pipe and that lubrication from the glass-sight oiler is dripping properly. Note the exposed lower unit gears (which require waterproof grease!) and the cylindrical fuel tank, which is mounted on a wooden steering handle. Ignition is via battery, spark coil, and timer. The Waterman was America's first commercially successful outboard motor, in the days when a "good" kicker was one that ran at least half the times you tried it! (Mercury Marine)

Late-teens Waterman clip art.

Waterman Porto
The Original Outboard Motor

made in Chicopee, Massachusetts, needed cleaning, and since the motor looked light, young Waterman carried the one-cylinder device up to his room.

After the revitalization, Waterman scanned the room for a place to brace the engine during a test run. Minutes later the Regal motor was sputtering away clamped to the back of a wooden chair. The future lawyer, an avid fisherman who judged rowing to be an activity that "stinks,"[11] suddenly pictured the rear of that chair as the stern of a small boat. The idea floated along with him through graduation.

Upon returning to his native Detroit, Waterman briefed his friend George Thrall (owner of the Taylor Boiler Company) on the outboard concept. The pair secured a Curtiss motorcycle engine, fastened it to the stern of a rowboat, and via a drive chain, rigged the motor to turn a propeller.

That experiment in the winter of 1905 was a limited success. The crude detachable rowboat motor was started a few times by way of a crank fitted into a stub on top of the engine's shaft, a protrusion that soon wore away. Consequently, the pioneer rig had to be enlivened by twirling its prop. More trial runs were enjoyed and everything worked OK until pieces of ice in the frigid Detroit River knocked the drive chain off the outboard's propeller sprocket.[12]

Waterman and Thrall discarded the chain in favor of an open drive shaft and bevel gears. They engaged the services of production engineer Oliver Barthel to help revise Waterman's "Coughing Sarah," which is what amused onlookers called it.[13] Once plans were on paper, a two-stroke, water-cooled Waterman outboard was built in the Detroit-based Caille Brothers Company tool room.[14] (Later this firm would enter the outboard field with its own unique designs.) This vintage kicker featured a horizontal external flywheel that teased its operator. A 1950 newspaper article quoting Waterman tells why:

> We began commercial production in 1905. Here's a catalog showing the motor. You see we had a drive shaft instead of a chain. However, we had this flywheel hung so low that every time the boat dipped, it hit water and gave us a shower bath. The next year we put the flywheel back inside the casing.[15]

By the way, the catalog mentioned in that article was one of a few thousand descriptive circulars that Waterman distributed at the 1906 New York Boat Show. Response from the modest promotion told Waterman his outboards would sell. In early 1906 Barthel's revised plans were taken back to the Caille factory where 25 air-cooled singles with enclosed flywheels were built.[16] Twenty-four were soon sold, with Waterman keeping the last one (from the Caille run) for himself.[17]

On an unseasonably warm September 1, 1906, he put his wife in a rowboat, hung the kicker on the stern, hopped in, and began a spin around the lake. After a while, though, the motor overheated

and conked out. The couple finally arrived home only after pouring water on the baking cylinder, causing steam to rise high in the humid air. This experience moved Waterman back to liquid cooling.

In the fall of 1906, he and engineer Barthel instituted a new water-cooled design for spring 1907 production. Simultaneously ads for the new motor appeared in a wide range of popular magazines such as *Rudder, Colliers, Scientific American, Popular Mechanics,* and *Outdoor Life.* Sportsmen bought up 3,000 of the vertical-cylinder, water-cooled rigs (with Lunkenheimer mixing valve) that year—a sales figure duplicated the following year (1908 motors wore a Schebler carb) and doubled in 1909.[18] The founder attributed this jump to Evinrude's 1909 entry into the outboard business. He speculated that folks seeing two (or more) aggressive players in the fledgling outboard field were more convinced of the device's usefulness.

Waterman was the first to use the words *outboard motor* in advertising. The phrase was coined by his friend, R. McDougal Campau, who had accompanied Waterman and Thrall on their "maiden" voyages in 1905. Trademark officials ruled, however, that the term was "too descriptive" to be held exclusively by one firm. As a result, Evinrude and anyone else in the business could call their product an outboard motor. And, of course, that is exactly what happened.

Incidentally, the Waterman Company also marketed an inboard marine motor based on its outboard powerhead. Similarly equipped generating plants (bearing the Waterman label) were offered to folks wanting electricity for light-duty rural applications.

As a young motor nut with very little grasp on accurate chronology, I sent a postcard to outboard pioneer Cameron Waterman. The note simply asked if he had any old owner's manuals that could be sent my way. Unfortunately Mr. Waterman had passed away years before that postcard arrived. His son and namesake, however, graciously answered with a manila envelope containing interesting articles and recollections. As a part of the parcel, Mr. Waterman Jr. wanted his young correspondent to know that in the early days there was no convenient flywheel magneto for spark:

> We used a battery ignition [on the first Waterman motors]. We would carry a black wooden box on the boat's rear seat. This box contained four dry cells and a spark coil.

The June 1969 letter revealed an example of informal research, which caused production changes back at the Waterman factory. Cameron Waterman Jr. noted his dad's outboards had a spark plug mounted close to the operator on the end of a tantalizing cylinder assembly. "I well remember hitting the spark plug with my hand and being rewarded for my clumsiness by a sharp poke!" Complaints to his father resulted in "later models having a rubber (spark plug) cover."

A couple of easygoing fishing buddies let their pre-1910 Waterman outboard take them to their favorite angling spot. Note that the battery to fire the sparkplug is on the stern seat. This early kicker publicity still was shot from a boat in tow. ("Ah, that's when a smoke was a smoke and cruisin' was cruisin'!") It now appears that far fewer than 3,000 1908 Waterman outboards were produced. A new interpretation of production figures suggests that accounts of "3,000 motors sold and double that the following year" refers to all Waterman engines produced that year. This includes Waterman inboards that were likely more plentiful than the outboard motors. (Mercury Marine)

By 1912 the Waterman outboards, long since dubbed Porto (as in *portable*) by the manufacturer, featured rudder steering and horizontal cylinders. The 1914 deluxe Porto outboards sported magneto instead of battery ignition.

Three years later intense competition caused the man who pioneered the outboard motor to sell his Waterman Marine Motor Company for $20,000 to the Arrow Motor and Machine Company of Newark, New Jersey. This firm, which marketed a twin-cylinder outboard of its own, floundered with the Waterman line and left the business altogether in 1924.

Cameron Waterman devoted the rest of his life to the legal profession. A few years before his 1955 passing, the grandfather of the American outboarding industry was forwarded a letter dotted with foreign postage stamps. A man in Panama wanted a new cylinder for a Waterman Porto.[19]

Notes

1. Wm. Taylor McKeown, "The Old Kicker and How it Got Slicker," *True* (April 1964), p. 110.
2. Harry LeDuc, "Detroiter Honored in NY as Inventor of First Outboard Motor," *Detroit News* (28 January 1950).
3. Gardner D. Hiscox, M.E., *Gas, Gasoline and Oil Vapor Engines for Stationary, Marine, and Vehicle Motive Power* (New York: Norman W. Henley Company, 1897), pp. 203–206.
4. Griffith Borgeson, *The Golden Age of the American Racing Car* (New York: W.W. Norton & Co., 1966), p. 202.
5. Ibid., p. 69.
6. Ibid., p. 65.
7. Ibid., p. 64.
8. Ibid., p. 65.
9. Ibid., p. 64.
10. Robert Brautigam, "Outboard World Rocked by New Discovery," *Antique Outboarder* (January 1983), pp. 44–45.
11. Red Smith, "Views of Sport: The Outboard Heresy," *New York Herald Tribune* (11 January 1950).
12. LeDuc, op. cit.
13. Ibid.
14. Hunn, Peter, "Letter from Cameron Waterman," *Antique Outboard* (January 1991), p. 66.
15. Smith, op. cit.
16. Robert Whittier, *The Outboard Motor and Boat Book* (Concord, MA: Voyager Press, 1949).
17. Smith, op. cit.
18. Ibid.
19. LeDuc, op. cit.

2

Evinrude

A young Milwaukee woman really wanted some ice cream. Coming from a hard-working, proper-minded single girl, such a craving had nothing to do with maternity, but it did serve as the mother of invention to a brand new outboard motor.

The lady fair, Bess Carey, and her lack of dessert during a warm August island picnic, caused suitor Ole Evinrude to hop in their rented rowboat and man the oars. A few miles later the love-motivated fellow finally reached a lakeside ice cream shop and, panting, placed the order. Upon his return, that ice cream (which most versions of the tale place in a cone, while a few others put it in a dish) had become sun-scorched, sugary soup.

Ole might have briefly thought, "Oh, *women!*" That, however, would make for lousy legend. So, according to the famous Evinrude soggy ice cream saga, Ole simply began thinking about ways to build a detachable rowboat motor.

Over the years details have been added to the incident's recounting. One source went to the extreme of identifying the ice cream as "double-dip caramel pecan fudge with chocolate sauce."[1] If the accounts of Harry Miller's 1898 outboard (Chapter 1) are accurate, Ole Evinrude (who was said to have seen Miller's motor in action) may have skipped all of the story's "perhaps I could invent the outboard motor" theme and deduced "why not rig up a portable gasoline boat motor like Harry's weird contraption?" In any event, following the picnic, Mr. Evinrude started piecing together a crude outboard motor.

Ole's confidence in tackling the project was rooted in his past successes with machinery repair, design, and construction. Ole grew up on a Wisconsin farm. Although his formal schooling was through only the third grade, he possessed a natural aptitude that earned him a reputation as a mechanical genius. At 16, Ole left the bucolic life in favor of larger communities containing machine shops and factories.

After mastering a number of the trade's finer points (at firms in Pennsylvania, Illinois, and Wisconsin), he settled in Milwaukee and marketed a single-cylinder auto engine of his own design. While the car motor was fine, Ole's infrequent attention to office details caused the venture's demise. Because of his fine

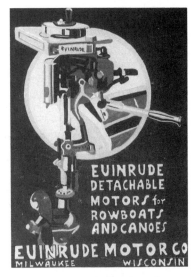

An undated Evinrude flyer sheet, this does not appear to be rendered in "factory authorized" style. It might have been painted by a dealer for local promotional use, or was a briefly distributed piece of official Evinrude literature.

Bess Evinrude, co-founder of two successful outboard motor companies (Evinrude and Elto), handled all the office responsibilities; husband Ole took care of product design and manufacturing. Bess often signed official correspondence "B. Evinrude" to keep those making materials bids from knowing they'd be dealing with a woman. She was always fair but never a pushover. Ole's motors were well received, but he cited his wife's expertise in business as the reason for the family's prosperity. (Outboard Marine Corp.)

Ole Evinrude put on his "corporate" suit for this 1920s publicity shot. He needed no extra promotion at the Milwaukee-based Elto plant; there wasn't an employee in the shop who didn't truly admire the soft-spoken outboard pioneer. (Outboard Marine Corp.)

mechanical record (especially as a pattern maker), the young man had little trouble gaining employment at someone else's shop.

Ole and Bess were married, and the new husband worked on a surprise in the basement. You can imagine a conversation something like this one:

> "Honey, come on down the cellar," said Ole to his bride. "Let me show you what I've done."
> "What's that unusual thing?" Bess asked. "It looks like a coffee grinder!" Alas, Bess was a practical woman and saw no purpose for such a gizmo.

Mr. Evinrude would undoubtedly have been distressed by his wife's lack of enthusiasm. Determined, Ole enlisted Bess's brother, Rob Carey, to help prove a point.

In April 1909 the pair toted Evinrude's kooky-looking kicker to the Kinnikinnic River and attached the contraption to a rented rowboat. Ole and Rob returned to Bess with reports of success.

Bess may have suggested that the little motor be improved, because a new prototype was concocted in 1909. This one (which was eventually retired to the Evinrude factory service department until getting accidentally discarded after World War II) ran better than the first.

Ole loaned the 2-cycle, water-cooled, forward-pointing, single-cylinder kicker to a friend embarking on a fishing trip. The angler came back wanting his own Evinrude motor and had orders for nine more. Soon patterns for the improved Evinrude went to the foundry, resulting in parts for 25 motors. Each was built by hand.

An old issue of *Fortune* magazine picks up the story:

[Evinrude] never visualized any business possibilities in the outboard beyond occasional sales to Milwaukee sportsmen, and it was Bess who kept after him to perfect the "coffee grinder" as she called it, and who sat down at her kitchen table one evening and wrote their first advertisement. DON'T ROW! THROW THOSE OARS AWAY! USE AN EVINRUDE MOTOR! This went into a motor magazine and pulled so many inquiries that there could be no doubt that a market for outboards existed.[2]

To grow in the burgeoning marketplace, Ole and Bess accepted $5,000 for a half interest in their Milwaukee-based Evinrude Detachable Rowboat Motor Company. Chris Meyer (owner of a tugboat firm) was the guy with the five grand; his money was used to rent a modest factory, acquire needed parts, and hire a small staff to help Ole build outboards. Bess (by then the mother of a toddler) worked overtime running the office and kept handing her busy husband orders for even more motors.

This was in 1911. Within a couple of years, not only were numerous battery-fired, flywheel-knob-started, Evinrude singles churning up American waterways, but many were exported. A few thousand were purchased by Scandinavian fishing fleets for more versatile net access. Every time the mailman arrived, it became clearer that boaters the world over were literally beating a paper path to the Evinrudes' door.

All this activity, while exciting, affected Bess's health and strained Ole's business relationship with Chris Meyer. Mr. Evinrude suggested he'd sell his half of the firm for $150,000. Meyer quickly arranged delivery of such a check. And, upon Ole's pledge to stay out of the outboard business for at least five years, the deal was closed (in late 1913), pushing the Evinrudes from the field they had helped pioneer.

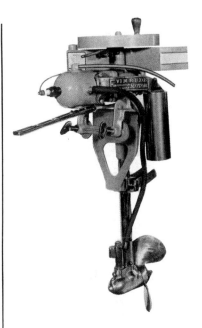

The famed Evinrude rowboat motor, circa 1912, with wooden "knuckle buster" starting knob on the flywheel. Note the rubber water tube. Earlier models had no name embossed into the exhaust assembly. Ole's first (1909) version, which someone at Evinrude accidentally threw away, reminded his wife of a coffee grinder. The lower unit on older rowboat motors had no skeg; the steering arm moved only the lower unit assembly, not the powerhead. (Outboard Marine Corp.)

Daylight illuminates the "motor assembly room" at Milwaukee's Evinrude factory. Once the rowboat motors were complete, each one was tested in the tank visible to the left of the facility's open door. A wooden mat prevented employees from slipping on a floor wet down by churning propellers. (Outboard Marine Corp.)

Make Any Rowboat A Motor Boat

The Evinrude Detachable Rowboat Motor does away with oars. Takes about two minutes to clamp it to the stern of any kind of a rowboat without alterations to the boat As quickly and easily detached. Powerful, reversible, two-cycle engine. Speed GUARANTEED 7 miles an hour. Simple weighs but 50 lbs.

EVINRUDE DETACHABLE ROW BOAT MOTOR

is compact, clean, smooth-running and weedless. Absolutely reliable and lasting. Used by the United States Government for Coast Survey, Light House Service and other work after passing a rigid test. Awarded special prize for ENDURANCE and RELIABILITY at Stockholm, Sweden Motor Boat Races, 1911. Also used extensively by the Scandinavian, Alaskan, Japanese and Australian Fisheries, as well as by prominent sportsmen. Write for Catalog. Shown, recommended, sold and money refunded if not satisfactory by—

The Fair Store, Chicago, Ill. Gimbel Bros., Milwaukee,Wis. New York Salesroom, 260 W.B'dway, New York, N.Y.,Dept.E

EVINRUDE MOTOR COMPANY
279 Walker Street, Milwaukee, Wisconsin

A 1912 Evinrude advertisement.

Ole and Bess departed on an extended vacation shortly prior to the establishment of a new outboard factory capable of turning out rowboat motors with much greater ease than before.

In 1912 Ole had started a guy called "Jump Spark" Miller (no relation to Harry Miller) working on what would become the flywheel magneto. The Evinrude company began outfitting its motors with flywheel mags for 1914. It also sold its invention to other outboard firms. A couple of these magneto-fired rigs went to Teddy Roosevelt. The former U.S. President reported great success with the Evinrudes, which were used on an expedition on uncharted South American rivers. TR did suggest that the motors would be more useful in primitive areas if they could be run on universally available kerosene.[3]

The Chris Meyer–controlled Evinrude company continued to enjoy the lion's share of the outboard market. It even sold boats, including a *sailing* dinghy!

Inadvertently, a real clunker was introduced for the 1916 model line. Someone in the firm felt a nearly 100-pound, 4-horse opposed twin employing the 4-cycle principle would prove irresistible to buyers. This darn thing had a flywheel mag and "distributor" to fire the two cylinders alternately. Even though it was 4-cycle, you still had to mix oil with the gas.

While the ads said, "Starting is easy and the motor picks up quickly and runs with a smooth hum," the PR department could have sold more of these nearly impossible-to-operate monstrosities by re-decaling them with EVINRUDE BOAT ANCHOR. The 4-cycle Big Twin was quickly discontinued in 1917, and the leading outboard maker returned to the promotion of its better running 2-cycle singles. All went well for the Evinrude company . . . for a while.

The real Evinrude family had been spending time touring the country by car and cabin cruiser. As Bess got healthier, Ole took more time toying with a new idea in portable boat motoring. New Orleans served as the Evinrudes' winter 1917 base.

"Ole spent most of his time locked up in a hotel room fooling around with plans for a new [lightweight] motor."[4] By 1919 the drawings led to a 47-pound opposed twin made mostly of World War I–proved aluminum. This revolutionary rig was presented to Chris Meyer at the outboard firm bearing the Evinrude name. Meyer was very skeptical and quickly shot down Ole's project motor.

Meyer's attitude seems to have been, Who'd ever want some wimpy lightweight thing like that when people can buy a hefty, iron and bronze, remarkably sturdy Evinrude Detachable Rowboat Motor?

Meyer's rejection turned out to be a tremendous blunder. The mistake soon caused his firm to lose a big share of the outboard pie to a newcomer. In 1921 this well-managed company began marketing Bess and Ole Evinrude's new Light Twin Outboards—Eltos. And, because the Elto was easier to carry, ran smoother, and started quicker than any other outboard to date, it sold like hotcakes.

An Elto Ruddertwin, circa 1924, being inspected by a trio of company models. Ole Evinrude had a hard time naming his aluminum kicker (he liked the description ''silvery''), so wife Bess came up with the acronym Elto, from Evinrude's Light Twin Outboard. Note the water scoop in the rudder of this battery-ignition product. Exhaust exited through the propeller hub. A clothesline tied to the rudder control assembly allowed for steering from any position in the boat. (Outboard Marine Corp.)

Meanwhile, back at the original Evinrude outfit, Chris Meyer got a great idea—*for people who want lighter outboards, design an aluminum one!*

The result was the Evinrude model K Lightweight. This poor thing, simply an aluminum version of the old rowboat motor, was rushed into production shortly after Meyer witnessed the less-cumbersome Eltos being snapped up by boaters, fishermen, and hunters.

Forged with castings appropriate only for bronze and iron, the aluminum model K was indeed lighter than its predecessors. Unfortunately, however, this reduction was often due to the fact many of the silver kicker's pieces cracked and fell off the motor.

Ads said the rig had been in the planning stages for seven years. Outboard historian Jim Webb observed that it was more like seven weeks or less. The 1922 Evinrude model K Lightweight was such a disaster that note of its existence is absent from most Evinrude specification booklets.

Meyer knew only too well that every Elto nameplate carried the message DESIGNED AND BUILT BY OLE EVINRUDE. Consequently, his products' decals began boasting THE ORIGINAL EVINRUDE. In 1924 this "original" firm introduced a nice 2½-hp Sportwin. It was a much better aluminum model than the K and helped the old company perk up a little.

In any event, Meyer had had enough and in 1925 decided to sell Evinrude to a fellow named Walter Zinn. Within a year of the purchase, this gentleman had lost $150,000. He quickly chalked up outboard making to experience and let the Evinrude company go (in early 1926) to August Petrie.

Owner of the Milwaukee Stamping Company, Petrie knew he'd have to put some money into the Evinrude firm in order to get it back on track. Koban, a longtime producer of twin-cylinder outboards, was acquired and closed by the new Evinrude management. With one less competitor (albeit a weak one), Mr. Petrie began revitalizing Evinrude.

Fuel tank ID plate for a 1929 High Speed (note ''H'' after serial number) Elto Speedster.

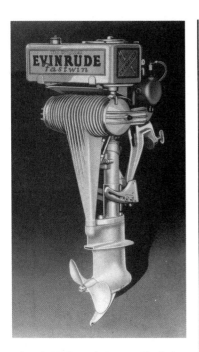

A late-1920s Evinrude Fastwin. The fuel tank decal says "The *Original* Evinrude," to distinguish it from Elto's "Designed and Built by Ole Evinrude" slogan. Mr. Evinrude had sold his "original" outboard company in 1914, but had reacquired it by 1930.

The venerable kicker firm's repair coincided nicely with an exciting increase of outboard speed. From 1926 to 1928 outboard motoring's clip improved from a putt-putt troll to a wave-jumping roar. The new president of Evinrude opened his 1928 catalog this way:

> The last few years have been especially important ones in the development of the Evinrude Motor. In a remarkably short span of years, speeds have increased unbelievably. This season [1928] will see unprecedented interest in speed contests. While this is going on, we shall be ever mindful of the majority of users of Evinrudes who do not engage in racing, giving them to the best of our ability, motors capable of maximum racing performance, yes, but giving besides, the utmost in instant starting, sturdiness, dependability, reliability, long life, up-to-date design—champions in every way. Our organization is dedicated to faithfully serve the users of our products, and these are built with the purpose of making them paramount in their field ever before us.

> Yours very truly,
> Aug. J. Petrie
> President, Evinrude Motor Co.

Certainly, by 1928 Petrie had placed Evinrude on surer footing. Although Ole's old rowboat motor (the 2¼-hp Utility Single) was still offered near the back of the catalog (some 150,000 of the A model rowboat motors were sold between 1909 and 1928), company advertising really featured the 2½-horse Sportwin, 6-hp Fleetwin, the 12-horse Fastwin, and Evinrude's main attention getter, the 16-hp Speeditwin.

This big motor, which had been introduced during 1927 (as an 8-hp rig) in freshwater and saltwater (with a bronze lower unit) versions, caught most other companies off guard and enjoyed a model year free of high-speed competitors. In 1928 the Speeditwin was joined by a few fast outboards from other firms (like the Elto Speedster and Quad). To most late-1920s boaters, however, it still represented a pretty flashy kicker. Evinrude was again riding high, and Mr. Petrie believed it was an opportune time to sell.

The eager Evinrude buyer was the Briggs and Stratton Corporation. This engine manufacturing outfit (known to almost anyone who's owned a power lawn mower) pumped nearly $400,000 of improvements into Evinrude, cutting sharply into profits. Some Briggs and Stratton officials wanted to retreat from the outboard business and prepared to put Evinrude on the block again.

Briggs and Stratton president Stephen Briggs had other ideas, including the establishment of a multi-companied, General Motors–type outboard firm. With Evinrude already in the fray, Briggs planned to acquire the respected Lockwood Outboard Motor Company. He then arranged a meeting with Ole and Bess Evinrude over at Elto.

Not all early outboard racers were male. In fact, some of the most daring and talented were women, as this 1928 shot shows. Their Speeditwin is equipped with a very limited production tractor lower unit that drives the propeller on front of the gearcase. (Antique Boat Museum)

Outboarding's first family said, no, they didn't want to sell Elto, which was in the second year of a great sales wave crested by very fast, easy-to-run, twin-cylinder Speedster and 4-Jug Quad motors. Briggs modified his approach, asking if, by chance, Ole had any interest in regaining the commercial right to use the Evinrude name. That query led to a deal which included Elto, Evinrude, and Lockwood. Ole got to be president of the merged companies (in March 1929), which were collectively dubbed the Outboard Motors Corporation (OMC).

Evinrude's Milwaukee plant was the best equipped, resulting in plans calling for all three of OMC's 1930 lines to be built there. Elto had been working on electric starting and was now in a position to share the outboard breakthrough with its new sister brands' deluxe 1930 models. All in all, OMC's divisions were ready for a remarkably bright immediate future. The immediate future, however, was anything but bright.

When my dad was a kid, there was a fellow across the street named Mr. Banker. This guy had done very well in the stock market, burned his mortgage, and paid cash for a 16-cylinder Cadillac touring car. The rest of the money went right back into Wall Street. He had great plans for the bundle sure to follow in late 1929–early 1930. Within a few months Mr. Banker was considered fortunate because, even though his stocks were now

Odd-lot motors were peddled here in the early 1930s to earn money for the company payroll. (Antique Boat Museum)

A 1934 Evinrude Lightfour Imperial, featuring engine cowling and rewind starter, helps a proud angler catch a really big one! (Outboard Marine Corp.)

worthless, he still had a home. With no funds for new tires or even gasoline, the big Caddy rested on blocks in the grassy driveway, and Mr. Banker drove a dairy truck to make ends meet.

Just like Mr. Banker, OMC was seriously affected by the Great Depression. Sales fell off instantly, outboard workers were sent home, and the quality Lockwood line was dropped after 1930. Ole Evinrude had his name and $25,000 salary taken off the payroll. Motors made from extra parts (as well as some new/old-stock models, i.e., unsold parts stock used to build new motors) were literally peddled in front of the factory in order to raise enough money to cover drastically reduced employee wages. It was not uncommon in the early Thirties for the OMC plant to operate less than 20 hours per week.

Banks wouldn't loan anything to OMC (which now consisted of Evinrude, Elto, and commonly branded models labeled Outboard Motors Corporation), so Ole kicked in $50,000 from his personal account. Things were very tight through early spring 1933, but Ole and Steve Brigg's company responded with every possible penny-pinching sacrifice.

The firm received another hardship with Bess Evinrude's May 1933 passing. Ole seemed lost without her, but his spirit revived a touch when planning a new concept in outboard design for the 1934 model year.

Having started in 1909, the Evinrude company in 1934 had been in business for 25 years. By this time, all the corporate scrimping began paying off and allowed for the introduction of a pair of Ole's newly designed outboards. These Imperial versions of the 5½-horse Lightwin and 9.2-hp Lightfour were the first truly shrouded outboards. When the optional rewind starter was ordered, the customer really had a modern-looking rig, unlike anything else on the water. In terms of the Depression, the Imperials sold well, and Ole was credited with another fine outboarding idea.

All the acclaim, however, could not make up for his loss of Bess. In this year, 1934, Ole died quietly in his Milwaukee home at age 57, outboard's most respected and best-loved personality.

Ole and Bess's son, Ralph Evinrude, grew up in the midst of outboard history and development. With positive attributes from both parents, young Evinrude began helping out around the factory while still in school. Ralph wasn't offered an automatic royal-family salary but was given the chance to learn the outboard business by working hard in a number of Elto (and then Evinrude/OMC) departments. During the late 1920s, it was Ralph who convinced his folks to build faster outboards. He pushed ahead in the development and testing of the Elto Speedster and Quad (released in late fall 1927), earning still greater responsibility at Elto.

When his dad died, Ralph was asked to serve as Outboard Motor Corporation's president. As it turned out, Ole and Bess would have been quite proud of their son, always leading (until his 1986 passing) the outboard firm in the right direction.

One of Ralph's first official duties was to introduce the 1935 OMC-Evinrude/Elto line. It included a 25-pound, predominantly die-cast, shrouded kicker called the Sportsman. This streamlined, 1½-hp motor was the first outboard sold with a reed valve fuel-vapor intake. Many a modern outboard motor subsequent to the Sportsman has used this valve design.

The mid-1930s were relatively prosperous for OMC. In fact, there was even enough extra money to consider the purchase of Johnson, a formidable (albeit faltering) competitor. Although motors wearing Evinrude or Elto decals had been available since the 1930 formation of OMC, most were primarily identified as Outboard Motors Corporation products. The 1935 catalog cover, for example, simply said, "1935 Series Outboard Motors." The OMC logo rested under the words "ELTO" and "Evinrude."

By 1936 Outboard Motors Corporation changed its name to the Outboard Marine and Manufacturing Company, after acquiring the Johnson Outboard firm. This new organization began concentrating on Evinrude and Johnson, leaving Elto to ride out the late Thirties and early Forties as the economy line. Evinrude advertising in 1937 featured Evinrude without much mention of Elto. Gas tank decals, model number plates, and (in most cases) rope sheaves finally dropped the OMC identification and returned to an Evinrude Motors ID. (Although the name changed, the company was and is still referred to as OMC, for Outboard Marine Company. OMMC never caught on.)

In 1938 each Evinrude, from the little 1.1-horse Ranger single to the 33.4-hp Speedifour, had underwater exhaust silencing, hooded powerheads, centrifugal water pump cooling, and copilot steering.

For 1939, Evinrude offered a tiny, ½-hp putt-putt called the Mate. This eggbeater began its retail life at $34.50 (later discounted to $29.95) and weighed about 10 pounds with a full tank of gas! The Mate's powerhead block was cast, from carb to cylinder, in one piece. Most of its sales were likely made to folks who thought the peanut kicker was irresistibly cute. Novel it was, but such is not the province of a very utilitarian product (on

Ralph Evinrude inherited his business and mechanical abilities from his parents. He hounded his folks to make fast outboards, which resulted in the legendary Elto Speedster and Quad motors. In this 1954 photograph, Ralph demonstrates an electric-starting Big Twin 25 that bears his family's name. (Outboard Marine Corp.)

The 1940, ½-hp Evinrude Mate weighed 10 pounds with a full tank of gas. (Antique Boat Museum)

About 1940, an Evinrude employee inspects a shipping crate ready for a 5.4-hp, 4-cylinder Zephyr. By the 1950s motors were shipped in cardboard boxes. (Outboard Marine Corp.)

which Evinrude built its strong reputation). When a Mate did start (the minuscule ignition coils and cylinder-piston assemblies were prone to quick wear), a brisk headwind would prove a conquering competitor. Even so, the Mate and her bigger sisters at Evinrude, Johnson, and Elto accounted for 60 percent of America's outboard output.

The long-lived Evinrude Speeditwin (first offered in 1927) was reintroduced in 1939 as the 22.5-hp model 6039. Thousands of these 30-cubic-inch-displacement, opposed-cylinder outboards were sold through 1950. Although usurped by an alternate-firing, 25-horse engine in 1951, a few company press releases included a shot of the Speeditwin. The implication that the old fashioned kicker was still current helped (from 1951 to 1953) move the stock of leftovers.

Another long-produced Evinrude making its (1940) pre–World War II debut was the 5.4-hp Zephyr. This approximately 10-cubic-inch kicker's claim to fame was its quad opposed-cylinder construction. Never meant to be more than a deluxe fishing motor, the Zephyr's four cylinders gave it a smooth-running quality but provided many prospective owners with the mistaken belief that with its two extra jugs it could easily outrace less-endowed 5-horse motors. Most outboard collectors would agree with the alliterative hyperbole that zillions of Zephyrs were turned out (some with silver-colored gas tanks, later ones with blue tanks or decals; a few had weedless lower units) through the late forties.

A typical Evinrude lineup of the prewar era—say, 1941— included the Zephyr, the half-horse Mate, the 1.1-hp Ranger, the 2-horse Sportsman, the Sportwin (a 3.3-hp rig), the 9.7-hp Lightfour,

the Sportfour (a 17.4-hp model), the old favorite 22.5-hp Speeditwin, and the big 33.4-horse Speedifour.

By summer 1941 it was inevitable the United States would enter World War II. Many materials crucial to outboard motor production had already been siphoned off to help Britain fight the Axis powers. A 1942 Evinrude model year was announced in late '41, but not many of these motors were turned out prior to America's December declaration of war. In February 1942 U.S. government officials ordered a freeze on the production of all nonessential civilian items in favor of military goods. Consequently, regular outboard manufacturing ceased.

Actually, Evinrude continued to make motors. It did so for the armed services via Zephyrs and Lightfours (often used to power emergency rubber rafts), as well as Speeditwins and Speedifours for larger craft. The most famous World War II kickers were Evinrude's 50-hp Storm Boat motors. These 60-cubic-inch hulks, designed from the old Elto 4-60 Quad, pushed thousands of troop assault boats to numerous strategic beachheads.

The war finally ended during the summer of 1945. So the next civilian Evinrude model year (after the abbreviated 1942 line) was officially the 1946 offering. Most of these were simply prewar-designed motors wearing postwar serial numbers. Such models as the Ranger, the Zephyr, the Speeditwin, and the Speedifour were in the catalog again. The only relatively new engine in the cache was the now army surplus (188-pound) Storm Boat motor, dubbed Big Four. Many of these 50-horse outboards, along with some Speedifours and Speeditwins, still had the unusual military-style lower unit featuring a tri-element skeg. In addition to the regular skeg fin under the gear case, these rigs had two other skeg "wings" on either side of the gear case. On some of the huge Evinrudes the two-side skeg pieces were cut off. Outlines on the gear case ofttimes served as evidence of the odd skeg's former presence. (A few 1980s heavy-duty commercial Evinrudes had this same arrangement.)

From late 1945 through 1947 there was such a release of pent-up demand for outboards that company officials could have made a profit selling electric mixers treated with Evinrude stickers. While Evinrude engineers were, no doubt, planning new models, motors sold through 1947 were still prewar single-cylinder and opposed multi-cylinder designs. With two exceptions, much of this "old style" line was retained for 1948. Unveiled that year were a 1.5-horse Sportsman single and 3.3-hp alternate-firing Sportwin, each with a silver shaded die-cast gas tank and classic blue Evinrude lettering. They set the stage for the firm's famous Fifties styling.

Evinrude showrooms of 1949 again included the Big Four, as Outboard Marine tried to use up its stock of the powerful, albeit outdated, bulky motors.

For 1950 a pair of alternate-firing, die-cast, blue and silver twins joined the fray. A 7½-horse Fleetwin had no reverse gear,

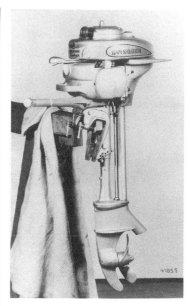

Evinrude's 1940 Zephyr 5.4-hp quad. (Antique Boat Museum)

Most of Evinrude's 1950 lineup. The 22.5-hp opposed cylinder Speeditwin, which would be replaced in late 1950, was absent from this ad. It was not a fishing motor.

but could be swung 180 degrees. Neutral was accomplished via a black plastic Duo-Clutch knob that was pulled up (from the top side of the gas tank) when disengaging was desired. This model had its share of shift problems but was well accepted, outselling most other Evinrudes by 1953.

A 14-hp Fastwin also made its 1950 debut. Although displacing some 20 cubic inches, the Fastwin really wasn't all that fast. The 10-horse Mercurys of the day could severely embarrass a Fastwin owner. Actually, the Fastwin's claim to fame is its being the first Evinrude equipped with a remote Cruise-A-Day fuel tank and full F-N-R gearshift.

Fastwin's poor speed record may have caused some concern at Evinrude, but officials were far too busy with a special project to worry about the 14-hp model. The assignment would serve as next year's big outboarding attraction.

Topping the "polychromatic blue" Evinrude marque for 1951 was a revolutionary 35.7-cubic-inch, 25-hp, alternate-firing Big Twin. Not only was this rig some 20 pounds lighter than the old opposed-cylinder, 22.5-horse Speeditwin it replaced, but it was also fitted with a complete (and relatively trouble-free) F-N-R gearshift. The new Big Twin could get a family-size runabout on speaking terms with 30 mph and would sit still for a bit of trolling, too. Unlike its large Evinrude predecessors, the Big Twin had an easy-to-operate twist-grip Roto-Matic synchronized spark/throttle speed control on the steering handle. A 6-gallon, pressurized, remote Cruise-A-Day fuel tank was standard, allowing the powerhead a sleeker look. This motor was clearly the star of the early-fifties Evinrude line.

A well-designed, alternate-firing Lightwin 3-hp was unveiled in late 1951 and quickly became the fisherman's standard. This 32-pound classic wore well-placed carrying handles and made perfect use of Evinrude's famous Weedless-Drive (developed in the

A stylish Feathercraft aluminum boat being pushed by a 1951 Evinrude Big Twin 25.

Thirties by Finn Irgens) and propeller. In an updated version this little kicker was still available in the 1980s.

When I was a kid, my neighbor loaned me a bumped-up '52 Lightwin (they seem to run better with a fist-size dent in the tank) for my 12-foot Sears plywood rowboat. That craft loved the little Evinrude, and they seemed perfectly matched to each other. Believing myself to be a junior underwater outboard propulsion researcher, I would jump out of the boat and cling to the side while tugging on the Lightwin's starter cord. She always came to life with about a quarter pull, allowing me to advance the mag/carb lever halfway and be gently pulled (via an old piece of water-ski rope) 25 feet behind the happy pair. Wouldn't the Coast Guard Auxiliary people have loved to witness that wonderful feat?

During 1952, materials needed for the Korean Conflict limited some outboard production, and the '51 motors, minus the 1½-horse Sportsman and 3.3-hp Sportwin leftovers (which were semi-officially part of the 1951 catalog), got carried over another year. The shortages left a few Evinrude dealers without enough products to satisfy every potential buyer.

In announcing their 1953 outboard roster, "Evinrude officials agreed that controls on metals [due to the war] would not be lifted in time to allow the supply to catch up with demand."[5] So the Lightwin, 7½-hp Fleetwin, and Big Twin were continued with little change.

Remember the slow, 14-hp Fastwin introduced in 1950? Evinrude finally received a chance to put the pokey thing to rest through the unveiling of the 1953 Super Fastwin. This redesigned, approximately 20-cubic-inch motor gained an extra horsepower (now 15) and truly had enough zing to pull junior water-skiers and keep up with other outboards in its class. Evinrude engineers chose the Super Fastwin to wear some of their recently developed noise-reduction technology, a water-sealed exhaust and a twin-chambered, acoustically tuned silencer aimed at the "complete elimination of high frequency sound factors." The quieter motor was also equipped with an Auto-Lift hood allowing the operator to un-fasten two clasps and easily raise the port side of the cover. Removal of a pair of screws made it possible to take off the entire hood.

The editor's Evinrude Fisherman 5.5 heads up the Tennessee River in the mid 1950s. (Babb photo)

Both the new Super Fastwin 15 and larger brother Big Twin 25 were finally factory-fitted with shift and speed levers that could (without modification) quickly accept remote (Simplex) controls and steering cables. For 1954 the well-selling 7½-hp Fleetwin (with its shear-pinless Safti-Grip propeller clutch) got a going over and was reintroduced as Super Fastwin's little brother. The new Fleetwin benefited from such modifications as a remote Cruise-A-Day Junior fuel tank and a full F-N-R gearshift. Universal connection points (such as those on Super Fastwin and Big Twin) allowed the easy addition of remote control operation.

Factory-installed electric starting became available for the 25. Powerhead isolation via springs and rubber mounts further quieted the 1954 Evinrude line (except the 3-hp), allowing the motors to be dubbed Aquasonic.

Evinrude catalogs of 1955 quietly noted one rather obscure newcomer called Ducktwin. Simply a Lightwin painted olive drab (and sporting a duck decal), this 3-horse product was aimed at the duck hunter market. It retained a tiny mention in Evinrude sales literature for years. The 1955 15-hp Super Fastwin was still a good motor, but its "Super" designation was dropped.

The pleasantly blue-colored Evinrude line expanded in 1956 with the addition of a 5½-horse Fisherman twin and a 10-horse Sportwin. The top-of-the-line motors went to 30 hp. Joining the Big Twin 30, a more deluxe Lark 30 (with electric starter and designer paint and trim) made its debut.

Things progressed quickly for 1957, with the old 30 moving up to 35 hp and the Fastwin going from 15 to 18 horses (with optional electric start).

All of these models were topped in 1958 with a 50-hp V-4 rig called the Four-Fifty, in plain trim, and Starflite, in deluxe form, with an optional 10-amp, heavy-duty generator. Evinrude's early V-4 engines were huge things nicknamed "Fat-Fifty." Although officially the first U.S.-production V-configured (with cylinders pointing aft) outboard, this model is better known for its heavy fuel consumption. At even half to three-quarters throttle, a Starflite could quickly drink dry a 6-gallon gas tank.

In 1958, some deluxe 35s, called Evinrude Larks, were treated with a boxy powerhead hood. Horsepower designation numerals attached to these grayish-colored covers looked like street address numbers from someone's front porch.

Evinrude celebrated its golden anniversary in 1959 with an attractively styled line ranging from 3 to 50 hp. These power brackets were identical to the previous year's. In honor of its fiftieth summer season, however, Evinrude fitted the 1959 line with blue fiberglass hoods accented in white and golden lettering. (Note: The little 3-horse motor retained an aluminum cowling.)

The "Fat-Fifty" was finally upgraded to a 75-hp model in 1960. Things went well for this big Evinrude until its conventional, two-lever shift/speed control was replaced in 1961 with an electro-magnetic gear changer. Initial difficulties with the Selectric push-

button shifter left a few Starflite 75 owners echoing "French" (as in *pardon my*) across North American waterways.

Conversely, folks who swore by the value of mid-size family motors quickly sung the praises of a beefed-up 35 that was promoted to 40 horses by 1960. The Evinrude 40, in standard or premium Lark form, became a true classic of 1960s outboarding.

Throughout the Sixties, Evinrude maintained a solid lineup. OMC's reputable blue motors were typically available in such sizes as 100, 90, 75, 60, 40, 33, 28, 18, 9 ½, 5 ½, and 3 hp.

Catering to the ever-growing family-leisure market, Evinrude's rigs represented a good, reliable value. In spring 1967 things got jazzed up just a bit when OMC entered the high-performance outboard arena for the first time since the early Forties. Evinrude introduced a limited-edition kicker called the X-115. (Johnson's version of the same 89.5-cubic-inch powerhouse was dubbed GT-115). This modified edition of the 100-hp model had a few powerhead differences, as well as a "new, slimmer lower unit." Because perennial horsepower leader, Mercury, offered up to 110 horses (in 1967), the flashy X-115 (hp) Evinrude put OMC on top of the power output scale for the first time in years.

Evinrude's appropriate slogan FIRST IN OUTBOARDS recognizes that its success is a result of an honest, hard-working couple who started with nothing more than a "coffee grinder" and a dream. Little did Ole and Bess know their long-ago picnic would be recalled today. Although no one keeps track, it's likely that an Evinrude has played a part in millions of enjoyable outings. Suffice it to say, a certain Evinrude kicker owns a warm spot in many a boater's heart—a memory warm enough even to melt ice cream.

The 1941 Evinrude "Midget Racer" was one of the last Class "M" products to leave the Milwaukee factory. There was also an Elto version with battery ignition. (Miville Fournier photo)

Notes

1. Red Smith, "Views of Sport," *New York Herald Tribune* (11 January 1950).
2. "The Put-Put," *Fortune* (August 1938), p. 55.
3. "The Facts Are, a President Liked His Evinrude," *Antique Outboarder* (January 1972), p. 54.
4. "The Put-Put," op. cit., p. 108.
5. "1953 Outboards," *Boating Industry* (January 1953), p. 80-G.

3

Johnson

Late in 1952 Chicago Johnson dealer W.L. Masters drove to Waukegan, Illinois, in order to get his picture taken near a couple of outboard motors. During that ride to the Johnson factory, Masters no doubt recalled a much earlier trek to Johnson's original South Bend, Indiana, plant. He'd been there in December of 1921 to pick up a motor and sign a paper making him one of the first Johnson dealers. Although it held little historical significance then, the new Johnson franchisee was invoiced for a small, shiny opposed twin wearing serial number 508.

Through good times and bad, Johnson continued to provide outboard motors for its dealers and boating public. The firm nearly collapsed in the early 1930s, but its quality reputation and subsequent acquisition by Evinrude pushed the company to the 1952 occasion attended by Mr. Masters. Someone had found old number 508 and placed it next to a brand-new green 10-hp Johnson Sea Horse sporting serial number 1,000,508. A photographer clicked his camera while the longtime Johnson dealer stood between milestones of one million outboard motors.

The Johnson motor got its name from four Terre Haute, Indiana, brothers, Lou, Harry, Julius (who wasn't officially active in the outboard project), and Clarence Johnson. While the oldest was still in his teens and without much mechanical training, the siblings built a small inboard marine engine. This 1908 homebrew powered a rowboat up the Wabash River to their favorite spot for gathering walnuts.

Scanning the tall black walnut trees must have lifted the brothers' thoughts into air because the Johnsons soon constructed a 2-cycle airplane engine. After an initial attempt at building a predominantly wooden plane to wear the motor, eldest brother Lou restructured much of it with alloy (although the single wood wing remained), enabling him (again, without formal instruction) to make America's first monoplane flight. This 1911 feat prompted the family members to open up the Johnson School of Aviation.

A storm destroyed the airplane enterprise and related engine shop in 1913. Over the next four years the Johnsons pieced together a portion of their building and began producing small, 2-cycle, air-cooled opposed twins of about 1½ hp. The motor was supposed to twirl an abbreviated airplane prop and push a rowboat

with air power, but the project didn't make much headway. They tried the propeller on a bike, too, but it proved both slow and very dangerous. Finally, the power plant was adapted to chain-drive the rear wheel of a bicycle. Tests went well, resulting in their Terre Haute shop's rechristening as the Johnson Motor Wheel Company.

The new firm, although not strong on marketing, began peddling motors (and complete motor bikes) to folks wanting inexpensive vehicles. The motor wheel engines worked pretty nicely except when they revved up and burned out their magnetos. A search for better fire power led the Johnsons to the Quick Action Ignition Company in South Bend, Indiana. Quick Action was controlled by Warren Ripple, who took a liking to the motor wheel idea. He helped beef up the Johnsons' young organization, subsequently joining the enterprise responsible for whipping up some 17,000 units. All went rather well until Henry Ford started selling Model T cars for about the same price as two-wheeled, powered transportation. Once the motorcycle market went bust around 1920, Johnson Motor Wheel needed to find another way to sell off those little engines.

Remember that one-lung inboard the brothers concocted in 1908? There had been other, bigger Johnson inboards too. In fact, a pair of the company's specially designed, 2-cycle, V-style, 12-cylinder engines were placed in a homemade runabout. This boat, known as the *Black Demon III* and carrying 360 hp, was said to be the first (circa 1913) craft to attain 60 mph on water.

After the motor wheel project was halted, Lou Johnson must have begun thinking about boat engines again. His brother-in-law, Warren Conover, was looking for something to do, so Lou suggested his relative should take an extra Johnson Motor Wheel power plant, "get an old Evinrude lower unit, make an adapter, and have a nice outfit to fish with."[1]

Although at the time Mr. Conover wasn't too interested in outboarding and forgot the recommendation, he easily recalled what Lou did next:

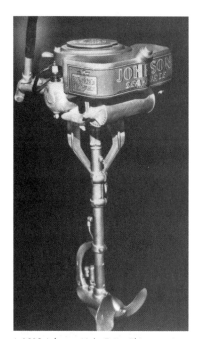

A 1922 Johnson Light Twin. This motor's easy starting and dependability won it many customers. Today the early Johnson Twins rank among the best-running antiques. Later versions (and those fitted with an accessory) wore a basic anti-cavitation plate. When operating their Johnsons in silty/salty waters, owners had to watch for clogging in the simple water pump assembly right above the gearcase. Sometimes referred to as "Water Bugs," these desirable kickers paved the way for the first Sea Horse-labeled Johnsons, which appeared in 1929. The Sea Horse decal on this kicker was mistakenly applied later. (Outboard Marine Corp.)

It was not so very many weeks later Lou came to our home one evening with a big roll of drawing paper and said, "Clear off that dining table. I got something here to share with you." I cleared the table, and he unrolled the drawing of the very first Johnson Outboard Motor, and it was not changed very much until after several thousand motors were built.[2]

Lou had enlisted Purdue University student Finn Irgens to help him with the drafting design. By the late spring of 1921 Conover and Lou, Harry, and Clarence Johnson worked the plans into a prototype. This kicker got tried out in a test tank. Unfortunately, the transom clamps loosened, causing the 2-cycle, water-cooled opposed twin to jump into the soupy drink. Clarence, the youngest brother, quickly hopped in the tank and rescued the outboard, but "swallowed a mouthful of oily water."[3]

Anyone appreciative of progress would verify that motor was worth the dunking. Loosely based on the old air-cooled Johnson Motor Wheel mill, the new, water-cooled Johnson outboard represented a great advance over most competitors. Unlike its 60- to 75-pound counterparts, the 2-cycle, 2-hp (at 2,200 rpm), opposed-twin-cylinder aluminum Johnson was really portable at 35 pounds. The simple Johnson-designed carburetor did not require the operator to possess great mechanical wisdom.

Not only were the little Johnson Light Twins (also called Water Bugs through 1923) reliably easy to start when new, but most, when rediscovered 50-plus years later by vintage-outboard collectors, can be brought back to life after cleaning the fuel strainer and tugging on the starter cord. All this from a motor built during an era when a "good" outboard might be coaxed to run half the time! The totable kicker could be tilted up for beaching (not many others had such a feature), swiveled 360 degrees for complete maneuvering, and came with a one-year guarantee. It was clearly a better outboard, a fact swiftly determined by those attending the 1922 New York Boat Show, where a few of the little motors were placed on display.

Actual production of this Johnson model A began at South Bend, Indiana, in December 1921. Serial numbers started with 500, and five Light Twin/Water Bug motors were considered "pre-production." So number 506 was the first Johnson sold to the public. Each was tested in the nearby St. Joseph River on boats representative of average fishing skiffs. Some 3,000 were eagerly purchased in the 1922 model year.

Positive word spread, and 7,000 of the $140 motors went to happy customers in 1923. Sales were even better the following year. For 1925 a notably lighter 27-pound model J-25 single joined the catalog. This 1½-hp rig also sold well, placing Johnson on the outboard industry's list of major players.

No one associated with other outboard firms had the Johnson brothers' brand of high-speed water travel experience. Understandably then, competitors were pleasantly surprised to learn (in the spring of 1925) Johnson was "wasting time" working on a big,

heavy motor. "After all," reasoned industry observers, "successes at Elto and certainly Johnson were completely based on light kickers, not fat, hard-to-lift hulks!"

Johnson's large, 1926 "flop" came in the form of an 80-pound, opposed-cylinder model P-30 Big Twin. While the heavy 6-hp (22.73-cubic-inch) outboard design ignored the scales, it lifted light boats up on plane at 16-plus mph, some 4 to 5 knots faster than most thought an outboard capable. By the end of 1926, tinkering pushed the P-30's rate past 23 mph.

References have also been made to an obscure, very large Johnson circa 1925 vintage. The two-cylinder Aqua-Flyer motor is said to have nearly 50-cubic-inch displacement generating some 15 hp. The big outboard was built into a special Johnson boat for show display purposes. Actual production figures, if any, are unknown.

Johnson was about the only outfit to offer a really quick motor from late 1925 through 1926. Outboard speed caught the public's fancy, and sales of all Johnson models (slower ones included) were brisk. In 1927 the old Big Twin was renamed P-35 and awarded more piston displacement as well as 2 extra horses (to 8 hp). This unit could push a boat over 32 mph! A new 6-hp offering, the K-35 opposed (17.33-cubic-inch) twin, was also introduced that year.

These new models were some of the first to forgo troublesome mechanical water pumps. A pressure vacuum pumping arrangement used propeller suction and forward motion to supply cooling water to the cylinders.

Meanwhile, all the successes caused Johnson to outgrow its South Bend, Indiana, plant. The outboard firm had a bit of trouble competing for workers with nearby Studebaker and other auto-related factories. When the local bigwigs complained Johnson was making too much noise, a piece of land in Illinois on Lake Michigan's shoreline was secured, and the motor company built the industry's finest outboard manufacturing facility. At about the same time Waukegan, Illinois, became Johnson's new home, a small Canadian plant was established for the production of kickers north of U.S. boundaries.

Anyone who has relocated knows that moving can expend a lot of one's energies. Similarly, Johnson's move caused the loss of some headway in the 1928 "big motor" scene. That year Elto officially unveiled its over-22-mph Speedster twin and four-cylinder, 40-mph Quad. These rigs were relatively easy to start and run, and typically performed very well. Evinrude was enjoying a second year of success with its Speeditwin, and Lockwood Ace and Chief models were also setting some racing records.

Unfortunately, Johnson's large 1928 offering came in the form of an impractically classic Giant Twin. Officially labeled model TR-40, this rig weighed in at more than 110 pounds and wore opposed cylinders displacing almost 50 cubic inches. The company had replaced its basic Water Bug/Light Twin A-25 with a restyled 2½-hp A-35 and simply "blew up" the design into the TR-40. It was

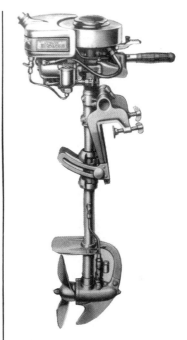

Model J-25, 1.5-hp motor, 1925-32.

almost as if someone at Johnson had put an A-35 on a photocopier and pressed the enlarge button, yielding a Giant Twin!

In any event, the noisy 25.75-hp monster was faster than previous Johnsons, but provided little all-around competition for motors like Elto's Quad. The Giant Twin found a few customers in 1928. Leftovers were offered in 1929. Thus now it had been Johnson that had underestimated the other companies. Something significant had to be done for 1929.

An advertising agency man named Carl Prell phoned Johnson before the 1929 model year:

> "I've got an idea," said Prell to his Johnson contact.
>
> "Well, we can sure use one," the Johnson man responded.
>
> "How 'bout you call your boat motors by a name representative of mighty waters and creatures exhibiting tremendous strength and stamina?"
>
> Oh, no, I hope he isn't going to recommend something like Ocean Oxen, thought the Johnson official.
>
> "Why not name those outboards"—Prell paused for effect—"something like 'Sea Horse' . . . the Johnson Sea Horse!"
>
> "Hey, that works for us!" came the relieved answer, and the new nomenclature was assigned to the 1929 line.

Fresh off the assembly line with Sea Horse decals were a pair of motors wearing an external, gear-driven (full-crankshaft-speed) rotary crankcase valve. This feature allowed for a greater efficiency in getting gas vapor into the engine. Rotary valves of this type were standard on the new 1929, 13-hp S-45 (approximately 20 cubic inches) opposed twin and the 4-cylinder opposed (approximately 40 cubic inches) 26-horse model V-45. Racing versions of these beautifully engineered kickers were designated SR-45 and VR-45 and checked in with 16 and 32 hp (at 5,200 rpm), respectively.

Lou Johnson, oldest of the Johnson brothers, in his Waukegan, Illinois office. His stern look in this 1932 photo may have been due to the outboard company's financial woes. Motor is a model P-50. (Outboard Marine Corp.)

The new Sea Horse logo appeared on these (and all other '29 Johnsons) looking a bit more like a ferocious dragon than an aqua-equine. No matter, the 1929 Sea Horses (with the exception of the holdover TR-40) were well received, pushing the company up where it wanted to be.

Throughout 1929, Johnson engineering research prospered. An approximately 30-cubic-inch, gear-driven, external rotary valve motor called the P-50 was developed (for 1930 release). This one sported an improved, half-crankcase-speed valve and operated so well the same technology was applied to the proposed 1930 Johnson V-50, 4-cylinder and the S-50 twin. (Leftover full-speed external-rotary-valved S-45 and V-45 motors would also be offered in 1930.)

While testing the four-banger model, one of the Johnson brothers released compression from a pair of cylinders and noticed the V-50 still ran pretty well. As spark plugs in the active bank of opposed cylinders ignited alternately, he wondered if such a firing order was responsible for the smoothness. Further experiments proved that hypothesis correct, and a new set of alternate-firing twins (4-hp model A-50 and K-50 8-horse motors) were developed for 1930 presentation.

Additionally, it was decided to market a line of Johnson boats that could be matched with various Sea Horse outboards. Inventories of boats and motors were stockpiled in late 1929. To let people know about everything Johnson had to sell, company president Warren Ripple pledged a block of the firm's stock and borrowed (from New York investment house Hayden-Stone) lots of promotion-earmarked funds. Six hundred thousand dollars were spent on advertising alone.

The stock market crashed in October of 1929. Even if someone wanted a mated Johnson boat-and-motor combo, he probably couldn't afford one. Johnson had put out huge sums of money, but wasn't taking in much at all. As a result Mr. Ripple lost the security stock to Hayden-Stone, and during 1930, control of the Sea Horses was rounded up by the financiers.

For some reason in 1931 (while Ole Evinrude's company was prudently pulling in the fiscal reins) the bankers let Johnson spend more money improving its existing racing models, adding an

"So easy to operate and maintain even a couple of girls in weird bathing suits can do it," a copy writer might quip. Indeed, the Johnson model J single was a good performer no matter who was at the controls. (Outboard Marine Corp.)

approximately 14-cubic-inch racer called KR-55, along with the obscure, approximately 50-cubic-inch, 50-horse XR-55 opposed, four-cylinder, high-speed rig weighing in at 144 pounds! A few dollars also went to develop an inboard/outboard stern-drive system.

While not commercially successful in 1931, these model SD 10 and SD 11 units (not to be confused with the SD 10 outboard of 1940) were actually 30 years ahead of their time. Wisely, some of the old opposed-twin parts were parsimoniously put together to form the outdated but utilitarian OA (3-hp) and OK (8-hp) two-cylinder outboards.

In 1932 Hayden-Stone had Johnson declare bankruptcy, submerging the once-proud outboard firm into receivership and reorganization. More Wall Street types were sent to Waukegan with financial cures. One new man got Johnson into the refrigerator compressor business, turning out chilly units under its own JoMoCo label, as well as for other firms such as Stewart-Warner.

Small 4-cycle Iron Horse utility power plants were also built at Johnson's Waukegan, Illinois, plant. Hayden-Stone even bought Johnson another factory in Galesburg, Illinois, to handle all the overflow in case the fridge and small-engine business went sky high. Unfortunately, everything kept going through the floor, with the Johnson Motor Company skating in the same direction.

It was probably about this time (1933 or 1934) when a deal—of which so little information remains that it was nearly forgotten—was planned between Johnson and Sears-Roebuck. The famous outboard maker was to provide Sears with a cheap opposed twin based on the model OK leftover motors. A few of these 8-hp opposed kickers were produced, each wearing the Waterwitch ID on its rope sheave plate. It appears that either Sears or Johnson canceled the contract before very many Waterwitches were brewed.

With a "just see if you can do anything with that disaster" attitude, Hayden-Stone kept bringing in and trying out new Johnson managers. The recruits had backgrounds in everything from the military to movie theater and clothes store operation.

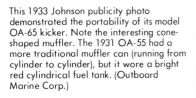
This 1933 Johnson publicity photo demonstrated the portability of its model OA-65 kicker. Note the interesting cone-shaped muffler. The 1931 OA-55 had a more traditional muffler can (running from cylinder to cylinder), but it wore a bright red cylindrical fuel tank. (Outboard Marine Corp.)

None knew much about running an outboard or industrial concern.

Stewart-Warner's association with Johnson (via their refrigerator compressor deal) led the diversified company to make a 1935 purchase order for the ailing outboard firm. Hayden-Stone quickly accepted, even reluctantly agreeing to take Stewart-Warner stock instead of cash.

A few weeks later Stewart-Warner told Charlie Hayden there could be a delay in the proposed transaction while the Securities and Exchange Commission looked into Stewart-Warner's stock values. Knowing the government never does anything fast (except raise taxes), Hayden was extremely aggravated. To make matters worse, he had taken sick and was "laid up in a New York City hotel room in fine temper."[4]

Johnson's chief competitor, Outboard Motors Corporation, had been pinching pennies since late 1929, and its principals, Ralph Evinrude and Steve Briggs, had saved a little extra cash. The pair had often discussed bringing Johnson into the family. Hearing rumors about the Stewart-Warner situation, Briggs headed to Hayden's New York hotel suite.

> "Do you want to buy Johnson?" the ill banker asked.
> "Sure," Briggs said, nodding.
> "I've got to get $10.35 a share for it," said Hayden.
> "OK," came the reply.
> "Well, then, it's yours," Mr. Hayden said in a rather relieved tone.
> And with that, he took a pen, a slip of paper, and wrote: "Steve Briggs and Ralph Evinrude agree to pay $10.35 a share for 80,000 shares (out of 102,000 outstanding) of Johnson Motor Company stock." Briggs scribbled his name on the tiny paper and took a train back to Milwaukee. In telling Ralph Evinrude the news, he smiled. "Johnson is going to be a perfect little gold mine."[5]

The famous company was finally back in the hands of people who knew outboards. Perhaps more importantly, Johnson was now operated by individuals who understood how to manage an outboard firm. Within a year after acquiring Johnson, officials at the newly named Outboard Marine and Manufacturing Corporation (covering Elto, Evinrude, and Johnson) cut Johnson expenses by doing things like "reducing the cost of directors' meetings from $8,000 to $250 annually."[6]

Johnson's expensive-to-produce, 4-cylinder opposed motors were never reintroduced, and by 1937 the firm began securing the position of quality fishing motor maker. In fact, Briggs's supposed "gold mine" prediction had almost instantly come true, as the 1937 Johnson gross exceeded Evinrude/Elto's by nearly $2 million.

Through the close of the 1930s, Johnson continued specializing in smaller fishing engines. In fact, 80 percent of its 10-model 1939 lineup came from motors 5 hp and under. These smooth-trolling "fishin' engines," such as the alternate-firing LT (Light Twin), were highly prized by anglers everywhere.

In 1940 a big 16-horse model SD was introduced. Johnson's first large "hooded" motor wore a fat 2½-gallon wraparound fuel tank, giving it the look of a prize pumpkin atop a lower unit. Engineers would soon agree that big outboards needed remote gas tanks. Another hefty Johnson of this vintage came in the form of the model PO. An approximately 30-cubic-inch opposed twin derived from a late-twenties design, this 22-hp kicker long enjoyed a following equaled by the similarly sized Evinrude Speeditwin.

In 1941 and 1942 Johnson updated the LT motors with a 5-horse model TS (TD Deluxe with rewind starting). Also introduced was a 2½-hp version called HS (HD). These nice-running outboards received modernization via shrouding. Their sales were quite brisk, and a surprising number are still in use today.

By spring 1942 World War II halted civilian outboard production and started many a GI wishing for the day a trusty Johnson would again take him to a relaxing fishing spot. The famous kicker company issued a wish list brochure promising it wouldn't abandon anyone who had such dreams. It admitted the Sea Horse motors shown in the little catalog were not then available, but "will be manufactured after the war is won. They are substantially the same as those which were discontinued in 1942."

By 1939 Johnson, under Evinrude ownership, had rebounded financially. This company outing included boat rides with Johnson outboards for power. One hopes that the mahogany *inboard* at the end of the dock is not Johnson property! (Outboard Marine Corp.)

The evolution of the Johnson Sea Horse logo.

1929

1940

1958

During World War II, Johnson honored defense contracts with products like modified 22-hp PO motors (model POLR), and water pumps based on the KR racing power plants.

At war's end Johnson did rerelease the HD 2½-, the TD 5-, the KD 9.8-, the SD 16-, and the PO 22-hp models. These products, most especially the two smaller units, sold very well, providing Johnson with a stable catalog offering through 1948. Sea Horses of this vintage began wearing a sea-mist green finish.

Johnson engineers were busy developing a "big" outboard "slenderized" by way of a remote Mile-Master gas tank. Most important, the new motor could be easily shifted into neutral, forward, or reverse. Debuting in 1949, this 10-hp model QD moved an important portion of Outboard Marine and Manufacturing into the state-of-the-art realm. The QD's premier was surpassed only by rival Scott-Atwater's trio of shift motors (4, 5, and 7½ hp), also introduced in '49. Nevertheless, the QD remained Johnson's star through 1950.

A quasi-shift model TN (*N* for neutral) replaced Johnson's old TD. The updated 5-horse favorite resembled its predecessor but had a neutral clutch.

Clear evidence that Johnson and Evinrude had common ownership surfaced with the 1951 introduction of the model RD Sea Horse 25. This instantly popular rig was mechanically identical to Evinrude's Big Twin 25 and contributed a new versatility to outboarding. Ads boasted "25 hp—Yet it trolls . . . and only 85 pounds!" Like many of this era's popular Johnsons, the first Sea Horse 25s sported motor rest wings along and forward of the cowling. The 25 allowed 1951's lineup to be simplified, and the chubby SD and heavy PO were dropped.

An Evinrude-based Johnson 3-hp kicker, dubbed the JW, began its run in 1952. Angle-Matic drive helped prevent the JW from snagging underwater vegetation. Designed to replace the old 2½-horse HD, this junior Johnson linked lots of fishermen and small-boat users with the Sea Horse logo.

> Sometime in late October 1952 workers on Johnson's assembly line were instructed to pay close attention to their products' serial numbers. On November 6, a couple of Sea Horse employees pointed at a 10-horse motor shouting, "That's it!" and ran for the foreman.
> "Yep, there she is," their supervisor confirmed.

They were talking about the 1 millionth Johnson outboard. The 1953 model QD milestone was subsequently "outfitted with special gold and chrome trim . . . and featured in major boat shows throughout the country."[7]

The year 1955 was when Johnson's cowling wings were moved aft. The 25 was updated and could be purchased with electric starting. (Johnson had last offered that convenience in the

The Johnson model QD 10-hp motor with remote "Mile-Master" fuel tank. The black knob on the lower front cowling shifts this Sea Horse from neutral to forward or reverse. In 1949, the only other outboard company to offer a gearshift was Scott-Atwater. Being a larger firm, however, Johnson got most of the credit for pioneering this convenience. (Outboard Marine Corp.)

early Thirties.) A 5 ½-hp model CD F-N-R shift outboard with Evinrude-influenced features replaced the old reliable 5-horse TN. Sea Horses rated at 3, 5.5, 10, and 25 hp represented the popular green (with white accents) 1954–55 Johnson line.

Rich maroon paint (with white detailing) signaled a change for Johnson's 1956 catalog. Again, Evinrude's influence contributed to the Sea Horse stable via new 7.5- and 15-hp offerings. The old 25 was upped to 30 hp, and came in both regular Sea Horse and deluxe Javelin versions. Like the fancy Evinrude Lark, Javelin served as Johnson's top-of-the-line product. Although always equipped with 6-volt electric starting, the chrome-trimmed Javelin differed only cosmetically from the regular Sea Horse 30 electric.

Javelin's manual-start cord grip was hidden behind a little white cover. When the cover was removed for emergency cranking, sharp edges of the clip, designed to hold it in place, caused salty words to shake from boaters with battery trouble! Such minor inconveniences notwithstanding, the deluxe Javelins were rewarded with a gold paint job (with chrome accents) and upped to 35 hp in 1957. Options included a heavy-duty 10-amp generator. There was also a maroon and white Sea Horse 35. The old 15 was promoted to 18 horses in 1957.

Javelins got tossed from Johnson's 1958 arena, leaving regular and Super Sea Horse 35 models. Top honors in 1958 went to a new white and gold V-4-cylinder hulk dreamed up with Evinrude. The Sea Horse 50, Johnson's version of the "Fat-Fifty," looked as if its 50 horses should perform better than they actually did. Had the motor run fast and consumed fuel slowly, all might have been well. Unfortunately, the opposite was true.

By 1960 the white Sea Horse line had a far superior leader. The new V-4 Sea Horse 75 had a much improved lower unit, was a bit easier on gas, and had an acceptable top end. It came in a two-

A late-1960s Johnson V-4 Meteor. (Outboard Marine Corp.)

lever remote-control version in 1960. Later models were sometimes plagued by bugs in a single-lever-controlled Electramatic, an electromagnetic lower-unit shifter.

Meanwhile, the vintage 35 had evolved into a 40-hp rig available in standard and Electramatic styles. Similar to the old 25s (on which they were based), the 40s became their era's leading family-size outboard.

The year 1964 saw the long-lived 10-horse Johnson dropped in favor of a low profile 9½. More than any other 1960s Sea Horse, the 9½ has an equal share of detractors and enthusiasts.

Few would disagree that the Johnson story is packed with many interesting, innovative, and, most important, dependable outboards. By the way, to illustrate the famous motor maker's accelerated popularity, its 1 millionth kicker from late 1952 was more than 30 years in the making. Johnson's number 2 million, however, arrived much faster, rolling off the line in 1959. By 1968 the 3 millionth Sea Horse presented one of the world's best-loved outboard motor makers with another remarkable photo opportunity.

Ad touting benefits of being a Johnson dealer.

Notes

1. Warren Mason Conover, "Early Johnson Engineering History," *Antique Outboarder* (April 1974), p. 7.
2. Ibid.
3. "Commemorative Edition," *Johnson Jottings*, (OMC, Johnson div. house organ), (1972), p. 3.
4. "The Put-Put," *Fortune* (August 1938), p. 115.
5. Ibid.
6. Ibid.
7. "Johnson," *Boating Industry* (January 1953), p. 82.

4

Kiekhaefer Mercury

Whether some nervous employee in a competitor's PR department did it, no one will ever know. The truth is, however, somebody started a Mercury rumor that has polarized outboarders since the late 1940s. The word was passed: "OK, Mercs might be speedy on tiny, impractical, non-family-oriented craft, but try to pull a skier with one on a real boat, and you'll see those noisy machines have absolutely no power."

The real force behind Mercury grew up on a Midwestern farm. Like Ole Evinrude, another native Wisconsinite, this fellow, E.C. "Carl" Kiekhaefer, was more interested in farm machinery than fields or livestock. Young Kiekhaefer left green pastures for a trade school specializing in practical and automotive electricity. Although this background soon helped him attain chief engineer status at a respectable firm, Carl Kiekhaefer was driven by a desire to run his own shop.

In 1938 the word was that the Cedarburg, Wisconsin, plant, which made Thor outboards, was about to fold. Located in Kiekhaefer's hometown, the Cedarburg Manufacturing Company's facility seemed a likely spot for his dream venture. With financial help from his dad and some townspeople, he acquired the defunct outboard factory and began deciding what kind of product to make.

The old sign saying CEDARBURG MFG. CO. was painted out and relettered KIEKHAEFER CORP. The word MAGNETIC was stuck on the firm's roof, touting Carl Kiekhaefer's expertise in electrical engineering. It also set the stage for the novice company to produce magnetic separators for the dairy industry.

Clean-up operations got under way but the separator idea was short-circuited by the discovery of some outboards in inventory. Kiekhaefer decided to sell them to raise a little capital for some manufacturing machinery.

The 300 or so silver kickers were small Thor singles re-labeled with red Sea King decals. Awaiting their fate, they stood in silent rows on wooden stands winding through the old factory.

Montgomery Ward had contracted Thor for a large stock of the low-cost, badge-engineered (motors that differ from others cosmetically, sold under different brand names) Sea Kings. Customer complaints about the poorly running engines caused the

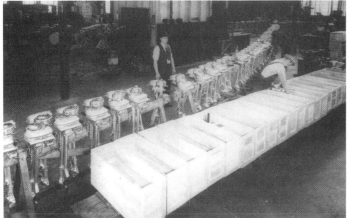

big catalog store to terminate the deal. Already beset by financial problems from the weak sales of Thor motors, Cedarburg was finished off by the Montgomery Ward situation.

Informal inspection of the outboards' fuel-air mixing valve caused Kiekhaefer to question his predecessor's engineering skill. To satisfy mechanical curiosity, the new plant owner postponed his call to the junk man and replaced a random kicker's mixing valve with an automotive-type float-feed carburetor. A factory test tank still holding gallons of oily water was fitted with the experimental Sea King. Three brisk pulls on the starter cord brought the motor to life and Kiekhaefer to consider phoning Montgomery Ward instead of the scrap dealer.

Initially skeptical, the Montgomery Ward buyer soon heard one of his store's erstwhile outboards happily purring with sales potential. The Kiekhaefer Corporation was quickly commissioned to revitalize the idle stock of Sea Kings for inclusion in the 1939 Montgomery Ward catalog. After most of the improved batch had been crated and sent to the Montgomery Ward warehouse, Kiekhaefer finally had time to count his fledgling outfit's receipts and return to the business of coming up with a good product to manufacture.

> "Line two for Mr. Kiekhaefer," paged a secretary. "Montgomery Ward calling long distance."
> Oh, no, what do they want? her boss wondered.
> "We sold all those Sea Kings," the guy on the phone stated, "and we want you to make us some more."

The old machines that had pressed out Thor/Sea King parts remained usable, so Kiekhaefer and his crew fired them up and satisfied Montgomery Ward's new order. Almost simultaneously, it was decided to print a 1939 Thor brochure and take another step into the outboard motor business.

Someone located the late model Thor's specs, patterns, and

The tilted powerhead on these Mercs was a province of carburetor placement less prone to "load-up" fuel. Forward-looking design on Merc's Mark 10 included a cover reminiscent of a fire-fighter's hat. Automatic transmission on this model was a neat idea but a real pain for repair shop personnel. Dealer ad is from 1957.

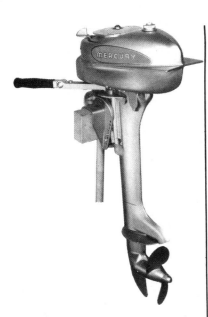

Products such as the 1940 Mercury Single placed the Kiekhaefer Corporation in outboarding's limelight. The firm's founder sought permission from Ford Motor Company to use the Mercury moniker. Ford gave the OK with the condition that the word *Mercury* be preceded by the Kiekhaefer name.

In the late 1940s and early 1950s, Merc's "Full Jeweled Power" logo always contained a little asterisk. Diamond studded pistons? No, indicated the note, just "ball and roller bearing throughout."

castings. Kiekhaefer made a few improvements, such as replacing the mixing valve with a workable carb, and offered a three-cylinder, in-line, 6.2-horse rig, an alternate-firing, 4.1-hp twin, and a 2.4-horse single. Because small motors accounted for most of the industry's business, Kiekhaefer concentrated on his one-lung model. While the lower unit still had Thor's characteristic steel stamping toy appearance, its fuel tank exhibited a new teardrop design. Such styling, complete with little wings and a tail fin, caused it to be dubbed Streamliner. During its brief production run, this kicker was never a common sight. Even so, the Streamliner set the stage for something unique in 1940.

The Cedarburg plant was about 20 miles outside of Milwaukee. Visitors were "welcome for inspection or actual boat demonstrations." Engineering and publicity purposes were served at the factory when Kiekhaefer had his staff run a "destruction test" on a Thor twin. They hooked it to that old test tank and kept it going full speed for an estimated 5,000 miles. Afterward, mechanics "tore it down, and the parts were in fine condition."

Not every employee at the Cedarburg facility was required to advocate Thor motors. Kiekhaefer knew the outboard design he'd acquired with the silent factory represented no long-term asset. So, as some of his staff built up more '39 Thors, the company president and a handful of select engineering associates worked to make their present product line shamefully obsolete.

Late in that final year of the decade, Kiekhaefer's workers were notified that Thor production would be discontinued. Seeing their boss packing things into his Plymouth coupe, numerous staffers wondered if they'd lose their jobs at Thor a second time. Although details were sketchy, rumor soon had it that the plant would actually get busier than ever.

Kiekhaefer's car headed away from the Cedarburg factory carrying a handmade display and a few interesting outboards. Curious service station attendants along the route to New York City might have caught a glimpse of the streamlined silver kickers on the backseat. A blanket protecting the motors could have moved just enough to reveal the word MERCURY on one of the outboard engines' gas tank.

These new models, taking their name from Roman mythology's speedy messenger god, were indeed far superior to the old Thors. Most striking on the 1940-debut Mercs was a "hydrodynamic designed [drive] shaft casing." Unlike most of its competitors, this piece "enclosed the drive shaft, water line, and served as a leak-proof underwater exhaust." Sales literature also claimed the whole unit was "designed like a streamlined airplane strut . . . knifing through water without resistance. The lower unit had no knobs or projections to cause turbulence. Clean, fast, weedless, and by far the strongest ever made."

Additional 1940 Mercury innovations included removable cylinder sleeves and water jackets. These features allowed saltwater boaters to clean the salt scale from the powerhead. Carbon deposits were also accessible for maintenance. A rubber

Rotex water pump eliminated the need for springs, plungers, valves, and other intricate parts found in most competitors' pumps. This facilitated constant cooling without concern for water or corrosion.

Folks attending the Boat Show watched Kiekhaefer highlight these aspects of his small Mercury exhibit. The notable little motors and their inventor's sales presentation netted 16,000 orders! Buyers had the option of the $52.95 Standard Single; the $59.95 De Luxe Single, with streamlined gas tank and powerhead cover; or the $89.95 Twin. Neither the 6-horse, two-cylinder rig nor the 3-hp singles had rewind starting.

The first Merc catalog also included note of a $42.95, 2 ½-hp single Mercury Special. While hawking Merc motors like this at the 1940 New York Boat Show, Kiekhaefer got word that Flambeau was trying to buy out his fledgling firm. He sped back to Wisconsin to nix the deal.

Kiekhaefer's outboard business got off to a good start and grew in 1941. Unfortunately, war clouds forced American officials to tighten the reins on civilian production items. Aluminum supplies for consumer goods, such as outboards, were redirected toward the military. With kicker production nearly halted, Mercury inventories disappeared by 1942.

Actually, the Kiekhaefer Corporation started getting busier. Defense contracting prompted nearly round-the-clock work designing and building "lightweight engines for military chain saws, pumps, compressors, generators, hoists, and target aircraft," according to the Mercury literature. Even a few outboards, wearing metal Kiekhaefer Corporation ID plates on the motor leg, found wartime assignments. Unlike many firms that got tapped by Uncle Sam to make goods completely foreign to their regular merchandise, Kiekhaefer's War Department contracts allowed over four years of research and development in its field of 2-cycle engine technology (ranging from 2 ½ to 90 hp).

Staffers were constantly reminded to think of ways that this war-products experience could be put to use in a postwar outboard marketplace. Mercury's "new kids on the block" image was kept alive from 1942 to 1945 as even the most vintage (1940) Mercs were only a few years old. This contrasted with other folks' potentially cantankerous 1930s kickers from Elto, Evinrude, or Johnson. When peacetime returned in summer 1945, the Kiekhaefer Corporation was ready with 1946 model-year Mercs.

Immediate postwar Mercs came in 3.2 single and 6-horse twin denominations and were called Comet and Rocket, respectively. "Special" versions of these silver motors wore rewind starters.

By 1947 a trio of new Kiekhaefer models began showing up in a rich, cedar green color. Although two of these rigs (3.6 and 7 ½ hp) had powerheads based on earlier Mercurys, they (along with a 10-horse big sister) visually outdated a whole crop of predecessors and competitors.

Star of this enviable triangle was indeed the approximately

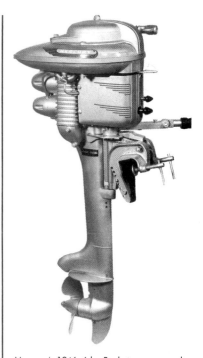

Mercury's 1946, 6-hp Rocket was a good seller for the Kiekhaefer Corporation. Note the ID plate on the motor leg. Early post-war Mercurys were silver, but golden versions were produced for Western Auto to sell under the Wizard name. (Mercury Marine)

This 1947 10-horse KE7 Lightning looks almost like its little 7½-hp brother, the Rocket KE4. Both models set speed records in their respective classes. The photo shows the original lower cowling, which is typically missing from old motors found today. The first few KE7 Mercs wore a rectangular ID plate with no mention of the term *Lightning*. Reportedly an early test caused someone to brag that "this thing goes like lightning!" Kiekhaefer heard about the comment and had the descriptive term added to subsequent label tags, which were semi-rounded off. (Mercury Marine)

20-cubic-inch model KE7 Lightning. Very conservatively rated at 10 hp, the 59-pound Lightning (on a light hull) often made quick work of much bigger Evinrude and Johnson 22-horse opposed twins.

While most outboard firms proudly fitted their products with lots of shiny control panel dials, motor rest wings, and carrying handles, Kiekhaefer built Lightning as sleek as a no-nonsense sports car. Its knifey silver lower unit and beautiful green powerhead, devoid of toting handles, was truly striking. An aluminum ring hugged the bottom edge of the ovalesque fuel tank. The mysterious word *Mercury* (with letters in descending size) was cast into both sides of this piece like teeth partially cloaked in a shark's mouth.

Kiekhaefer's liberal use of ball and needle bearings allowed Lightning to run in rpm ranges dangerous for lesser-engineered outboards. The rather compact green Merc inspired the Michigan Wheel Company to develop special two-blade bronze racing propellers called Aqua-Jet. These props, appropriate for small, planing hulls, made Lightning even faster.

There was something wonderfully strange about the first generation Lightning. It was clearly not the type of motor a respectable family man would long consider. Still, Kiekhaefer's plan to offer an outboard capable of becoming a legend was quickly realized. Non-Mercury dealers scoffed at the glossy green 10s as a hot-rodder's province. Others speculated, "If that's a 10, I sure would like to see a Merc 20 or 25!"

The year 1949 gave curious outboarders just such a view when the four-cylinder, in-line Mercury model KF9 was introduced. This approximately 40-cubic-inch Thunderbolt sported a bright chrome rope-start flywheel slightly above its cedar green powerhead covers. Thunderbolt's cowling said MERCURY 25, but like the underrated Lightning, it generated much more zing than advertised. In fact, small print in Kiekhaefer's parts booklets lists this one's horsepower as "25+*." The asterisk refers to a reminder that Thunderbolt's horsepower varies with revolutions per minute. Enigmatically, no rpm rating is given. Adding to the 25's mystique, a "deadman's throttle" grip positioned on the tiller handle was designed to slow the green giant if its operator got thrown out of the boat. The Mercury 25 Thunderbolt was easily 40 hp and could "blow the doors off" craft powered by the larger 50-horse Evinrude quads of the late 1940s.

Carl Kiekhaefer was bugged by the accepted notion that Ole Evinrude had actually invented the outboard motor. Various versions of the famous "ice cream story" (noted in Chapter 2) continually surfaced, honoring Evinrude as the most valid kicker company. So in late 1949 Kiekhaefer hired an investigator to research documents in the U.S. patent office.

Dusty paperwork discovered in Washington predated Ole's ice cream incident and sent the researcher scurrying for the telephone. It seemed that Cameron Waterman was selling outboards before Evinrude ever set up shop.

Seventy-one-year-old Waterman was located in Detroit and invited (along with his wife, of course) by Mercury for an all-expense-paid trip to the upcoming New York Boat Show. There, the elderly gent was honored as outboarding's real inventor. Many prominent outdoors writers and just about all of the New York newspaper columnists were invited, too.

The resulting publicity was a tremendous PR coup for Mercury. The Evinrude people didn't say much. Mr. Waterman smiled a lot, got an official "outboard inventor" plaque and a new 1950 Merc 25. A copy of the plaque turned up years later in a West Coast junkyard.

Leftover KE7 Lightnings were offered through 1949 (and probably later at smaller dealers). The approximately 20-cubic-inch motors were also marketed that year with a few internal updates and convenient carrying handles. Labeled Super 10, KF7, these Lightnings tread water nicely while a hotter "10+ hp*" Merc was on the drawing board. The little one-cylinder Comet 3 ½ was upgraded a touch and represented a pretty nice fishing engine. Although some of these singles sold in 1949 and 1950, a new 1949 Super 5 twin, priced only a few dollars over the Comet, frequently eclipsed its smaller sister and fast became one of Mercury's most popular products.

Late 1940s economic progress required more space for the Kiekhaefer Corporation. A Fond du Lac, Wisconsin, dairy farm, once renowned for its prize-winning cattle, was acquired and converted into Mercury's new manufacturing, marketing, and training center. By 1951 most Mercs were tagged with their ID plates in a big barn comprising the Fond du Lac plant. It must have seemed strange to see trailer trucks displaying the Mercury outboard logo picking up goods from a siloed structure boasting, in huge letters, CORIUM FARM—HOME OF FAMOUS GUERNSEY COWS.

That old Cedarburg property received the temporary honor of serving as Kiekhaefer's engineering and administrative head-quarters. Once additions were completed in Fond du Lac, the original Thor/Mercury factory's "home office" status quietly ended. Funds were allocated for a parts and service division at Beaver Dam, a research plant at Oshkosh (both Wisconsin), as well as a saltwater test site in Sarasota, Florida.

Meanwhile, racing enthusiasts were squeezing even more miles per hour from their fast Merc-powered boats. Sometime during 1949 or 1950, the factory released a handful of extra speedy KF7-HD (approximately 20-cubic-inch) and (approximately 40-cubic-inch) KF9-HD motors. The *HD* stood for "heavy-duty," signifying these rigs had reinforced castings and larger carbs. HD outboards most likely found their way to promising racers planning a run in some important event such as the Albany to New York (City) Marathon.

Shortly after the HD engines were produced, Kiekhaefer introduced the long (15-inch) Quicksilver racing lower unit. Early versions of this "Quicky" were available for the 10-horse KE7 and KF7, as well as for the 4-cylinder KF9 and subsequent KG9

In 1949, big motors produced by other companies lacked rewind starting, so Kiekhaefer officials decided to save time by releasing their revolutionary Mercury 25 Thunderbolt with a simple, rope-start flywheel. The 1949 KF9 was the first 4-cylinder, in-line production outboard. Subsequent Mercs with similar appearance were the KG9, the KG9-1 (with rewind start), and the Mark 40 (on which the side cowling simply read "Mercury"). That squeeze grip on the 40-cubic-inch powerhouse's steering handle operated spark/throttle and would idle if released (or if the driver flipped out of the boat). While most of these rigs were cedar green, some literature shows bare aluminum models. Introductory ads featured a non-ribbed cowl with no lettering. A few KF9s (which apparently had weak crankshafts) and KG9s came through the factory painted red. This underrated 25 was neck-snapping quick. (Mercury Marine)

HEAVY duty

conversion kits (for pushing house-boats, barges, big fishing boats and other heavy loads with KE 7, KF7 and KG7 models.)

The rugged construction, reserve power and stamina of Mercury KE-7, KF-7 and KG-7 models make them capable of propelling enormous loads. However, for heavy duty work, such as propulsion of barges, houseboats and heavy fishing boats, it is necessary to compensate for abnormally high mounting position of motor by extending lower unit downward so propeller can operate deep enough in the water; also, it is advantageous to use a large diameter low pitch propeller which will develop maximum thrust at low forward speeds, yet will allow engine to operate at normal R.P.M.

Each heavy duty conversion kit contains a special driveshaft housing extension and an extra long drive shaft, plus all parts required to make the conversion. It does not include the propeller.

NOTE: For gross loads between 1000 and 1500 pounds, a 9'' x 7'' propeller will be found most efficient. For gross loads over 1500 pounds, a 9'' x 6'' propeller is recommended.

M-50-1191 for KE-7, less propeller $13.45
M-50-1182 for KF-7 and KG-7, less propeller 18.01
M-50-1132 9'' x 6'' propeller, KF-7 and KG-7 . . . . 9.90
M-50-1133 9'' x 7'' propeller, KF-7 and KG-7 . . . . 9.90
M-50-1134 9'' x 6'' propeller, KE-7 . . . . 9.90
M-50-1135 9'' x 7'' propeller, KE-7 . . . . 9.90

Heavy-duty conversion kits for Mercury model KE7, KF7, and KG7 model motors.

(featuring a stronger crankshaft). Actually, the Quicksilver unit was really built with a new generation of Merc 10 in mind.

The approximately 20-cubic-inch Super 10 Hurricane model KG7 of 1950 would soon outshine Lightning in Kiekhaefer's crown. (The short-lived KF7-HD was probably a preproduction KG7 Hurricane.) Boaters wanting extra zip offered by a Quicky had to buy a stock motor and then purchase the super-sleek Quicksilver lower unit as an accessory. When a Merc dealer was asked to replace the standard unit with the Quicksilver piece, factory rules authorized him to stamp a little letter Q on the motor's ID plate, hence, KG7Q or KF9Q, and so on. Not everyone bothered with this detail.

The 15-inch Quicksilver lower-unit equipped Q motors worked well on racing runabouts, but owners of hydroplanes (tiny boats with transoms shorter than those on utility craft) often placed broken pieces of yardsticks under the motor clamp yoke in order to raise their Mercs to a competitive operating level. Kiekhaefer reps observing this practice prompted the 1950 or 1951 introduction of a new Quicksilver lower unit colloquially known as the Hydro-Short Quicky. This Hydro or H lower unit had only one (instead of two) anticavitation plates and was 2 inches shorter than the old 15-inch Quicky. While the gearfoot design remained the same, a slightly abbreviated drive shaft was used.

Motors mated to the Hydro-Short units came that way from the factory and had an H after the model designation. The first H Mercs were the hot Hurricane over-10-hp KG7H and the new approximately 15-cubic-inch 7½-horse Rocket Hurricane KG4H. For the latter, the powerhead was taken directly from the "standard" 7.5-hp KG4 advertised as a fishing engine. Interestingly, in fall 1952 one could select from three 7½-horse Merc "fishin' motors." There was the old reliable 11-cubic-inch KE4, its updated (1953) sister, the Mark 7, and the KG4.

During the mid-Eighties, I purchased a KG4 that appeared to have just come out of the factory packing carton. In late 1952 a gentleman retired to a little lake hamlet in Georgia. As a retirement gift, his familiy went to the local Merc franchise in search of a nice 7.5-horse fishing motor. They had their choice of the functional KE4, a generic Mark 7, and as the dealer stated, a "top-of-the-line seven-and-a-half-horsepower model, KG4 Rocket Hurricane." Wanting only the best for their elderly loved one, a shiny green KG4 was selected.

Although the KE4 and Mark 7 rigs were 11-cubic-inch garden-variety fishing models, the larger displacement KG4 was never made for trolling. It was probably offered on a standard lower unit only to prove the KG4H production run economical.

Well, the KG4's high compression made it nearly impossible for the poor old fellow to rope over. When his son was summoned to get the gift going, the younger man had a tough time, too. Little idling was accomplished on that maiden voyage, and brave bursts of throttle practically stood the senior citizen's 10-foot aluminum

jonboat on end! Needless to say, oars were used until the subsequent presentation of a more suitable Sears-Roebuck putt-putt. The sassy KG4 waited out her next 30-plus years in a garage corner.

Carl Kiekhaefer continued bristling at charges his Mercs were simply show-offs' motors. By 1951 Evinrude and Johnson began selling hundreds of their versatile 25-hp twins. Admittedly, Mercury's KG9 (especially with lower race unit) 25-hp rig was much sexier and faster than OMC's offering, but Kiekhaefer's motors lacked one important Evinrude/Johnson detail: a gearshift. Without this function, a bigger outboard became tricky to handle, especially when docking or water-skiing. So, an F-N-R Merc was quickly planned for fall 1951 release. Time constraints, however, allowed only the new "shift" lower unit to be ready for the '52 catalog. As a result, available approximately 20-cubic-inch Hurricane powerheads were mounted on these parts.

The whole product was officially dubbed the Super 10 Hurricane Cruiser, model KH7. Some advertising showed the Cruiser towing a pair of water-skiers or pushing an outboard cabin cruiser. Because the Hurricane power plant got much of its punch from high rpm provided by light loads, outstanding operation under such applications may have been an adman's wish. A good motor, but no real competition for the OMC 25s that had more torque, Merc's Cruiser served primarily as a "transition motor" and was gone by 1953.

A new pair of shift motors was soon introduced, and simplified model designations became Kiekhaefer's 1953 trademark. Merc's K nomenclature (as in KE7, KG9, etc.), used since 1940, gave way to motors known as "Mark" something. The two F-N-R engines, bred from the old KH7 Cruiser, were the 10-horse Mark 15 (so-called for its approximately 15-cubic-inch, KG4-type powerhead) and the 16-hp approximately 20-cube Mark 20. These rich green and silver outboards made use of a remote fuel tank system and featured styling so sleek it masked the power plant's capabilities.

Also available for 1953 were a popular 5-horse Mark 5; the updated KE4; a 7½-hp now called the Mark 7 (a brief factory memo offered dealers new Mark 7 ID plates in exchange for KE4 identification, which enabled 1947–52 new/old-stock KE4 motors to be sold as 1953 Mark 7 products); and the old 40-cubic-inch Mercury 25, KG9, renamed Mark 40. Most exotic of the 1953 Mercs was a neck-snapping Mark 40H. Company brochures correctly referred to this kicker as "the winningest thrill mill on water!"

In 1954 a batch of successful Mark 20 motors had their Tillotson carburetors replaced with Carter carbs, were given some strengthened parts, some gold accents, and a side-mounted spark advance lever, and were mounted on a Hydro-Short Quicky lower unit. The resulting Mark 20H kickers became the most popular stock racers in competitive outboard history.

Kiekhaefer's high-volume sales hopes, however, were pinned

The author displays his 1952 Mercury KG7H with Hydro-Short Quicksilver racing lower unit. (Gas tank color should be cedar green.) This was the motor to beat in the early 1950s. Notice that the lower cowling is gone. Most of these covers were removed and discarded by racers wanting a "meaner" look and faster access to engine components.

Early 1950s Mercury ads. They came to
the dealer several times a year in a packet
of Kiekhaefer promotional materials. Motor
price and dealership info were added at
the newspaper office.

to the brand-new 1954, four-in-line, 40-horse Mark 50. With a full
gearshift (finally!), optional electric start, and remote controls, it
clearly did OMC's 25-hp motors one better. A small gold crown
affixed to the Mark 50's face signaled Mercury's royal entry into
the profitable family-oriented water-skiing/cruising market. This
marked the first time Mercury offered a bigger shift motor than did
Evinrude and Johnson. While Carl Kiekhaefer owned the company,
it was a race Merc would always win.

Appropriately, 1955's big Mercury was labeled Mark 55.
Available with electric start (MercElectric Mark 55E), this 40-horse
rig's color scheme departed from traditional Merc green, making
its debut in a coral tint. Also updated for 1955 was the 20-cube
Hurricane, now in the form of a Mark 25 (and electric-starting
Mark 25E), wearing an 18-hp rating. A Mark 6 (5.9 hp) made its
entrance that year too. (Note: In many fall 1955 Mercury
showrooms, you could find a Mark 5, 6, and 7.)

Would there be a Mark 56 in 1956? No. The Mark 55 was
simply carried over from the previous year. New in that 40-cubic-
inch range, however, was the Mark 55H racer. Those wanting to
compete in the 30-cube outboard class were treated to the Turbo-

Four Mark 30H Mercury. A standard Mark 30 (as well as electric-start Mark 30E) provided small cruisers and family runabouts enough zip to handle extended ranges and pull a few water-skiers. It could be equipped with a steering arm for local control. Mark 25s of 1956 were rerated at 20 horses.

The company responsible for those legendary old green motors became increasingly design conscious, offering buyers an authentic Fifties choice of "Two-Tone Merchromatic Colors," like Sarasota Blue, Sand, Silver, Mercury Green (the original cedar green), Marlin Blue, Sunset Orange, Tan, and Gulf Blue.

Kids fond of arguing which motor was truly fastest sent a "Wow, keen!" Mercury's way in 1957. Mr. Kiekhaefer's 2-cycle engine research, begun for the government in World War II, led him to continue with the in-line cylinder format. Six such cylinders, yielding approximately 60 cubic inches of displacement, made up the sparkling new Mark 75E Marathon-Six. Johnson and Evinrude's premium 35s fell far short of this tall kicker's 60 hp. Folks thinking the Mark 75 actually had 75 hp understand why the PR people recommended such labeling.

Along with their great ideas, many famous inventors have embraced a clunker or two. Thomas Edison was long convinced that disc records were simply a flash in the pan compared to his cylindrical recordings.

Similarly, Carl Kiekhaefer held unusual convictions about reversing a big outboard. Perhaps the gearfoot failures of giant kickers like Riley and Fageol caused Merc's father to insist that such powerhouses would always rip up a standard reversing gearshift system. As a result, the huge Mercs were given Direct-Reverse. When backing, this mode actually called for the motor to be momentarily shut off and restarted in reverse! Even so, the Mark 75, with the industry's first single-lever remote control, was quite a machine.

Besides mass-producing the world's first six-cylinder, in-line, 2-cycle outboard, Mercury also put together a few Mark 75H racers. In 1958, a Quicksilver-lower-unit-equipped 75H on a little wooden hyro that was designed and driven by Seattle aircraft engineer, Hugh Entrop, "set a new official outboard speed record . . . [at almost 108 mph] returning the title to the United States for the first time since 1937. *Science & Mechanics* offered $5 plans for a somewhat similar 75H-powered boat.

The late Fifties were a time filled with the essence of "new." Old was getting squarer, outer space would soon be entered, and only items as sleek as rockets were perceived to have a future. Merc designers worked overtime shaping modern powerhead covers. A Trol Twin Rocket, Mark 10 model was fitted with a red top resembling a futuristic fireman's helmet. Engine exhaust shot through the propeller hub.

This 10-hp motor and 22-horse Mark 28 were the first Mercs to receive the "on your mark, get set" look in which the power-head seemed to be leaning forward with lower unit angled out in anticipation. Such a design reduced the possibility of snagging

When competitors Johnson and Evinrude unveiled their 1957 twin cylinder, 35-hp, top-of-the-line motors, Mercury took them by surprise with a tall, 6-cylinder, in-line Mark 75. This Marathon-Six sported 60 cubic inches and 60 hp. The Dyna-Float on the lower unit is a small shock absorber. (Mercury Marine)

In 1964 Carl Kiekhaefer celebrated his firm's 25th anniversary. Shown with a '64 3.9 h.p. single and one-lung 1940 Merc, the founder smiles for a publicity shot.

The first (1955) Mark 25 Mercs generated 18 horses. By 1956–57 this model was jumped to an even twenty. These quick little powerpacks came in a variety of cowl colors.

TRADE IN NOW
for a '57 Mercury!

MERCURY

Mark 25
MERCURY
20 h.p.-2 Cyl.

AS LOW AS
$**00**DOWN
Up to 24 months to pay

See us today for highest trades on the new '57 Mercurys with a *new kind of performance!*

DEALER IMPRINT

underwater weeds. Dyna Float suspension rubber-mounted the motor leg for smoother operation. In keeping with the modern theme, these outboards came with spring-loaded, automatic F-N-R transmissions. When they worked, they were OK, but few Merc repair shops enjoyed getting one that didn't. No other manufacturer had such a shifter.

Needless to say, you could always tell a Mercury from its competitors. For 1958 OMC dealers were shipped chubby V-4, 50-horse engines, but Mercury bested its rivals by 20 hp with its lanky new Mark 78E.

Motors from six-cylinder versions to the Mark 6 twin were tested at Kiekhaefer's Lake X. Fabled to be secret, this private Florida waterway was equipped with jump ramps, obstructive logs, and anything else that might stress an outboard. A couple of Mark 75A (60-horse) powered runabouts spent 68 days on Lake X in continuous operation, racking up 50,000 miles each. The boats were refueled, food provided, and drivers switched while in motion. The "record endurance run [meant to represent many years of typical outboard use] . . . at an average speed of 30.3 mph was certified by the U.S. Auto Club." That way, OMC couldn't dispute it.

Although Carl Kiekhaefer successfully augmented Mercury's performance image via factory-built racing models, he was well aware the fast little power plants set few sales records. Johnson and Evinrude produced no competition outboards from World War II through the later Sixties, but were very busy turning out thousands of family-oriented motors. Kiekhaefer aimed for a greater degree of that lucrative leisure market and decided to make 1958 the final year his firm would offer a Quicksilver racer. Consequently, the approximately 30-cubic-inch Mark 30H became the last 1950s' Mercury of its type. Those looking hard enough, however, discovered a tiny scattered stock of leftover Mark 20H, 55H, and 30H rigs through the very early 1960s. The Kiekhaefer Corporation completed the Eisenhower decade still on top of the horsepower hill with their six-cylinder, in-line, 70-horse Mark 78A.

As 1960 Mercurys were ushered in, the well-worn model nomenclature *Mark* was shown the back door. Kiekhaefer borrowed an old Martin motor ID technique in which engines are named with their approximate horsepower and an extra zero. Thus, the 10-horse motor became Merc 100; the new 80-hp powerhouse was called Merc 800, and so on. (Exceptions included the likes of a 22-hp Merc 200 and a 35-horse model known as Merc 300.)

With the updated designations came a complete de-emphasis on exotic color schemes. Most Mercs of the late Fifties and very early Sixties were clean white. By 1962 the first black Mercurys would debut.

Kiekhaefer still had hopes for his big Direct-Reverse models. The 70- and 80-hp motors were offered with this drive system in 1960 and 1961. A gearshift version was available in 1961, and logically, soon replaced direct-reversing Mercs.

The year 1962 became one of the most notable in Mercury outboard history. First, all models got equipped with Jet-Prop, through-the-propeller hub exhaust. (The firm's major boat show displays included a gigantic silver prop turning slowly and blowing colored streamers via a hidden fan attached to the hub.)

Finally, the world's first 100-hp production outboard, the big Merc 1000, was unveiled. Something about all those zeroes captured the public's fancy, and even die-hard Evinrude/Johnson fans (OMC's top motor had 25 fewer horses in 1962) couldn't help but salute Mercury's notable achievement.

Kiekhaefer had decided in summer 1961 to merge his company with the Brunswick Corporation. A recreation-oriented conglomerate with interests in everything from a pop record label to bowling equipment manufacturing, Brunswick was happy to acquire Mercury's expanding consumer marine propulsion niche. This amalgamation brought extra fiscal strength to Merc but quickly placed its iron-willed founder in an environment where he no longer called the shots.

Within a few years, Brunswick deleted the vintage Kiekhaefer Mercury logo in favor of a Mercury Marine nameplate, and in 1970 Carl Kiekhaefer left what was once his organization.

Prior to this departure, a pair of interesting, limited-edition, competition Mercs was introduced. One, the 7.2-cubic-inch Merc 60J, wore a pint-size edition of the old Quicksilver lower unit. It was meant to be raced by kids and petite women and could get a mini hull going 40 mph. The other rig came in the form of a 125-hp powerhouse suitable for rugged, offshore races.

Meanwhile, Brunswick concentrated on marketing a wide range of consumer outboards and MerCruiser stern drives. The big company's methodical promotion was quite successful but lacked Kiekhaefer's "let's take a chance on this one" flair.

Perhaps wanting to do to Brunswick's Mercury what Ole Evinrude did with Elto to his former firm, Mr. Kiekhaefer started a company called Kiekhaefer Aeromarine Motors. While a few Aeromarine kickers were developed for auxiliary sailboat power, and some snowmobile engines were built for Bolens, Kiekhaefer's second dream didn't materialize. The outboard pioneer, who ran a prominent boat motor concern with greater nerve and individuality than anyone before or since, passed away in 1983.

The "aftermarket" Cyclone exhaust stack from a small, Midwestern manufacturer dresses up a Merc KG-7Q—and makes it a lot louder too.

5 | Private Brands

On a Monday morning in 1913 some guy at Sears-Roebuck told coworkers about a very strange sight. He had witnessed two fishermen hang an unusual metal contraption on the stern of a little rowboat. One angler cranked the thing's top, causing smoke to sputter from the device, which proceeded to move their craft right past the other fishing boats, allowing first dibs on the big ones.

"We'd better look into that," suggested one of the mail-order store's buyers. "Could be something to it. . Somebody see who can make a few for us."

The next year's Sears catalog included a genuine Motorgo (built by the Lockwood-Ash Company) rowboat motor, and the private-brand outboard was born.

A private-brand motor is any kicker designed and constructed by one company for sale through some other firm. Breweries often do this type of thing by producing beer (complete with a custom label) for a grocery store chain. Private-brand outboards, like those brewed supermarket counterparts, are generally intended to be a little less chic than their name-brand cousins. Consequently, their price tags are smaller.

The lineage of many private-brand engines is clearly recognizable. Uniqueness in these badge-engineered rigs is found only in a decal, a paint scheme, or a minor, cosmetic cowling feature. Other rigs were made of a major's stock of leftover or obsolete parts. While these models' appearance contained a hint of their better-known kin, they retained a specific distinction.

Outboard makers often viewed private-brand contracts as financial blessings. Not only did such agreements mean the certain sale of a large block of motors, but shelves of theretofore surplus parts began producing revenue. A strong desire to keep the wholesale purchasers happy resulted in some pretty good and attractively priced outboard motors.

The early Sears Motorgo outboards were soon followed by Montgomery Ward's (Caille-produced) Hiawatha rowboat motors. Other vintage marques, such as Sweet, Anderson, Blakely, and (some

Sears ad featuring a Caille-built 1930 Motorgo outboard.

The Old Outboard Book   48

Caille-built) Gray kickers, were most probably private-brand motors. This book's outboard list (see Chapter 11) provides more detail.

By the early 1930s Outboard Motors Corporation, later Outboard Marine and Manufacturing, began taking on private-brand contracts for the likes of Montgomery Ward and Canada's Eaton stores.

During the late Thirties, Thor, a struggling marque in its own right, badge-engineered some Sea Kings. Unfortunately, these poor performers contributed to the firm's demise. A stock of the rejected motors, however, gave birth to the Mercury outboard line.

Scott-Atwater got its start building Champions (originally sold through Firestone stores) and then Firestone-brand kickers.

Waterwitch, Sear's outboard name plate from 1936 to 1945, had numerous origins. The most unusual actually came from the world's most prolific outboard company—Johnson! Built from aging stock, the Model 550.75 Waterwitches by Johnson lingered in Sears catalogs from 1938 to 1940. Neither Sears nor Johnson retained much information about the motor (which was actually an OK-75 Johnson). Information concerning other rare Thirties private brands, such as the little Kingfisher, has been largely forgotten.

It appears the Great Depression created another sort of private brand. Reportedly, a number of outboard dealers, struggling to survive the broken economy, made their own motors from spare parts. Typically, these rigs wore a brand name (like Evinrude or Elto), but didn't look exactly like anything in the current catalog. Any "weirdo" from about 1931 to about 1936 just might be such a concoction. Of course, the outboard manufacturers were not happy with this practice, but it served as a trade-off for Depression-era bargain motor sales held at factory showrooms.

In 1938 things brightened up a bit, and Outboard Marine and Manufacturing shifted much private-brand work to its Gale Products Division. Montgomery Ward's Sea King and Western Auto's Western Flyer were just two marques to originate at this Galesburg, Illinois, facility.

Post–World War II kicker demand sent OMC's private-brand plant into high gear, and by 1951 the busy factory was cranking out 3-, 5-, and 12-hp motors in seven badge-engineered versions. A few more (short-lived) private-brand contracts, such as Aimcee Wholesale Corporation's AMC Saber, sent the Gale staff into overtime.

During this era, one-third of all outboard motor sales was attributed to private brands. Thousands of that number came from the West Bend Aluminum Company and were marketed under Sears's Elgin label.

The Fifties' "bigger is better" philosophy increased many private-brand offerings to full-range (1.5-hp to over-35-hp) lines. Scores of family runabouts and cruisers got powered by large Elgins, Buccaneers, Sea-Bees, Firestones, and Brooklures. Even so, private-brand horsepower ratings were traditionally a bit lower

Logo for the Sears Waterwitch, which was built by Kissel.

The Wizard, circa 1946, built by Kiekhaefer Mercury.

than comparable major-brand models. For example, Gale Products' 1955 top-of-the-line units produced 22 hp, compared to the conglomerate's Evinrude and Johnson 25.

Flashiest of the Fifties private brands was no doubt the Wizard. Made for Western Auto by Kiekhaefer Mercury, Wizards shared Merc's fast "ball and roller bearing power" design. While other private brands' modest literature featured practical aspects of owning a nice, low-priced motor, Wizard's 1953 brochure boasted two world's speed records!

> In races run under supervision of the National Outboard Association at Memphis, Tennessee, a Wizard 10 skimmed the measured mile at 48.8 mph to set a new world's record for class "B" modified service runabouts. A Wizard also won the class "A" race—on the same day [7/20/52]—establishing a new world's record for that classification of 45.1 mph. Both records [were] officially recognized by the NOA.

The pamphlet indicated these Wizards were "modified for racing," which probably means they rode on high-speed Mercury Quicksilver lower units.

The aforementioned records were obtained "legally" in sanctioned events. Racing legend holds, however, that some class "A" racers (officially restricted to outboards with piston displacement less than 15 cubic inches) disguised the "look-alike" 18.34-cube Wizard 10 powerhead under a Mercury (class "A") gas tank. When such a rig was mated to the Quicksilver lower unit, it gave an unfair cylinder-size advantage over those who followed rules. Because this practice was allegedly pulled off below the Mason-Dixon line, such a motor got dubbed a "Southern A."

Unlike most private brands, Wizards were nationally advertised in such publications as *Field and Stream*, *Sports Afield*, *Outdoor Life*, and *True*. Western Auto even commissioned a 16-mm motion picture called *Sea Chasers*. This half-hour film about exciting professionals who search oceans to stock Miami's Seaquarium featured shots of sharks, dolphins, and working Wizard outboards. Civic clubs and sports groups could borrow a copy by writing to Western Auto.

After 1957 the "Medium (pea soup) Green" (with red decals) Merc-built Wizards were no longer marketed, although a few remote, independently owned Western Auto stores had leftovers through the early Sixties. Going out in style were some Wizard Super 10 rigs. They had finally been given remote fuel tanks, upped to almost 20 cubic inches (using the noted Merc Hurricane block), and supplied with special crankshafts from Mercury's recently discontinued Mark 20H racer![1]

No one appears certain why Kiekhaefer stopped Wizard production. Some say growing sales of its name-brand Mercury models simply required more and more manufacturing space. Suggestions have also surfaced indicating Mercury dealers wanted Kiekhaefer-built Wizards off the market. They realized the generic, lower-priced Wizard actually had an uncomfortable number of

thoroughbred Mercury features. Private-brand motors were meant for a marketplace somewhat less sophisticated than the marina/boat store clientele. When Wizard began acquiring a reputation, it stepped over a sacred boundary.

Significant line changes in the early-to-mid-Sixties outboard industry affected private-branding. OMC's Gale Products' Gale-Buccaneer closed up shop in 1964. Along with it went the last of its private-brand contracts. McCulloch, which evolved from Scott-Atwater, acted as this era's leading private-brander, producing the final Elgin and subsequent Sears and Ted Williams marques. It even gave Western Auto a late-Fifties–early-Sixties spin with nicely stylized Wizards (featuring PowerBail automatic bailing). West Bend, so renowned for its fine Elgin contributions, eventually made some Wizards and then sold out to Chrysler.

Large auto-related retailers (Firestone, Goodyear, and B.F. Goodrich), once eager to market a complete line of private-brand kickers, decided to get back to basics. As a result, they either dropped their outboard line entirely, or went with a drastically reduced offering of a couple of fishing motors. When the latter occurred, a small company, such as Clinton or Eska, usually gained the contract. Remaining late 1960s private brands were largely the province of minor producers. Single-cylinder, air-cooled Tecumseh powerheads were the standard fare.

By the mid-1970s foreign-made kickers appeared at large American retail chains. Additionally, major U.S. outboard firms, such as Mercury, began obtaining Japanese motors to sell under their own and subsidiary (such as Mariner) labels.

Over the years, parts and service problems have plagued private-brand owners. Many major brand's franchised repair departments prejudicially view such rigs as troublesome orphans. I recall visiting a busy big-name outboard dealership when a man carried in a private-brand rig that "wouldn't idle too good." The shop's three mechanics rolled their eyeballs. After superficially examining that 5-horse twin, one technician recommended, "Do yourself a favor; go into our showroom and trade up to a real motor!"

In reality, of course, private-brand kickers are as authentic as any brand-name motor. And most importantly, since 1914 they have been responsible for an impressive amount of outboarding pleasure.

1. Lawrence Carpenter, "Antique Corner—Wizard," *Trailer Boats* (January 1989), p. 164.

Lockwood Chief-type Sea King 15

Outboard Motors Corporation raised much needed early 1930s capital by relabeling some of its product for Montgomery Ward. In 1932, late-model Elto Quads, Lockwood Chiefs, and Evinrude Speeditwins, among others, were marketed by Wards under their Sea King banner.

Evinrude Speeditwin-based Sea King 22

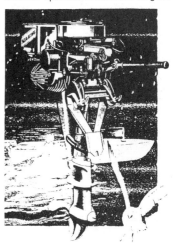

Notes

6

Where Have All the Old Outboards Gone?

Down South a fellow noticed the strangest looking tree. It had three large trunks originating at a lumpy, rooty base. Wedged between and grown firmly into the rough trio was a knot or something shaped like an outboard motor. No one seemed to be home, so the curious individual jumped a rickety fence for a closer inspection.

Suddenly, an elderly lady appeared in the yard and verified the "bump" in the tree's middle was indeed an Evinrude motor. Her late husband had, years ago, leaned it there. Over time the tree had grown around the outboard. She said the leaves were a nuisance and anyone having the tree completely removed could take the Evinrude free of charge.

Up North lived new owners of an old lakeside cabin. All fall they'd been feeding a stony fireplace with cordwood found on their recently acquired side porch. During one quick evening trip to the chilly veranda, four or five logs were gathered. A cold, medium-size stick for kindling seemed stuck to the floor. Hearty tugs were exercised, toppling the surrounding wood onto the ground. That man fetching fuel for the fire was surprised to be grasping a contraption complete with copper gas tank. It was a 1913 Waterman outboard, buried under chopped wood for nearly half a century.

Not every motor lives long enough to create such tales. The vociferous scrap drives of World War II and the Korean Conflict claimed tons of early examples.

As a kid, I witnessed a frustrated fisherman echo discouraging words across our lake. His ancient Sea King single had caught fire in the sunset, and he finally claimed victory over the perpetually balky eggbeater by loosening its lone transom clamp and waving "bye-bye." If waterways had rubber drain plugs that could be pulled up, we'd all find a tremendous stockpile of rusty relics.

For decades boat shops and marinas were great places to locate classic outboards. Establishments with questionable storage sheds featuring broken windows provided obvious havens for wayward motors. By the late 1970s, however, the pleasure-boating industry became so upscale that those little old boat and motor places, if occupying some key waterfront locale, were revamped and divested of their iron goodies. Most of the legendary one-man motor repair shops simply went the way of the wind. Tiny "junque"-filled outboard dealerships, usually the home of some second-string brand, have also become a rarity.

A spring 1975 college outing led me to Boston. There I spied a time-worn outboard store which turned out to have a cellar full of old motors. Minutes later and $35 lighter, I carefully walked upstairs with a nice little Clarke Troller. My vow to return for other classic iron was thwarted that summer, however, when urban renewal flattened the place. No one seemed to know what had happened to the proprietor and his classic kickers.

Even when it's impossible to locate a remarkably run-down rural boat shop run by some guy with poor sentence structure, don't assume that the old motor stream has dried up. While many models are scarce, enough old "bread and butter" outboards still exist for everyone to enjoy.

Actually, the best place to find old kickers continues to be the outboard dealership. Usually, antique motors displayed in a marine outlet are not for sale, but their presence often sensitizes customers to the fact that vintage rigs shouldn't be discarded. By the same token, marina owners need floor space for stuff normal people buy, and they can't accept every old putt-putt coming through the turnstile. As a result, the local boat place is a good spot to obtain castoffs, or at least good old-engine leads.

A local radio station swap-shop show and weekly paper's classified sections always provide outboard collectors paths toward old iron. Amidst badly spelled ads for FREE HOUSE BORKEN PUPPIES and SIZE 14 WEDDING GOWN, NEVER WORN, a WANTED—OLD OUTBOARD MOTORS request may command attention.

Serious engine enthusiasts sometimes spend a few dollars printing up their desire on business cards (or on photocopied slips of paper). You never know who'll see one of these cards posted in a restaurant, shopping mall, or laundromat. They also can be handed out at gas stations, junkyards, hardware stores, small engine repair shops, and the like. The more folks who know you're nuts about old motors and think you'll actually pay cash for Uncle Waldo's corroded fishin' engine, the faster your collection will grow.

Unlike classic cars, aged outboards take up little space and have been stacked away in peculiar places. While waterside communities hold the best discovery bets, old motors have even popped up at flea markets held in desert towns. Throughout burgs with more grass, lawn sales frequently provide point-of-purchase eggbeater opportunities.

The author's "business" card advertises his hobby.

Old phonebooks are a good resource for tracking old dealers.

Although they don't usually grow on (or in) trees, vintage kickers yet to be found are out there, and in the craziest locations.

"My neighbor is in big trouble and could really use your help," a business associate told me. He recounted the story, one heard all too often, and I sprinted for the car.

"You're here!" the distressed fellow exclaimed as I pulled into his driveway. "It's hidden in the garage," he whispered.

While walking toward the building, the guy recounted how his compulsive behavior at a bar and subsequent weekend auction had placed him in authentic hot water.

"Bought myself an old outboard motor and a heap of yelling from my wife! If you'd just give me what I got in it and get the stinkin' thing outta here quick, I could probably patch things up with her."

The poor fellow's rather violent-looking spouse gave us the evil eye from a back-porch vantage point. She was aggressively operating one of those pulley clotheslines.

"Are you at all interested in the motor?" the desperate man asked. "See, I've been sleeping on the couch since last Saturday."

He paused briefly to rub his lower back while I inquired, "What kind of outboard is it?"

"Oh, someone said it's a Clinton . . . a 4-cycle, cylinder electric-starting Clinton. But actually," he stated, crestfallen, "I don't know and wouldn't even know where to look."

Typically, Clinton specialized in small, garden-variety, 2-cycle, single-cylinder kickers. Such a mysterious assessment, coupled with an electric-start description, really threw me for a loop! It must have had the same effect on a few other old-motor nuts who phoned prior to my arrival. The generic Clinton ID had kept them away.

Well, the strange Clinton turned out to be a Johnson VA-50, a very limited-production, electric-starting model dating back to 1930. The deluxe rig was meant to be mated to a classy Aqua-Flyer boat and today represents the rarest of four-cylinder Johnsons.

My glowing account brightened the fellow's face, and he was, no doubt, about to boost the asking price significantly. As fate would have it, however, the wife's other clothesline pulley was hooked to the garage. Its sharp, vicious-sounding squeak startled the fellow into divulging he'd actually paid only $10 for the old engine. That unlubricated squeal prompted my host to offer free, next-day delivery. The VA-50 was the first misidentified putt-putt I'd taken on for humanitarian reasons.

In retrospect, that unusual Johnson might have produced a greater interest level had the contraption been properly advertised to collectors. But as its erstwhile owner noted, ready knowledge of make, model, and year was the critical factor he lacked.

My first vintage kicker, assumed to be a 1922, was later identified as a '28. The misidentification was corrected only after writing the manufacturer with a model number.

Nowadays, letters to most old outboard firms will come back "address unknown." The remaining companies seldom have the archival staff eager to research aged motor topics. As a result, the ability to locate basic outboard data is crucial to enjoying vintage motors.

Few companies set out to hide the identity of their products. A well-running outboard emblazoned with a bright gas tank decal held great promotional power. Unfortunately, these labels were often worn away by years of having fuel spilled on them. If your rig still sports a decal, though, you've probably got a good idea as to its manufacture.

Model and serial numbers are very important, and on many kickers may be found stamped into the flywheel's rope sheave plate. Regrettably, many a rope sheave, removed to inspect or service the magneto, got dropped overboard or was simply misplaced. Because plates from other motors would sometimes fit, there are plenty of old kickers wearing incorrect identities.

Some companies wisely stamped the serial number (and model) on the engine block. (Be careful not to confuse them with casting part numbers.) If those digits disagree with the rope sheave (or fuel-tank-based ID stamp), something got switched somewhere.

Remember, most of these motors came from a time when people went to great lengths to repair, fix up, or modify a tired engine inexpensively. Typically, money was scarcer than time. If a part that would *sort of* fit could be scrounged for a few dollars, there were plenty of tiny machine shops and backyard mechanics willing to complete the job.

I once found a battery-ignition early-Thirties Elto Quad elaborately fitted with a 1929 Johnson V-45 flywheel and magneto. It sure looked weird, but it apparently worked. Also in that category was a bargain-basement Sears Waterwitch single that some talented tinkerer had equipped with a lower-unit gear shifter—years before such mechanisms were commercially available.

Owners of racing motors were often the chief switcheroo offenders, as provocative modification in competitive circles was part of the fun. If some guy's championship racing engine had been treated with a purple cylinder head and no muffler, similar modifications would soon proliferate. By the way, the stock mufflers probably got tossed. In any event, whether you have a service motor or racer, a little enjoyable detective work will usually reveal a rationale for the refitting.

1938–40 Sears Waterwitches, produced by Johnson. This rare private-brand kicker differed from Johnson's OK-75 motors only in its rope sheave plate cover. Consequently, to satisfy the Sears contract, Johnson simply cast new rope sheaves with the Waterwitch marque. Few were put into circulation. A Johnson version of this outboard, produced in its Canadian plant, had detachable cylinder heads and lots of power. It was a favorite in remote areas of Canada. Johnson's "Eskimo Motors" were available through the early 1950s.

Best Bets for Locating ID Numbers

Brand	ID Number Location
Champion	Many post-World War II Champ products are identified by small transom clamp bracket ID plates.
Elto	Earlier models: Fuel tank should have metal ID plate. Serial number also stamped into engine block. Later models: Small ID plate should be on transom bracket or steering arm support.
Evinrude	Many early models had alloy tags soldered into gas tank. Look for some model numbers stamped into front of engine block. Identification is also found on plate mounted to steering arm or transom bracket. (Note: On post-1929 Evinrude, Elto, and OMC motors, model number is first three or four digits of designation. Serial number occupies the figure's remainder. Thus, Evinrude #1770015 is the fifteenth motor in the model 177 series.)
Johnson	Early Johnsons featured rope sheave plate IDs. Vintage electric-start models (i.e., the VA-50) had model stamped into the starter motor cover's thin rim. Most Johnsons had serial number stamped into the block. Motors that had rewind but no rope sheave plate sported the ID and the model designation on the block. By the Fifties, most Johnson numbers were put on transom bracket plates.
Lockwood	Rope sheave plate usually tells the story.
Martin	Look for a small plate on steering handle or (Martin 200) on motor leg.
Mercury	Early Mercs had some numbers placed on rope sheave. Throughout the years some got tagged on motor leg. Most of the classic "green" models were ID'd on the tank rim plate. (KF9/KG9 plates were put on front cover.)
Scott-Atwater	The important numbers are usually found on a transom bracket plate.

Each outboard maker had its own model and serial number code. Some, like the Koban (noted in the motor list chapter) and post–World War II Scott-Atwater, revealed the kicker's year through its numbers. For example, a model *473* is a 1947 Scott-Atwater. A *509* comes from 1950, and so on. Model numbers from 1952 through 1957 had the final two digits of the year reversed in the last pair of the four-numeral model designation (e.g., 371*25* would be a 1952 motor). Just like life, there were exceptions to these and other manufacturers' ID rules.

In 1925 the Johnson people gave their outboard model designations a logical -25 suffix (e.g., A-25, J-25). They added five to that figure in 1926, so new model designations were suffixed with -30 (e.g., P-30). This "plus five" practice continued through 1936, when an -80 suffix was issued. Most 1937 Johnsons wore a -37 suffix; 1938s a -38; and '39s a -39. It was -10 for 1940 and, typically, -15 in 1941.

Again, there were numerous violations of this rule. Some A-35 (1927) Johnsons, for example, were 1928 motors. There were also pre–World War II Johnsons designated model 100, 200, and 300, not in keeping with the suffix system.

The letter *B* in a Johnson model name (such as PB-30) usually signified a bronze lower unit (suited for ocean use). There was a model B Johnson, however, that sported a standard aluminum lower unit which *bolted* to the boat instead of being affixed via transom clip thumbscrews. Getting back to the high seas, 1920s Evinrudes containing an *S* in their model names (e.g., TS, NS) were bronze lower unit versions meant for saltwater applications.

Johnson and Lockwood stamped an *R* in the model description of their racing outboards. The fast version of Johnson's alternate-firing twin K was dubbed KR. Please note, however, that Johnson made a military version of the 22-horse PO called POLR. It was *not* a racing engine. Post–World War II Sea Horse 25s model RD rigs were not racers either. So not everything fit into the "R = racing motor" lexicon.

Elto's high-speed models often had an *H* stamped after the serial number. Merc's H outboards were racers, too, but that *H* stood for the Hydro-Short streamlined lower unit.

About the only quasi-universal nomenclature was the *L*. Typically, such a designation at the conclusion of a model description signifies a *l*ong-shaft lower unit.

Some kickers, especially old, private-brand, catalog store models, are now virtually devoid of ID. And more than one old-outboard enthusiast has encountered a real mystery motor. Fortunately, such challenge is another enjoyable aspect of the antique outboard hobby.

Be advised there are still a number of homebrew rigs out there. Few are more than a discarded lower unit fitted to a lawn mower or garden tractor engine. Even though none existed commercially, both John Deere and Wheel Horse outboards pop up occasionally.

In any event, keeping this info at hand may allow you to help a troubled neighbor getting static for bidding on some dusty old Johnson PBL-30. You'll quickly deduce it's a 1926 *l*ong, bronze-shaft, and will drive away with a classic little outboard gold mine!

"Oh, it's you again," the busy outboard dealer sighed into his multi-line telephone.

An elderly woman's feeble voice stated, "Yes, I'm

How much is it worth?

calling for the old motor appraisal you promised me."

"OK, ma'am," the marine store proprietor said, while reaching into a bottom desk drawer for a dusty booklet. "What kind of outboard you say it is?"

"Well . . . there's a little sign on it that looks like it says Buccaneer."

"OK, any numbers on it?"

"Well . . . there's a 12. Twelve horse . . . power."

"OK, what year?"

"Oh, my goodness, well . . . my late husband bought it the year President Eisenhower . . . right around 1953. What do you feel it's worth?"

"That's hard to know, ma'am, but this 1960 used outboard motor guide I'm looking at says a good one would have brought sixty-five bucks back then. 'Course that was years ago."

"So you're saying it has increased in value?"

"Uh . . . well, you know how much prices have gone up on antiques. Some of that old stuff probably sells for 10 times what it's worth."

"Ten times you say?"

"I guess. . . ."

"Thank you, young man," said the widow.

That phone call helped her decide that anything less than $650 for the weathered Buccaneer would be an insult to her husband's memory. Because nobody wanted the motor at anywhere near that price, it was a recollection she long held.

Although there are some classic outboards which command a good dollar, most contain greater sentimental than monetary value. Back in the Sixties only an exceptional kicker would bring more than $15 to $25. Five-dollar motors were commonplace. Many overloaded dealers would calculate a "scrap" price, selling you the kicker and loose parts by the carload.

Thirty years later, a few $500-plus motors have been noted, but their $10 counterparts are still available (especially from bulging collections). For most tinkerers, it's the reasonable-ticket aspect of old outboarding which makes such a pastime enjoyable.

Perhaps you'll feel this chapter is geared more toward the buyer than the seller. But for quite some time, there have been more old outboards looking for homes than people interested in housing them. Until this supply and demand quotient shifts, antique motors can fit into most any budget.

Without insulting the owner, an old-outboard seeker should ask the following questions:

1. *Is it a "freshwater" motor?* The majority of engines used in salty waterways have seriously corroded parts. Unless the saltwater motor has been flushed regularly, is a special bronze-lower-unit

saltwater model, is otherwise scarce, or was owned by a past President, it might not represent a good buy.

2. *Does the motor have all its parts? Are there any damaged, cracked, or broken parts?* As in automotive circles, the sum of an outboard's parts is often greater than its total price. The innocent-looking $25 motor, missing a rewind starter assembly, propeller, and gas cap, isn't really a $25 engine.

3. *Can you rotate the flywheel?* If a motor is stuck, chances are its piston(s) are bonded to the cylinder wall. A complete overhaul may be required. Note: Should the motor "turn-over" with some resistance, or do so with lots of play (from side to side) in the crankshaft, major repairs are likely to be needed.

4. *Is there good compression?* With a finger-tight spark plug and lubricated piston-cylinder assembly, a promising motor will demonstrate some compression "bounce."

5. *Is there any spark?* Don't ask the seller to hold the plug wires while you pull the starter cord. Although, if you do ask and he refuses, chances are that motor has run in his lifetime. Ask to remove the spark plug, ground it against the cylinder, and quickly rotate the flywheel. You should see a spark jump between the plug's gap. (Battery-ignition models require a 6-volt DC source.)

6. *What is the condition of exterior finish, including decals?* Because a "nice, original" condition motor is considered more valuable than a restored rig, everything from faded paint to gasoline-worn starting-instruction stickers comes under consideration here. More than a few vintage putt-putts have been brush-stroked red by some well-meaning fixer-upper. If authenticity is your goal, however, three coats of house paint will not make your job easier.

7. *Is there original equipment or accessories?* Find out whether the owner retained any instruction booklets, sales literature, a motor stand, the original packing case, and so on. The answer is usually no, but it never hurts to ask.

8. *Does the outboard run?* Remember, every motor "worked the last time it was used," so don't get caught up in that infamous play on words. Someone with an operating engine will usually provide a brief demonstration. Even if the thing is "fired up dry" (on a sawhorse) for 5 or 10 seconds, you'll know it has compression, spark, and quasi-complete carburetion. Multi-family mouse nests under the cover can also tell you something about this topic.

9. *Do you really want this particular motor?* This is a very subjective question not always easy to answer. I usually ask myself, If the old motor doesn't fit in with the rest of my valuable equipment, can I pass it along to someone else for the same price?

When purchasing an old outboard, never attempt stealing the thing through intimidation. Comments like "What a piece of junk!" or "You called me out here to see this?" will leave a sour taste. A better way to soften the reality that the seller's '51 Martin isn't the only old kicker known to exist might be to show a snapshot of

Motors from bygone days, ready to come out of retirement.

some rigs in your collection. Perhaps point out that although it's a nice example of a vintage motor, there are some parts missing and it has an incomplete decal. The seller will sometimes take exception to such assessments, but remember that afore-mentioned widow. She wasn't selling a tinny eggbeater as much as offering a cherished memento. You may see a bashed-in gas tank; the seller visualizes Uncle Louis sputtering to some long-forgotten dock with a full stringer of perch.

Speaking of fishermen, there are plenty who'd gladly pay $200 for a nice-running old outboard that is worth $50. Because a new 5-horse fishin' engine can produce sticker shock, a good vintage model is typically worth more to an angler than it is to a collector.

In deference to the average-condition kicker, super-nice motors make me nervous. Because I fear "scratch and dent" incidents, primo motors in my collection seldom see water. Come to think of it, beat-up Elgins, incapable of idling on both cylinders, have provided a more relaxing brand of fun than my "nearly mint" originals. Everybody approaches old outboarding differently, but it seems the hobby is best supported by a rig (albeit hopelessly weathered) receiving regular exercise.

Placing an exact dollar value on old motors is very difficult. Obviously, the person wanting a certain outboard the most will pay the highest price. Anyone who has spent a bundle, however, knows that the weekend after you do so, some guy in your church will clean out his basement and present you with one just like it!

Sellers claiming they've just turned down 10 grand for their motor often sing a new tune when you demonstrate that your collection contains three similar models . . . and then ask for the $10,000 bidder's phone number.

As previously noted, well-cared-for, original-condition motors top the value list. Although such popularity is cyclical, good 1950s

models command interest. Factory racers and hot-rod motors are prized by collectors. Outboards wearing a lot of brass parts receive attention. Very old (pre–World War I) examples are also popular with some antique buffs. In general the big brand old-timers seem to generate the most conversation. Because many Johnson, Evinrude, and Mercurys were sold through the years, lots of people remember them and seek such products today.

Finally, the tiny ½-hp eggbeaters and novel Clarke Trollers often bring buyers. These motors are easy to handle (but seldom run very well) and produce a focal point in a showroom or basement display. Conversely, huge rigs like Johnson's TR-40 Giant Twin and the Cross Radial have their following.

Old outboards probably shouldn't be purchased only as "big investments." Although it's been tried, no one having done so has received recognition from Wall Street. A vintage kicker is best acquired by someone who will obtain pleasure from its history, repair, care, and use. Pride demonstrated by new owners of everything from rare twin-carbed racing engines to garden-variety Scott-Atwater singles is the fuel that makes the antique outboard world go round. Here, fortunately, value is predominantly in the beholder's eye.

Parts department

In 1929 the Detroit-Parks Airplane Company built eight model P-2A Speedster biplanes. Years later, author Richard Bach acquired an operable member of this tiny production run and did a bit of old-fashioned Midwestern barnstorming. During that 1966 recreation, he met a friend in Palmyra, Wisconsin, who asked to give the rare plane a try.

Unfortunately, upon landing, the friend cracked up the vintage craft. Pushing the damaged biplane to within 10 feet of a little hangar, they set about making repairs. But it was no use. A wing strut, 100-percent unique to the original eight P-2A airplanes, was hopelessly shot.

An old guy watching from the nearby weathered hangar called out, "Need any help, fellas?"

Mr. Bach shook his head, saying, "Not unless you have a left wing strut for a 1929 Detroit-Parks Speedster biplane model P-2A!"

The onlooker began rummaging through his hangar and soon emerged with the factory-original replacement part.

It surely would be neat if that kind of thing always happened to everyone. How rewarding it would be simply to head to the local outboard dealer and pick up, say, a crankshaft for some 1940 Clarke Troller 2.7-hp twin . . . or even gaskets for a 1961 Evinrude.

Fortunately, there are times when critical parts do show up. They usually appear in one of four ways:

1. *New/old stock.* These new, but obsolete, components have been sitting around (taking up room) for years. Because they're small, new/old-stock stuff can hide in most any shop.
2. *Used.* Often a result of a "parted-out" motor, used parts run a close second to new, more difficult to obtain pieces.
3. *Reproductions.* A few critical outboard parts are now being manufactured by old kicker buffs. Included in this category are decals, Elto Speedster timer cam bushings, and the like.
4. *Parts motors.* Some old outboards are simply too shot (or salt-ridden) for restoration. Generally available for a few bucks, these "junked car" counterparts frequently contain pieces usable on similar models.

The Antique Outboard Motor Club's *Newsletter* (mailed eight times annually) is a great tool for parts searchers. Members can place free ads, while nonmembers pay only a nominal fee. The publication's readers hold literally tons of old outboard parts from 1910 to 1980. Like the old fellow in the airplane hangar, many AOMC people enjoy surprising kicker fixer-uppers who believe they're stuck.

Parts Sources

The first two editions of *The Old Outboard Book* contained a short list of parts sources that readers generally found helpful. With an "evergreen" book like this, though, particularly in our fast-paced economy, such lists are quickly outdated. Instead, get on the Internet. One useful Web site is Antique Outboard Motor Club, www.aomci.org. Anyone considering the revitalization of a vintage kicker should access this site, join the Club, and take advantage of its member services. One of the AOMC home page's favorite venues is its free classified section where people try to buy, sell, or swap motors. There's also an opportunity to ask questions about vintage outboards. No true AOMC'er wants anyone to get ripped off. To that end, there will usually be "old time" collectors who will gladly try steering novices in the right direction. It's always best to correspond with experienced buffs in order to get a sense of a motor's or part's worth and availability.

When I was just starting out, my 1930s Johnson needed a propeller. Perhaps sensing my over-the-barrel predicament, a marina offered me a rather chewed-up wheel for $22.50 in a "take it or leave it, kid" deal. Serendipitously, at an AOMC meet a few days later, a guy with a pickup filled with old iron sold me a decent prop for ten bucks and included the Johnson it was attached to. Suddenly, my Sea Horse collection had doubled. Not everything works out like that, but the AOMC site allows you the luxury of doing some homework and becoming a more informed old outboard enthusiast. It also offers an ever-lengthening list of outboard-related links and happily makes this chapter's job much easier and more effective.

7

Outboard Accessories

True or false? A well-known kicker company actually marketed a thing with wheels on which groceries or its motors could be mounted. While this question will probably never pop up on a TV game show, the answer is yes, and it was called the Evinrude Cart. That early 1920s wooden device, wearing 16-inch, rubber-tired spoke wheels, was, in the words of Evinrude's sales literature, "designed particularly for those who want to haul their motor (or other stuff) a considerable distance." Even though it had a "staunch axle," a 2-hp Evinrude single was the cart's carrying limit. An optional canvas motor cover would make onlookers more curious. The aforementioned buggy was just one of many offerings in a vintage catalog of outboard motors and accessories.

Circa World War I, Evinrude (often collaborating with outside suppliers) realized a proprietary accessory line provided another way to put food on the table. Many of the first ancillary outboard items were simply updated parts for retrofitting older motors. Primary examples included flywheel magnetos (replacing the entire battery ignition system), reversing lower-unit attachments, and rope-start sheaves. Those wanting kits converting a regular-shaft Evinrude rowboat motor into a short, through-the-bottom-of-the-craft canoe motor had such an option. There was also a vice versa kit for folks fed up with power-canoeing. Instructions with the rowboat-to-canoe package suggested purchasing a special "outboard canoe exhaust" system piping motor fumes through the canoe's side.

Among the host of promotional items available to Merc dealers were ice bags, playing cards, hats, T-shirts, and matches. These fire sticks date to 1954.

Close Cover Before Striking

MERCURY mark 50

KIEKHAEFER

America's most Powerful PRODUCTION OUTBOARD

Power Power Power Power!

KIEKHAEFER

MERCURY
mark 50

40 HORSEPOWER, FORWARD, NEUTRAL, REVERSE. ELECTRIC STARTER & GENERATOR OPTIONAL

MERCURY
K

The mark of a true sportsman...

Universal Match Corp., Milwaukee

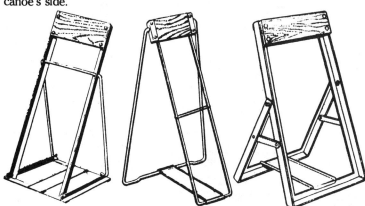

Various motor stands.

A 1920s Evinrude stove ad.

Prevent Fires!

Use a real, he-man Camp Stove! Evinrude in developing the Evinrude Camp Stove, drew on the full, ripe experience gained through years of serving sportsmen well. We offer a Camp Stove 100 per cent safe, a camp stove with a blue gas flame so much hotter than ever achieved before that it amazed even skeptical University Engineering Laboratories, a camp stove that is a model of compactness and practicability.

We are proud of the Evinrude Camp Stove—three seasons beyond experiment. As safe a buy as a key of ten-penny nails or a dozen league baseballs. Buy it! Try it! Write for Booklet.

EVINRUDE MOTOR CO.
CAMP STOVE DIVISION

Milwaukee   Wisconsin

Stove, utensils and all fit snugly in it's carrying container

A complete kitchen is on hand

Some early Evinrude owners suffering from pounding headaches bought a "maxim silencer" muffler baffle. A few extra bucks netted a deluxe water-cooled version which, according to company literature, caused hot gases, led through water jackets, to say simply "puff-puff" upon emission. Speed demons could activate the unit's "cut-out." Outboard buffs buffeted by their motors' hitting bottom were targeted for a tilt-up attachment. Without such an accessory, early Evinrude-powered boats could not be beached completely. Anyone finding an Evinrude rowboat motor wearing a 14-gauge brass rudder (clamped over the drive shaft tube) has a nice factory-authorized accessory.

Proud Evinruders could consider a wooden motor stand, gray motor enamel, and motor polish to keep that kicker "clean and bright." Evinrude grease and lubricating oil (with "full directions on each can") were always the "proper density for Evinrude motors." The latter substance "prevented carbon deposits."

Occasionally, a vintage outboard surfaces in its own special protective case. For the 2-horse rowboat motors, Evinrude offered a "full length" white pine shipping case, as well as a trunk. Covered and lined with "vulcanized fibre," the (38-inch by 13½-inch by 17½-inch) Evinrude trunk was built of "3-ply veneer lumber, securely bound in brass and fitted with a high grade lock." It could be conveniently checked on a train as baggage or lashed to an automobile running board.

Some pioneer gadgeteers equipped their rowboat motors with an Evinrude "magneto-electric lighting system." An extra coil, a switch, 32 feet of waterproof wire, and a searchlight (on a stand)

"Official" outboard accessories included brand-name engine oil.

got power from the kicker's mag. "Unusual weather conditions due to dense saltwater fogs of the ocean" called for the use of the magneto Booster. Its dry-cell battery, enclosed in a waterproof case, was wired to the magneto coil and could be switched on if the mag didn't have sufficient zing.

Through the years, most outboard companies pushed at least a page or two of "official accessories" aimed at helping the outboarder get more utility from his motor. Scott-Atwater offered everything from remote control and its own brand of 2-cycle motor oil to the obscure Green Hornet high-speed lower unit and racing throttle kit for its 16-hp twin. Private brands like Elgin, Sea King, and Wizard marketed a handful of accessories. Gas cans, engine covers, oil, and shear pins were chief among them.

Martin published a four-page accessory flyer offering standard outboarding fare. Items like motor safety cables ($1 for regular and $2 for the deluxe, stainless steel version) and canvas engine carrying bags graced its 1948 cover. The Upland Manufacturing Company of Upland, Indiana, made Martin some chubby outboard covers. If trouble struck, these items doubled as life jackets. Generic storage stands, also produced by an outside firm, were offered in three sizes ranging in price from $2.98 to about $12 (for the one with wheels). Saltwater boaters could get a special "Martin designed cooling system flushing attachment." The dollar-and-a-half rubber tip screwed into a garden hose and was stuck into a lower-unit water-intake port.

Martin 60 owners with high transom craft had the option of a $10, 5-inch "lower unit extension set." Those taking pride in their National Pressure Cooker Company–produced kickers were invited to brighten up for the new season with a complete Martin decal set. At 20 cents each, it's a shame they're not available today!

By the mid-1950s Mercury's Quicksilver accessory line had developed into a nice sideline for its dealer organization. Because Mercs were never as generic as other brands, accessory catalogs featured many interesting, uniquely Mercury items. Chief among them were the Quicksilver racing lower units and high-speed, two-blade propellers.

Although a standard (family runabout) front-mount steering-cable motor bracket was offered, rear-mounted racer's steering bars were prominently touted. They could be quickly bolted to any Merc competition model. In any event the Kiekhaefer Corporation pioneered hydraulic steering and pushed its Ride-Guide system for single- or dual-engine installation. Wheels came in a choice of such shades as "Marlin Blue," "Desert Sand," and "Sunset Orange." Regular (rope and pulley) steering wheels received less catalog space.

Steering handles with twist-grip speed control could be purchased for the big four-cylinder Mercs of the day. Dual-lever Quicksilver remote controls were marketed to boaters desiring "armchair comfort . . . fingertip control" of shift, throttle, and electric starting. Single-lever units debuted in 1957. A fuel-pump conversion kit adapted one-hose tanks to the older (Mark 50)

Mercury's dandy little shear pin kit sold for 35 cents.

A generic ad for Mercury outboard accessories.

Twist Grip Throttle Control

Just a "Twist of the Wrist" is all it takes to control the speed of the boat when your Mercury is fitted with this steering handle incorporating the ingenious twist-grip throttle developed by Kiekhaefer Mercury engineers. It's simple and reliable; a rotatable grip is connected to the throttle linkage through a flexible control cable. Handle can be set in vertical carrying position without upsetting throttle adjustment.

For safe, sure, split-second, one-hand control of Mercury Horsepower in any emergency and under all conditions of operation, the twist-grip throttle is ideal. It can be fitted to KE-4, KE-7, KG-4, KF-7 and KG-7 models. Handle bracket supplied with kit is adapted to use of steering bar. Kit includes all necessary attachments and fittings. M-60-588............................ $10.50

Keep the stern of your boat
SPIC and SPAN
with this mercury drip pan

Every outboard operator knows that, over a period of time, even the most neatly kept boat will eventually show the deteriorating effects of gasoline and oil drippings. You can keep the stern of your boat spic and span with this nicely finished aluminum drip pan which attaches to the transom and is provided with a drain tube leading to the outside of the boat.

An additional feature of this drip pan is the rib at the top edge, designed to prevent motor from coming off of transom if clamp brackets should accidentally work loose during operation. M-60-5034................................ $4.63

More Mercury accessories: "Twist of the Wrist" throttle control and aluminum drip pan.

This OMC accessory made it possible to control steering and throttle at the motor.

STEERING HANDLE

For 28 H.P., 33 H.P. and 40 H.P. motors (except electric shift). Permits steering and throttle control at the motor. Installation instructions are furnished.

Part No. 377949 $11.00

pressurized system. Cooling system flushing attachments were available for a wide range of Merc motors.

Fastidious boaters could keep leaking fuel from gumming up their hulls by getting an official Quicksilver aluminum drip pan. Sort of a cookie sheet bent at a 45-degree angle, it attached to and protected the transom. The Merc got clamped over it. The unit's top rib would catch the clamps should they vibrate loose. Lots of utility for $4.63!

Older Mercurys sporting integral gas tanks could be fitted with an interesting "fuel transfer cap." This piece resembled its standard counterpart except for a horizontal, ¼-inch hose-fitting on top. A tube running from this fitting to an ordinary gas can refilled the motor's tank whenever the auxiliary gas can was pumped or raised above the kicker. A check valve prevented overfilling. Marathon racers used these $2.95 items religiously.

Truly one of the nicest Merc accessories was a custom motor stand. Constructed of heavy cast iron, the black and silver (some were all black) unit featured a prominently embossed Kiekhaefer Mercury logo. They were equally at home with a one-lung putt-putt or a six-cylinder giant.

Mercury nuts, especially those who raced the legendary power plants, were asked by the accessory catalog to "wear the emblem and fly the pennant." Deck pennants, sweatshirts, hats, and $1.25 T-shirts were marketed. Mercury's famous logo, in 65-cent and $1.15 sizes, could be sewn on an enthusiast's clothing to "boost his motor." Championship hydroplane racer Bill Tenney bought one of the bigger emblems. He gained worldwide outboarding notoriety with a very fast 1930s-era Johnson model SR. That aforementioned accessory patch was added to text carefully embroidered to his racing togs. The results read something like I HAVE NOT YET SUCCUMBED TO KIEKHAEFER MERCURY!

Evinrude, Johnson, and Gale Products outboard owners of the 1960s could yield to desires to dress up their motors via genuine OMC accessories. Among the featured gear were single and traditional two-lever remote controls. (Evinrude's was dubbed Simplex, while Johnson's said Ship Master.) Gadget-minded, large-horsepower skippers could choose from generator, electric starting, power tilt, and radio-noise-suppression kits. Operators of the little 3-horse OMC twins were offered a $9.75 fuel pump kit, allowing the integral tank to be retired in favor of a heftier remote unit. A lengthy, 15-inch lower-unit extension package was also available for the 3-horse. Five-horse OMC products used in the fall or in cold climates could be fitted with a $2.80 thermostat so the motor would warm up rapidly. Many salty, sandy, or silty water outboarders had the option of OMC's chrome water-pump kit, said to resist damage from foreign particles. Of course, an assortment of auxiliary fuel tanks, hoses (up to 100 feet!), official OMC lubricants, engine cleaner, and rust preventative were offered. A clever "spare propeller kit" was marketed on an almond-shaped base. This handy rig (which mounted in the boat) included everything, from pliers to prop nut, for a quick emergency wheel change.

Most universal of all OMC accessories were its classic engine stands. Although lightweight, they were very sturdy. Their aluminum tube legs pulled out for easy transport. Today, both regular (for motors up to 40 hp) and jumbo-size OMC stands are favored among outboard collectors.

Outboard makers were not the only firms producing motor accessories. In fact, dozens of "factory-authorized" pieces (such as Evinrude Cruise-A-Day fuel tanks) were built by outside sources. Most frequently these were motor stands, locks, remote controls, and lower-unit–mounted trolling plates.

Many times, some little "aftermarket" company pioneers technology eventually adopted by the majors. A tiny Midwestern outfit offered electric starting kits (linking starter motor to flywheel via a bicycle chain and ratchet) for OMC 25s a few years prior to the concept's 1954 "factory equipped" reintroduction. Small, belt-driven DC generators were also available.

Circa 1948, another pint-size manufacturing concern worked up a steering handle twist-grip throttle control for early Mercury Rockets and Lightnings. Merc began adopting this principle in 1952. Mercury 10 owners could also acquire the Tescher Automatic Fuel Pump and install a remote gas tank. Similar kits were available for the Evinrude Fleetwin 7 ½ hp and Martin 100 (10 hp) outboards. This pump employed a safe, nonpressurized, single-hose system some years before the big firms decided that that process was best.

The Quincy (Illinois) Welding Works sold hop-up accessories directly and through Mercury distributors. Lucky motor buffs may still find an old Merc sporting a Quincy exhaust stack, manifold cut-out shutter, or other items.

Perhaps one of the most elusive pieces of this genre was designed for Johnson, Evinrude, and Gale Products (Buccaneer, Sea King, Sea-Bee, etc.) 35-horse models. In 1958 a small Bartlesville, Oklahoma, company marketed JET-PAC Dual Carburetion for the aforementioned outboards. Apparently the second carb mounted on the cylinder assembly and added "5 HP with no increase in fuel consumption."

Collectors who gobble up outboard accessories might like to find a juice-can-sized device hooked to their motor. Labeled Retriev-a-Buoy, this canister was clipped to the kicker's transom clamp thumbscrew or bracket-mounted to the steering arm. If the outboard ever fell overboard, Retriev-a-Buoy's airtight cartridge on a 120-foot nylon line would float to the surface. The submerged motor could thus be rescued.

Those who save old motors should keep an eye open for their pastime's associated products. A vintage putt-putt dressed with some official accessory is truly double the treasure.

DUAL CARBURETION

A tiny company in mid-America marketed their "Jet Pac dual carb" device to folks wanting to hop-up their OMC "Big Twin" type motors. The modification served more as an auxiliary intake breather than a second carburetor.

8

The Antique Outboard Motor Club

"Oh, no!" moaned my cousin Jim, "someone's coming! Quick! Hide this magazine in your shirt!"

I stashed the publication on my person just as Aunt Sarah opened the door.

"Why don't you boys get some fresh air?" she suggested.

As I began following my young relative, that questionable magazine slid down to the top of my socks. Only an exaggerated limp prevented its untimely appearance.

"Is your leg all right?" Aunt Sarah inquired.

"Sure it is!" Jim chimed in with a slap on my shoulder. "Pete just has an old football injury."

"Your cousin Peter plays with old motors, not footballs," she reponded suspiciously.

"Well . . ." I stammered, "I played football once and got tackled."

After we were safely outside, Jim rewarded my ad hoc clandestine cooperation by explaining the hot pages were "sorta borrowed" from a friend's dad. The magazine's ownership then passed to me with a blessing, "There're some pictures in there I know you'll love!"

My cousin was right on target. Those photos were, indeed, eye-opening. They also defeated my fears that I was the only one who thought about such things. After being shown the magazine, my folks expressed shock.

"You mean to tell us," they gasped, "*Popular Mechanics* actually found other people who collect antique outboard motors!"

The famed publication's March 1966 issue not only featured old kickers, but introduced an organization called the Antique Outboard Motor Club. In those days membership was $5. I promised to do extra chores as my skeptical mom wrote out a check. It was a wise use of five bucks.

The idea for an antique outboard club probably got its start in a Florida Ford dealership. Assistant service manager George Ralph enjoyed pre–World War II kickers and often compared his hobby to vintage car collecting. Old car clubs were flourishing, and members paid dues, and bought publications and promotional materials. Mr. Ralph believed outboard collectors would do likewise.

During the spring of 1959, he formed the Antique Outboard Motor Club of America. A local advertising agency helped prepare ads aimed at acquiring membership. The desired enrollees were supposed to establish club chapters and pay small annual royalties for this affiliation. By 1962 one of the modest ads appeared. Unfortunately, only about 50 motor buffs replied. A few short club magazines were published, but none were printed after 1963. Subsequently, the Antique Outboard Motor Club of America faded out.

One of that outfit's disappointed members was a graduate student named David Reinhartsen. On a semester break he visited club founder George Ralph, only to discover there was little hope Ralph's club would be reactivated. Taking names from the old outboard magazines, Reinhartsen contacted a handful of collectors and decided to start a new organization. This one, called simply the Antique Outboard Motor Club, meant only to help anyone interested in vintage kickers, and had no profit motive.

During the formative years, Reinhartsen and his wife, although busy with other things, handled most of the club's workload. A better brand of magazine was introduced. Soon a few other buffs pitched in, allowing the Antique Outboard Motor Club continued growth.

Today, several thousand enthusiasts from coast to coast and around the world are members. Many participate in various indoor swap and outdoor "wet" meets. Some contribute articles to the quarterly *Antique Outboarder* publication, or buy and sell old motors and parts through the club's regular newsletter.

A.O.M.C. logo.

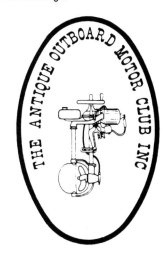

A display of restored Johnson outboards at an Antique Outboard Motor Club Meet. Some enthusiasts like to find "basket case" outboards and turn them into beauties like these.

Anyone who enjoys this book and its topic would be very happy with membership in the Antique Outboard Motor Club. Most AOMC people vividly recall how singular they felt before realizing there was a whole club full of folks sharing their unique interest. As a result, veteran members helping new ones is commonplace. Whether you're seeking a propeller for a '56 Firestone 5-hp or need starting instructions for some battery-ignition kicker, the best source has long been this fine club.

From time to time, the AOMC address changes with a shift in officers. Should you desire more information, write me in care of the publisher. Or, better yet, contact the Antique Boat Museum, 750 Mary Street, Clayton, New York 13624. This excellent Thousands Islands–area repository (which has an extensive old-outboard display) can give you the Antique Outboard Club's current mailing address. Or, get full details about joining the club by visiting their Web site, www.aomci.org.

9

The Big List

In 1951 Edwin Hodge composed a doctoral dissertation for Indiana University. His scholarly work, entitled "A Study of the Outboard Motor Industry," contained a historical listing of U.S. outboard manufacturers. That interesting roster was updated by Jim Webb and Robert Carrack in their 1967 *Pictorial History of Outboard Motors* and has received revisions from members of the Antique Outboard Motor Club.

Based in part on the aforementioned works, the following list attempts to identify all known American brands of gasoline-powered outboards. Engines from the beginning of the industry through the early 1960s are included. Many of the entries outline producers from the World War I era. A majority of their machines were of the 2-cycle, forward-pointing, single-cylinder variety. More often than not, each gave about 2 hp via a modest (under 1,000) rpm rating. Most were rather obvious copies of Ole Evinrude's already famous rowboat motor.

When you think back to the late 1970s consumer scene, you'll recall everybody trying to break into the promising home computer market. Dozens of companies quickly put a little computer into production, or more commonly, marketed a relabeled model from someone else's factory. Many of those early junior electronic setups, with their modest keyboard, cassette player drive, and $89 black-and-white TV monitor, looked about the same. By the late '80s the normal business shakedown had converted most pioneer home computer firms into a footnote in American business history, and assigned remnants of their first-generation wares to the trash, or more mercifully, neighborhood lawn sales.

Similarly, the years 1913 to 1919 saw many manufacturers taking a chance in the growing outboard motor marketplace. While a few companies came up with original designs, the majority either duplicated (with the possible exception of adding rudder steering) Mr. Evinrude's early motor, or marketed a batch of badge-engineered outboards produced by some other outfit. In any event, those not wholeheartedly committed to weathering economic storms in which supply was usually far greater than demand silently submerged.

71

The Big List

After World War II, the economy strengthened, and many people seemed to be interested in buying a lot of outboards. To fill this need, the majors strengthened their lines, and dozens of small companies entered the field. This flurry of activity continued through most of the 1960s. (Note: As a result of this activity, acquisitions, and badge-engineering as well as public preference, many outboards were known by several names. In the Big List, these other monikers appear in parentheses after the engine's proper or most common name.)

Rather than preface this directory with a list of excuses, suffice it to say, the more I researched, the greater my "content confidence" was shaken. There are probably some outboard examples that escaped my typewriter. Should you come across something not listed here, I would be most happy to receive your correspondence via the publisher.

Admiral

Boaters who valued their feet were, no doubt, swayed by Affiliated Manufacturers Company advertising. The Milwaukee concern said its Admiral detachable rowboat motor would "fit any boat like an old shoe."

The Admiral, which looked quite like the Anderson and some Blakely models, was available with either a gear-driven magneto or battery ignition. An underwater exhaust tube could be substituted for the "can" muffler at no extra charge. The lower-unit gear case was said to be "small and streamlined" and contained the water pump. Rather than use a shear pin or key, the propeller was taper fitted.

Like the Anderson and some Blakelys, the Admiral sported a relatively prominent, unusually shaped skeg, called a "skag [*sic*] rudder" (but the motor was not rudder-steered).

Affiliated Manufacturers had its foot in the outboard industry door between 1914 and 1916.

Aeromarine

After leaving Mercury, Carl Kiekhaefer reactivated his Aeromarine marque, specializing in snowmobile power plants. Reportedly, some small Kiekhaefer Aeromarine outboards were on the drawing board. The name was also associated with a California firm that built erstwhile McCulloch kickers. See the Back Rack chapter for details.

Aerothrust

Aerothrust outboards were not designed to get wet! That is to say, their props were like airplane propellers and pushed boats by means of air thrust.

It appears the Chicago-made motors debuted in 1915 and were not produced much after 1920. (One source does indicate Aerothrusts were built through 1925, but research into old advertising conflicts with the report.)

These products, generally in the form of 2-, 3-, or 5-horse twins, were air-cooled and available with either battery or magneto ignition. Some Aerothrusts came through with the crankcase and both (opposed) cylinders cast in a single assembly.

A front-mounted flywheel got "turned over" with a removable hand crank. Once the engine started, the operator was to pull the crank from the catch fitting, adjust the float-style carb, and prepare to get whisked away.

During its production run, Aerothrusts were equipped with two-blade props composed in various formats. Some looked like a pair of laminated wooden paddle blades, while others had a sharper appearance and were fashioned of alloy.

A few Aerothrusts never saw liquid waterways but were mounted on 45-mph ice sleds.[1]

Air-Boy

First produced in 1954, the Air-Boy consisted of a small air-cooled engine driving an airplane-style prop. Air thrust from the propeller pushed the boat. Airboats, Inc., of Denver made the Air-Boy through the 1960s. The single-cylinder machines were available in 2, 3 ½, 4, and 5, 9, 12.9, and 18 (twin) hp denominations.

Airdrive

An early attempt to market a fan-prop type outboard rig came from the Kemp Machine Works in Muncie, Indiana. The Airdrive was sold from 1918 through 1922. Some advertising called this one the Kemp.

Aldens (Pathfinder)

Available in 3-, 5-, and 7-hp enominations, private brand outboards from the Aldens stores wore a Pathfinder label. Reportedly they were marketed from 1961 through 1969. Eska made it.

AMC Saber

Another Fifties private-brand outboard, the AMC Saber, was produced by Gale Products for Aimcee Wholesale Corporation, New York, New York.

The AMC Saber made its debut in 1955 with 3-, 5-, 12-, and 22-hp models. For 1956 the 22-hp was replaced with a 25-hp. Even so, officials at Aimcee decided the AMC Saber marque just couldn't cut it and discontinued sales at the close of the year.

American (1)

The 1896 American outboard is covered in Chapter 1, page 3.

American (2)

Not to be confused with the 1896 American outboard, this rig, built in Detroit by the American Engine Company, generated 2 hp at 900 rpm. Most models had a gear-driven magneto and rudder steering. The flywheel-knob-start, 62-pound single was produced between 1913 and 1918.

American Marc

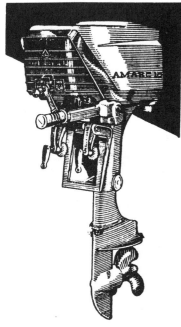

Artist's rendering of 9¼-hp AMARC diesel outboard prototype. Production version of this obscure offering was too unorthodox and complicated for most boaters.

Would you buy an outboard requiring no carburetor, no valves, no magneto, nor even a single spark plug? What if this motor, minus said troublesome components, sported one cylinder and a pair of pistons? Sound weird? Well, such an outboard, a diesel, was actually made.

Around 1959 American Marc, Inc., of Inglewood, California, advertised a line of diesel outboards ranging from 7½ to 22 hp. Early ads, however, showed only the American Marc 10 (not to be confused with the Mercury Mark 10 of similar vintage). The single-cylinder, opposed-dual-piston model produced 9¼ hp at 3,500 rpm. The lower unit was reminiscent of a Merc or Oliver, and its twist-grip steering handle looked 100-percent Mercury.

The California company's prototype may not have actually gone into production, as subsequent literature covering its restyled AMARC 10 identified the motor as "the first diesel outboard."

Although the AMARC 10 could go without parts vital to gas outboards and could cruise "twice as far as a gasoline engine of comparable size on the same amount of fuel," its unconventionality kept customers away. Even in its faint heyday, the AMARC 10 was a rare sight. It was much more so after being discontinued in the early Sixties. (It should be noted that American Marc, Inc., also marketed its own line of boats in lengths from 14 to 30 feet.)

Amphion

Most companies without aggressive sales organizations seldom put a dent in the marketplace. Such was the case with Clarence Allen's Milwaukee, Wisconsin, outboard business.

Allen knew Ole Evinrude and admired the success of Ole's rowboat motor. Consequently, he decided to build a couple of small inboard marine engines, and in 1915 mounted an in-line, alternate-firing twin on an outboard lower unit. (This represents one of the earliest alternate-firing two-cylinder outboards.) The strange-looking rig, called "Amphion," was on the market (so to speak) until 1919.

Unfortunately, Mr. Allen lacked a strong dealer network, and his biggest orders were said to have come from "one enterprising salesman who'd load up his Model T Ford truck and go to nearby Wisconsin lakes and peddle the Amphions."[2]

In 1926 Allen advertised a weird-looking 3-to-4-hp model "D.O." outboard. Its odd appearance was a primary result of the

cowl-like rudder covering most of the prop area. This feature was identified as the McNabb Kitchen Rudder and was said to lack "freakiness."

A short time later Allen sold all the remaining Amphions, patterns, tooling, and parts to fellow Milwaukeean A.J. Machek. This guy assembled some of the motors, and a few more Amphions made it to the waterways. The firm was sold at the close of World War II, and the Amphion stuff (tooling, patterns, etc.) was donated to the shop department of a Wisconsin high school.

In the 1960s a member of the Antique Outboard Motor Club found some old Amphion goods, including what turned out to be a late Twenties unfinished Amphion Dreadnought kicker. After some machining, adjusting, and balancing, the opposed twin went to work. While not the smoothest or lightest 6-hp of its day (circa 1928), the Dreadnaught's horseshoe-shaped gas tank is not afraid to sport a beautifully cast oval Amphion logo, reminding us of its company's interesting place in outboarding history.

This 1914–18 vintage 2½-hp rowboat motor was available in either battery or gear-driven magneto models. The Anderson, complete with its ornately shaped skeg, looked a lot like the Admiral and Blakely. It was made by the Anderson Engine Company of Chicago.

The Damac Corporation of Roslyn, Long Island, New York, served as U.S. distributor for a line of English outboards called British

Like many historical accounts of vintage businesses, our Amphion chronology has come into a new light. Several old boating annuals have surfaced showing A.J. Machek as Amphion's original owner and Allen running the company in the 1920s. Our original description was received by an Evinrude exec who knew Allen. It may be that he simply juxtaposed the dates.

Anderson

Anzani

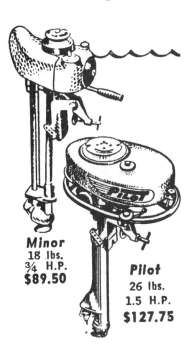

Minor
18 lbs.
¾ H.P.
$89.50

Pilot
26 lbs.
1.5 H.P.
$127.75

A pair of small Anzani singles from late 1953.

Anzani. Minor, a ¾-horse putt-putt was said to "drive a dinghy as fast as two men can row." There were also 1½- and 4-hp singles, as well as 10- and 15-horsepower "uni-twins." Damac targeted 1950s upscale yachtsmen, touting Anzani motors as "light, rugged, gadget-free . . . easy to stow, start, and maintain." They never really caught on in the States. Anzani's racing outboards, however, were a little more successful in the U.S.

Aqua-Jet

"Pull the starter," says an Aqua-Jet ad, "and you're on your way to fishing spots you could never reach with an ordinary motor." This jet pump outboard from Farrow Manufacturing Inc., of Elmore, Minnesota, used a single-cylinder, air-cooled Tecumseh powerhead and was easily carried by means of handles both front and back. The Aqua-Jet water intake was "covered by a shield which kept debris out and allowed an unrestricted flow of water in." The 5-hp rig was advertised as the motor that "would take you where you want to go"; however, its mid-Sixties production went but a few years.

Arrow (1)

A 1908 Waterman outboard

Most remembered for a 1917 acquisition of the pioneer Waterman outboard firm, the Arrow Motor and Machine Company (sometimes called Newark Motor and Machine) had been marketing its own kickers for two years prior to absorbing Waterman.

Arrow's main offering was a flywheel-knob-start, 4-hp, opposed-twin-cylinder model with adjustable propeller. As a special "anti-backfiring" feature, Arrow cylinders were drilled with double ports.

Also originating in a Newark, New Jersey, factory were the National and Federal twins. Because of the similar venue and like appearance, I'll bet there was some connection between the three motors.

Although Arrow's mechanical claim to fame was its two-cylinder status, some dusty listings mention a 2½-hp Arrow single.

It is generally believed that Arrow and sister line (as of late 1916) Waterman went totally out of business in 1924. Apparently, however, ownership eventually passed to the Pausin Engineering Company of Newark, and a small stock of motors was still available into the early Thirties. Reportedly, Pausin was getting requests for Waterman (and possibly Arrow) outboard replacement parts though the 1940s.[3] Some of these requisitions came from exotic ports in Africa and China.

Arrow (2)

The 1960s-vintage Arrow linked "Canada's finest outboard with the famous [air-cooled, 2-cycle] American-made Tecumseh power plant." Painted in "heat- and gasoline-resistant off-white," these rigs wore a front-and-back carrying handle assembly.

Rather than the typical "pin"-style motor angle adjustment, Arrow's transom bracket had a knob on the end of a bolt which

could be tightened into the proper position. The transom clamp bracket's height could also be adjusted. Its collar, securing it to the motor leg, slid up and down. This allowed the operator to obtain the desired lower-unit length.

Arrows were identified with Indian names and wore such model designations as Iroquois (3 hp), Mohawk (4 hp), Seminole (5 hp), Mohican (6 hp), Navajo (7½ hp), and Apache (9½ hp). Arrow, primarily a Montreal, Quebec, firm, also maintained an office in New York, New York.

Atco Boatimpeller

Although distributed by an American firm, Atco Motors of New York, the 1950s straight-shaft (like a Caille Liberty Drive) Atco was built by Charles H. Pugh, Ltd., in Birmingham, England. Two versions (1⅓ hp and 2½ hp) of the air-cooled outboard were available.

Bantam

Not much is remembered about this 1946 offering from the Bantam Products Company of New York City.

Barracuda

This air-cooled, 4-hp Barracuda "standard" outboard, circa 1960, was picked up at a swap meet. This rig is identical to various Mono, Eska, and My-te models.

Imagine that it is early August, 1961; a fellow walks into a New Jersey Mercury dealership looking for a fishing motor bargain. The proprietor quickly shows him a shiny new 6 horse Merc but is met by an objection:

> "No, no! Too expensive!"
> "Well sir," the outboard dealer says, "over here, we have a nice little economy model. . . ."
> "How much?" the customer interrupts.
> "This 5.1-cubic-inch single lists for $92.50."
> "Still too much!" the customer retorts.
> "Wait a minute sir. I quoted the suggested retail price. Today this particular gem happens to be on sale for . . . only $76.00"
> "Seventy-six, you say?"
> "Just 76 bucks; yes, sir."
> "I'll take it and pay cash," comes the reply. "Now what kind of kicker did I just get?"

Actually, I don't know if the original owner of Barracuda outboard motor, serial number 4705, was a true skinflint. I concocted this hypothetical scenario based upon a nearly forgotten sales slip. It is likely, however, the 4-hp Barracuda was purchased largely on the basis of price.

Accompanying literature from the Barracuda Outboard Company of Aurora, Illinois, boasted that its product is "a machine of the finest quality . . . found to be in perfect mechanical condition." Even so, the firm warned: "Do not contact us if you experience engine difficulties." Of course that's because the Power Products Corporation (lawn-mower–type) engine could be serviced at any one of the many local small engine shops authorized throughout the U.S. and Canada.

Identical to other low-priced brands (such as Mono, Eska, My-Te, etc.), Barracuda featured an air-cooled powerhead and water-cooled lower unit exhaust assembly and engine base. Standard (with small cylindrical, exposed fuel tank), and Deluxe (wearing a plastic powerhead shroud) versions were available. By mail, the little outboard concern also offered (for 30 days after motor purchase), "a rugged chromium-plated" storage stand ($4.95), as well as a spare, $2.50 prop (plus 50¢ postage). A white "Barracuda" decal (typically on a blue engine) distinguished this mini-marque from its previously noted and very similar competitors.

Whether the Barracuda Outboard Company really built the lower unit and attached the powerhead is a mystery. Perhaps the entire package came from another source with Barracuda simply acting as a private-brand marketing agent.

One thing for sure is the likely existence of other such tiny brands not presently known by the author. The Barracuda was yet another cute, lightweight, which served a limited, but valid, boating public.

Bearcat

See the listing for Fageol.

Beaver

A 4-horse kicker of unknown origin, the Beaver logged a tiny bite of American outboard history in the 1960s.

Bendix

A relatively rare marque, known for its air-cooled, 2-cycle powerhead, was the Bendix. Produced by the Bendix Aviation Company of Newark, New Jersey, the Bendix Eclipse outboards were actually built in the firm's South Bend, Indiana, facility.

Two basic powerheads were available: a 2¼-hp single, and a 4½-hp opposed twin. Usually a tiny ID plate riveted to the transom bracket assembly carried easy-to-interpret model codes like TMD (Twin-Magneto-Deluxe), SMD (Single-Magneto-Deluxe), SM (Single-Magneto), and SB (Single-Battery). An *L* indicated "Longshaft."

The Bendix outboards were marketed from 1936 to about 1940. Parts were supplied through the early post-World War II years.

Around 1938 Bendix worked up a unique four-piston, in-line prototype with a "wobble plate" supercharger. While it seems likely this was an air-cooled rig, one source says liquid did the trick. Technicians ran the big Bendix in the shop, but for reasons lost to time, the approximately 15-hp outboard never saw production.[4]

It is not uncommon for a wayward Bendix to be discovered minus some of its skeg. This component was a rather thin casting that broke easily with carelessness.

The top on this streamlined, air-cooled 1936 Bendix got "flipped" so the operator could wrap the starter rope around the flywheel. Once this battery-ignition kicker started, adjustments to a choke lever dangerously close to the flywheel required strict attention. Not a motor for OSHA inspectors!

Bendix production ceased in 1940. Bendix owners with motors needing parts or service were directed to Pozgay Welding Works on Long Island, New York.

Blakely

The Blakely Engine Company of Muskegon, Michigan, was in the outboard business from 1914 to 1918. During that run, it offered a standard battery-ignition rowboat motor with above water "tin can" exhaust, as well as a deluxe, gear-driven, magneto version that sported a below-the-waterline exhaust tube. Some of the rigs were offered for $39.50 "while they last." Both standard and deluxe models looked nearly identical to the Admiral and Anderson singles.

Many believe that Blakely, which primarily was involved in race car engines, built kickers for other firms. Mr. Blakely reportedly held the rights to a flexible drive shaft outboard design. While some Blakely-labeled motors of this style were marketed, most were sold by Detroit's Gray Motor Company. Whether Blakely actually produced Gray Gearless outboards or licensed Gray to construct them is unknown.

Blue Jet

Blue Jet is somewhat of a mystery motor. I speculate it was a jet-thrust outboard painted blue. Three- and 5-hp versions were available from 1961 to 1963.

Bourke-Cycle

A couple of motors with weird mechanical properties appeared briefly on the outboard racing scene in late 1954. These 2-stroke engines, affixed to Mercury class "D" Quicksilver high-speed lower units, came from B.R. Bourke Research of Portland, Oregon.

The Bourke-Cycle outboards had only two moving powerhead parts: the piston/connecting-rod assembly and the crankshaft. Glow plugs, rather than spark plugs, were fired by battery ignition. Motorcycle-style cooling fins covered the cylinders. The Bourke engines had no flywheel and were available in two sizes: the two-cylinder Bourke-30 and a four-cylinder rig called the V-4-60. "The single throw crank of the 2-cylinder model had no connection to the pistons, and the engine functioned more like a high pressure turbine than like a reciprocating engine."[5]

Bourke claimed its approximately 30-cubic-inch twin could do 15,000 rpm and produce 114 hp! Reportedly, the first Bourke experiments were done in the 1930s through an Evinrude racing lower unit whose gears the Bourke tore up.

British Sea Gull

Although not an American product, British Sea Gull outboards are mentioned here because they've long been distributed in the U.S. Their primitive appearance (with square-blade prop, non-shrouded gas tank, and rope-start flywheel) might cause a novice outboard collector to believe his find is a real antique. Like the small Anzanis, Sea Gulls were primarily pushed to an upscale sailing crowd looking for a quality foreign name in auxiliary or dinghy power.

These rugged kickers had their start in the late 1920s at the Sunbeam Motor (cycle) Company in Wolverhampton, England. Through the 1930s, Marston (named for their designer) Sea Gulls became known for resistance to saltwater corrosion. The manufacturer sold his outboard interest to a firm eventually called the British Sea Gull Company, Ltd., of Poole, Dorset. American sailors in England during World War II were exposed to the product's reliability, perhaps promoting U.S. importation of Sea Gulls, which began by the 1950s.

Brooklure

Spiegel, Inc, the famous Chicago-based mail-order house, decided to get into the outboard business in 1950. Motors wearing the Brooklure label were manufactured by Outboard Marine's Gale Products Division, of Galesburg, Illinois.

Over its production run, Brooklure outboards came in sizes from 1½ to 25 hp. Records show the 1958 Brooklures made up the last of their line.

Buccaneer (Gale)

Buccaneer's freebooter logo. OMC originally planned to call this line Fleetwing.

In the late Forties Outboard Marine and Manufacturing, producer of Evinrude, Johnson, and half a dozen private-brand outboards, saw another niche it might fill. Wholesalers serving sporting goods and hardware stores sought a small line of low-priced outboard motors they could offer their clients. Many of these retailers were already in someone else's Evinrude or Johnson franchise area, and they wanted just a simple outboard that could be added to their outdoor-related inventory and sold informally.

Because Outboard Marine's Gale Products Division was already building a series of 3-, 5-, and 12-hp generic kickers, a decision was made to badge-engineer another brand for direct sale to the aforementioned wholesalers. The new line was dubbed Buccaneer and was debuted in 1950.

Over the years the brand name was changed to Gale, with Buccaneer becoming a model designation. Like many of its private-brand sisters, this product offered boaters on a budget their first opportunity to own a reliable outboard.

The last Gale Buccaneers and more deluxe Gale Sovereigns were marketed in 1963. This line included motors from a 3-hp single to a V-configuration, four-cylinder, 60-horse job.

Bundy

The Detroit-based Bundy Tubing Company imported a line of outboards from its Milan, Italy, subsidiary. Bundy motors were actively marketed in the United States from about 1961 to 1964.

I have heard tales of brand-new, new/old-stock Bundy 40-horse outboards (complete with fuel tank and a few spare parts) being offered in a Connecticut marina as late as the mid-1980s. Although clearance-sale priced comparable to a fishing motor, these particular "never been run" rigs drew little more than customer conversation.

Burroughs

"Let Burroughs Row for You," suggested 1916 ads for the Time Manufacturing Company's new single, forward-pointing-cylinder

rowboat motor. The Milwaukee firm (with a factory in Oostburg, Wisconsin) said its knob-start, rudder-steered rig was "so powerful that you can go anywhere and pass them all." A fancy-looking variable-pitch prop mechanism may have caused its producer to believe its motor could give small boaters a life in the fast lane.

Although the outboard "typified 100% efficiency, being as nearly troubleproof as human ingenuity permitted," the public's satisfaction with other motors caused the Burroughs marque to fade after 1918.

At least two years before Ole Evinrude began seriously marketing his rowboat motor, the Burtray Engine Works of Chicago quietly introduced a primitive but relatively practical outboard. The Burtray wore a vertical, air-cooled cylinder, sight oiler, and Lunkenheimer valve-lift-type carb. On the prominent flywheel (positioned horizontally over the transom clamps) was mounted a large wooden starting knob. The Burtray's gas tank sitting vertically next to the cylinder, looked like a "family-size" flask. The battery-fired power plant rested atop a cast aluminum lower unit and swung a hefty 12-inch, three-blade prop reminiscent of an electric fan. An adjustment allowed the Burtray operator to change the outboard's transom angle easily. Although the Burtray had an exaggerated skeg/rudder, encompassing a good portion of the lower unit, the motor was pivot-steered like its present-day counterparts. First available in 1907, the Burtray had been discontinued by the close of the 1909 boating season.

A motor called the Walnut (bearing properties nearly identical to the Burtray) also appeared on the scene a couple of years prior to the Evinrude. One wayward Walnut was discovered in the 1950s by a prominent Connecticut outboard collector. That machine differed from the Burtray only with respect to being minus the skeg/rudder and the metal shells covering the upper and lower bevel gears.

The Walnut Machine and Brass Foundry Company of Toledo may not have placed shells over its outboards' gearing, or the coverings simply may have been missing from this particular machine; the issue is open to question.

No one would blame you for wondering if the Walnut and the Burtray, being so distinctively designed for the day, were dreamed up by the same guy, or actually came out of a common factory, or something of that nature. Coincidentally, the Walnut lasted for the exact length of time as the Burtray, silently fading from the early outboard marketplace in 1909.

To add to the interesting confusion (which may never be straightened out), another Chicago firm offered a detachable boat motor it sold as the Water Sprite. That model was available only in 1910 and strongly resembled both the Burtray and Walnut!

A fellow named Sidney Helm was probably the most unusual Caille outboard owner. In 1925 he bought a direct-drive Liberty twin

Burtray(Walnut, Water Sprite)

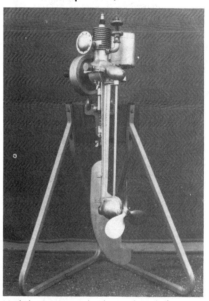

Made by someone who'd never heard of radio, World War I, or potato chips, this 1907–09 Burtray is one of the oldest surviving outboard motors in existence. Its undersized fuel tank might lead to the impression long trips were not expected.

Caille

Two views of a 1930 Caille Class "B" 5-speed outboard. Raising or lowering the steering arm bracket would "shift" the propeller pitch through five speeds: reverse, neutral, and three forward speeds. (Most of the smaller outboard models had two reverse positions, a neutral, and two forward settings.) Steering arm motion swiveled only the lower unit, not the powerhead. These motors were dubbed Caille Red Heads in honor of their red gas tanks.

model, affixed it to a floating mattress, and putt-putted over 200 miles from Keokuk, Iowa, to St. Louis.[6]

Without anticipating such antics, Adolph and Arthur Caille formed the Detroit-based Caille Perfection Motor Company. This was in 1910, and the chief product was to be inboard marine engines. The brothers had been in other businesses together for nearly 20 years. Successes making coin-operated phonographs, scales, and slot machines provided capital for the marine engine concern.

By 1913 outboard production was begun, and it didn't take long for the kickers to eclipse Caille's interest in its inboard line. Even Montgomery Ward bought some early Caille outboard motors for resale (under the Hiawatha banner) in its mail-order catalog.

Early on Caille set its agenda with distinctive-feature outboards. The Liberty single's and subsequent Liberty twin's long, direct-drive shaft was easily recognizable. The firm also came up with a five-speed, adjustable propeller system said to offer neutral, two speeds forward, and two in reverse. In the mid-Teens Caille bought some prominently labeled magnetos from Evinrude. Consequently, these models could be mistaken for Evinrude rowboat motors.

When outboard racing began attracting national attention, Caille joined the field with such motors as the "Flash" and "Streak." Some of these wore tractor lower units (pulling props mounted in front of the gear housing) and dual carbs.

Caille powerheads remained stationary on the boat, as the tiller handle steered only the lower unit. On the bigger twins this arrangement lessened the effects of engine vibration but made high-speed (high-torque) steering a muscleman's province.

The Caille organization quickly built a quality reputation and advertised in upscale publications such as *National Geographic*. The firm's early Thirties "Red Head" (with bright red gas tank) outboards, some with the five-speed prop feature, enhanced that swanky image.

Meanwhile, impecunious boaters desiring Caille craftsmanship could pay a little less for the firm's product sold under Sears's Motorgo label. (A Caille-style motor minus flywheel rope sheave plate labeling is probably a Motorgo.)

By 1932 the Depression had taken its toll on Caille. In an effort to weather the storm, company officials pushed their more basic outboards. A good example of this redirection came in the form of the model 79, so named for its modest $79 price tag. A few other Cailles were renamed to reflect their attractive sales price.

Early the following year control of the once proud, family-owned outboard maker passed to a large holding company called Fuller Johnson. This outfit "owned a number of important manufacturing companies in the east and middle west," and "predict[ed] a bright future for Caille."[7] Unfortunately, that

forecast was off the mark. From 1933 to 1935 Fuller Johnson did little to spark up Caille's line. The marque's catalog offered pretty much the same motors for three years, and Caille outboard production was quietly discontinued by the end of 1935.

Vintage motor buffs may be interested to know that the Caille Motor Company, although long out of the kicker business, was still operational (in Minerva, Ohio) during the 1950s.[8]

The Caille Liberty Twin had its own group of devoted followers. Typical satisfied users operated their motors in calm, shallow waters.

Cal-Jet

While writing this chapter, I showed it to a fellow anxious to see his old outboard in print.

"Where's the listing for Cal-Jet?" he asked.

"Uh-oh, never heard of it," came my reply.

Seems back in the mid-Sixties a coworker offered this gentleman a brand-new, genuine, gasoline-powered fishing motor for $50! He was directed to an evening rendezvous behind some guy's house (in the nearby Syracuse, New York, area). Fifty bucks were produced, prompting a backyard wholesale entrepreneur to open his garage door.

Reportedly, the place was filled with Cal-Jet outboard motors. Memory indicates the small jet-thrust kickers were powered by single-cylinder, 2-cycle, West Bend and Tecumseh air-cooled engines. Produced only in 1965 by California Jet Marine and Air Research, Inc., Cal-Jet models included 4-hp Econojet (E-4), Ramjet (R-4), and 8.8-horse Jetmaster. Some had crank and release starters. The firm's short-lived offices were located in Beverly Hills.

Campbell

Among the many Minneapolis-built outboards was the 2½-hp "Baby Campbell" rowboat motor Campbell Motor Manufacturing Company specialized in marine, inboard engines up to 125 hp, but offered "immediate shipment" and "special prices" on its "absolutely guaranteed" rudder-steered outboard motor. The Campbell's cigar-box-shaped gas tank looked a bit larger than those of its contemporaries. The company was always looking for "agents" to sell the "Baby Campbell" during its 1914 to 1918 production run.

Cary Jet

Cary Enterprises of Huntington Station, New York, entered the jet-thrust outboard field in 1963. Its fishing-motor-sized product with its Italian-built powerhead was offered for only a few years.

Champion

The Champion outboard label was founded by a guy out in his St. Paul, Minnesota, workshop, Sig Konrad's 1926 Champions (and the less expensive Monarch motors) were the first Champ outboard products. Champions bearing low serial numbers (yes, they started with #1) were of the water-cooled, 2-hp, single-cylinder, 2-cycle variety. They had a small, square exhaust housing

New Home of Champion Motors
MORE THAN 4½ ACRES UNDER ONE ROOF ·

Post-World War II Champion factory.

Champion began producing the Blue Ribbon line of motors in its own plant after agreement with Firestone retailers expired.

leading to the lower unit and timing marks you could use to realign (in the event of hitting an underwater obstruction) the keyway-less flywheel and crankshaft.

A rather deluxe 4-cycle, water-cooled Champion was produced in limited quantities. This model featured a dipstick and a pair of spark plugs in its single cylinder. Should one plug foul, the spark wire could be moved in order to give the other one a try! Much of the early Champion output was sold close to home by a St. Paul boating store.

In 1935 Mr. Konrad decided to leave the outboard business and let the Champion name go to Earl DuMonte (who hoped the marque would someday make him a millionaire[9]) for $500. Another fellow, Stanley Grey, became a partner in the new venture.

DuMonte, a veteran outboard racer, moved his new Champion Outboard Motors Company a few miles to Minneapolis. Actually, the young firm had no way to make motors and existed only as a sales organization offering Scott-Atwater-built outboards, primarily through Firestone retailers.

The Scott-Atwater "Champion" engines date from 1935 to 1942. Firestone's agreement began around 1939 and ended with the United States' entry into World War II. During wartime the Champion folks envisioned newly designed kickers constructed in their own factory.

Following the war a new production facility was built. Ralph Herrington, a top Scott-Atwater engineer, joined Champion, and the firm's dreams of independence began to be realized. Within a short time a small line of new Champion Blue Ribbon motors was rolling off the assembly line.

The late Forties saw great consumer acceptance of the well-built, reasonably priced motors. To expand the line, private-brand versions called Majestic and Voyager were introduced around 1949 or 1950.

Also at this time DuMonte unveiled his pride and joy, the Champion Hot Rod special stock outboard racer. The Hot Rod has been compared to the old Johnson KR racing engine of the 1930s, but featured state-of-the-art improvements. Its gear ratio, 14 to 19, was superior to the KR's 12-to-19 figure. The Champion also wore a more sophisticated and streamlined lower unit. Because the Hot Rod's prop turned opposite of the KR, special propellers had to be developed and tested.

By the mid-Fifties a few of the available Hot Rods showed up to compete in class "B" (approximately 20-cubic-inch displacement) races. Quickly, the "B" Hot Rods began to embarrass owners of high-speed Mercury rigs. Postwar Mercs had enjoyed an easy dominance of the stock outboard racing scene and were not too happy with DuMonte's buzzing challenger. Some say politics came into play, causing victorious Hot Rods to be dismantled by inspectors and then disqualified on construction technicalities. In the face of this battle, race officials gave Mercury permission to

replace the veteran Quicksilver drive-shaft housing with a turned exhaust "Howler" unit. This gave the Merc 20-hp high-speed jobs an advantage over the pretty blue Champions. (The Champs weren't allowed to modity the exhaust.) Also in competition were class "J" (9.66 cubic-inch) and "A" (14.96-cubic-inch) versions.

By 1955, with all the unfortunate Hot Rod setbacks, sales of the service (fighing/pleasure motor) Champion lines also began to slow. While the major manufacturers could sell you a 25-or 40-horse outboard, Champion's top offering registered just 16 ½ hp. Admittedly, this approximately 20-cubic-inch "Blue Streak" twin (sister to the Hot Rod) was a good performer, but it didn't have nearly enough zing for family cruising or serious water-skiing.

In order to stem the tide while deciding whether to retool for the expensive production of bigger motors, Champion modified the prop rotation on a small stock of 16 ½s. By matching a couple of 16 ½-hp motors, the pair (complete with Y-shaped gas tank hose) could be marketed as a Tandem 33. As it worked out, the pair idea didn't catch on well enough to give Champion a marketable "full-line outboard maker" image.

This failure again raised the urgent question: should Champion spend the money to develop bigger outboards? It had just put out a sizable sum for a new factory in 1955. The company bank account answered "no," leaving the firm with few viable options. As a cold economic result, the 1957 Champs were the last (although some late '57s were called '58 models).

By early 1958 the Champion name and patents were sold to Western Tool and Stamping. Western figured it could save the well-known marque and built some very contemporary, 25-, 50-, and 75-hp prototypes. (These looked a little like the big West Bends or Scotts of the day.) Alas, money again became an issue, and the powerful Champions never saw the showroom. The brand's trade name and all remaining outboard assets were then sold to a small manufacturing firm in the summer of 1962.[10]

Incidentally, all of the Hot Rod stuff had been sold to Swanson's Outboard Service of Crystal, Minnesota For many years Lyle Swanson built Hot Rods from old stock, and subsequently, newly manufactured parts. The racer was renamed the "Swanson Hot Rod" and was available new into the 1970s. By the mid-Eighties a redesigned "Hot Rod" (which won many races) was available from a firm that had purchased the Swanson interests. At about this time a garage full of new/old-stock Champion fishing-motor parts (since 1958 they had gone from one small firm to the next) were advertised for sale.

In retrospect it is interesting to note some of the many cleverly nutty promotional stunts staged during Champion's heyday. For example, two Midwestern fellows, one seven and the other eighty-three years young, were taken to a little Minnesota lake in June 1947. Neither had ever operated an outboard, but

Champion's 1955, 16½-hp Blue Streak. The factory would also sell you a pair of these models with counter-rotating props, under the name Tandem 33.

This 1955 Champion Midget Hot Rod's 9.66 cubic inches could push a small hydro to 40 mph-plus.

after basic instructions, both easily passed the "One-Pull Test" with a Champion. The following year Champ employees placed one of their motors in a specially designed steel hoop. They started the outboard in –21-degree weather and rolled it down an icy road. When the hoop stopped, the Champion (now upside down) was still running. The promo tricks took a wrong turn, however, when a motor that was supposed to be dropped from an airplane into a lake was ejected too soon. The engine landed, gas tank first, on a farm!

Chris-Craft

Chris-Craft
10 h.p.   Chris-Craft
5½ h.p.

THE CHOICE OF EXPERTS

Chris ★ Craft

OUTBOARD MOTORS
2000 BEVERLY, GRAND RAPIDS 9, MICH.

A 1951 Chris-Craft ad. If the line had continued, their mid-1950s ads would have likely included a full gearshift 25-hp Chris-Craft that was on the drawing board when the outboard division closed circa 1954.

In the late 1930s Jay W. Smith began work on an outboard motor design. Ordinarily, a fellow with a common surname involved in such a project wouldn't seem too significant. This Smith, however, was the son of Chris Smith, the master boatbuilder responsible for the legendary Chris-Craft inboards.

The younger Smith observed post-Depression America seeking recreation but understood that not everyone could afford even the smallest mahogany-decked Chris-Craft. Consequently, the firm planned for a line of outboard-powered craft, the most modest of which (an 8-foot pram) sold for $42!

To power these new Chrises, while keeping the customers in the family, the famous yacht producer offered a couple of newly designed outboards of its own. The rich blue Chris-Craft motors came in the form of a 5½-hp "Challenger" (introduced in 1949) and 10-horse "Commander." Beginning in 1950 these products, aided no doubt by their famous nomenclature, sold rather well, and some 15,000 were manufactured in 1950. The firm was rumored to be planning an expanded outboard line featuring larger power motors.[11]

Chris-Craft outboards were nicely built and performed very satisfactorily. The 10-hp model was comparable to similarly rated Mercury Lightnings and Hurricanes. Some said the design comparisons were too coincidental and talked of possible litigation.

Suddenly, perhaps to avoid the courtroom, the attractive Chris-Craft outboard line was discontinued at the end of 1953. A short time later the Grand Rapids–based company sold its outboard division to the folks who made Oliver farm tractors.

Chrysler

Chrysler Motors Corporation had been in the marine inboard engine business since 1927. By 1965 the famous auto firm saw its chance to expand via a pair of purchases. It acquired the Lone Star Boat Company and bought West Bend's outboard division.

The first Chrysler kickers (or the last West Bends, depending how you view it) were the 1965 "West Bend by Chrysler" models. While most of the subsequent 1966 Chrysler line came from West Bend's vintage drawing board, Chrysler engineers came up with new three-cylinder, 75-hp, and four-cylinder, 105-hp outboards. Over the years several Chryslers, including the 105, were also offered in racing versions (complete with exhaust stacks!). The

motors, with the distinctive white with blue and gold accents, sold rather well.

In some cases the outboards drew more customers to Chrysler Corporation showrooms than did the autos. In the late 1970s, with Chrysler, Dodge, and Plymouth on the verge of bankruptcy, management decided to sell the outboard division to the Force people. During Chrysler's tenure building outboard motors, their plant in Barrie, Ontario, filled Canadian orders.[12]

> An amazed-looking guy quickly entered a small, main street, upstate New York shop. The proprietor could already guess what was to come next.
> "Is that little outboard in your window display for sale?" the fellow asked.
> "No! And you're only the twelfth person today to ask me!"

That diminutive old motor was a Clarke Troller, produced in small quantities between 1937 and 1941. It was the brainchild of one D.R. Clarke and his Clarke Engineering Company in Detroit. At 10½ pounds and just 21 inches high, it certainly was the most portable of all outboards.

Reportedly, a balky conventional outboard led Canadian-born Clarke to invent his own kind of motor. Indeed, the Clarke Troller represents the pinnacle of individualist thinking. The top of the unit contained the coil, fuel metering device, and gas tank. (Some models had a one-piece tank, while others were fitted with a tank made of a pair of castings.)

New York outboard collector Phil Kranz, who is knowledge-able about Clarkes, explains, "The motor incorporated several unusual engineering features. The powerhead operated completely underwater (facilitating simple water cooling) and there were no bevel gears, as the crankshaft was also the propeller shaft. The rope starter sheave was on the propeller end of the crankshaft, with the motor tilted out of the water for starting. There was no magneto, so a battery was used to provide electric current to the coil. The motor was made largely from polished aluminum castings."[13]

In all candor, the Clarke approximately 1.2-hp power plant was equal in zing to a model airplane engine and even used the tiny Champion (⅜-inch-thread) spark plug popular with modelers. While the Clarke's parts were fabricated in the United States, actual construction took place in both Detroit and Toronto.

The motor sold for about $35, and came complete with a canvas carry-bag. Accessories included a canoe bracket, a 6-inch-long shaft extension, and a strange clock-spring thing hooked to a rod. This item, called a "chicken starter," would be wound up, cocked, placed over the prop's starter sheave, and released. The bronze prop on some Clarkes had a variable-pitch feature. No matter what the propeller adjustment was, however, once a

A 1939 Clarke Troller advertisement. Circa 1962–63, D.R. Clarke reentered the outboard business with a bargain basement 2½- to 3-hp (at maximum rpm) putt-putt. It was a far cry from the first Clarke Trollers and wore a Tecumseh lawn-mower–type powerhead, which featured a steel strap carry handle on top of the rewind assembly. This Clarke incarnation, dubbed OB-42 or Kompac 3, had an old-style two-tube lower unit and apparently was designed for Canadian distribution.

running motor was eased into the water, it usually quit—a victim of too much theory and not enough power.

Hoping to curb some of his machine's capriciousness, Clarke announced the advent of a twin-cylinder version. Few of these have surfaced.

From a collector's point of view, the Clarke is a gem. In fact even folks who don't know they like old outboards enjoy looking at one of these trinkets of the waterways.

Clay

A forward-pointing, single-cylinder rowboat motor, the Clay came from Cleveland in 1914. It was a Spinaway clone.

Clinton (Chief, Peerless, Apache)

Clinton Engines Corporation, of Maquoketa, Iowa, along with its predecessor, Clinton Machine Company of Clinton, Michigan, had been marketing single-cylinder, air-cooled saws, mowers, and inboard marine engines prior to its circa-1954 introduction of a low-priced outboard motor. (Early Clintons were distributed by Fageol.)

The Clinton outboards, available through the years in almost every color from light green to gold, were just about the simplest, dependably understandable motors you'd find anywhere. Clintons bore model names such as Sprite, "J-9," Peerless, Apache, and Chief.

A member of the Antique Outboard Motor Club drove five hours to follow a lead on "an old Chief with a red gas tank," assuming it to be a rare 1929 Lockwood Racing Chief. He came home with a garden-variety Clinton!

Left: In an effort to economically devise another private-brand marque, or to modernize an existing power plant, Clinton made use of shroud styling. This late-1960s Sprite used the famous little Clinton lower unit also worn by the likes of Eska and Mono. (Clinton Engines Corp.)

Right: This 1969 Clinton Chief 350 delivered 3.5 hp. Over the years, similar-looking outboards with various color schemes and model names (such as J-9 and Apache) left the Clinton factory. The Starling-Jet water thrust outboard version of this rig wore a jet lower unit. (Clinton Engines Corp.)

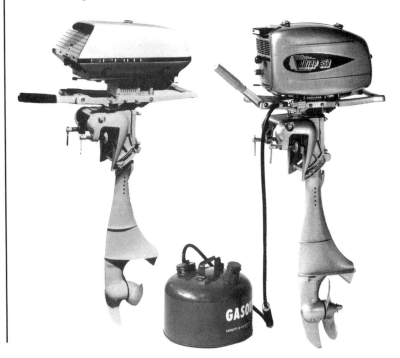

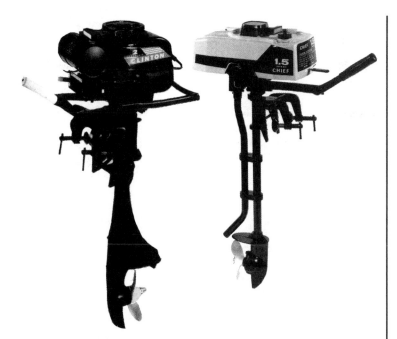

Some Clintons were available with a red, remote, 3-gallon fuel tank, a lower unit whose shaft was 5 inches longer, a neutral gear, and a lighting coil. The latter feature developed 42 watts at 4,000 rpm and could fire a 6- or 12-volt trouble light when connected via the optional "handy plug-in receptacle on the control panel."

Generally in the 3-to-5½-hp range, Clinton outboards were also wholesaled to a number of other firms that marketed them under their own private-brand labels.

By the early 1980s Clinton signed a temporary pact with rival Eska agreeing to limit the sale of Clintons in certain markets.

There used to be an old fisherman near my summer place on Lake Champlain who every evening faithfully outboarded to a distant fishing spot. Curious about the brand of his busy-sounding little fishing motor, I finally asked.

"Uh, it's a *good* one," he responded, subsequently admitting he forgot who had made it.

Later I discovered it was a Clinton and realized that not everyone needs to buy a motor from one of the big manufacturers.

Coast-to-Coast

A 1965 offering of the Midwestern Coast-to-Coast variety stores, these small motors were marketed in 4- and 6-hp sizes.

Columbian (Cullen)

"Unlimited enjoyment at very little expense" is essentially what the Cullen Motor Company of Chicago offered its outboarding customers from 1913 to 1918. Like many of its contemporaries, the 2-hp (at 900 rpm) Columbian (also labeled Cullen) resembled Ole Evinrude's standard rowboat motor. The later Cullen (or Columbian) models had a flywheel magneto.

In the final production year the Cullen Motor Company equipped its outboards with an aluminum piston, thus "reducing the weight of the motor... and its vibration while running." The firm advertised its pride in marketing the motor "with a get-there come-back reputation."

Commando

See the listing for Milburn.

Commodore

Essentially a relabeled 2-hp West Bend fishing motor, the Commodore was available around the time President Kennedy took office. Bigger Commodore-brand outboards came in such sizes as 7½, 10, 18, and 40 hp.

Continental (1)

Added by late 1932 to the long list of former Detroit outboard makers was the Continental Motors Corporation. It had begun production in 1926. This outboard is not to be confused with the small post-World War II single from California.

Continental (2)

See the listing for Milburn.

Corsair

In 1948 Scott-Atwater began producing a line of private-brand outboards for the Corsair Outboard Motor Company, of Minneapolis, Minnesota.The outboards were distributed by both Skelly Oil Company and Pure Oil Company. When Scott was acquired by the McCulloch people in 1956, the new management briefly continued the construction of Corsairs. The line was discontinued in 1957.

Crescent

Direct from the "maybe, who knows?" department comes an early World War I-era rowboater called the Crescent. Actually, this listing was almost omitted, but a fellow old-outboard collector is pretty sure he saw an old brochure—somewhere—advertising such a forward-pointing single. The motor was said to have been built by a long-forgotten outfit in Scotia, New York. For years a river bend in that community has been known as the "crescent." Perhaps there's a connection?

Crofton

See the listing for Fageol.

Cross (Cross Radial, Sea Gull)

A family business on Detroit's waterfront, the Cross Gear and Engine Company had roots in the manufacturing of brass marine accessories. The firm branched out into the production of inboard engines and by 1928 began building a 73-cubic-inch, 35-hp outboard called the Cross Radial. The giant, 4-cycle kicker got its name from the powerhead arrangement with "5 cylinders placed radially around the shaft, the axis of the cylinders being horizontal." Not designed for fishermen seeking a trolling motor, the 135- to 160-pound Cross Radial appealed to a few high-speed enthusiasts desiring an outboard larger than any other. Either a tractor or pusher lower unit could be furnished, and

"the gear ratio could be made suitable for racing or ordinary service."

Cross Radial owners filling the 3-gallon (around the flywheel) gas tank and 1-gallon oil reservoir were ready to be treated to "lightning acceleration." Those behind the big outboard were treated to a roar, as no muffler was used. Speeds of 45 to 50 mph were targeted by the manufacturer.

The Cross firm recognized that its water-cooled radial model (which soon had been beefed up to 50 hp) was not for everyone. Consequently, in 1931 it introduced an outboard motor promised to be "smooth, alert, simple, perfect for your wife and kiddies to handle." This gentler offering came in the form of the 40-cycle, 29.68-cubic-inch "Sea Gull 29." The masculine-looking, two-cylinder motor, in service form, generated between 20 and 25 hp.

Its racing sister with twin carbs and battery dual ignition (two spark plugs for each cylinder) wore a gas tank with a pair of filler caps. As on the service Sea Gull 29, about three-quarters of the tank held gasoline, while the other quarter was an oil reservoir.

Most old-motor enthusiasts agree the Sea Gull 29 racer, complete with ultra-streamlined lower unit, was one of the most beautiful motors ever produced. The 76-pound rig had aluminum pistons and no-nonsense open exhaust stacks. Racers were rated at 28 hp at 6,000 rpm.

Although of the opposed-cylinder configuration, Sea Gull 29s were alternate-firing engines. Believing people would be fired up to buy these motors, production was said to have been increased 300 percent for 1932. (Of course, that wasn't too difficult in light of small 1931 production runs.)

Cross Radial and Sea Gull 29 motors were built through 1933. The previous year the outboard division (renamed Cross Motor Sales Corporation) told prospective dealers that the Cross franchise would "be even more valuable in the years to come!" Early Thirties economic troubles got the better part of that claim. The business was reduced to three members, and no new Cross outboards were marketed after the close of 1933.

The once-ambitious firm sold its outboard interests to the Detroit Outboard Products Corporation of St. Clair Shores, Michigan. Although the racing twin and radial designs were permanently retired, this new organization resurrected the Sea Gull 29 service model as a 1940 motor called the Detroiter.

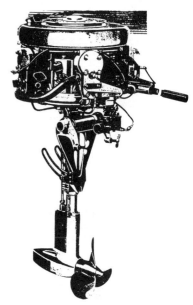

For 1928, the Cross Radial equipped with "tractor" lower unit was designed for serious speed enthusiasts.

Cunard

A rowboat motor marketed by Russell A. Reed of New York City, the Cunard was available during 1916. The single-cylinder kicker was rated at 2½ hp at 675 rpm.

Cyclone

It's hard to believe anyone would have the nerve to name an approximately 2-hp motor the "Cyclone"! That's just what the folks at the Bellevue Industrial Furnace Company did, however, when labeling their "new patented detachable rowboat motor, specially designed for fishing and pleasure trips."

The water-cooled, forward-pointing, single-cylinder engine wore a knob-start flywheel, a tin-can muffler (positioned under the gas tank), and a reversing lower unit. Both sides of the cylinder had spacers and wing nuts holding brackets connected to the transom clamp assembly. You could loosen the wing nuts, tilt the motor angle, and retighten after reaching the desired position.

Filled with the usual exaggeration of the day, Cyclone brochures claimed its special features would drive an ordinary rowboat about 11 mph. (I bet "about" is the key word here!) The literature also made it clear that anyone who attempted to steal the company's patents, such as the mysterious "non-vibrating device," would not escape prosecution.

One of the many "troubles [that would] cease when you own a Cyclone" was fouling by water vegetation, as the outboard wore a weedless prop. Actually, this wheel looked very much like the useful weedless props of post-World War II Evinrude/Johnson 3-hp fame. The propeller could be replaced with an accessory pulley "for running different kinds of machinery." (Coolant water would have to be supplied by a garden hose.)

The Cyclone was advertised at around $100. Apparently, few customers with money to burn felt the Detroit-based furnace firm's offering was hot enough. Although little Cyclone information exists today, it appears the outboard was made around 1914.

I can't help but wonder if George Thrall (the Detroit boiler factory owner who was said to have helped develop the early Waterman) had something to do with the Cyclone.

Davis (Experimental)

The Davis outboard was a 1930s prototype. Its water-cooled, 4-cycle, five-cylinder, radial-type powerhead got mated to a Caille lower unit. The 29.96-cubic-inch Davis was said to develop 27 HP at 6,500 rpm. Although Wllliam Morris Davis worked up an operable outboard and spare powerhead, his plans to produce the class "C" racer never went any further.[14]

Detroit

Logically, the Detroit was produced in its Michigan namesake. The front-pointing single with a knob-start flywheel was offered in both 1914 and 1915.

Detroiter

When the "new" Detroiter was introduced as "1940's outboard sensation," the poor thing was already about 10 years old. Although modified here and there, the 18-hp Detroiter was obviously a reincarnation of the old 4-cycle Cross Sea Gull 29.

Convinced boaters would love to say "good-bye to chatter, stink, and stalls" of 2-cycle outboarding, Detroit Outboard Products (based in St. Clair, Michigan) purchased the rights to the early Thirties Cross 4-cycle kicker. As had been said of the Cross in 1931, it was claimed that the Detroiter would give performance equaling "the smoothness of the modern motor car." Detroit Outboard Products also stressed the 4-cycle's tremendous oil savings, another big sales point made by Cross.

One readily discernible external difference between the two related motors was the gas tank. The Detroiter's tank was somewhat more rounded than that of the Cross Sea Gull 29.

Detroit Outboard Products really tried to entice potential dealers by offering to protect them "fully." The company swore that no direct factory-to-owner sales would ever take place "without paying full commission to the dealer controlling the territory." In addition the firm pledged to increase the product line by quickly following its 18-horse model with 5- and 10-hp versions, which were allegedly completely designed and ready for production. Furthermore, said the new company, with a Detroiter rig "the old bang-bang days are gone from outboarding." Boaters, they promised, would wait in line to buy its products.

Flyers for Detroiter claimed their (proposed) 10-horse motor got its power via four cylinders. Exhaust was piped through a hollow propeller shaft. At 49 pounds, the Detroiter Four (which apparently never saw production) was designed to compete with Evinrude Zephyr. The 1940 Detroiter Four brochure did not specifically state 4-cycle operation.

By the next year, however, customer acceptance was still about as imaginary as mermaids, which were depicted swimming around the Detroiter's logo. The company's limited outboard production concluded with America's entry into World War II.

Dragonfly "Troller" consisted of Power Products lawnmower engine and truck radiator fan mounted on transom clamp brackets. (Miville Fournier photo)

Dragonfly

Like its direct competitors in the air-prop outboard avenue, the air-cooled, single-cylinder Dragonfly was most attractive to swamp and shallow-water boaters. Aptly named by Robertson, Hedges, Inc., of Kansas City, Missouri, these mechanical dragonflies enjoyed a 10-year manufacturing run beginning in 1954.

The Dragonfly came in two sizes: 4.7 and 8.0 cubic inches. Over the years they generated power in the 2-to-5-hp range and sported model names like Troller and Cruiser.

Durkee

A 1930 motor, the Durkee was marketed by Durkee Manufacturing Company, which was based in Grassmere, New York.

Eclipse

See the listing for Bendix.

Elgin

Every old-outboard nut knows the feeling. Someone professes to have a real vintage boat motor for sale—maybe, if the offer is right.

"Been in the family for yeeeaars! And it ran the last time we tried it, too."
As you walk toward the guy's old shed, you inquire what color the engine is.
"Uh, kinda medium green,"
Yes, there under a torn tarp is an *Elgin!*

One of the first outboards to wear a fiberglass hood was the 1953, 16-hp Elgin, produced by West Bend and sold by Sears.

Although most Elgins are not at all rare, the marque's survivors serve as a tribute to its reliable design and construction.

Elgin outboards first hit Sears stores and catalogs in 1946. They were eagerly supplied by the West Bend Aluminum Company (Hartford, Wisconsin), which led the premier with a 2-cycle, single-cylinder, air-cooled, 1¼-hp job. This rope-start, green Elgin with a yellow-gold decal was widely accepted and set the stage for subsequent, water-cooled one- and two-cylinder versions in 2½- to 7½-horse denominations.

A sturdy 16-hp twin (with shift) was added in 1949. The 16 had many innovative features, including a fiberglass hood and rewind starter knob at the base of the cowling. Such placement provided a lower center of gravity and prevented the outboard from kicking up when the cord was yanked.

Among the 1955 Sears outboard offerings was an interesting pair of "variable-horsepower" Elgins. The West Bend–produced Elgin 12- and 25-hp models featured Regu-Lock, a key-activated switch to vary the outboard's horsepower. Sears's Compact Elgin 12 could be key set "at 5 hp for rental boats, 7½ for youngsters, and 12 hp for full action speed." The Power-Packed Elgin 25 Regu-Lock limited throttle advance to key in 7½, 15, or 25 horses. It was a novel effort in customizing the motors' horsepower "to suit type and condition of boat, or for use by young or inexperienced operators."

In the mid-Fifties some other Elgins were equipped with gearshifts and electric starters (1956), and sported attractive colors ranging from light green with gold accents, to coral and copper. Power on the top-of-the-line motors was faithfully increased.

Beginning in 1959 the Elgin line was a mix of West Bend– and McCulloch–produced outboards. McCulloch's involvement lasted through the time the Elgin name was switched to "Sears." The final West Bend Elgins were produced in the early Sixties.

For most boaters with a memory, the Elgin essence is embodied in a beat-up 5½ twin—the one wearing that little *Sears* script on its bare aluminum rope sheave—the one you could even start with a piece of clothesline and with a few pine needles floating in the gas tank. Until the last aluminum rowboat disappears from some little lake somewhere, there will always be Elgins. (See also West Bend, McCulloch, Waterwitch.)

Elto

Ole Evinrude's wife Bess became ill around 1913. Because nothing meant more to Mr. Evinrude than his spouse, he decided to sell his portion of the famed outboard company (bearing the Evinrude name) in order to devote all his time to Bess's recuperation. After six years of leisurely auto and yacht travel, Mrs. Evinrude was restored. Ole's thoughts returned to motors.

By 1919 the outboard pioneer had come up with a 2½- to 3-hp kicker composed largely of war-proved aluminum. This

Amist billboards touting Atwater-Kent radio sets, Yellow Cabs, and men's drawers, a 1925-era 4-hp Super Elto Light Twin (Ruddertwin) is loaded onto a Model T Ford delivery truck. The "Propello" sign on the lower right of the building refers to Elto's cooling water intake system. Words on the top right of the store identify Elto as "Ole Evinrudes fastest motor!" At that time, the rival Evinrude company was not owned by the Evinrude family. (Outboard Marine Corp.)

Elto's ad agency probably purchased the "catch" pictured in this 1925 catalog photo at a local fish market. The motor is an Elto Ruddertwin with battery ignition (note the wires wrapped around the clamp bracket/carrying handle assembly). The aluminum flywheel "knuckle buster" starting knob was spring-loaded; it retracted when it wasn't being cranked. (Outboard Marine Corp.)

opposed-twin-cylinder rig weighed in at just 47 pounds, representing greater portability than the old rowboat motors. Excited by the new project, Mr. Evinrude offered it to his old partner, who now owned all of the Evinrude Outboard Motor company. Surprisingly, the plan was quickly rejected, leaving Ole nearly heartbroken.

Bess encouraged her husband to reenter the outboard business himself. After all, his 1913, five-year noncompete clause with the Evinrude firm had expired.

> "But, Bess," he reminded her, "the commercial use of our name was sold with the old company."
> "Well, then, let me come up with something catchy," Bess suggested. "Maybe a clever, easy to remember name like Kodak."

So, identifying Ole's new motor as *E*vinrude's *L*ight *T*win *O*utboard, the creative woman coined the acronym ELTO, and a major outboard label was born.

The Elto motors were an instant hit, making Ole and Bess's new company profitable by its second year (1922). Elto's first offering was dubbed "Ruddertwin" (although its shiny aluminum exterior caused Ole to call it "Silvery") because it steered with a rather large rudder. After a few years of a thin, solid rudder, this model said good-bye to its traditional water pump and got a hollow, water-scooping rudder in 1924. Ignition was generated via battery and Atwater-Kent timer. The flywheel-knob-start Ruddertwin was upgraded to 4 hp in 1926.

By the late 1920s Ole and Bess's college-age son, Ralph, urged his folks to enter outboarding's new high-performance avenue. This plea was met in late 1927 with the two-cylinder. 7-hp Speedster, and the four-cylinder, dual-carbed Quad. Speedsters could plane a boat over 20 mph, while a good Quad would put a light hull on speaking terms with 40! Both products helped revolutionize the outboard industry by taking it out of the "putt-

Almost identical to its American-made 36-cubic-inch Gale Products brothers, this 1955 Elto 22 was built at OMC's Ontario factory. Tiny maple leaf decal on cowl accent boasts of national origin.

putt" realm. Eltos of this era wore Atwater-Kent timer-fired battery ignition and could be "started with a quarter turn" of the "knuckle buster" flywheel knob.

The Quad got updated in 1929 with more cubic inches and fancy cylinder covers. It and the '29 Speedster were available in standard and high-speed (with auxiliary air intakes, aluminum pistons, etc.) versions.

When Elto merged with Evinrude, and then with Lockwood in late 1929, Ole found himself in charge of three major outboard firms. The new corporate umbrella was named Outboard Motors Corporation (OMC), and Mr. Evinrude, his family, and associates opted to simplify advertising by highlighting the merger. A late-Thirties issue of *Fortune* provides some Monday-morning quarterbacking on the topic:

> The [new] company set out to impress upon the public that here was the ultimate fount of all outboarding wisdom. In a great institutional advertising campaign the grandeur of Outboard [Motors Corp.] as a merged entity was stressed, rather than the existence of its products [Elto, Evinrude, and Lockwood], and this was a mistake since it tended to wash out the name value of the separate lines. It also caused intense dismay among the several thousand Elto and Evinrude dealers who for years had been in competition.[15]

Actually, since the merger idea developed quite rapidly (in 1929), Elto had already planned a 1930 line of its own. This model year featured seven Eltos, from 2¾ to 35 hp. The two small Elto motors, the 2¾-hp Foldlite (which was actually an Outboard Motors Corporation engine) and 3½-hp light-weight, were twin-cylinder rigs which folded for portability and storage.

The well-tried standard (or Service) Speedster, touted as Elto's 7-hp "fast rugged utility model," could be ordered with rudder steering and optional underwater exhaust silencer. A new member of the 1930 Elto line checked in at 14 hp wearing the Senior Speedster decal. This beauty had standard underwater exhaust and optional electric starting.

Topping the Elto lineup was a 35-hp Quad. Like the Senior Speedster, it could be purchased with an electric starter, but was manually cranked by a cord instead of the Senior Speedster's flywheel knob.

For 1931 OMC began advertising Elto's trademark by touting "ELTO—BATTERY IGNITION OUTBOARD MOTORS." That year the popular Service Speedster was given 1 hp more (making 8 hp) and sold for $165. With an additional five-dollar bill, one could get the new 12-horse Special Speedster. This motor was somewhat of an amalgamation of OMC parts stock as were several other Eltos during the Great Depression.

Also introduced in 1931 was Elto's Junior Quad 18-hp motor, as well as an Evinrude Speeditwin takeoff called the Super C 25-hp

model. "Tucked away in its crankcase [was] a new-type rotary valve that works marvels in performance and economy." The 35-horse Quad of 1930 was boosted to 40 hp for 1931. Electric starting was available for it, the Super C, Junior Quad, and Senior Speedster.

The year 1932 was a pretty tough one economically, but the Elto division of OMC came up with a new Super A 11-horse twin and a 4-hp Fisherman twin with a weedless prop.

Most folks could hardly pay the rent, let alone purchase a new outboard. As a result, ads shouted, "Here's ELTO quality at the lowest prices in ELTO history!" The retail price of some models (such as the Special Speedster) was actually reduced from the previous model year.

Eltos of 1933 still sported battery ignition, but switched to a new way of measuring horsepower. Sample Eltos were taken to the Pittsburgh (PA) Testing Lab, where they got rated for horsepower certified by the National Outboard Association. This new method provided an accurate standard but dropped the advertised output of most models. (OMC then affixed a little gold "certified NOA HP" medallion to its products.) The Senior Quad got bumped back from 40 to 31.2 hp; the Super C went from 25 hp to 21.1; while the Junior Quad, previously 18 hp, dropped to 16.2. Also affected by the new measurements was the Super A, going from 11 to 8.5 horses. By the way, this rather small (by today's standards) twin could be upgraded via an optional electric starter. New to the

Half-hp Cubs being tested prior to shipment to dealers. Motors numbers 3, 4, and 9 have conked out. Notice the starter cords in the upper left. (Shipyard Museum)

A 1936 Elto Ace.

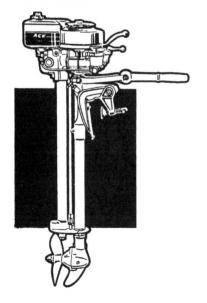

1933 line was a nonfolding Lightweight 5.1-hp twin and Super Single, a 2.2-horse rig sporting front-mounted fuel tank.

Ole's wife Bess had passed away in 1933, and Ole was often clouded in a fog of loneliness. There were times, however, when he'd put the final touches on a new concept in outboard styling. A couple of shrouded, or Hooded Power, outboards were introduced for 1934. They gained positive attention and were the major focus of OMC's desired modernization direction.

Ole died during the summer of Elto's 1934 model run, signaling a de-emphasis on the Elto line. Around this time, Elto and Evinrude motors began being sold in the same dealer showroom. Advertising often linked the pair, urging boaters to move up to a new Evinrude-Elto. Magazine ads running at about the time of Ole's passing simply featured this theme and even included a little coupon you could fill out concerning your present (old clunker of an outboard) motor. After receiving such particulars (make, model year) and noting an X next to "Good ____, Fair ___ , or Poor ____" condition, OMC would mail you back an appraisal along with a new Evinrude-Elto catalog.

By 1940 Elto had clearly taken a backseat to Evinrude as its economy line, and separate Elto-only advertising was not common. Eltos of this era had (with a few exceptions) been upgraded with flywheel magneto ignition, but usually lacked the fancy shrouding of Evinrudes.

A good example of this rested with the tiny ½-hp Elto Cub. The 8½-pound baby Elto differed from the similarly endowed Evinrude Mate in that the Cub had no powerhead covers. Believe it or not, when "ELTO put a new price tag on the world's handiest motor" in 1940, you could pick up a new Cub for $26.50!

OMC had been renamed (Outboard Marine and Manufacturing in 1936) when Johnson was acquired by Evinrude. Consequently, the Elto ID plate now said Evinrude Motors instead of Outboard Motors Corporation. (This change indicated the close, literal family relationship between the Elto and Evinrude divisions, as well as flagged the Evinrude division as a strong influence on, perhaps even the seat of, engineering and marketing forces within OMC.) Late-Thirties and early-Forties advertising for Evinrude's bargain stable plainly stated, "Every motor in the complete Elto Line is designed by Evinrude engineers and built to Evinrude standards of dependability, starting ease, and smooth, quiet operation." That standard 1940 Elto offering included the Cub; the 1.1-hp Pal single; the one-lung, 1.8-horse Ace; the 3-hp Handitwin; the Lightwin 5 hp; and the 8.5-horse Fleetwin (which had always been an Evinrude name).

As it became clear America would be embroiled in World War II, Evinrude officials placed Elto on the back burner. Elto ad literature coasted to a stop after about 1940.

Evinrude management opted not to return Elto to the immediate postwar lineup. In 1949, however, the Elto name made a very brief American reintroduction. These Eltos were based on a

standard pair of economy kickers out of OMC's Gale Products plant. Labeled Sportster was a 5-horse, twin two-cylinder Elto, while a 12-hp twin got tagged with the famous Speedster model designation. This small family of Elto motors was mostly offered through Evinrude dealerships as the economy line. Elto disappeared from U.S. outboard catalogs the next year. Perhaps with OMC's 1950 introduction of the Gale-built Buccaneer, there was no need to have two budget brands.

The Elto line was produced and marketed in Canada for some time after World War II. Evinrude's Ontario factory turned out badge-engineered Eltos identical (except for decal and trim) to Gale's Buccaneer, Sea King, Brooklure, and others. In 1956, for example, Canadian-built Eltos (a rare sight in the States) ranged from a 3-hp single to an electric-start, 25-hp, 35.7-cubic-inch twin.

By the late 1960s, although no longer on the market, Elto began to enjoy another round of success. I wonder if Ole ever imagined his Silvery Ruddertwins, Speedsters, and Quads becoming some of the best-loved (and most desirable) kickers in today's antique outboarding scene.

Emmons

It looks like officials from the Emmons Specialty Company of Detroit sent their delivery wagon across town to pick up some relabeled Caille rowboat motors. The 1913–1916 2-hp Emmons "Oarsman" outboard was a deadringer for an early fold-up rudder Caille.

Ensign

Even though other makers unveiled numerous 1933 kickers, Van Blerck Marine of Newark, New Jersey, advertised that it had "the only MODERN outboard." The 4-cycle, four-cylinder (arranged like those of a Volkswagen Bug engine) Ensign power plant put out 30 hp and employed a "tractor" lower unit. This drive mechanism placed the propeller in front, instead of at the rear, of the gear case.

Ads said you could troll with the huge electric-starting outboard, but invited purchasers to open the Ensign's throttle, too. Obviously, any outboarder interested in this "car engine perched on a sleek lower unit" was more apt to buy such a rig for the latter suggestion. Not very many customers showed up, though, so the big Ensign did not return in 1934.

Eska

Ask a six-year-old kid to draw a picture of an outboard motor, and you'll most likely be presented with a good representation of an Eska These single-cylinder kickers were perhaps more generic than any other and offered would-be yachtsmen an opportunity to forgo oars.

The first (1960) Eska motors were simply relabeled stock purchased from Clinton. Within a few years the Eska Company of Dubuque, Iowa, duplicated some of Clinton's tooling and began manufacturing its own lower units. On top of these, Eska put 2-cycle, air-cooled powerheads secured from the Tecumseh small engine people.

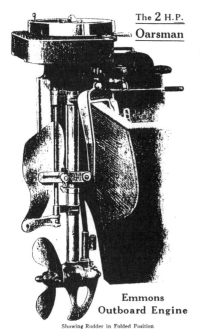

The 2 H.P.
Oarsman

Emmons
Outboard Engine

Showing Rudder in Folded Position

Evansville

Evinrude

Fageol
(Crofton, Homelite, Bearcat)

The 1963 Homelite 55 evolved from a Crosley car engine and the Fageol outboard.

HOMELITE
4-Cycle-55 hp Outboard

Eska initialed an agreement whereby it would pay Clinton (which backed off some of its outboard production) a royalty for every Eska sold.

Because a merchant needed only to commit to a couple of these "bargain-basement" motors per year, it was not uncommon to see little Eska franchises in country hardware and sporting goods stores.

In addition to marketing outboards under its own name, Eska supplied private-brand motors for the likes of Sears and Montgomery Ward. Over the years Eska called its various models names such as Golden Jet and Pathfinder.

Faced with foreign competition, a drop in the low-priced, gas-powered outboard market, and the desire on the part of some of its officers to retire, Eska closed up shop in the mid-Eighties. Fortunately, the company stayed in business long enough to provide motors for a lot of kids and the young at heart.

Emmons outboards looked suspiciously identical to some Caille engines. You could get a battery ignition model for seventy bucks, and a magnet version for twenty dollars more. Also available from Emmons (which probably got their stuff from nearby Caille) were carrying cases, underwater exhaust housings, canoe motor brackets, and steering handle/tiller arms.

The Evansville dates from 1933 to 1946. Not much is remembered about this outboard once offered by the Evansville (Indiana) Gas Engine Works.

See Chapter 2 for background and details for Evinrude outboards.

Anyone saying a Fageol outboard looked like a small car engine would be right! The unusual Fifties rig was, in fact, comprised of a 44-cubic inch Crosley auto power plant mounted vertically on a beefed-up Scott-Atwater lower unit. (Inboard versions were also available.)

Legendary inboard racer Lou Fageol flipped his competition boat at 120 mph in 1955 and was laid up in the hospital. While recuperating, Fageol got his outboard idea. The 4-cycle, in-line, four-cylinder, 35-hp, Crosley-powered Fageol went on the market the following year. This premier model was dubbed FAGEOL 44 and was purchased by boaters wanting 4-cycle power and fuel economy.

In 1957 the 44 was joined by a more powerful GOLD CUP 60 model. This 60-cubic-inch motor developed 55 hp.[16] While the 1956 Fageols had a rounded top with a wraparound, Mercury-like ribbed center cowl, the 1957s wore a fiberglass top (with Merc-style ribs), covering only three-quarters of the twin-carb powerhead. Consequently, many complete Fageols looked as if important parts were missing. By 1957 Fageol's deluxe single-lever remote-control had been introduced. Dubbed the "One-Arm Bandit," this unit actually sported two levers (one for starting) but used a single stick for speed and shift.

The 1958 Fageol line included 35- and 40-horse versions. During this production run, however, Mr. Fageol passed away suddenly, and the project (which had been plagued by a weak lower unit design) lost its impetus.

By 1959 the Kent, Ohio, based Fageol Products Company (a division of Twin Coach Co.) was sold to the Crofton Manufacturing Company in Los Angeles. This firm had been marketing auto-related Crosley engine products, so the connection was natural. Even so, Crofton let its acquisition go after only two years of offering a handful of Crofton-labeled Fageols. This sale opened the way for the best remembered incarnation of a Crosley powerhead outboard when Textron's Homelite Division used its purchase as the base of the 1962 to 1966 Homelite 55-horse, four-cylinder, 4-cycle kicker. Rights to the Homelite motor were sold to Fisher Pierce Company, Inc., of Rockland, Massachusetts (maker of Boston Whaler boats), in 1966. Fisher Pierce called their product "Bearcat 55." Using engines from the English, Coventry Climax auto, they soon raised their offering to an 85-hp model. Ironically, some Crosley enthusiasts are now buying the Bearcat and Homelite 55s and converting them to automobile use. These outboards generate more power than a standard Crosley engine.

I once found an old FAGEOL 44 in a remote upstate New York marina. The huge thing showed very little use, as the instruction tags were still affixed to the battery cable. True to form, the rig's lower unit was missing.

"A guy on vacation paddled in with this years ago," the marina operator recalled. "Wanted a replacement lower unit part or something. Asked him, 'Are you kiddin'? Parts for that weird thing way up here?' Sold him a new 40-horse Johnson, and he went on his way."

My castoff treasure was to cost me $10—or $25 if I required the marina man's services to help me get the 175-pound beauty into my trunk!

Federal

The U.S. capital was home to the Federal Motor and Manufacturing Company. During 1914 and 1915 this firm, through its Newark, New Jersey, factory, built an interesting twin-cylinder, 3-hp, knob-started outboard with a "tilt-up" transom bracket. This was one of the first motors to offer the convenient tilting feature. (Although some early Evinrude owners enjoyed the same effect by removing their motor angle adjustment bolt.)

Instead of the traditional tiller handle, a pair of cords maneuvered the Federal. Grips on the cords' ends held additional line for control toward the bow of the boat. You could get the Federal with battery or gear-driven Bosch ignition. An underwater exhaust tube was optional. The lower unit could be turned around for reverse operation. Spark plugs pointed to the front and were parallel with the water's surface.

A summer 1915 *Motor Boating* advertisement for the Federal emphasized the twin's smooth running characteristics (as

compared to the era's one-lungers). The ad showed a guy holding up an operating Federal and indicated the feat was done while the engine was turning 1,700 rpm! Nevertheless, the company took a turn for the worse and was bankrupt by the end of that year. (Note: This classy looking rig may have been revitalized in 1916. See National.)

Fedway Saber

See the listing for Saber.

Ferro

"Don't go rowing, go FERROwing!" suggested advertisements for this 2½-hp (at 850 rpm), single-cylinder outboard produced by the Ferro Machine and Foundry Company. Ads for the Cleveland, Ohio, firm's rowboat motor also pictured a pair of small boats headed for shore during a thunderstorm. One was being rowed by a sweaty, exhausted fellow (with his necktie unceremoniously undone). The other was being quickly "Ferrowed" to safety with a well-dressed, attractive woman at the controls! (I enjoy old outboards but, in that situation, would prefer oars.)

Some Ferros were adapted to canoe use by installing them in a special "well" one could cut into the center of one's craft. The "carpenter's plans" were available free from Ferro.

While many of its counterparts had simple fuel-mixing valves, Ferro bragged about a "genuine float feed carburetor." This was a major reason why Ferro said its motor was so dependable even "a girl can run it!" To give ears of any gender some quiet (without sapping the engine's power), a "scientifically constructed," water-cooled muffler was standard. A rudder, attached to the torque tube, turned with the lower unit for "propeller and rudder steering."

Ferros were fitted with a pair of petcocks. One, labeled a "priming cup," was tapped into the cylinder. The other, situated in the bottom of the crankcase, served as a drain. Some of the antique-looking motors stood on a "skeleton" skeg (while others were solid).

Buyers could choose between battery ignition or Bosch gear-driven, high-tension magneto ignition. The flywheel-knob-started Ferro was on the market from 1914 to 1917.

Firestone

The first outboards from the Akron. Ohio, Firestone Tire and Rubber Company were actually Scott-Atwater-produced kickers wearing the Champion label. During this time (1932–1942) the Champion outfit was little more than a middleman marketing organization.

After World War II Champion decided to build its own motor factory. So Firestone turned directly to the Scott-Atwater people for a newly designed private-brand engine. The Firestone nameplate hit the water in 1946 and developed a respectable following among fishermen.

By the mid-Fifties the Scott-Atwater-built Firestones gained more horsepower and features. Most notable of the latter was the

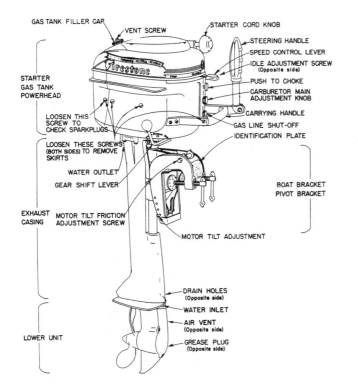

GAS TANK FILLER CAP
VENT SCREW
STARTER CORD KNOB
STARTER
GAS TANK
POWERHEAD
STEERING HANDLE
SPEED CONTROL LEVER
IDLE ADJUSTMENT SCREW
(Opposite side)
PUSH TO CHOKE
CARBURETOR MAIN
ADJUSTMENT KNOB
LOOSEN THIS
SCREW TO
CHECK SPARKPLUGS
CARRYING HANDLE
GAS LINE SHUT-OFF
IDENTIFICATION PLATE
LOOSEN THESE SCREWS
(BOTH SIDES) TO REMOVE
SKIRTS
WATER OUTLET
GEAR SHIFT LEVER
BOAT BRACKET
PIVOT BRACKET
EXHAUST
CASING
MOTOR TILT FRICTION
ADJUSTMENT SCREW
MOTOR TILT ADJUSTMENT
DRAIN HOLES
(Opposite side)
WATER INLET
AIR VENT
(Opposite side)
LOWER UNIT
GREASE PLUG
(Opposite side)

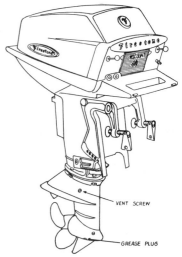

Left: Early-1950s, 7.5-hp Firestone.

VENT SCREW

GREASE PLUG

Above: West Bend-produced Firestone 40 Viscount.

Anyone for a Flambeau "sandwich?" Pictured are left and right halves of Metal Products twin cylinder motor with crankshaft, driveshaft, bevel gears, prop shaft, lower cylinder, piston, and connecting rod installed.

Knotometer on the 1956 5-, 10-, and 16-hp models. The Knoto-meter, a water speedometer, was built into the transom bracket assembly and dialed boat speed in knots as well as miles per hour. The handy device's pilot, or water pickup, was discreetly mounted in the leading edge of the lower unit. The Knotometer was exclusive to Firestone. It's strange that others haven't adopted such an accessory.

In the late Fifties the big tiremaker contracted with West Bend for its outboard supply. West Bend's successor, Chrysler, honored the remainder of the Firestone agreement.

By 1963, however, what had been a relatively complete line of motors was reduced to a few fishing engines when Firestone had Clinton take over the last two years of production of its outboard marque. These engines were identified as the Firestone Featherweight.

Here's an intriguing outboard you could "open up" two ways—by advancing the spark lever, or by placing the motor on its side, removing some screws, and literally opening the little kicker in half! The Flambeau's major components, from lower unit gears to top crankshaft bearing, fit into and were held together by two castings: a right and a left half.

This sandwich motor, made in Milwaukee by Metal Products Corporation, was introduced in 1946. Metal Products' president,

Flambeau

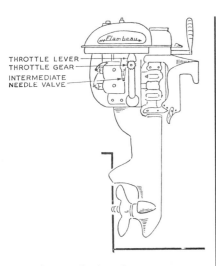

THROTTLE LEVER
THROTTLE GEAR
INTERMEDIATE
NEEDLE VALVE

Early-1950s Flambeau Twin

The complete 1952 Flambeau line, single and twin. The motors were built in two parts, then "sandwiched" together. In 1940, before designing these interesting motors, Flambeau execs tried to get their Milwaukee company going by offering to buy Mercury. In 1954, Flambeau planned a gearshift model, but never followed through.

George Kuehn, was an experienced outboarder, having been a class "C" amateur hydro-racing national champion in 1933. His company, however, never got into the production of fast motors.

Flambeaus were typically of the 2½-hp single-cylinder or 5-hp twin design. The 1950 models were rated at 3- and 6-hp, respectively, but dropped back to the lower figures the following year. The interesting little motors came standard with rope start, but rewind starters were available. Their unusual name may have come from Wisconsin's Lac du Flambeau Indian Reservation.[17] Native Americans in full regalia were sometimes pictured in company advertising. In addition to the trade name, Metal Products owned all of the Flambeau machining dies, but the casting, forging, and stamping were done by outside sources. [18]

The Flambeau ("the *TRULY* outboard"), which sat on the boat, had most of its powerhead mounted outboard. This resulted in very little fuel dripping inboard. (Of course, the waterway got an extra snootful.) On top of the gas tank (of some motors) was a knurled knob geared into a carb adjust mechanism.

From 1946 to 1949 the rig's exterior was unpainted aluminum with a yellow decal background. From 1950 Flambeaus wore a burgundy color. Flambeau twins of 1953 and later sported a lower-unit cavitation plate.

Metal Products got caught in the same bind as many other small outboard makers: it needed a larger power motor in order to compete in the growing postwar watersport scene. The firm did work up a 10-hp prototype (looking just like an overgrown 5-horse model) for boat-show exhibition. Retooling costs and lack of consumer interest probably prevented actual production.

In the early Fifties some 1,000 retail dealers handled Flambeau (mostly as a sideline). About 10 percent of total production was exported. In any event sales, which had never been remarkable, dropped further. This left little for Flambeau's promotional budget. Ads for the motors are virtually nonexistent past 1954, and Flambeau, "the Aristocrat of Outboard Motors," finally disappeared between 1956 and 1957.

Fleetwing

Color catalog pictures of familiar-looking 1½-, 3-, 5-, and 12-horse outboards sure seemed like Buccaneers. But on the page, plain as day, was a puzzling Fleetwing logo. Small rubber-stamp imprints on the very early Gale Products brochure help solve the mystery. "Please note," the additions warn, "the Fleetwing name is discontinued in favor of Buccaneer. New circulars will be avail-

Ever heard of an OMC Fleetwing? The name lasted only a few months before being switched to Buccaneer for the 1950 boating season.

able with the Buccaneer name." Apparently, some OMC bigwig (circa 1949) had second thoughts about the barely launched Fleetwing moniker. Outboard collectors might want to keep an eye open for an escaped pre-production (Buccaneer) Fleetwing. Maybe one or two actually left the Galesburg, Illinois, plant.

Offered in 1968 and 1969, Flying-O outboards were made in horsepowers such as 3½, 5, and 7.

An early-to-mid-Sixties private-brand marketed by J.C. Penney, the Foremost was produced by West Bend. These outboards were available in sizes such as 3½, 6, and 9.2 hp.

Another limited-production, private brand, the 3- and 5-horse Furies made a mad dash for outboard recognition in 1961.

See the listing for Buccaneer.

The year 1920 saw the Gierholtt Gas Motor Corporation of Marine City, Michigan, introduce its "direct-drive" outboard. The single-cylinder motor could shed its gas tank and long drive shaft for easy carrying (via a snow-shovel-style handle) like "a handbag." Also, anyone realizing he really didn't want a Gierholtt outboard after all could convert his adaptable machine to inboard use.

The Gierholtt folks said their "outboard of no inconveniences" solved the starting, shallow water, and weed problems. Unfortunately, it wasn't able to do anything about the no-customers problem and went out of production two years later.

Gierholtt sold the outboard business to the Hess Motor Corporation from Algonac, Michigan. Hess gave its relabeled version of the Gierholtt a try from 1926 to 1928.

Gierholtt's early-1920s "direct drive" kicker

Flying-O

Foremost

Fury

Gale

Gierholtt (Hess)

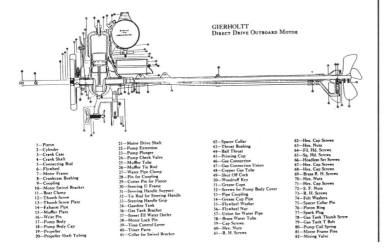

GIERHOLTT
DIRECT DRIVE OUTBOARD MOTOR

1—Piston	21—Motor Drive Shaft	42—Spacer Collar	62—Hex. Cap Screws
2—Cylinder	22—Pump Extension	43—Thrust Bushing	63—Hex. Nuts
3—Crank Case	23—Pump Plunger	44—Ball Thrust	64—Fil. Hd. Screws
4—Crank Shaft	24—Pump Check Valve	45—Priming Cup	65—Sq. Hd. Screws
5—Connecting Rod	25—Muffler Tube	46—Gas Connection	66—Headless Set Screws
6—Flywheel	26—Muffler Tie Rod	47—Gas Connection Union	67—Hex. Cap Screws
7—Motor Frame	27—Water Pipe Clamp	48—Copper Gas Tube	68—Hex. Cap Screws
8—Crankcase Bushing	28—Pin for Coupling	49—Shut Off Cock	69—Brass R. H. Screws
9—Coupling	29—Cotter Pin for Piston	50—Woodruff Key	70—Hex. Nuts
10—Motor Swivel Bracket	30—Steering U Frame	51—Grease Cups	71—Hex. Cap Screws
11—Boat Clamp	31—Steering Handle Support	52—Screws for Pump Body Cover	72—S. F. Nuts
12—Thumb Screw	32—Tie Rod for Steering Handle	53—Pipe Coupling	73—R. H. Screws
13—Thumb Screw Plate	33—Steering Handle Grip	54—Grease Cup Pipe	74—Felt Washers
14—Exhaust Pipe	34—Gasoline Tank	55—Flywheel Washer	75—Spacer Collar Pin
15—Muffler Plate	36—Gas Tank Bracket	56—Flywheel Nut	76—Piston Ring
16—Wrist Pin	37—Street Ell Water Outlet	57—Union for Water Pipe	77—Spark Plug
17—Pump Body	38—Motor Lock Pin	58—Brass Water Tube	78—Gas Tank Thumb Screw
18—Pump Body Cap	39—Time Control Lever	59—Cap Screws	79—Gas Tank T Bolt
19—Propeller	40—Timer Parts	60—Hex. Nuts	80—Pump Coil Spring
20—Propeller Shaft Tubing	41—Collar for Swivel Bracket	61—R. H. Screws	81—Motor Frame Pins
			82—Mixing Valve

Early-1920s Geirholtt diagram.

Gilmore

Gopher

Gray

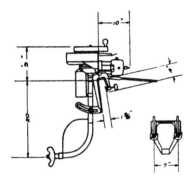

Gulf Queen

Guppy

Harrison

The Gilmore Marine Motor Corporation briefly entered the outboard business in 1920. By the following year the Marine City, Michigan, concern had left the field.

Designed by a mechanical engineering professor at the University of Minnesota, the Gopher outboards were actually produced (except for spark plugs and carbs) by college students. Two versions of the Gopher were built. The first version, from 1925, looked somewhat like a generic, forward-pointing, single-cylinder rowboat motor. More distinctive features included crank steering (similar to the Wright) and rounded gas tank.

By 1929 the professor simplified things and redesigned the Gopher as a direct-drive-style outboard (akin to the Palmer, Gierholtt, and Caille Liberty).

Over 100 "class project" Gophers were constructed. Some of the approximately 2½-hp outboards were sold to the public (for $75 to $80). Students with a spare twenty-dollar bill could take home their "assignment" for the cost of materials.[19]

In 1914 the Gray Motor Company of Detroit decided to try its luck in the fast-growing outboard motor market. Some 500 Gray Gearless outboards were produced between 1914 and 1917. This 52-pound, 3-hp (at 1,000 rpm) outboard was unique in that it used a flexible drive shaft to turn the prop on the end of a curved, "gearless" lower unit. Gray Gearless owners started their motors with a flywheel knob.

The Gray Motor Company also bought a few outboards from Caille, relabeled them, and sold the motors under the Gray nameplate. Gray's moniker has long been associated with the manufacture of 4-cycle inboard marine engines.

Gray Gearless outboards were produced from 1914 to 1917.

My guess is that this small 1960s outboard was a private-brand supplied by Clinton.

See the listing for Lancaster.

During the late Sixties, Birmingham (Ohio) Metal Products, Inc., manufactured a mean-looking pair of racing outboards. These Harrison class "A" (approximately 15-cubic-inch displacement) and "B" (approximately 20-cubic-inch) motors were designed for easy, quick disassembly and reassembly. Harrison lower units featured a "removable lower skeg and drain plug." Spark was available with "flywheel or battery ignition."

The Harrison racers' most prominent feature was a curved horn-of-plenty-type exhaust tube. This thing looked a bit like a saxophone and played its alcohol-burning tune just above the

waterline. Birmingham shipped the Harrisons "completely tuned" for competition performance.

The manufacturer indicated one of its "B" models powered a hydro at over 88 mph. The firm also boasted of National Outboard Association straightaway records.

Hartford

In the last years before the Great Depression, 311 interesting outboard motors found their way out of an old brick building in Hartford, Connecticut. These Hartford STURDY TWIN engines, just shy of 20-cubic-inch displacement, were touted as "exceptionally fast motors for class B racing enthusiasts."

The Hartford, offered by Gray and Prior Machine Company, was designed by partner George Prior. The first year for the Sturdy Twin was 1927. Production continued through much of 1929, with the bulk of the marque being constructed in 1928.

Although marketed for a scant three years, the outboard saw numerous changes. The muffler was modified a couple of times, finally ushering in an underwater exhaust tube in 1929.

Early gas tanks attractively stamped with the Hartford name were, by mid-1928, replaced by tanks bearing decals. A change of magneto called for a different size flywheel. Later Hartfords wore Tillotson (instead of Gray and Prior) carbs. An early water pump didn't work too well and was replaced by a water pickup scoop in back of the prop area (The old-water-pump models could be returned to the shop for modification.)

Cast-iron cylinders and pistons gave way to a cast-iron-cylinder-aluminum-piston combo. This finally opened the route in 1929 for aluminum pistons and aluminum cylinders wearing steel sleeves (a real innovation at the time).

Not enough of these quality Hartfords were produced to compete seriously in the changing outboard industry. Consequently, near the end of 1929, when the nearby Indian Motorcycle Company of Springfield, Massachusetts, expressed interest in entering the boating field, Gray and Prior sold the cycle firm all of the Sturdy Twin patterns and tooling for some $15,000.

The first year of the new decade would see a transformed Hartford wearing the legendary Indian Silver Arrow nameplate.

Should you ever have the good fortune to scout out a Hartford, the serial number's last two digits will tell you its vintage.[20]

Henninger (H.A.)

One of a few early West Coast outboards, the Henninger was produced by the Henninger and Ayers Manufacturing Company of Portland, Oregon. Mr. Ayers got his initials mentioned in some Henninger ads when the motor was referred to as the H.A. No matter the motor had two names, as it was sold only a single year, 1918.

Hiawatha (1)

Montgomery Ward and Company's first private-brand outboard was the rudder-steered Hiawatha. This forward-pointing, single-cylinder rowboat motor developed 1¼ hp. The 2-cycle, flywheel-

knob-start rig could be purchased from "Monkey Wards" with either battery ignition ($38.95) or flywheel magneto ($52.90).

According to the mail-order house's 1916 catalog, this kicker would be shipped to you "from a factory in Southern Michigan." Only Ward's officials were supposed to know it was the Caille outboard motor factory.

Hiawatha (2)

Gamble-Skogmo, Inc., a large Minneapolis-based retailer, first ordered a line of private-brand outboards in 1941. These Hiawatha motors were secured from OMC's Gale Products Division.

By 1956 Hiawathas were being built by the Scott-Atwater (subsequently McCulloch) people. This 1956 series, from 3.6 to 30 hp, was finished in an eye-catching aquamarine color. The larger motors featured a Scott-Atwater-introduced automatic boat bailer (working in conjunction with the water pump) called Bail Master.

Gambles, "the friendly store," ran beautiful multicolor ads in fishing magazines (very unusual for a private brand) and offered "big trade-in allowances" for those moving up to a Hiawatha motor.

The marque moved out of the outboard picture at the end of the 1961 boating season.

Hi-Speed

The Hi-Speed Motor Company of Chicago began offering an Evinrude rowboat-motor-type clone in 1914. By today's standards the Hi-Speed was anything but! Production, however, did come to a fast halt two years later.

Homelite

See the listing for Fageol.

Hubbell

When Evinrude and Johnson resumed outboard production following World War II, neither firm decided to reenter the racing scene. This move made it difficult for racers with prewar high-speed rigs to obtain new parts. As a result, OMC's chief marques were happy to sell Randolph Hubbell the rights to cook up factory-spec replacement racing-motor components.

A 1961 Hubbell KR racer on a Mercury Quicksilver drive shaft housing. The lower gearcase is missing. Tuned exhaust motor burns alcohol fuel.

Within five years Mr. Hubbell was making so many parts that (with the exception of items such as carbs and mags) he had enough stuff in his South El Monte, California, shop to build complete, new/old-stock style racing motors. Pretty soon, fast outboards, looking a lot like old Johnsons but bearing the Hubbell name, were showing up in competition. Most famous was his class "C" (Johnson PR) C-52 model.

Hubbell was obsessed with keeping the old class "A" Johnson KR racer competitive. Through the early Sixties he offered alcohol-burning versions of the "Hubbell KR" mounted on

a sleek Mercury Quicksilver lower unit. The "Hubbell SR" class "B" opposed twin was similarly marketed. Hubbell also made outboards called Mercury "Wildcats." Using stock, gas-powered KG4H, KG7H, and Mark 20H Mercs, the Hubbell shop converted them to full-race, alcohol-burning, modified Mercury powerheads (on Quicksilver lower units). Wide, clear plastic fuel line, and a Hubbell cat (wearing a sailor hat) logo distinguished (externally) these super-high revving rigs from regular "H" model Mercurys. Anyone owning a Hubbell has a good example of a quality, limited-production racer.

Husky

A low-priced, mid-1960s outboard, the Husky was marketed by Ward International, Inc., of Studio City, California. (See Milburn).

Indian

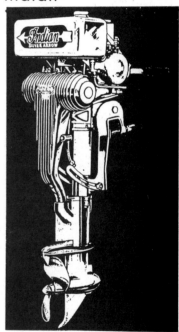

The Indian "Silver Arrow" was based on an earlier outboard called Hartford "Sturdy Twin." Both legendary motors were short lived.

Seeing the success of Elto and Johnson, the Springfield, Massachusetts, based Indian Motorcycle Company thought it might like to branch into the outboard business. Its opportunity came when the nearby Gray and Prior people decided to part with their inventory of Sturdy Twin outboard stock and related tooling and patterns.

This was in economically troubled late 1929, but Indian went ahead with a few Sturdy Twin modifications, turning the old predominantly aluminum Hartford into a shiny new 1930 Indian Silver Arrow. Most striking was the large, beautifully cast muffler assembly. It sported the famed Indian logo and was tastefully ribbed almost down to the water line. The Silver Arrow's throttle twist grip was borrowed from the firm's motorcycle parts bin.

Today the few remaining Indians certainly gain visual attention at vintage outboard meets, but most don't seem to run too well. Probably due to the fact the Indian was rushed into production and marketed only briefly, the little bugs never really got worked out of its design.

The failing early-Thirties economy, along with Indian's logical commitment to concentrate on cycles, caused the firm to bow out of outboarding in 1931. Similar to the premature passing of a pop personality, the Indian Silver Arrow's short life and royal lineage quickly made it a minor legend.

Johnson

See Chapter 3.

Joymotor

From 1915 to 1923 people at the Joy Engineering Company (later called Joymotor Manufacturing Company) of Chicago produced a run of interesting single-cylinder rowboat motors. Only a very few are still known to exist.

One Joymotor was found in the late 1960s by an Antique Outboard Motor Club member. He reports "the flywheel rim, muffler, magneto, water lines, and the entire lower unit were

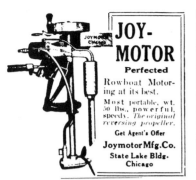

Joymotor ad, 1919.

The 1923 Joymotor model 7.

Jules

Karboater

Kemp

Kermath
Screw-Ball

nickel plated. The exhaust manifold and crankcase (with removable bronze bearings) were excellent aluminum castings and were highly polished. Original colors were red tank and flywheel, blue cylinder, and black transom bracket. Ignition (on this model) was by an American-made Dixie magneto which sits on top of the squared cylinder and is geared directly to the crankshaft. Also mounted on the cylinder was a plunger-type water pump."[21]

Joymotors were available with battery, or, previously noted, magneto. Canoe owners could get an optional mounting bracket or a special Joy Low-Down canoe model. This adaptation, designed for nautical safety, featured a Joymotor with a very short torque tube. A hole was drilled through the bottom of the canoe, and "a board flange on the bottom of the tube pressed up against the bottom of the canoe, through the ⅞[-inch] board and then through the base of the bracket which supported the motor. A large nut came down around this tube and tightly clamped canoe, board and bracket in one solid piece. A rubber gasket prevented leakage."[22] This placed the Joymotor inside the canoe with its flywheel just above the gunwale, making for a more stable craft.

Joymotor ads often detailed a reversing feature. When the tiller handle was swung to the extreme left or right, the lower unit would rotate 180 degrees, allowing the prop to push the boat backwards. Dialing the tiller grip a half turn would lock the driveshaft housing in any desired position. By the way, this housing, or torque tube, could "telescope" to fit transom heights from 17 inches to 21 inches deep.

The original water pump, situated at the powerhead, and the Joy Exhaust Silencer muffler (running directly under the fuel tank), were apparently redesigned in the late teens. A 1921 brochure pictured the silhouette of a model 7 Joymotor. This rig had a muffler pointing toward the water, as well as a hose to carry water up from the lower-unit-based pump. If ever there was an old outboard suitable for window display in an antique shop, the early Joymotor would get my vote.

A 4-cycle job out of a long-defunct firm called Jules Motor Corporation of Syracuse, the Jules was shipped from its central New York State port of entry from 1932 to 1933.

A Chicago firm, Karboat Manufacturing Company, produced this rare outboard in 1926.

See listing for Air-Drive.

These rigs weren't actually outboard motors, but looked like they could have been. In the 1950s, boaters had the option of drilling a hole through the craft's bottom and installing a Kermath (with large vertical powerhead inside and lower unit underside). This concept was akin to the early outboards permanently mounted in a canoe. Kermath Screw-Balls were available in a number of large

horsepower ratings. Fageol kickers of the late '50s could also be purchased in such a format. The Fageol version was dubbed V-I-P, for vertical-inboard-power.

Kingfisher

A very obscure outboard from the 1930s, the Kingfisher was produced by the Loos Machine Shop of Colby, Wisconsin, for a now-forgotten Minneapolis retailer.

It is estimated that 500 of these air-cooled, ⅝-hp motors were built, but a fire at the shop claimed all detailed specs.

The Kingfisher was meant to be a rock-bottom low-priced outboard, and its designers were penny-wise in providing no opening for the addition of gear grease to the cast-aluminum lower unit. This economy also offered the Kingfisher owner no way to drain off any water that might have entered via the prop shaft. Consequently, many Kingfishers stored in freezing weather burst their lower units. It is also noted that the magneto spark lever could not be completely advanced unless the gas tank cap had its air vent screwed closed.[23] This is akin to a hiccup cure which requires a patient to hold his breath indefinitely.

Klepper

This straight-shaft (Caille Liberty drive style) 3-hp outboard featured a spotlight on the fuel tank. The air-cooled rig was sold by a New York City firm specializing in folding boats but was of European manufacture. Klepper motors were introduced in the U.S. in 1955.

Koban

What's in a name? Well, in the case of Koban, America's first successful two-cylinder outboard, portions of its creators' names constituted the logo. Milwaukee residents Arthur *Ko*ch and Walter *Ban*non designed their heavy-set rowboat motor in late 1913. This 1914 model featured detachable finned cylinder heads and battery ignition.

The next year's model, available with battery or magneto ignition, was minus a starting knob on its "steering wheel-like" rimmed flywheel. The firm said the thing was so easy to get going, who needed a cumbersome knob? By 1918, however, the starting knob (and it was a good-sized one) was back, sitting on top of a 14-pound flywheel! A flywheel-mounted magneto was offered.

On some Kobans the cylinders and crankcase were cast *en bloc,* or in one piece. With the exception of the earliest model, Koban cylinder heads were smooth, lightly rounded, detachable components bearing the brand name. The rounded fuel tanks on these motors look too small for the rest of the engine. Not too small, though, was the bulk of this twin.

By 1920, after some six years of production, Koban actually increased the iron content of its hefty cylinders. That made a 3-horse (at 900 rpm) portable rowboat motor weigh in at 85 pounds. Contributing to the bulk were bronze rudder steering mechanisms and optional underwater exhaust tubes. Cooling water was pumped to the cylinders by means of a couple of ball

bearings acting as a check valve. The H_2O was coaxed into the valve via an exposed lower unit gear, which "twirled-in" its chilly prey. (Sounds great for weedy, sandy, or saltwater applications!)

As you can imagine, except for a few conservative diehards wanting a motor husky enough to survive getting run over by a bus, not many people were enchanted by Koban's weight. When the aluminum Eltos and Johnsons hit the early Twenties boating scene, the Koban became much less marketable. Koch and Bannon had already bailed out, selling the Koban Outboard Motor Company to Messrs. Schellin and Hoth.

In 1926 Koban, which was figuratively on its last heavy bronze lower-unit "legs," was sold by these partners to the Evinrude people. For a while Evinrude offered Koban parts and service, but opted not to continue Koban outboard production. It is possible the price of the Koban firm was low enough to warrant buying the company in order to rid the marketplace of another (albeit weak) rowboat-motor maker.

Recently discovered Evinrude documents list a model "100; Koban outboard motor assembly." It appears that, following Evinrude's 1926 purchase of the Koban firm, a few "leftovers" and/or Kobans made from parts obtained in the transaction, were offered for sale (on an informal basis) from 1927 to 1929. There doesn't seem to be any evidence that the Koban line was officially continued after 1926. Consequently post-1926 Kobans may have been peddled at the Evinrude factory store or at some of its more enterprising dealers.

If you find a Koban, the first digit of the serial number will tell the last digit of its year (up to 1919). In the case of 1920 to 1926 models, the first two numbers should reveal the Manufacturing date. [24]

A Lancaster Guppy found in a New England scrap yard. No gas cap, and a piece of rag for a spark plug. Drive tube is actually a length of plumber's pipe.

Lancaster Guppy

Large companies are always seeking diversification. During the early 1960s, the Lancaster (Pennsylvania) Pump and Manufacturing Company decided to use its respected pump technology and venture into the low-power-outboard business. The firm designed a lower unit complete with a small jet water pump (that propelled the boat via water pressure) and attached it to a Tecumseh lawn-mower-type powerhead. The result was called a Guppy model 30.

The novel motor steered with a U-shaped tiller rail, not unlike the top section of an aluminum lawn-mower handle. A change in the crank-to-driveshaft connection caused subsequent Guppy models to be classified as the 30A. The small jet outboard was finally taken off the market after 1967.

Some years ago, curiosity about the obsolete little Guppy led me to contact its former maker. The folks in Lancaster quickly indicated they retained no records covering their outboard products.

"Furthermore," someone there said, "just about all of the 500 or so Guppies had been sold to a supplier in Singapore." The

mental picture of the tiny Guppy pushing a Chinese junk only strengthened my resolve to locate a Lancaster. (Perhaps such is the lure of the old-motor hobby.)

In the 1990s more than a few of these cute, one-cylinder, 2-cycle rigs have surfaced in various regions of the U.S.

The five Danish Lauson brothers set up shop in Wisconsin and by the close of the 1800s began experimenting with engine building. Light, high-speed farm tractors were but one of the product types developed by the Lauson Company. After making small, air-cooled, 4-cycle power plants for pumps, garden equipment, and motor scooters, the firm began considering other outlets for its technology.

In 1940 Lauson introduced a 2½-hp, 4-cycle, air-cooled, single-cylinder outboard dubbed the Sport King. While understandably not keeping pace with the sales of major brands, the little Lausons did gain a following. Saltwater boaters enjoyed an air-cooled product devoid of corrosion-prone water pumps and cylinder jackets. Because 4-cycle engines seem to idle well, anglers liked the way the Lausons could troll.

The year 1941 saw the introduction of a pair of Lauson outboards consisting of an air-cooled, 4-cycle, lawn-mower-style powerhead mated (under a circular collar) to either a standard or a long-length lower unit. Checking in at 2¼ and 4 hp, these particular Lausons, wearing small cylindrical gas tanks, were offered only one year.

After World War II the 2½-hp single was reintroduced. It was replaced in 1948 by an upgraded, 3-horse, rewind-start model and joined by a new opposed twin (also with rewind) generating 6 hp. In the early Fifties the bigger Lauson was offered with an optional

Lauson Company's Sport King

MODEL "S-300"
4-Cycle Air Cooled
Single Cylinder Sport King 3 H. P. Outboard

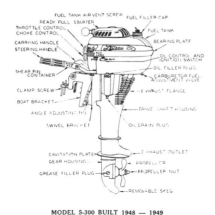

MODEL S-300 BUILT 1948 — 1949

A 1956 model Sport King. By 1958 Lauson's new owner, Tecumseh, grew tired of stocking parts for a product it chose not to produce. Remaining Lauson distributors were notified: "You're on your own." To soften the disappointment, Tecumseh invited former dealers to come to the old Lauson factory via station wagon or truck and cart home any outboard motor parts they could find . . . for free!

F-N-R shifter. Unlike most other outboard shift mechanisms, Lauson placed its unit between drive shaft and powerhead (instead of making it integral with the lower gears). The shift Lauson didn't work too well. Consequently, a 6-horse twin was introduced, having forward and neutral via a clutch. This rig, as well as the standard, forward-only Lauson, were better performers.

An old Lauson employee reported motors were tested on the factory's front lawn. There, 40 newly built Lauson outboards mounted on saw horses would take their turn being test-run. Some of these air-cooled kickers operated in the great outdoors eight hours per day for weeks. Their mechanical symphony drew a fair amount of attention from folks and livestock in Lauson's hometown.

My father recalls seeing, at a late-Forties New York boat show, Lauson's air-cooled, 25-hp prototype. He remembers it being painted brown and said the need for a flywheel cooling fan made the 4-cycle thing a real giant. No one else I've met ever mentioned viewing the big Lauson. A few lines of small print near the bottom of a 1940s (possibly 1941) Lauson outboard ad, however, promised "Coming! New Lauson 3-cylinder, 4-cycle Radial model outboard. Watch for details!" Perhaps this was the rig displayed at the show.

The company evidently realized that its largest market consisted of fishermen and opted not to enter the big-motor arena.

My grandfather was a bona fide Lauson enthusiast, finally trading in his trusty old 2½-hp Sport King for a bright blue 1950 6-horse model. He loved it, and as a Yale Ph.D. in chemistry, had numerous convincing arguments for Lauson ownership. That new motor ran great—until his passing, after which the chubby Lauson never worked right again. Really, you could pull and pull, drifting for miles, getting a couple of pops now and again. Experienced outboarders would borrow the Lauson for vacation and return it in the midst of bad words I'd never heard before. No cause for the motor's behavior was ever discovered. Perhaps it just missed its true owner.

Coincidentally, it was about 1956, right around the time my grandfather died, that Lauson's parent company (Hart-Carter of New Holstein, Wisconsin) decided to sell out to the Tecumseh small engine people. Tecumseh never reactivated Lauson's outboard motor division.

Lionel (Airex)

By the late 1950s America's most famous electric train maker realized that toy train sales were fast declining. Lionel had stepped into diversification by acquiring controlling interest in the Airex fishing tackle company and figured the introduction of an outboard motor could revive revenues. About $50,000 was spent—with an Italian firm—on the kicker's development, but severe money trouble as well as a nationwide recession halted the project. Consequently Lionel's proposed low-horsepower fishing outboard, which likely would have been marketed under the Airex name, never came down the track.[24a]

Published a few short months before the merger with Evinrude and Elto, a 1929 Lockwood catalog proudly boasted of the status connected with being the "oldest marine engine manufacturer in the outboard motor business." Lockwood had built up its plant and held a good supply of "working capital." The firm's factory and equipment were "situated on a tract of land sufficient for any future expansion." Less than a year later, however, the Lockwood facility was closed.

At the turn of the century the Lockwood brothers formed a Jackson, Michigan, company. This outfit was engaged in everything from electrical wiring jobs and spark plug manufacturing to fixing and selling bicycles. Within a few years the Lockwoods had acquired an Oldsmobile car dealership franchise. In between selling and servicing autos and their other activities, they began building 2-cycle, single-cylinder inboard marine engines. By 1914 a Mr. Ash had entered the fray, and the busy little company went into the outboard motor business.

Lockwood-Ash's first outboard effort was a forward-pointing, single-cylinder rowboat motor. In addition to "customer-direct" sales, the 1914 battery ignition, rudder-steered Lockwood-Ash kicker was wholesaled to Sears-Roebuck and offered under the Motorgo label. A couple of years later flywheel magnetos were available on the little motors. At the close of World War I, Lockwood-Ash began backing off inboard production and introduced outboards with an optional rope-start flywheel sheave.

In the early Twenties Mr. Ash passed away, and his heirs eventually sold out to the Lockwoods. By 1924 a new Lockwood two-cylinder (model T) outboard motor was unveiled, and the inboards, along with other business interests, were dropped in favor of the outboard division.

The 1926 (model 62T) and 1927 (model 72T) twins attracted a good deal of attention, as the little 4-to-5-hp units could put a light boat on speaking terms with 20 mph. Although it seems elementary today, Lockwood pioneered copilot steering (you could let go of the tiller and the motor would stay on course) under the trademark Lockwood-Pilot.

With such innovation taken into consideration, a young neighbor of the Lockwoods was shocked to see one of the firm's founders buying a Sears outboard! The lad's disgust was calmed only after he learned that Lockwood was still supplying Sears with motors, and the purchase had been made for test purposes.

An extremely talented young engineer named Finn T. Irgens joined the growing outboard company in 1925 and played an important role in the development of the stirring 1928 Lockwood Ace (class "A" model 82A) and Chief (class "B" model 82B). These were fast engines and became instant hits. The 50-pound Ace made over 27 mph in time trials, while a Chief-powered speedboat traveled faster than 35 mph. One unusual Ace and Chief feature was the skegless lower unit. (A skeg could be installed as an

Lockwood (Lockwood-Ash)

The 1929 Lockwood Silent Chief featured underwater "quiet" exhaust.

Someone replaced the twin carburetors on this 1929 Lockwood Racing Chief with a single carb. This suggests that after the motor was retired from serious competition, whoever ended up with it opted for simplicity of operation over an extra mph or two. Even with one carburetor, though, the Lockwood Model 92BR represented a pretty neat cottage racer.

option.) Propellers for these motors had a small cavity in each blade through which cooling water exited.

The 1929 (model 92A) Ace didn't get much modification over the previous year's offering, but its big sister (model 92B) received an underwater exhaust, making her the Silent Chief. A transparent Bakelite gas gauge graced the front of the gas tank. Carb and steering handle updates were also evident on the new Chief.

Although the original Chief's speed records were set with a service (or pleasure use) motor, Lockwood saw fit to augment its 1929 line with a model 92BR Racing Chief. This rig developed 30 percent more horsepower than the regular Silent Chief, and test runs pushed boats near the 40-mph mark. The Racing Chief was produced (in limited numbers) with "an entirely new type of [red] gasoline tank of pleasing but unusual appearance to add distinction and prevent confusion as to the exact type of motor." This beauty also wore dual carbs and a Lunkenheimer glass sight oiler automatic lubricating system " so that fresh, undiluted oil is fed from a duplex drip cup directly to the main and connecting rod bearings." (Note: Some 92BR models had a pair of oilers—one over each cylinder.) Its smaller flywheel and magneto came from the Ace.

While the 1929 line was being introduced, Lockwood engineers were busy working on a class "D" (approximately 40-cubic-inch) racer to be called the Flying-Four. The big rig's 4-cycle, flat, opposed, four-cylinder powerhead (like the old VW auto engine) sat atop a modified Chief lower unit. By the time the Flying-Four was to be released, Lockwood was seriously considering a merger with Elto and Evinrude. Additionally, company technocrats realized their unconventional outboard would be too cumbersome to compete with similarly rated 2-cycle motors. Some prototypes were worked up, but the model never saw production.

The 92BR racer became a one-year offering and didn't get much of a chance to show off, either. By the fall of 1929 Lockwood had merged with Elto and Evinrude, creating a new organization known as Outboard Motors Corporation. The Jackson, Michigan, factory was locked up, and its employees given the option of moving to Milwaukee.

A 1930 Lockwood catalog, featuring a Silent Electric Starting Chief, was released by the new firm. In the grips of the unfolding economic depression, however, the marque was quietly discontinued.

Interestingly, some spec sheets list a 1931 Lockwood "4-60" racer. If, in fact, ever marketed, this rare item differed from the famed Elto 4-60 (four-cylinder, 60 cubic inches) high-speed outboard in decal and model number only. Also, according to a few vintage references, a handful of "B" Lockwoods may have made it to the 1932 model year. Otherwise, a small stock of lonely Chiefs was reclassified as Montgomery Ward's Sea Kings. These

The 1928 Lockwood Ace was a favorite of pioneer Class "A" racers. The motor could be equipped with an accessory skeg.

final Lockwood products, some fitted with strange crank-up, spring-loaded "inertia starters," were stripped of their true identity and sold through Ward's mail-order catalogs—a humble end for a once proud marque. Reportedly, though, as late as the 1950s people were contacting the Evinrude office requesting Lockwood "literature, parts, and dealer franchises."[25]

Majestic

Badge-engineered Champions wearing the Majestic label premiered in 1950 (although some early Majestics might be considered as 1949s). Outboard Motor Brands, Inc., headquartered at a post office box in Minneapolis, marketed this marque, referred to as "King of the Outboard Motors."

Because of common ownership, Majestic simply disappeared with Champion at the close of 1958.

Mann's Troller

This interesting, albeit generic, private-brand outboard was marketed, not by some national chain store retailer, but from a sporting goods shop in Pinckneyville, Illinois. Ad sheets out of Mann's Sporting Goods targeted resort owners, commercial fishermen, and sportsmen to consider its 5-hp "quiet-strong" outboard motor called the Mann's Troller M5T.

At 29 pounds, this 2-cycle, air-cooled outboard featured a remote 3-gallon "handy stowaway gas tank" and 360-degree "swivel" steering. Its single-cylinder powerhead carried a 90-day warranty, while the lower unit was guaranteed a full year. This time difference was due to the fact that these two major parts came from separate manufacturers.

Meant to be a very inexpensive way to get a small motor on your fishing boat, the Mann's Troller differed from a number of its private-brand sisters (such as Mono) in name sticker only.

Mariner

Although sharing a name with the 1970s–1990s Mercury-marketed motor, this 1950s Mariner was sold through the Mariner Outboard Motor Company in Minneapolis. It was produced by Scott-Atwater, and finally by Champion.

Martin

"Slow down a little," my wife said, "this might be it."

"Let's see," I answered, glancing at directions scribbled hastily on the back of a new Johnson motor catalog. "Looks like we should turn in here."

Seconds after our car bumped down a dirt driveway, a bathrobe-clad senior citizen appeared at the screen door.

An hour earlier we'd stopped for ice cream at an Adirondack, New York, restaurant. I spotted a Johnson outboard dealership next door and walked over in search of old treasures.

"No, there's no vintage motors around here," the owner sternly noted. "But if you want some Martins, I will tell you where to find an old dealer. After Martin went under, this place just seemed to stop in time . . . still has some stuff for sale. You head down Route 8"—he pointed—"and take the first drive after the

1947 Martin ad targets fisherman.

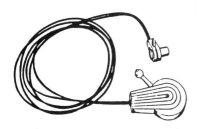

The end of Martin's remote speed control simply plugged into the spot that normally accepted the twist grip tiller handle. This accessory fit the company's 20-horse twin.

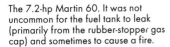

The 7.2-hp Martin 60. It was not uncommon for the fuel tank to leak (primarily from the rubber-stopper gas cap) and sometimes to cause a fire.

lake becomes visible through the pine trees."

I explained all this to the gentleman in the bathrobe. He smiled and led me toward an unpainted shed. When the small structure's weathered doors swung open, it became evident this excursion had been no wild-goose chase.

There, disguised as a rickety garage, was a full-fledged, albeit modest, Martin dealership—frozen in time for nearly 35 years. On the wall, near a window wearing a crinkled green shade, hung dozens of Martin gaskets, each on a marked display board. A workbench, horseshoed around the building's back portion, contained tools appropriate for Martin repair. New/old-stock Martin and Evinrude parts were stacked in small boxes. Overflow from this cache filled seven or eight worn bushel baskets.

A handy rack of outboard oil and grease leaned against the side wall. And next to the big workbench vise rested a pair of official Martin motor stands. A tired-looking single-cylinder Martin 20 had a customer tag affixed to the spark lever. The brittle paper indicated its owner was some 25 years overdue. A red, combo life jacket–motor cover (complete with yellow Martin logo) topped the other engine.

My host slowly raised the motor covering the way a proud chef reveals his most tasty dish. There she was, a beautiful 1954 Martin 100.

"It's a 10-horse," he said, beaming. "We got it in here shortly before the home office called it quits. Used it a bit as a demo, but I'll bet there's no more than five or six hours on the old gal."

It was so exciting to be able to walk out of a bona fide Martin dealership over three decades after the motors had last been produced, with an almost-new Martin! It was so noteworthy, in fact, that we'd hardly turned onto the main road before I began to tell my wife the whole story of the Martin outboards.

That model 100 was one of about 300,000 Martins built between 1946 and 1954. The inspiration for these outboards came to engineer and former professional outboard racer George W. Martin. In the late 1930s Mr. Martin began planning a revolutionary new outboard using mechanically controlled intake poppet valves. "Mechanical timing of these valves meant equal fuel distribution making possible uninterrupted acceleration, ranging from the slowest, sputter-free trolling speed to full throttle in a matter of only a few seconds."[26] Having secured a U.S. patent on these valves, George Martin interested National Pressure Cooker Company of Eau Claire, Wisconsin, in financing an outboard-motor manufacturing project. An agreement was composed in 1943 providing the inventor with a royalty for every poppet valve engine sold.

After World War II the first couple hundred Martins (serial numbers began with C-5000) were "practically hand built" in an erstwhile printing plant.[27] The line's premier model was the Martin 60, so labeled because its designers figured the 11-cubic-inch powerhead would generate 6.0 hp. Prototypes, however, put

out some 7.2 horses, and the smooth-running Martin started gaining a good reputation. Some of the early 60s did have a problem or two. I've encountered a number of these vintage rigs with cracked or broken transom clamp brackets, or other supporting cast pieces. This type of thing caused concern, and clearing up such weaknesses became a top priority.

Soon Martin manufacturing facilities were moved to a bigger site, and the line was expanded in 1947 with the two-cylinder, 4½-horse Martin 40. A 2½-hp Martin 20 single was added in late 1948.

The Martin 20 was a perfect little fishing motor. Robert Grubb, veteran outboard retailer and Test Editor of the Antique Outboard Motor Club, tried a tiny (1949) Martin 20 in 1984 and reported:

> This is the slowest trolling motor I have yet tested. It went so slow that on one attempt to make time runs, the current in the river was going faster than the motor. Noise level at idle is also very impressive. It gets down to a very low level, more like the sound of a 4-cycle Lauson than any other 2-cycle I know of.[28]

By 1950 Martin entered the larger (for that time) motor province via introducing the 10-hp Martin 100. (Early versions were called Commando.) Like all of its sisters (except the subsequent 200), this rig had 360-degree steering. It also featured a third thumbscrew (between the two transom clamp knobs), which facilitated motor angle adjustment while under way. Many Martin models were fitted with a clever transom bracket that allowed the motor to be tilted up and swung inboard for lower-unit or propeller repair.

Unique to certain 100s was a neutral clutch and an "Aquamatic" button on the end of the tiller handle, which, when pressed, would instantly slow the motor. After the wave, approaching boat, or other obstacle passed, the button could be released, returning the engine to higher speeds. The 100 and 200 motors had a gas gauge on the front of the fuel tank.

During this era Martin had half a dozen salesmen on the road contacting and helping dealers and potential franchises. "Two servicemen worked in the field, holding service schools both at [regional] distribution points, and at the home plant."[29]

The year 1950 was Martin Hi-Speed 60's second catalog year. This tiny powerhouse (more than just a fishing engine hooked to a racing lower unit), beefed up with special steel rods and needle bearings, enlarged ports, and a steel high-compression cylinder head, was a real thoroughbred. George Martin's pet project pulled 16 hp on the factory dynamometer at 6,000-plus rpm.[30] The Hi-Speed 60's sleek lower unit was made for Martin by the Mayberry-Edwards Company in Florida and helped the racer achieve 5 to 7 mph more than a similar motor simply equipped with the standard fishing lower unit.

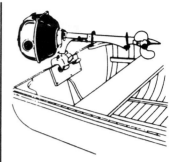

MOTOR IN SWIVEL POSITION

Martin's swivel feature.

Martin Aquamatic.

1 The Aquamatic Control button operates only when the speed indicator lever is in the upper half of the speed range.

2 By pressing this button, speed is reduced to ½ full speed.

3 Upon releasing the Aquamatic Control button, the motor speed returns to that point at which the speed indicator lever is set in the high speed or upper range.

4 This device permits you to face forward and steer while you have complete control of your motor speed, and is an added safety feature.

5 The Aquamatic Control is non-operative when the speed indicator lever is in the lower half of the speed range.

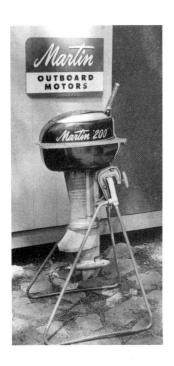

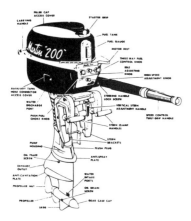

The exhaust section of the Martin 200 could be replaced with a piece 3 inches shorter for racing.

At 11 cubic inches, however, the Hi-Speed 60 didn't really fit well into any American Power Boating Association stock outboard racing class, and the busy little rig (sometimes fueled on alcohol) never really got the attention it deserved. Following the release of this limited production engine, Mr. Martin parted company with the National Pressure Cooker people.

By 1951 the firm was advertising heavily in publications ranging from *National Geographic* and *The Saturday Evening Post* to *Boys' Life*. Dealers were offered cooperative promotional funds in order to place local ads. Martin officials announced their desire to develop a full-line outboard offering. To start this trend, a big, 17-horse Martin 200 motor was unveiled to the press in 1951. When it became apparent these engines would not be ready for production, Martin PR men quietly indicated the Korean War had caused aluminum shortages that postponed the project.

Meanwhile, a Martin 60 derivative, the 66, spent 1950 in the catalog. The roster of 1951 included a 7½-horse updated version of the Martin 60 and 66 called the 75. Like some of the 100s, a number of these wore the Twistshift logo and could be popped into neutral. (Reverse was accomplished by swinging the motor around 180 degrees.)

The lineup in 1952 included the trio of Martin 45 (a revised 40), 75, and 100. On the surface the 1953 model year seemed to hold lots of promise for Martin, as the firm had begun hyping its finally ready Martin 200 in the fall of '52. This Silver Streak 200, unlike the proposed 17-horse '51 edition, was rated at a full 20 hp. Its nonshift Torpedo lower unit rivaled Mercury's Quicksilver racing gear foot. By late 1953 or early 1954, a more pointy, streamlined gear-case cap and a 3-inch-shorter exhaust section could be ordered from the factory. These accessories made the regular Martin 200 (which was a pretty quick motor) into a real weekend racer.

The 1954 Martin family, much like the previous year, had the 20, the 45, the 75, the 100, and the 200. Press releases promised a gear-shift version of the 200, dubbed "Silver Liner." Although a demo motor or two were built, apparently none ever got into circulation.

The 200 series had actually been National Pressure Cooker's last-ditch attempt to transform its outboard division into a full-horsepower-range line, offering the boating public everything from fishing to waterskiing.

Around 1952 workers and management within the firm began squabbling about ways best to produce the rather complex poppet-valved Martins at a price appropriate to its ranking under Johnson, Evinrude, and Mercury. National Pressure Cooker started wondering if it was worth all the trouble. Once-strict factory standards began to slide. "Inspections became less rigid, and some bad motors got by, hurting sales."[31]

While most National Pressure Cooker brass were planning to phase out their outboard division, some Martin engineers were

shooting for the future. Reportedly technicians in Eau Claire connected a pair of 20-cubic-inch Martin 200 blocks, built upon a four-cylinder crankshaft, and shrouded the creation with a tall black and silver cowl labeled Martin 400. The powerhead rested on a shift lower unit borrowed from a rare Martin Silver-Liner.

One of the outboard maker's devoted Midwest dealers visited the factory around the summer of 1953 and asked about the giant Martin he spied waiting on the transom of a test boat.

"Oh! Uh, uh, actually you didn't see that," his host might have winked. "Officially speaking there is no 40-horse Martin 400 prototype down there at the test dock."

Predating Martin's clandestine quad experiments, an obscure outboard listing appeared in a pleasure boat handbook. It mentioned a 75-pound, twin-cylinder, forward-only, 16-hp motor called Martin 80.

When I met Bill Allard, co-author of the 1948 *Handbook of Outboard Motorboating*, I quickly sought additional information on the previously uncharted Martin 80. "Just a mistake," Allard instantly responded. "No such motor ever hit the showroom."

It now appears, however, that the 80 note was based in some fact.[31a] An 8-hp Martin prototype, which looked identical to the firm's 1950–1954 10-hp 100, was unveiled in a factory bull session. Company big shots liked the engine's appearance but queried the marketing logic of having both the 7.2-hp Martin 60 and the 8-horse 80. Engineering staffers speculated two more horses could be squeezed from the powerhead; they were instructed to make it so. Sales executives then began working on catalog copy for the new Martin 100. The would-be 80 was fast forgotten.

By mid-summer 1954, rumors of Martin's demise were confirmed and most of the workers got sent home. A few top Martin plant staffers were put in charge of supplying replacement parts for the thousands of motors still in use. Reportedly, though, a whole freight train full of Martin carbs, gas tanks, and powerhead shrouds was simply sent to the scrap yard.

During this period a dealers' used-motor trade-in publication warned that

> there were many closeouts on Martin Motors after the factory announced [it] would discontinue manufacturing outboard motors. This makes our survey on Martin not in accord with usual estimated prices.[32]

In the mid-Sixties National Pressure Cooker finally sold the remains of its Martin parts to a fellow in Rice Lake, Wisconsin. The remnants of that extensive stock passed into the hands of a small Nebraska firm, which reports doing a brisk mail-order business. It is evident that lots of George Martin's little poppet-valve motors, with a new part here and there, have no desire to slow down.

Just when we thought all the various incarnations of the little Milburn Cub outboard were already documented, the Master Cub

Martin contracted the Shakespeare fishing tackle people to private-brand lures for dealers to offer as giveaways. Besides the *Silver Streak* (named for the Martin "200"), there was the smaller *Marty's Mouse*.

Master Cub

McCulloch

A pair of 3-cylinder, 1964 McCulloch outboards. The one on the left is a racing version.

turns up. This motor, just like its California sisters (such as Continental, Commando, Sport, etc.), was a bargain-priced, sand-cast single. It was sold by Water Master's, Inc., in Los Angeles.

The Los Angeles-based McCulloch Corporation was already well known for its 2-cycle chain saws and kart engines when it went looking for ways to diversify. In 1956 McCulloch acquired Minneapolis outboard producer Scott-Atwater and jumped right into the boat motor business.

McCULLOCH 590 AND 630   McCULLOCH 75

In 1964 Scott-Atwater's name (which had unofficially been shortened to Scott) was dropped entirely to make way for the McCulloch label. Around this time Sears-Roebuck also renamed its Elgin line. McCulloch produced outboards using the Sears label.

While most of the newly tagged McCullochs actually received their start as Scott-Atwaters, some, like the larger horsepower, three-cylinder models and the *OX* gas and diesel heavy-duty work motors, were designed by McCulloch engineers. Most memorable of the mid-Sixties McCulloch outboards were an air-cooled (although water quenched the hot motor leg exhaust section), 4-hp fishing motor and a series of low profile, 7½- and 9-horse fishing motors advertised as being "shorter than a striper, or shirt-sleeve." Some of these compact rigs even sported electric starting, making them about the smallest electric-start outboards in the industry's history.

McCulloch also marketed a couple of limited edition racing outboard motors (most notably a class "F" 60-cubic-inch model). The three-cylinder, triple-carbed, coverless hot rods had bright red powerheads sitting atop white, streamlined lower units. Despite such efforts, McCulloch began drawing away from the outboard picture, offering just a few fishing motors prior to closing its marine operations in the late 1960s.

See Chapter 4

Michigan Wheel Company, the well-known, Grand Rapids–based propeller maker, took a brief spin in the early rowboat motor market. Its Michigan outboard was current in 1916.

A Mr. W.H. Schnacke of Rural Route #4, Evansville, Indiana, formed a little company to build "the newest in outboard motor design, versatility, safety, and economy." Schnacke Manufacturing Corporation called its Midwestern jet outboard product the Mid-Jet.

Like many of its competitors, the Mid-Jet used an air-cooled, 2-cycle Tecumseh Power Products powerhead especially designed for outboard-motor application. The lower unit, as described in a Mid-Jet service manual, was an aluminum casting.

> The one-piece drive shaft rides in a sealed ball bearing at the lower end and the 3-blade, 5-inch propeller screws directly on the end of the drive shaft. The propulsion unit is simple in construction and completely enclosed. A small amount of water entering the water housing is diverted through a water tube to cool the lower unit housing and exhaust gases. The remainder of the water is ejected at high speed through the discharge opening to propel the boat.[33]

The 27-pound, single-cylinder Mid-Jet came in models ranging from 2.4 to 5 hp. The larger power promised the shallow-water boater 65 pounds of thrust at 4,200 rpm.

Mid-Jets were available between 1961 and 1965. A June, 1969 letter in my files from the company founder indicates that although his firm had gone out of business, he still at that time had a few lower-unit parts on hand for Mid-Jet owners.

See the listing for Neptune.

Back in the late 1940s, somewhere in southern California, a guy ("experienced in nautical and aviation engineering") sat in front of a small drawing board and designed a pint-size outboard. Little did the fellow know that the history of his straightforward motor would one day be a source of confusion for old-outboard collectors.

First advertised in December 1948 as a potential Christmas present for lucky sportsmen, the subject motor began its life as the Milburn Cub. The H.B. Milburn Company of Los Angeles (with a New York City office tucked away in a Rockefeller Plaza room) tried to entice folks with the promise of a 30-day guarantee, and 1-to-6-mph performance from its 2½-hp (at 3,750 rpm) rope-start motor. Additionally, the manufacturers promised their air-cooled outboard would "never conk out because of water pump troubles." The Milburn Cub was identified solely by a small

Mercury

Michigan

Mid-Jet

The 1960s Mid-Jet, a water-jet thrust outboard.

Mighty-Mite

Milburn Cub, Continental Commando, Husky, Master Cub and Comanco

(See also Budbilt, The Kit, Sea Lion, and Wego in the Back Rack chapter.)

nameplate screwed to the front of its 2½-quart, cast-aluminum fuel tank. The skinny tiller handle seemed to be mounted to the wrong (left) side of the cute 2-cycle powerhead.

Conspicuously absent was a choke for the Milburn Cub's cast-aluminum carb. Because most operators had thumbs they could stick over the air intake while starting a cold motor, company officials didn't view the lack of a real choke mechanism as a problem. A copper tube from the tank to the carburetor might have been cut too long and consequently had a loop in it. The lawn-chair-gauge underwater exhaust tube, giving clearance for about 180-degree steering, was standard. For an extra three bucks you could get a model with exhaust piped through the torque tube, allowing 360-degree turning.

Early Milburn Cub ads included a tiny coupon (like those on the side of a breakfast cereal box offering Superman sweatshirts for $3.97) which read: "Enclosed is $_____ for which please ship_____ Cub motors" at $69.50 each.

Just how many coupons were sent in is unknown, but sometime in the mid-Fifties it was evident that the Milburn was being handled by an L.K. Products of Culver City, California. This company apparently sold the outboard business to an outfit called Continental Manufacturing Corporation, also in Culver City. Continental put out a new 2½-hp motor called the Continental Commando, which weighed in at about 20 pounds and looked exactly like the deluxe (exhaust through the torque tube) Milburn. (Note: Some references call this motor the Sport.) New was a rewind-start model for $99.95, a 10-spot over the cost of the standard rope-start edition.

By early 1957 Continental ventured into an interesting marketing avenue by offering the little outboard in kit form, which saved the boater 25 percent of a finished motor's price. Instructions claimed "The Kit" outboard could be assembled on a fence or back of a chair, and you'd need only an adjustable wrench along with a couple of household-grade screwdrivers to do the job. Folks getting started on the Continental kit read:

> You have just purchased the finest light outboard motor in its field. [Of course, it was the *only* one in the kit genre.] All parts have been designed to aircraft specifications by aircraft engineers and manufactured to precision standards. Each part you have received has been meticulously inspected and if proper assembly instructions are followed will fit with its mating part. No forcing is necessary and care should be taken not to strip the threads.

In the early Sixties somebody told me about a "real cheap" outboard you could make yourself. As a kid seeking a very fast way to convince my dad to buy me a boat motor, "real cheap" were operative words. I borrowed a faded picture of a Continental ripped out of a boating magazine and wrote to the firm identified in the caption. Sometime in April 1964 a letter from Comanco, Inc.,

of Culver City, California, came my way heralding the 1963 air-cooled, rewind-start Commando VII outboard motor. The lower unit was identical to the Milburn and other Commandos (models V and VI), but the Tecumseh powerhead's shroud was sheet metal (like that of a power motor), and a cylindrical gas tank was hooked to the front of the thing. This time, the tiller handle was on the right side. Its funny-looking throttle lever was described as "pistol grip." The rig weighed about the same as its predecessors but developed 4 hp at 5,400 rpm. The typed brochure suggested that

> there's no need to let the Commando VII sit idle after the fishing and duck hunting season. Put it to work as a stationary engine to run pumps, saws, generators, even lawn mowers or go-karts.

Wow! I imagined, *outboards, saws, and go-karts, and all for just $99.95!*

Still, my parents took one look at the bargain-basement Commando and immediately decided to buy me a new Mercury—for which I've always credited the Comanco people.

The late Sixties saw me sentimentally inquire about my favorite little engine. A promotional letter finally came back from McMar, Commando Motor Division, Newport Beach, California. Pictured was that distinctive Milburn Cub–type lower unit under a Tecumseh single-cylinder, air-cooled, 2-cycle, "loop scavenged" powerhead. Both a Commando 500 (at 5 hp) and 750 (at 7½ hp) were offered. Each sipped fuel from a remote tank. A solid-state ignition could be ordered for the larger motor. Buyers were given their choice of three shaft lengths: 9, 18, or 24 inches.

I lost track of the little motors after that, but am reminded that none of the ads for any of the Milburn Cub–based products ever actually pictured the kicker in motion. One flyer, however, showed a kid *carrying* the thing, but it was not stated where he was taking it.

Adding a bit of intrigue to the Milburn/Comanco lineage was Ward International, Inc. This Studio City, California, firm was listed as producing a small outboard during the mid-Sixties called the Husky. A few Comanco parts lists mention the Husky (with that classic Milburn Cub lower unit) as a sister motor to the Commando. According to my notes, the Husky was marketed in 1963, 1966, and 1967. Perhaps Comanco provided the motors (with Tecumseh powerheads) to Ward International.

Miller (1)

A bit longer-lived than many competitors, the Miller Gas and Vacuum Engine Company of Chicago marketed rowboat motors from 1914 to 1923. Miller outboards were available with battery or gear-driven Bosch magneto ignition. An adjustable propeller was optional. Millers looked similar to Evinrude rowboat motors.

Miller (2)

Auto racing legend Harry A. Miller was said to have built a workable outboard in the late 1890s. By 1932 his Miller Motor

Company of Los Angeles entered the realm of portable boat motor production with an intriguing four-cylinder (horizontal), in-line rig.

Like the previously marketed Submerged and subsequent Clarke, this product's powerhead rode completely underwater. Reportedly, problems with the complex castings let lubrication out and water in. This limited issue Miller was a one-year motor.

Miller (3)

Getting its early 1960s start at the Miller Engineering Company, in Shawnee, Oklahoma, this Miller was one of those air-prop fan outboards. From 1964 the Miller was offered by the Arrow Propeller Company of Memphis.

Mini

One of the most fact-filled leaflets in 1960s outboard advertising indicated this tiny motor was ideal for senior citizens. Weighing less than 9 pounds, the Mini outboard motor came as a "result of many years of testing and designing a multitude of combinations to achieve the smallest, lightest, most economical, least expensive, yet practical outboard motor attainable." Knight Distributing Company of Springfield, Massachusetts, was proud to acknowledge its air-cooled product as 100-percent manufactured and assembled in the USA.

Because Americans relate to empirical data, the model 10-S Mini outboard motor's "unbelievable propelling power" was verified in an "actual speed test." The pint-size kicker was "clocked at 4.2 mph with three men in a twelve-foot aluminum boat." For some long-forgotten reason, however, the photo captioned with these statistics showed a man and a woman in a sailing dinghy named the *Two-Teds*. The craft was inching along under power from an engine with no rewind starter or plastic powerhead cover (unlike the one prominently featured on the front of the informative brochure).

The single-cylinder, 2-cycle Mini outboard motor featured an adjustable shaft length and a 14-millimeter "shorty" spark plug. Its polycarbonate, semi-weedless propeller had a lifetime guarantee against breakage. Exhaust exited the cylinder through a piece of flexible gooseneck pipe before traveling to the water via a little rigid tube.

Customers purchasing the small motor had a little time to try it, and if not completely satisfied, return it within seven days. "Any damage or misuse of the product by the customer would be deducted from the purchase price." At $99.95 the 1-hp (at 6,300 rpm) outboard cost about the same as the garden weed whackers that its powerhead resembled.

Minn-Kota

This Minnesota-based firm has been a leading manufacturer of electric trolling motors since 1932. Reportedly Minn-Kota planned to introduce a gasoline-powered fishing outboard for 1951. Actually, the "gas" Minn-Kota motor was supposed to be a small

engine that could be mounted interchangeably on the company's flexible "cable drive" electric outboard lower units. Apparently one could switch powerheads from electric to gas (and vice versa), depending on fishing conditions. Although there's only a single reference for the gasoline Minn-Kota Troller, it is possible some got into circulation.

Monarch

A sister motor to very early Champion outboards, the Monarch was the tiny Champ firm's low-priced offering.

Sig Konrad, who founded the Champion marque in 1926, built the first Monarch a short time later. The little motor's stately brand name was cast in large letters into the top of its fuel tank. SAINT PAUL, MINN. graced the rope sheave plate. About 600 of the water-cooled, $39.50, 2-hp Monarchs were produced. It is believed some 100 air-cooled versions were also marketed.

While some of the production wore a pair of piston rings, a few single-ringed rigs went through the company's door. Rather than mate the flywheel to the crankshaft with a keyway, the two were aligned with a simple timing mark (on each piece). This reduced the risk of powerhead damage due to running into rocks.[34]

The Monarch name disappeared after Mr. Konrad sold his Champion company rights in 1935.

Mono

Look for a powerhead diagram on a Mono outboard parts list, and you won't find it. That's because the Mono Manufacturing Company, based in Springfield, Missouri, got the 2-cycle engines for its outboards from the Tecumseh people.

Mono began marketing these single-cylinder, 360-degree-steering, low-priced fishing motors around 1963. Early Monos had exposed power plants with front-mounted cylindrical gas tanks. Later models wore plastic shrouds. Some came with a neutral clutch and a remote fuel tank resembling a 2½-gallon lawn mower gas can. Generally occupying the 3-to-7½-hp range, many Monos, although primarily air cooled, had a small tube protruding from the lower unit which supplied water to cool the muffler.

The Mono was essentially a private-brand-style outboard rivaling the Eska, the My-te, and the obscure Mann's Troller. Because the power plant came from Tecumseh, a firm with thousands of authorized repair shops, the Mono could be serviced in a wider range of locations than most major outboard products.

Motorgo

Probably the first serious private-brand outboard, the 1914 Motorgo, built by Lockwood, was sold by Sears-Roebuck. Although the Lockwood-made Motorgos were offered until about 1928, other well-known makers, such as Caille and Muncie, produced Motorgo-labeled outboards for the giant Chicago-based retailer.

It was not unusual for the Caille Motorgo rigs to lack identification except for a difficult-to-spot serial number stamped onto the block or transom clamp assembly. Some of these designations begin with *M.* If you come across a Caille with no name on the flywheel rope-sheave plate, you most likely have a Motorgo. Sears retitled most of its outboards Waterwitch by late 1933.

Early-30s, 10-hp Sears Motorgo, made by Caille. Note the priming cup on the front of the cylinder. The steering arm only turned the lower section.

Motorow

Although on occasion Uncle Sam has spent good money on items that don't work, the Motorow Engine Company of Chicago proudly advertised that the U.S. government purchased some 1915 Motorow outboards for "coast work."

Built from 1913 to 1918 by a "trained force of men," the single-cylinder, tin-can-mufflered Motorow featured "a pinion at the top of the drive shaft housing meshing into a segment gear at the end of the tiller handle, enabling one to steer perfectly and reverse instantly."

The company claimed ownership of the basic patents on this "positive mechanical reversing device." It also touted "velvety" smooth running because of a secret, exclusive (and unexplained) "vibration absorber."

The skegless Motorow was indeed an interesting World War I-era engine. Its claim, however, as "the *only* rowboat motor that reverses instantly . . ." should be more like: "the only one that reverses and is spelled with a capital *M.*" Finally, while no old-outboard enthusiast has come up with an exact count, the Motorow people were fond of saying their product had "fewer parts than any other motor on the market."

Motor Troller

The Motor Troller Company of Westport, Connecticut, offered a post-World War II fishing outboard in 1947.

Muncie

See the listing for Neptune.

Munco

Circa 1933 the Munco Sales Company of Muncie, Indiana, tried to interest impecunious boaters by offering a $44.50, 2-horsepower, single-cylinder outboard motor kit.

"All you have to do," said Munco's tiny ads, "is assemble this tested outboard. No machining—a 12-year-old boy can put it together with a screwdriver and wrench."

The Munco kit outboard looked exactly like a 2-hp Neptune-brand kicker of similar vintage. It would seem likely that the Munco Sales Company was simply a small marketing arm of Neptune's parent, Muncie Gear Works. A little coupon on the bottom of Munco's advertising asked folks to send for "complete details concerning the assembly of the MUNCO OUTBOARD MOTOR."

Because no mention was made of Neptune or Muncie Gear Works lineage (except to say Munco's design was "tested"), it is possible this very obscure kit motor came with MUNCO cast into the rope sheave plate. Consequently, the Munco may be considered an autonomous marque.

My-te

City Engineering Company, Inc., an Indianapolis firm specializing in electric winches, hoists, and 6- to 12-volt trolling motors, marketed a 4-hp, 2-cycle, air-cooled outboard called the My-te IV. This early-Sixties, 29-pound rig was a good example of a simple, 2-cycle lawn mower engine mated to a generic lower unit.

The My-te IV was meant to compete with the majors' fishing models on price, as it sold for just under $100. This rig looked a lot like a Mono.

National

The National outboard, built from 1916 to 1918, had more cylinders than most contemporaries. The National Marine Motor Company of Newark came up with an ornate, opposed twin featuring an adjustable (forward-neutral-reverse pitch) propeller and a gas tank resembling the front of an old cash register drawer. Topping off this very antique-looking rig was a large fluted flywheel that would remind you of a church collection plate.

Note: Because the similar twin-cylinder Federal was actually built in a Newark factory during 1914 and 1915, one could speculate a connection between the Federal and the National. Even the names had a similar "solid" (at least back in those days) ring.

Neptune (1) (Caille)

From 1917 to 1925 the Caille outboard people marketed a bargain-price line dubbed Neptune. This offering was similar to Evinrude's lower-cost Buccaneer lineup of the Fifties. Single-cylinder Neptune rowboat motors came in 2- and 3½-hp sizes and sported such exotic model names as Czar, Czarina, Prince, King, Queen, and Empress. Both battery and magneto-ignition styles were available.

Additionally, Caille-built Neptunes (2 hp only) could be purchased in regular or canoe (mounted through a hole in the bottom of the craft) versions. According to sales literature, one of these rigs pushed the canoe *Hiawatha* 16 mph! This figure is akin to Johnson's famed 1925 publicity about its 6-hp Big Twin. The Neptune claim seems rather questionable.

Neptune (2) (Muncie)

The Muncie (Indiana) Gear Works was established in 1907. During its various evolutionary reorganizations it became well known in the young auto industry for the manufacture of gears and transmissions. Muncie entered the outboard business in 1930 via its

NEPTUNE

OUTBOARD
M·O·T·O·R·S

for

1935

Muncie Gear Works' Neptune logo.

A 1948–49, 10-hp Neptune. As most of these rigs were sold through the mail, few were purchased. This design was suspiciously close to popular small Johnsons of the day.

Neptune Ned sez:

By cracky th' feller that ketches fish is th' one that keeps fishin' stead of rowin' and wishin'! Brother, buy a NEPTUNE!

Circa-1946 "Neptune Ned" logo.

NEPTUNE
OUTBOARD MOTORS

own Neptune line. In addition the firm private-branded thinly disguised Neptunes to Sears-Roebuck (some relabeled Water Witch, others with a Motorgo tag), as well as to small sales organizations under the Portage and Sea-Gull nameplates.

A typical pre-World War II Neptune lineup included the Master Twin, a 16-hp opposed twin wearing the look of a poor man's Caille. This big rig with detachable cylinder heads had a tiller that turned only the lower unit and was built with "the liberal use of ball and roller bearings." Also available were alternate-firing 9½- and 6-horse twins, a 4-hp opposed twin with removable cylinder heads, the 2-hp Neptune single, and a Junior single producing 1.2 hp. This tiny, 17-pound putt-putt was the great-grandfather of the famed Neptune Mighty-Mite. Muncie's advertising stressed "outstanding quality, superior design, and skilled workmanship." In fact Neptunes, especially the early alternate-firing models, were rather well designed and should not be lumped into the outboard picture as just also-rans. In the area of weaknesses, however, Neptunes, like many of their contemporaries, quickly succumbed to the ravages of salt water.

Following World War II, Muncie jumped back into the outboard field through its ads featuring an old fisherman (cartoon character) named Neptune Ned. The firm promoted a 1945-46 line ranging from 1½ to 9½ hp. The stable of 1947 offered only 1½-, 2-, and 3½-horse products.

But the following year Muncie unveiled its newly designed/styled, shrouded, alternate-firing Twins, such as the 10-hp model AA10. (There was also a shrouded single.) These metallic-green (occasionally maroon) motors with red tiller grips looked somewhat like Western Auto's Wizard outboards and the more expensive Johnson fishing motors of the day.

The new Neptunes would offer a boat shop unable to secure a major-label outboard franchise a good alternative line. Then for some reason, in 1949, the manufacturer "tried to sell these motors by mail order. This practice cost dealer support, and Muncie was not able to secure adequate dealer outlets in 1950–51 to warrant continuing in the outboard field."[35]

By 1951 the company's outboard motor promotion largely consisted of a small exhibit at the New York Boat Show.[36] Of course, this era also saw the Korean War, and Muncie's production

facilities were tapped by the U.S. government to make jet engines. So there were no Neptunes in 1952 or 1953.

After completion of Defense Department work, Muncie decided to attempt a comeback into the kicker picture by filling a niche in the low-priced, micro-power outboard slot. It reintroduced the tiny (now 1.7 hp) single in 1954. Three years later the firm moved to Cordele, Georgia, and dubbed its little motor the Mighty-Mite. Although available as a sideline through a few marine and sporting goods stores, most Mighty-Mite purchases were transacted through factory-direct orders. Muncie's promotion was now the province of tiny folders touting the portability (especially for children and women) of the under-$100 putt-putt. For years this outboard was the best known (albeit outdated, with separate drive shaft and exhaust tubes) of all "basic eggbeaters." It was even offered as a top prize for junior super salespeople peddling the most novelties, seed packets, or *Grit* newspaper subscriptions.

The Georgia-based Muncie company was sold in 1969, and in time the outboard operation moved to Florida (where senior citizens assembled some of the motors). Following a few more transfers, it ended up in Connecticut. In the 1980s a 2-horse updated derivative (in complete or kit form with rewind starter and 360-degree steering) of the 1930s Junior single and the more recent Mighty-Mite was still being offered.

Because of such lineage, the new Mighty-Mite firm can be called the second oldest American maker (after OMC, with Evinrude and Johnson) of gasoline-powered outboard motors!

The famed 17-pound, 1.7-hp Neptune Mighty-Mite. Over the years this rig became America's most famous putt-putt.

Niagara

Buffalo, New York, was home to Niagara Motors Corporation, producer of the Niagara rowboat motor. Introduced in 1918, the Niagara fell off the market by the end of that year.

Nichoalds

Little is remembered about this 1916 Detroit-produced rowboat motor. The 2-hp putt-putt wore a round gas tank.

No-Ro

In 1913 the No-Ro Motorworks of Boston (West Roxbury), Massachusetts, set out to save its potential customers from purchasing a single-cylinder rowboat motor "blunder," with those "disastrous vibratory effects." Keeping this in mind, the company came up with a 4-cycle, 3-to-4-hp opposed twin called the No-Ro Presto Motor.

In an effort to protect further its future clientele and its machinery "from dirt," the power plant (except the protruding cylinders) was enclosed. This arrangement gave the No-Ro some of the round Spinaway look and made the unusual kicker appear as if some important parts were missing. Alas, most early outboarders made the "mistake" of purchasing a single-cylinder, causing No-Ro to fold after 1916.

Northwestern

From 1912 to 1918 the Northwestern Motor Company (Eau Claire, Wisconsin) produced a 62-pound, 2-hp rowboat motor. The

Northwestern was available with battery or gear-driven Bosch magneto ignition. A buyer could also choose between tin-can mufflering or underwater exhaust.

Northwesterns came with a bronze rudder-style lower unit and were handsomely painted in dark maroon and given a "piano finish." It appears the crankshaft extended a few inches above the knob-start flywheel. This may have allowed the introduction of upper main bearing grease in a way similar to that of the Wilcox-McKim motor.

Although elementary by modern standards, the Northwestern placed a rubber cover over the boat end of the spark plug. Anyone who has accidentally bumped into a bare-plug wire connection can appreciate such protective innovation.

Like many early outboard firms, the Northwestern folks sold their motor on a 30-day free-trial basis. Noting the average vacation was only about two weeks, this might have proved a risky business practice.

Notre Dame

Like the student-built "Gopher" outboards, Notre Dame kickers were projects of an engineering class, bearing the name of the university where they were designed and built (circa 1935). It is estimated less than 100 of the one-lung outboards were produced at the famed South Bend, Indiana institution. "Fighting Irish" engineering scholars also turned out a few single-cylinder inboard engines of similar vintage. There were some twins, too.

Nymph

The Nymph Motor Company offered an outboard motor from 1914 to 1916. Not much else is known about this Cleveland-based firm or its engine. The Nymph may have been copied from the Ferro, which was also built in Cleveland.

O & R

For years, the Ohlsson and Rice folks were famous for their nice-running, ignition-type model airplane engines. Sometime in the late 1960s, several firms, like Mini-Motor, offered a 1-hp outboard suitable for a dinghy or canoe. They used O&R-powered heads.

Oliver

The well-accepted Chris-Craft outboards had been in production for only a few years before the famed boat maker closed its kicker division in late 1953.

A year later press releases from the executive offices of the Oliver Corporation announced the firm's purchase of the silent outboard factory, along with the rights to "two basic motors which are currently tooled and known to the public as Chris-Craft."

Attached to the typed statement was a publicity photo of what had been a Chris-Craft 5½-horse Challenger motor. Someone in the PR department retouched the picture so the Oliver name appeared on both sides of its gas tank. If any of these badge-engineered Chris-Craft/Olivers were marketed, it probably wasn't many.

Actually, Oliver promised to completely modernize these engines before releasing them to sales outlets.[37]

The old line farm machinery manufacturer began making good on its pledge by learning which updated features outboarders might appreciate. Survey results prompted Oliver to provide its new models with a full gear shift (an F-N-R prototype Oliver lower unit got tested under an old Chris-Craft 10 powerhead), twist speed-control tiller handle, and a Tenda-Matic remote fuel tank. The 1955-premier Olivers wore the old ChrisCraft model names. The new outboard division's 5½-hp motor was designated ("J") Challenger, and the bigger one, upgraded from 10 to 15 horses, sported the ("K") Commander tag.

The rigs were painted in rich blues, yellows, and reds; ads for them made the motors seem larger than life. In fact the actual outboards, with nicely accented fiberglass covers, were as attractive as any motor of the era.

For 1956, model names were dropped and an electric-start version of the 15-horse made the catalog.

When Oliver first contemplated getting into the boat-motor business, it knew additional models would be added to round out the line. It had hoped to release 25- and 30-hp motors by late '55. All research pointed toward the need for bigger engines. As a result, the 35-hp, electric-start Olympus was introduced in 1957. Also tuning up the roster was the announcement that the old 5½ and 15 would gain ½ horse and 1 hp, respectively.

Oliver brochures of 1958 again offered 6-, 16-, and 35-hp models. New that year, however, was an electric-start option on the 16.

For 1959 the Mohawk model name was assigned to the 6-horse motor. Oliver's 16 became the Lancer (with optional electric start and long shaft), with the 35 (long shaft available) remaining Olympus. In an effort to compete with the major brands' big motors (the 50-hp OMC and the Mercury 70), Oliver offered twin 35s with factory-matched, counter-rotating propellers (like Champion's dual 16½ Tandem 33) generating a combined 70 horses of boat thrust.

Oliver began searching for ways to make its outboard production more cost-effective. By 1960 the Oliver line was being manufactured in Great Britain. Advertisements of this period pictured an Oliver-powered cruiser rippling the coastal waters of a sleepy English village. The slogan "American designed—British built," had a nice ring to it, but did little to jingle the front doors of Oliver outboard dealerships.

In 1961 New York City designer Richard Arbib worked up some futuristic Oliver motor sketches. Although a few of the cosmetically engineered Olivers got into circulation, the venerable tractor firm decided to pull out of the water and closed its outboard division around the time President Eisenhower left office.

An old issue of the *National Sportsman* listed this mysterious manufacturer as having produced outboards from 1918 to 1926.

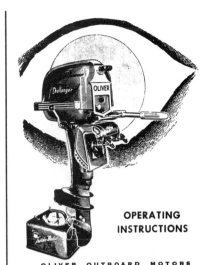

OPERATING INSTRUCTIONS

OLIVER OUTBOARD MOTORS
BATTLE CREEK, MICHIGAN
DIVISION OF OLIVER CORPORATION

A 5½-hp, 1955 Oliver Challenger. Two years later the biggest Olivers (35 hp) featured poppet valves designed by George Martin, formerly with the firm bearing his name.

A.E. Olmstead & Sons

Nine model years of motors should have added up to more information than a single, dusty magazine listing. No one ever came up with any other documentation, or even a brand name for the Olmstead outboard, and that made me suspicious. In any event, the original citation identified the phantom kicker as having been built in Pulaski, New York. As that locale was near my home, some detective work was in order.

A phone call to A. E. Olmstead's daughter revealed that, to the best of her knowledge, the small firm made an inboard, but not an outboard motor.

What makes this hobby interesting, however, is that now someone will probably send me a picture of four of them!

Otasco

Products of 1968–69, Otasco outboards pumped out 3½, 5, and 7 horsepower.

Otterbine

This is a 1960s jet-drive outboard powered by a 2-hp Briggs and Stratton engine. Reportedly some had 4-horse Briggs motors.

Outboard Jet

Like many of its water jet-propelled sisters, the Outboard Jet used an air-cooled Tecumseh powerhead. Outboard Jet, Inc., of Indianapolis, Indiana, should get credit, however, for placing the generic engine under a contoured shroud.

While most jet outboards shot thrust underwater, this one's push exited above the water line, thus "producing more efficient thrust, a more level ride, and greater fuel economy." The Outboard Jet could deliver 100 pounds of thrust, and all this without any portion of the lower unit extending below the boat's bottom. The "instant reversing," single-cylinder, 2-cycle Outboard Jet was supplied with a 3-gallon remote fuel tank. Options included a weed sweeper for passing through heavily vegetated waters, as well as a water hose attachment used in conjunction with the Outboard Jet's pump. This feature allowed lawn sprinkling, car washing, or fire fighting.

A model designated J-55 was introduced in 1963. An updated J-55B was manufactured from 1964 to 1966. Unfortunately, even though this product was advertised as "more fun than any 5½-hp motor you've ever tried!" not many folks gave the Outboard Jet a try.

Undaunted, the manufacturer was convinced it was on the right track and introduced an ambitious update by 1967. The new offering came in the form of a more sophisticated (compared to the previous engine) water-cooled 2-cycle twin, labeled Outboard Jet OJ200. One owner of the 9½-hp unit reported its performance barely matched a conventional 6-hp prop-driven rig. Weeds (often a feature of shallow water, where one would tend to need a jet outboard) got caught on the water intake screen and caused problems. The stream of cooling water diverted from the jet pump diminished at low rpms and allowed the powerhead to get too hot.

Most outboard shoppers were still cool to the idea of water jet propulsion and continued to ignore this product.

In 1929 three major outboard firms merged. Combining Evinrude, Elto, and Lockwood, this merger probably saved the first two firms (the Lockwood name was quietly dropped by 1931) from the ravages of the Great Depression.

Motors wearing the OMC,or Outboard Motors Corporation, name were produced predominantly in Milwaukee and bore a strong likeness to various models in the Evinrude and Elto lines.

One of the most notable Outboard Motors Corporation models was the 1930 Foldlite. This 29-pound, 2¾-hp fishing motor had a hinge in the middle of the drive shaft housing that allowed the very portable motor to fold up when not in use. Also atypical of most of its contemporaries was the front-mounted Foldlite fuel tank.

The Outboard Motors Corporation ID was also well represented in the low production 1930 Speedy-Bee Racer, and the OMC 460, a four-cylinder, 60-cubic-inch racer. Ads assured the few fortunate Depression-era outboardrs who could come up with $450.00 that the OMC 4-60 was readily availabel at "Elto, Evinrude, and Lockwood dealers throughout the world."

One of only a few New England–built outboards was the 1921 to 1922 Direct-Drive model from the Palmer Brothers Engine Company of Cos Cob, Connecticut. The single-cylinder, air-cooled Palmer featured an unusual transom bracket with a thumbscrew clamp on the outside of the boat. The Palmer outboard was a very limited production item.

Polar Motors, Inc., of La Crosse, Wisconsin, tried to warm up potential outboard customers with its 1964 ice boat outboard motor. The project was given the deep freeze by the following year.

An obscure 1930s outboard, the Portage single, was identified as a product of Outboard Motor Sales and Service of Indianapolis, Indiana. In addition to a pair of tubes holding the drive shaft and exhaust, a third tube, running from powerhead to lower unit, housed the motor's waterlines. My guess is the 2-hp (at 2,800 rpm) Portage was simply a private-brand built for its seller by the Muncie (Neptune) Gear Works.

After World War II boaters could consider the purchase of the new Power-Pak outboard from Propulsion Engine Corporation of Kansas City, Kansas. Power-Paks are described in greater detail in the Back Rack chapter.

The Production Foundries Company, Ann Arbor, Michigan, sold its motor minus a catchy brand name. This firm's outboard division was operational in 1923.

Outboard Motors Corporation

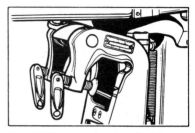

Many OMC post-war engines had ID plates on the clamp assembly. By then, though, OMC stood for Outboard Marine Corporation as opposed to the firm's earlier Outboard Motors Corp. name.

Palmer

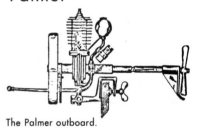

The Palmer outboard.

Polar

Portage

Power-Pak

Production Foundries

Quincy Looper

Quincy (Illinois) Welding Works began making aftermarket high-speed accessories for Mercury outboards in the late Forties. Small items such as open exhaust stacks and throttle/spark stop pieces gave way to larger Merc-oriented components.

Because it cast many of its own parts, Quincy was eventually able to come up with a complete Mercury derivative racer that scavenged fuel via the "loop charged" instead of the deflector method. These Quincy Loopers were made in small supply for exacting late Fifties and early Sixties outboard racing enthusiasts.

The alcohol-burning motors came in a variety of sizes such as class "A" (at 15 cubic inches), "B" (at 20 cubic inches), "C" (at 30 cubic inches), and "F" (at 60 cubic inches).

Raabe's "Marine Traction Motor"

A strange-looking contraption built by sea captain Henry E. Raabe might just qualify as one of the oldest outboards. Circa 1890, Raabe (who died in New Jersey around 1966) concocted a 90-degree device with a three-blade prop on one end and a small steam engine on the other. By the turn of the century, an air-cooled, single-cylinder (reportedly kerosene or gasoline) powerplant replaced the original engine. Because the rig had no transom clamp, it simply hung over a boat's stern with the motor portion resting on or near the craft's rear seat. Surviving photos show a bulky, but rather professionally constructed unit. It was apparently experimental, however, and never went into commercial production.

Racine

In the 1960s a lucky member of the Antique Outboard Motor Club discovered a rusty Racine tucked away in a New Jersey barn. That forward-pointing, single-cylinder engine built by the Racine Motor Oars Company of Racine, Wisconsin, features rudder steering and its name ornately emblazoned on its cast-iron knob-starting flywheel.

Racine rowboat motors ran 2 hp at 800 rpm. Though available from 1913 to 1918, they weren't in *Motor Boating*'s 1916 listing.

Red Top (A/C—Auto City)

Daily output at Mercury or Evinrude easily outdistanced the 250 or so total outboard production from the tiny Auto City Outboard Association, Inc., of Detroit. Actually, the small firm made its single-cylinder Red Top motors in a modest, cement-block factory near Pontiac, Michigan.

The Red Top outboard, which generated about 4 to 5 hp, came with a rewind starter on top of its red gas tank and featured a unique steering system. A small tiller handle extended a few inches from the bottom of the powerhead and was connected at a 45-degree angle with another short handle sporting the plastic tiller grip. To turn the lower unit (the Red Top powerhead remained stationary), the up-pointing tiller grip was moved in an arch fashion down to the right or left.

It is believed the Auto City Outboard Association firm consisted of former staffers of the Packard car company. While the years have faded the facts surrounding the Red Top, a Caille-like appearance of some of its castings, as well as the red gas tank

(many 1930s Caille outboards wore a red fuel tank and were dubbed Red Heads), leads one to speculate about a Caille connection. Caille, also a Detroit company, stopped outboard production in 1935. Perhaps some of the old Caille parts and castings were acquired by the Auto City Outboard Association people for use in their Red Top project.

A surviving member of the group guessed he had about two dozen coworkers in the tiny outboard firm.

The Red Top was said to outrun the Johnson fishing motors of the day. It was produced sometime during the close of World War II.[38]

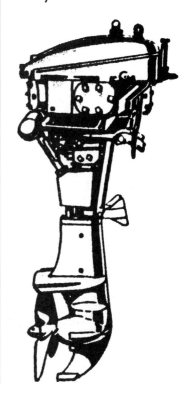

Reveley

An early 1960s jet pump propulsion outboard, the Reveley came from the Meadville, Pennsylvania, Reveley Corporation.

Revere

Here's a mystery motor that may not be an outboard at all. An Ohio engine buff came across a vintage metal name tag stating: "Revere. Detroit Outboard Motors, Inc. Detroit, Mich." It's possible the firm didn't even make outboard motors and the ID plate came from some other device. My guess is, however, that the Revere was a limited production, early World War I–era rowboat motor of the Waterman style. Perhaps more detailed info, or an actual Revere kicker will someday emerge, solving this puzzler.

Riley

During the mid-1950s, outboard cabin cruisers became quite the rage. For much less than the price of a stuffy yacht, one could get a nice 20-foot outboard cruiser, motor, and trailer. But craft such as these liked large motors—the bigger the better.

Johnson and Evinrude's top-of-the-line models were in the 25- to 35-hp range. Merc was up to 40 horses in 1954. Imagine a cruiser owner's surprise when he heard that some California outfit was selling an outboard actually capable of 75 hp!

The giant motor was from the George Riley Company of Los Angeles, and cooked up that power in a 4-cycle, five-cylinder, radial, flat-head engine. Tipping up the monster's fiberglass top revealed a British Lucas 12-volt electrical system. Pistons and bearings were said to be of Harley-Davidson motorcycle origin. An oil tank was mounted to the side of the cover. The face of the Riley looked at you through a pair of round gauges (oil pressure and amps), and the ignition key fit into an assembly between the two. A skipper could operate his 55-inch-tall giant outboard at the cruiser's steering console via a single-lever remote control.[39]

The Riley 75 hp was America's biggest mid-1950s outboard offering. The 250-pound motor consumed 6¼ gallons of gas per hour at full throttle. Very few of these 5-cylinder radials were sold.

First marketed in 1954, the Riley's bulk couldn't compete with its competitors' better looks and established dealer/parts organization. Weaknesses with the lower unit also caused

Row-No-More

Royal
(Atlas Royal)

Saber

Salisbury

Savage
Scott-Atwater

problems. This King Kong of the consumer outboard jungle disappeared after 1956.

Reportedly a World War I–era rowboat motor that looked suspiciously similar to one of the Wisconsin Machinery and Manufacturing Company's outboards, the origins of the Row-No-More are unknown.

Any happy motorist wanting to get on the water could ask his Esso gas station attendant for info about the Royal outboards.

First offered for the 1947–48 model year, the Gale Products–built Royal was distributed by Atlas Supply Company of Newark, New Jersey, to Esso (and Humble) related retailers connected with Standard Oil of New Jersey, Kentucky, and Indiana. The 3-, 5-, 12-, and 25-hp 1956 line was Royal's last.

Outboards bearing the Saber name decal came from the Galesburg, Illinois, Gale Products Plant and were sold through various branches of the Minneapolis-headquartered Fedway Stores. These motors, also called Fedway Sabers, were available only in 1953. They came in denominations of 3, 5, and 12 hp.

Chicagoan Wilbur S. Salisbury entered the fledgling outboard world in 1892 with an electric kicker that he marketed under his name. A similar device surfaced as the 1897 Allen. The next year (circa 1898) Salisbury advertised a gasoline-fired "portable boat propelling motor." This 4-cycle, rear-pointing single looked enough like the legendary 1898 American (except for a semi-submerged oil tank braced to the lower unit) to make one wonder about a possible connection.

See Chapter 1.

"The Adirondack resort had a whole fleet of wooden rowboats," explained my elderly friend, Sidney Tripp, "and each one of 'em wore a green and gold Scott-Atwater seven-and-a-half horse outboard. As camp manager, I had to help any guests who couldn't run the motors right. One particular outboard was a hard starter. Those Scotts had gearshifts, so we used to tow the rowboat behind our inboard runabout, get it goin' maybe twenty, twenty-five miles per hour, and throw the balky kicker in forward. She didn't like it much, but it got her goin' every time!

"One evening 'round nightfall," my friend continued despite the protest of rolling eyeballs, "we rescued a family stranded near the Four Brother Islands, 'bout three miles out from camp. I had them taken back in the inboard while I stayed to fix that very same Scott-Atwater. Knowing the finicky thing

Scott-Atwater ad, about 1949.

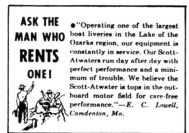

liked a hot spark, I advanced the mag, stood up, and really yanked.

"Well, sir, don't ya know, it roared to life on the second pull. Only thing was, the jack-rabbit start got the best of my footin' and I somersaulted into the lake!

"As mentioned earlier, it was gettin' pretty dark by then, but I was able to see the motor's direction as the renegade Scott sprayed me with her rooster tail and sped my boat away. Calculatin' the area of reentry," he smiled, "I swam to where the boat should eventually be comin' around. And nearly an hour later, I hear this distant *HMMMMMMMMMM, HMMMMMMMMMMM.* It was the old Scott. She was bringing that boat back to me after all! Soon my opportunity came. So grabbin' onto the side of the speeding craft, I boosted myself on board, and pointed an accusin' finger at that Scott outboard. Could have sworn she kinda stuck her choke knob out at me. Anyhow, I decided to ignore it, and without saying a word let the old gal push me home."

Even as a kid, I was never quite sure about the authenticity of those Scott yarns. Actually, at the 1946 introduction of its own outboard motor line, Scott-Atwater faced somewhat of a credibility problem. Although few knew about it, the firm had been making motors since 1935, and in 1941 was considered the second largest (after Outboard Marine) U.S. outboard producer.

The Minneapolis company was started in 1932 (as a small tool-making and punch-press operation) by C.E. Scott and H.B.

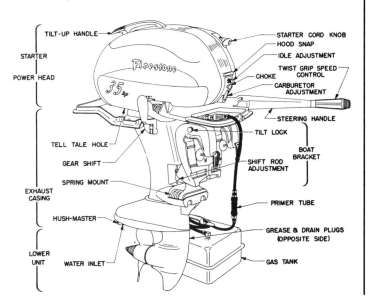

Firestone 35-hp Twin, built by Scott-Atwater.

A 1949 advertisement for Scott-Atwater's new gearshift motors.

Atwater. The pair eventually obtained contracts from local establishments, such as Gold Medal Flour, for the production of promotional trinkets and advertising premiums. This worked well when the flour customers were attracted to the specials. Any marketing flop, however, would allow Scott-Atwater's employees to take a continual coffee break.

A Mr. DuMonte walked into the little factory in 1935 and asked if the firm could possibly help design and build a simple outboard motor for him to sell. Messrs. Scott and Atwater saw this request as a way to get steady work and soon presented DuMonte with a sample kicker. This putt-putt (offered at about half the price of its nearest competitor) was exhibited at the New York Boat Show, and "orders were placed for several hundred."

Right after the show Scott-Atwater turned most of its shop into an outboard factory. Some Champion decals were ordered and affixed to the little motors before Mr. DuMonte came by to pick them up for distribution. Still a bit apprehensive about the success of this venture, Scott-Atwater kept coming up with those little advertising items whenever Gold Medal Flour called.

But this nervousness was ended in 1939 when DuMonte secured a contract from Firestone Tire and Rubber Company. The agreement called for Firestone to distribute Champions in its stores and franchise outlets (such as gas stations). Between 1939 and 1942, this marketing avenue sold all the Scott-Atwater–built Champions that the once-nervous little manufacturing concern could produce.

During World War II, Scott-Atwater was immersed in defense work, but frequently considered its postwar outboard options. Mr. DuMonte indicated he'd like to set up his own factory to build a new Champion line. Firestone wondered about its outboard motor status and went directly to Scott-Atwater with a request for kickers wearing its own Firestone label.

In 1946 both Scott-Atwater and Firestone motors hit the recreation-hungry marketplace. Larger facilities capable of handling the extra output were obtained.

Scott-Atwater didn't require its dealers to maintain an exclusive franchise. As a result marine shops with other makes were signed up. (This reasonable practice, which often placed Scott-Atwaters next to Mercurys on the showroom stands, allowed the line to expand its sales network quickly.)

Scott-Atwaters of 1946 were 3.6-horse, water-cooled singles (with optional rewind starter). In 1947 and again in '48, a 7½-hp twin was included in the lineup. Motors of this family received a rich, dark green paint job.

The company had been very busy working on an innovation it believed would set the firm apart from all competitors. The Scott-Atwater F-N-R gearshift was finally ready in 1949. Although Johnson had introduced a 10-horse shift model, Scott-Atwater offered a trio (4, 5, and 7½) with the shift feature. The line of 1950 contained all of these plus a new 16-hp shift rig. Scott-Atwater was

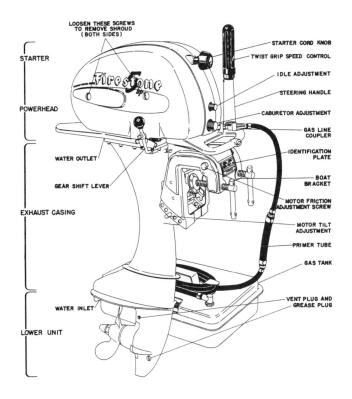

LOOSEN THESE SCREWS
TO REMOVE SHROUD
(BOTH SIDES)

STARTER

POWERHEAD

WATER OUTLET

GEAR SHIFT LEVER

EXHAUST CASING

WATER INLET

LOWER UNIT

STARTER CORD KNOB

TWIST GRIP SPEED CONTROL

IDLE ADJUSTMENT

STEERING HANDLE

CABURETOR ADJUSTMENT

GAS LINE
COUPLER

IDENTIFICATION
PLATE

BOAT
BRACKET

MOTOR FRICTION
ADJUSTMENT SCREW

MOTOR TILT
ADJUSTMENT

PRIMER TUBE

GAS TANK

VENT PLUG AND
GREASE PLUG

The 1956, 5-hp Firestone motor, built by Scott-Atwater, had a thin, Gold Pennant profile.

also serious about its products' appearance and had the motors' external features done by New York industrial designer Francisco Cullura.

The 1951 lineup was unchanged except for the addition of a 10-hp model. Speed designations were serving as unofficial model names. For example, the big 16 was supposed to go 1 to 30 mph; hence, it became the 1-30. The basic 3.6 single (nonshift) could cover 1 to 12 mph and was labeled the 1-12, and so on.

The outboards started gaining positive attention, and Scott-Atwater, recalling its involvement with the flour company promotions, knew the importance of publicity. Besides actively participating in every major boat and sport show, as well as advertising nationally, the firm would pay up to 50 percent of the cost of local dealer ads.

Furthermore, Scott-Atwater not only provided dealerships with an "extensive mat service" (mats are newspaper/magazine ad sheets suitable for easy use in any publication), but also offered recorded (usually on big 16-inch transcription discs) radio commercials which could conveniently be tagged by a local station announcer with the dealer's address. This was an aggressive practice on the part of a relatively small, early Fifties company. Still more unusual in that radio and newspaper-oriented era was Scott-Atwater's offer to cover half the dealers' cost for airing video versions of outboard ads on local TV stations. A 1951

Scott-Atwater touted their "Aquablade" lower units as being markedly thinner than Evinrude or Johnson. In fairness to OMC, its "Big Twin" 25 was compared with Scott's smaller 16. Besides, most of OMC's bulk is above the water line.

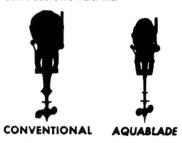

CONVENTIONAL   AQUABLADE

Note clean, sleek lines of
Aquablade underwater unit.

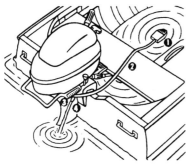

HERE'S HOW *BAIL-A-MATIC* WORKS

A vacuum pump pulled water through Scott-Atwater's "Bail-A-Matic" motors and then shot it out of the boat (at 150-gph maximum). This water did not circulate through the engine's cooling system. Even so, outboard repairmen have spent many hours fixing this "convenience."

survey found Scott-Atwater to be the only such organization to have prepared 60-second TV commercials "for dealer distribution."[40]

Ads in 1952 dropped the 4-hp rig, as the line included motors in 3.6-, 5-, 7½-, 10-, and 16-horse denominations. In 1953 two very unusual-looking Scott-Atwaters, dubbed Gold Pennant motors, were unveiled. These green-and-gold 7½- and 10-horse kickers had remote gas tanks and wore little chrome accent ears on each side of the two-piece cover shell. Because the Gold Pennant's profile was remarkably thin, you could get the idea the poor thing had been squished. Although well promoted, Gold Pennant motors (which some folks called pumpkin seeds) did not return the following year. The skinny styling was revised on Scott-Atwater's private-brand Corsair and Firestone outboards.

Scott-Atwater had tooled up for a new series of green (bottom shroud) and gold (top cover section) motors aimed at giving boaters the most useful nautical feature in marine history—a mechanical bailer. Unfortunately, this strong sales point eventually caused some folks to shake their heads in disgust.

All of the 1954s (except the 3.6 hp) had a little hose attached to a small rectangular aluminum assembly. The other end of the hose went to the motor. The green aluminum gizmo got placed in the bottom of the boat, and as a trademark (Bail-A-Matic) proudly emblazoned on the motor cover presumed, would automatically rid your craft of water.

Numerous problems with early Bail-A-Matic water pumps (also assigned to cool the cylinders) caused many a salty word to echo over worldwide waterways. As luck would have it, these parts were not easy to access and fix, either. In addition many Scott-Atwater repairs required special tools and a working knowledge of outboard innards, a pair of prerequisites seldom held by motor owners.

Bail-A-Matic, which was a darn good idea anyway, got heavily promoted through 1956. Although it remained on some subsequent models (even on Scott-Atwater's mid-Sixties successor, McCulloch), the system was de-emphasized from its original "top-feature" status.

The Scott-Atwater people had always planned on joining the full-line outboard producers and finally did so in 1955 with a 30-hp unit. This rig was upped to 33 horses in 1956.

Meantime, Messrs. Scott and Atwater were approached by McCulloch Corporation about the possibility of selling the outboard company. A deal was closed in 1956.

McCulloch discontinued the private-brand Corsair line (the old firm had been producing this badge-engineered product since 1948) and began referring to its outboard division as Scott. Even though the full Scott-Atwater name remained for a time on engine hoods, the shortened Scott title came as a relief to many who could never remember the second part anyway (kind of like *Sears* and Roebuck).

The new management enlarged the 1957 line by souping up the old 33 for a nice round 40 hp. It was offered in manual or electric start and could be equipped with a long shaft for large runabouts and cruisers. The 16-horse motor had an optional electrical start. Some of the Scott line's fiberglass hoods were available in a choice of eight colors.

Some McCulloch brass felt publicity generated via outboard racing was a good way to promote Scott. A 14-foot utility boat with twin Scott 40s won the 120-mile Malibu Beach open marathon during early 1957. In another California event the executive vice-president of McCulloch used a pair of 40-horse Scotts to push his 16-foot runabout to victory. These gains caused McCulloch to institute a "competition development" department. There was even hope Scott would produce a line of racing motors suitable for National Outboard Association and American Power Boat Association stock outboard classes. (At that time only Mercury and Champion offered a few such kickers.)

Rather than introduce a utilitarian 20-cubic-inch class "B" stocker, however, Scott decided to shoot for the world's outboard speed record of just over 100 mph. The company came up with a special gear box linking two of its soon-to-be-unveiled three-cylinder Flying Scott 60-hp powerheads. This rig, mounted on an unconventional Italian-built di Priolo lower unit, was dubbed the Scott-Atwater Square Six. Its torque tube protruded back of the motor at about a 30 degree angle and had triple anticavitation plates and an overdrive gear requiring a gallon and a half of SAE 90 lubricant per run! The Square Six was supposed to provide Scott with a "braggin' rights" display at the 1958 New York Boat Show. While it easily zipped a custom designed hydro to 80 mph, the six-cylinder, six-carb power plant didn't quite hit the desired 101.12-mph mark. Still, industry observers hoped the motor would serve as a catalyst for more racing outboards from Scott.[41]

The year 1958 saw the McCulloch-designed three-cylinder, in-line, 60-hp Flying Scott officially introduced. It was also the year that Scott-Atwater motors were offered with electric power steering enlivened by the boat's 12-volt battery, an option that was somewhat ahead of its time when first introduced. Electric-starting models now came with a generator for more dependable battery use. Model names of the late Fifties Scotts took on a psychographic tone with nomenclature such as Thrifty, Fishing, Family, Special, Sports, Super, and Royal.

The McCulloch management was really into experimentation. Soon after buying Scott-Atwater, these fidgety folks started cooking up new designs, and by late 1959 built a 90-cubic-inch, four-cylinder radial outboard, which hung behind the transom on a special mounting bracket. Electronic controls steered the lower unit and changed propeller pitch from high forward through neutral to reverse.

Apparently this model, the Scott R-120, used 4-cycle combustion in addition to being turbo-supercharged and fuel-injected. The

125-hp space-age kicker never saw mass production but made the rounds at 1960 boat shows.

During the early Sixties, most Scotts received a clean white paint scheme. The McCulloch people also offered custom fiberglass boats matched to their various outboards. The 1961–62 line ranged from 2.6 to 75.2 hp.

Popular during this era was the low-profile Fishing Scott. This uniquely shaped motor (positioned predominantly outboard like the old Flambeau) weighed but 40 pounds and measured only 30 inches high.

Scott, never one to pass up a useful feature, debuted its Shallowater Drive as standard equipment on the Royal Scott Custom 40 and Flying Scott 75.2-hp models. This remote tilt mechanism, operable from the front of the boat, used engine thrust to tilt the motor. This item could be used at higher speeds and allowed effective and safe cruising in 6 inches of water.

Also belonging to the early 1960s were a few hardy Scotts known as *OX*. These strong rigs (most of which occupied the 14-hp range and wore red covers) could be ordered with either a standard or geared-down lower unit for houseboat pushing and/or industrial applications. Thermostat cooling was added to later models. Diesel power was also an option.

By 1964 Scott's owners decided to relabel their motors with the McCulloch name, and another well-known Forties and Fifties marque faded into outboard history.

The Sea-Bee 5-hp motor featured a genuine Evinrude/Johnson look. It was made by OMC's Gale Products division.

Sea-Bee (1)

The fighting Seabee military men racked up many honors during World War II. So in 1946, when the Goodyear Tire and Rubber Company of Akron, Ohio, wanted a good name for its private-brand outboard line, Sea-Bee fought its way to the top of the suggestion list. Sea-Bee motors, made by Gale Products Division of Outboard Marine, were marketed through 1959.

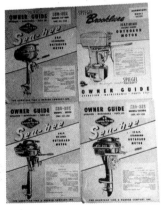

Owner's manuals printed for auto and catalog stores retailing Gale-made private-brand outboards.

Sea-Bee (2)

This 1960s marque had no connection with the earlier Goodyear Sea-Bee. A trio of small engines in 1½-, 3-, and 4-hp denominations made up the Sea-Bee outboard line marketed by Robert T. Boomer of Venice, California The 2-cycle, single-cylinder motors wore such model names as "Minor" and "Super 3." Some were available in long-shaft versions for auxiliary-power sailboat use.

This 7-hp model came on the market in 1966.

Not to be outdone by its tire competitors at Goodyear and Firestone, the BF Goodrich Company of Akron, Ohio, purchased a 1952 (some were considered 1951) stock of private-brand motors from Gale Products Division. The following year Goodrich's sea-green color Sea-Flyer outboards were being built at the Champion factory. By 1955 the Sea-Flyer had flown the coop.

See listing under Cross, earlier in this chapter.

Muncie Gear Works was under contract from the 1930s through about 1941 to supply outboards to the National Outboard Motor Company of Marshall, Michigan. To fulfill this agreement, Muncie's complete "Neptune" line from 1.2 to 16 hp was simply relabeled with the Sea Gull nameplate. These Sea Gulls had no relationship with the better-known British motors bearing the same moniker.

"Only the finest motors have Sea King features," boasted a late-Forties Montgomery Ward and Company catalog. Its claim was based on the fact that Ward's Sea King outboards were typically supplied by the industry's major players.

"Just my size!" A youngster proudly displays his Montgomery Ward Sea King Midget Single eggbeater, which sold for $27.95 in 1941. Postwar inflation pushed the price of a 1947 version to $49.50. That was still a bargain for an OMC-built motor.

The big Chicago-based mail-order house's first rowboat motor came in the form of a Caille-built, World War I–era kicker called Hiawatha. Montgomery Ward changed its marine line's name to Sea King and purchased product from the Evinrude-controlled Outboard Motors Corporation. During the early Thirties, OMC had an odd stock of idle class "B" Chiefs from its discontinued Lockwood line. The firm honored part of its Montgomery Ward contract by sticking Sea King decals on these interesting motors. Some of the 15-horse twins had electric starters. A very few were equipped with unusual Bendix Eclipse crank-up inertia starters. (Today, these make up the rarest Sea Kings.)

By the late Thirties, Montgomery Ward (which also bought some Muncie-built outboards) purchased a supply of catalog engines from the Cedarburg (Wisconsin) Manufacturing Company. These erstwhile Thors, relabeled with the Sea King name, didn't run very well and gave Montgomery Ward a black eye. Meanwhile, Carl Kiekhaefer bought the Thor factory, fixed up some rejected Sea Kings, and earned a new contract with the large retailer. As a result, the early 1940s Sea King line comprised a mix of smaller Kiekhaefer motors and outboards produced by Evinrude's Gale Products Division.

Sea Breeze
Sea-Flyer

Sea Gull (1)
Sea Gull (2)

Sea King

Years ago I spotted an old Spring–Summer 1947 Montgomery Ward catalog peeking out from under a wicker rocker on the screened-in porch of a vintage lakeside cottage. The publication's Sea King section pictured a 1-horse "midget single," a 2.9-hp "large single," standard and deluxe (full-pivot reverse and rewind-start) 3.3-horse opposed twins, 5-hp standard and deluxe alternate-firing twins, a "super" 8½-hp, and "giant" 15.2-horse opposed twins. The 2.9-hp rig came from Kiekhaefer, with the remainder originating at Gale.

While the smaller motors could be mailed through the post office, large models were shipped by freight or express from Montgomery Ward's warehouses in Baltimore or Albany, New York. Sea Kings were sent with "full instructions and complete parts list." Spare parts were "carried in stock at your nearest Ward mail order house and at the motor factories."

By the early Fifties, Gale supplied the Sea King line via its standard stable of private-brand outboards: a 3-hp single, a 5-horse with neutral clutch, and a 12-hp gearshift-equipped alternate-firing twin. In 1955 the top Sea King had 22 hp, a remote Bo'sun fuel tank system, and optional electric starter. The next year the 22 was upped to 25. In addition a neat 12-hp electric-start outboard was introduced into the '56 Sea King lineup. Two years later, this smaller power-start model was gone, and a 35-horse twin was added to the roster. Early Sixties Montgomery Ward catalogs showed a few changes in power range. For example, a 15-hp twin and 60-hp quad were introduced.

Montgomery Ward made a bigger switch for the 1964–65 Sea King line by contracting with West Bend to supply its watersport section. Typically occupying the 3½-, 5½-, 6-, 8-, 9-, 20-, and up to 80-hp brackets, these mid-Sixties engines made up the final Sea Kings in our area of interest.

If you ever wonder why someone would buy an outboard from a catalog, convenience constitutes most of the answer. Prior to the 1960s not every locale was served by a marine store. Montgomery Ward catalogs brought the marina to rural customers. More importantly, huge retailers like Montgomery Ward allowed items to be purchased on credit. That previously mentioned 1947 "midget single" was available through the mail to anyone willing to commit "$4 a month (or about 13 cents per day) on terms" for a Sea King sporting features found in "only the finest outboard motors."

Sea Pacer

Introduced in 1962 the Sea Pacer offered small boaters a 4-cycle powerhead The air-cooled outboard in the 3-hp range featured a front and rear carrying handle assembly and Clinton-style lower units.

Sears

About 1964 America's largest retailer dropped the Elgin marque from its outboard line. The predominantly McCulloch-produced motors of this vintage simply bore the Sears name.

Skipper was a rather rare private-brand built in the late 1940s and early 1950s by Muncie Gear Works (the Neptune people). It appears the company marketing Skipper outboards also contracted for some kickers from Outboard Marine's Gale Products Division. Regardless of their various origins, Skippers were constructed in 1½-, 3-, 5-, and 12-hp denominations.

Skipper (1)

The 1962–67 Skipper is an Eska-built air-cooled, 3-hp single. Typically, these wore a "juice can" fuel tank.

Skipper (2)

Metalex Ltd. of Richmond, in Vancouver, British Columbia, Canada, began marketing its Spartan V outboard in 1959. Presumably, this obscure motor was of the low-horsepower, fishing variety.

Spartan

A letter in my files dated July, 1969 says 'We have not been in the business of manufacturing this equipment for more than seven years and are unable to supply you with anything [information] in this regard." A Spartan that turned up in the U.S. Pacific Northwest consisted of a 1-cylinder, air-cooled Lauson lawn mower powerhead on a basic outboard lower unit.

We sell "the motor that puts the *TING* in boating!" claimed a Spinaway advertisement. With ad copy like that, it is doubtful its author lasted to the 1924 end of the Spinaway production run.

Spinaway (Speedaway)

Officially, the earliest Spinaways (1911) were called Speedaways, originating from the Speedaway Boat Motor Company, Freeport, Illinois. Three years later, the Hoefer Manufacturing Company owned the young rowboat motor firm and renamed it Spinaway Boat Motor Company.

Hoefer reminded small-boat owners that Roman soldiers once chained slaves to galley oars and suggested the modern equivalent of such harsh activity could best be avoided by purchasing a Spinaway.

One of the forward-pointing single's most prominent features was its round gas tank (of about equal size to the flywheel). Owners found a funnel was needed to fuel-up via the tank's small, side-mounted spout. Ignition was available from a battery or gear-driven Bosch mag. By the later Teens Spinaways could be ordered with a flywheel-enclosed magneto. In fact some wore an Evinrude flywheel and mag. (This could cause a Spinaway to be mistaken for an old Evinrude.) The rudder-steered Spinaway was finished in a moss green color, accented by various bronze and polished-aluminum parts.

Many examples came through the factory with nice identification detailing on the exhaust assembly. Early models had an underwater exhaust tube. Later ones simply used a rear-pointing muffler (in which case, the brand was put on the gas tank). Some Spinaways had starting knobs that recessed in a small flywheel cavity when the motor was either idle or spinning away.

During the final two years of production (1923 and 1924), a number of Spinaway opposed twins were produced. The '23

A World War I–era Spinaway outboard and logo.

Circa 1923 Spinaway "Superb Twin" was available in battery or magneto ignition version. Although most documentation indicates the Spinaway firm was gone by the mid-1920s, a recently discovered factory letter to a potential customer is dated September 1929. Perhaps it was a misprint, or correspondence from someone who bought the remnants of the company and was trying to peddle a few leftovers.

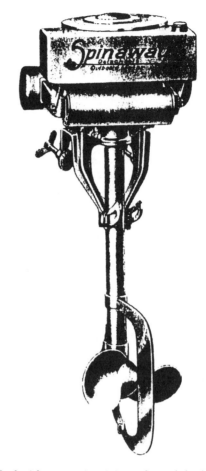

metered fuel with a generic mixing valve, while the '24 sported a Zenith carb. As was the case with some of the last singles, mag ignition was often from Evinrude. And then after that "all of the fun, pleasure, and wholesome diversion" from Spinaway came to a close.

Starling Jet

"From Propulsion Research, Inc. in Minneapolis, heart of the outboard country, came America's first production line jet propelled outboard." So stated the 1965 introductory brochure for the model P-500 Starling Jet "complete fishing motor."

Actually, other U.S. companies (such as Lancaster Pump) had similar products predating the Starling Jet, but this firm's Marine Jet Division was probably aiming at wider distribution. The 5-hp, air-cooled, single-cylinder powerhead was built by Clinton Engines Corporation of Maquoketa, Iowa, and looked identical to Clinton's own outboard power plant. The jet lower unit was of Propulsion Research's design and drew water through a grill into a small turbine. This internal turbine created "super hydro thrust" and pushed a jet stream through slots where a propeller would be

on a regular outboard. The 29-pound, 2-cycle rig was marketed to fishermen wanting to maneuver in weedy, shallow waters. Safety-minded swimmers and skin divers were also targeted in ads stressing "prop-less" action.

At 6,800 rpm (a lot of revs for the lawn-mower-style powerhead), the Starling Jet gave 82 pounds of push. The company, however, suggested an operating range of 3,900 to 5,000 rpm.

This novel little motor came with a 3-gallon remote fuel tank and was available in "Jet White" for fishermen or "Olive Drab" for duck hunters. Neither group really responded to the thrust of Propulsion Research's message, and the Starling Jet was grounded a few years later.

Added to the list of circa World War I forward-pointing, single-cylinder rowboat motors was the St. Lawrence. Its manufacturer, the St. Lawrence Engine Company, equipped the (1916) motor with a knob-starting flywheel and rudder steering.

St. Lawrence

Sometimes called the Strelmotor, this 1914–16 Detroit-built outboard's most striking feature was its long, direct-drive lower unit. The powerhead could be separated from the drive shaft assembly for easier carrying. The Strelinger Marine Company's offering generated 2 hp at 800 rpm.

Strelinger claimed the motor would run six hours on a gallon of gas, and also guaranteed it for five years, but went out of business before then. This direct-drive kicker predated the similarly styled Caille Liberty drive.

Strelinger

See Chapter 1.

A little bit of hearsay and a touch of faded memory put this mystery kicker on the list. Apparently the circa-1910 Sunbeams looked like one of Submerged's gasoline-powered outboards from Menomonie, Wisconsin. One old motor buff heard that Sunbeams were private brands marketed by the well-known home appliance outfit.

Submerged
Sunbeam

See listing under Champion.

Rather than a firm with a full-fledged outboard factory, the Sweet Manufacturing Company might actually have been an early private-brand motor distributor. From 1914 to 1916 the Detroit concern marketed a 4-hp (at 1,000 rpm) single that was virtually indistinguishable from a forward-pointing, horizontal-cylinder Waterman Porto.

It would be nearly impossible to tell a Sweet, minus its ID plate, from a nameless Waterman of similar vintage, Because Sweet and Waterman both hailed from what would become the "Motor City," it's unlikely Sweet simply copied Waterman's design without prior approval. My guess is that Sweets were built by Water-

Swanson
Sweet

Sweet motors were almost identical to Watermans. Both companies were located in Detroit. Sweets had more brass than Watermans, though.

4 H. P. MOTOR
Call and see a Sweet Row-Boat Motor

Ted Williams

Terry Troller

Thor

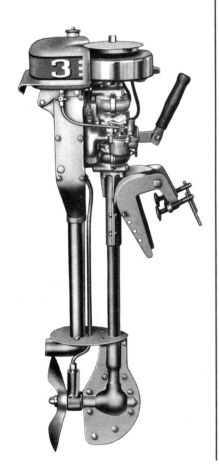

man, then sent to Sweet for labeling and distribution. Or, perhaps Sweet purchased pieces from Waterman and built up the motors in its shop. Whatever the case, there had to be some connection.

By the way, Sweet also offered a 2-hp (at 700 rpm) single that was a dead ringer for an Evinrude rowboat motor.

The famous Red Sox hitter lent his name to a McCulloch-produced 1960s fishing motor sold by Sears. The Eska company also made some of these private-brand outboards.

Meant to be a fishing motor, the 4-cycle Terry Troller from Terry Troller Manufacturing, Inc. (West Frankfort, Illinois) was on the market from 1960 to 1963. One of its most interesting features was a lawn-mower-style "wind-up and release" crank starter.

Thor Hansen often said, "Go ahead, drop any Thor outboard on cement! You will not harm it." Mr. Hansen, president of Cedarburg (Wisconsin) Manufacturing Company, even invited Thor owners to stick "a pencil into the carburetor air intake hole [breaking away any oily film] to assure quick starting."

Steel stampings comprised portions of this 1938–39 Thor Pyramid-3, in-line outboard. Alternate fire on this 3-cyclinder, 2-cycle, 6.2-hp model was touted as being as smooth as a 6-cylinder auto engine. A few of these rigs were fitted with cast lower gearcases. (Mercury Marine)

Thor outboards, introduced in 1935, had a very "basic" appearance. The motors incorporated pressed-steel, cadmium-plated stampings for crankcase, gear housing, main stem, clamping bracket, and steering handle. This stuff was supposed to be "rustproof," but was in fact vulnerable to the elements—particularly salt water. The 1935, 2.4-hp single was advertised as "sturdy, simple, and quick starting!" While the first two claims were indeed true, the latter could, at best, be euphemized as a wish. Hansen's nearly featureless mixing valve/carb was usually the culprit.

In 1936 it was claimed that Thor outboards would "again astound the outboard world" with a 4.8-hp, two-cylinder version. At $42.50 for the single and $62.50 for the opposed twin, these motors were priced within the "range of every fisherman and sportsman."

By 1938 the angled lower-unit skeg, fashioned from steel stampings, was given a rounded look. Hansen had a little bit of luck selling a few of his motors. Then Montgomery Ward's catalog stores gave him a chance to use the "same engineering genius that upset all former standards of outboard value" and make up some motors to be sold under the Sea King label. Having purchased Sea Kings to push a boat, as opposed to pound cement, however, Montgomery Ward customers registered numerous complaints. That dissatisfaction, coupled with sagging Thor sales, caused Hansen to go out of business.

The closed-up Cedarburg Manufacturing Company was soon purchased by E.C. Kiekhaefer, who decided to rename it Kiekhaefer Corporation. The new firm was supposed to make electromagnetic auto components, but a lack of capital caused Kiekhaefer to rebuild the remaining stock of faulty Thor-Sea Kings. Montgomery Ward was so pleased with the results that Kiekhaefer figured he'd temporarily remain in the outboard business.

Under Kiekhaefer management the 1939 Thor line included a 2.4-hp Streamliner. Complete with new carb, this remnant of the old Thor single wore a streamlined, teardrop fuel tank. It is a rare and highly desired motor today. Also offered were alternate-firing, in-line two- and three-cylinder outboards. At 6.2 hp, the Pyramid 3 was the first of its configuration.

By 1940 Kiekhaefer opted to stay with the outboard industry, but dropped the Thor name in favor of his new Mercury marque.

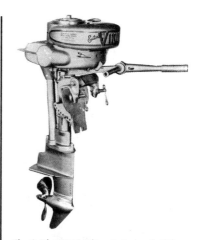

The 8.5-hp 1940 Viking Twin was built by Evinrude for Canada's Eaton department stores. (Antique Boat Museum)

Valley

A rowboat motor from Saginaw, Michigan, the Valley dates back to 1914.

Versatool (Aqua-Sport Outboard Attachment)

While not an antique, wayward examples of this rig could throw an outboard enthusiast for a loop. Consequently, the Versatool is listed herein. Noting the proliferation of chainsaws, Versatool, Inc., of Sun Valley, California, developed a wide range of accessories that could be mated to a chainsaw engine.

Among the firm's hedgetrimmers, pumps, generators, and drills was the Versatool VT600 Aqua-Sport Outboard Attachment. Early 1980s Versatool brochures indicated you could remove your saw's chain, mount the outboard converter (steer with the saw handgrip), and "in seconds be ready to take your chainsaw fishing." A 6-gallon (OMC) remote fuel tank could be fitted to the saw's carb for greater range.

At just under $100, this clever product represented an economical way for chainsaw owners to go outboarding. Because the outboard unit could be matched to an array of chainsaw brands, including those sharing outboard motor names (such as Western Auto-Wizard, Homelite, and McCulloch), one needs to be aware the resulting kicker is a conversion.

Viking

Like Sears, its American counterpart, the T. Eaton Company of Toronto, Ontario, offered a line of private-brand outboards. Over the years (from the 1930s to the 1960s) Eaton's Viking motors were supplied by manufacturers such as Muncie, Evinrude, Gale, and West Bend.[42]

Voyager

Relabeled 1950 Champions made up the first Voyager line. The thinly disguised Champs, like their sister Majestic outboards, were sold through Champion's subsidiary, Outboard Motor Brands, Inc., of Minneapolis, Minnesota. When Champion faded from sight in 1959, Voyager disappeared too.

Walnut
Waterman
Water Sprite
Waterwitch

See the listing for Burtray.

See the listing for Arrow (1).

See the listing for Burtray.

Sears-Roebuck got into the retail outboard business about 1913 or 1914. Its Motorgo kickers were produced by a number of firms. Around 1934 Sears switched its outboard name to Waterwitch. Muncie made some, and interestingly, even Johnson built a very few Waterwitches that were based on its 8.1-hp OK series motors.

When its 1930–36 outboard supply agreement with Muncie Gear Works was expiring, the big retailer turned to Kissel Industry Company of Hartford, Wisconsin, for help. This Kissel organization had been salvaged around 1930 from the remnants of the bankrupt Kissel Automobile Company. These folks were more than happy to contract with Sears, and from 1936 to 1942 came up with a rather wide selection of Waterwitch outboards.

Understandably, to the uninterested all Kissel Waterwitches look the same. Actually, however, these rigs ranged from a ¾-hp, air-cooled putt-putt, to a rare (about 600 built) 1941, 10-horse, alternate-firing twin. Its deluxe 5.75-hp model came with a rewind starter and a receptacle on the front of the gas tank into which a small light (or other accessory) could be plugged. Some of the most exotic Waterwitches, with their "twin-pod" fuel tanks, were styled by designer Raymond Loewy. Futuristic looks or not, many of these classics ran poorly, and Sears, ever mindful of customer satisfaction, recoiled under complaints.

Near the close of World War II the West Bend Aluminum Company purchased the Kissel plant, and Sears asked West Bend to come up with a new Elgin outboard by 1946. Even though the last Waterwitches officially rolled off the assembly line in 1942, it appears West Bend put together a few thousand from remaining parts stock in 1945. Actually, during the war, the government ordered a small run of 3½-hp Waterwitches for essential use by various domestic authorities. Note: The first Waterwitch motors were of Muncie manufacture and date from late 1933 to early 1937. They came in denominations from 2 to 16 hp.

Also a point of Waterwitch interest: The story line for Robert McCloskey's famous children's book *One Morning in Maine,* included one of the famous Sears motors. The darn thing wouldn't start in the book, either.

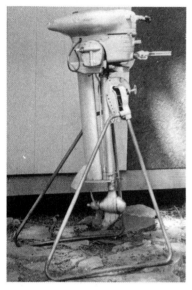

The 1942 Sears Waterwitch 5¾-hp Twin had rewind start and a tiny generator and receptacle plug for attaching a fishing light. Looks like it could come up the cellar stairs at night and attack somebody! As a Waterwitch footnote, a 1939 document has surfaced showing a Waterwitch "twin pod" fuel tank–equipped motor, and captioned "Design for an outboard motor for boats" with a patent granted to a Mr. John R. Morgan. No Raymond Loewy?

Wayman
Aqua-Jet

Toronto Engine Works owner Charles Wayman developed a jet-thrust outboard called Aqua-Jet Miner in early 1947. A streamlined version with rather attractive styling was prepared circa 1948 to 1949. Wearing a Tillotson carb and Eiseman magneto, the one-lung, two-stroke Wayman delivered 3 hp. Rowboat tests showed a speed capability of 3 to 8 mph. Unfortunately neither Canadian jet outboard saw actual production.

Many people had been depending on the West Bend Aluminum Company's outboards for some 10 years before realizing the firm was ever in the boat-motor business. The story starts in 1944, when the famous kitchen utensil concern bought the (Hartford, Wisconsin) Kissel plant. That factory came with a Sears contract to produce outboard motors.

Although West Bend built a few Sears Waterwitch motors from existing stock, its engineers were asked to develop a completely new outboard for debut after World War II. They did, and the famous Elgin line sold like hotcakes from 1946 until ties with Sears were loosened in the early 1960s.

Meanwhile, West Bend's contract with the big retailer allowed for the relabeling of some Elgin motors. These green, badge-engineered rigs got to wear the West Bend name and were considered exports.

In 1955 the firm used a paint scheme different from the Elgins and offered West Bend outboards to the domestic market. The public demand for higher-horsepower motors caused West Bend wisely to offer a full line. This stable, which began at 2 hp, went to 25 hp, and soon 40 horses, culminated (in 1961) with an over-5-foot-tall, four-cylinder, in-line Tiger-Shark powerhouse rated at 80 hp. This piece was also offered in a modified form as the Shark-O-Matic inboard/outboard. West Bend assigned "fishy" names to many of its motors. Various models were labeled Shrimp, Pike, Muskie, Shark, and Barracuda.

During this era, West Bend really began concentrating in the home appliance avenue, shifting some executive interest away from the outboard division.

By late 1964, after the unchanged 1965 models were announced, West Bend accepted a purchase order from Chrysler. Consequently, the 1965s were called WESTBEND—by CHRYSLER.

In retrospect West Bend always seemed to be lumped in with the also-rans of the day. This labeling was very unfair, however, as its outboards showed considerable reliability and innovation. West Bend–produced motors were the first to have a vacuum fuel system, a three-phase super-alternator generator, a low-level reduction gear starter, cushion mounting, V reed intake valves, an acoustical leg chamber, and a fiberglass motor cover.[43] All these features were available at pricing often lower than Mercury, Johnson, or Evinrude.

Perhaps if West Bend had enjoyed a stronger dealership network, its undue second-stringer image would have disappeared. In fact Chrysler's desire to buy West Bend's outboard division was heightened from evidence suggesting the product was, indeed, a quality marque suffering from being undersold.[44]

In 1941 and 1942 Outboard Marine's Gale Products Division of Galesburg, Illinois, produced this 2½- and 5-hp fishing-motor line for the Kansas City–based Western Auto Supply Company. World War II stopped Western Flyer production. Following that conflict,

West Bend

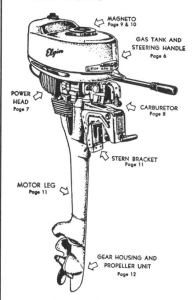

West Bend produced this 1¼-hp, Elgin air-cooled outboard for Sears in 1946.

Late-1950s West Bend logo.

This boat is fitted with an 80-hp, 1964 West Bend motor.

Western Flyer

Whirlpool

the famous auto parts and hardware chain came out with the Wizard outboard.

Not exactly the kind of old motor you'd expect to spot at a garage sale, the 4-cycle Whirlpool outboard was an experimental, three-cylinder, radial model. Built by the famous Whirlpool home appliance people in Los Angeles, this rig could be thrown into neutral by raising the tiller handle. The approximately 30-cubic-inch–displacement Whirlpool outboard motor was probably constructed in late 1927 and received rave reviews from folks who watched it race in California. Kudos aside, company execs decided to stick with machines capable of handling America's laundry, and hung any further plans for the Whirlpool outboard's production out to dry.

Wilco

A Chicago firm marketed an Evinrude rowboat motor look-alike called the Wilco. Not to be confused with the Wilcox-McKim, the Wilco was available only in 1914.

Wilcox

Saginaw, Michigan, was home to the Wilcox-McKim Company, makers of the Wilcox (some were labeled Wilcox-McKim) outboard from 1914 to 1916. The 2½-hp, 70-pound engine was sparked by a gear-driven Dixie magneto. The flywheel starting knob rested in a cavity when not in use.

Interestingly, the very top of the crankshaft was hollow and extended an inch or so above the flywheel. Wilcox owners packed the crank top with grease to satisfy the upper main bearing.

The Wilcox steered with a rudder and had an underwater exhaust tube identical to the early Spinaway single.

Wisconsin

In a large field of quickly exhausted also-rans, the Wisconsin Machinery and Manufacturing Company made a relatively long-lived series of one-cylinder rowboat motors. The famous farm and industrial engine builder reminded potential customers that "the primary fact to observe in buying any mechanical device is the experience and reputation of its maker."

On patents issued late in the summer of 1913, Wisconsin began offering its 2-stroke, water-cooled outboards the following model year. Most Wisconsins were variations on two basic themes: a 2-hp Junior kicker (sometimes called model J, K, L, or M) and a 3½-horse rig (model N) especially adaptable for commercial use on fishing and livery boats, as well as tenders.

The smaller Wisconsin could be ordered with a battery ignition or a gear-driven Elkhart magneto (said to produce a good spark at 50 rpm). Owners of the 2-hp had the option of rudder or conventional propeller steering. The latter method's tiller could be twisted one quarter turn, allowing the operator to lock in a specific direction.

A 1922 Wisconsin rowboat motor ad.

Typically, the 3½-hp version came with a magneto and rudder steering. Wisconsin described its products as "simple, compact, capable of delivering wonderful power."

By the mid-1920s these rowboat motors were hopelessly outdated. (Note: Evinrude offered diehards a basic rowboat motor through 1928.) Even so, Wisconsin remained in the outboard business to 1930, possibly offering the few patrons of that era motors from new/old stock. Since the Milwaukee-based firm continued manufacturing its other product lines, parts and service for the Wisconsin outboards were available for a good number of years thereafter.

Before World War II, the fledgling Kiekhaefer Corporation entered the outboard business via supplying Montgomery Ward with some Sea King motors. After the war its recollections of that profitable relationship caused the manufacturer of Mercury outboards to get back into private-branding.

In 1946 Western Auto Supply Company of Kansas City, Missouri, contracted Kiekhaefer to relabel some basic 3.2- and 6-horse Mercs with Wizard decals.

By 1949 Western Auto catalogs listed a more deluxe 6-hp Super Twin. The following year Wizards took on a light green color and were offered in 6- and 10-hp sizes. A shift version of the 10 was added for 1952. This top-of-the-line Wizard rig was upgraded to 12 hp in 1954 and joined the standard 6 and 10 in the expanding line.

For 1955 the old 6 was replaced with a Super 5. The following year Kiekhaefer supplied Western Auto with a slightly tuned-down version of its four-cylinder Mercury Mark 30. This Wizard Super Power 25 was also available with electric start.

Wizard

The 1956/57 Wizard 25.

The 1953 Western Auto Wizard had definite Mercury traits.

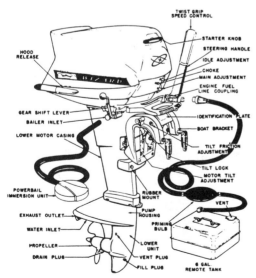

Early-1960s Wizard logo and 1961, 14.1-hp Wizard by Scott.

For some reason an Oliver-built model, dubbed **Powermatic 15**, showed up in Wizard's '57 line. The 1958 series (5½, 15, and 35 hp) were all from Oliver.

For 1959 the catalog store went with Scott (McCulloch) and offered a stable of these products wearing the Wizard name, 3.6 to 40 hp.

Finally, the last of the full-line Wizards were Chrysler outboard products ordered from mid-1960s Western Auto catalogs.

Wright

Where other rowboat motors had tiller handles, the Wright had a crank, which the operator turned for steering, or complete reversing. This 2-hp (at 675 rpm) forward-pointing single had a knob-start flywheel but no lower-unit skeg.

The Wright could be ordered with battery or flywheel magneto ignition and sported an aluminum crankcase, torque tube, and transom bracket.

A product of the C.T. Wright Engine Company of Greenville, Michigan, the Wright "attachable" (as compared with everyone else's "*de*tachable") rowboat motor was marketed between 1914 and 1917.

Here's a rare early twenty-first-century boating scene! This old motor buff was probably the only person in the world that day actually operating a Flambeau.

A single-cylinder Outboard Jet in operation.

For over a century, boaters have been using electric outboards successfully. As a complement to the list of American gasoline-powered kickers, the following roster chronicles U.S.–made electrics and even a couple of "people-powered" models.

Here is a true milestone motor. The 1895 Allen Portable Electric Propeller was America's first generally advertised and mass-produced outboard. Well, *mass produced* is probably stretching numbers a little, but Frank S. Allen's New York City–based firm (sometimes referred to as the Electric Boat Company) made enough of a splash to plant the seed for America's lucrative outboard motor industry.

It appears Allen got his idea from an 1892 patent granted to Chicagoan Wilbur Salisbury. The government paperwork for the Windy City man's "Boat Propelling Apparatus" contained drawings remarkably similar to Allen's 1895 electric outboard.

Allen's product featured an electric power plant that drove a propeller via a flexible bronze shaft through a long, angled tube. For smooth running, the operator filled a portion of that torque tube with oil.

By today's standards, ads for the early outboard are pretty humorous. Claims such as, "Can go forward, stop, and steer. No fire explosives or engineer. No danger possible," might make us smile. But 1890s sportsmen, taking a first glance at the thing, probably didn't have a clue about what it did or how it worked.

The Allen weighed 35 pounds. Associated batteries, however, could add more than 250 pounds to the package. Consequently, ad copy saying that a Portable Electric Propeller "requires no strength" on its owner's part was somewhat understated.

Allen motors were marketed through 1899, and at least one survives today. Perhaps there's another hidden away in a dusty attic or vintage boatyard.

Electric and Other-Powered Motors

Allen

One of the first outboard ads is this one for the 1895 Allen.

Ashbrook

A World War I–era electric outboard, the Ashbrook came out of Chicago. It was available circa 1918.

Bantam

This mid-1960s troller was marketed by Phantom Products, Inc., of Kansas City, Missouri.

Bendix (Eclipse)

From 1937 through about 1940, the Bendix Marine Products Company of South Bend, Indiana, offered an electric troller. A very ruggedly constructed battery-powered outboard, the Bendix Eclipse electric (along with its gas-fired sisters) was touted as "modern dinghy power." The 6- or 12-volt trolling motor featured an underwater powerhead sealed in a black case. The relatively good-sized linoleum knife-shaped skeg on the bottom of the Eclipse electric was a bit sturdier than those on gasoline Bendix kickers.

Bucol

Buc-O Manufacturing Company offered an electric troller called Bucol. Buc-O began selling these motors from its Lake Alfred, Florida, headquarters in 1964. It's not known how long Bucol trollers were available.

Electro-Jet

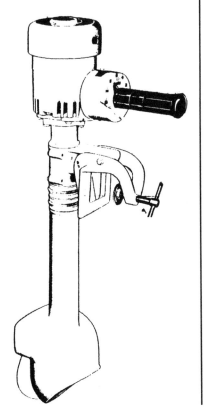

One of the most novel electric trollers came from the tiny W.H. Schnacke Company in Evansville, Indiana. Unlike most of its competitors, Schnacke's Electro-Jet propelled the boat via water (jet) thrust. A 1/3-hp electric power plant activated a three-blade (5-inch diameter by 2½-inch pitch) prop enclosed in a hefty aluminum alloy casting. Six speeds, ranging from 500 to 2,250 rpm, originated in a 12-volt battery wired through a combination voltage switch/tiller handle.

An early 1960s Electro-Jet troller. It ranks among the most unusual electrics.

The firm's Electro-Jet was companion to a gasoline-powered Mid-Jet. Both were designed for safety (with no exposed propeller blades) and unimpeded operation in weedy or shallow waters. Anyone who has used a small jet-thrust outboard, however, can testify to the unit's rather anemic and noisy performance. Electro-Jet's micro-horsepower motor probably gave very little push. Additionally the nature of jet thrust was sure to scare away marine life—not a great attribute for a fishing motor.

Electro-Jet, along with optional battery and charger, came on the market sometime in the early 1960s and faded from the scene a few years later. A neat idea on the drawing board, these bright, white trollers with cherry red steering grips looked more like an extraterrestrial's weapon than anything of practical interest to an angler.

Through the years, the giant Chicago-based mail-order retailer marketed a number of electric trollers. As was the case with its gas outboards, Sears sold electrics made by a number of different firms under the corporate banner, as well as Elgin and Ted Williams marques. Circa-1950s Elgin trollers came from the Silver Creek Precision Corporation (maker of the Silvertrol).

Elgin (Sears)

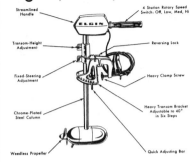

Sears and Roebuck's Elgin of the late 1950s-early 1960s era was made by Silvertrol.

Evinrude

Nineteen thirty was to be the year of convenient electric starting. Major makers such as Evinrude, Johnson, and Caille rushed to introduce the "modern" key-activated feature, figuring it would greatly expand the ranks of outboarding public.

In reality the units were bulky, balky, and simply needed to go back to the drawing board. In order to get rid of all the leftover starter motor assemblies, Evinrude connected some of them to lower units (from their small, gas-powered kickers) and called the results Evinrude All-Electric. They made the 1932 catalog.

A few saw use in a special lagoon at Chicago's 1933 World's Fair. The April 1934 issue of *Power Boating* magazine shows families and kids in small Evinrude electric-powered runabouts. These boats were motoring through little cement-lined rivers at a theme park. The article indicated these "electric outboard motors . . . so simple to control . . . have proved extremely popular for amusement park use in various parts of the country."

Fisher

From Fargo, North Dakota (a home of Minn-Kota trollers), the Fisher Manufacturing Company offered its 1937 electric outboards. Whether or not Fisher had any connection with Minn-Kota is unknown, but the "silent cushion-mounted" Fisher motor, weighing less than 13 pounds, looked just different enough (than Minn-Kota) to suggest one-upmanship. The encased powerhead drove a three-blade bronze prop through a gentle L-shaped "rust-proof Monel metal propeller shaft." A selective speed switch on the powerhead gave options of two speeds on one power pack and double that number from two batteries.

NEW 1937 FISHER
EECTRIC OUTBOARD MOTOR
SILENT CUSHION MOUNTED
Backed by twenty five years of practical experience in all phases of Electric Motor Service.
Most economical to operate, due to lowest POSSIBLE Battery consumption.
Weighs less than 13 pounds.
MORE FISHING HOURS AT LOWER COST.
Three Blade Bronze Propeller, Rust Proof Monel metal Propeller Shaft, Noiseless grease packed Flexible Propeller Shaft.
Selective Speed Switch, 2 Speeds on one Battery
4 Speeds on two Batteries
All Speeds Within CASTING AND TROLLING RANGES.
Write for full particulars to
Fisher Manufacturing Co.
Dept. 2, Box 22,
Office 723—2d Ave. North
FARGO, NORTH DAKOTA

Fortunately, 1937 Fisher motors worked better than their ads were spelled. Someone left out the "L" in electric. Perhaps it was used to make the drive shaft.

Grimes Electric Oar

What a simple idea! This looks like something someone concocted in the basement. That's what you might say upon discovering a 1933 Grimes. Production line workers at Grimes Electric Oar Company simply mounted an electric motor, shaft, and propeller

H-S

Hatch

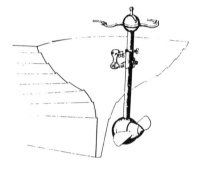

Hav-A-Ride

Hydro-Fin

Next to the oar, Hydro-Fin is the most basic "outboard device."

on the edge of a sturdy wooden oar. An oarlock served as mount. Steering was accomplished by directing the oar. The Grimes firm was based in Syracuse, New York.

One of but a few outboard motors partially comprised of wooden parts, the Grimes-style electric oar relaxes near a telephone pole. Perhaps they came from the same tree.

Here's a listing that almost didn't make the book. Except for a brief mention in an out-of-print publication, not much is remembered about this motor. The H-S electric outboard was reported to be a 1933 product of a J.L. Howarth, Inc., of Florida Street in Long Beach, New York.

During the spring of 1899, Chicago resident Tracy B. Hatch sought a U.S. patent for his "propelling mechanism for boats." Judging from the drawings, it appears Mr. Hatch's "new and useful" electric boat propeller is very similar to the Submerged outboard described on page 192. Instead of a thumbscrew arrangement, however, the Hatch outboard is bolted or screwed to the transom through a mounting bracket. Hatch indicated water flowing past the well-sealed, submerged motor case would keep the unit from overheating.

Patent drawing for T.B. Hatch's 1899 electric outboard bears some resemblance to many of today's trolling motors. This rig was produced as the Submerged Electric and promised boat speeds of up to six miles per hour. Batteries were said to last at least 20 miles before needing a recharge.

The inventor received his patent by late May 1900 and assigned the rights to the Submerged Electric Motor Company of Menomonie, Wisconsin, which is where the outboard was put into production. Whether or not any early Hatch versions (or prototypes) of this rig were built is unknown.

Another obscure 1933 electric, the Hav-A-Ride was a product of the Rochester, New York, Hav-A-Ride Motor Company.

"Row and wish or Hydro-Fin and fish!" For years readers of outdoors-oriented magazines were exposed to this clever slogan. The tiny ads showed a skimpy-looking outboard with absolutely no powerhead. It was the Hydro-Fin, offered by an Aurora, Illinois, firm. Using the same principle as a fish tail, Hydro-Fin was "wiggled" via a tiller to propel a small boat or canoe.

In the early 1980s, a New Hampshire outboard buff spotted a bunch of Hydro-Fins at a yard sale. Turned out the homeowner once had a modest bait and tackle shop and Hydro-Fin dealership. The old outboard enthusiast bought the lot of yard-sale Hydro-Fins for a song and passed one on to me. You know, the thing really works!

It would be difficult to chronicle a specific Hydro-Fin. The ones from the late 1940s look like those in a 1970 leaflet. In the later literature, there was a Standard ($19.20) Hydro-Fin with a flat fin and a Deluxe model wearing a "heavy-duty cast-aluminum boat clamp with (blue) enamel finish and removable or interchangeable rust-resistant plated steel fin with corrugated edges that retard water from slipping." (In other words, a "high speed" version!) It sold for $21.95, freight and taxes extra.

Some brochures claimed there were more than 80,000 Hydro-Fin users, so some of these devices are probably still available on the used market. However, who would want to sell an outboard that will always start?

Jewel Electric

Gas-powered rowboat motors of the circa–World War I era had two main problems: they didn't always start and they were pretty slow. Jewel Electric Manufacturing Company officials hoped to compete head-to-head with these smoky rigs by offering an electric-powered outboard that started instantly and was about as quick as its fuel-fired counterparts. The Chicago-based company began offering their outboard product in 1913 and apparently continued marketing the kicker through the 1920s. Jewel also handled other electric motor–based items, such as decorative water-pumping fountains for use in the backyard.

Lazi-Trol

A 1960s product of Byrd Industries of Ripley, Tennessee, Lazi-Trol motors were designed primarily for the expanding angling market. In one listing, five Lazi-Trol models were available with various shaft length options.

LeJay (Electrol)

If you bought a brand-new 1936 LeJay electric outboard, the Minneapolis manufacturer didn't expect you'd need another LeJay product until the early '60s. Judging from the simplicity of the first LeJay trollers, the company's claim that its outboard "is built to give satisfactory service for 25 years" seems quite reasonable.

LeJay Manufacturing Company specialized in items such as windmill-powered generating units fashioned from old automobile generators. The firm entered the outboard business in the mid-1930s with a long kicker powered by a Model T Ford generator. It drove a cast-aluminum, machine-balanced propeller through a hollow brass shaft. There were no gears—the early LeJay used

In addition to some interesting electric outboards made from old car generators, LeJay offered plans for a wind-operated power plant. They'd send you all their know-how for 10 cents.

The first (1936) LeJay outboard was a straight-shaft electric fashioned from a surplus Model T Ford generator. If you couldn't afford a complete factory-built unit, LeJay offered parts and do-it-yourself plans.

Early 1950s LeJay waits patiently for a boat, battery, and eager fisherman.

direct drive with the propeller some three feet aft of the boat. LeJay brochures invited folks to drive to a "favorite lake or stream, take out the car battery and run the outboard as long as (they) wished. Then replace the battery in your car and recharge it as you drive."

The 1936 price for this motor was $24.50, a good chunk of change during the Depression. LeJay officials knew this, and for the impecunious offered a variety of cheaper options. Anyone inquiring by mail would receive LeJay's "Plan 20," detailing how one could "build your own electric outboard motor from an old Ford Model T generator. Easily done in a few hours' time." Advertisements claimed it could push a rowboat up to 8 mph via a 6-volt battery. To help with this do-it-yourself project, LeJay sold a kit for rewinding a Model T generator as well as factory-wound armature and field coils, and a complete factory-built Model T generator motor for outboard use. In addition to "stock" LeJays, there are probably still a few interesting examples of their homemade counterparts somewhere.

After World War II, LeJay featured a series of more traditionally appointed outboards. Some had a lower unit with bevel gears; other LeJays spun a prop via a flexible shaft in a curved torque tube.

The company dubbed its trollers Electrol and advertised its products as "unsurpassed in performance as well as beautiful in appearance." Actually, the classic flexible-shaft LeJays for this period had a funny/cute styling all their own. The contoured powerhead cover and tinny webbed skeg fins gave them a "froggy" look. Other Electrols were more ordinary, with a standard lower unit and cylindrical powerhead shell.

For a while LeJay seemed to be a perennial player in the electric outboard field. Their products were solid, dependable performers. By the early 1960s, however, the firm was gone. True to the promise in their original brochures, however, many of the little motors were still in service.

Man-U-Troll

A hand-powered outboard, the Man-U-Troll came from Jacksonville, Florida's, Universal Projects, Inc. It made a 1964 debut.

Millican Pedal-Oar

Even secret agent James Bond might approve of Challenge Gauge and Tool Company's outboard device. Their Millican Pedal-Oar could be unfolded from a "lightweight (approximately 30 pounds)

An angling owner of this Millican Pedal-Oar outboard device had to eat his catch in order to be "re-fueled" for another day's outing.

carrying size" and installed on most small boats within two minutes. The Indianapolis, Indiana, firm's manual kicker was designed to be pedaled backward or forward, and sold for $39.85.

*Minn*esota is way up there near North Da*kota*. A fellow named O.G. Schmidt used a portion of each state's identity to coin a moniker for his new company. Minn-Kota began making farm implements and in 1932 introduced electric fishing motors. The first Minn-Kotas (1932–33) had an underwater powerhead. By 1934, though, the motor was top-side and ran a prop through lower unit bevel gears. The following year, Minn-Kota's classic flexible drive shaft appeared, remaining the standard-bearer for decades. (A bevel-gear model made a brief reintroduction in 1962.) Circa 1950, Minn-Kota marketed a heavy-duty troller with dual motor/prop drive. The firm also announced plans for a model with interchangeable gas-to-electric powerheads. The fuel-fired engine would quickly get you to your favorite fishing spot. Then the gas motor could be replaced with an electric powerhead for trolling. Apparently none were produced.

The first Minn-Kotas came from Fargo, North Dakota. Then manufacture moved to a plant in Moorhead, Minnesota. According to an official Minn-Kota profile, for quite a while the firm "lacked good financial management and floundered until the mid-1960s" at which time it was treated to a series of monied takeovers. By 1970 Minn-Kota became the property of the Johnson Wax people and later relocated to a Mankato, Minnesota, factory (where Johnson fishing reels were also being constructed).

Since the late '60s, Minn-Kota's owners have concentrated on the large trolling motor market in the southern United States. Over the years, Minn-Kotas have been offered in a wide variety of shapes under their own banner as well as via a number of private brand labels. The marque's tenacity and reliability has long given Minn-Kota the status of best-known electric outboard motor.

Every manufacturer hopes to find a niche for its product. In the case of the Herschede Hall Clock Company, feet fit nicely into the picture. The Starkville, Mississippi, firm based its Motor-Guide outboard's focus on foot-operated control. Renowned angler Homer Circle, quoted in a 1969 catalog, said, "At last, a fishing motor designed for the fisherman. The Motor-Guide is truly an enjoyable and practical motor. I enjoy the foot control. It lets me use both hands for fishing."

Motor-Guide literature frequently pictured a bow-mounted arrangement (with a conventional gas outboard on the stern). The operator used a pedal to activate the electric motor encapsulated underwater. The maker indicated its Motor-Guide rig, capable of 2 to 10 mph (which seems a little optimistic), was "built like a fine clock"—a play on the company's reputation as America's oldest and finest maker of grandfather clocks. Herschede Hall's letter-head sports a crown logo and touts: "Makers of fine floor, mantel, table and wall clocks."

At the time, Herschede Hall was successful in getting their motors into the hands of professional anglers. Consequently their brochures were often headlined "Motor-Guide, the foot-operated

Minn-Kota

THE NEW 1937 MINN-KOTA
ELECTRIC OUTBOARD
Having pioneered in the Electric Outboard field, our many years of experience is concentrated into the superior features of our 1937 model. OUR ELECTRICS ARE IN USE FROM THE EVERGLADES OF FLORIDA TO THE NORTHERN WATERS OF CANADA. PLENTY OF POWER—Sufficient to drive a boat loaded to capacity. ROTARY SPEED CONTROL SWITCH—3 speeds on six volts and 3 more on twelve volts, forward or reverse. ITS SILENT OPERATION and selective speed range from just barely moving to ten miles per hour makes it ideal for trolling or silently gliding along the water on a pleasure cruise. The motor is equipped with life time grease sealed bearings, air-cooled, and out of the water, with no chance for condensation. EFFICIENT—QUIET—uses famous gearless cable drive to propeller, which permits economical operation on ordinary car battery. See the MINN-KOTA Electric Outboard Motor at your dealers or write direct for further details. DEALERS—Here is your BIG SELLER—NATIONALLY ADVERTISED—Write at once for attractive dealership proposition. MINN-KOTA MFG. CO., Dept. 9, Fargo, N. Dak.

The lines on this late 1930s troller are classic Minn-Kota and were copied by other makers.

Motor-Guide

My-te

A reconditioned auto generator served as powerhead for the My-te electric outboard. The manufacturer had hoped to compete head-to-head with small gas-powered motors on the market.

trolling motor used by fishing champions." The company also made a cast for less demanding sportsmen by marketing a manually operated (via a switch on the steering assembly) standard transom clamp troller called Bass Tracker.

Fred Seiger enjoyed tinkering and inventing. In the mid-1940s, he bought a little Indianapolis firm called City Engineering Company and went to work refining and producing a variety of products, including electric winches and hoists. By the late '50s, Mr. Seiger's interest in small boats got him thinking about adding an outboard to City Engineering's line. He envisioned a motor suitable for the thousands of ponds where only flea-power or electric kickers were allowed.

A lower unit with strong bevel gears and solid steel drive shaft was designed. Mr. Seiger then contacted an automobile starter rebuilder in Georgia for a good price on hefty generators that could serve as electric outboard powerheads.

The aluminum casting work was farmed out, but actual assembly of the new offering (dubbed My-te) took place at City Engineering's Massachusetts Avenue plant. Completed units looked quite sturdy, with an oversized rear carrying handle (through which the motor wiring ran) and dual grip steering bar. Seiger's idea of a rugged little outboard (and battery) one could tote to the lake, river, or pond and use all day was realized in his My-te electric outboard motor.

Seiger also came up with a "simple do-it-yourself modifica-tion of a standard 12-volt auto battery" to get both 12- and 6-volt outputs. Via this plurality, four speeds could be obtained: two on 6 volts and another pair on 12. Touting My-te's full-service abilities, the manufacturer's sales literature stressed: "When it is necessary to hurry to shore, change to 12-volt operation and you will be delighted with the higher traveling speed."

This was an electric outboard on a par with small gasoline-powered counterparts and sold for a few dollars more than most. In fact, even City Engineering marketed a less expensive 4-horse, 2-cycle kicker.

Sales began in 1959 and went in spurts. A Baltimore distribu-tor sold lots of the more than 1,000 My-te electrics produced. Many also were bought by a German firm for European sale. If no dealer could be "found in your area," noted a brochure, "order direct from the factory. Freight will be prepaid anywhere in the USA."

While certainly useful for fishing, this rig was not merely a troller. Most folks seeking a small outboard, however, went with traditional gas-powered units.

During the late 1960s, tooling and casting molds for My-te's parts were showing signs of wear. City Engineering executives decided against an expensive revamping. As a stern-mounted electric generating remarkable thrust, My-te was in a league different from the growing number of popular foot-controlled,

bow-riding bass fishing motors. In addition company officials felt their product's robot-like appearance wouldn't translate well next to another firm's streamlined troller in a Wal-Mart sporting goods aisle. Consequently My-te Electric production faded out about 1970. But, you know, every so often someone calls My-te Products (formerly City Engineering) hoping to find a replacement part for one of Fred Seiger's interesting electric outboards.

Pflueger

An Akron, Ohio, firm called Pflueger (the *P* is silent) pronounced their line of Phantom trollers, "America's best-selling electric motors." Like many other brands, the actual motor was encapsulated underwater with the prop attached directly to the motor's shaft. Pflueger's late-1960s catalog indicated: "All Phantom motors are Duo-Sealed, or double sealed, around the prop shaft with non-water-soluble lubricant between seals. Prop hub recessed in tube keeps fishing line from the seal." A telltale feature on many Pflueger Phantoms is a two-piece motor housing with a raised seam around the center. The deluxe models sported a horizontal tilt-lock and dual thumbscrew transom clamp, unusual features for an electric troller. The firm labeled most of their products with a model designation that began with an *M*.

Pioneer

A scan of some old fishing magazines reveals tiny ads for the Pioneer Manufacturing Company of Middlebury, Indiana. This outfit's primary focus was metal fishing boats, so an outboard offering was a natural extension of the line. Pioneer's electric troller featured a flexible drive shaft and looked just like a basic Minn-Kota model. It appears the Pioneer was a relabeled Minn-Kota built for the Hoosier-based boat concern. One source indicated that Pioneer was marketed from 1963 through the end of the decade. I'm going to speculate, however, that the earliest Pioneer motors were 1950s products.

Rayfield Propel-Power

Probably the most deluxe of all "people-powered" outboards, the 1948 Rayfield Propel-Power unit came from the C.L. Rayfield Company of Chicago. The contraption was activated by pedals that drove a two-blade prop with a 3-to-1 "step-up ratio." Rayfields could be operated forward or backward. Steering was accomplished by swiveling in a seat hooked to the outboard unit. The novel Propel-Power, sporting bright decals on its top, was concocted by the same firm that made Rayfield carburetors and oil burners.

Ro-Peller

The Shelbyville, Indiana, Ra-Sco Manufacturing Company's hand-cranked outboard device could be compared to a giant kitchen egg beater. The crank doubled as a tiller that directed a good-sized (9-by-10-inch) three-blade prop. Ro-Peller primarily was promoted in fishing publications and aimed at "anglers, guides,

and old-timers who realize necessity for quietness . . . no disturbing boat vibrations . . . no churning water."

This unit was "geared-up" to give the propeller more rpms than provided by the cranker. But even a hearty fellow who had just eaten vegetables couldn't make Ro-Peller a consistent match for a gas- or electric-powered outboard.

These outboard devices first appeared circa 1931 and were initially offered by the Connersville, Indiana–based, Ro-Peller Manufacturing Company. During the early to mid-1930s, they sold their 14-pound product factory-direct for $16.

Primarily a product of the 1930s, Ro-Peller was designed for short commutes or easy trolling on sheltered waters. It was also one of the only kickers whose "powerhead" could be refueled in a coffee shop. Cruising speed was advertised at 2 to 4 mph . . . depending on the size of one's breakfast.

Salisbury

This circa 1892 electric probably saw limited production under the Salisbury label. W.S. Salisbury was granted an 1892 patent for his "Boat Propelling Apparatus." The flexible shaft of coiled wire wound up a bit when its propeller hit a rock. After the obstruction passed, the shaft uncoiled. Salisbury-like motors showed up in the mid-1890s bearing an Allen nameplate.

Sea King

Montgomery Ward, like Sears, its chief competitor, purchased electric trollers from various manufacturers and offered them in the boating/fishing section of Ward's catalogs and showrooms. The Sea King name was borrowed from "Monkey Ward's" well-received line of boats and gasoline-fired outboards.

Silver Streak

Silver Streak is an obscure electric from 1931. The company's ad pushed canoes with their custom mounted outboard.

A New York City firm known as Mayfair Boats marketed an electric outboard that could be ordered for either canoe ($145) or rowboat ($155) use. Mayfair also sold a "complete $375 outfit, including (electric motor) highest type of sponson canoe and batteries."

The Silver Streak outboards (named for their polished aluminum finish) were of the submerged powerhead style (looking a bit like the 1900 Submerged electric kicker). They were fixed-mounted via special brackets to canoe or square stern craft. Steering was facilitated through a pulley/cable arrangement.

It was evident from their promotional literature that Mayfair was primarily interested in selling canoe/custom-mounted motor packages. Ads touted Silver Streak electric power boats to be "the aristocrats of pleasure boating . . . ideal for boat liveries, women and children."

It's unknown whether or not the motors sported any ID plates or self-contained nomenclature. Silver Streak electrics (not to be confused with the postwar, gas-powered Martin 200 Silver Streak) were offered in 1931.

Submerged

About 10 years before Ole Evinrude started building gasoline boat motors in Wisconsin, a little factory in that Midwestern state

began turning out electric outboards. Mr. Tracy Hatch occupied an erstwhile lumber mill on the banks of the Red Cedar River in Menomonie, figuring it would be a good place to produce his Submerged Electric Motor Company kickers.

The product got its name from the shiny aluminum football-shaped motor enclosure that rode underwater. The Submerged Electric spun a twin-blade, 9-inch prop and looked a bit like some of the trollers available today. Specifications indicated the electric could push a small craft at 3 to 6 mph via a pair of 6-volt battery packs. It appears the wires from the top of the unit to the batteries also served as steering cables.

The Submerged electric, introduced circa 1900, sold well enough to allow the small firm to add a gasoline version six years later. Extra competition in a quickly changing marketplace, however, caused the company to close in 1909.

Touromarine

Electrical Industries Manufacturing Company in Red Bank, New Jersey, marketed the Touromarine electric outboard in 1937 and 1938. Not much literature remains on this particular offering.

Troll-King

Similar to other electric trollers of the 1950s, either 6 or 12 volts would drive Troll-King adequately. A product aimed at fishermen, it was offered by Troll-King of Jacksonville, Florida. The buyer took home a three-item package containing motor, battery, and charger.

Wizard

During the '50s, Silver Creek (New York) Precision Corporation built some trollers with the Wizard nameplate. The motors were sold through Western Auto Supply of Kansas City, Missouri. No doubt, Western Auto stores also sold electrics from other manufacturers.

Notes

1. Phil Kranz, "The Aerothrust," *Antique Outboarder* (July 1971), pp. 22–24.
2. W.J. Webb, "Of Historical Interest, Amphion History," *Antique Outboarder* (October 1972), pp. 9–10.
3. Harold Polk, "A Waterman Story—My First Outboard," *Antique Outboarder* (January 1980), p. 27.
4. Sam Vance, "An Interesting Prototype," *Antique Outboarder* (April 1973), p. 13.
5. "It's News," *Boat Sport* (September 1954), p. 27.
6. *Motor Boating* (September 1925), p. 134.
7. Edwin R. Hodge, Jr. "A Study of the Outboard Motor Industry," (Ph.D. diss., Indiana University, 1951).
8. Ibid.
9. *Antique Outboarder* (January 1985), p. 21.
10. Glen Ollila, "The Champ," *Antique Outboarder* (October 1970), pp. 27–31.

11. Hodge, op. cit.

12. Don Peterson, "The Chrysler Story," *Antique Outboarder* (April 1976), pp. 39–43.

13. Phil Kranz, "Mini Outboard," *Antique Outboarder* (April 1975), p. 38.

14. Dave Batchelder, "Davis Experimental Radial Outboard," *Antique Outboarder* (July 1980), pp. 19–24.

15. "The Put-Put," *Fortune* (August 1938), p. 112.

16. Donald Peterson, "The Fageol Story," *Antique Outboarder* (October 1973), pp. 25–26.

17. Richard A. Hawie, "Notes from the Curator," *Antique Outboarder* (October 1985), pp. 12–15.

18. Hodge, op. cit.

19. LeRoi Russel, "The Minnesota Gopher," *Antique Outboarder* (October 1981), pp. 76–77.

20. Bill Andrulitis with Bob Zipps, "Hartford Sturdy Twin," *Antique Outboarder* (April 1975), pp. 32–37.

21. Paul Strot, "The Joymotor," *Antique Outboarder* (July 1976), pp. 38–40.

22. "Special Feature Articles—Joymotor Canoe Model Low Down—Safety *First,*" *Antique Outboarder* (April 1988), p. 26.

23. Wayne Schoepke, "The Kingfisher," *Antique Outboarder* (October 1979), p. 41.

24. J.L. Smith, "The Koban Twin: 1914–1926," *Antique Outboarder* (October 1975), pp. 30-33.

24a. Ron Hollander, *All Aboard!* (New York: Workman Publishing, 1981), p. 227.

25. Hodge, op. cit.

26. Ibid.

27. Chuck Sundby, "The Martin Motor," *Antique Outboarder* (January 1984), pp. 25–28.

28. Bob Grubb, "Test Editor Tests the 1949 Martin 20," *Antique Outboarder* (January 1984), pp. 22–24

29. Hodge, op. cit.

30. Sundby, op. cit.

31. Ibid.

31a. Ronald Lietha, "The Martin 80?! Yes-No," *Antique Outboarder* (April, 1993), p. 69.

32. *1956 Outboarder Dealer Trade-In Guide* (Mishawaka, IN: Abos Publishing Co., 1956)

33. *Outboard Motor Service Manual,* 4th ed., Vol. 1 (Mishawaka, IN: Abos Marine Div. Technical Publications, 1967), p. 131.

34. T. Kilcoyne, "A Minnesota Milestone," *Antique Outboarder* (July 1983), pp. 5–8.

35. Hodge, op. cit.

36. Ibid.

37. "It's News—Oliver Outboard Motors," *Boat Sport* (February 1955), p. 3.

38. Bob Lomerson, "Mystery Outboard Somewhat Less of a Mystery," *Antique Outboarder* (April 1988), pp. 24–26.

39. Don Peterson, "Collector's Gallery, Riley," *Antique Outboarder* (July 1974), pp. 14–15.

40. Hodge, op. cit.

41. Hank Wieand Bowman, "Will it Top 01.12 Miles an Hour?" *Aqua Sport* (June/July 1958), pp. 21–36.

42. Art Doling, "Viking Outboard Numbers," *Antique Outboarder* (January 1989), pp. 70–71.

43. James L. Smith, "Tiger Shark, West Bend's Big Iron," *Antique Outboarder* (April 1979), pp. 8–10.

44. Peterson, "Chrysler Story," *Antique Outboarder* (April 1976), pp. 39–43.

|10

The Back Rack

It just so happened that the riverside village's only traffic light turned red the instant our new 1963 Rambler was heading through town. During the momentary stop, something through a half-raised garage bay door of the corner gas station caught my eye.

"Hey Dad!" I yelled in my most enthusiastic, fourth-grader voice, "That place is filled with old outboard motors!"

But, it was no use. The light changed, and we were off for what seemed an interminable day trip. During the next several weeks, I pestered my parents to take me back to that garage where I'd glimpsed a stately row of fine antique kickers.

"Knock yourself out, kid," the amused service station proprietor laughed, gesturing me to what he pejoratively called "the back rack."

Though my mind was spinning at the colorful kaleidoscope of outboard relics situated among oily, splintered, two-by-four stands sagging from one wall to the other, I heard the guy tell my father that most of the motors had been there a decade earlier when he'd bought the place.

"Used to be a small Studebaker car dealership . . . sold outboards and a rowboat here and there, too. I bought it for the gas and auto repair business. Got lots of that, but don't got time to do no outboard work. Never fails, though. Every spring some old-timer will insist on leaving his ailing fishing motor for me to get to it when I can. That Lockwood over there is still waiting for a carb part . . . since about '56," he laughed. "It's just more junk I'll be forever tripping over. I think I just read that the old fellow who owns it died."

To me, however, the garage's dimly lit recesses appeared full of life. Forty-seven com-plete engines resided there. This didn't count a couple of dozen "possibles" hospitalized sans vital components, ranging from just a missing fuel tank to a bunch of "outboard stalks" minus so many appendages that it took me a while to identify their pedigrees. To be sure, that back rack harbored a smattering of garden variety Evinrudes, Johnsons, and a couple of sexier green Mercs, but the most intriguing were provinces of obscure branding and short-lived ventures.

"That's why they never made it out of here, kid," the garage man mused, with my Dad concur-ring. "You need a special part for some weird motor that nobody's ever heard of, and it's 'good night Nellie' for that poor little putt-putt."

He then obliged us by checking the rem-nants of grimy paper claim tags still hanging on a bunch of outboards that looked the most valuable to me. The guy speculated in a mumble that any motor not retrieved by the customer after ten years was probably "OK for selling."

"How about this one-lung job for five bucks?" he smiled. "I bet it'd like a good home after being stuck on the back rack for longer than you've been around."

Over my Dad's polite protests, a second "gem"—as the generous proprietor laughingly labeled the inmates of his accidental outboard col-lection—was thrown into the deal.

"That's much better," he announced after kicking the contraption my way over the cracked cement floor. "I won't hafta walk around that one no more."

Such a serendipitous experience, like those of many other vintage outboard buffs, has long led me to frequent boat and motor dealership show-

rooms only as a means of gaining access to the establishments' most forgotten mechanical inventory, often shackled to some subterranean or otherwise exiled back rack. Since the 1980s, though, marinas, small engine fix-it shops, and gas stations with back racks have almost entirely evaporated. They were part of an era when decisions were made more slowly, and old outboards in the back of the shop were simply old things that service business owners tolerated as they might an elderly aunt. Besides, they never knew when some nut might come along on a slow Saturday and offer a little off-the-books cash for the junk.

Fortunately, the back rack genre still exists in collectors' sheds, basements, garages, and barns where "to-do" project outboards anticipate revitalization. Because the definition of "old motor" keeps creeping into the upper decades of the twentieth century, many of the orphaned kickers arranged alphabetically in this chapter's "back rack" might not seem that vintage to some outboarders. A majority of the readers' letters to *The Old Outboard Book* HQ now seek info about "old" motors from the 1960s and 1970s.

One might well consider the Back Rack an addendum to *The Old Outboard Book*'s main showroom, the Big List chapter. A surprising number of recently discovered vintage gas, electric, and even a few hand-powered mills found their way to the third edition. In any event, the rows of motor makes included herein are representative of the kind of iron that just might appear at the next local yard sale. As always, the author enjoys hearing from readers who happen to discover a brand—at least twenty years old—that's not yet part of this volume.

Note: As is the case in the Big List chapter, numbers following a heading indicate that it is one of several motor makes using the same brand name. An example is Hiawatha (4). Between this chapter and the Big List chapter, there are five Hiawatha-branded outboards covered. Each has a lineage either slightly or completely different than the others and is distinctly annotated.

Acco

This multiuse product consisted of a lower-unit accessory that mated to a 2 ½ hp lawnmower powerhead. After a day on the water, Acco owners could remove the four-stroke, air-cooled power plant from the outboard lower unit and bolt it to an Acco mower deck that was included in the deal. American Chain and Cable Company offered the engine, outboard driveshaft housing and lower unit, and mower with push handle as a $150 package. Circa 1960 that wasn't a bad price for a new brand kicker and cutter. But, even then, turning the mower into an outboard (and vice versa) was probably viewed as a lot of rigmarole by all but the most eccentric prospective buyers. Besides, who wants grass clippings all over a boat?

Aero Marine

This company is no relation to Kiekhaefer Aeromarine, Inc., or Kaminc, as was suggested in the earlier editions of this book. These early 1970s models (possibly late 1960s stock) were largely left-

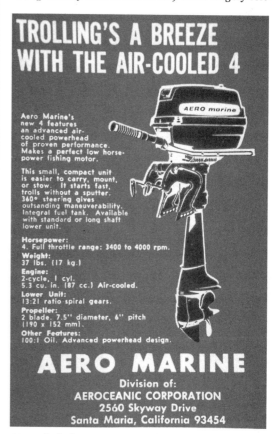

Here is half of Aero Marine's early 1970s brochure. The other side simply pictured an old pipe-smoking guy in a porkpie hat trolling along with an Aero Marine 4 on his 12-foot aluminum boat.

over McCulloch motors bought by the Aeroceanic Corporation of Santa Monica (and Santa Maria in some listings), California, following McCulloch's decision to exit the outboard business. Then they were simply relabeled Aero Marine.

While typically the likes of the old air-cooled McCulloch 4 hp fishing engine, some slipped through in 5, "shorty" 7.5, and 9 hp versions. The 1970 motor trade-in *Blue Book* shows this line's 5 hp engine (model AM-5000E) equipped with an electric starter, making it one of the industry's tiniest motors with such a convenience. An old upstate New York outboard dealer recalled seeing some low-horsepower Aero Marine kickers with Clinton or Tecumseh powerheads. He suggested that the Aero folks got into the business with private-branded models made by Clinton or Tecumseh, et al., and then graduated to building their own products via the purchase of McCulloch's stock and outboard tooling. Advertising for the West Coast brand is scarce, making chronology difficult. It appears, though, that the marque was gone by the latter part of the 1970s. During the small firm's foray into boating, though, Aero Marine even offered its own brand of outboard oil, as well as gasoline and diesel marine (inboard) engines, and an Aero-Jacuzzi Jet Propulsion drive!

Aikenhead. See Kompac-3.

All Sport

A bit of a mystery motor as the only reference the author has seen comes from the 1982 Champion Spark Plug list. It simply refers to an All Sport with either "14 or 18 mm plugs."

America's Best

An electric troller that looks to be private-branded by Minn-Kota, America's Best came through the Moore-Handley Hardware Company. The firm's model AB ran on either 6 or 12 volts, had a flexible driveshaft, and was probably marketed during the 1950s and/or early 1960s.

Apache

When the July 1957 issue of *Motor Boating* announced Clinton's "new low priced 5 hp motor," the Apache, it noted that the Clinton Machine Company (then of Clinton, Michigan) "has for years

manufactured other name outboards." Such was a euphemistic way of saying that Clinton liked to reinvent its line via a new name and maybe a touch of cosmetic restyling. At $149.50, though, the air-cooled, two-stroke, single-cylinder Apache and its 3-gallon remote fuel tank were priced about the same as a 3 hp Evinrude or Johnson.

For the casual outboarder, the Apache was not a bad deal. Clinton penetrated the novice market with low prices and a gizmo feature or two. The motor's "special speed control dial" serves as an example. With this mysterious device, the Apache could be operated at seven different speed levels by presetting the desired speeds ahead of your trip. Without the Apache nomenclature on the cowling sides, it would be difficult to distinguish it from other Clinton marques, like the Chief, the Peerless, or the J-9. (See also Clinton and Chief.)

Aquabug

SeaBorne Systems of Island Park, New York, utilized O&R (Ohlsson and Rice) brand single-cylinder powerheads to enter the microhorsepower outboard category of the 1970s. The company's Aquabug (sometimes split into two words) was a direct descendent of the Mini Motor (see the Big List chapter). An electric powerhead was also available, as was a larger gas powered model called the SuperBug.

SeaBorne offered a standard lower unit with interchangeable gas and electric powerheads. And, you could buy an Aquabug Gas or an Aquabug Elec-

A small Simsbury, Connecticut, Johnson dealer (who probably got hit up by a sales rep from Mini Motor's nearby southwestern Massachusetts factory) was one of the initial purchase points for the circa 1970 Mini Motor shown here. The 8-pounds-and-change outboard was restyled over the original Mini Motor by way of a bit of lightweight plastic cowling. Aquabug owners can probably see some Mini Motor resemblance in their little outboards.

tric separately. The fuel version could get you to your favorite fishing spot and, with a quick power-head change, could transform into an electric motor that would provide a few hours of quiet trolling. For the real gadget lover, there was the Aquabug/System 1, "the world's first gas/electric outboard motor system." With this set, you could quickly make either a gas or electric Aquabug and mount the gas powerhead onto an Aquabug 6- to 12-volt generator capable of charging the electric outboard's battery or powering small camping accessories.

Like the similarly low-priced Milburn/Continental motors, Aquabug seemed to go from one manufacturer to another. SeaBorne Systems reincarnated with a Chicopee, Massachusetts, address. Aquabugs also appeared from the Roper Corporation of Bradley, Illinois. Some of these were equipped with extra long shafts and Japanese Tanaka power plants.

Aqua Scooter

Here's a 2 hp, submersible unit that can pull a swimmer or, with an accessory called a boat bracket, be turned into an outboard. Marketed by a Springfield, New Jersey, firm, this jet-thrust gizmo was probably of foreign manufacture.

Armsco

This hand-powered sculling device from Detroit-based Armsco Manufacturing Company looked a lot like the Hydro-Fin (which is annotated in the Big List chapter).

Beaver

Beaver Motors, of Norwell, Massachusetts, offered a line of outboards that were clearly based upon Clinton and Eska products. Touted as "rugged, dependable, and economical," Beavers came in 2, 4, 5.5, 7.5, and 9.5 hp models. One version of the 7.5 featured a neutral clutch, while the biggest Beaver was fitted with forward-neutral-reverse (F-N-R) gearing. The firm promised "complete unit service at more than 12,000 authorized service outlets." Of course, this generous number included the many locally operated small engine service shops authorized to work on the Clinton and Tecumseh (often used by Eska) power plants so prevalent in 1970s lawnmowers and fishing motors.

Briggs & Stratton

In 2002, Briggs & Stratton did something that rural legend said the company had already been doing for decades—they built an outboard. Prior to the 21st century, though, no kicker was ever officially manufactured and marketed by the B&S folks. That's not to suggest that several small outboard makers didn't use B&S powerheads. Otterbine serves as an example. In fact, the simple Otterbine outboard jet's most prominent above-water feature was a B&S mill co-opted from rotary lawn-mower use. The recoil starter cord angle on these motors required the tiller to be swung hard to one side so that the little rubber starter handle could be pulled straight towards the bow of the boat. There was also the Polar ice outboard that drove a spiked wheel.

More than a few homebrew outboards—sometimes dubbed "hillbilly" motors—were fashioned from junk parts and a bit of welding with erstwhile B&S mower engines. One bucolic classified ad touted a kicker as an "Old 3 hp Briggs & Stratton outboard. Ran good the last time it was used. $75 or b.o." It may indeed be a good runner, but unless that mill is an official Otterbine or Polar, vintage motor buffs should smell something funny.

Brooks

In its 1921 catalog, the Brooks Boat Company offered a Brooks 2-hp, 5-Speed Outboard Motor." This was obviously a badge-engineered, one-lung Caille rowboat motor. Also featured in the pages touting Brooks' line of motorboats were several single- and twin-cylinder Waterman inboard engines, which were also advertised as Brooks products.

Budbilt

The Budbilt Cub is another mysterious Milburn clone. This approximately 2 ½ hp air-cooled fishing motor came out of the Budbilt Manufacturing Company of Los Angeles sometime during the 1950s (maybe even 1949). It's likely, though, that the motor was produced for Budbilt by whoever controlled the Milburn Cub parts, molds, and tooling at the time. Then again, it could be that Budbilt actually produced these bargain-basement kickers either immediately preceding or succeeding the Wego Motor Company, also of Los Angeles,

From a few paces away, it's pretty near impossible to tell a Budbilt Cub from its Continental Sport, Watermaster Cub, and Wego clones. They all look like the circa 1949 Milburn Cub and vice versa. The left photo actually shows a Continental fitted with a Tillotson carburetor instead of the no-name carb often included with some of these bargain-basement kickers. The right photo shows the front view of a Continental (in back) and a Watermaster Cub with a single transom clamp and simple Milburn carburetor.

which marketed Wego Junior, yet another Milburn look-alike. Budgetary constraints dictated sand-casting (even the propeller was a rough molded piece) and allowed for a Budbilt to be priced at less than half the cost of a comparable Evinrude, Johnson, or Merc. (See also Milburn in the Big List chapter, and Wego later in this chapter.)

Bull Dog

This name appeared on the rewind starter of some small air-cooled outboards. It is the brand of the starter, not of the motor.

Century

Here's a nearly forgotten brand rediscovered on eBay, the Internet auction site. The seller's photo showed a jet outboard bearing similarities to the Cal-Jet. Dubbed Century Ram-Jet, this product of Leeder's Pacific, Ltd., from Westminster, British Columbia, appears to feature a 2 ½ hp powerhead

by Tecumseh. Starting is of the rewind type. My guess is that it's of early to mid-1960s vintage. Reportedly, Leeder's made a bigger version for boats used in commercial log boom work.

Chief

A Clinton product, Chief outboards were marketed as a brand autonomous from Clinton and the firm's other kickers the likes of Apache or Peerless. Through badge-engineering and sometimes a bit of cosmetic modification, Clinton could reinvent or extend its outboard product line. Typically, this was done to give a retailer, such as a hardware or sporting goods chain, a unique motor brand it could sell in its marketing region. If another store in that area also wanted to sell outboards made by Clinton, an additional brand name would be established. That's what brought Chief into the Clinton tribe.

Clinton made no mention of itself on the cover of this owner's guide for badge-engineered Chief outboards. The company extended its product line several times by rebranding Clinton kickers with names like Chief or Apache and conveying the suggestion that they were separate entities from the main Clinton marque.

Clay

A flywheel mounted "safety starting handle" ranked among the top selling features of the Clay Engine Company's Clay Noiseless Detachable Motor. From the looks of 1914 ads for the Cleveland, Ohio, firm's forward-pointing, single-cylinder rowboat motor, this cast metal, fold-into-the-flywheel "knuckle buster" seems to be a thinly-disguised Spinaway. The battery ignition version sold for $65, while the deluxe magneto-fire model went for $78.

According to vintage publicity, both came with "noiseless underwater exhaust, lock to hold rudder in position, and extension shaft to permit raising and lowering propeller." Clay's ad also included small print hoping to attract "*live* dealers . . . in open territories." Even though that opportunity probably spanned just about every place except downtown Cleveland, chances for such entrepreneurship died not long thereafter, as Clay soon disappeared from the scene.

Colt

A Champion Spark Plug chart lists the Eska-controlled Colt line as having 3 and 5 hp fishing motors for 1963. Eska equipped the smaller one with their usual Tecumseh-built power plant and fit the larger one with a Clinton mill. This short-lived marque is typical of the seemingly ubiquitous, albeit low production, private-brand outboards of that day.

Craig

Some of the fun in crafting *The Old Outboard Book* listings relates to obscure and enigmatic brands reported to have been built but lacking physical evidence. The Craig outboard is included herein as an interesting "maybe." In the 1999 edition of *Hydro Legends* (a publication of Seattle's Hydroplane and Raceboat Museum), it was briefly mentioned that "the Craig Motor Company manufactured an early 8-horsepower outboard motor in 1909." While 8 hp seems a bit much compared to the typical 1 to 2 hp output of other circa 1910 outboards, the informal information is worthy of further study.

Crofton

Circa 1959, Fageol, one of the Eisenhower era's strangest looking outboards, got a new lease on life under the Crofton banner. The 190-pound Crofton 53 (cubic inch displacement) from Crofton Marine Engine Company of San Diego, California, yielded 45 hp through its bored-out Crosley auto power plant. Crofton ad people claimed their partially hooded outboard had enough "magnificent appearance [to] add beauty to any boat." From a distance, a Crofton appeared to be a fat Mercury with a hernia. To its real credit, it had four-cycle economy capable of significantly reducing typical outboard fuel and oil costs, thus "increasing cruising range." While too big for most vintage outboard collectors and their boats, this is a rare motor! (See also Fageol in the Big List chapter.)

Cruise 'n Carry

This 1.4 hp, air-cooled, two-stroke single was part of the late 1960s to early 1970s "micro outboard" wave. Standard (forward only) as well as neutral shift models were offered by HMC of Torrance, California.

Cruise 'n Carry management indicated their 22.5 cc forward-pointing single was "wondrously easy to start [and could be] tested on land for instant use in water." The gearshift on Model 6500 (as opposed to standard Model 6000) was controlled via a tiny push-pull knob mounted on the tiller. Actually, it was simply a neutral clutch, as a full pivot accomplished reverse. Cruise 'n Carry may be compared to Mini Motors and Aquabugs of similar vintage.

Detroiter (World War I–era twin)

A fleeting e-mail to *The Old Outboard Book*'s HQ sought information about a 1917 opposed twin with a variable-pitch propeller. Reportedly, the motor was labeled Detroiter. There was a World War 1–era Detroit brand rowboat motor, but that one is assumed to be a single-cylinder machine. The only other Detroiter twin hailed from the early 1940s. So, the motor in the e-mail is either a heretofore unknown circa 1917 brand, or maybe it

is a two-cylinder version of the Detroit with an illegible decal. Either way, it sounds like a rare machine.

Dynamic

Tackle Industries of Shreveport, Louisiana, made ¾ and 1 hp electric trollers circa 1967.

Dyk

Six- or 12-volt electric trollers from Groendyk Manufacturing Company of Buchanan, Virginia, first showed up in 1968.

Electra Pal

Osborn Engineering in Bloomington, Illinois, offered a variety of electrics beginning in the 1960s. Circa 1969 models wore fishy names the likes of Texas Marlin and Tarpon.

Electric Sportsman

A sturdily built, battery-powered outboard, the Electric Sportsman was designed to keep up with small gasoline-fired kickers. This (presumably) late 1950s product of the Citrus Machinery Company, Orlando, Florida, had a car starter motor powerhead and a real outboard (probably from Clinton) lower unit. Translucent green or red knobs on either end of a bar directly under the powerhead steered the lower unit 360 degrees if desired. Electric Sportsman may be compared to

This Electric Sportsman was found in a flea market still in its wooden shipping crate. Possessing a hefty automotive starter motor powerhead and a lower unit identical to those found on some gas-powered outboards, the Florida-built kicker was designed to be a cut above the average electric troller.

the My-te in that both were meant to replace—rather than supplement—traditional putt-putt fishing motor competitors the likes of a 1.7 hp Mighty-Mite.

Elk Marine

An English firm exported a number of air-cooled, low-horsepower outboards through the Robert Boomer Agency of Torrance, California. Offerings in 1961 included the 1.5 hp Cub, the 3 hp Cadet, and the 4.5 hp Captain. Boomer's company also marketed a line of budget-priced motors under the Sea-Bee banner. [See also Sea-Bee (2) in the Big List chapter and Sea-Bee in the U.K. section of An Empire of Vintage Outboards.]

Elliot Power Paddle

A Binghamton, New York, firm marketed this elfin, air-cooled, 21.1 cc, flexible driveshaft, weed whacker–type outboard in the early 1980s. Designed with an automatic centrifugal clutch, the single cylinder Elliot Power Paddle was dubbed "the versatile outboard motor." Plastic parts, like the fuel tank and skeg, kept the weight down to about 9 ½ pounds. Rather than trying to compete with other small gasoline-fired kickers on a horsepower basis, the Power Paddle's maker advertised it in terms of 24 pounds of prop thrust exerted via the motor's three-blade bronze wheel. Actually, the mnemonic comparison to a handy paddle served as the little mill's best marketing strategy.

Empire Invincible

During the World War I era, New York City's Empire Engine Works investigated the mechanical virtues of various forward-pointing, single-cylinder outboards in order to come up with one that had "no superior in any detachable rowboat motor no matter at what price." The resulting 2 hp Invincible featured a cylinder-mounted priming cup, rudder steering, and flywheel knob starting. It could be purchased with battery or magneto ignition and with above- or underwater exhaust. Because "under no circumstances" did Empire "want a dissatisfied customer," it guaranteed the Invincible forever. Broken or wornout parts, the fault of poor workmanship or defects, would be replaced free, provided the old component was sent to the factory "post paid." Empire's offer came with the

greatest implications, however. It stated: "In lots of 12 and upwards, we will brand these motors with the buyer's name or trademark as may be desired." The 1919 outboard probably also appeared under private-brand marques even more obscure than the Empire Invincible. This mill possessed striking similarities to the Lockwood-Ash rowboat motor of World War I vintage.

Eska (electric)

Trollers from this budget-priced outboard producer featured ten speeds with 12-volt operation. Hailing from the 1960s and 1970s, they also appeared with J.C. Penney, Seaco, Sears, and Wizard labels.

Explorer

A badge-engineered addition to the Eska line, Explorer boasted economy-priced outboards in the 3.5 to 15 hp range. Eska's 30 September 1987 production halt finished Explorer's run.

Fairbanks-Morse

F-M built rewind starters for a few small kickers the likes of Continental Sport. Don't confuse the label with an actual brand of outboard.

Federal

From 1968 to the 1970s, Federal badge-engineered these Eska-based, low-horsepower singles and wholesaled them to various retailers.

Fisherman's Delight

The model FD-1 was an offering of Lake Alfred, Florida's Sportsman's Delight. An electric troller circa the 1960s, this one had an underwater motor "permanently lubricated and sealed in a one piece pod."

Flodin

Nels Flodin of Marquette, Michigan's Lakeshore Engine Works, spent his spare time between 1896 and 1898 working on an outboard of his own design. Reportedly, during the summer of 1898 he ran it on a rowboat in Marquette's lower harbor. Although relatively successful, the historic Flodin outboard never left the prototype stage. Sketchy details and a grainy photo—showing a primitive kicker with exposed lower unit gearing and a four-spoked "steering wheel" flywheel—are all that remain of this pioneering machine.

Florida Sneaker Blade

A small Jacksonville, Florida, firm, Whidden Welding, offered this hand-powered sculling device in the 1950s.

Ford

A 1963 book, *Young Henry Ford*, notes that Henry and a friend built two "gasoline engines for boats" in 1897. It is mentioned here in case anyone discovers a nineteenth-century prototypical outboard with some sort of Ford nomenclature cast into it. What's more likely, though, is that the motors mentioned were of the inboard variety.

Fussomatic

Maybe this one is too obscure to ever get hitched to our back rack. Nonetheless, a goofy-looking outboard prominently festooned with such nomenclature was featured in a late 1940s Mercury promotional film. The cartoon-esque kicker had a red gas tank the likes of an Anzani Minor that looked like a hat Robin Hood would have worn. It had silver opposed cylinders and a bevy of handles and complicated carburetor controls. It was supposed to represent a troublesome brand X motor that the folks at Kiekhaefer invited viewers to trade in for a new, shiny green, easy-to-use Merc.

Rather than a completely redesigned machine, however, this mill was probably a late model Gale Products or Waterwitch engine covered with the funny top for use as a movie prop. Because odd things happen in the vintage engine hobby, it isn't beyond the scope of possibility that the Fussomatic will turn up at a yard sale, perhaps on the lawn of someone associated with the disposition of the movie set. This doesn't qualify as a true marque, but is being noted to keep some lucky collector from needlessly racking his or her brain. Of course, one could complicate matters by obtaining a videotape of that Merc movie and concocting a Fussomatic replica. Internet auction bidders beware!

Gambles (Neptune)

This listing resulted from a motor called the Gambles 100 auctioned on eBay. While the Gambles chain stores are best known by old outboard

enthusiasts for their mid-1950s Scott-Atwater-produced Hiawatha motors, it appears the retailer also offered kickers with the Gambles moniker. In this case, the Gambles 100 appears to be a badge-engineered (possibly a model 17A1) 1 ½ hp Neptune single. That would make it a 1947 model, but one that might look current to novice outboard buyers through the early 1950s. If there was a Gambles 100 (with a blue and yellow logo on a red fuel tank), it's likely a few other Neptune models were turned into Gambles versions, too.

Genie

In 1970, Fisherman's Genie Manufacturing Company of Vivian, Louisiana, introduced this electric troller.

Glideaway

Influence from Wisconsin Engine Company, Evinrude, and Lockwood is clearly evident in this World War I–era single. The Glideaway "portable rowboat motor" was sold by the W. H. Mullins Company of Salem, Ohio. Mullins indicated the kicker was "manufactured for"—as opposed to having been "built by"—them. Consequently, the parts may well have come from one of those aforementioned better known outboard makers.

Golden Jet

Sometimes also called the Eska Golden Jet, this marque ran from 1962 to 1969. Enigmatically, it is reported that Golden Jets didn't necessarily have water "jet thrust" drives but were fitted with standard propeller lower units.

Grant (1)

One of several motors labeled Grant, or possibly Grant's, this Eska-built outboard was reportedly offered in the sporting goods department of the long-defunct W. T. Grant 5&10 chain stores. That's not to say these bargain-brand kickers could actually be purchased for a nickel and a dime. It is believed Grants offered them in the late 1960s through early 1970s. (See also Seacruiser-Grant.)

Grant (2)

Using specially cast parts, as well as components from other makers' engines, a Mr. Grant of Memphis, Tennessee, had his mechanics build custom "alky" alcohol-fired racing outboards. The Grant name was included in the motors' fuel tank casting. These parts were also available for sale to fellow speedsters who incorporated them into their own motor projects. Because Grant was connected with country singer Johnny Cash—famous for tunes like "Ring of Fire"—he featured the hit song's title (incorporated into a fiery logo) on his race boats.

Handi-Trol

A manually propelled crank outboard with open lower unit gears, the Handi-Trol appears to be a product of the early 1950s. It's reported that the brand name was cast into a transom bracket thumbscrew.

Hanimex

Dating from approximately 1968 through the 1970s, this Eska-based private brand was available with a one- or two-cylinder Tecumseh powerhead.

Harley-Davidson

Legend has it that America's most famous motorcycle firm produced a prototype rowboat motor in the World War I era. Dusty historical outboard documents say the founders of H-D had dropped into the shop of fellow Milwaukee resident, Ole Evinrude, for some cycle-related small engine carburetor improvement advice. It's quite possible they noted the outboards and considered adding such an item to their product line. Arguably, the project never got beyond a few experimental machines and extremely limited production. There is also the scenario that H-D simply figured to offer a Harley-branded kicker produced by Evinrude or another nearby maker.

Hiawatha (3)

One of the Eska-based private-brand lines featuring several sizes, this circa 1969 incarnation of the seemingly ubiquitously used Hiawatha outboard name was offered in 3.5, 5, and 7 hp models.

Hiawatha (4)

This version of the mid-1950s Scott-Atwater-built Hiawatha definitely had no relationship to the American Midwestern Gambles stores. In fact, it wasn't even built in the U.S. A surviving 5 hp motor with this unique lineage is simply tagged "Hiawatha. Made in Canada. Mfd. Under U.S. Patent

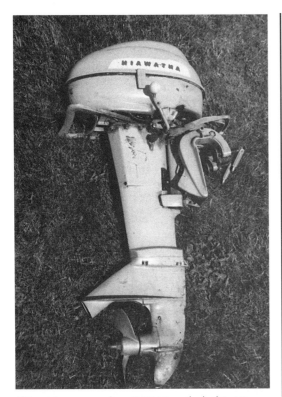

This might appear to be a 1956 Hiawatha built in Minneapolis, Minnesota, by Scott-Atwater for the Midwestern Gambles department store chain, but its ID tag says "Made in Canada" and makes no mention of Gambles.

NOS. 2.553.935., 2.659.454., 2.548.762., 2.536.118. Distributed by (in Western Canada) Macleods Ltd., Winnipeg, Manitoba; (in Eastern Canada) Wood Alexander, Ltd., Hamilton, Ontario." The tan, full F-N-R gearshift twin is proof that one could collect quite a few variations of Hiawatha outboard motors.

Hiawatha (5)

Admittedly a nuanced listing, but this Hiawatha might *not* have a connection to the big retailer Gambles, for whom most of Gale Products' badge-engineered Hiawathas were produced. This annotation originated with an early 1950s cardboard in-store display placard picturing a Gale Products–built 5 hp Hiawatha. Its copy says: "Nationally advertised in *Outdoor Life* and *Sports Afield*. Hiawatha, the sportsmen's choice! Big action motoring at thrifty prices!" The suggested price and terms

could be written in a little box near the motor's picture. And the words "Exclusive Hiawatha Distributors" sat on the advertising card's bottom ¾ inch or so. Nowhere was there a mention of Gambles. The latter is germane to our interests because it allows for the possibility that there were some Hiawathas with other retailers' names on the identification tag. On the other hand, the placards might simply have been the product of Hiawatha Outboard Motors, Galesburg, Illinois (home of Outboard Marine Corporation's Gale Products Division).

Hydro–Meteor (or Hydro-Kart)

This do-it-yourself kicker required any McCulloch kart engine, a few wrenches, and the Hydro-Meteor drive unit. Once the 16-pound complete lower unit—from transom clamp to skeg—was mated to the air-cooled kart motor, you would have an outboard "adaptable for racing, fishing, or auxiliary" purposes. The $149 piece (less the McCulloch power head) was marketed around 1965 by Hydro-Meteor of Torrance, California. Without great success, Acco had tried this kind of thing five years earlier. Another company, Versa-Tool, resurrected the "adapter" outboard concept in the early 1980s.

Jetmaster

Released during the early 1960s hydro-thrust outboard craze (or should that be "crazette"?), Jetmaster was fitted with an 8 hp West Bend Super Bee powerhead. That mill earned this outboard the model name Jetmaster 8.

J.C. Penney

Private-brand electric trolling outboards for the Penney's chain were provided by Eska. During the 1960s, the retailer also marketed gasoline-powered motors, typically under the Foremost name, but later they may have slipped a few gassers, simply bearing a J.C. Penney label, into its eventually phased out sporting goods departments.

Kaufmann

During the tail end of the 1950s, Buck Kaufmann of Sioux City, Iowa, built a line of racing motors based on 15-, 20-, 30-, and 40-cubic-inch Mercury engines. Actually, he modified Mercs by equipping them with rotary valves instead of the standard

reed valve fuel induction system. His finished products were branded the Kaufmann K-15, K-20, K-30, or K-40, and ranged from $550 to $650. During January 1960, an official spec sheet was submitted by Kaufmann Motors to the National Outboard Association's racing engine specification committee with the hope that NOA officials would legalize these obscure mills for use in sanctioned regattas.

Keller-Craft

This was a barely disguised Clinton marketed in the early 1960s by the Keller Hardware Company of Pottstown, Pennsylvania. The Clinton folks would badge-engineer their small fishing engines for any firm willing to order an acceptable number (possibly a minimum of ten) of the low-priced kickers. It's quite likely other very limited edition marques were built for sundry hardware, discount, or sporting goods stores (see Mans Troller in the Big List chapter). It's not unusual for an outboard buff to encounter such a motor with no distinguishing ID other than a Clinton, Eska, Power Products, or Tecumseh marking on the powerhead. No doubt some private-brand decals provided to the retailer by Clinton (or Eska, et al.) were plain, small, and printed on generic bumper sticker material that tended to peel off after coming in contact with gasoline. It's also likely that such private-brand motor makers simply packed those decals in the owner's manual envelope, making their application a responsibility of store personnel or the outboard buyer. If this was the case, it's no wonder that many bargain-brand nametags never made it to the motor cowling.

Keystone

The lightweight Keystone single generated 1 hp @ 6,500 rpm. It was a private brand made by Japan's Tanaka Kogyo of Japan and was offered circa 1974. There may have been other models in the budget-priced Keystone line.

The Kit

Vociferous *Old Outboard Book* readers may well be tired of seeing the oft-cited Milburn Cub name, but its mention here is imperative. That's because the economy outboard, introduced for 1949, resurfaced in kit form some seven years later. By then, Los Angeles-based Milburn (and successor L. K. Products) had sold to Continental Manufacturing

Corporation in nearby Culver City, California. This firm's first marine offering and biggest publicity getter was the $59.95, 2 ½ hp, knocked-down version of the original Milburn. Miniscule ads promised that construction would only take two hours for folks possessing an adjustable wrench and screwdriver.

After assembly, all that distinguished The Kit from a Milburn, the factory-built Continental Sport, or the host of other Milburn clones, was the front-mounted, rectangular nameplate that doubled as a seal and covering for the fuel tank's sand-cast core cavity. Instead of Continental's standard brand designation Sport, these were embossed with "THE KIT," qualifying it for a distinct listing herein.

The kit outboard idea seemed to play well in the do-it-yourself, family project–crazed 1950s, netting Continental Manufacturing decent promotional coverage in publications like *Popular Mechanics*. Because the instruction booklets for The Kit seem to surface more often than the related motors, it may be that some Kits were shipped with standard Continental Sport tags. In fact, one buff restoring his Sport discovered that the flip side of the motor's ID tag said "THE KIT," further confusing the issue.

Kompac-3

The 1938–42 Clarke Troller is arguably antique outboarding's most unique motor. That's why the generic nature of Douglas R. Clarke's second kicker project seems so surprising. Circa 1960, Clarke endeavored to create a small inexpensive outboard to be initially offered in his native Toronto, Ontario, region. Instead of designing a completely new powerhead, though, he decided to go the quick route and purchase a stock of air-cooled, single-cylinder, two-stroke engines from the Power Products/Tecumseh organization in Wisconsin.

Rated at 2 ½ to 3 hp, these mills, originally designed for a rotary lawnmower, were fitted with a front-mounted "juice can" fuel tank, a large grass and dust filter covering the carburetor air intake, and a rectangular sheet metal carrying strap bolted (in conjunction with the rewind-start assembly) to the shrouding. The powerhead rode atop a basic lower unit composed of a separate exhaust tube and driveshaft housing, simple for-

ward-only gears, and a two-blade prop. According to publicity, a diaphragm (floatless) carburetor was employed so that the motor could be operated "at steep angles or in rough water." Of course the real reason for this big deal about steep angles had more to do with the Power Products' engine being able to mow hilly lawns than it did with outboarding up a waterfall. But hyperbole was often employed when trying to sell a bargain-basement kicker to novices.

Initially advertised in a "smart yellow and black" color scheme but also noted in white or cream, this Clarke was dubbed the Kompac-3. Actually, the earliest of these motors (1961–62) did not wear Kompac-3 nomenclature. They were marketed exclusively through the Aikenhead hardware store in Toronto and had a D. R. Clarke Model 3HP decal and were simply identified in advertising as an "Aikenhead Outboard Motor." Whatever the first identity, few of them sold, so by 1963 Clarke struck a distribution deal with Longwood Equipment Company in Don Mills, Ontario. Officials there coined the Kompac-3 name, but this

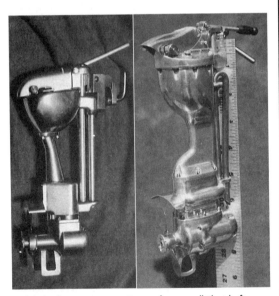

While built circa 2000 in Europe for a small Florida firm and thus not officially "old" outboards, these Clarke Troller scale models are worthy of note in this book. They operate on the glowplug-model airplane engine principle and are the spittin' image of the real things. The ⅓-scale single is comparable in size to a $5 bill. The replica of the rare Clarke Twin is about 9 inches.

minor remake was no more effective in attracting customers than the hardware retailer's attempts. It's doubtful whether new Kompac-3 Clarkes were assembled after about 1964. Impecunious boaters could, however, coax a dusty one out of Longwood's existing stock for several years thereafter. Even so, Kompac-3 is a less common vintage motor find today than its older, temperamental, more intricate, and less dependable but highly sought after sibling.

Lakeland Turbojet

This appears to be a restyled, thinly disguised Clinton-powered Starling Jet (see the Big List chapter). Ads for the 7.5 hp water-jet thrust outboard from the Minneapolis-based Lakeland Turbojet outfit appeared in 1967.

Leisure Products

Joining the "tiny kicker" fray for the 1971 boating season was a 1 hp outboard of about 9 pounds. Leisure Products, the Swampscott, Massachusetts, firm marketing the motor, advertised features like the "positive rewind starter, twist grip throttle, and adjustable length shaft." Interested parties could send a postcard to a P.O. box for a leaflet showing an unmarked (no noticeable logo or decal) clone of the Mini Motor and look-alike Cruise 'n Carry model. It may be that there was no actual brand on Leisure Products' engines.

Man'll Motor

A hand-powered outboard device of the 1990s, this offering of Water Mate (Crystal Lake, Illinois) is included here because its unusual mode may make it appear to be older than it actually is.

Marine Motors

This Towson, Maryland, firm entered the fishing motor fray with a four-cycle, 3 hp outboard around 1961. The 35-pound, air-cooled kicker probably featured a lawnmower engine.

Maxwell

From a Canadian port of call, the Maxwell was powered by an air-cooled, four-cycle Tecumseh mill. Some sources date this 5 hp fishing outboard to 1954, but Maxwell's plastic lower powerhead shrouding actually makes it appear to hail from the early 1960s.

Nassau 5

A Clinton-built fishing motor with an aquamarine paint job and stick-on lettering was noted at an Antique Outboard Motor Club swap meet. Unfortunately, its pedigree seems to be lost to time and minutia. No other identification could be detected. Perhaps the single-cylinder kicker was a Clinton that became the victim of some blue-green spray paint and stick-on labeling in connection with "cabin number five" at some Bahamian (or Long Island?) resort. That being too far-fetched, maybe our mystery Nassau 5 is akin to the Keller-Craft and those extremely limited private-branding arrangements mentioned earlier in this chapter.

While Nassau 5's Clinton heritage is apparent, no one seems to recall if Nassau was an "official" outboard brand. Clinton would badge-engineer motors for customers ordering lots of about twelve or more, and that may have been the case here. Of course, buffs would have to uncover eleven additional engines labeled like this early 1960s mill to prove the point.

Nip-N-Tuck

A tiny ad in the August 1946 *Sports Afield* introduced a pair of electric trolling motors branded Nip-N-Tuck. Swanky anglers were invited to mount Nip on one side of the boat and attach Tuck to the other. A foot-operated switch left the fisherman's hands free to cast and reel while Nip-N-Tuck's forward-reverse, push-pull options gently glided the boat into just about any position. For $98 you could buy both Nip-N-Tuck (left and right) motors from H. G. Gentry & Company of Chamblee, Georgia. The trollers (each looked like a flexible shaft Minn-Kota electric) folded together for easy carrying on a "keeper" handle or mount, which was included in the standard price.

Anglers would do well to be ambidextrous with the feet and hands for smooth Nip-N-Tuck operation. Otherwise the foot-controlled troller twins (with a spring-return to center position) could make for some frustrating maneuvering. The motors mounted on each side of the boat rather than on a craft's transom.

Pacemaker

Not really a brand per se, the Pacemaker label was affixed to factory "remanufactured" Mercury motors that had originally been loaned by Merc for short-term use in movies, TV shows, or for use by large dealers and distributors engaged in promotional or charitable projects. This identification was meant be a seal of approval for those officially reconditioned late-model Mercs that were sold for less than similar looking new engines. The Pacemaker name was important enough to the jealous folks at Kiekhaefer Mercury for them to initiate legal action against Champion Outboard Motors when Champion inadvertently adopted the Pacemaker model designation for its 1956 line.

Pathfinder

Also referred to as an Aldens, the Eska-built Pathfinder's most unusual model was the 400, a 1962 four-cycle job. Reportedly, it represents Eska's only four-stroker. Even Eska's service litera-

ture couldn't identify the powerhead make. The repair bulletin simply lists it as "unknown." Also air-cooled, there were Pathfinders in a more traditional two-cycle format. These had remote fuel tanks and Tecumseh engines. During the late 1980s through the 1990s, one kept showing up at the Thousand Islands Antique Boat Museum's annual show and flea market. Every so often during that weekend-long event, someone would tell me they saw a motor that wasn't listed in my book. I referred them to Aldens, but thought it a good idea to give Pathfinder an alphabetized spot. Maybe I should've simply bought the motor?!

Pausin (Waterman)

The Pausin name might be of special interest to vintage outboard buffs focused on the venerable Waterman line. In May 1924, *Rudder* magazine ran an advertisement for Pausin Engineering Company of Newark, New Jersey, stating that Pausin had purchased (from Arrow Motor and Machine Company) the parts and manufacturing rights to Arrow and Waterman motors. Starting in 1916, Arrow had offered a nicely engineered opposed twin-cylinder, 4 hp outboard, in addition to a 2 ½ hp single.

During the next year, Arrow bought the Waterman assets and added them to the catalog. These included Waterman outboards, as well as their inboard models, which were probably the better sellers. Up until 1929, *Rudder*'s annual "marine engines" roster indicated that Pausin still marketed Waterman products. By that time, most of the Pausin Watermans in the inventory were probably the hopelessly outdated model C-21, last built (by Arrow) in 1921. Of course, other leftovers might have been available, too. And it's possible they were identified as Pausin outboards or that they even left Pausin's warehouse sans nomenclature. The latter scenario makes sense if the motor was purchased by a late 1920s to early 1930s bargain hunter who cared little about pedigree.

Perfection

A 1916 Caille-like rowboat motor with rewind start accessory showed up in Canada bearing a nameplate that reads "Perfection Motor Company, Montreal." It appears to be a relabeled Caille for the Canadian market and may have been assembled from there (from mostly U.S. components) to take advantage of a trade tariff issue.

Power-Pak

An air of mystery surrounds this circa 1945–46 offering first promoted by the Meyer Corporation and then by Propulsion Engine Corporation of Kansas City, Kansas. Originally guessed to be someone's generic lawnmower engine mounted on a fishing lower unit, it now appears Power-Paks were unique to their maker(s). Listed in *Motor Boatings*'s 1946 boat show edition specifications, models A-5 through C-5 ranged from 4.4- to 42-cubic-inch piston displacement. This included a single-, two twin-, and two four-cylinder models. Each Power-Pak was equipped with rewind starting, reverse gearing, and a Power-Pak-built carburetor and ignition system. The line spanned from about 2 to 26 hp and was arguably sleeker and more dramatically modern than Mercury's streamlined late 1940s products.

Actually, a Merc/Power-Pak connection was in the works in 1950–51. Food Machinery and Chemical Corporation, the California conglomerate that owned Power-Pak's maker, Propulsion Engine Company, was very close to striking a deal to acquire Mercury's Kiekhaefer Corporation. No doubt, the extensive promise of that 1946 Power-Pak outboard lineup (albeit prototypical), the palpable postwar boating boom, and Merc's rapid advances in the outboard industry made FMC covet Kiekhaefer's product line and collective acumen. There's no telling what a Mercury/Propulsion Engine marriage would have yielded. A series of communication delays and miscues, however, caused the proposed sale to go cold. What actually happened regarding those 1946 plans to launch "America's finest line of outstanding outboards" is rather fuzzy, as it's unknown whether or not any Power-Paks ever found their way to dealer showrooms.

During the late 1990s, a Pennsylvania outboard collector bought an odd-looking gas tank from a flea market junk pile. Later the buff studied its faded decal and recognized the Power-Pak logo. Was the part from one of these very rare outboards? The April 1947 issue of *Popular Science* magazine contains a 2-by-3-inch advertisement for a Mow-Master rotary lawnmower from Propulsion Engine Corporation of Kansas City. The mower's vertical shaft engine looks to be rounder than a typical Briggs & Stratton mill. The ad states that the Mow-Master is "powered by a 2 HP Power-Pak

It isn't certain that Power-Pak motors like the one depicted here were ever built, but the line's 1945 ad suggested that aggressive planning was underway for what would have been America's most modern, feature-filled stable of outboard motors.

gasoline engine with muffler." This makes the fuel tank a possible lawnmower orphan. However, scrupulous examination of weathered printing on the tank appears to say something about lower unit grease. No mower tank would include that wording.

Pozgay

While probably never getting involved in palpable promotion of such a fact, the Pozgay Welding Works of Long Island, New York, reportedly built some 1940 Bendix singles and twins from existing parts it acquired from Bendix the previous year. It's also logical to assume that they did so for the 1941 and 1942 boating seasons. Consequently, there just might be some Pozgay brand markings on very late Bendix singles and twins. (See also Bendix in the Big List chapter.)

Production Engineering (Propeloar)

This Berkeley, California, firm obtained the rights to build a "man-powered" outboard invented by Clarence Allen of San Francisco. Initially shown in the August 1950 issue of *Mechanics Illustrated*, Production Engineering's manual outboard, called the Propeloar, was equipped with a seat that rested on a rowboat's middle seat and foot pedals that could steer and turn the machine's propeller. It was primarily targeted to freshwater fishermen for use on calm rivers and lakes.

Rocket Racing Products

This marque was a private brand, sort of. Reportedly, a small U.S. outfit picked up some (used?) 1950s-era Mercury Mark 6 outboards, tossed the cover, did a bit of souping-up, and marketed them for novelty bathtub boat racing. Reworking included enlarged intakes, a "built-up" block, and padded cylinder heads for extra compression. A pair of stickers on the flywheel identified the "hopped-up" Merc as a bona fide Rocket Racing Products machine. The engine's throttle was activated by gently pulling a cord attached to the carburetor butterfly valve. A Michigan Wheel racing propeller completed the ensemble and made this mill just right for the 8-foot plywood Minimax hydroplanes many fathers and sons built during the late 1950s to early 1960s.

Ro-No-Mo

An electric, the 1960s troller came from Lisk Fly Manufacturing Company of Greensboro, North Carolina. Don't confuse it with the No-Ro four-cycle job mentioned in the Big List chapter.

Roper. See Aquabug.

Schnacke (Mid-Jet)

Officially, Walter Schnacke retired and closed his outboard firm (Schnacke Manufacturing Company, makers of the Mid-Jet/Electro-Jet) during the late 1960s.

This Midwestern gentleman, who got his professional start around 1915 with the Hercules Gas Engine Company, passed away in the summer of 1995. Reportedly however, up through about 1989, Mr. Schnacke was still casting aluminum components and building an occasional jet outboard in a backyard shed. The last Mid-Jets (perhaps with no labeling) were said to be Briggs & Stratton powered. When assembled, the fishing motors were likely sold directly from the enterprising senior citizen's outbuilding.

Seabreeze

From about 1965 to 1968, Seabreeze was a private brand that originated at the Eska factory.

Seaco

Here's a modest group of 1960s to 1970s Eska clones that each wore a Tecumseh powerhead. You could choose a single- or twin-cylinder model.

Seacruiser-Grant (SeaCruiser)

This listing originated from an e-mail sent my way by someone requesting info on a SeaCruiser 7.5. "It wasn't in your book," the fellow complained. "Never heard of such a thing," I admitted, but postulated it was "probably an Eska or Clinton clone from the late 1960s to 1970s of the plastic shrouded, bargain fishing motor genre." Turned out that the now-defunct W. T. Grant discount department stores retailed one- and two-cylinder models from Eska using the SeaCruiser and Sea Cruiser-Grant marques. Like most other Eska private-branders, Tecumseh provided the powerheads. Some of these kickers were simply tagged with "Grant" or "Grants." Arguably, neither the manufacturer, retailer, nor thrifty shopper spent much time focusing upon these bargain motors' exact pedigrees.

Sea Hawk

Just like the aforementioned Seacruiser-Grant, these 1960s to 1970s fishing motors were badge-engineered for some now-forgotten retailer by Eska.

Sea Horse. See Johnson in the Big List chapter.

Sea Lion

One of the many budget-focused outboards stemming from the Milburn Cub, Continental Commando, Comanco, et al., the Sea Lion was actually the 1968 model designation for a Commando 23-pound, 7.5 hp single. Its $179.95 sticker price was some $122 less than Evinrude's 52-pound, 6 hp twin from that same year. In some used motor guides, Sea Lion was listed as a distinct marque and may have been represented by some enterprising retailer (who figured no one would connect it to the equally obscure Commando) as a private brand.

Seapower Outdrive

While not an outboard motor, this late 1950s to early 1960s product looked a bit like one. Swein-hart Equipment sales of Los Angeles marketed the Seapower Outdrive unit with the pitch that it could be driven by "any automotive, industrial, or marine" engine. A tiny publicity photo suggests the unit's head—with decorative fins and scripted nameplate—contained some serious gearing. A three-blade prop, protected by a curved bar from the skeg to the anticavitation plate, played an important role on Seapower's "tractor" (prop in front) gear foot.

Seeling

Modern industrialists might argue that a total output of just two dozen motors does not constitute a "mass produced" outboard brand. Maybe so, but the twenty-four engines reportedly built by John Seeling during the early 1930s are amply sufficient to qualify this La Crosse, Wisconsin, marque for a permanent harbor in *The Old Outboard Book*. Actually, the nascent brand was rediscovered in the 1990s by Antique Outboard Club member Gene Church, who tracked down one of the Seeling 6 (presumably denoting 6 hp) mills. The surviving motor is a water-cooled, opposed twin, with above-water exhaust, a Tillotson carburetor and detachable cylinder heads.

In a July 2000 article for the *The Antique Outboarder*, Robert Peterson reported that Seeling, who had a day job as a machinist with a local railroad, was "listed in La Crosse's 1930 city directory as the manufacturer [of] Seeling Outboard Motors." His small organization also built small steam engines, likely doing so on an ad hoc, per order basis. The surviving Seeling kicker exhibits nice lines and a skilled machinist's detailing. While designing and building an outboard line is certainly no easy endeavor, successfully marketing the resulting machines in profitable numbers is arguably tougher. It may be assumed that such was Seeling's barrier to continuing his brand beyond the original twenty-four motors. Perhaps, though, this tiny production run was constructed and retailed (by word of mouth and right from the maker's shop) over a period of several years.

Shakespeare

In addition to having made some promotionally packaged Marty Martin and Silverstreak lures for the Martin Motors people, this Kalamazoo, Michigan, company marketed electric trollers branded with its famous fishing tackle firm's name. Early versions can be dated to about 1969.

Silvertrol (electric)

A major player in the electric trolling motor industry's early years, Silver Creek (of Silver Creek, New York) Precision built their first trollers in 1946.

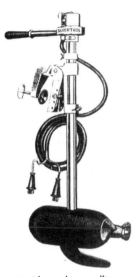

By the late 1940s, Silvertrol was selling enough electric outboards to be on a par with then leaders LeJay and Minn-Kota. The upstate New York manufacturer even had a promising distribution in England. This is one of Silvertrol's circa 1950 models that employed the same "sealed motor pod" technology as the 1930s Bendix electric troller.

Typically, Silvertrol configured its electric motor in a capsule-shaped submersible compartment. That way, the propeller could be attached directly to the motor's drive output, eliminating gears and flexible shafts. The sealed motor pods could overheat if run out of water, as Silvertrol's owner's manuals were quick to instruct. Some of Silver Creek's first models had the word "Silvertrol" cast into the steering handle. The firm also private-branded for the likes of Sears and Western Auto.

Snow's Electric Trolling Motor

Available fully assembled in kit form or via do-it-yourself plans, these rugged trollers originated in the tiny Snow's Electric Shop in Au Sable Forks, New York, sometime during the 1940s and 1950s. Mr. Snow's daughter recalls her dad placing an ad the size of a postage stamp in publications such as *Popular Mechanics* and then putting a troller together whenever an order trickled in. Even the mailman was excited about one request from China. Reportedly, Snow's favorite powerhead source was an Adirondack auto junkyard flush with Chevrolet starter motors.

Spencer

"Motor cooled without pump, water jacket, pipes or valves," boasted a 1912–13 Spencer Motor Company ad. This unusual rowboat motor from Montreal, Quebec, featured a vertical cylinder positioned (a la the Clarke Troller) underwater. There was also "a device to elevate the motor when you desire to land." The heavy-duty contraption certainly did not look like any of its American contemporaries, and it was likely a Canadian original. It's also possible is that the Spencer might have been private-branded by a European firm.

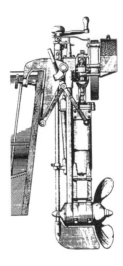

"Buy it because it's a better motor," urged ads for this Montreal-built outboard. It appears that the unique motor's vertical cylinder was just below the waterline (to facilitate cooling) and its driveshaft (running under the crank handle) traveled ahead of what would be the driveshaft-tower housing in a typical outboard. The 11-inch propeller was described by Spencer to be "weedless," but it appears able to do some serious snagging. Note that the flywheel is directly in front of the fuel tank. Spencer might have been current through about World War 1, as a vague 1915 company listing suggests.

Spirit

When the Japanese manufacturer Suzuki first came to the U.S. with an outboard offering (circa 1978), it wore the Spirit name.

Sportfisher

From about 1968 through the 1970s, Eska labeled a few batches of its single-cylinder outboards for private-brand marketing under the Sportfisher name.

Sports–Jets

With its aqua and white color scheme, similar castings, and air-cooled Tecumseh powerhead, the Sports-Jets motor leads one to speculate about a connection to the late 1960s McMar Commando. But

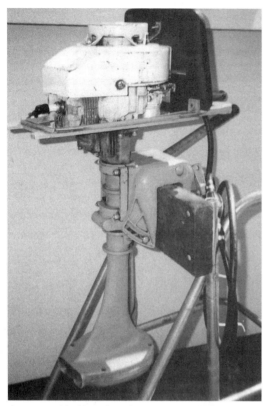

The aqua and white color scheme, transom clamp castings, and Tecumseh engine on this Sports-Jets are very similar to those of the McMar Commando of Milburn Cub lineage. Had the powerhead cowling been present when this classic back rack example was found, more information about the heritage of water-thrust outboards would be available. It was not unusual for a budget-brand, propeller-drive motor to subsequently appear with a hydro-jet thrust lower unit, and vice versa. Examples of jet drives that were also available as standard outboards with regular horizontal gear cases include Blue Jet and Starling Jet.

the Commando uses a conventional propeller motor and Sports-Jets drives with water thrust. A black faceplate and powerhead shroud also distinguish it from Commando. Even so, the aluminum transom clamp bracket castings are similar enough to cause speculation that Sports-Jets could be a subsequent incarnation of the McMar motor (which sprang from the mysterious Milburn Cub). One Sports-Jets found hanging on a back rack has an identification tag touting Sports-Jets Industries, Minneapolis, Minnesota. The owner estimated it was built in 1963, however, making any McMar connection unlikely.

Sportsmaster

A LeJay clone, the Sportsmaster electric troller probably dates from the late 1940s to early 1950s. Via either 6 or 12 volts, it drove a little two-blade propeller through regular lower unit bevel gears. Some might have been made with a flexible (curved) driveshaft. It's quite possible that LeJay built Sportsmasters and then wholesaled them to the Sportsmaster Products Company. A July 1946 ad calls the Sportsmaster a "Trolmotor," the same name later used by LeJay.

Starling Troller

Probably not an autonomous brand, but Starling Troller's main difference from its relative, Starling Jet, is worth mentioning. Instead of a hydro-thrust (impeller) drive like Starling Jet, the Troller was fitted with a regular (propeller) outboard motor lower unit. Both versions had Starling's P-500 logo on the engine shroud. (See also Starling Jet in the Big List chapter.)

Stewart & Stevenson

The spouse of any outboard collector who brings home an S&S would probably go through the roof. That's because this V-16 cylinder Detroit diesel-powered "kicker" stands taller than most chimneys. In fact the motor's three-blade prop checks in with a diameter of 5 ½ feet! A number of these giants were produced by Houston-based Stewart & Stevenson for use on barges. Early examples (circa 1960s) were offered in a 540 hp size. Updated turbocharged S&S outboards delivered something like 700 horses!

Superbug. See Aquabug.

Tackle Industries

This Shreveport, Louisiana, firm purchased LeJay and its related brands in the late 1950s. While there are electric trollers with Tackle Industries and Electrol nomenclature, there may also be some branded with both Tackle Industries and LeJay or Trolmotor.

Tempo-Troll

New for 1967 was a mostly aluminum electric outboard with stainless steel motor shaft from the Tempo Products Company of Cleveland, Ohio. The firm's well-known aftermarket marine

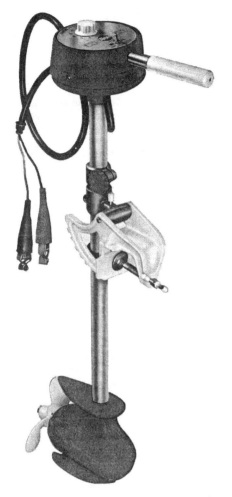

Improved electric motor-battery technology, advanced metallurgy, and stronger plastic parts helped make modern trollers lighter and more versatile. Exhibiting these characteristics, the 1967 Tempo-Troll encouraged competition anglers to rely on electric motors.

troller had a host of features, like a ten-speed motor control dial, a seven-position tilting bracket, and an anticavitation plate. A bright red lower unit (with sealed motor), a height-adjust knob, and top-control head assemblies colorfully distinguished the Tempo-Troll from a growing number of rivals.

Traveler

In the late 1980s, the Yugoslavian Tomos firm renamed some of their motors Traveler before aiming for the American outboard market. For the most part, the export venture went the way of the $3,995 Yugo automobile from the 1980s.

Trolmotor

On several occasions, the LeJay Manufacturing Company reinvented its electric trolling motor line via a name change and/or simple feature. The 1951 Trolmotor illustrates this point. LeJay told *Rudder* magazine (in July 1951) that its new troller would be "marketed under the name of Trolmotor." The company had also offered similar products under the LeJay and Electrol banners. What made the Deluxe Trolmotor different than its relatives was a "steering brake [to] hold the motor on its course" when the operator lets go of the tiller. *Rudder* explained that this steering brake was actually just a thumbscrew through the transom clamp-swivel assembly that could be tightened against the driveshaft. Reportedly, there was also a standard Trolmotor without such a thumbscrew, making it very similar to the regular line of LeJays and Electrols. It may be, however, that Trolmotor came only in a flexible driveshaft configuration (like the one pictured in the Big List's LeJay section.) Electrols were typically marketed with a standard bevel gears lower unit arrangement. Then again, some left the factory with the flexible driveshaft.

Suffice it to say American industry and consumers like "new" things, and if that may be accomplished with a simple product name change, so much the better. LeJay made quality trollers, no matter the particular nomenclature. Incidentally, the company's 1938 catalog not only offered electric kickers, but it also included gas-fired Neptune outboards.

Tryton

A reader contacted me about his mystery 3 hp engine labeled Tryton Outboard Motor Company. Though it looked a bit like the Canadian Arrow (because of Tryton's black water faucet type transom clamp thumbscrew wheels) or the American Eska and wears a single-cylinder, air-cooled Tecumseh powerhead, no further lineage could be determined from the puzzling little orphan. The surviving example's serial number reads "71030," perhaps denoting a 1971 engine.

Twin-Fins

According to a 2-inch ad in the May 1959 issue of *Sports Afield*, "anyone [wanting to] handle a boat like an expert" needed to buy Twin-Fins from a small company at P.O. Box 27 in Philadelphia, Mississippi. This manually powered unit was kind of a double Hydro-Fin. Operated by a hand lever that worked up and down (in about a 30-degree arc), the Twin-Fins flapped outward like frogs' legs. This action caused "no noise or splash" while moving "your boat in any direction with an easy one hand motion." Probably more of a threat to Kermit the Frog's ego than to any design engineer in the outboard industry, Twin-Fins were a novel idea few looked into.

Yard sale shoppers, be on the lookout for the quintessential garage-cluttering device: Twin-Fins. Actually, one of these unusual hand-powered outboards would make a very interesting manual-visual focal point for any motor collection.

Voyager (2)

Eska produced this low hp, low-cost 1961 private-brander.

Wayne Metalcraft Hand Cranked Propeller

For just under $13 in 1948 you could be the contented owner of Wayne Metalcraft Company's manual prop and associated rudder. The ultimate in basic outboard power, the Wayne was essentially a necker's-knob equipped steering wheel that drove a straight shaft that extended to a two-blade prop. For maneuvering, the Detroit firm's

Two hands and a knee were required to operate Wayne Metalcraft's propeller and rudder while fishing. Ads claimed, however, only one hand was needed (as the separate but related rudder could apparently be thumbscrew-tightened into a particular position) to operate the direct-drive propeller, thus eliminating a "pesky motor" or "noisy oars."

"Steer Strate" rudder device (that looked somewhat like a Hydro-Fin) was included, or it could be purchased separately. Duck hunters and fisherman were seen as the unit's potential market.

Wego

Produced around 1950 in a tiny California factory, this is just one more badge-engineered version of the Milburn Cub. Typically, a single feature differentiates Milburn clone motors from the real McCoy—the nameplate. In this case, the nameplate is front-mounted with four screws (later Continental brand Milburn-esque motors were fitted with six ID plate screws) onto the red fuel tank, carrying the Wego name in a breezy pennant. Under the flag, in smaller letters, the Junior model is designated, as is "Wego Motor Co. Los Angeles,

You're looking down the barrel of a low production Wego Junior. It likely hails from the early 1950s. It's of Milburn Cub lineage and includes the proprietary carburetor. Its left-hand (as you face the powerhead) tiller is situated opposite of most other outboards.

CA." Unlike most of the known private-label, Milburn-esque outboards, the Wego has provisions to be secured to a transom via two clamp screws—a la the Milburn/Continental—rather than just one. It is not known whether the Wego was private-branded by the Milburn people or if Wego Motor Company had purchased Milburn's business and actually built Wego outboards on its own.

One Wego Junior surfaced with the serial number 49 H 928, reminiscent of the early, albeit enigmatic, Milburn serialization coding. We might suppose it to be a 1949 motor from August (the eighth month, "H" being the eighth letter in the alphabet), and the 928th motor Milburn built in 1949, then private-branding it for the now-forgotten Wego people.

Wiljo

Another small horsepower Eska clone for private-brand marketing. Like its counterparts (Sea Hawk, et al.), a decal or sticker was all that stood between these brands and their sister Eskas. It's believed more than a few left stores with no unique marking whatsoever.

Willis

Circa 1908, the E. J. Willis Co. of New York City offered a vertical single-cylinder outboard that was obviously a badge-engineered Waterman. Willis' catalog of motorboat supplies calls this rig "our Special Fisherman's portable rowboat motor." List price was $120, but you could buy it for just $65 if you sent cash with your order. Early (about 1910) in the life of Evinrude Motor Company, E. J. Willis' name was featured prominently on Ole and Bess' four-page ad folder. The Willis folks were identified as Evinrude's "eastern representative." This probably meant their Waterman-clone days had ended.

11

An Empire of Vintage Outboards

In 1915, someone at *Rudder* magazine got the idea to do an introductory article about the then new universe of detachable boat engines. With that objective in mind, a search was on for names, addresses, and descriptions of every outboard maker the world over so that the article might be coaxed to run at least a couple of pages. When I compiled an historical annotated worldwide outboard roster in 2001, trying to squeeze the resulting text into the framework of this edition proved impossible. Therefore, an editorial compromise was reached to offer details about two of the globe's most prolific outboard-producing countries—Australia and the United Kingdom.

Note: In this chapter, most piston displacement figures are reported in cubic centimeters. Quoted material is typically either from a magazine article or derived from the actual adverting copy.

Australia

Incredibly diverse during a short burst of marine entrepreneurship, the Australian outboard motor industry was partly a result of surplus aluminum. The American military had seen to it that huge stockpiles of the versatile alloy were shipped there during World War II. When Japan surrendered without the Allies having to use Australia as an invasion staging area, the ready-to-use metal was simply left behind for the Australian government to use at its pleasure. Aussie officials practically gave it away to any firm promising to use the aluminum for local production and the creation of industrial jobs. By the late 1940s, several small companies cast the stuff into parts for their new

outboard designs. Almost all resulting motors were of the prewar style—rather basic, but quite serviceable. Some three dozen brands called Australia their home. Most ended up being relatively low production and were gone from the marketplace by the 1960s. Typically, these kickers were lawnmower engines co-opted for waterway use. Most had English-style throttle controls cabled to a lever on the tiller handle.

According to Australian outboard historian Steve Green, of all the local makes, Riptide was the strongest, most fertile, and best equipped to survive. But it too submerged circa 1965, and today an old Riptide is a rare sight in its native milieu. Undaunted, Green thinks his continent still contains lots of vintage motors that are hiding in garages and backyard sheds. While many are likely U.S., European, or Japanese imports, undoubtedly some—bearing the exotic branding chronicled below—wait for discovery throughout that mammoth island.

Aqua-Vic

Powered by a Hurricane lawnmower engine, the Aqua-Vic was a low production kicker from a now-forgotten manufacturer.

Ascoy

Reminiscent of a cute American Elto Pal, the nicely shrouded Ascoy checked in at 1 ½ hp @ 2,500 rpm. Aeronautical Supply Company of Melbourne was said to be Ascoy's manufacturer, but it's more likely that the firm served as a distributor. The brand appeared in January 1948 *Seacraft* magazine ads, ranking it as one of a handful of Australian outboard pioneers.

Atom. See Waterboy.

Blaxland

A longtime maker of boats and (mostly inboard) motors, Blaxland Rae Pty., Ltd., of Camperdown marketed a simple, water-cooled outboard circa the 1950s. It is described as a "4.5-hp model, ideal for 12 foot ply or fibreglass craft." The Blaxland single swung around to be fully reversible. Blaxland Rae said its outboard wore a "heavy duty [lower unit] gearbox," but it looked no different than that of its numerous standard duty competitors. A recoil starter, tiller-mounted throttle lever, and small, rear-positioned "juice can" fuel tank, defined the Blaxland outboard's putt-putt look.

Cheetah. See Gold Cheetah.

Cheras

A sturdily shrouded single with "modern" one-piece driveshaft housing and exhaust leg, Cheras hailed from the 1950s.

This 1950s Cheras appeared much more contemporary than many of its local competitors. Some ads might refer to Cheras' relatively streamlined design as "the American look." No matter the imitation, this marque was short-lived. (Loch-Sport Antique Marine Engine Museum)

Clinton

The retailer Boan's of Perth imported U.S. bargain-brand Clinton J-9 kickers. Clinton was thought to have had licensing agreements with several overseas companies that called for the motors to be shipped in pieces and then assembled by light-duty manufacturers. This may have been the case at some now-forgotten facility hired by Boan's.

Then again, Clinton might have exported its J-9 motors ready-to-run.

Clipper

Another versatile outboard that could double as lawnmower power and vice versa, the Clipper lived the same 1950s to early 1960s life of many of its plentiful competitors. Clipper Products out of Carlton, New South Wales, developed a simple torque/exhaust tube lower unit (with 3:1 reduction gearbox) on which it fitted mills like the 82 cc Kirby Hi-Torque engine. Over its run, slight changes to the basic 2 hp kicker included power-head cowling. Clipper's "juice can" fuel tank eventually morphed into the improved shrouding. While it's not certain why Clipper got cut from the market, one might speculate that the outboard simply had trouble finding sufficient customers in Australia's overcrowded low-horsepower outboard industry.

Commando

Arguably one of Australia's first domestic outboards, the Commando appeared in consumer form during early 1948 as an unbranded offering of Stokoe Motors Pty., Ltd. The Melbourne firm's 3 hp @ 2,400 rpm, two-stroke single had originally been designed for World War II military use, so it had been built for applications calling for slow but powerful operation. An interesting Commando feature was a small canvas cover bagged over the "waterproof Lucas ignition." Early ads touted the outboard as being "built to Army and Navy specifications . . . [and the right] unit for men who want to breast the current, speed when required, and dependability. Easy to install . . . Can be removed in a couple of minutes. Ideal for barges, fishing craft or pleasure boats." Knowing that the Commando stood a good chance of saltwater use, Stokoe Motors bragged that the cylinder cooling passages on its 102-pound kicker had a "very large water space" supplied by an ample water pump. The utilitarian outboard swung a 10-inch prop, driven by 12:7 reduction gearing.

C-Powa

A play on the action-packed words "sea" and "power," C-Powa was an early 1950s outboard brand name that's easy to recall. Perhaps remem-

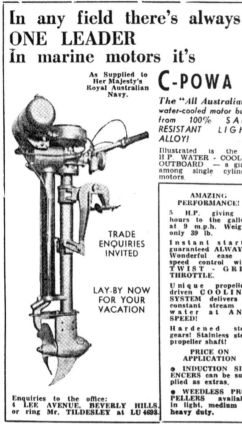
It's easy to see why the C-Powa might be mistaken for a British Seagull. Both had "juice can" tanks and a salt-resistant exhaust tube and lower unit components. This 1953 model with a twist-grip throttle and propeller-driven cooling system was like ones used by the Royal Australian Navy. The manufacturer advertised that it would consider trade-ins on any new C-Powa.

bering the success of British Seagull kickers, the C-Powa people designed their motor to strongly resemble that famed U.K. boat motor. More than a knockoff, though, C-Powa sufficiently impressed officials in Her Majesty's Royal Australian Navy for them to order some motors. The outboard's components were indeed sturdy, saltwater resistant, and nicely finished. Representative of C-Powa output from the maker's Beverly Hills (Australia) factory was a 5 hp model that weighed just under 40 pounds. Though a quality local product, C-Powa production ran out of gas during the early 1960s.

Cromac

"America's design. Quality built in Australia," headlined Cromac outboard ads of early 1959. At that point, Cromac Pty., Ltd., offered a 4 ½ hp "marine designed motor." It sought to distinguish itself from the many local competitors who concocted lower units from lawnmower engines. Bullets in typical Cromac publicity often touted:

- Automatic rewind starter and famous Baily magneto gives one pull start.
- Completely enclosed waterproof ignition system.
- Positive action clutch for easier starting and better boat handling.
- Adjustable, rubber bushed and padded mounting, means NO vibration.
- No old-fashioned shear pin. Rubber mounted propeller allows slip when obstruction is met.
- Constructed of non-corrosive alloys for lightness and long life.
- The sleek, streamlined Cromac is dependable and safe.

In fact, Cromac was a decent looking product and came from a Melbourne company that

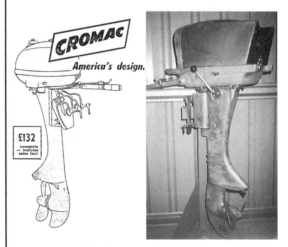

Left: Even simple advertising sketches of Cromac emphasized its American design. It did look a bit like a small Scott-Atwater. Few U.S. motors, though, had the bicycle shifter–type lever that Cromac used for a throttle control. *Right:* The 10 hp Cromac was prototyped in 1959, but it never went into production. The motor's styling is reminiscent of a late 1950s Scott of similar size.

seemed quite serious about outboarding. Dealer-ships were established in all of Australia's capital cities and country centers. Most importantly, though, the firm understood that in order to be truly competitive, they needed to developed a full line of Cromacs. To that end, engineers worked up very contemporary (for circa 1960) 10 and 50 hp prototypes. Alas, claims that they would soon be in dealer showrooms did not prove accurate. Stiff competition from other American designed out-boards—such as those from Mercury, Evinrude, Johnson, and West Bend—probably thwarted the ambitious Cromac expansion project.

Dependable

A footnote on an obscure specification sheet sim-ply identifies the Dependable outboard brand as having been equipped with Hurricane grass-cutter engines. It's another low-power, low production motor from the 1950s.

Close examination of this Dependable kicker reveals the sizable exhaust manifold piped down to the motor leg. Also evident is the mill's heritage as a lawn-mower engine. Note how the shrouding falls short of the cylinder head and spark plug. (Loch Sport Antique Marine Engine Museum)

Dolphin

A 7 hp motor was considered pretty big stuff for a 1950s Australian outboard, and Dolphin had one in its line. Cambridge Manufacturing in Bowen Hills, Brisbane, equipped its Hi-Power Dolphin 7 with a 180 cc air-cooled mill, a 2 ½:1 lower unit reduction gear, and a high-pitched, four-blade propeller. That combo yielded just 10 to 12 knots, but it delivered respectable power. Also in the line were the Dolphin Standard 4 (horsepower) and Deluxe Four, also with air-cooling. Originally, both sizes

1959 seemed to hold enough promise for Cambridge Manufacturing to take out full-page ads in Australian boat-ing magazines for its Dolphin outboards. British-built J.A.P. mills were used for Dolphin power. The line's deluxe kicker was interestingly shrouded, making space for a generous exhaust manifold on the engine's air-cooled cylinder.

were set atop basic lower units with separate drive and exhaust tubes. The fours could be ordered without rewind start and exhaust pipe, allowing for 360-degree steering. By 1959, a pleas-antly streamlined lower unit—with full reverse swiveling—got fitted to the 4 and 7 hp motors. Cowling on the Hi-Power Dolphin received a bit of a facelift, too. Regardless, the brand began por-poising and then dove under around 1964.

Ell-Den

"Motor-mow on Saturday, then motor-boat on Sun-day," suggested Ell-Den Industries' 1960 advertis-ing. Actually, the Sydney firm didn't market a whole outboard. Rather, it offered parsimonious boaters a simple lower unit and a "rapid conver-sion kit" to adapt lawnmower engines from Victa, Villiers, Hurricane, Pope, or Kirby Motor Mower to the Ell-Den outboard drive.

Evenride

Like opening a new hamburger place and calling it McDonnell's, the Evenride outboard people probably hoped to receive a bit of status conferral from the world-renowned Evinrude name. While undoubtedly functional, the Evenride was a world apart from its U.S.-based, quasi-namesake. In fact, Evenride models were really a province of a very generic lower unit and various air-cooled lawnmower engines, such as the 2 hp British J.A.P., the 3 ½ hp Victa, or the 4 ½ hp English Villiers. In July of 1958, Evenride advertising noted that one manufacturer—Lawrence Brothers of Peakhurst, New South Wales—also offered kits to adapt one's mower engine to an Evenride lower unit. With the kit came an "extended carburettor manifold for protection from heavy seas." How placing the carburetor further from the engine helped keep it away from salt spray is unknown. Possibly, though, the extension facilitated some sort of air intake water resistance. Customers could pick from two or three-blade props that were driven via a gearbox of "hardened nickel steel gears, four bearings, and two seals." The Lawrence Brothers assured Evenride buyers that "life-long service and spares" would be available. Even so, the brand with that familiar-sounding name was discontinued sometime in the early 1960s.

Gold Cheetah

Close your eyes and picture how exotic an outboard named "Gold Cheetah" might look! The actual motor might not match your expectations unless you're partial to "juice can" fuel tanks and air-cooled lawnmower engines on two-tube lower units. Appearances aside, the Gold Cheetah was a sturdily built kicker sporting a 7 ½-cubic-inch motor that yielded 125 pounds of propeller thrust (as opposed to a horsepower rating). McPherson's, Ltd., the company who carried these motors, suggested that "if after years of running you require an engine overhaul . . . replacement powerheads [were] available at extremely low cost."

Horton

H. S. Horton of Toronto, New South Wales, wrote to an Australian boating magazine to say he owned a locally produced electric outboard. At first the publication was "disinclined to believe him," but a snapshot of the troller in use on his rowboat con-vinced the editors. It turned out that Horton invented and built the Aussie electric kicker so that he might find a manufacturer interested in producing the straight-shaft outboard. Interestingly, Horton's (circa early 1950s) electric motor was yoked to a bracket that mounted on the boat's stern seat.

Hurricane

It's not certain whether Hurricane-branded kickers were actually built. Instead, the author speculates that Hurricane lawnmower engines fitted to lower unit conversion kits might have been referred to as an actual Hurricane outboard motor.

King

Oddball motor buffs would smile at the sight of a 1957 King outboard from Alec's Boat Centre of Mascot. That's because it was unashamedly a forward-pointing, single-cylinder, air-cooled lawnmower engine clumsily crowned on a modest lower unit. King's rear-mounted "juice can" fuel tank hung high over a little aft steering bar, and a fat exhaust pipe stuck out of the cylinder and then connected to the top of the lower unit. Reportedly, there were King outboards in 2, 3, and 4 hp denominations, with a 16 hp version "in preparation." It's doubtful that the big motor ever made it past the proposal stage.

Kingfisher

Ads bragged that the new 1958 Kingfisher model 82 was "undoubtedly the finest outboard ever designed." That's big praise for what was ostensibly a 2 hp Kirby Hi-Torque mower engine atop an American Clinton or Eska-style lower unit. Savvy outboarders probably enjoyed a chuckle from Kingfisher's advertised features, which included the universal claim to saltwater boaters: "Can be hosed down after use!" Hipsleys Ltd., of East Sydney assembled the Kingfisher, which—all exaggeration aside—made for a decent little (33 pounds) outboard package. Some circa 1960 sources identify Kingfisher as a product of the marine retailer Kopsen's.

Marlin

Even surpassing the "old college try" of Riptide, the Marlin outboard line was one of Australia's most ambitious. In 1959, for example, the brand

The 1959 Marlin model 346 yielded 18 hp.

took the form of a respectable looking 18 hp alternate-firing Sportwin, as well as a well-built 5 hp. With its fiberglass hood and relatively streamlined lower unit, the bigger one was reminiscent of a comparable U.S. product. Sportwin was arguably the nation's most powerful homegrown outboard. Marlin Outboard and Watercraft Company hailed from Geelong, Victoria.

Mermaid

Another all Australian putt-putt, Mermaid emanated from the Smithurst and Son plant in Caringbah. By spring 1957, the firm marketed Mermaid by advertising that its powerhead was actually an air-cooled, 125 cc Victa lawnmower engine. In fact, Smithurst would be happy to sell boaters a complete, ready-to-run Mermaid or a "special conversion unit available to owners of Victa Mowers." For information regarding the latter applications, customers were simply asked to send Smithurst the Victa engine number from their cutter. Some

The Mermaid folks made no attempt to disguise their kicker's lawnmower power. Instead, their ads touted the 125 cc Victa brand mower engine that crowned Mermaid's basic lower unit. A few loosened nuts would separate the two.

versions of Mermaid got mated to Hurricane power mower engines.

Nowa

Plastic powerhead cowling gave this low-powered kicker an economical hat over its air-cooled, single-cylinder head. Probably also offered as a conversion kit, as well as a ready-to-run outboard, Nowa was current in the 1960s.

Olympic

Sometimes called the Australian Olympic, this British Seagull-like single wore a slow-but-sure four-blade propeller. The little engine was water-cooled.

Pathfinder and Penguin

Research is ongoing into the histories of these outboard brands.

Randall-Albatross

Not much is recalled about this low-power outboard, which sported a Hurricane lawnmower engine.

Riptide

The Riptide Outboard Motor Company of Bexley, New South Wales, produced one of Australia's most complete outboard lines. Their top model was a handsome alternate-firing twin. Its cast aluminum and corrugated sheet metal cowling resembled an American Mercury Mark 30 or Mark 55. This Riptide Sportsman began life (circa 1958) with 7 hp, got rerated at 7 ½, then went to 8 hp by 1960. It was one of the only locally built outboards to sport a remote fuel tank. All three models of this

serious marque were touted as being genuine, water-cooled marine engines, as opposed to converted lawnmower motors. Each had its own little advertising poem. This is Sportsman's:

> Riptide "Sportsman" saves you wishing
> For those extra knots you need
> Sweet to hear the bow waves swishing
> "Sportsman's" got both power and speed.

Smaller and lower priced was the Riptide Boatman, a 2 ½ hp single designed in the British Seagull style. Also in the tradition of simplicity, ruggedness, and easily accessed parts was the Fisherman, which wore detachable heads on its opposed twin cylinders and generated 4 hp. A deluxe version of the Fisherman made use of the Merc-like top cowl of the Sportsman, so the fuel tank could be shrouded and a rewind starter could be attached. Cut to fit Fisherman's opposed jugs, this use of what was originally a Sportsman part made the smaller motor look a bit like a little kid with big ears wearing an oversize baseball cap.

It is apparent that Riptide had every intention of being a long-lived presence in Australia's small boating milieu. In 1956, Len Sheltrum, who managed an automotive engineering firm, envisioned building an Australian outboard that "compared favorably with the best from the United States." The Merc-like Sportsman resulted. As the March 1959 issue of *Seacraft* reported, "outwardly this motor looks like an American production. It is

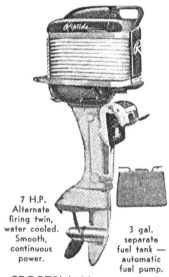

7 H.P.
Alternate
firing twin,
water cooled.
Smooth,
continuous
power.

3 gal.
separate
fuel tank —
automatic
fuel pump.

SPORTSMAN

Riptide "Sportsman" saves you wishing
For those extra knots you need.
Sweet to hear the bow wave swishing.
"Sportsman's" got both power and
speed.

Riptide officials were not shy about imitating the styling of their favorite American outboard. The company's Sportsman twin mimicked a Mercury Mark 30, but it possessed two fewer cylinders than that Merc and was 23 hp less powerful.

A 1959 Riptide Sportsman. This one offered 7 ½ hp.

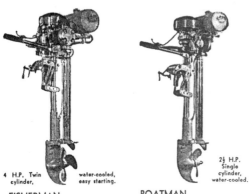

4 H.P. Twin cylinder, water-cooled, easy starting.

FISHERMAN

Riptide "Fisherman's" got power.
All-weather use on fishing waters.
Speed? Six to eight miles an hour.
Fun for self, wife, sons and daughters.

2½ H.P. Single cylinder, water-cooled.

BOATMAN

Riptide "Boatman" is the right mate
For your dinghy, skiff or tender,
30 pounds, so just a lightweight.
You should see the "Boatman" send'er.

While Riptide's crown jewel, the Sportsman, looked like a Mercury, the rest of the line consisted of kickers designed for boaters with an eye for the simple and rugged style of British Seagull outboards.

streamlined, finished in two tone baked enamel and is entirely enclosed. However it is not a copy of an American motor. [But, Sheltrum's Riptide] Company purchased one of each of the four leading Yankee engines—Mercury, Johnson Evinrude, and Scott—and minutely examined every component in each motor." While this reverse engineering resulted in a Mercury-esque top, the lower unit appears to be borrowed from Scott.

Of course, looks alone don't make a motor great. Service was a focus of almost every Riptide ad, such as this one: "Service and spares for all Riptides are Australia-wide. Every Riptide buyer receives two warrantys. One entitles him to free after sales adjustment service from any [of the numerous] Riptide dealer or Distributor. The other is the maker's warranty. Only Riptide gives you this dual nation-wide after-sales service." Unlike the promotional literature its local competition, company publicity also showed rows of completed

motors and the tank in which they'd been tested. In one photo, over twenty Fisherman motors appeared, proving that legitimate production efforts were undertaken at Riptide. By the summer of 1960, though, the Riptide Outboard Motor Company had sold out to Wescott, Hazell Industries, and moved manufacturing to its Sydney plant where production lasted only a few years.

Riverside

"For a smoother ride, choose Riverside!" shouted ads for the Riverside 3 ½ hp outboard motor. A single offered by Sydney's Cameron and Sutherland Sales, this kicker featured "recoil starter and pulley, strong one-piece [tower housing] body, case-hardened steel gears, heavy ball races [bearings] and Torrington needle races sealed against water, and propeller-driveshaft to the latest overseas style." While it's unclear how a mundane prop shaft exudes a particular style, fuzzy photos in Riverside literature hint that ad writers meant to tout Riverside's lower unit shape. It looked slightly more "overseas" than many of the kicker's local counterparts. Reportedly, the motor was current in the 1960s.

Riverside ads liked to tout the "overseas styling" of its lower unit. This Riverside is circa 1959 and exhibits decent motor leg and gearcase streamlining. Atop that assembly, though, is standard lawnmower power. (Loch Sport Antique Marine Engine Museum)

Seacraft. See Tornado.

Sea Hawk

New for 1972, the Sea Hawk used a 125 cc Victa T-S powerhead to enliven its basic lower unit. Notes in Sea Hawk ads pointed to a "3-blade propeller . . . Powerful, very easy starting with recoil starter . . . Australian made motor separates in a few minutes from leg assembly for compact stowing . . . Parts always available . . . Full 12 months guarantee, a genuine terrific bargain . . . Sent rail freight collect . . . 1000s [already] sold." Sea Hawk wore a power rating range in that it was called a 4 to 5 hp outboard motor. Because the brand's advertising often emphasized its price ($112 Australian dollars in 1972) with the largest print size, it seems that price was the little motor's most compelling feature.

Seamaster

One of Australia's cutest putt-putts, the Seamaster hit waterways circa 1947. This very early Aussie outboard produced 3 ½ hp (some sources say 3.3 @ 3,000 rpm) via an air-cooled mill. Seamaster's puffy little streamlined cowling lent it an endearing cartoonish look. Depending on how the motor was positioned when rope-starting, though, the cowl's front-mounted fuel cap could be in a direct path with the pull cord. Seamaster had a sister motor called Seasprite. Though water-cooled (compared to Seamaster's basic air-cooling), it was slightly cheaper and came without the nice shrouding.

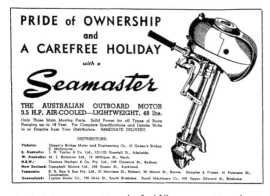

A 1948 Seamaster. Note the fuel filler cap positioned directly in front of starter pulley. The motor would need to be roped over carefully so as to not catch the cord on that cap.

This exposed a rather homely powerhead. Both were products of Australian Marine Engine Company of Melbourne. They were sold by retailers like A. W. Pryor of South Brisbane.

Sea Ride

Not much is currently remembered about Australian outboards branded with the Sea Ride moniker.

Seasprite

Anglers were targeted in most Seasprite advertising. That's because the seller of the 3.5 hp @ 3,000 rpm motor, A. W. Pryor of South Brisbane, figured them to be the likeliest market for their little kickers. Originally tagged with a 3.3 hp rating, the earliest Seasprites (circa 1947) were products of Melbourne's Australian Marine Engine Company.

In 1952, Seasprite was touted as "Australian made [so that] all parts [would] always be available [locally]." Reliability was said to have stemmed from a "flat top piston, variable jet carburettor, precision workmanship, only the best materials, special flywheel polar inductor magneto, and positive water-cooling."

By late 1958, a new Seasprite—looking identical to the original—was promoted by Pryor as "the measure of fishing pleasure." Reportedly, improvements included a "redesigned petrol tank, carburettor, choke assembly, and crankshaft." The maker always stated that Seasprite's Australian design and construction made the 40-pound outboard "an outstanding performer . . . and the obvious choice for the wise fisherman." In some ad layouts, depictions of fish were larger than an accompanying sketch of the motor. (See also Seamaster.)

The Seasprite was sister to the Seamaster. Though Seamaster was treated with streamlined shrouding, it was the stripped-down Seasprite that featured water-cooling. A smidgen of shrouding was added to this 1958 model to cover the spark plug.

Sea Tang

A rather extensive line—in terms of the 1960 Australian outboard industry—Brisbane's Owen Cox and Company offered four Sea Tang models. They included the 3 to 4 hp Tiger, the 4 hp Deluxe, the 4 to 5 hp Sea Tang, and a 10 to 12 hp Sea Tang. All were single-cylinder engines, and all but the largest were air-cooled.

Simplex

Simplex outboards from Hardman and Hall of Sydney mirrored the chronology of the lion's share of Australia's outboard makers. The motors were available from the late 1950s to the early 1960s. Typical of the air-cooled marque were the rope-start, 2 hp @ 3,000 rpm model S2 (introduced in the summer of 1957) and the more deluxe, rewind-equipped model S4.

Though gas, the S2 was reminiscent of a ¾ hp electric washing machine motor on a lower unit. A prominent starter pulley and "juice can" fuel tank completed the styling. The S4 was treated to more traditional component shrouding. Both models, however, sported a basic lower unit assembly with separate drive and exhaust tubes. The Australian maker proudly noted that Simplex's "only foreign components are the Bledetley carburetor and Wyco magneto—both famous English brands."

Speed

Introduced in late 1947, the Speed outboard was a 2.2 hp @ 3,750 rpm, water-cooled single. Davey's Auto Service in Melbourne and Sports Craft Company in Gladesville, New South Wales, are listed (in vintage publications) as makers, but it's likely they simply served as distributors for the 32 ½-pound kicker. A unique characteristic of this model was a cast flip-up top that could expose the flywheel. When closed, the hatch blended into the rest of the motor's streamlined shroud. Speed may be considered one of Australia's oldest locally made outboards.

Tasman

"Small, cheap outboard!" announced a little blurb for Stanmore's Tas Manufacturing Company, Pty., Ltd. It heralded that the Tasman was concocted by Tas via mating the most basic of outboard lower units with a 1 ½ hp two-stroke, air-cooled power-head. According to the presumed 1960 article, that power plant was a lightweight Japanese mill originally intended for modest lawnmowers and chainsaws. Tas co-opted it for their outboard package that weighed in at a nicely portable 23 pounds.

As a footnote to Tasman history, some sources list the kicker as a British product. What is likely, though, is that Tas Manufacturing did a bit of exporting as well as importing the engines from Japan.

Tornado

A British 75 cc Trojan engine provided power for the little Seacraft Tornado 75, offered by Seacraft Manufacturing Company of Mordialloc. Seacraft had a connection with the Ezycut Tool company and heralded their motor as "the most popular and efficient lightweight available." Tornado was fitted with an Amal carburetor—named for the *amal*gamation of a number of British carburetor makers—"with single lever control, Wico magneto, and built in fan to supply adequate draft of cooling air." Outboard shoppers were assured that a pulley, on which to wrap the starter cord, would be provided, and that the lower unit's 2:1 reduction drive gears had been "fully enclosed and run in grease." Like those of many local competitors, Tornado's castings had been fabricated with "L-33, a well known salt resistant [silicon aluminum] alloy." Seacraft Tornados were on the market from about 1952 to 1960.

Triton

As readers can ascertain from various narratives in this volume, vintage advertising often provides the only remaining documentation for historical outboard research. That understood, the claim that the Triton was "made by one of Australia's most experienced engineering firms, except for [the motor's] English Solex carburettor and English Wico Pacy magneto," is a bit baffling. Triton outboards were most certainly badge-engineered British Motor Boat Manufacturing Company, Ltd., (BMB) Britannia Swordfish motors of British origin.

An opposed water-cooled twin with detachable cylinder heads, the 165 cc, 5 hp @ 3,000 rpm Triton (née Swordfish) was, as ads headlined, "built as an outboard, not a [lawnmower engine to lower unit/adapter] conversion." Boat Supplies Pty., Ltd., of Sydney and Drummoyne, New South

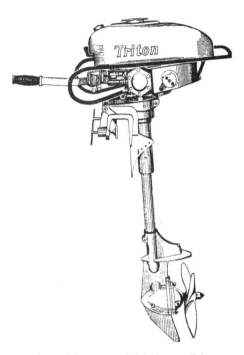

Triton began life as an English-built Swordfish. Removable cylinder heads on the opposed twin facilitated water jacket servicing.

Wales, handled Triton, reiterating that it was the "best outboard ever made locally." It's possible that, rather than a relabeled U.K. import, Triton got built under license by BMB or some successor. Perhaps the Boat Supplies people acquired the British firm's outboard rights and/or assets. There are also summer 1960 references to the Triton being a proprietary brand of retailer Kopsen. These folks also handled the Kingfisher.

In any event, Triton got treated to a pretty "aquamarine enameled fuel tank with chrome guardrail, stainless steel torque tube, drive shaft and propeller shaft, cylinder liners . . . and kit of tools [including a] grease gun." Though presented as a sure shot in the late 1950s, Triton sales ran out of ammunition in the early 1960s.

Verity

Rivaling the Commando for the honor of being the first Australian-built outboard, Verity arrived on the boating scene during the summer of 1947. Its manufacturer, A. V. Sale, Ltd., got interested in entering the outboard business during World War

The 1948 Verity was one of Australia's first homegrown outboards. Its front-positioned fuel tank cap could play havoc with the starter rope.

II when the firm "maintained and serviced hundreds of different types of outboards for the Defense Department." While such numbers are hyperbolic, Verity was born from that experience and was purported to have the best of leading overseas (such as Evinrude and Johnson) designs. In fact, the motor looked a bit like a Sears Waterwitch, Muncie Neptune, or prewar Champion.

The water-cooled, opposed-twin motor developed between 3.3 and 5 hp @ 3,800 rpm. No doubt Sale engineers noticed that other motors suffered from saltwater residue–clogged cylinder cooling jackets. Consequently, the Verity got fitted with removable cylinder heads and "exceptionally large water jackets. The company seemed quite proud of their motor's "scientifically designed submarine exhaust which produce only a pleasant purr at low speeds." It appears, though, that this device was simply an exhaust pipe running from the muffler to the water. Verity's designers chose a steering arrangement by which the tiller turned only the lower unit. There, depending on their hull's weight, customers could opt for either an 8- or 9-inch two-blade propeller.

Victa-Jet

Unlike the most basic hydro-thrust outboards, Victa-Jet employed a lower unit water output positioned to shoot slightly above the lake or sea surface. This gave it more zip than units exiting the

water several inches under the boat. Victa-Jets' model CJ 920-A4 from about 1970 serves as an example of the marque. Its power came from a single cylinder Victa lawnmower engine with the "fabulous *Zip* starter" that the firm was already producing for the homeowner market.

Waterboy

"For pleasure, work, or emergency, it's Waterboy for boating joy," promised 1960 ads for Atom Distributing Company (a Dangar, Gedye, and Malloch sudsidiary) in Burwood, Victoria. At first glance, North American outboarders might mistake these kickers for a small, air-cooled Elgin, West Bend, or Chrysler. While indeed air-cooled (but with a water-cooled exhaust chamber), Waterboy outboards were powered by two-stroke engines unique to Australia. At least four models made up the line: a 2 hp (with Trojan powerhead), as well as 3, 5, and 6 hp versions using Hurricane-brand mills. The marque had been introduced in the 1950s to be sold "in gay colour tonings . . . at all leading stores throughout Australia." Although given the opportunity for wide distribution, Waterboy sales never grew large enough, and the company submerged during the 1960s.

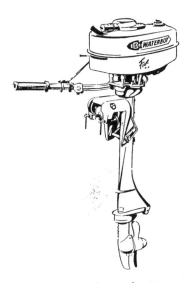

Though externally a dead ringer for a 1950s U.S.-built Clinton or West Bend, Waterboy's internal power originated from the smaller Trojan and Hurricane engines often found in English and Australian outboard and mower applications.

United Kingdom

"In view of the demand that exists for outboard motors in this country," editorialized a 1919 issue of the English maritime publication, *The Motor Ship and Motor Boat*, "it is a little surprising that hitherto only one model has been built in the U.K., and this, so far as we know, was never manufactured on a commercial scale." By late spring of that year, however, Watermota outboards, clones of the forward-pointing, single-cylinder American Waterman, were being manufactured in a modest U.K. machine shop. During the 1920s and 1930s, at least a dozen new British outboard brands hit the local market. And one, produced at the Sunbeam motorcycle plant, morphed into British Seagull, which became the U.K.'s most loved outboard export.

World War II ensured that little in the way of pleasure boating would be enjoyed anywhere from the early to mid-1940s. The British Isles' urgent need for scrap metal surely consumed most of the country's stock of antique outboards. At hostilities' end, though, the English outboard industry started rebuilding with a modest offering (such as the Ferrier) here and there, as well as through a few relatively aggressive lines such as British Anzani and Perkins. Quietly, though, and without much notice from other business sectors, the 1950s saw the entrepreneurial production of dozens of English outboard models. Much of this ignition was fueled by the heavy import duties that made American outboards very expensive in Britain's "export or die" immediate postwar economy. Some buffs say circa 1948 through the early 1960s was the most vibrant in the U.K.'s outboard history. Unfortunately, the glory dimmed considerably when tariffs began easing in about 1959, and U.S. motors suddenly became less expensive to acquire. Eventually, only British Seagull survived, but it had its share of rough times near the close of the twentieth century.

The following offers a glimpse into each known English outboard brand. Many have been "rediscovered" via tattered listings in old magazines. The author is especially grateful to British boating historians Peter Allen, Rod Champkin, and Colin B. Wilson for their research efforts. They contributed mightily to this chronicling of the U.K.'s rich outboarding past.

Ailsa-Craig

A mysterious World War 1–era marque, The Ailsa-Craig Motor Company in London was said to have marketed an outboard in 1914. Enigmatically, British outboard history as outlined in the 12 February 1932 issue of *The Motor Boat* makes no mention of Ailsa-Craig and identifies Watermota as the earliest English outboard motor. It is known that the firm did offer high-speed diesel marine (inboard) engines, and they either had a dalliance in outboard production or badge-engineered someone else's kickers in order to test the detachable market.

Anzani. See British Anzani.

Apex. See Coventry Apex.

Aquajet

One of the world's very first water-thrust outboards, Aquajet Minor hit the U.K. boating market in 1946. It was described as a 98 cc, water-cooled, two-stroker capable of 3 to 3 ½ hp @ 3,000 rpm. This powerhead was enclosed in a teardrop-shaped (when observing it from above) cowl treated to dye anodization. *Motor Boat & Yachting* editors tested an Aquajet in their May 1946 issue and found it "specially pleasing . . . smooth and vibration-free running especially for a single cylinder unit. They also noticed "the complete absence of exhaust smell."

As one might gather, the unit's model name, "Minor," left the door open for a larger, or "Major" version. By 1948, there was another Aquajet with a slightly bigger engine but no gain over Minor in

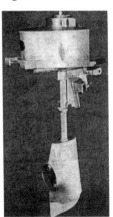

Britain's Aquajet was about a decade and a half ahead of the slew of U.S.-built small hydrojet thrust "squirters" that sought outboard market share during the early 1960s. Aquajet's first incarnation looked a bit like a province of the home workshop, but its powerhead cowling gained a more professionally contoured appearance by 1950.

actual horsepower. R. M. Parkinson, Ltd., of Cheltenham, was listed as the producer of this 3 hp @ 3,000 rpm squirt. Like the first one, its single-cylinder, 123 cc engine drove a horizontal impeller to quicken the water. One might say Aquajet's bulky lines are crude by today's standards, but the 50-pound, full-reverse, swivel-steering motor was an admirable effort for a small U.K. firm not long after World War II. By late 1949, the novel motor had received more sophisticated cowling and a new maker, Kenneth Long and Company, Ltd.

Aspin

A smartly styled motor in the midst of many mechanical-looking competitors, the Aspin Five-Point-Five was British built by F. M. Aspin and Company, Ltd. The Elton, Bury, Lancashire, firm debuted its nicely contoured outboard around 1957. A surviving example is serialized 59 L 0138. Such coding can't hide the suggestion that Aspin was a low production, short-lived product, with perhaps only 138 built in or by 1959.

Possessing a single, air-cooled cylinder, the powerhead was advertised as an Aspin engine and was not an outsourced mill. Other useful features were the twist-grip throttle control, remote fuel tank, and full F-N-R gearshift. Externally, Aspin was reminiscent of the slightly larger and notably streamlined Medina, which also hailed from the late 1950s.

Atco

After World War II, many British manufacturers enthusiastically sought suggestions that might lead their companies into sensible diversification.

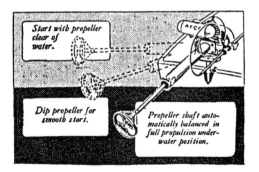

Though employing a simpler propulsion system than conventional (lower unit geared) outboards, Atco's direct-drive operation was often explained in its ads.

When first marketed, the Atco Boatimpeller was usually mentioned alongside its maker's Motor Mower as the lawn care machine, and its network of parts and service dealerships was well known throughout the U.K.

At lawnmower maker Charles H. Pugh, Ltd., someone said an outboard motor would be a natural extension of Pugh's Atco product line, and a little kicker with an extended lower unit was designed. One of the firm's mowers received power from a spunky, two-stroke, air-cooled, 79 cc Villiers mill.

During 1946, they proposed to adapt this reliable engine to a direct-drive lower unit. Execs imagined that such a simple outboard would become the worldwide standard. Tests on the resulting prototypes were conducted throughout Europe, beginning in 1947. Bugs were worked out, and the Birmingham-based concern put its new Atco Boatimpeller into production in the fall of 1948. Weighing 44 pounds and producing just 0.6 hp, the Boatimpeller possessed one of the heaviest weight-to-horsepower ratios in the business. In practice, though, it made for a useful package that could be easily carried after quickly disconnecting the Villiers powerhead from the matching Atco lower unit. When assembled, the novel outboard measured 64 inches from rope-start flywheel to

propeller protector cage. Atco sold an accessory self-priming pump, which could be conveniently substituted for the outboard drive. It would clear over 3 gallons per minute from flooded cellars, or (with optional spray jet) it could be used for horticultural spraying.

By 1950, Charles H. Pugh, Ltd., had collected correspondence from hundreds of satisfied Atco Boatimpeller users, including a fellow in the Shetland Islands who used his to ferry sheep. Holiday resorts (with "hire" boats) also reported in, expressing pleasure about the motor's ease of use and reliability. And in 1949, when the River Avon flooded out parts of Warwickshire, an Atco-powered dinghy maneuvered an inspection party through the countryside, coping nicely with flotsam and slightly submerged fences.

In fact, it was Boatimpeller's ability to navigate shallow or weedy water that earned it praise. That's not to say scores of them didn't get used in the ocean, but the product's biggest fans were shallow water boaters tired of changing shear pins on their conventional outboards. The author had occasion to use a 1950 model in the shallows of a river reservoir and was delighted with the motor's adjustable pivot balance feature that allows for easy steering. When the tiller is released, a properly adjusted Atco keeps its prop just beneath the water's surface. (As Atco information predicts, that's "about 30 degrees to the horizontal.") There was no torque to fight. The outboard started easily, plus it took the 12-foot aluminum rowboat anywhere it could float. Even a stubborn hunk of weeds was easily cleared after shutting off the engine and swinging the lower unit inboard for quick untangling.

The new ATCO BOATIMPELLER

The 1950 Atco Boatimpeller. Ads promised it would work well in just 4 inches of water.

By the early 1960s, several Atco Boatimpeller sizes were offered, including a 70 cc, 1 ¼ hp model dubbed the AB-Two-and-a-Quarter, and the 147 cc, 3 hp job called the AB-Five-and-a-Half. It's not known why those letters and numbers were chosen, but it might have been to give the impression to outboard shoppers that they were bigger than their actual rated horsepower. Actually the 147 cc version had been introduced (albeit with just 1.8 hp) in 1951 with the more sensible moniker, "Atco Boatimpeller 147." No matter what Pugh called it, most outboard buyers gravitated towards motors sporting conventional lower units. Circa 1917, officials at the Detroit-based Caille outboard factory predicted that their Atco-like Liberty Drive outboard would cause the geared-type kicker to become obsolete within a decade. Of course, their prophecy failed. Years later, the Atco folks came to the conclusion that this was simply not going to be the case for their product either. Although they catered for a long time to a loyal niche market, Atco decided it would be better for business to discontinue the manufacture of the Boatimpeller around 1965.

Bantam. See J.S.L.

Basil Engineering

For 1962, Basil Engineering Company, Ltd., advertised a trio of single-cylinder outboards: a 76.4 cc, 2 to 2 ½ hp @ 3,800 rpm model, a standard 105 cc kicker producing 4 to 5 hp @ 3,800 rpm, and a deluxe version of the latter with neutral clutch. As was the case with most small (and large) British outboards, one could order a long shaft option.

Bermuda

The vintage Scott motorcycle power plant got recycled in the form of 1959–63 Bermuda outboards from the B.R.D. Company, Ltd., of Aldridge, Staffordshire. While several sizes (from 395 cc with 22 hp to 695 cc with 45 hp) of the water-cooled, two-cycle, alternate-firing twin were transplanted into the Bermuda, nicely representative of the offering was the Bermuda Mark III-Electric. This 1963 outboard sported the 675 cc (41-cubic-inch) erstwhile motorcycle mill, developed 40 hp, started electrically, and charged its own battery. Reportedly, the powerhead—fitted with a Solex downdraft carburetor—could be removed from the

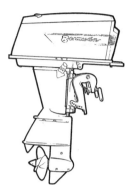

Looking a bit like the early 1960s Evinrude Lark 40 or the Johnson Sea Horse 40, the Bermuda was actually based on a motorcycle engine. Its manufacturer, B.R.D. Company, touted the outboard as "all British, trial tested, and race winning." The latter claim referred to the eighteen speed trophies the motor won and to the week-long endurance runs that the motor participated in during its first year of sales.

lower unit by simply loosening three bolts. Single- or double-lever remote controls were available.

Also notable was the 1961 Bermuda 2-40 (two cylinders, 40 hp). Descriptive model names included the 22 and 40 hp Workman (with low ratio lower unit gearing), the 45 hp Skeeman (for high-speed waterskiing), and the Sportsman, which was described as "the super speed engine for racing and skiing." Its advertisements cheered, "Powerful Fun! All British and proud of it!," and often depicted the motor's use in family outings. This contrasted with many other local makers' ads, which simply showed the engine and its specifications.

B.R.D. strove for customer satisfaction, so it publicized its 12-month guarantee and promise to render spare parts to Bermuda owners on a 24-hour basis. The plant also maintained a repair shop and conducted off-season overhaul service. Though thoughtful on the part of the manufacturer, its target market was attracted to big U.S. outboard manufacturers almost immediately after English import tariffs were lowered.

Berning

Colorful brochures for Regina outboards from Outboard Motors, Ltd., of Whitstable, Kent, appeared around 1954. Drawings of these machines looked to be straight off the sketchpad of some futuristic industrial designer. In fact, the only comparable rocket-age renderings belonged to the mysterious American brand Power-Pak. The company was not the manufacturer but served as Regina's U.K. distributor. The motors actually came from Europe where they sold under

the Regina name. Outboard Motors' circa 1960 catalog showed the same ultrastreamlined motors, but they carried the Berning brand. Reportedly, the Regina name was too closely connected to the Queen of England's moniker, necessitating a quick rebadge job. Four models are touted:

- Model 100: 4.5 hp @ 4,500 rpm (single cylinder)
- Model 125: 5.6 hp @ 4,500 rpm (6 hp on the Berning version, single cylinder)
- Model 250: 15 hp @ 4,500 rpm (alternate-firing twin, full gearshift, remote 4-gallon tank, electric starting, generator, and plug for 6-volt lighting)
- Model 250SS (racer): 18 hp @ 6,000 rpm (alternate-firing twin with dual Amal carburetors, remote 4-gallon tank, optional electric starting)

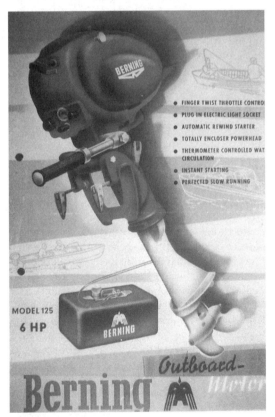

The Berning line was produced in Europe as the Regina. That moniker's similarity to a royal name of the Queen of England, however, necessitated the change to Berning.

Central to these elaborate outboards was a built-in (to the front cowl) thermometer "to show the temperature of the (cooling) water which can be adjusted to climatical conditions." From an outboard lover's point of view, though, even in the coldest seawater, these machines looked hot!

BMB. See Britannia.

B.R.D. See Bermuda.

Britannia

The Britannia outboard epic begins in 1932 and includes several trade names for what was essentially the same Depression-era motor. Actually, the brand started with the formation of the London-based British Motor Boat Manufacturing Company, Ltd. Dubbed BMB for short, this organization was founded by boat racer Hubert Scott-Paine, who endeavored to sell small boats and American Elto motors and who possibly made hulls and outboards.

Under the engineering guidance of executive J. W. Shillan, and chief engineer C. H. Harrison, the firm had developed by late 1932 the 4 hp @ 3,000 rpm Britannia Light-Twin, a quality-built, reliable water-cooled, opposed twin that ads claimed "you can flog without failure or trouble." Shillan tried to get a U.S. company to build motors in England but was rebuffed. For that reason and under the influence of a nationalistic "Buy British" campaign, he set out to create the Britannia. Interestingly, early publicity for Britannia often included a little space

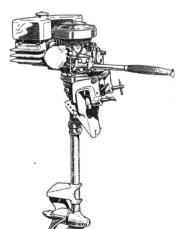

The 1932 Britannia yielded 4 hp and spawned several other outboards that used its basic opposed-twin powerhead.

For small boaters preferring inboard power and a nice steering wheel, Britannia offered its outboard in this "through-hull" inboard style. While it might seem that most mariners would recognize the greater logic of outboard simplicity, more than a few opted for Britannia's Middy inboard model.

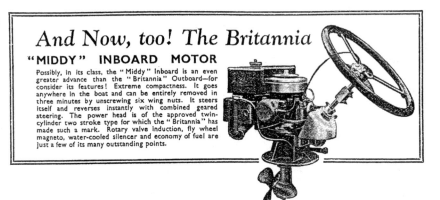

And Now, too! The Britannia

"MIDDY" INBOARD MOTOR

Possibly, in its class, the "Middy" Inboard is an even greater advance than the "Britannia" Outboard—for consider its features! Extreme compactness. It goes anywhere in the boat and can be entirely removed in three minutes by unscrewing six wing nuts. It steers itself and reverses instantly with combined geared steering. The power head is of the approved twin-cylinder two stroke type for which the "Britannia" has made such a mark. Rotary valve induction, fly wheel magneto, water-cooled silencer and economy of fuel are just a few of its many outstanding points.

to plug some Elto that BMB was marketing as part of their distribution deal with the U.S. company. They even expressed interest in accepting trade-in motors from their Elto or Britannia shoppers. In time, promotion appeared for inboard versions of Britannia's powerhead. The most notable, a vertically mounted inboard, got dubbed BMB Mariner, and it rotated when steered with a wheel geared into the column connected to the motor base.

During the 1930s, slight internal changes were made in the Britannia powerhead. These included better rotary valving that allowed for a 5

THE *New* OUTBOARD

Britannia's successors might not have reinvented the wheel, but circa 1950, they dressed-up their twenty-year-old outboard design with a modern fuel tank and cowl assembly and new name—Swordfish.

hp version in 1934. Cooling water intakes were repositioned and a three-blade prop made available. In 1937 its initial 172 cc displacement got eased back to 165 cc, and the motor was rechristened the 4 hp Britannia Ensign. To modernize its appearance, circa 1948, Britannia used a streamlined fuel tank that encircled the flywheel, replacing the original rear-mounted unit. In this form, the motor mimicked a late 1930s Evinrude or Sportwin.

Around 1949, BMB was acquired by Brockhouse Engineering, Ltd., which quickly indicated that the "BMB" would now stand for "British Made by Brockhouse." They revamped Britannia into the Swordfish, "a new outboard motor conserving all the fine qualities of the famous BMB Britannia and embodying also some very attractive additional features." These, like the new spray shield/shroud (though the rope start flywheel sheave still stuck out), were mostly cosmetic. Customers could choose their Britannia Swordfish in a range of three colors: light green, cambridge blue, or sky blue. Knowing that Swordfish engines were often used live in salt water though, Brockhouse continued using phosphor bronze for all underwater bearings, plus a stainless steel driveshaft. It advertised both Britannia and Swordfish models, the former being the "conventional [1930s exposed powerhead] design." Swordfish got promoted as the "streamlined" version, and a Swordfish Mark IIIA Deluxe model was likely fitted with rewind starting or some other easily adaptable convenience.

It appears that Swordfish was current through about 1957–59, at which time a reincarnation labeled Triton appeared in Australia. This one

wore detachable cylinder heads and somehow gained horsepower (to 5 hp @ 3,000 rpm) over its predecessor. The motor lived on into the 1960s. Not a bad run for a 1930-style outboard that was simply redecorated several times.

Brit Engineering

A mid-1950s to early 1960s product, Brit's outboard wore a 79.9 cc, J.A.P two-stroke, air-cooled single. It generated 1 ½ hp @ 2,500 rpm and was typically equipped with a rewind starter. Introduced during the fall of 1956, the little kicker came from Brit Engineering in Bridport, Dorset, a firm that had produced inboard engines since about 1905. Touted on the debut Brit was its "telescopic tiller," which was equipped with throttle control and maintained the boat's optimal plane. Savvy about seawater, the motor maker fitted its "juice can" fuel tank outboard with a stainless steel propeller shaft. Especially interesting was Brit's centrifugal clutch assembly, which was positioned between the powerhead and the driveshaft.

British Anzani

The British Anzani Engineering Company, Ltd., began as a U.K. repair shop for airplanes with French Anzani engines during World War 1. By the 1920s, the firm named for engineer, motorcycle racer, and engine maker Alessandro Anzani, was operating as an autonomous company. It produced power plants like a V-Twin cycle engine. Perhaps noting some motorcycle companies' diversification forays into the outboard market (Sunbeam/Seagull and Dunelt, for example), British Anzani (sometimes simply referred to as Anzani) executives got involved with the pursuit.

By 1950, they were offering a respectable line of outboards, including the beautifully shrouded tiny Minor (though, sans cowling, its 1949 incarnation featured a front-mounted, kidney-shaped tank, and only ½ hp instead of the subsequent ¾ hp rating). Also notable for 1950, the 4 hp, forward-pointing, single-cylinder Super Single was co-opted from the old Sharland line. Originally fitted with a chain-drive external magneto, the Sharland was upgraded by Anzani via a more tenable flywheel magnet.

During this early postwar era, Anzani's Hampton Hill, Middlesex, plant turned out the first

of its several respectable racing outboards. The firm's May 1950 advertising identified the British Anzani 14 hp Sports Twin as the "first post-war racing engine to be produced in this country [England] or America." And, except for a few competition motors from Randolph Hubbell's fledgling California shop, this was indeed true. What made the Sports Twin racer (and standard service version) unique were the twin forward-pointing cylinders on separate crankshafts that geared into the driveshaft.

During the later 1950s, Anzani engineers dropped this unorthodox, albeit successful in its initial days, design so that an in-line, alternate-firing, twin-cylinder arrangement could be followed. The resulting Unitwin models of 10 and 15 hp with 15- and 20-cubic-inch displacement, proved themselves good performers. And souped-up, streamlined lower unit versions, dubbed Competition Unitwins, set speed records for class A (15-cubic-inch) and class B (20-cubic-inch) engines.

Joining the late 1950s Anzani lineup was one of the strangest looking production outboards of all time. The Magnatwin, an 18 hp electric starting model based on the bigger Unitwin, wore a bulky, bulbous shroud that caused it to appear either homemade or like a refugee from a sci-fi movie about evil robots. Few of the other Anzanis (except the remarkably cute ¾ hp Minor) were sold with cowling, so officials must have figured that goofy shrouds wouldn't cause problems. Magnatwin's "bigger than a breadbox" bonnet and separate exhaust and driveshaft tubes, however, were bound to cause some folks to wonder, "What the . . . ?" After all, streamlined, one-piece lower units on larger motors were considered a "must" by most circa 1960 outboard buyers.

Decades ago, a wayward British copy of J. Lee Richardson's *Outboard Boating* fell into the hands of the author and his outboard expert buddies. A Magnatwin-powered cruiser floated on the book's cover. After sustained laughter, we agreed we'd never seen a weirder outboard. Of course, in vintage motor collecting terms, the Magnatwin is now a sought-after item. Incidentally, early Magnatwins had a 12-volt electrical system. By 1962, new versions were being fitted with 24-volt components and had separate batteries and a remote 4 ½-gallon fuel tank. All that junk was stuffed under the original Magnatwin hood. And, like early

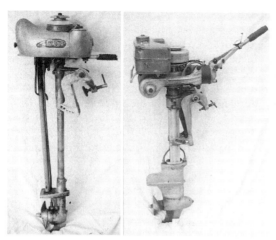

Left: Some call this Anzani Minor "Britain's cutest outboard." Introduced circa 1949 as a ½ hp mill with no cowls, it was soon upgraded to a ¾ hp kicker and fitted with a little "elf's hat" shroud. (Champkin collection) *Right:* British Anzani's Super Single of the 1950s was a redux of the old 4 hp Sharland. These are among the only outboards in which the tiller is connected to a cylinder head. (Champkin collection)

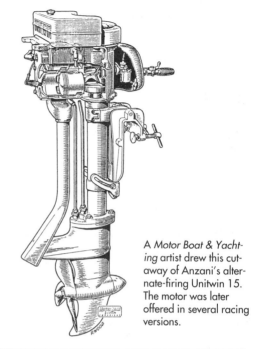

A *Motor Boat & Yachting* artist drew this cut-away of Anzani's alternate-firing Unitwin 15. The motor was later offered in several racing versions.

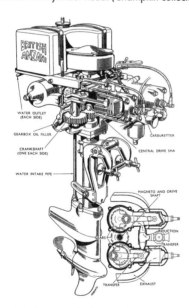

Two crankshafts, two cylinders, and a gearbox! This 14 hp 1950 Anzani Sports Twin Racer was developed from a pair of the firm's forward-pointing singles. Most marine history buffs consider it to be the world's first post–World War II competition outboard. Hubbell of California was also there in 1950 with his Johnson PR clone, but it's a photo finish. (Drawing rendered by *Motor Boat & Yachting* staff artist)

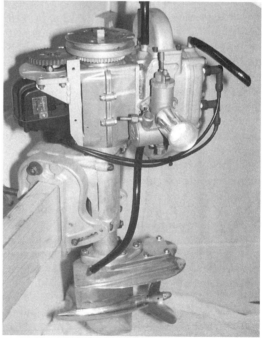

A gear under the flywheel meshes with the magneto drive cog to spark this 1959 Anzani Mark II racer. When fired up, these mills are mighty fast and loud. Rubber hosing carries cooling water. (Champkin collection)

six-cylinder Mercury "dockbusters," to back up your boat, you had to stop the motor, and then restart it in reverse.

With a penchant for high-speed equipment, Anzani officials kept calling for big motors to add to their line. Among the most interesting was an alternate-firing, three-cylinder, 492 cc mill that appeared by 1962. This 30 hp @ 4,500 rpm Triton was concocted from "individual cylinder blocks superimposed on a built-up crankcase." It came with electric starting, a generator, and a voltage regulator. On Triton's control panel, an ignition key switch and electric system warning light were installed. These could be operated remotely with accessory wiring. Like all British Anzanis, the Triton was water-cooled and two-cycle. In fact, few got into the marketplace. During the early 1960s Anzani was acquired by a metal company in Maidstone, Kent.

When Perkins shut down its outboard operation in 1963, it got picked up by the Rootes car group where it floundered (under the Rootes Outboard banner) and was sold off to the aforementioned Maidstone firm to be marketed as an Anzani product. For a time, this must have seemed like quite a coup, and it made Anzani the undisputed leader of full-line British outboard production. Brochures from 1965 show Perkins' top-end, 40 hp model with an Anzani label. The heady days were relatively short-lived, though, as Anzani became highly vulnerable to increasing sorties from foreign outboard makers. Cutbacks came to British Anzani by the early 1970s, when only a few of their singles remained in the catalog. Several years later (circa 1975), the company's outboard venture was history.

British Seagull

A testament to this brand's ubiquity, British Seagull has already received editorial space in the Big List chapter. There it's noted that British Seagull began life as the outboard arm of John Marston's Sunbeam Motorcycle venture in Wolverhampton. This 1931 debut gave boaters a glimpse of an outboard line that, to the untrained eye, never really changed. Such constancy, along with Seagull motors' respectable reputation, gave outboard buyers the confidence to keep on buying the simple little kickers and to continue recommending them to their friends.

The British Seagull began life with the name Marston, as noted in the motor's original logo.

The author recalls a frustrated owner of a generously shrouded, full gearshift, fuel pump–equipped, gadget-laden outboard trying desperately to get his motor fired up. Meantime, a neighbor with a battered old Seagull on a dinghy hopped into that pram, wrapped a piece of wet, frayed clothesline around his modest engine's flywheel sheave, pulled once and was off with a broad smile. "Well, of course your funny little outboard runs!" the aggravated fellow yelled as the dinghy rode by. "That @#$%&! primitive thing isn't sophisticated enough not to start!"

The first simple Seagull (then dubbed Marston Seagull or Sunbeam Seagull) was a 78 cc

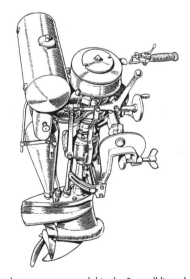

Perhaps the least common model in the Seagull line, the 340 cc, alternate-firing twin produced 10 hp. It was full of gadgets, including a transmission (mounted between the powerhead and the lower unit) and a shifting linkage (located in front of the carburetor).

" 4½ knots in comfort . . . smooth and seamanlike with respect for others afloat "

model. Like all subsequent Seagulls, it was water-cooled. For 1932, the company began promoting a motor that even some die-hard Seagull fans never knew existed. This was the 340 cc, alternate-firing, in-line, twin-cylinder model (weighing 85 pounds) rated at a full 10 hp @ 4,500 rpm. Marston officials were well aware that outboard racing had been capturing attention in early 1930s Britain. Their idea was to enter the fray with a 10 hp motor that would "propel a light speed dinghy at 20 to 25 mph." One equipped with a full F-N-R gearshift was prototyped and exhibited at England's 1931 Motor Boat Show. It offered the characteristics of most early Seagulls—a rear-mounted cylindrical fuel tank and an exhaust leg shaped like an exaggerated baseball bat (with the wide end at the exhaust ports).

The 102 cc Model 102 was the most successful of the pre–World War II Seagulls. It became a cornerstone in 1937, when some of Marston's associates acquired the outboard business and pledged to focus on simple singles. A move from Wolverhampton to Poole, Dorset, in 1938 came on the heels of a company name change to British Seagull. The "British" was added to distinguish it from the plain "Seagull" name then recently utilized by Cross Gear Works in the U.S. and on some badge-engineered U.S. Neptune motors. Several hundred thousand of the Model 102 British Seagulls were sold for work, pleasure, and even military use. Along the way, external design changes included a uniformly shaped exhaust tube and a flattening out of the line's trademark glossy black fuel tank.

Using 1962 British Seagull specifications as an example, we see that besides the beloved 102 (available with optional neutral clutch and rated

between 3 ½ to 4 hp @ 3,800 rpm), the following British Seagulls appeared:

- Forty Minus: 1 to 1 ½ hp @ 3,500 rpm
- Forty Plus: 1 ½ to 2 ½ hp @ 4,000 rpm
- Century Model 100: 3 to 4 hp @ 3,800 rpm
- Century Model 100 Plus: 3 ½ to 5 hp @ 4,000 rpm
- Model 102 Plus: 3 ½ to 5 hp @ 4,000 rpm

The company was happy to accommodate sailors needing a long shaft or a four-bladed (or more), power-propped Seagull. And eventually, neutral clutches, remote fuel tanks, and even rewind starters found their way to many models in order to better compete with the growing number of non-U.K. makes—especially from Japan—infiltrating the British Isles. But many outboarders felt such add-ons sapped the spirit from the original Seagull values of ultimate simplicity and reliability. Many other boaters, however, were not enchanted by basic motors handicapped by so many exposed hot and oily parts. They liked their outboards fully shrouded, quiet, and clean. By the 1990s, British Seagull officials were battling even harder to adapt to the changing marketplace. Design modifications like electronic ignition and loop-charged fuel induction, as well as parts and complete motors supplied by other makers, took the British Seagull line a long way from the basic machines of the 1930s. Still, the brand holds significance to thousands of boaters who appreciate functional simplicity combined with quality.

Cavender & Clark. See Peter Pan.

Comet

"Speed and comfort without an ounce of personal effort," promised a late 1922 pitch from Comet Marine Motor Company, Ltd., for its Comet detachable motor. Considering that date, the ad showed a rather primitive forward-pointing single. It was equipped with a sizable rudder, knuckle-buster starting, and an external gear-driven magneto. Reportedly, Comet motors from this Long Ditton, Surrey, firm were on the market between 1921 and 1929. Though the Comet, with its stardust trail fuel tank decal would make a wonderful antique find

This motor's literature promised, "Fit your skiff with a Comet and enjoy the pleasures of speed without an ounce of personal effort." That was the proper English way of saying what early Evinrude ads shouted: "Don't row! Throw away the oars!" Comet buyers probably needed a bit of a stiff upper lip when they realized their heavy single-cylinder outboard was old-fashioned compared to the light aluminum twins introduced around the same time as Comet's early 1920s debut.

today, outboard shoppers of the time, comparing the heavy kicker to the likes of a rival aluminum Elto Ruddertwin, probably found it rather old-fashioned.

Cormorant

Taking its name from a sea bird, the Cormorant looked a bit like a British Seagull, but it was offered to satisfy a midrange horsepower gap that its maker believed the competition had ignored. No doubt an organization with some active weekend sailors, F. B. Thomas Engineers, Ltd., of Ivybridge, South Devon, came up with the two-stroke, water-cooled, 7 hp @ 3,300 rpm single for the few extra horsepower critical to pushing craft larger than a dinghy. In fact, its testing was conducted on a heavy 16-foot sailboat.

Cormorant's cast-iron, rear-pointing cylinder wore a detachable head so that just about anyone could remove salt deposits from the water jackets. According to an introductory magazine piece on the 40-pound (weight) Cormorant, ignition came from a Miller flywheel. That September 1956 article ended with this blessing: "There should, in our opinion, be good scope for the sale of the [203 cc] Cormorant in both the home and overseas markets." Even so, it now seems few of these sturdy-looking birds with cylindrical fuel tanks ever flew out of the factory.

Coventry Apex

Not to be confused with the Coventry Victor chain-drive motor, these Coventry products were sometimes referred to simply as Apex. They are listed as follows:

- Canoe Engine: 1 hp, 34 cc (direct-drive/inclined shaft)
- Model 50: 1½ hp, 56 cc (water-cooled)
- Model 75: 2½ hp, 76 cc (water-cooled)
- Model 85: 3 hp, 79.7 cc (J.A.P. engine)
- Model 80: 3 hp, 82 cc
- Swampmaster: 3 hp, 79.7 cc (65-inch direct-drive/inclined shaft)
- Dynapower 5: 4 to 5 hp, 125 cc twin (neutral clutch, fiberglass cowls, and rewind starter)

All, except the Dynapower 5, were single-cylinder motors. Some were air-cooled. During the late 1950s to early 1960s, Coventry Apex Engineer-

ing of Coventry, Warwickshire, made these and a few other low-power outboards like the Mallard. In fact, by the summer of 1957, the tiny Mallard line, which the firm had originally built for C. H. Haley, was fully advertised as a Coventry Apex product. Adding enjoyable confusion to this mix is another magazine ad (presumably from 1957) showing the 1 ½ hp Coventry Apex Model 50 and 2 ½ hp Model 75. These have old style quasi-wraparound fuel tanks and possess a prewar look. It's likely, though, that they're Mallards fitted with different tanks and Coventry Apex decals. The U.K.'s outboard industry was relatively fraternal, facilitating acquisition of engine lines and badge-engineering (the sticking of a differently shaped cowl or tank on an engine). And voila, another new marque would be born.

Coventry Climax

From 100 yards away, the Coventry Climax might be mistaken for a tall Mercury. Except for the four in-line cylinders though, this was no Merc! Coventry-based Coventry Climax Engines, Ltd., issued an introductory brochure for its outboard in 1959. The Godiva 40 was "an outboard motor of advanced design developed from the sports car engine [originally a fire pump powerhead] that has been so successful in events all over the world." The organization also touted its offering as "the world's first lightweight high performance 4-cylinder, 4-stroke

Dubbed the Godiva-40, the Coventry Climax was based upon a famous fire pump engine that was also used in a sports car. The motor had a connection to the U.S.-built, four-stroke Fisher-Pierce Bearcat outboard.

outboard motor." Actually, those kudos belonged to the Fageol-44 in America, but the two would eventually meld anyway.

Specs for Coventry's Type F.W.M engine included water-cooling, an overhead camshaft, all aluminum construction, a remote fuel tank, a gear-driven oil pump, electric starting (with emergency recoil starting), dual carburetion, and 39.9 cubic inches (652 cc) of piston displacement. Originally projected to yield 35 hp, the Godiva 40 ended up with a horsepower rating of an even 40, just over 1 horsepower per cubic inch. Flyers claimed the big motor could be steered with a twist-grip-throttle tiller, handrail controlled, or fitted with a remote speed and shift unit.

It's unknown how many of the Godiva 40s left the Coventry factory. The fact is, though, that a few years after the big motor's debut in the British boating press, the same Coventry Climax power plant appeared in the Fisher-Pierce Bearcat 85 outboard. That American marque descended from Homelite and the aforementioned Fageol-44.

Coventry Victor

Available as early as December 1928, the Victor (or Coventry Victor) represented a sharp departure from competitors. These outboards employed four-stroke engines and chain drive from the powerhead to the actual propeller driveshaft. This was described as a pair of "noiseless chains running in an oil bath and provided with a simple double eccentric adjuster." While bulkier than standard driveshaft outboards, the chain method so impressed the British Admiralty that they placed repeat orders for Coventry Victors. The engine's magneto was external—it did not mount under the flywheel. A gear-driven pump circulated oil from a dedicated tank. Operators started their Coventry Victors with a "car-type crank handle." A 1932 roster lists three horizontally opposed, twin-cylinder models (688 cc with side valves, a similarly valved 749 cc, and an overhead valve 749 cc mill) of 13, 16, and 30 hp, respectively. All were water-cooled.

In 1948, a pair of Coventry Victor twin-cylinder models was offered through Coventry Victor Motor Company, Ltd. Both the 6 ½ and 7 ½ hp outboards were originally rated at 3,300 rpm. By 1960, only the smaller one remained in Coventry Victor's catalog and showed a 6 ½ hp @ 3,000 rpm

specification. This was a unique product that primarily attracted industrial users and the occasional eccentric pleasure boater.

Dolphin (M.H.H.)

Circa 1960, M.H.H. Engineering Company, Ltd., had two Dolphins in its little lineup, the Standard, with 2 ½ hp @ 3,500 rpm and the Super, with 3 ½ hp @ 4,000 rpm. Both of these singles had cylinder displacements of 79.7 cubic centimeters. The air-cooled kickers emanated from M.H.H. Engineering's Bramley (near Guildford), Surrey, shop.

Dunelt

In the spring of 1929, *The Yachting Monthly* heralded the Dunelt outboard this way: "The relationship between outboard motor boats and those with inboard motors is very similar to that between motorcycles and cars. It is only natural, therefore, that the makers of motorcycles should turn their attention to outboard motors." With that, the magazine indicated that Messrs. Dunford and Elliott of Dunelt Motorcycles in Sheffield had logically added outboards to their repertoire.

First off, the line was a forward-pointing single employing a doughnut-shaped warmed-air breather (on the cylinder head) for its Amal carburetor. A spring-loaded steering mechanism caused the tiller to activate just the lower unit, then return to a "straight-course position if let go." The Dunelt two-stroke single appeared to be a beautifully finished quality product, and was offered in an 8 ¼ hp @ 3,400 rpm general utility version as well as a 10.6 hp @ 3,800 rpm racing version. Dunford and Elliott became so enthralled with outboarding that they proposed a line of Dunelt boats and trailers. Among the planned hulls was a 10-foot, single-stepped hydroplane that would do 30 mph with their 10.6 hp mill.

In the midst of such high-flying activity, the firm built a few glossy black and silver hot-rod racers that are now considered some of Britain's most beautiful vintage outboard models. Officially released in January 1930, this opposed 30-cubic-inch twin sported an Amal carburetor on each of its black enameled cylinders. The cylindrical fuel tank was also black. In contrast, its removable cylinder heads were polished aluminum, and some parts received chroming. To the casual observer, a Dunelt might look like a 1929 Lockwood Racing

One of several outboard lines offered by English motorcycle companies, Dunelt motors were full of interesting features, like the intake air warmer on this Dunelt single's cylinder head.

Chief, but it is actually far more svelte than that legendary model. A regular service model with underwater exhaust, the Silent Speed 500 cc Dunelt also received catalog space.

In 1930, the electric-starting craze hit outboard makers in the U.S. and Europe. Most of these starting units came from the U.S.-based Dyneto firm and replaced the motor's flywheel with the starting unit. This is mentioned here because the large Dunelt (in its standard service lower unit form with removable skeg) was one of several outboards to be so equipped that year. With the electric start option, the motor was also fitted with spark plug covers, remote control, and

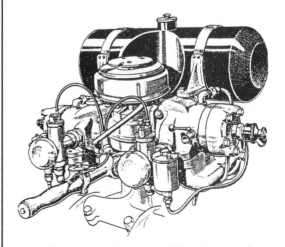

Arguably Britain's sexiest pre–World War II outboard, the Dunelt 500 cc racing twin wore dual carburetors and delivered 20 to 25 hp.

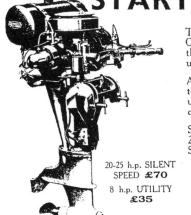

steering cable eyes attached via the cylinder head bolts.

Alas, all these goodies didn't attract many customers. According to the 12 February 1932 issue of *The Motor Boat*, Dunelt had "decided to stop manufacture temporarily, although a few engines [were] still available." That hiatus never ended.

Excelsior

English boating literature for the early 1960s notes the presence of 20 and 30 hp outboards from Excelsior Motor Company, Ltd. The firm offered its 20 hp size in either air- or water-cooled models. This was a rather unusual option in engines over 5 horsepower. Excelsior's 30 hp outboard could only be supplied with water-cooling. This one also featured a Siba Dynastarter that not only enlivened the motor but also served as a 90-watt generator. Reportedly, some of the Excelsior 20s were also factory equipped with that convenience.

Ferrier

New for the U.K.'s 1950 boating season was the 3.9 hp @ 3,500 rpm single from Ferrier Marine of Whitstable, Kent. Rounded off to 4 hp for advertising's sake, the Ferrier Seacub 120 (cubic centimeters) had what one British antique outboard enthusiast likes to call "an agricultural equipment look." That is to say, like many of its local competitors, Ferrier

exposed much of its plumbing. Acceptably streamlined, though, was Seacub's shrouding, which covered about 80 percent of the powerhead. The manufacturer knew many of its customers would use their motor in salt water. Consequently, it was designed with a detachable cylinder head and enough room to clean crusty water jackets. Ferrier promised to individually balance each crankshaft-connecting rod-piston set prior to final assembly. An Amal (type 261) carburetor came standard and helped produce a test performance quite satisfactory to a trio of *Motor Boat & Yachting* magazine officials who ran it on a dinghy in Chichester Harbor. During the entire day of typical cruising (at 7 mph) and on the eight separate occasions that they wrapped a cord around Ferrier Seacub's Miller magneto-equipped flywheel, it sprang to life on the first pull. "Generally," those writers mused, "[our] Ferrier outboard motor strikes us as being a thoroughly well-made job, without any unessential complications . . . [except for having] no means of reversing."

Sales of Ferrier never matched its high rating from that article, but the company seemed undaunted. In fact, several years later, they doubled a Ferrier engine in order to produce the 240 cc Model 240 (horizontally opposed) twin-cylinder version capable of 8 hp @ 4,000 rpm. Both models had water-cooling and optional long shafts. Though very functional kickers, neither appeared

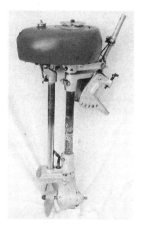

This 120 cc Ferrier single from about 1953 was designed to be rugged yet provide relatively light-weight outboard power for use along Britain's many miles of seacoast. A 1955 version with a cylindrical fuel tank looked like the 1956 Cormorant. The two were related. (Champkin collection)

"Take the wheel of the outboard while I go below deck!" could be a captain's order if his craft were powered by a 1920s Fortis opposed twin. The wheel maneuvered only the lower unit on this obscure machine.

to be very contemporary by the early 1960s, nor were they able to carve a sustainable niche in the face of British Seagull name recognition and colorful American imports.

As a footnote, the September 1956 issue of *Motor Boat & Yachting* reported that Ferrier (then of Buckfastleigh, Devon) was hoping to produce a new model. A picture of one of the prototypes looked quite a bit like several other British low-priced, low-horsepower kickers engulfing the U.K. dinghy motor arena. This new kicker "consists of the marriage of an 80 cc J.A.P. air-cooled engine to the [sturdily built] Ferrier lower unit," the magazine explained. The Ferrier-J.A.P outboard was an exercise in product line extension and was offered alongside the brand's water-cooled models. (*Note:* Ferrier's original Seacub designation should not be confused with a circa 1960 Mallard redux also dubbed Seacub.)

Fisherman

Research continues on this outboard brand once noted in a mildewed listing. From its name, though, one might assume Fisherman motors were lightweight, low-power kickers.

Fortis

Less than a decade after being offered to British mariners, the unique Fortis motor had been so forgotten that even a 1932 historical treatise on England's outboards passed it by. No matter, the Fortis should now be recalled as one of the U.K.'s earliest homegrown kickers and join the likes of Watermota in our outboard hall of fame. While scarce, surviving references to this Manchester-

produced marque hint that the first Fortis was offered in 1920.

A 1923 ad for its maker, Power Engineering Company, Ltd., depicts the 2 ½ hp outboard as having opposed twin cylinders and an external Bosch magneto driven by gearing on the crankshaft. The flywheel ("knuckle-buster") knob-starting is evident, as is Fortis' most distinguishing feature—a steering wheel where the tiller arm would typically be positioned. "Reverse and steering by swiveling propeller," the advertising states. This suggests that the steering wheel facilitated 360-degree rotation of the lower unit.

Power Engineering also marketed their engine as an inboard, as did a number of other outboard firms during this era. In that mode, the powerhead was mounted on a base adaptable to the craft's floor (or motor boards). Gearing in the pedestal of this base transferred power to a prop shaft also available from Fortis. It's likely that Fortis sold more inboards than outboards. Though not a commercial success, the Fortis outboard deserves a comfortable resting place in British outboard motor chronology.

Gaines

The Gaines outboard line appears to consist of relabeled Caille motors imported for sale in the U.K. Examples include the 1916 Five-Speed Gaines with self-starter, which was clearly a Detroit-built Caille wearing the Gaines decal.

Gary Jet

During the early 1960s, Stuart and Payne, Ltd., offered a 40-pound, four-horse, water-jet thrust outboard touted as "particularly well suited to boats used in shallow waters, in weed infested lakes and rivers, and on the sea where there are shingle beaches and bathers." The thought of a little Gary Jet 4–propelled dinghy heading far out into the English Channel can bring a smile to anyone who has experienced the lackluster performance of that era's hydro-jet kickers. Stuart and Payne fitted its product with a two-stroke single that revved out at 4,500 rpm.

Godiva 40. See Coventry Climax.

Gregg

Research continues on the Gregg outboard, said to have flashed in the English pleasure boating pan around 1925.

Harbormaster

The editors of a 1963 British boating annual played it safe and cautioned outboard shoppers that Harbormaster Ltd., of Harlow, Essex, did not make ordinary kickers. "These are not outboard motors in the generally understood sense of the term," noted the contributing writer. "They are four-stroke diesel engines installed inboard with geared outboard drives and are intended for heavy duty and for towing." Of course, weighing 14,000 pounds, few Harbormaster motors would get mistaken for a portable putt-putt. Those giants produced 130 hp @ 1,500 rpm through six cylinders. Two "smaller" Harbormasters were rated at 65 and 42 hp @ 1,800 rpm and had four cylinders. Starting for each needed to be electric. Cooling was via radiator, making Harbormaster a unique footnote in this outboarding history.

H.E.

The Motor Boat noted that this outboard brand was slated for a March 1930 debut. Reported as a three-cylinder radial, four-stroke motor, the H.E. never hit the market and was likely a victim of worldwide economic storm clouds gathering at the time of the engine's proposed release.

Jet

A novel trio of 95 cc, 2 ½ hp @ 3,800 rpm outboards were available to early 1960s British boaters. Stockdale's Engineers of Balsham (near Cambridge) offered these pivoted, direct-drive units for sideboard or stern installation. There was the Canu Jet for canoes, another Canu Jet (probably a stern-mount version) for dinghies or punts, and a Dingi Jet equipped with a built-in neutral clutch. Power came from an imported Clinton engine. The literature mentions nothing about any of Stockdale's products possessing hydro-jet (as opposed to regular propeller) drive. Why anyone would call such putt-putts "Jet," or label one of the Canu models a dinghy-punt motor, are good essay questions for a business school exam.

Johnson (U.K. import)

Though an American make with a Canadian subsidiary, Johnson is listed here because a few of its products were built specifically for sale in the U.K.

From Johnson's earliest years, the company arranged for English distribution. This 1930 advertisement for its London-based importer depicted speedy Johnson-powered craft racing past an historic High Street riparian milieu. In contrast, a typical U.S. ad showed boats on a mountain lake surrounded by pine trees.

The 1933 Johnson Junior serves as an example. Editors of *The Motor Boat* enjoyed a 28-mile test run for a 5 May 1933 article about the 3 hp @ 3,000 rpm Johnson Junior Sea Horse that was "produced specially for the British market." Knowing that saltwater use was a given in the U.K., Johnson engineers back in Illinois fitted this model with a muffler can, an exhaust tube, driveshaft housing, and a lower unit fashioned from brass.

J.S.L. and Bantam

During its early 1930s heyday, the J.S.L. had the distinction of being England's smallest F-N-R shift outboard. Of course, in that era, any kicker with such versatility was novel. This 128 cc, opposed twin from Joseph Stubbs, Ltd. (hence J.S.L.), in Manchester, pulled 2 ½ hp @ 3,000 rpm. Actually, the shifter (and detachable underwater exhaust) was an option on the new J.S.L. Bantam, a kicker the manufacturer introduced in late 1930 to replace its Mobo brand.

Reportedly, Bantam's 10-pound gearbox-clutch-shift lever assembly—sandwiched between the engine and lower unit—could be removed at will to lighten the package to an even 30 pounds. The pipe creating an underwater exhaust could also (via one screw) be taken off. A cooling water pump got built into the cavitation plate casting. Lucas-built ignition hid under the flywheel, but carburetion was a province of Joseph Stubbs' proprietary design. It all made for a neat package and a very maneuverable little outboard. (See also Mobo.)

Pre–World War II outboards with gearbox reverse were much more common in the U.K. than in the U.S. The popular J.S.L. 128 cc twin serves as an example. For 1932, it could be fitted with a transmission between the powerhead and lower unit. Note that the shift lever is parallel to the tiller.

Kelston. See Peto.

Knight

If the Knight had actually been produced somewhere in the U.K., it would be a strong contender for the title of "earliest British outboard." It appears the Knight Outboard Motor Company, Ltd., was established around 1917 in order to import opposed, two-cylindered Swedish Archimedes outboards to its swanky-sounding Riverside, Hampton Wick, Kingston-on-Thames, address. Much of the motor was fashioned from brass or bronze. This included the motor's svelte flywheel into which was embossed the Knight nomenclature and company locale. When polished, it was suitable for display in a High Street jewelry store. Also notable are the brackets that attached the powerhead and lower unit to the transom clamp assembly. Two wing nut releasable brackets clamp to the ends of the cylinders, allowing for motor angle adjustments.

Often dubbed "balanced twins," early batches of Knights were marketed as 2 ½ hp machines. By 1923, another horsepower had been added, though early and late Knights looked the same on the outside. No matter how valiantly the Knight company crusaded, outboard customers cut paths to other brands. Little literature exists about the marque past the mid-1920s, so we can assume it was around then the Knight Outboard Motor Company finally laid down its sword.

As a footnote, the 10 February 1928 issue of *The Motor Boat* stated: "For some years the [Archimedes] engine was known in this country [England] as the Knight, although a comparatively recent reversion has been made to the original name."

KS

Under the names KS or Skinner, a fascinating group of direct-drive kickers arrived on the mid-1950s to 1960s English small boating scene. They were intended only to match the power of "two good paddlers." Each weighed about 15 pounds and offered just ⅓ hp @ 2,300 rpm or ½ hp @ 2,500 rpm via a two-stroke, J.A.P. air-cooled, 34 cc single. Marine engineer K. Skinner of Lincoln marketed the KS34, KS34B and KS34C (denoting the inventor's initials, the engine size, and the series) with the following explanation: "Model KS34B is a side-

board engine specifically designed for use with kayak-type canoes. Model KS34C is a similar unit designed for use with Canadian-type canoes. It has a small balanced rudder. Both [of the latter models] have recoil starting." To solve the canoe motor mounting problem, Skinner equipped his kickers to a little "bracket that can be bolted to a [scrap lumber] wooden crossbar held by hook bolts to the craft's cockpit coaming." That positioned the direct-drive tail shaft/propeller shaft at a 22-degree angle to the waterline. When clocked, Skinner and a boating magazine writer attained 6 mph with the prototype KS34 on a homemade decked canoe.

Mallard

From a distance, one might easily mistake the 1 hp @ 3,000 to 3,300 rpm Mallard single for a British Seagull or maybe a pre–World War II Elto Pal from

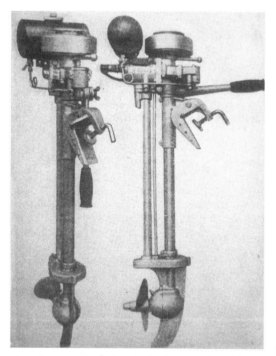

Upon its 1950 introduction, Mallard received lots of favorable boating press. It was a capable little kicker built in the "simple, but durable" British Seagull mode, but it seemed to have some difficulty differentiating itself from the better-known Seagull marque. Maybe outboard shoppers figured that motors named for ducks and seabirds were pretty much the same.

America. For Mallard's 1950 introduction, however, maker C. H. Haley and Company of Leicester noted that the 32 cc, 19-pound kicker possessed some pretty nifty features. Among them was a "leak-proof" carburetor that would not spill a drop of fuel even when the motor "was lain down or stood on its head." Gas and oil for this two-stroker originated in a two-pint "juice can" tank. Miller flywheel ignition was employed, and saltwater-resistant stainless steel was used in making the toque tube, driveshaft, and propeller shaft. Indeed a competently cute kicker, but the 1 hp Mallard never achieved a market share near that of Seagull.

As a result, Haley updated his outboard to a 54 cc version yielding 1 ½ hp @ 3,600 rpm. It wore a semiwraparound fuel tank and detachable cylinder head. The stock propeller had three blades, as opposed to the earlier Mallard's two. It was explained in a February 1957 introductory article that Haley's motors were actually being built and sold by the Coventry Apex Engineering organization (see listing in this section.) Finally, an undated but presumably early 1960s advertisement for Mallard outboards mentions 1 ½ and 2 hp models. "Stocks arriving," noted the ad copy for the air-cooled, 2 hp Mallard. A fuzzy depiction shows a cheapo kicker not worthy of being compared to the sturdy little water-cooled Mallards of 1950 and 1957.

Marston. See British Seagull.

Medina

Here's a circa 1960 departure from the many single-cylinder putt-putts typically offered by modest outboard firms in the U.K. The 7 ½ hp @ 4,250 rpm Medina was designed to be comparable to the then growing number of U.S. imports in the 5 to 10 horsepower range. Its water-cooled, 200 cc, twin-cylinder powerhead got treated to stylish shrouding. A full F-N-R gearshift and a 3 ¼-gallon fuel tank were conveniences often sought by serious outboarders. J. and F. Poole, Ltd., of Hayle, Cornwall, offered the space-age, 50-pound Medina in standard and long shaft (adding a bit of weight) versions. It should be noted that Poole bought Medina from the Saunders-Roe organization that developed the motor around 1958–59. Its launch came just in time to be adversely affected by the British Board of Trade's "token import" outboard

scheme, which began cracking the protectionist walls that had made U.S. outboards prohibitively expensive in the U.K.

Mobo

Debuting in February 1929, Mobo—"the all British outboard"—wore a distinctive cylindrical fuel tank. Two versions of the 498.8 cc, opposed twin were released. A 16 hp @ 3,500 rpm, one-carburetor edition was branded as "standard," while a dual-carbureted racer checked in with 20+ hp @ 4,500 rpm. On this speed model, only one of the Amal carburetors was needed for cruising, but the second could be set to kick in for extra zip as desired. Mobo (presumably short for *motor boat*) users held a tiller that only turned the lower unit. Though a handsome mill, Mobo production was discontinued by 1932 and then replaced with the much tamer J.S.L. outboards, which were products of Joseph Stubbs, Ltd., of Manchester.

The 1929–32 Mobo could be ordered in either single or dual carbureted form. The latter model was a promising British racer, but its sales were few. Its Manchester-based manufacturer let Mobo sink in order to concentrate on the introduction of a smaller motor called the J.S.L.

Outboard Motors, Ltd. See Berning.

Perkins

The Big List chapter contains an entry on Oliver outboards and notes that by 1960 they were being built in England. That's because the Chris-Craft outboard line was sold to Oliver in 1954. Oliver, in turn, was acquired by British-based Perkins Diesel circa 1959. The Peterborough-based industrial engine maker figured it could entice U.S. outboard buyers and carve out a decent share in the U.K. market as well. To this end, Perkins invested a fortune in seeking to improve the trio of Olivers (6,

OLIVER

Precision built in England for dependable and all around service to American boatmen

American designed... British built

The English are a practical people. The products they make are built to last. The 1960 line of Oliver outboard motors are economical, durable and painstakingly made . . . a perfect example of British craftsmanship. They are American designed for light weight and compactness, with cat-quick get away, high load carrying ability and top speeds. Hundreds of owners have testified that Oliver outboards have outperformed higher horsepower competitive models. Top-flight engineering and craftsmanship produce smooth, precise motor operation. Many years of faithful service at lower operating costs will confirm your wise decision in favor of an Oliver. 1960 models include 6 hp, 16 hp, 35 hp and twin counter-rotating 35s for 70 hp. Finished with durable baked marine type (epoxy-resin) paints in turquoise with white trim. See your Oliver dealer or write for full details.

Visit us at the National Motorboat Show, New York Coliseum, Booths A-71 and 72, First Floor.

OLIVER OUTBOARD MOTORS
33 HAMBLIN, BATTLE CREEK, MICHIGAN

Division of Oliver Corporation

Perkins outboards resulted from the British diesel maker purchase of the American Oliver tractor company's outboard division. This 1960 transitional ad shows an "American designed/British built" Oliver. Perkins motors looked the same as they were badge-engineered. The Oliver name was subsequently discontinued in favor of Perkins, but that outboard moniker died a few years later.

16, and 35 hp) it received in the deal. Reportedly, nearly one thousand design changes were recognized and implemented.

One asset of the transaction was the licensing agreement for the George Martin "poppet valve" system granted to Oliver after Martin had a dispute with National Presto Industries (erstwhile maker of Martin motors). These efficient fuel induction devices were built into Oliver's 35 hp model and sustained by Perkins in its version of the 35 and its subsequent revamp, the Perkins 40. Perkins Outboard Motors, Ltd., continued its predecessor's 6 hp models and added a poppet-valved 30 hp model (in a heavy-duty "commercial" edition), and a 4 ½ hp model. For 1963, the old 6 became a 6 ½, while Perkins morphed their 16 into an 18 hp motor. All were of the twin-cylinder, water-cooled variety. Long shafts could be ordered

on any Perkins. Electric starting was available on all Perkins of 16 hp or more.

During the early 1960s, Perkins (having dropped the Oliver moniker) marketed motors in the U.S. But it was no use. Evinrude, Johnson, and Mercury had much of the customer base, which left Perkins trying to establish its name and scrounging for buyers willing to shop second-string U.S. brands the likes of West Bend, Scott/McCulloch, Gale, Sea King, and Sears/Elgin. Also problematic was the line's need for a "big" motor. Though relatively sizable when Perkins bought Oliver, the 35 (later 40) horsepower machine would soon be considered only a middle-range motor as U.S. boaters began seeking higher power engines. With ample quantities of second-string American outboard makes readily available, even those motor shoppers not fixated on buying a Johnson, Evinrude, or Merc had plenty of domestic products to choose from.

On home turf, however, early 1960s Perkins outboard sales proved somewhat more respectable. Regardless, after the firm was purchased by Massey-Ferguson, executives decided to close their outboard division in 1963. But that wasn't the end of the line. Still having value in the English marine milieu, the Perkins outboard assets passed to the Rootes automobile group and then onto the Maidstone, Kent, firm that had also acquired British Anzani.

Peter Pan

Called a "sideboard" (as opposed to an outboard), the Peter Pan drove its propeller via a 39-inch inclined shaft. Introduced for the 1955 boating season, the debut Peter Pans buzzed up to 3,000 rpm to give its 49 cc, air-cooled, two-stroke single about 1.3 hp. In its Series 3 form (1960), this 18-pound mill was an air-cooled, 98 cc, single-cylinder, rated at 2 ¼ hp @ 3,800 rpm. A 1963 listing for the Series 5 Peter Pan notes a 1 hp @ 3,200 rpm, two-stroke engine of just 34 cubic centimeters that still weighed 18 pounds, but it was equipped with recoil starting.

Cavender and Clark (at the Granta Works) in Cottenham, Cambridge, was responsible for the kicker with the fairy-tale name. The 1963 notation, though, seems to indicate that this firm also claimed the moniker Granta Folding Boats Company. Literature promised that Peter Pan would be "supplied complete with fixing bar and bracket for folding and non-folding canoes, [underwater exhaust tube], a tilting device enabling the propeller to be raised from the water for starting, and two locking positions when running." The machine could also be separated into several parts for toting. Reportedly, one Peter Pan test pilot got the little mill to put his folding boat on speaking terms with 10 mph! Hopefully, the craft was unfolded during that trial.

Peto

Kelston Engineering Company, Ltd., indicated that its water-cooled Peto outboard could be equipped with a long shaft, recoil starter, and remote controls. The latter seems an ambitious accessory for the motor's modest 4 ½ hp @ 4,000 rpm rating. Peto's water-cooled powerhead had a single cylinder and a piston displacement of 99.75 cc. It was introduced in 1957, came with a neutral clutch, and the Bristol manufacturer offered a reverse gear option. *Motor Boat & Yachting* editors tried one and touted it as "a smart looking engine with notable features," such as the oversized transom bracket that "is tightened and released by a single hand wheel." The magazine also reported Peto's designers had considerable experience in the aircraft industry. While a similar claim by the American producers of the 1949 Milburn Cub seemed euphemistic, in Peto's case, the attention to detail inferred a fine design.

Pierce

The Jim Pierce outboard that appeared in the May 1930 edition of *Motorboat—The Trade Journal* looked fast, exotic, and likely of British origin. This motor was a two-stroke, opposed twin, and

This 30-cubic-inch racer was fitted with a tractor lower unit, a flywheel nut tachometer drive, and a transom clamp assembly that allowed the Pierce twin to be "tilted horizontally and swung through an arc of 180 degrees [to] permit propeller changes from the security of the hull."

wore a nicely streamlined tractor-type lower unit. Research continues on the racer.

Pilco

Possibly identified as Pilco or Pilco-Caille outboards, motors from G. C. Pillinger and Company, Ltd., of Westminster, were U.S.-made Caille products.

Prince

The 4 November 1927 issue of *Motor Boat* magazine listed two outboards handled by J. J. Beckett of South Wales. Wearing the Prince moniker, they yielded 3 hp in the single cylinder version and double that in a twin. Both were rated @ 900 rpm. Their actual place of manufacture is unknown. It's believed that Beckett simply served as Prince's importing agent.

Puffin

Leicester's Basil Engineering Company, Ltd., produced a small line of outboards with the Puffin brand. Circa the early 1960s, the firm offered a trio in the following sizes:

- Puffin 75: 2 to 2 ½ hp @ 3,800 rpm, 76.4 cc (some sources say 75 cc)
- Puffin 105: 4 to 5 hp @ 3,800 rpm, 105 cc (also came in a deluxe version with a neutral clutch)

The 5 hp Puffin 105s (both regular and deluxe) could be fitted with long shafts. All Puffins were single-cylinder outboards fitted with Basil Engineering's unique propeller assembly that facilitated shear pin changes without tools.

Queenie

In one British outboard buff's loft is a mysterious powerhead clearly marked "Queenie Outboard Motor." It is all that survives of a marque assumed to be of English origin. The opposed twin of about 250 cc is fitted with a gear-driven magneto, and it is estimated to have been made sometime between 1914 and 1920.

Regina. See Berning.

Roness

Released in January 1928, the exotic Roness Silent 4 was designed to satisfy outboarders who wanted

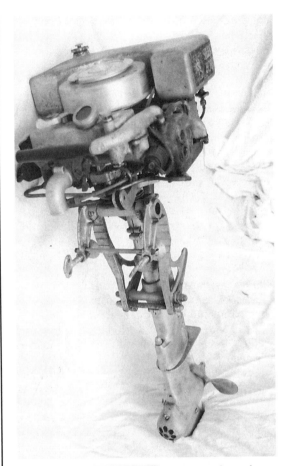

Two views of one of England's rarest vintage outboards. The Roness Silent 4 was called "silent" because of its underwater exhaust that wasn't standard equipment on most other outboards in 1928. The "4" denoted Roness' four-cycle engine. This twin had a four-cylinder sister, few of which have surfaced. (Champkin collection)

the economy and power of a four-stroke engine. Two Roness sizes (248 cc and 498 cc) sprang from powerheads built by the J.A.P. engine works. November 1927 introductory specifications promised that the smaller model, an opposed twin, delivered 3 ½ to 4 hp, while the bigger model, an opposed quad (doubly earning the "4" in Silent 4), generated 9 hp. A few months later (March 1928), however, rosters included twins (possessing the aforementioned displacements) with 5 ½ hp @ 3,500 rpm and 7 hp @ 5,000 rpm, a quad bearing 14 hp @ 3,500, and an unrated four-cylinder racer capable of 5,000 rpm. All Roness models were mechanically and visually beautiful products of E. Roness, Ltd., of Littlehampton, Sussex, but they vanished from the market by the end of 1928.

Rootes

Rootes Marine, Ltd., of Maidstone (a division of the Rootes automobile concern), had an impressive passel of outboard models in its 1963 and 1964 catalogs. After that, though, the line was gone. All were designated with a nicely transparent code that began with "RM" (for Rootes Marine) and was followed by horsepower range, starting type, and shaft length. The smallest engine in its stable had the designation RM/4.5/MS, indicating that it was a Rootes Marine 4.5 hp outboard with manual start and short shaft. Rootes' largest model was the 40 hp, electric-start, long shaft model RM/40/EL. Other models included engines in 6.5, 18, and 30 hp denominations. Rootes customers could select either a 2 ¾- or 5 ½-gallon remote fuel tank.

Actually, the Rootes line was simply a result of a car group's acquisition of Perkins, and the resulting motors were simply badge-engineered. Rootes' outboard business was subsequently sold to the company that had also bought the British Anzani marque.

Safix

Circa 1920 (and quite possibly earlier), an outboard bearing the Safix label appeared on British waterways. Its maker, Safix Marine Engine Company, Ltd., of London, cataloged two British-made outboard motors: Type A, with a single water-cooled, forward-pointing cylinder, generated 2 ¾ hp; Type B, an opposed twin, generated 5 to 6 hp. Both were two strokers, wore an external gear-

Parsimonious outboard shoppers were welcome to call a representative of Safix Marine Engine Company, Ltd., and ask about the availability of used motors. The representative might have confirmed an offer Safix advertisement suggested: "A few slightly soiled but good as new demonstration models at specially reduced prices." This 1922 ad shows a rowboat motor that would stop a collector's heart today, but it was rather outdated when compared to the new Elto Ruddertwins or Johnson Waterbugs then arriving in the U.K.

driven magneto, had been topped with a big "church collection plate" rim-start flywheel, and swung a variable-pitch propeller.

A full-page November 1921 advertisement for Safix devoted some space to the firm's line of Miller petrol-paraffin (inboard) marine engines. Also noted is another ad in an Australian publication that promoted the Safix-Miller outboard. That picture showed a badge-engineered 1915 American Miller rowboat motor with a forward-pointing single cylinder. This provides a clue that Safix might have been an importer of U.S. engines that it relabeled and sold around the British Empire. As a further footnote, the 15 November 1926 issue of

The Motor Boat shows an opposed twin, knob-start flywheel, magneto-equipped powerhead captioned "The Safi outboard motor." There seems to be a misstrike between the "i" in "Safi" and the "o" in "outboard." Maybe it said "Safix"? If so, it must have been the Type B and rather outdated for a mid-1920s product.

Saunders

E. E. Saunders, Ltd., was reported to have built outboard motors in its Isle of Wight plant about 1920. Little else is remembered about such a product, making it another rather mysterious British brand.

Scott

Somewhere in England there just might be an old outboard adapted from a 1920s high-speed Scott Motorcycle Company engine. Early in 1929, the cycle firm planned the introduction of such a machine. Scott was known for its twin-cylinder, water-cooled engines in denominations like 299, 497, and 598 cc. Headlined, "Outboard Motors for 1929," *The Motor Boat* for 22 March 1929 lists a 596 cc, two-cylinder Scott outboard ("from the Scott Motorcycle Co., Ltd.") rated at 6 to 30 hp with a maximum rpm of 6,000 revs. For some now-forgotten reason, though, Scott officials decided to stay focused on land transport. It is believed that this Scott never actually went into production. Three decades later, though, an incarnation of the famed motorcycle power plant turned up in the Bermuda outboard. (See also Bermuda.)

Sea-Bee

One of England's most attractive late 1950s to 1960s outboards was the Sea-Bee 5 from Austin Burrell, Ltd. The author makes such an assessment based upon American-oriented external appearance standards, though. There are opposing judgments from sundry British vintage motor enthusiasts who consider the Sea-Bee 5 to be generically bland (and akin to the plastic-shrouded loved-hated 1 ½ to 2 hp Evinrude Mate or Johnson Sea Horse 2 "throwaway" kickers of the 1970s). Perhaps that's due to Sea-Bee's brief burst of seeming ubiquity on U.K. waterways and their appearance today as the lone "antique motor" offerings at English marine swap meets (or *jumbles*).

On the inside, this 5 hp @ 4,500 rpm Sea-Bee sported a single-cylinder, water-cooled 106 cc engine and weighed in at 42 pounds. Sea-Bee's Leicester-based manufacturer also offered a ¾ hp @ 4,250 rpm, 34 cc Minor (reminiscent of the British Anzani with the same model name) as well as a 2.6 hp @ 4,000 rpm, 80 cc dubbed Sea-Bee 3.

You deserve the best . . . .

. . . and the "Sea Bee" Outboard gives it!
Greater power with greater economy at lower cost!

Powered by an 80 cc Air Cooled specially tuned J.A.P. engine in the 3 h.p. category it is built to withstand long arduous work. Fitted with recoil starter as standard equipment.
The streamlined underwater unit is of stainless steel and corrosion resistant alloys, and incorporates the exhaust outlet to give a high degree of silencing.

For any size of dinghy or as a spare engine for craft up to 14 feet the "Sea Bee" is ideal. It has, in fact, all the features you look for, yet costs only **£32.0.0**

Sea ❋ Bee
OUTBOARD MOTORS

Write today for free illustrated leaflet to:—
AUSTIN-BURRELL LIMITED · Abbey Park Road · Leicester · Phone: 21235

Austin-Burrell, Ltd., made clever use of promotional mascots. In 1957, the firm's ads depicted a bee and a salty admiral. Though the bee motif didn't last, the navy man survived throughout much of the marque's life. No doubt outboard buyers thought it cute that there could be any connection between the Royal Navy and a tiny air-cooled putt-putt.

Leaning against the proverbial English garden shed, this old Sea-Bee waits to be planted on the stern of a nice little dinghy.

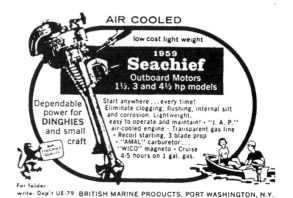

AIR COOLED

low cost light weight

1959 Seachief
Outboard Motors
1½, 3 and 4½ hp models

Dependable power for **DINGHIES** and small craft

Start anywhere...every time! Eliminate clogging, flushing, internal silt and corrosion. Lightweight, easy to operate and maintain! • "J. A. P." air-cooled engine • Transparent gas line • Recoil starting, 3 blade prop • "AMAL" carburetor... "WICO" magneto • Cruise 4-5 hours on 1 gal. gas.

For folder write: Dep't UE-79 BRITISH MARINE PRODUCTS, PORT WASHINGTON, N.Y.

This Seachief's J.A.P. powerhead with a curved fuel tank gave it a similar look to some of its rival Sea-Bee outboards, which employed the same engine.

The smaller models featured air-cooling. Austin-Burrell debuted the line in early 1957 with the 80 cc putt-putt. Actually, it was only 79.7 cc, but it opened the door for a host of other Sea-Bees in 1961, including the stylistically shrouded Sea-Bee Hurricane (130.8 cc, 6 hp) and Tempest (3 hp). Both were sold with a remote 2 ½-gallon fuel tank and a comprehensive tool kit. Air-cooled motors with water-cooled exhaust, these deluxe Sea-Bees were said to have "embodied the very latest design features plus a marvelous new power unit by Aspera of Turin."

The Sea-Bee's relative ubiquity might be compared to that of the Eska in the U.S. Giving the marque an even greater appearance of market penetration was its competitor, Seachief. This brand not only had a similar name, but it was often fitted with similar J.A.P. engines (with the characteristic "drooping" fuel tank styling). In fact, sans an ID tag, it's difficult to distinguish between a late 1950s Seachief single and a Sea-Bee Super 3. Perhaps there was a connection.

Seachief

Another late 1950s to 1960s marque (which is sometimes derided by old local outboard buffs) is the once widely distributed Seachief. Elk Marine (or Toogood and Jones, Ltd.) of Whitsable, Kent, made the machine. Seachief sales even made American incursions through British Marine Products of Port Washington, New York. Most common in the line were the 34 cc Seachief 1, a 1 to 1 ½ hp @ 4,250 rpm mill; the Seachief 2 with an 80 cc pow-

erhead and 2 ½ to 3 horses @ 3,500 rpm; another 80 cc model, the Seachief 3, equipped with a full F-N-R gearshift; and finally, the Seachief 5, the Excelsior-powered, 120 cc, 5 to 6 ½ hp @ 5,200 rpm with shift and 3-gallon remote tank. Not often seen was the Super Seachief 5, factory-fitted with electric starting and remote control hookup. Truly rare today are bigger Seachiefs like the 10 (9 to 10 ½ hp @ 5,000 rpm) and the notable 328 cc Seachief 20, generating 18 to 20 hp. Strict speed limits—sometimes capped at 6 mph or at no-wake speed—on many inland lakes and rivers, as well as corrosive ocean salt in coastal waterways, make vintage outboards of large cylinder displacement tough to find. While the biggest Seachief employed two cylinders, the others were singles. And, all—even the Seachief 20—had air-cooling! Elk Marine made electric starting standard on the 10 and 20. A 5-gallon remote fuel tank came with these two outboards.

One notable cosmetic Seachief feature was the "drooping" fuel tank used on a few of its lower-power models. A long oval-shaped container, it appeared to have been lain on top of the motor in scorching direct sunlight, its aft end left to melt down from the powerhead. Some rival Sea-Bee models—also with J.A.P. powerheads—had the same look, perhaps causing Seachiefs and Sea-Bees to be lumped into one visual genre.

Seacub

"Can be used by women and children," bragged a 1960 ad for Seacub, "the world's greatest outboard

value." It appears that this 20-pound (weight), 1.7 hp, water-cooled single with a "juice can" fuel tank was simply a Mallard redux. It wasn't uncommon for the rights to a low-power kicker from some tiny maker to get shuffled from company to company and then reinvented via a new name. Warehouses full of new and old stock offered willing retailers the opportunity to badge-engineer their own engines. Seacub came from Outboard Motors, Ltd., of Whitstable, a firm that had handled a number of different minor brands. However, not enough women and children responded to Outboard Motor's sales pitch to make Seacub a familiar sight on English waterways.

Sharland

In 1931, His Royal Highness the Prince of Wales went outboard shopping and picked up a 347 cc Sharland racer. Perhaps it was the opposed twin cylinders, overhead valve, and four-stroke power-head that enticed him. Then again, Sharland's chrome-plated fuel tank probably moved the monarch. With an 8:1 compression ratio, this mill developed 22 hp @ 5,600 rpm. A service version of the 20-cubic-inch mill turned 5,000 revs for 17 hp. There was also a tuned-down 15 hp version along the way. A 1932 *The Motor Boat* article bragged that the 120-pound Sharland racer included "twin camshafts, twin Amal carburetors, a centrifugal engine-driven water pump, and pressure lubrication on the dry sump principle with a quart oil

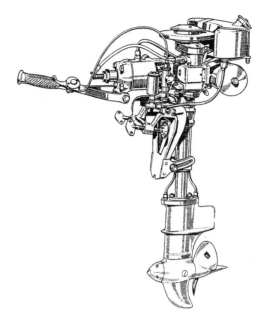

The 1932 Sharland single delivered 4 hp from 158 cc. This motor morphed into a popular British Anzani model.

tank provided with cooling fins." Reportedly, only about eighty Sharland competition engines were produced.

The Sharland 347 cc powerhead was built for Sharland Motors, Ltd., of Tipton, by the J.A.P. (J. A. Prestwich) engine firm, best known for its various motorcycle power plants. A former Dunelt

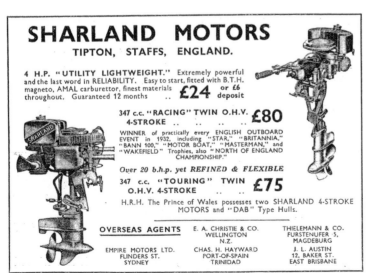

One of England's fastest racing outboards of the early 1930s was the 347 cc OHV twin pictured in the lower left-hand corner of this summer 1933 Sharland advertisement. The four-stroker cost a king's ransom to manufacture and could be afforded by only a few posh customers, like the Prince of Wales. He bought two.

design engineer started this outboard business with a racing compatriot who went on to win several important trophies with the product.

To capture the fishing and cruising market, Sharland quickly introduced a 158 cc two-stroker, pulling 4 hp @ 3,000 rpm. This forward-pointing single employed a horseshoe style B.T.H. magneto and an Amal carburetor. The latter's throttle level provided the motor's only necessary speed control. Pressure vacuum cooling via the propeller stream (and water holes in the prop) was employed in this Sharland. The well-built 48-pound motor had a wider customer base than did the larger models. Never having pulled much of a profit on any of these endeavors, the firm sold out to a retailer, Outboards of Isleworth, Ltd., around 1934. By this time, the racer and related standard twin had been discontinued. Outboards of Isleworth pressed forward with the single, offering it until the onset of World War II. Following hostilities, the old 4 hp Sharland was revamped under the Anzani moniker, becoming that marque's popular Super Single.

Skinner. See KS.

Spartan

Another early U.K. make currently lost in the historical haze, the Spartan was only produced in 1914. A dusty archive lists Goodrich, Hamlyn, and Arnand of London as the Spartan's manufacturer.

Supercraft Airboard

An impressive range of air-propeller "pusher" outboards were made by Supercraft, Ltd., of London. The 1935 lineup of Airboards fitted with airscrews included a 2 hp, 147 cc single; 5 hp, 249 cc and 7 hp, 348 cc twins; and five larger models up to 28 hp! Reportedly, the smallest Supercraft was a two-stroker, while the others employed the four-cycle principle.

Swordfish. See Britannia.

Tasman. See listing in Australia section.

Tidemaster

The 1950s brought U.K. boaters numerous lines of modest air-cooled outboards. One grouping wore the Tidemaster brand and came from Tidemaster Motors, Ltd., of Whitstable. London-based Heddon-Smith Engineering handled the sales. All air-cooled, they included 2 and 3 ½ hp Tidemaster singles and an alternate-firing twin. July 1956 debut ads show the 2 hp Tidemaster with an 80 cc J.A.P. engine. These looked rather "lawnmowerish" with plenty of exposed parts and a little "juice can" fuel tank bracketed to the rear top shroud. The starter pulley stuck out significantly.

Fiberglass cowling was increasingly used by the late 1950s to stylize an otherwise insignificant kicker. Tidemaster bedecked their 3 ½ and 5 hp models with this material. The latter also got treated to rewind starting, while the small Tidemasters required a knotted rope. Curiously, ads for the 1957 Tidemaster ("The outboard motor which has really efficient cooling.") make the featured shrouded model look like it's covered with a construction hard hat. The 1958 models, including a 3 ½ hp Deluxe with full F-N-R gearshift, had more official outboard motor cowling.

T-S-D (or T.S.D.)

Indeed an unusual configuration, the earliest T-S-D motors wore forward-pointing "superimposed" (or over-and-under) alternate-firing cylinders. Production on these twins began in the summer of 1929 for both the 248 cc and 348 cc sizes. Interchangeable cylinder blocks allowed owners to switch between these displacements. Furthermore, one could quickly remove a T-S-D powerhead from its lower unit via three thumbscrews. A horseshoe-type (M.L. brand) magneto delivered spark to the T-S-D, and a ported sleeve gave the engine its optimum fuel mixture. Engineers designed it to operate by an eccentric from the crankshaft so that the sleeve would remain open only for the fuel intake period. Reportedly, this provided for easy starting and fuel economy. Both models weighed 72 pounds, but they possessed different horsepower specs. The 248 cc "pleasure/utility" T-S-D gave 8 hp @ 3,500 rpm, while its speedier 348 cc counterpart pulled 14 horses @ 4,500 rpm. According to obscure details unearthed by English marine historian David Pugh, they were actually designated Bulldog and Greyhound, respectively. T-S-D Outboard Motors, Ltd., of Littlehampton, built these outboards until about 1934.

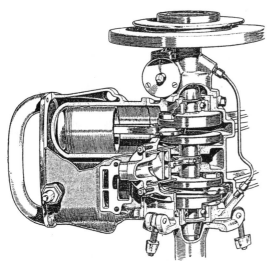

Details of the crankshaft assembly and sleeve-valve induction system.

Streamlining is evident on the 1930 T-S-D forward-pointing, alternate-firing twin. So is some intricate workmanship. Note the exhaust manifold, the oversized cylinder head, and the gear-driven magneto.

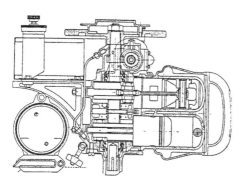

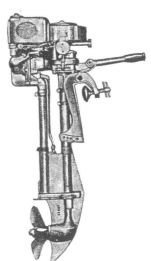

The T-S-D people discovered that big, fancy, expensive outboards might have received a lot of magazine coverage during the 1930s, but they didn't make the cash register ring very often. That's why the firm began concentrating its efforts on a more affordable kicker in 1933. The T-S-D Pup found its way to more transoms than the larger models, and it became a favorite in the 3 hp range.

Sketches of a 1929 T-S-D show how the forward-pointing twin was designed. Three easily unfastened nuts hold this T-S-D's powerhead to its driveshaft housing.

The company had taken part of its name from proprietors Trotman, Smith, and Doe. Trotman provided the engineering talent, and in 1933 he and his partners realized that the exotic T-S-D models would find few customers in the era's engulfing economic depression. Trotman got out his sketchpad and came up with a 124 cc, 3 hp @ 3,000 rpm single that could be affordably built and sold. Through the late 1930s, a good number of these little Pup outboards moved out of the T-S-D factory and into the hands of eager buyers.

The motor's lower unit received strengthening via an aluminum web cast between a length of the exhaust and driveshaft housing tubes. It looked as if the skeg simply kept going up in order to form a crude one-piece motor leg. This results in the model's most visually defining characteristic. Collars on the aforementioned tubing allowed for adjustable shaft depths. Still, there was more. The Pup's novel "fold-twist" folding propeller could be adjusted for pitch, or it would collapse horizontally if the lower unit smacked into something. For some reason, T-S-D itself folded not long before World War II. Pup tooling and manufacturing rights were then acquired by Lowestoft-based Brook Marine Company.

Turner-Bray (also Turner)

Considered to be a sideboard rather than outboard motor, the Turner-Bray was introduced to British boaters in the early spring of 1930. Early ads identified it as the "Konig-Bray Motor," and it had an astonishingly low price. During the previous summer, Arthur Bray, Ltd., on London's famed Baker Street, had imported an 83 cc Konig sideboard. The motor delighted the importer, which sought a license from Berlin-based Konig so that the design could be copied and built at a British plant in Wolverhampton.

By 1932, dubbed Turner-Brays and touted as "perfectly silent," the resulting single-cylinder, water-cooled kickers generated 1 ¼ hp @ 1,800 rpm. Propeller action came through a long shaft connected to a hand-operated friction clutch and a direct-drive dog clutch that was worked by a lever on the tiller. To draw cooling water, a rubber pipe was tossed over the boat's side and enlivened with a diaphragm pump. Turner-Bray offered its motors with a "bed-plate" to facilitate bolt mounting through the side of the hull, but the

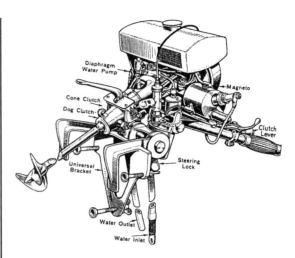

That break in the driveshaft (just above the propeller) was the sketch artist's way of showing that Turner-Bray's driveshaft extended farther than page space would allow. The 1 ¼ hp sideboard began life as a German-built Konig commissioned by a London marine dealer.

motors also came with a conventional transom bracket.

In late 1932, some sources simply listed this as an 83 cc, 1 hp sideboard from Turner's Motor Manufacturing in Wolverhampton. A 90.5 cc sideboard version was also available, but it yielded the same horsepower as the smaller one. To satisfy conservative putt-putt enthusiasts, the company offered the 90.5 cc mill on a conventional outboard lower unit.

Viking (four-cycle)

In May of 1929, *The Motor Boat* ran tests on a twin-cylinder, four-stroke outboard dubbed Viking. A gear drive aft of the powerhead allowed this outboard to ride lower in the boat, thus achieving a safer center of gravity than other "large" models of the era. This outboard sported many unique features including a horizontal crankshaft, a neutral clutch, and twin Amal carburetors. Additionally, as a 1929 *Yachting Monthly* reported, "a loose starting handle engages the flywheel boss (but provision is also made for cord starting). Splash oiling has been adopted from troughs under the crank [throws], which are filled by a rotary pump. The oil is both strained and cooled during its circuit. A saddle-shaped petrol tank covers the magneto and other parts likely to be affected by bad weather.

The main bearings and those for the camshaft are of the ball type. By slackening off four nuts the engine can be taken off the clutch housing and gear case, and slid off the clamping bracket on guides provided for this purpose."

The design allowed Viking's powerhead to be rigidly affixed to the boat while bevel gears connecting the engine to the lower unit helped the latter to tilt. The magazine saw this as a "blessing in disguise." The maker, British Outboards, Ltd. of Victoria Street in London, planned to include with the Viking three shaft lengths (24, 27, and 32 inches from transom to propeller shaft). Though given excellent coverage in the boating press, public interest wasn't sufficient for actual commercial introduction of this incredibly novel 8 hp @ 3,600 rpm outboard motor.

Like the Coventry Victor, the 1929 Viking four-cycle outboard consisted of a horizontal crankshaft-equipped opposed twin on a beefy outboard lower unit. Although it could be started by either a crank or with a rope, sales of this unique motor never made much of a spark.

Viking (Southend)

Another 1950s to early 1960s offering, Southend Engineering Company's Viking was designed for economy. Its Leigh-on-Sea, Essex, maker claimed the water-cooled, 43 cc single's ½-gallon fuel tank wouldn't run dry for four hours at cruising speed. That couldn't have been too fast, though, as Southend was loath to release an actual horsepower rating for inclusion in boating publications. In fact, the company recommended the Viking (sometimes called the Viking 3) as a troller "for lengthy periods [so as to be] particularly useful to anglers."

The little motor's 9 ¾-inch diameter by 14-inch pitch propeller (typically a three-blade) was operated with "an adjustable clutch . . . and an extending tiller which—through a system of

"The indestructible rectangular outboard" made a good advertising slogan for the Viking from Southend Engineering Company. Its "toolbox" style powerhead shrouding yielded a bulletproof look unique to this brand. Viking had an offset gear case imitated by a few rivals, too.

cams—controls the throttle, magneto, and clutch." Seven control options were cast into the cowling: "Stop, Idle, Start, Move Slowly, Troll, Rev." It isn't clear whether the latter activated reverse or high-revving speed. Advertised as "The ultimate in dinghy control . . . plus the world's quietest and highly efficient dinghy motor," the major focus was not particularly on speed. This Viking also had 360-degree steering and a rewind starter, thus making a geared reverse curious.

Truly eccentric, though, were the model's "stove enameled" rectangular powerhead shrouds (with hinges on the side so that the cover could be flipped open) and offset lower unit gear case affixed to the side, instead of the center, of the driveshaft housing. It made for a very mechanical-looking, bulletproof package. In fact, some have described the Viking 3 as a "toolbox perched atop a lower unit." Incidentally, 1953 ads mentioned a 1 ½ hp version with the same external appearance as the bigger model.

Warren Jet

Other than a quarter-page advertisement in a July 1962 boating magazine, little documentation remains on the Warren Hi-Thrust Jet outboards. Warren Marine Jets, Ltd., of Westminster, offered 2, 4, and 10 hp models equipped with "ahead, neutral and astern maneuvering."

Waterman Marine of London (or Waterman Marine Motor Co.)

This obscure subsidiary of the famous American outboard company might not have been noted here unless an old engine buff in Warwickshire hadn't spied a small brass ID tag at the Maritime Institute of Ireland. What looked to be a standard U.S.-built 1914–15 Waterman model C-14-X wore an original label indicating it had come from Waterman Marine of London, 14 Leicester Street, Leicester Square, London, WC. Further, the single was branded No. 142073, Type C14X. Perhaps the serial number signifies the 2,073rd motor made in 1914 . . . but by whom? If it came from Waterman in Detroit, why would they select a British carburetor? The motor was fitted with a carburetor from Brown & Barlow, Ltd., Birmingham, England.

It is known that circa 1914–16 Walter D. Fair and Company (by 1919, the makers of the Waterman clone, Watermota) offered imported Water-

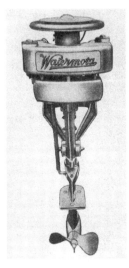

Watermota's maker never varied from the forward-pointing, single-cylinder format it first encountered when importing low rpm American Waterman outboards. Even so, it developed some pretty sophisticated machines in that cylinder placement style. The 1930 8 hp utility depicted here serves as an example. There was also a 4,500 rpm racing version that hit about 40 mph!

man products (with U.S.-made Kingston carburetors) through an office at 43 Leicester Square, not far from the Waterman Marine of London address. In 1912, Waterman's U.K. distribution had been handled by the Auxiliary Motor Installation Company of South Molton Street, London. Such shifting leads one to assume that a Waterman could be secured from several British venues concurrently. Adding to the confusion is a 1917 note in a British boating periodical indicating that a Mr. John A. Marine (as in "Waterman Marine"?) served as agent for Waterman outboards in what was then known as Mesopotamia. Suffice it to say research is continuing on this enjoyable conundrum.

Watermota

Even the moniker "Watermota" hints of a connection to the American pioneer of outboard motors, Waterman. In fact, Watermota's maker, Walter D. Fair and Company, Hampton Wick, Middlesex, had imported Waterman products starting around 1911–12. During the summer of 1919, and reportedly at the behest of the British Admiralty, Fair's firm began manufacturing a clone of the circa 1916 forward-pointing cylinder Waterman, dubbing it the Watermota. This was perhaps a serendipitous slight departure from the familiar Waterman name and a play on the words "water" and "motor" (or "mota," as it's pronounced in some British circles). The 5 September 1919 issue of *The Motor Ship and Motor Boat* reported that a batch of one hundred U.K.-made, 3 ½ hp Watermota Mark 1 out-

boards were then "going through the shop" and that the company planned to build one thousand per year.

During the mid-1920s, an influx of faster, sexier imported outboards motivated Fair to upgrade the original Watermota so that it might be more suitable for the lighter weight, higher speed, and outboard-friendly hulls just entering the marketplace. Fair's son, Colin, who by 1926 was a devotee of the fledgling sport of outboard racing, was likely the catalyst. The younger Fair convinced company engineer Shingi Yano to help create a competitive machine. Around 1926, the duo revamped their 292 cc, 3 to 4 hp @ 900 rpm Watermota Mark I from a relatively sleepy putt-putt into a 347 cc, 15 hp @ 4,500 rpm racer that put its small hydroplane on speaking terms with a then unbelievable 40 mph! Also incredible was the continuance of the ancient forward-pointing, single-cylinder design and externally-mounted, horseshoe-style magneto.

When Yano drowned during a time trial sponsored by *The Daily Mirror*, much of Fair's outboarding enthusiasm died, too. Reportedly, he decided to get away for a while and traveled to America where he called on his counterparts at the Johnson and Evinrude facilities. In both Waukegan and Milwaukee, Fair was humbled by the tens of thousands of outboards each company expected to manufacture for the coming year. Comparing these numbers to the one hundred or so Watermota outboards slated for 1930 production, he lost additional zeal for devoting time to the constant research and development that would have been required to keep Watermota on a par with American advances.

Back in England, Fair's company continued to offer a pair of 347 cc outboards. It produced the Silent Utility Eight, which had 8 hp @ 2,150 rpm as well as the Silent Speed Eleven, which gave 11 hp @ 3,500 rpm and a remarkable 18 hp when allowed to rev up to 4,800 rpm. In racing form, the Silent Speed Eleven had a flywheel magneto (as opposed to the external, horseshoe type) and vacuum cooling (rather than the gear-case mounted water pump). A separate lubrication system on all the models ensured adequate oil supply, though gas and oil still got mixed for the tank. Each came with a detachable (from the cylinder) water jacket. The tiller steered only the lower unit, and an "impulse" starter could be ordered as an accessory. Electric

This ad shows where Walter D. Fair and Company's focus was circa 1930. Sales of their Watermota inboards were bigger than their outboard revenues. Many of Fair's inboards were motors from the U.S.-based Waterman, and varied little from Waterman's World War I–era design.

starting was also available in 1930 via the same unit fitted on American motors of the period.

This information was found in a 1932 *The Motor Boat* outboard motor review. The publication found that little had changed from the previous year, nor would there be much news for the next annual. By the mid-1930s, Fair felt it futile to compete with the growing list of British makers, let alone Evinrude and Johnson. It's likely that, had Yano been alive, Fair could have been persuaded to develop a twin-cylinder (or maybe even a quad) Watermota outboard. That not being the case, though, the company quietly let its quickly aging outboard line sink. It did, however, continue marketing inboard engines for some time.

Water-Spryt

The 2 hp, air-cooled Water-Spryt appeared on the scene in 1949 and looked like the kind of outboard one might see in an old Warner Brothers cartoon. This cute kicker with bulbous cowling was a product of Brockhouse, the firm known for Britannia motors.

Woodson

One of the world's few diesel outboards, the Woodson hit the market in 1961. Its manufacturer, Woodson Marine, Ltd., of Slough, utilized a single-cylinder, 447 cc, two-stroke Hirth-brand diesel that pulled some 6 to 7 hp @ 2,200 rpm. Actually, this air-cooled machine wasn't really an outboard motor, because the bulk of the powerhead rested inboard of the stern. Belts transferred power to the outboard drive, and Woodson's tiller moved a rudder on the tiltable lower unit instead of swiveling the whole rig. Hardly the type of kicker an angler might stow in a car trunk, the Woodson weighed 285 pounds. An optional Siba Dynastartelectric starter-generator added another 15 pounds, but it sure beat the hand-cranking method!

Zenith Tiller Boat Motor

This motor was probably never built, but any British outboard from the early 1900s that even made it to the drawing board is worthy of inclusion in this volume. The story goes that in 1903 a

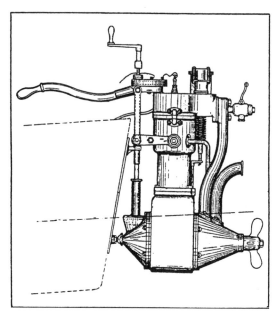

An underwater crankcase is a distinguishing feature of the 1903 Zenith. It's doubtful, though, that any of these "tiller boat motors" ever surfaced in real life.

F. W. Barnes of Zenith Motors, Ltd., designed a gasoline-powered "Tiller Boat Motor" while visiting a friend (C. T. Crowden) from Leamington. Slated as a four-stroke single, this unit designed to have a partially submerged crankcase. Perhaps remains of the prototype are hiding in someone's garden shed.

12

Price Guide and Rarity Rating

A Word About the Price Guide

Shortly before the second edition of *The Old Outboard Book* was published, word leaked out that it would contain a price guide. This prompted numerous complaints and even an anonymous fax to the publisher demanding that such inflammatory material never be released. Understandably, these salvos came from folks fearful that a price guide would turn our sleepy little "for fun only" old outboard motor collecting hobby into the likes of the big dollar-driven toy train pursuit. Once the book was available, several readers quickly contacted me about the price guide. Some complained that the prices were too high. At least as many, however, seemed upset that my suggestions appeared to be "way too cheap." In almost every case, the partisanship accurately aligned with those either in a buying mode or people hoping to sell profitably. Thankfully, there has also been a rather steady stream of centrist correspondence from novices who've used the guide for pricing comparisons, from veteran collectors finally able to reasonably acquire a motor from an antique dealer who, prior to seeing a figure in the book, believed it was "worth thousands," as well as from a widow happy to know what to ask for her departed husband's Sea King single.

Truth told, though, I liked the old informal system, and never wanted to do a price guide. I'd been scared off by the attitudinal changes at some toy train shows. There, seemingly due to the introduction of pricing booklets, the dynamics had shifted from the pleasant camaraderie of fond Lionel memories to a sense that the hobby was now all about finding dupes from whom you could buy cheaply and then "get high book" for the stuff from some starry-eyed neophyte. The rarity rating was my attempt to offer informative delineation between a common old kicker and one much more sought after by most buffs . . . all without committing to actual dollar values. My publisher thought that was useful, but insisted on adding some related numbers. As a result, I consulted a group of active antique outboarders and we came up with the guide. Of course, the economy boomed during the late 1990s, making some of the second edition's estimates seem miniscule. "Hunn's book plus 35 percent," someone who didn't know me announced when I asked about a motor in a pile of battered kickers at a 1998 nautical flea market. It made me breathe a sigh of relief that I hadn't been completely responsible for increasing the cost of outboard collecting.

By early 2000 any remaining derision about "Hunn prices" morphed into shock about what even the crummiest old kicker went for on eBay. The Internet auction site's arrival quickly mated a large variety of outboards—often touted as "extremely rare"—with electronic shopping convenience, chance, and every dynamic in human nature. Some sellers discovered that a garden-variety kicker of little interest to veteran collectors could pull bids exponentially higher than its upper price-guide level if marketed on the Web to potential buyers who were not aware of the engine's commonality in AOMC circles. For example, the same month that a guy in New York paid several times the original price (plus shipping and handling) for a 1970s Eska (missing its rewind starter), *The Antique Outboarder* ran a story about a motor meet at which buffs staged an "Eska

toss," a gag event to determine how far off a dock a bunch of the "rare" outboards could be thrown. That's not to say that eBay is bad for old motor nuts. Quite the opposite is true because, like this book, it can serve as a research tool. And, homework is the key to any hobby. In such a spirit, our third edition price guide is offered. Please remember that none of the prices herein relate to restored motors. Still typically the case are the following points.

- Factory-built racing motors, and pre–World War I engines are highly valued. The closer an outboard motor is to "as-from-the-factory stock," the better. Like hot rod cars, customized engines (with fancy paint jobs or chrome plating, etc.) do not necessarily appeal to a broad segment of collectors.
- Small motors can be lifted, stored, and utilized by a larger numbers of people than big outboards. This is especially true for older buffs in retirement settings, and likely impacts supply and demand of little kickers.
- There are still many more "garden-variety" 1930s–70s fishing engines (like a 1949 Johnson TD-20 Sea Horse 5) available than there are vociferous buyers for them.
- Someone who knows little about old outboards—except that he or she might like one—is more likely to pay more for common (or customized) motors than a knowledgeable collector will.
- Certain models with sporty or classic lines (such as the 1952 Mercury KG-7 Hurricane or Martin "200") will probably remain popular even after those who remember them from childhood are no longer buying.
- America's large senior demographic is well represented in the vintage outboard hobby, meaning it's likely that groups of motors from several major collections will hit the market annually.
- Through the 1970s, many buffs considered 1950s engines "too new" to be of interest to collectors. By the mid-1980s, though, certain Eisenhower-era motors were among the most sought. It may be that this trend—of motors becoming "collectible" after twenty-five years—will continue. Certain motors are hot collectors' items one year, then a bit cooler the next. By the way, when suggesting to dealers how much money they should offer for a

1928–29 Model TR-40 Giant Twin (highly prized today), Johnson's official *1940 Recommended Trade-In Value* booklet simply stated "NONE."
- Any interested kid with twenty bucks of birthday money should always be able to find a decent "starter" outboard (and lots of advice) at an AOMC meet. (Go to www.aomci.org for more information.)
- When buying an old motor, seek one that has only been used in freshwater, possesses all of its parts (unbroken), turns over smoothly (with good compression "bounce"), and has spark. If you're looking to get into the hobby economically, it's OK to be less picky about fuel tank dents and missing lower cowls.
- Rescuing and revitalizing a 1966 Eska can be just as rewarding as doing so with an expensive 1910 vintage motor. Besides, few aluminum rowboats filled with eager passengers can tell the difference.
- And finally, here's the most important piece of vintage outboard motor collecting and pricing advice: "Love people and use things . . . never the other way around."

Pricing—in this guide as well as in practice—depends on certain conditions, which are somewhat fluid since some of the older motors fit into more than a single category. For freshwater motors, the four major conditions are:

- **Condition 1: Nice original.** A really pretty outboard that runs well.
- **Condition 2: Complete.** A kicker that might be dirty, might have minor dents and worn decals, and may need a water pump impeller and plug wire-ignition coil-condenser replacement, but otherwise is all there and could be put in running order with ordinary mechanical skill and tools.
- **Condition 3: Mostly there.** An outboard missing cosmetic parts, such the cowling or knobs, etc., that also possibly has some broken or missing external mechanical components such as a carburetor or steering arm. (An incorrect replacement is equivalent to an absence.)
- **Condition 4: Bare bones.** An outboard that typically is rusted, corroded, missing lots of parts, and may have pistons seized in the cylinders. Many of these units show the effects of being left outside or in a wet basement.

Price Guide Estimates for:

Bendix

Model	Condition: 1	2	3	4	Comments
Battery-ignition single	$175	$100	$45	$30	1936 is least common. Make sure ignition coil is present.
Single Magneto Deluxe (magneto-ignition)	$150	$75	$40	$30	Bendix fuel tanks are often dented.
Twin	$190	$100	$60	$30	Less common than 1937–40 single; all models prone to suffer broken skeg.

Caille

Model	Condition: 1	2	3	4	Comments
5-speed rowboat motor	$400	$225	$150	$85*	Is the prop present? Does the propeller feather through its 5 settings?
Conventional-drive rowboat motor	$250	$175	$90	$75	
Liberty single or twin	$450	$275	$150	$100	Single-cylinder version was produced for longer period than twin.
Class B and C service twins 5-speed/Standard	$225	$125	$75	$60	
	$400	$200	$125	$65	Working electric starting models are rare.
Pennant 5-speed	$250	$130	$90	$65	Make sure prop feathering action works.
Racing models	$500+	$300	$200	$150**	"Tractor" lower unit is most desirable. Dual carbs is also a coveted feature.
"Depression" models like 79, 109, etc.	$175	$100	$60	$30	Caille's "bargain" motors—more common than most other Cailles.
"Companion" take-apart twin	$175	$100	$60	$40***	Is the carrying crate present?
Class A service twins 5-speed	$250	$110	$60	$40	
Standard	$150	$75	$50	$25	

*w/ lower unit & prop
**w/ lower unit & carbs
***w/ lower unit

Champion

Model	Condition: 1	2	3	4	Comments
1926–35 prewar models	$175	$100	$65	$50	Early "non-Scott-Atwater" produced (pre-1935) models are least common; 1942 Electra twin is best of Scott-made Champion engines.
1935–42	$125	$75	$50	$20	
Postwar 15 hp or more	$300	$150	$85	$40	Most interesting is the Tandem 33 setup with a pair of 16 ½ hp motors w/ common fuel tank and remote controls.
Hot Rod models (including Special Racer)	$500+	$400	$250*	$150	Midget and pre-1953 models are least common.
All other postwar singles or twins	$90	$70	$45	$20	As always, look for lower shrouds and cowling.

*w/ lower unit

Elgin (West Bend–produced)

Model	1	2	3	4	Comments
			Condition:		
1 ¼ hp single	$125	$60	$25	$15	Some of these air-cooled motors overheated. Make sure compression is good and engine turns over smoothly.
16 hp twin	$350	$150	$75	$20	Motor has no handles or rests, so the fiberglass cover is often faded and marred.
Circa 1955 models w/ key-selectable hp	$200	$125	$75	$30	25 hp model is worth double. Is the key there?
Other singles & twins 12 hp or less	$75	$50	$30	$15	Sears sure sold lots of the little pea-green Elgins. Water pump impellers are problematic.
1957–58 30/35 hp	$200	$110	$55	$25	Is Elgin remote tank present?
All others over 12 hp	$120	$70	$40	$25	Is cover scuffed or cracked?

Elto

Model	1	2	3	4	Comments
			Condition:		
Ruddertwin	$250	$150	$80	$60	Some very early (1921) versions are designated model F or have no model lettering. Thin, solid rudder motors are older than those with hollow rudder.
Speedster	$300	$200	$80	$50	Those w/ serial #s under 60999 are least common; 1929 w/ underwater exhaust or rudder is very unusual.
High-Speed Speedster	$400	$300	$200	$100*	Look for little H stamped after serial #.
Quad	$700	$400	$250	$120	1928 and 1929 models are most coveted. On all battery-ignition Eltos timer & coil(s) must be working.
High-Speed Quad	$1,000	$700	$400	$200	Single-carb version is extremely rare.
Senior Speedster	$400	$300	$200	$120	Much harder to find than standard Speedster.
Senior Speedster w/ electric start	$500	$400	$250	$150	
Lightweight	$110	$60	$50	$30	Double the value for folding version.
Foldlight	$210	$120	$70	$35	
Junior Quad	$350	$200	$100	$60	
Super C	$420	$250	$150	$75	
4-60 Racer	$1,000+	$700	$400	$200*	Is propeller present? Decals usually not intact because of alcohol fuel.
Super C Racer	$750+	$500+	$350	$200*	Is propeller included?
Super A	$150	$100	$60	$20	
Fisherman	$150	$100	$60	$20	Some have bronze lower units and these are @ 20% more valuable.
Super Single	$140	$80	$60	$20	
Imperial series	$120	$85	$30	$15	Is shrouding present?
Cub	$350+	$250	$150	$75	Any spark or compression? This smallest Elto is a favorite of some collectors.
Pal	$150	$100	$75	$40	More available than Cub.
Ace	$65	$45	$30	$25	Elto sold lots of these!
Handitwin	$120	$75	$40	$25	Fairly common.
Lightwin	$120	$75	$40	$25	"Weedless/Fisherman Drive" lower-unit option is a nice feature.
Fleetwin	$200	$150	$80	$60	

Model					Comments
Midget Racer	$500+	$400	$250	$150*	Elto version may have battery ignition.
1949 Sportster	$100	$50	$25	$15	
1949 Speedster	$120	$80	$50	$25	Less common than Sportster.

*w/ lower unit

Evinrude (Pre–World War II)

		Condition:			
Model	**1**	**2**	**3**	**4**	**Comments**
Rowboat Motor	$300	$180	$120	$65	Early "skegless" models with no name embossed on exhaust are least common; later (circa 1928) versions also unusual. 3 ½ hp version is more rare than standard.
Model K aluminum Rowboat Motor	$325	$190	$125	$70	This model was beset with production problems and prone to broken parts.
Model N Sportwin	$200	$120	$80	$40	
Model U Speeditwin	$350	$200	$100	$50	
Model T Speeditwin	$300	$200	$120	$65	Saltwater version (Model TS) w/ bronze lower unit is a real find. Bronze could be @ 50% more valuable.
1930 Speeditwin Racer	$700+	$500	$300	$150**	There are different versions of this one. Exhaust and lower unit styles vary, but it should have twin carbs.
1931–38 Speeditwin	$300	$200	$150	$70	Lots of variations with this famous Evinrude model.
6039 model Speeditwin	$275	$195	$140	$60	Are spark plug covers present? See post–World War II Evinrude Speeditwin note.
Class C Hex-Head Speeditwin Racer	$1,000+	$750	$500	$300*	Has external rotary valve on front of crankcase.
Midget Racer	$500+	$400	$250	$150*	Skeg is usually cut off and muffler missing. Are optional exhaust stacks present?
Mate (½ hp)	$500+	$400	$200	$100***	Are cowls present? Spark & compression is typically poor.
Scout	$175	$150	$100	$50	Some Scouts (9/10 hp) were sold as the Fishinrude Kit w/ case to hold motor and fishing equipment.
Lightwin	$120	$75	$50	$20	Note: Bronze weedless lower unit on 1937–42 Evinrude/Elto motors makes these rigs more valuable than standard offering.
Sturditwin	$150	$125	$45	$25	
Fleetwin	$150	$125	$45	$25	
Fastwin	$175	$125	$50	$25	
Sportfour	$150	$85	$45	$10	
Foldlight	$210	$110	$60	$30	
Zephyr	$100	$70	$40	$25	These are very underrated little engineering gems w/ numerous variations.

*w/ lower unit
**w/ 4-60-style lower unit
***w/ cowls

Evinrude (Post–World War II)

Model	Condition: 1	2	3	4	Comments
Ranger	$130	$75	$40	$20	
Sportsman	$130	$75	$40	$20	
Zephyr	$130	$75	$40	$20	1949 has weedless Fisherman-Drive lower unit. Some say this is the best Zephyr. See pre–WWII Evinrude Zephyr note.
Lightfour	$150	$80	$50	$25	Also applies to pre–WWII version.
Speeditwin	$250	$150	$70	$50	Some gear cases have side-skeg "wings." Others appear to be shaved off or were never there. Are spark plug covers present?
Speedifour	$300	$125	$80	$35	See gear case note above. Are spark plug covers present?
Big Four	$350	$175	$90	$50	See Speeditwin gear case comment. 1946 and 1949 models should have plug covers.
Lightwin (3 hp)	$200	$100	$40	$15	This is a good example of an older outboard that has more "used motor" value than actual worth to a collector.
Fleetwin (7 ½ hp)					
Neutral clutch	$150	$85	$40	$10	Early version (sold well) has neutral clutch knob. Later Fleetwins have full shift.
Full gear shift	$250*	$125	$80	$20	
Fastwin (14 hp)	$125	$75	$30	$15	Make sure you get the fuel tank and connectors.
Super Fastwin (15 hp)	$210	$120	$50	$20	As is the case with all pressure-tank fuel systems, make certain all components are present and in working order.
Fastwin (18 hp)	$200	$120	$50	$20	See comment for 15 hp Super Fastwin. Some have optional electric start.
Big Twin (25, 30, 35 hp)	$250	$125	$55	$20	See 15 hp Super Fastwin comment. Pressure tanks are not easy to replace. Most useful is version with steering handle.
Fisherman (5 ½ hp)	$200	$120	$50	$20	Needs fuel tank; often worth more to a regular outboard user than to a collector.
Sportwin 10	$150	$90	$50	$20	Is fuel tank present? A motor of this ilk (like most OMC products) is fit for regular use.

*w/ fuel tank

Flambeau

Model	Condition: 1	2	3	4	Comments
Single	$130	$90	$35	$20	1950 model is 3 hp; others are rated at 2 ½ hp. Rewind version is a bit more attractive.
Twin	$120	$80	$30	$20	1950 twin is 6 hp; others are @ 5. 1953–57 models should have cavitation plate. Rewind-start version is slightly more attractive.

Johnson

Model	Condition: 1	2	3	4	Comments
A	$160	$100	$75	$40	Earliest have 3-digit serial # and no cavitation plate (although one could have been added as accessory).
A-25, J-25	$125	$85	$50	$15	
AB, BN	$200	$125	$75	$25*	Has bronze lower unit.
A-35, A-45	$100	$60	$40	$10	A-35 sold very well.
PB-30	$500	$275	$150	$75	
P-30, P-35, P-40, P-45	$300	$125	$75	$50	
TR-40 Giant-Twin	$1,000	$500	$300	$200	Is skeg still there? Usually missing original lower unit.
K-35, K-40, K-45	$125	$85	$40	$25	Opposed-twin type.
S series	$300	$125	$75	$50	S-50 onward were more popular than S-45.
SR series	$500+	$350	$200	$100	These were typically converted (at home) to run on alcohol. Factory-stock gasoline version is a bit more unusual.
P-50 onward	$500+	$350	$150	$100	
PE-50	$500	$300	$150	$100	Electric start.
PR series	$750+	$500	$400	$150	See SR notes. PR Johnsons are still being raced in antique outboard circles.
V series	$300	$200	$100	$50	
VE, VA	$400	$250	$125	$50	
VR series	$1,000	$500	$200	$100	Twin-carb version is uncommon.
A-50, A-65, A-70, A-75, A-80	$100	$75	$50	$25	Alternate-firing twin.
K-50, K-65, K-70, K-75, K-80	$100	$85	$50	$25	Alternate-firing twin.
KR series (alternate-firing twin)	$600+	$500	$400	$150	See note for SR series. Skeg is typically cut off, muffler is missing, and motor probably has Tillotson instead of Johnson carb.
OA series	$120	$85	$60	$25	OA-55 has cylindrical fuel tank.
OK series	$120	$85	$60	$25	Some were post–WWII products of Johnson's Canadian factory. Most interesting have removable cylinder heads.
PO series	$350	$200	$75	$50	Post–WWII models are more common.
Models 100, 110, 200, 210, 300	$100	$60	$35	$10	Some models (like 300) had cowls and instrument panel. Are all parts present?
MS series	$200	$125	$100**	$40	The little MS horseshoe/sausage gas tanks are often dented. Is cowling present? MS-38 & MS-39 are most desirable. MS-20 doesn't have sausage tank.
MD series	$100	$60	$30	$15	
LS series	$80	$45	$20	$15	
DS series	$100	$60	$30	$15	
F series	$80	$60	$40	$15	
HA series	$80	$35	$20	$15	
HS series	$80	$35	$20	$15	
HD series	$90	$45	$25	$15	
DT series	$100	$50	$25	$15	
LT series	$90	$50	$25	$15	
AT series	$90	$65	$35	$15	
TD series	$95	$55	$35	$15	
TN series	$100	$60	$45	$15	Has neutral clutch.
KD series	$125	$55	$35	$15	

Model	1	2	3	4	Comments
KA series	$125	$55	$35	$15	
SD series	$125	$65	$35	$15	Are the knobs on front control panel present?
QD series	$200	$110	$50	$20	Must have fuel tank to be complete.
JW series	$200	$110	$40	$25	A usable motor of this type could easily make your local dealer's used motor rack.
RD series	$250	$125	$55	$25	Must have fuel tank to be complete. Some models are equipped with steering handle.
CD series	$200	$125	$50	$20	Is fuel tank present?

*w/ lower unit
**w/ tank

Lauson

Model	Condition: 1	2	3	4	Comments
Prewar single	$100	$60	$20	$15	Lawnmower engine style rated to lower unit via collar is more interesting version.
Standard single	$75	$45	$15	$10	Valve problems can cause poor compression.
Deluxe single (such as S-300)	$100	$65	$25	$15	Seems to be less common than standard 6 hp twin.
Twin	$100	$65	$25	$15	Look for oil gauge and lower cowling.
Twin w/ shift	$125	$75	$35	$15	Shifting mechanism (between motor and leg) is sometimes troublesome. Twin w/ neutral-forward only is said to be better performer.

Lockwood

Model	Condition: 1	2	3	4	Comments
Single-cylinder rowboat motor	$300	$150	$70	$50	Includes similar Sears Motorgo models.
1924–25 L-A twin					
w/out brass lower unit	$275	$135	$70	$30	Rudder models must have rudder intact.
w/ brass lower unit	$350	$200	$100	$50	
Models 62T or 72T					
w/out brass lower unit	$175	$100	$60	$20	
w/ brass lower unit	$400	$300	$75	$35	
Ace					
w/out brass lower unit	$375	$200	$100	$75	Accessory skeg is a nice find.
w/ brass lower unit	$400	$200+	$150	$90+	
Chief					
w/out brass lower unit	$400	$300	$150	$75	Accessory skeg is a nice find. Drip pan is sometimes broken. Check for excessive bearing wear by feeling play in flywheel; side-to-side wiggle is a sign of a problem.
w/ brass lower unit	$500	$350	$200	$150	
Racing Chief	$750+	$500+	$300	$200	Should have dual carbs, glass "drip" oilers, and cylindrical fuel tank.

Martin

Model	Condition: 1	2	3	4	Comments
20	$200	$100	$50	$30	Not as common as other small Martin models, these require lower cowls.
40/45	$100	$55	$20	$10	Like other Martins of this size, the 40/45 motors can be very good runners. They require lower cowls.

60 & 75	$100	$50	$20	$15	60 is Martin's most common model. It requires lower cowls.
66	$250	$150	$50	$30	Least common of 7.2 to 7 ½ hp series, the 66 needs lower cowls.
100	$150	$65	$40	$10	Lower cowls often are missing. Does the neutral clutch and/or Aquamatic speed reduction button work?
200	$500+	$300	$200	$100	Plastic-coated ignition coils are often cracked, consequently no spark. Rewind start is easily broken at mounting screw. Are lower cowls present?
200-S (factory racer)	$500+	$400	$225	$125	This 1954 limited-production item has spark advance lever and throttle cable hookup. Is remote fuel tank present?
60 Hi-Speed (w/ racing lower unit)	$500+	$400	$225	$125	Only about 150 of these were built. They have no lower cowls or steering handle. Real high-speed powerhead has serial # on front of crankcase.

Mercury

	Condition:				
Model	**1**	**2**	**3**	**4**	**Comments**
Pre–WWII Singles	$150	$95	$50	$25	Mercury Streamliner with cowls is worth @ 50% more.
Pre–WWII Twins	$150	$95	$50	$25	
Post–WWII Singles (silver)	$100	$70	$40	$20	Requires cover over carb to be complete.
Post–WWII Twins (silver)	$120	$75	$45	$20	On many early Mercs, the spark plugs were covered with little "bra-cup" style castings. These are often missing.
KE3 & KF3	$200	$125	$50	$25	Are water jackets intact? Lower cowls present?
KF5	$150	$95	$50	$25	Is gear case cracked? Are lower shrouds present?
Mark 5	$200	$135	$70	$35	See KF5 comments.
KE4 & Mark 7	$130	$80	$40	$20	Check for lower cowls.
KE7 Lightning Deluxe	$300	$155	$80	$40	Is lower cowling present? Earliest version has rectangular ID plate w/ no mention of Lightning.
KF7 Super 10	$310	$160	$80	$40	Less common than KE7. Are lower cowls present?
KG7 Hurricane (service lower unit)	$375	$180	$90	$45	Are lower cowls present and exhaust leg intact?
KH7 Cruiser	$410+	$210	$120	$60	Are lower shrouds present? Early motors had fewer water intake holes and small water pump; some overheated.
KF9 Thunderbolt	$500+	$350	$150	$100	Must include fuel tank, connectors, and steering handle to be considered complete.
KG4 Rocket Hurricane	$325	$165	$85	$45	Are lower cowls present? Standard service lower unit is rather uncommon as most motors were put on racing lower units.
Mark 15	$350	$250	$120	$60	The 15 must have fuel tank & connectors to be considered complete. Is Mark 15 emblem on front cowling present? It's scarcer than Mark 20.
Mark 20	$350+	$250	$120	$60	Same as Mark 15, but emblem says Mark 20.
Mark 25	$300	$200	$100	$40	

Model					Comments
Mark 30	$350	$200	$100	$40	Steering handle adds value.
Mark 40	$500	$350	$150	$100	Needs fuel tank & connectors to be complete.
Mark 55	$350	$200	$100	$60	Are remote controls present?
Mark 75 (and early 6-cylinder models)	$375	$150	$75	$40	Needs remote control to be complete.
KG7H, KG4H, Mark 20H	$750+	$500	$250	$150	Lower cowls (KG7H, KG4G) are usually missing. To be authentic, ID plate must have H designation. W/ regular powerheads on lower units, Quicksilver are @ 10% less. Pre-conversion Mark 20H fuel tank is @ 3 gallons and is 2-hose pressure type. Conversion model is more common than original green/gold 20H. Original has Carter carb and KG7H-style Quicksilver motor leg. Conversion wears fat, tuned-exhaust motor leg, and Tillotson carb. Cowls no longer fit and are usually gone. Make sure the rewind starter works well.
KG9H, Mark 30H, Mark 40H, Mark 55H	$750+	$500	$300	$150	It's nice to get the high-speed propeller with the motor. Usually racers kept 2 or 3 props. Are extras present? Real H Mercs will say so on ID plate. Standard Mercury powerhead on Quicksilver lower unit worth is @ 10% less.
Mark 10, 15A, 28 and other auto/transmission models	$200	$95	$60	$30	

Scott-Atwater

Model	Condition: 1	2	3	4	Comments
Nonshift single or twin	$60	$30	$10	$5	
Gold Pennant series (7 ½ to 10 hp)	$125	$75	$20	$10	Bail-A-Matic models have lots of problems w/ water pump.
Shift single or twin (up to 10 hp inclusive)	$100	$70	$20	$10	
Early 16 hp twin (1950–53)	$150	$100	$25	$15	Is lower shroud still there?
Later 16 hp twin (1954+)	$125	$75	$20	$10	Bail-A-Matic models are difficult to keep pumping water. Are bailing components present?
30 & 33 hp twin	$130	$85	$25	$10	Some had steering arm. See also Bail-A-Matic notes.

Thor

Model	Condition: 1	2	3	4	Comments
Thor/Sea King single	$150	$100	$35	$15	Original Thor/Sea King decals seldom are found intact.
Thor single	$160	$110	$40	$20	A little more interesting with the word *Thor* cast into carb cover; serial # might begin with S for single.
Thor opposed twin	$200	$125	$75	$30	Serial # could have T for twin.
Thor alternate-firing twin	$250+	$150	$100	$50	Uncommon.
Thor Pyramid-3	$500+	$375	$200	$150	Some had stamped steel lower gear case while others were cast aluminum.

Model	1	2	3	4	Comments
Thor Streamliner	$400+	$300	$200	$100	Must have teardrop-shaped tank and lower cowls, or could be confused with much more common Thor single made prior to 1939.

Waterwitch

Model	Condition: 1	2	3	4	Comments
¾ hp	$100	$50	$25	$10	Water-cooled model is less common than air-cooled style.
Raymond Loewy "twin-pod" fuel-tank styles	$150	$100	$40	$15	Sometimes referred to as Mae West motors.
3 ½ & 5 ¾ hp Deluxe Twin	$100	$75	$35	$10	This must have shrouds. Is generator in working order? Accessory light & plug present?
10 hp Kissel-built model	$250	$100	$55	$40	Lower shrouds should be included.
All other Kissel-built models w/ 571.XX model numbers	$60	$35	$20	$5–10	There are still lots of generic Waterwitch motors.
Muncie-made models (early 1930s)	$60	$35	$25	$10	Similar to Muncie's Neptune outboards.
Johnson-produced model 550.75	$300+	$200	$100	$75	Must have Waterwitch rope sheave plate.

Various Makes

Model	Condition: 1	2	3	4	Comments
Air-Boy	$150	$100	$50	$20	Fan blades and fan cage should be intact.
Brooklure (22+ hp)	$200	$100	$50	$25	It's good to find one still sporting the steering arm.
Brooklure (all others)	$75	$50	$25	$10	
Buccaneer/Gale (22+ hp)	$200	$100	$50	$25	Is steering arm present?
Buccaneer/Gale (all others)	$75	$50	$20	$5	
Chris-Craft (5 ½ hp)	$125	$100	$40	$15	
Chris-Craft (10 hp)	$250	$125	$55	$20	Are lower cowls present? A few of these had racing lower units—very desirable and double value.
Clarke (single)	$400+	$300+	$125	$75	Long shaft is a nice option. Motor must have spark plug cover, cavitation plate, and coil to be complete. Some have adjustable pitch prop, canoe bracket, carrybag, & wind-up starter "wand."
Clinton	$50	$35	$15	$5	Like many "modern-era" fishing motors, Clintons are probably worth more to an angler (for use) than to a collector.
Corsair	(See values for similar size Scott-Atwater.)				16 and 30 hp versions are a bit more desirable than smaller models.
Cross Radial	$1,000	$500	$150	$75+	Model w/ tractor lower unit is most desirable.
Cross Sea Gull	$400+	$250	$100	$75	Dual-carb-equipped racer is most desirable and @ 50% more valuable.
Detroiter (18 hp)	$400	$200	$95	$50	
Dragonfly	$100	$75	$25	$10	Fan cage and blade must be intact.
Eska (under 9 hp)	$50	$35	$10	$5	See notes concerning Clinton.
Fageol	$225	$125	$45	$20	Needs controls, cowl, and fuel tank to be complete.
Firestone (16+ hp)	(Values same as comparable Scott-Atwater models.)				Some have Knotometer water speedometer.

Firestone (under 16 hp)	$75	$50	$15	$5	Look for Knotometer on deluxe models. Otherwise this is a very generic outboard that sold reasonably well.
Guppy	$75	$50	$20	$7	Complete examples come with garden hose pump nozzle attachment for lower unit.
Homelite	$175	$100	$40	$20	Must have gas tank and remote controls to be complete.
Indian	$800	$400	$200	$100	Values are inflated due to interest of vintage motorcycle collectors.
Koban	$400	$200	$120	$75	
Majestic	(See post–WWII Champion listing.)				Majestic Hot-Rod is rare.
Mighty-Mite	$75	$50	$20	$5	
Milburn Cub, Continental Commando, Husky	$100	$50	$25	$10	Some have underwater exhaust accessory.
Mono	$50	$35	$15	$5	See notes in Clinton section.
Neptune 16 hp Master Twin	$150	$100	$40	$15	
Neptune-Muncie (all other pre–WWII)	$60	$40	$20	$10	
Neptune (post–WWII)	$90	$50	$25	$15	Shrouded (typically green or maroon) models are most desirable. Of these, 10 & 10 ½ hp are least common and worth @ 50% more.
Oliver (5 ½ & 6 hp)	$100	$60	$30	$10	Is fuel tank present?
Oliver (15 & 16 hp)	$175	$75	$40	$15	Is fuel tank present? Some 16 hp motors had electric start.
Oliver (35 hp)	$200	$110	$50	$20	Are fuel tank & remote controls present?
Royal (22 & 25 hp)	$200	$100	$50	$20	Should have steering arm.
Royal (all others)	$75	$50	$20	$10	
Sea-Bee (22, 25, 35 hp)	$200	$100	$50	$20	22 and 25 hp models need steering handle to be complete.
Sea-Bee (all others)	$75	$50	$20	$10	
Sea-Flyer	$70	$45	$20	$5	
Sea King (Thor)	$100	$70	$35	$15	
Sea King (15 hp; Lockwood Chief)	$275	$150	$75	$50	Add @ 25% w/ Eclipse inertia starter.
Sea King Folding	$200	$110	$60	$35	
Sea King Midget-Single	$120	$75	$20	$10	Motor needs little "chipmunk-cheeks" side covers to be complete.
Sea King 15.2 hp Giant Twin	$150	$100	$40	$20	
Sea King (post–WWII, less than 22 hp)	$75–100	$60	$20	$10	
Sea King (22+ hp)	$200	$100	$50	$20	
Voyager	(See post–WWII Champion listing.)				
West Bend (less than 12 hp)	$75–100	$50	$15	$5	
West Bend (12 hp or more)	$125–200	$75	$20	$10	Pre-1955 West Bend motors were made for export. They're uncommon in the U.S.
80 hp Shark	$350	$200	$100	$50	Needs controls.
Wizard 10 & 12 hp (Mercury-based)	$200	$75	$50	$35	On remote fuel-tank models, be certain tank & connectors are present. Is shrouding still there?
Shift models	$300	$125	$85	$35	
Wizard (Oliver- or Scott-based)	(Values @ 20% higher than comparable Oliver or Scott models.)				Is automatic bailer on Scott-based Wizard?
Wizard Super Power 25	$350	$200	$100	$50	Is fuel tank present?
Wizard (all others)	$75–100	$50	$25	$10	Is lower cowling present?

If you are like most motor collectors, at one time or another you have had a dream that features a long descent on creaky stairs. As you reach the bottom step, an old guy, who just sold the land on which his ancient dealership sits to a mall developer, flips a sparky light switch. This clicks on a string of dusty bulbs whose light keeps you from tripping over 75 or 80 vintage outboards. Double row racks along the far wall faintly smile with weathered tank decals. Cobwebs connect motor after unfamiliar motor. Every fourth or fifth lower unit is identifiable, however, causing your heart rate to accelerate with disbelief.

The elderly fellow says, "Take your time, and if you find anything worth twenty bucks or so to ya, just holler." In no time you glance at your watch and nearly two hours have gone by.

Admittedly, old outboarding is a truly personal endeavor. Generally speaking, however, off-brand engines one would love to discover in the aforementioned proverbial kicker cache might include a Cross Radial or Cross Sea Gull Racer, Clarke Twin, primitive Burtray/Walnut, Indian Silver Arrow, Koban, Allen or Submerged electric, Submerged gas, and 1896 American. In fact, any early minor marque rowboat motor such as a Wright, Joy Motor, Federal, National, Gray, Spinaway, Ferro, Amphion, Strelinger, Blakely, or Wisconsin would be a notable find.

Although Waterman was once the outboard industry's front-runner, it's included here because the brand has a certain rare mystique with outboard buffs because it is on the Antique Out-board Motor Club's logo. Vertical-cylinder models seem to be the favorite.

Accurately pricing these pieces is difficult at best because so few have been sold or traded. And strange as it may seem, while minor-make "stars" are often admired at meets, often interest in buying and using the more common old outboards is greater. Perhaps this is due to the fact that favorites are typically ones most fondly remembered by collectors. Hence, the green Merc 10 or maroon and white Johnson 7½-hp seem a more useful acquisition than an elaborate 110-pound Cross Radial. Different strokes for different folks makes for a wide variety of "dream motors," keeps costs in line, and treats vintage outboarding as fun.

Outboarders digging up an air-cooled Bendix usually find a Single Magneto Deluxe or "SMD" model (with a busted skeg). The battery-fired singles follow in availability. Harder to find are the twin-cylinder Bendix engines. A four-piston/two-cylinder, 15-horse prototype was tested in the Bendix factories. (Each connecting rod held a pair of pistons.) Whether or not this super-rare Bendix still exists, is unknown.

By the way, Bendix also offered their outboard powerheads linked to small transmissions for inboard use. Plans for the big 15-cube, 15-hp Bendix reportedly were modified for inboard marine and midget race car applications.

Minor Makes

Rarity Rating
Bendix

During a 1937 flood in the Kentucky/Indiana region, Bendix shipped about 300 of its single-cylinder motors to emergency workers. The engines' air-cooled feature performed well in the silty, mud-laden flood waters. Perhaps some of these "hero" motors are waiting to take a place in an outboard collection.

Bendix production, which began in Indiana during 1936 was reportedly shifted to the firm's Brooklyn, New York, facility by late 1938.

Caille

The 1931 Caille Model 50 racer with tractor lower unit and twin carbs is a very rare motor today. Still, there could be one waiting for discovery in someone's garage.

If there were any such thing as a common Caille, it might be one of the small 1930s budget engines, such as the Model 79 or 109. Rowboat motor enthusiasts look for the early 1915–1925 5-speed singles. In fact, all of Caille's 5-speed propeller kickers rate a little extra. One without a prop, however, makes restoration frustrating.

The straight-shaft Liberty Drive singles and twins also have a following and are prized by some collectors. Caille racers, especially with twin carbs and tractor lower unit, count as rare outboards. The larger (15-plus-hp) Red Head twins seldom show up anymore.

Almost every Caille left the Detroit factory with a little priming cup on each cylinder. Often they're missing, having been replaced with a small bolt.

Caille is pronounced "KALE," but no matter how you say it the quality outboard firm had some classy logos.

Champion

Anyone intrigued with ornate aluminum castings would find the few remaining 1926 Champions (and sister Monarch) interesting. A number of the late-1930s Scott-Atwater–produced Champs are almost as available as the ubiquitous Waterwitch. An exception is the more unusual 1942 Champion Electra alternate-firing twin.

After 1945, Champion motors—which had been offered through Firestone stores coast to coast—were then sold via a spotty fledgling dealer network. Consequently, the newly designed postwar Champs are much more available in a locale once featuring a Champion Outboards franchise.

The large 15-plus-hp twins are not very easy to find. Hot rod racing models are typically considered the rarest versions of this

marque. Badge-engineered Voyager and Voyager Majestic private brand models are a bit tougher to find than their Champion counterpart. This includes Majestic class "BU" and "JU" hot-rod racers, reportedly marketed in 1955.

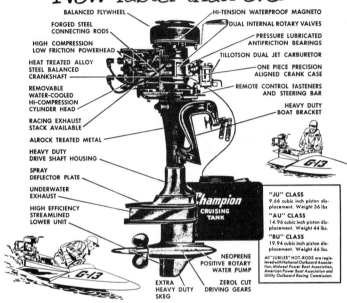

"JUBILEE" Hot-Rods
Now faster than ever

BALANCED FLYWHEEL
FORGED STEEL CONNECTING RODS
HIGH COMPRESSION LOW FRICTION POWERHEAD
HEAT TREATED ALLOY STEEL BALANCED CRANKSHAFT
REMOVABLE WATER-COOLED HI-COMPRESSION CYLINDER HEAD
RACING EXHAUST STACK AVAILABLE
ALROCK TREATED METAL
HEAVY DUTY DRIVE SHAFT HOUSING
SPRAY DEFLECTOR PLATE
UNDERWATER EXHAUST
HIGH EFFICIENCY STREAMLINED LOWER UNIT

HI-TENSION WATERPROOF MAGNETO
DUAL INTERNAL ROTARY VALVES
PRESSURE LUBRICATED ANTIFRICTION BEARINGS
TILLOTSON DUAL JET CARBURETOR
ONE PIECE PRECISION ALIGNED CRANK CASE
REMOTE CONTROL FASTENERS AND STEERING BAR
HEAVY DUTY BOAT BRACKET

Champion CRUISING TANK

NEOPRENE POSITIVE ROTARY WATER PUMP
EXTRA HEAVY DUTY SKEG
ZEROL CUT DRIVING GEARS

"JU" CLASS
9.66 cubic inch piston displacement. Weight 36 lbs.

"AU" CLASS
14.96 cubic inch piston displacement. Weight 44 lbs.

"BU" CLASS
19.94 cubic inch piston displacement. Weight 46 lbs.

All "JUBILEE" HOT-RODS are registered with National Outboard Association, Midwest Power Boat Association, American Power Boat Association and Utility Outboard Racing Commission.

Late 1940s-early 1950s Champion Hot-Rods were built for action. They provided Champion with a proving ground on which the Minneapolis firm refined it's circa-1956 Class "B" Hot-Rod and gave Mercury fits!

Well-built and nicely designed, Elgins were sold by the thousands at Sears. Many from showrooms and the famous Sears and Roebuck catalog are still in service. These West Bend–built Elgins aren't hard to find and have often surfaced with bargain price tags at lawn sales and swap meets.

In terms of collectibility, notable light-green Elgins are the 16-horse twin and the tiny 1¼-hp single. Another interesting West Bend–produced Elgin is the 1955 multi-horsepower outboards that could shift to different power ratings with a key-controlled switch. All others might be said to be as common as hot dogs. Not much interest has been exhibited for the late-1950s/early-1960s Scott- and McCulloch-made Elgins, but that doesn't mean there's anything wrong with them.

Key in upper left hand section of front panel switched-in different horsepower ratings on Sears 1955 Elgin (12 and 25 HP) motors. Lower settings were recommended for younger operators. Once dad took over, the Elgin power-key could be quickly dialed to the engine's full shot.

Elgin

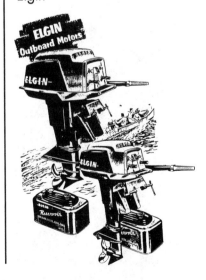

Elto

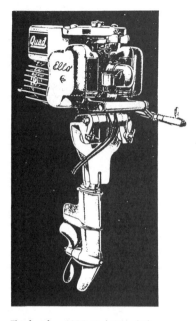

The first few 1929 High-Speed Elto Quads had just one carb. An early race caused factory officials to decide single carburetion was not such a good idea. Once replaced, the carb and manifold got tossed off the dock.

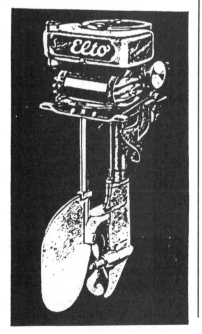

The Elto Speedster for 1929 had water intake scoop that could accept a rudder.

From the time of their late-1921 introduction, Ole Evinrude's Elto Ruddertwins gained quick popularity. Thousands were sold, and many are still around today. Considered unusual are later engines (circa 1931) in this series. Elto's Speedster makes a first-class antique outboard due to its vintage look, light weight, knuckle-buster starting, and lively performance. It is not as common as Ruddertwin (especially the mid-1927 to 1928 engines with a serial number under 61000) but it certainly is not rare. *H* designated High Speed Speedsters (1929) are a much more difficult find.

Jumping up two cylinders, the Quad is considered a pinnacle of Elto engineering. Both 1928 and 1929 versions are coveted by most collectors. Because Elto produced fewer Quads than Speedsters, they're not as common now. The H model High Speed 1929 Quad is truly an unusual find.

Incidentally, a few early 1929 Quad racers came through the factory with one carb instead of dual carburetors. They were given a test in the Albany to New York Marathon but didn't run well at the start. According to legend, Elto officials hurriedly replaced the single-intake manifold with a dual-carb-equipped spare. The rare original pieces were tossed from the dock into the Hudson River.

By the early 1930s, the top-of-the-line Elto was a factory racer called 4-60. Some even came with double ignition (two sparkplugs in each cylinder). One of these would make most old racing outboard buffs' hearts jump. In fact, any 4-60 is a remarkable find.

Other 1930s Eltos of note include: Racing "C," Senior Speedster, Elto Speeditwin with battery ignition, Elto Midget Racer, and ½-horse Cub. The latter model was practically a toy, wore out fast, and, when found today, typically lacks spark and compression.

Battery-fired Eltos usually require attention to their coils and timers. Coil wires are often frayed or broken, condensers sometimes conked, and pot metal timer bushings seized and cracked. Spring tension in Elto poppet valve-type carbs sometimes is out of spec, causing slow performance. In any event, revitalized Eltos make dandy runners. And with a little attention to the ignition system, they really do (as their ads claimed) "start with just a quarter turn" of the flywheel!

A moment's glance at an Evinrude rowboat motor triggers estimates of antiquity. Ole's most vintage-looking, legendary product was produced between 1909 and 1928, and a fair number of the run survives. Less common engines in this series are the earliest examples, circa 1909–1911 (senior at present is #780 from 1910) and late-1927–1928 versions. A larger, 3½-hp single-cylinder rowboat motor, designed for heavy-duty commercial use, is not as common as the 1½- or 2-horse styles.

There were a few attempts at building an opposed-twin Evinrude rowboat motor. They are hard to find. Evinrude began making Speeditwins in 1927. The first examples (especially with bronze or tractor lower unit) are rather unusual. Dual-carb-equipped 1930 Speeditwin Racers count as extremely uncommon. Evinrude's sister line, OMC, made a 20-cubic-inch SpeediBee racing motor in 1930. It, too, is remarkably rare.

Mid-1930s Evinrude Hex-Head competition models (with Johnson-type external rotary valve) are a great find. Speaking of fast kickers, the Milwaukee company's Midget Racer is not a regular sight. There was also Evinrude's version of the big 4-60 high-speed motor. Like other performance models, it's relatively rare. A fishing motor from this period that doesn't surface often is the Foldlight. Yes, its hinged mid-section was for folding and easy toting.

In 1934 Evinrude's 25th anniversary fleet included motors like Lightwin and Lightfour with "Hooded Power." These products ushered in the era of engine shrouding and dependable rewind starting. They're seldom found still wearing their cowls and starter.

Most collectors have room for Evinrude's tiny ½-hp Mate. Built just prior to World War II, Mates found today usually lack compression and spark. Light-duty products, they simply wore out quickly.

Vintage motorcycle buffs go crazy over small displacement four-cylinder bike power plants. Interestingly, though, boating's most famous little quad, Evinrude Zephyr, has long been ignored by most outboard people. With numerous versions, such as the 1949 angled-drive Weedless lower unit, Zephyr just might grow in popularity. And there have always seemed to be more than enough to go around.

A few years before World War II, Ole's firm refined Speeditwin and modeled the old Elto Quad into Speedifour. Some were later used in combat. During this time, 4-60 was worked into a military Storm Boat Motor (later dubbed Big Four). These rigs were subsequently sold (circa 1946–1950) for civilian use. Although too large for some collectors, model 6039 Speeditwin, the Speedifour, and Big Four do have a definite following. Some of the Speeditwins were converted into "C Service" hot rods. The 60-cube Big Fours also saw some racing. And Speedifours make great antique water ski motors. They're not super-rare, but getting harder to find in decent shape.

Newly designed post–World War II Evinrudes of note include well-preserved examples of Big Twin 25 with pressure fuel tank and steering handle. Other blue and silver Evinrude models from the

late-1940s to the mid-1950s, such as the Fastwin 15, aren't particularly rare but are nice to find in clean, running condition. Perhaps the most unusual "modern" kicker bearing Ole's brand is the 3-horse Ducktwin. The low production run, olive-drab color variation of the popular alternate-firing Lightwin was produced well into the 1960s. It also came in a folding version.

True devotees of the Evinrude line might seek examples of the firm's non-outboard power equipment. Centrifugal pumps, rock drills, and ice saws (based on the rowboat motor) are now seldom seen. The 1930s Evinrude bicycle, micro-horsepower Speedibike motor, pumps, Shop King lathe, and Lawn Boy Power Mower are out there somewhere but are less common than the outboards.

Flambeau

Not a very common motor, even during its original Truman/Eisenhower–era production run, a Flambeau typically pops up in the Midwest or in spots where the firm's tiny local dealerships existed. Seldom found in operating condition and sometimes stuck, the Flambeau twin seems to be more prevalent than the single. Both rope-start and rewind models were offered. The 1950 versions of single and twin with 3- and 6-hp ratings, respectively, were one-year motors. Actually, however, it's difficult to date Flambeau engines. Some rules of thumb: 1946–1949 models are silver; 1950 on up sported burgundy-color powerheads; 1953–1957 twins wore cavitation plates.

In the 1970s, a golden, 10-horse twin prototype (missing its ignition system) was acquired from a former factory employee. It dates from the late 1940s and is probably the rarest Flambeau. Whether or not other 10s were cast is open to speculation.

Like many minor makes (and old outboards in general) Flambeau values are highly dependent on finding someone with keen interest in that particular brand. And sometimes that's harder than coming up with the motor.

Waterstained engineering drawings discovered in a pile of factory remains indicate this Golden Ten Flambeau twin was built circa 1948. The motor wears layers of gold automotive-type paint, appears to be tacked together with a minimum number of bolts, and has no flywheel or ignition system. Apparently, the Ten was fabricated just to get carted from one boat show to the next in hopes enthusiastic outboarders would place their orders for a king-size Flambeau. Although these rigs were touted in early 1946 brochures, it looks like this is the only one. (Miville Fournier photo)

Johnson

Dozens of owners of vintage Johnsons were once convinced theirs was the oldest, rarest surviving motor. As soon as other collectors enter the equation, though, those early Johnsons begin to add up. Over the years, the Johnson people manufactured more outboards than anyone else. So it stands to reason a greater number of these kickers (as compared with other brands) is still around. It's somewhat like Ford's Model T and Model A cars. Today you seldom see them on the side of the road or rusting in a farmer's field but in antique auto circles they are plentiful.

In all fairness to Johnson buffs, some of the marque's limited production and low serial number motors are considered scarce.

But anyone starting out in old outboarding with a hankering to find, say, a 1928 A-35 classic LT from 1937, postwar alternate-firing KD or TD, will most likely have his or her desires fulfilled.

Early Johnson (Waterbug) Lightwins with exposed water pump originally sold like crazy. Later A-25 versions met success, too. It's not unusual for one to be found in operating condition, following a cleanup. An A with a low (506–750) serial number would be a nice find. Models B̲N, A̲B̲ (*B* for bronze lower unit) and A̲C̲ (*C* for canoe-mount bracket) are harder to find than the standard models.

Perhaps the most legendary 1920s Johnson is the TR-40 Giant Twin. This 25-hp brute might be considered a must-have for Sea Horse and/or racing motor collectors. So far, only a handful have been discovered. Late-1920s Johnsons with an *F* following the first letter in the model designation (such as: KF-45) are uncommon F̲ull-pivot reverse rigs. The V series, especially V-50 onward (with half-speed external rotary valve) are popular with collectors willing to lug big four-cylinder iron. S and P series Johnsons (again, especially 1930 onward with half-speed rotary valve) are good finds. Thirty-cubic-inch P motors of the early-to-mid-1930s era are more desirable. Electric-starting variations (SE, SA, PE, PA, VE and VA) have a small, dedicated following. Any prewar Johnson racer (with an *R* in the model code), such as PR-65, could very easily find a new home.

In order to reduce production costs, Johnson quit its intricate external rotary valve motors (S, P, and V) but resurrected the Class "C" series P as the PO in 1937. Made through 1950, a good PO is certainly not rare but is typically valued higher than smaller engines of the marque.

A die-hard Johnson collector might seek examples of the firm's 4-cycle "Iron Horse" power plants. These single-cylinder, air-cooled, landlubber motors were used to quicken everything from lawn mowers to washing machines. Some were mated to a 300-watt, 12-volt generator for use at summer camp or farm yet untouched by the Rural Electrification Administration. They sometimes show up at stationary engine auctions. Johnson also made refrigerators labeled Jo-Mo-Co in the early 1930s. Later versions (1937) wore a Briggs (as in Steve Briggs, who bought Johnson with partner Ralph Evinrude) nameplate.

Following World War II, the Waukegan, Illinois–based outboard plant turned out more kickers than any other facility. Running, super-clean (Condition 1) examples of this era's Sea Horse are getting snapped up. This is especially the case with 10- and 25-horse Johnsons with steering handle and a working pressure-feed fuel tank.

Perhaps the most unusual Lausons are the pre–World War II models with a lawn mower engine connected to an outboard lower unit under a collar ring. Reportedly, a huge 25-hp prototype Lauson was slated for market. My dad recalls seeing one at a 1940s New York Boat Show. That prototype would be valuable to a Lauson enthusiast. Postwar, 6-horse, non-shift twins and the 2-and-change-hp singles with separate drive shaft and exhaust tube are still around. The T-300 single with

A 2½-horse single was one of Lauson's first post-WWII offerings. Its 4-cycle design made fueling and trolling easy.

Lauson

Lockwood (Lockwood-Ash)

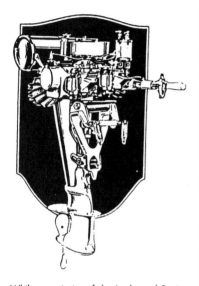

While a majority of the Lockwood Racing Chief outboards wore a glass, drip oiler on each cylinder, this rendering from a 1929 Scandinavian language Lockwood catalog featured one large oiler. Throttle control consisted of a lever on the tiller handle.

Martin

more streamlined lower unit is a little harder to locate. Shift versions of the Lauson are not quite as common, either.

Like Caille, its contemporary competitor, Lockwood didn't produce any outboards that are considered common today. The Jackson, Michigan, firm's 1926 (62T) and 1927 (72T) twins seem to be more plentiful than most of their other models. An earlier 2-cylinder Lockwood-Ash fitted with rudder steering is considered unusual. World War I–era singles had a respectable share of the fledgling outboard market. Some were sold under Sears's Motorgo banner.

By 1928 Lockwood's two basic models, the Ace and the larger Chief, were winning races and had earned reputations as major industry players. "Silent" versions (1929) featured underwater exhaust. Both years are prized by most collectors. If such a motor comes through with accessory skeg and/or saltwater bronze lower unit, it's a notable find. According to most buffs, however, Lockwood's real gem was their 92BR, the 1929 Racing Chief. These motors wore red, cylindrical fuel tanks, glass sight drip oilers, and dual carburetors. Some period literature shows the 92BR racer with a single carb (which was probably easier to control), but the real McCoy will still wear a pair. (Note: Finding replacements is very tough.) An authentic racer also has a three-digit serial number on the crankcase.

Post-1929 Lockwoods were products of Outboard Motors Corporation and typically represent badge-engineered (differentiated only by a decal) Elto/Evinrude motors. The Lockwood Foldlite folding twin is a good example. The unique engine in this genre is probably the Lockwood version of OMC's 4-60 racing motor.

Evinrude/Elto did offer a few models with Lockwood's own design, such as the Silent Electric (start) Chief. Numerous leftovers were unloaded to Montgomery Ward to be sold during the Depression as Sea Kings. Locating one with the weird Bendix inertia (wind-up spring) starter would make for a happy day.

Outboard motors in the Lockwood stable were rather "oil-intensive." Inadequately lubed examples often seized, blew up, or made wobbly work of important bearings. Some motors were equipped with a "drip pan" on the transom bracket. Carelessly tilting up the engine often broke this feature.

It's surprising just how many Martin outboards still ripple the waterways. Lots of parts motors, as well as a supplier (see page 83) with a large stock of Martin components, ensures this marque's continuation.

Easiest to acquire are Martin's 7.2-horse 60 and 75. In terms of commonality, next on the Martin roster are the 45, 100, and 20 respectively. However, you don't see that many 66 models. Rather coveted by Martin nuts are the remainders of the original 150 or so of the 60 Hi-Speed motors, as well as the 200 Silver Streaks (especially the 200-S racer). Plastic ignition coils for the 200 are often found cracked and inoperative. Some 200 owners are retrofit-

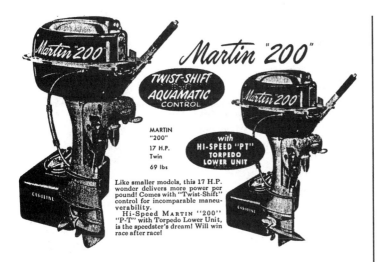

Martin "200"

MARTIN "200"
17 H.P.
Twin
69 lbs

TWIST-SHIFT
AQUAMATIC
CONTROL

with
HI-SPEED "PT"
TORPEDO
LOWER UNIT

Like smaller models, this 17 H.P. wonder delivers more power per pound! Comes with "Twist-Shift" control for incomparable maneuverability.
Hi-Speed MARTIN "200" "P-T" with Torpedo Lower Unit, is the speedster's dream! Will win race after race!

It's unknown whether or not any of the 1951 Martin "200" motors were actually produced. These 17-hp versions had transom clamps, instrument panel, spark advance lever, and "Aquamatic" steering handle button like a Martin "100." Documentation of a demonstration, as well as a fuzzy photo of a shift lower unit (in a boating magazine) indicates a gearshift Martin "200" did exist. Reportedly 10 were built but none has ever surfaced.

ting their motors with the cloth- and varnish-covered Martin 60 coils.

Most elusive is the pre-production 1951 200 with 100-style instrument panel and, of course, the 200 Silver-Liner with full gear shift. Reports of a four-cylinder, 40-hp Martin 400 have surfaced. That phantom prototype would be a neat Martin to find. Martins are often missing their lower shrouds.

Mercury

Nearly half of all correspondence generated by the first *Old Outboard Book* concerned Mercury. It seems this marque's beautifully styled, fast motors, along with the maker's colorful history, have sparked a lot of interest.

In terms of rarity, 1940 first-year Mercs in the K1 through K5 series are not very common. When found, their sheet metal fuel tanks are often rusty.

Kiekhaefer featured cast-aluminum gas tanks on its (1941–42) KB1 through KB5 models. Unfortunately, the seam sealer (between the two tank halves) dried out or oozed, causing leaks. The sand-cast tank surface was just rough enough to stymie decal adherence.

A few olive-drab color versions of early Mercs have surfaced. They wear U.S. military ID plates, denoting armed forces (1943–45) ownership.

The first post–World War II Kiekhaefer Mercurys, such as KD3 and KD4 (S models have rewind starter), are easier to obtain than early 1940s versions, but their spark plug covers and lower cowling are typically long gone. Many of these outboards were sold under Western Auto's Wizard name. In some parts of the country where a Western Auto store was very active, the Wizards are more plentiful than their Kiekhaefer counterparts.

Never a big seller, Merc's (1947–50) KE3 and KF3 Comet singles are not readily available. (And KF3 is less common than earlier KE3.) They suffered from easily corroded or cracked water jackets. As is the case with any motor originally sold with cosmetic

New Twin

MERCURY
MARK 28

New Slant

22 h.p.
SUPER
HURRICANE TWIN

big motor ski power!

only $00 down
24 MONTHS
TO PAY!

Here's 22 h.p. in the smallest package yet! — with patented Glide-Angle Design, Prop-Jet Exhaust, scientific powerhead tilt and *automatic transmission* with one-hand twist-grip control! Full Jeweled Power*!

* Ball and roller bearings throughout.

Thru-prop hub exhaust, automatic transmission-equipped Mercury Hurricane Mark 28 had many more features than Merc's first Hurricane KG7. Most collectors, however, prefer the original 10- version over this 22-horse model from 1958.

covering, Comets are often found minus their lower cowling. Tolerance/seal troubles often caused grease to exit the lower unit, while allowing water to enter. A nice-running Comet, however, is a joy to own. They're light, start quickly, use little fuel, and have that distinctive "old green Merc" look.

The 7½-hp Rocket KE4 (1947–52) and subsequent (1953–55) Mark 7 represented a big success at Mercury. Lots were sold and show up regularly in vintage outboard circles. Water jacket corrosion and splitting seem to be problems of these series.

Like the Rocket fishing models, Kiekhaefer's 5-horse KF5/Super 5 outboards were very well accepted. Look out for cracked lower unit gearcases. The Mark 5 is similar to the other 5s but wore a wire-operated neutral clutch. Check to see whether this feature still functions. Cracked gearcases and busted water pumps are also a problem here. Apparently, poor lower unit seals allowed in some water. Consequently, an undrained motor stored in freezing conditions usually popped its gearfoot. By the way, Mark 5's slip clutch (on the propeller hub) was subject to rust and corrosion.

In catalogs KG4 Rocket Hurricanes were only 7½ hp. Actually, however, the horsepower rating was followed by an asterisk that reminded operators that the horsepower varied with the rpms. Kiekhaefer understated KG4 at 7½ hp to keep it from bumping into the firm's underrated 10-horse model. Built predominately for high performance, KG4 powerheads often wound up on Quicksilver racing lower units. A number of them, originally sold with the standard "fishing" leg, eventually found their way to racers' spare engine piles. This 15-cubic-inch model might be considered the least common green Merc. It should not be confused with the rather plentiful 11-cube 7½-hp KE4/Mark 7 Rocket.

Diehard Kiekhaefer enthusiasts often go after Mercury's one-year offerings, such as the 1953 Mark 15. This 15-cubic-inch twin was very similar to a KG4 (powerhead) but had a remote fuel tank and gear shift. Not many were sold, and the ones that survived a few years often had weathered cannibalization by Class "A" racers. Mark 15's pressure tank, hoses, and fuel line connectors are hard to find in good shape.

The 20-cubic-inch (Class "B") Mercs are arguably Kiekhaefer's most "classic" products. KE7 Lightning models were very good sellers. Earliest versions starting with serial numbers 191 wear a rectangular ID with no reference to the Lightning name. Reportedly, in 1947 about 2,000 of these 10-horse motors were built each month.

KF7 Super 10s were a bit more sophisticated, with gas tank handles top and rear (although you could buy factory retrofits for KE7). They were not, however, as plentiful as the first Lightning motors.

KG7 moved from Lightning to Hurricane designation and was faster than its predecessors. These motors aren't scarce, but folks seem to hang onto them. Often missing are the lower cowls. In an effort to gain extra punch, some KE7/KF7/KG7 owners (especially

second or subsequent owners) cut off the end of the lower unit exhaust housing. Some models were equipped with a splined prop shaft, which worked a slip clutch. These are often found rusted or corroded. Lucky old outboarders might find a stainless steel shear pin-type prop adapter. It uses a pair of shear pins mounted parallel to the propeller shaft.

Kiekhaefer's 1952 KH7 Cruiser was an attempt to enter the growing Forward-Neutral-Reverse outboard shift market. While the gears were OK, Cruiser's lower unit had not been adequately "field-tested," causing water pump/cooling problems. Most surviving KH7 motors (not that they're very common) have a modified lower unit. The original had a small pump impeller and limited water intake holes. Another trouble spot, albeit cosmetic: the lower cowling is often missing.

The Mercury Mark 20 was probably the sexiest of all 1950s mid-sized outboards. They were handsomely svelte and energetically structured like a petite ballerina. About the size of a competitor's 7½, the Mark 20 with its highly pitched and cupped two-blade wheel bit the water like nobody's business. On a 12-foot aluminum rowboat with a 150-pound driver, the Mark 20 Hurricane engine delivered top-end performance that could have been considered dangerous! This model sold well but is hard to find with a working pressure-type fuel tank.

Twenty-cube Mark 25 models were available in a variety of styles and color schemes. They're more plentiful (except slower seller Mark 25E electric-start) than most other Mercs of similar displacement. Fitted with a fuel pump, Mark 25 isn't bothered by a problematic pressure feed system. One trouble spot here (and it's common to a number of 1950s Mercurys): ignition coils get leaky and/or shorted and require replacement.

The four-cylinder Mercurys debuted in 1949 as KF9. This 25-plus-hp in-line quad suffered from weak connecting rods, poor magneto venting, and spotty factory production. Numerous engines reportedly flunked factory inspections and had to be rebuilt two or three times before getting shipped to dealers. Not too many survive today. Because it's easy to put a KF9 shroud on a later KG9, one must make certain the serial number on the KF9 cover and engine block agree.

Subsequent KG9 and KG9-1 models were built better, helping Merc pick up more early 1950s sales. Initial examples have exposed chrome flywheel (although a rewind start retrofit kit was later available) and are more popular.

To most owners, a good Mercury 25 (KF9 or KG9) is like a '55 Thunderbird and not easy to part with. Watch for broken cylinder head bolts, cut-off exhaust legs, and missing or chopped-off steering handles. Such items, along with cowling and early fuel-line–to–motor connectors are difficult to replace.

Mark 40 is an updated version of KG9. Any of these big motors would make a great addition to a post–World War II outboard collection.

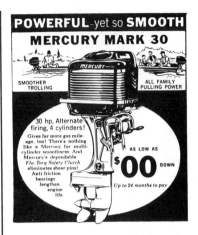

Small drawings in 1956 ad depict Mark 30 with tiller handle. Some Merc nuts are wild about this feature on a big motor.

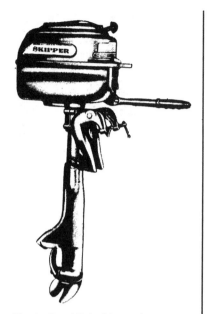

Muncie Gear Works (Neptune) manufactured Skipper outboards for "private brand" marketing in the late 1940s. Thinly disguised, this Skipper model BB2 differed from its 3.3-horse Neptune sister in decals only. In fact, a diagram photo in the Skipper operating instructions and repair parts catalog wears a Neptune logo.

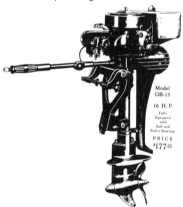

Model OB-15

16 H. P.

Fully Equipped with Ball and Roller Bearings

PRICE $177.50

1930s vintage Muncie Gear Works' top-of-the-line Master Twin was fitted with ball and roller bearings, as Mercury would be in the next decade. The ring on end of tiller arm was for optional steering rope.

Muncie/Neptune

Another of Kiekhaefer's single-year motors, the Mark 50 was the firm's first large, family water-ski engine equipped with full rear shift, electric start, and remote control. Too big and "new" for the tastes of some vintage outboard buffs, who prefer steering handle operation, this rig, due to production/delivery delays (some dealers didn't get one until midsummer 1954), is an unusual sight. Motors equipped with pressure fuel systems must have a good tank and workable controls.

Mercury racers armed with Quicksilver lower units are prized by many old outboard collectors. In order for these motors to be considered authentic, their ID should include a painted *H* (for hydro) after the model designation, or a stamped *Q* following the serial number. H Mercs' lower units have one cavitation plate, while earlier Q versions wear two. Incidentally the serial numbers on the tank ring (or in later models on the transom bracket) must match ID numbers on the engine block. If they don't match, you have a service powerhead on a racing leg (which isn't quite as official). Trouble spots on these fast kickers include water pump impellers (there's a special tool for replacement) and ignition coils.

As is the case with all Mercury models originally shipped with little lead seals on the powerhead bolts, these telltale tags will be intact if the motor hasn't been dismantled.

Even though Merc racing motors are not necessarily common, many survive. Kiekhaefer enthusiasts often have amassed a half-dozen or so per collection, which is where these motors are likely to remain. If they all went on the market at once, perhaps there would be more sellers than buyers. Then again, other collectors would no doubt race to snatch them up.

Early six-cylinder Mercurys, such as Mark 75, Mark 78, Merc 700, Merc 800, and even the 1962 Merc 1000, have a special following among collectors who have lots of storage space and a strong teenager to help with the lifting. Of this series, the Mark 75H racer is by far most coveted. Few older motors of this brand liked salt water. Avoid Mercs used in the ocean.

Kiekhaefer also made chain saws (circa 1942–53) bearing the Mercury name. Single- and twin-cylinder models were marketed by Disston, a Philadelphia saw manufacturer. In addition to cutting machines, the Merc folks also offered gas-powered generators and small aircraft engines for World War II– and Korean War–era target planes. The saws aren't common but pop up now and again. A few of the aircraft engines survive but are often found sporting bullet holes or shot-up cooling fins.

In terms of outboard collecting, Muncie products traditionally have not been in high demand. Even so, the 1930s model OB-2 quasi-racer with tractor lower unit conversion is an interesting item. Prewar 16-horse Master Twins have a small following. Some of the

rarer Muncie-produced Neptune kickers are the late-1940s shrouded models. Seen in light green or maroon, these rigs were available for a short while through a very modest dealer network and finally via mail order. Ten- and 10½-hp versions are the hardest to find. Muncie also did a private-brand version of some of their cowled kickers under the Skipper banner.

The tiny Muncie/Neptune Mighty-Mite singles are often identified as "real old motors." Though primitive in appearance, variations of this roughly 1.7-hp eggbeater were sold through the 1970s and are fairly common (especially in pieces).

Scott-Atwater

In certain areas of the U.S., Scott-Atwater had a respectable share of the outboard market. Its engines sold for less than Evinrude/ Johnson without being completely considered a minor make. Scott officials didn't insist its dealers carry only their motors. Nor were they overly critical with an establishment's size. Consequently Scotts were peddled in boat shops marketing a variety of outboard brands, and by little hardware stores and gas stations, as well as seasonal backyard small engine repair shops featuring the marque as their only outboard line.

Scott-Atwater often went after commercial accounts engaged in the motor rental business. They targeted campsites, boat liveries, fishing clubs, and resorts. This explains why collectors generally have found Scotts to be rather plentiful and in some pretty out-of-the-way places.

Less common models of this marque include first-year (1949) shift motors. Non–Bail-A-Matic 16-horse twins are a little hard to come by. This engine with Green Hornet racing lower unit is truly rare, more so if it has dual carbs. The heavy-duty diesel Scott (and successor McCulloch) OX doesn't show up much. McCulloch's three-cylinder (590/630) racers also could be considered a find.

Scotts were not known for their adaptation to salt water. Motors of this (and most every) marque used in the ocean should be scrutinized.

Sea King

Since the World War I era, Montgomery Ward has offered outboards from a variety of makers such as Caille, Lockwood, Evinrude/Gale Products, Thor, and Mercury. Most were marketed under the Sea King banner. Some early-1930s Ward's kickers were large, leftover Lockwoods. A rare, exotic example is a wind-up, inertia starter-equipped, 15-horse, erstwhile Chief model. The 1932–34 Folding Sea King is an uncommon 3-hp motor. The late-1930s Thor/Sea Kings, as well as early-1940s Kiekhaefer-produced singles, are sometimes popular with Mercury enthusiasts. Post–World War II 12-hp electric-starting Gale Products twins are rather unusual.

Like Sears's Elgin, many of Ward's Sea Kings sold well and are still plentiful. As is the case with the minor makes and private brands (like Sea King) in general, the higher the horsepower (especially 20-plus hp), the fewer motors produced.

Thor

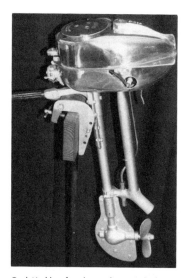

Carl Kiekhaefer dressed up a clunky-looking Thor with an aircraft-esque fuel tank. With the addition of a reliable Tillotson carb, he made his 1939 Streamliner into a better performer. This was the stepping stone motor between Thor and Mercury.

Famous for loose, rattling parts, Thor's quirky performance and mechanical toy-like appearance probably caused scads of them to be scrapped prior to the age of serious outboard collecting.

Picture a greasy, rust-spotted one leaning in the corner of someone's 1950s garage. During a Saturday spring cleaning, the wife asks, "What's that? Does it work? Will you ever use it?" Loving hubby slowly admits he probably doesn't need such a device. So either the mechanically inclined kid next door inherits the darn thing or the poor Thor is piled onto a squished lamp shade with the rest of the trash at the curb.

Of the Thor products escaping similar fates, single-cylinder Thor/Sea Kings are most plentiful. Thor—and later Kiekhaefer—apparently produced more "Monkey-Ward" kickers than the standard Thor model. By the way, Thor/Sea King serial numbers typically contain a *W* (for Ward's). Late Sea King versions (circa 1939) carry a *WK*, designating Ward's-Kiekhaefer.

Most manufacturers number their first motors in the hundreds of thousands. The result is that those who buy an early version don't know that they are getting motors that didn't yet have the bugs worked out. Thor folks, however, opted for honest simplicity and apparently began labeling their motors for Mongomery-Ward with #1. The numbering went like this:

Thor/Sea King

Year	Serial Number Spread
1936	W1–W2580
1937	W3000–W6302
1938	W7000–W9000
1939	W9001–W11000

Look for Thor/Sea Kings in rural areas where folks bought lots of catalog stuff (on credit). Following Thor/Sea King motors, the standard Thor singles come next in terms of availability. They'll vary in carb position (front or side mount), skeg type (rounded or angled), and some have the word *THOR* cast into the carburetor cover. It is believed more Thor singles with Sea King labels were produced than single-cylinder outboards bearing the Thor marque. Water pump arrangement differs, too, as some are right in front of the prop, while others have pick-up tubes piping H_2O to the pump.

Harder to come by than the single is the opposed twin (also with its share of variances). In a tie for rarest Thor might be the alternate-firing twin, Pyramid-3 (triple-cylinder, in-line) and the teardrop-shaped (gas tank) Thor 1939 Streamliner.

Waterwitch

During the early days of outboard collecting, Sears's Waterwitches were considered nuisances. Most vintage outboard meets during the mid-Sixties sported a pile of wayward Waterwitches. Even with $2–$15 price tags, not all found new homes. I recall seeing a motor buff politely turning away a free Waterwitch. In the 1980s, however, a glitzy magazine article on American style linked famed industrial designer Raymond Loewy with a certain Waterwitch model, and all

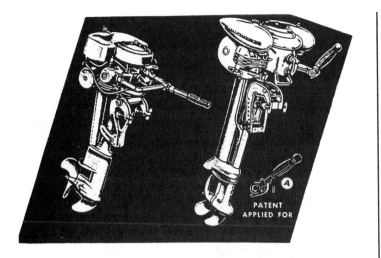

PATENT APPLIED FOR

of a sudden they got a little hotter. Of approximately 128,000 Kissel-built Waterwitch motors, most unusual is a three-cylinder radial experimental. Sears apparently saw the prototype but decided it was too unconventional.

Kissel's rarest Waterwitch actually offered by Sears and Roebuck has to be the 10-hp alternate-firing twin. A 5¾-horse opposed-twin with little internal generator and light plug probably comes in second. Johnson made an 8½-hp Waterwitch twin offered by Sears between 1938 and 1940, which is rather unusual. Muncie produced a few Waterwitch outboards, and they are a bit harder to find than most Kissel versions of the well-known prewar marque.

More than almost any other private brand, Wizard has achieved an antique outboard following. The Kiekhaefer Corporation's role in Wizard production no doubt contributes to the marque's popularity. In communities where strong Western Auto stores existed, Wizards sold well and still pop up on a relatively regular basis.

In terms of rarity, the least common Wizard is the four-cylinder, Mercury-based (Mark 30) Super Power 25. Another great Western Auto outboard is the 10-horse WM-7A. It's reputed to be built with some Mercury racing motor parts.

Be on the lookout for any Wizard wearing a Mercury Quicksilver racing lower unit. Western Auto catalogs never showed their motors available in such a form, but some high-speed enthusiasts made the modification. It's a nice find.

By 1958 the Oliver tractor people, as well as Scott, were making Wizard outboards. These products do not seem to be as plentiful as the catalog store's earlier models.

Wizard

A Note About The Model/Year Guide

The old 27th Street Evinrude plant in Milwaukee included everything from offices to assembly lines. By 1959, the crowding there eased a bit when much of Evinrude's engineering department got reassigned to the Johnson HQ in Waukegan, Illinois. Remaining was Dick Bayley, who became the company's Service Promotion Manager, a new position aimed at assisting busy Evinrude dealers. Having seen the Evinrude Model/Year Guide represented in the first two editions of *The Old Outboard Book*, Bayley recalled in a 1988 letter his role in creating the frequently consulted motor ID document:

"That job of Service Promotion Manager had to be the best job in the world as I could pretty much develop things as I wanted. The Model/Year Guide idea came to me soon after I started [as manager] because the number of calls and letters from dealers seeking motor identification was phenomenal. Customer inquiries were also numerous. I mentioned the problem to [Evinrude Vice President] Jim Webb during some watercooler conversation and he gave me a rough list of just the model numbers that started in 1916 and finished around World War II. I then started bugging everyone, especially the older guys, for serial numbers. Some of the pre-1916 numbers came from handwritten notes found in bottom drawers of our old timers' desks. There were many serial numbers I was never able to locate. I guess the Evinrude people at the time [didn't worry about documenting that kind of thing because they] never gave a thought to their machines lasting so long!"

An old gentleman, Walter Hoth, who had been with Koban when it was taken over by Evinrude in 1926, assisted Bayley. Hoth was about to retire, and Bayley wanted to get some identification information to dealers ASAP, so in the interests of time, the duo pieced together the 1909–59 section of the list printed herein. Shortly after its 1959 distribution, several dealers called about old motors (like the 1922 Evinrude "K," or 1927 Koban model 100) noted in their shops but not on the list. Bayley wished his detective work had yielded sufficient information to include such obscure motors in the subsequent 1965 Model/Year Guide update, but by then other priorities beckoned, leaving little time for tinkering with nuances. He did collect a significant body of old Evinrude service department model and serial numbers, features, and manufacturing dates ultimately considered too esoteric for inclusion on a quick-reference guide. Those notes got shelved for future reference. But "much of that paperwork," Bayley ruefully admits, "was sent to a warehouse in Milwaukee during the late 1960s, was more or less ignored, and has since disappeared."

Happily, a few nuanced statistics of interest to old motor buffs made their way to an odd service bulletin or two. And some other numbers (such as Johnson's heretofore unknown P-25 and Canadian Sea Horse serialization) have also surfaced. Those and several more Model/Year listings have been added to this edition at the end of this chapter. It just may be that they'll help clarify the identity of the next old engine that you discover.

Appendix A
Model/Year Guide

Evinrude, Elto, and Some Lockwood, Sea King, and Viking.

By the early 1960s, most Evinrude dealerships had their share of customers seeking parts or information about obsolete outboard motors. Because it was not uncommon for owner and dealer alike to have little more than a guess about the old kickers' true model name, year of manufacture, horsepower, etc., tracking down parts or pertinent details was a chore. In 1965, Evinrude released a Model/Year Guide, compiled from dusty factory paperwork, to assist dealers in locating other reference material about replacement parts. The Evinrude people indicate "all available records were researched to keep multiple-year listings at a minimum. In some instances, this could not be avoided. Should the model's years be given as 1927–31, for example, no closer identification could be provided." Some obscure Evinrude models were omitted from the 1965 guide. Most were extremely limited-production, early 1930s racing motors that only differed from some other rare racer in that one had an underwater exhaust or a similar long forgotten nuance. Also missing were a few "bombs," like the 1922, all-aluminum, Model K rowboat motor.

Very few Evinrude rowboat motors were actually produced in 1909. In fact, 1910 was probably the first year of real commercial production. As of 1990, the oldest known Evinrude wears the serial number 780. It came out of Vermont and has no skeg and no Evinrude logo lettering on its exhaust manifold. It is most likely a 1910 or 1911 motor.

By 1915, Evinrude had enough variations of its 2- and 3½-hp motors that rowboat motor sub-categories "A" through "H" were tacked onto the standard model designations. In most cases, these differences were slight, and records of the secondary classifications got overshadowed by time and subsequent model nomenclature. Therefore, there probably are Evinrudes (and other brands) which do not correspond with any list.

A curious lack of engineering data on some early Evinrude/Elto models and model changes leads me to believe many designs, developments, and modifications were informally drawn up by Ole Evinrude and implemented by factory staffers at the earliest convenience.

Notes: An "X" stamped after the serial number of an Evinrude/Elto usually signifies a factory-rebuilt motor.

Some Evinrudes, such as 4006, had an identical model number, but were different vintage motors. Numbers 2001-plus follow the 1959 listing.

Year	Model	HP
1909-12	---- / Single, #1 to 9,999	1.5
1913	---- / Single, #10,000 to 19,000	2.0
1914	---- / Single, #20,000 to 49,999	2.0
1921	---- / Twin, Elto, #1,000 to 1,920	3.0
1922	---- / Twin, Elto, #1,921 to A6,519	3.0
1915	A / Single, #3,000 to 3,999	3.5
1916	A / Single, #4,014 to 4,660	3.5
1917	A / Single, #4,661 to 4,950	3.5
1918	A / Single, #4,951 to 5,480	3.5
1919	A / Single, #5,481 to 6,050	3.5
1920	A / Single, #6,051 to 6,700	3.5
1921	A / Single, #6,701 to 6,908	3.5
1922	A / Single, #7,000 to 7,200	3.5
1915	A / Single, #50,000 to 54,999	2.0
1916	A / Single, #90,000 to 92,499	2.0
1917	A / Single, #95,000 to 96,998	2.0
1918	A / Single, #97,000 to 101,899	2.0
1919	A / Single, #101,900 to 103,799	2.0
1920	A / Single, #103,800 to 111,199	2.0
1921	A / Single, #111,200 to 116,980	2.0
1922	A / Single, #117,000 to 121,999	2.0
1923	A / Single, #122,000 to 123,999	2.0
1924	A / Single, #124,000 to 124,999	2.0
1925	A / Single, #125,000 to 126,349	2.0
1926	A / Single, #126,350 to 127,299	2.0
1927	A / Single, #127,300 to 127,959	2.0
1928	A / Single, #127,960 and up	2.0
1923	A / Twin, Elto, #6,520 to 12,000	3.0
1916	AA / Twin, (4-cycle) #53,420 to 54,415	4.0
1917	AA / Twin, (4-cycle) #54,416 to 54,819	4.0
1915	B / Single, #5,000 to 5,199	3.5
1916	B / Single, #5,200 to 5,374	3.5
1917	B / Single, #5,375 to 5,430	3.5
1918	B / Single, #5,431 to 5,580	3.5
1919	B / Single, #5,581 to 5,749	3.5
1920	B / Single, #5,750 to 5,850	3.5
1921	B / Single, #6,701 to 6,908	3.5
1922	B / Single, #7,000 to 7,200	3.5
1915	B / Single, #55,000 to 55,999	2.0

Year	Model	HP
1916	B / Single, #56,000 to 56,644	2.0
1917	B / Single, #56,645 to 57,299	2.0
1918	B / Single, #57,300 to 57,799	2.0
1919	B / Single, #57,800 to 58,699	2.0
1920	B / Single, #58,700 to 59,249	2.0
1921	B / Single, #59,250 to 59,499	2.0
1922	B / Single, #59,500 to 59,649	2.0
1923	B / Single, #59,650 to 65,000	2.0
1924	B / Single, #124,000 to 124,999	2.0
1925	B / Single, #125,000 to 126,349	2.0
1926	B / Single, #126,350 to 127,299	2.0
1927	B / Single, #127,300 to 127,959	2.0
1928	B / Single, #127,960 and up	2.0
1923	B / Twin, Elto, #6,520 to 12,000	3.0
1916	C / Single, #61,000 to 61,465	2.0
1924	C / Twin, Elto, #12,001 to 20,000	3.0
1925	C / Twin, Elto, #20,001 to 20,999	3.0
1916-24	CC / Single Cyl. Inboard	2.0
1923-26	CCV / Single Cyl. Pressure Pump	2.0
1916	D / Single, #66,000 to 66,799	2.0
1924	D / Twin, Elto, #12,001 to 20,000	3.0
1925	D / Twin, Elto, #20,001 to 20,999	3.0
1916-27	DD / Twin Cyl. Inboard	4.5
1916-27	DDR / Twin Cyl. Inboard (reverse)	4.5
1923-29	DDV / Twin Cyl. Pump	4.5
1915	E / Single-Canoe, #10,000 to 10,128	3.5
1916	EE / Twin (4-cycle), #59,000 to 59,056	4.0
1928	F / Fleetwin, #F1001 to F4000	6.0
1929	F / Fleetwin, #1F001 to 4F300	7.0
1928	FV / Twin Cyl. Pump	6.0
1926	G / Twin, Elto, #30,000 to 44,900	4.0
1928	H / Fastwin, #H1001 to H2500	12.0
1929	H / Fastwin, #1H001 to 13H250	14.0
1913	H / Single (bat) #1 to 299	3.5
1914	H / Single (mag) #300 to 2,999	3.5
1926	H / Twin, Elto, #30,000 to 44,900	4.0
1927	J / Twin, Elto, #45,000 to 54,799	4.0
1928	J / Twin, Elto, #54,800 to 56,859	4.0
1929	J / Twin, Elto, #56,860 to 59,999	4.0
1927	K / Twin, Elto, #45,000 to 54,799	4.0
1928	K / Twin, Elto, #54,800 to 56,859	4.0
1929	K / Twin, Elto, #56,860 to 59,999	4.0
1923-26	L / Big Twin	4.0
1923-26	LA / Big Twin	4.0
1923-26	LAT / Big Twin	4.0
1923	N / Sportwin, #N1,500 to N3,499	2.5
1924	N / Sportwin, #N3,500 to N8,499	2.5
1925	N / Sportwin, #N8,500 to N10,499	2.5
1926	N / Sportwin, #N10,500 to N13,499	2.5
1927	N / Sportwin, #N13,500 to N14,499	2.5
1928	N / Sportwin, #N14,500 to N14,750	2.5
1929	NF / Sportwin-Folding, #1N001 to 2N001	2.5
1923	NS / Sportwin, #NS1,500 to NS3,499	2.5
1924	NS / Sportwin, #NS3,500 to NS8,499	2.5
1925	NS / Sportwin, #NS8,500 to NS9,999	2.5
1926	NS / Sportwin, #NS10,000 to NS10,999	2.5
1927	NS / Sportwin, #NS11,000 to NS11,999	2.5
1919-29	P / Centrifugal Pump	2.0
1927	R / Fastwin	4.0
1927	RS / Fastwin	4.0
1927	RV / Twin Cylinder Pump	4.0
1927	T / Speeditwin	8.0
1927	TS / Speeditwin	8.0
1928	U / Speeditwin, #U1001 to U5200	16.0
1929	U / Speeditwin, #1U001 to 15U000	20.0
1925	52T / Lockwood Twin	7.0
1926	62T / Lockwood Twin	7.0
1927	72T / Lockwood Twin	7.0
1928	82A / Lockwood Ace	7.0
1928	82B / Lockwood Chief	11.0
1929	92A / Lockwood Ace	7.0
1929	92B / Lockwood Chief	14.0
1929	92BR / Lockwood Racing Chief	14.0
1929	142 / Centrifugal Pump	6.0
1929-32	143 / Speeditwin	20.0
1929-33	145 / Fastwin	14.0
1930-34	156 / Speeditwin	22.0
1930-34	157 / Speeditwin—6" Longer	22.0
1930	160 / Lockwood Chief	11.0
1930	161 / Lockwood Ace	7.0
1930	162 / OMC Foldlight	2.75
1930	163 / Lockwood Chief-Electric	11.0
1930	167 / Speeditwin-Electric	22.0
1930	168 / Speeditwin-Electric—6" Longer	22.0
1930	176 / OMC Speedibee Racer	20.0
1930	177 / Speeditwin Racer	----
1930	178 / OMC Four-Sixty Racer	----
1930	179 / OMC Racer	----
1931	183 / Sportwin	2.5
1929	300 / Elto Service Speedster, #80,000 to 89,999S	7.0
1929	301 / Elto Service Speedster, 5" Longer, #80,000 to 89,999S	7.0
1929	302 / Elto Hi Speed Speedster, #80,000 to 89,999H	11.0
1929	303 / Elto Hi Speed Speedster, 5" Longer, #80,000 to 89,999H	11.0
1929	305 / Elto Service Quad, #75,000 to 79,999S	25.0
1929	306 / Elto Hi Speed Quad, #75,000 to 79,999H	25.0
1928	307 / Elto Service Quad, #70,000 to 74,999S	18.0
1928	308 / Elto Hi Speed Quad, #70,000 to 74,999H	18.0
1929	309 / Elto Lightweight, #90,000 to 99,999	3.5
1930	310 / Elto Senior Speedster	14.0
1930	311 / Elto Senior Speedster-Electric	14.0
1930	312 / Elto Sr. Speedster—5" Longer	14.0
1930	313 / Elto Sr. Speedster-Elec.—5" Longer	14.0
1930	314 / Elto Quad	30.0
1930	315 / Elto Quad-Electric	30.0
1930	335 / Elto Hi Speed Quad (50 cu.in.)	35.0
1930	336 / Elto Hi Speed Quad (60 cu.in.)	40.0
1929	340 / Elto Special Speedster	9.0
1930	344 / Elto Hi Speed Quad (50 cu.in.)	40.0
1930	348 / Elto Hi Speed Service Speedster	7.0
1928	355 / Elto Service Speedster, #60,000 to 69,999	7.0

Year	Model	Value	Year	Model	Value
1931	358 / Service Twin	4.0	1933	444 / Lightweight	5.1
1931	359 / Service Twin 5" Longer	4.0	1933	445 / Lightweight 5" Longer	5.1
1931	360 / Special Lightweight	3.5	1933	446 / Lightwin — Full Reverse	5.1
1933	361 / Senior Speedster	13.7	1938	447 / Sea King #8763	1.8
1933	362 / Senior Speedster 5" Longer	13.7	1933	448 / Lightweight Full Reverse	5.1
1933	363 / Senior Speedster	13.7	1938	449 / Sea King #8764	2.8
1933	364 / Senior Speedster 5" Longer	13.7	1939	449 / Sea King #8766	3.0
1934	365 / Senior Speedster	13.7	1933	450 / Fleetwin	8.5
1934	366 / Senior Speedster 5" Longer	13.7	1933	451 / Fleetwin 5" Longer	8.5
1940–41	367 / Sea King #8813	1.8	1933	452 / Fleetwin Electric	8.5
1940–41	368 / Sea King #8814	3.0	1933	453 / Fleetwin Electric 5" Longer	8.5
1940–41	369 / Sea King #8815 Deluxe	3.0	1933	454 / OMC Midget Racer	----
1940–41	371 / Sea King #8816	5.0	1933	456 / Super 'A'	8.5
1940–41	373 / Sea King #8817 Deluxe	5.0	1933	457 / Super 'A' 5" Longer	8.5
1940–42	375 / Sea King #8818	15.2	1933	458 / Super 'A' Electric	8.5
1941	377 / Sea King #8822	1.0	1933	459 / Super 'A' Electric 5" Longer	8.5
1941–42	378 / Sea King #8823	3.3	1933	460 / Lightwin	5.1
1941–42	379 / Sea King #8824 Deluxe	3.3	1933	461 / Lightwin 5" Longer	5.1
1946–47	379 / Sea King #9008 Deluxe	3.3	1933	462 / Lightweight	5.1
1946–47	381 / Sea King #9002	1.0	1940	463 / Viking	1.8
1931–35	400 / Sea King #9186	4.0	1933	464 / Sport Single	2.2
1931	401 / Lightweight	4.0	1939	465 / Viking	1.8
1931	402 / Lightwin	4.0	1939	466 / Viking	5.0
1931	403 / Foldlight	2.75	1939	467 / Viking	8.5
1931	404 / Foldlight	2.75	1933	468 / Lightwin Full Reverse	5.1
1931	405 / Lightweight 5" Longer	4.0	1939	469 / Sea King #8809	1.0
1931	406 / Lightwin 5" Longer	4.0	1940	469 / Sea King #8812	1.0
1932	407 / Lightwin	4.0	1933	470 / Lightweight Full Reverse	5.1
1932	408 / Lightwin 5" Longer	4.0	1939–41	471 / Sea King #8811	8.5
1932	409 / Sportwin	4.0	1933	472 / Sport Single Full Reverse	2.2
1932	410 / Sportwin 5" Longer	4.0	1933	474 / Super Single Full Reverse	2.2
1932	411 / Lightweight	4.0	1940	475 / Viking	5.0
1932	412 / Lightweight 5" Longer	4.0	1933	476 / Sportwin	4.0
1932–33	413 / Fisherman	4.0	1939	477 / Sea King #8765	1.8
1932–33	414 / Fisherman 5" Longer	4.0	1933	478 / Fisherman	4.0
1932–34	415 / Sea King-Folding #9200	3.0	1933	479 / Fisherman 5" Longer	4.0
1932–35	416 / Sea King #9186	4.0	1933	481 / Electric Troller	----
1932–34	417 / Sea King #9194	8.0	1933	483 / Sportwin	4.0
1932	418 / Fleetwin	11.0	1933	484 / Fisherman	4.0
1932	419 / Fleetwin 5" Longer	11.0	1934	489 / Sea King #8390	2.2
1932–33	420 / Sturditwin	5.8	1935	490 / Sea King #8800	2.2
1932–33	421 / Sturditwin 5" Longer	5.8	1935	491 / Sea King #8801	4.0
1932	422 / Super 'A'	11.0	1935–36	492 / Sea King #8802	8.5
1932	423 / Super 'A' 5" Longer	11.0	1937–38	492 / Sea King #8808	8.5
1932–33	424 / Service 'A'	5.8	1936	494 / Sea King #8803	4.0
1932–33	425 / Service 'A' 5" Longer	5.8	1936–37	495 / Viking	4.0
1932	426 / Lightwin	4.0	1936–37	496 / Viking	8.5
1932	427 / Lightwin 5" Longer	4.0	1936	497 / Sea King #8802 5" Longer	8.5
1932	428 / Lightweight	4.0	1937	498 / Sea King #8806	2.5
1932	429 / Lightweight 5" Longer	4.0	1937–38	499 / Sea King #8807	4.2
1932	430 / Service 'A'	5.8	1939	499 / Sea King #8810	5.0
1932	431 / Service 'A' 5" Longer	5.8	1934–35	500 / Sea King #8394	11.0
1933	432 / Sport Single	2.2	1931–33	500 / Sea King #9188	15.0
1933	433 / Sport Single 5" Longer	2.2	1931	600 / Sea King #9190	21.0
1933	434 / Sport Single Full Reverse	2.2	1931–33	601 / Speeditwin	25.0
1933	436 / Super Single	2.2	1931–33	602 / Speeditwin 5" Longer	25.0
1933	437 / Super Single 5" Longer	2.2	1931–33	603 / Speeditwin Electric	25.0
1933	438 / Super Single Full Reverse	2.2	1931–33	604 / Speeditwin Electric 5" Longer	25.0
1933	440 / Sea King #8300	3.0	1931–33	605 / Super 'C'	25.0
1933	441 / Viking	4.0	1931–33	606 / Super 'C' 5" Longer	25.0
1933	442 / Lightwin	5.1	1931–33	607 / Super 'C' Electric	25.0
1933	443 / Lightwin 5" Longer	5.1	1931–33	608 / Super 'C' Electric 5" Longer	25.0

1931	609 / Speeditwin Racer	----	1931	806 / Big Quad Electric	40.0
1931	610 / Super 'C' Racer	----	1931	807 / Big Quad Electric, 5" Longer	40.0
1931–32	615 / Sea King #9190	21.0	1931	808 / Big Four Electric	40.0
1931–32	616 / Sea King #9150	21.0	1931	809 / Big Four Electric, 5" Longer	40.0
1931–32	617 / Sea King #9196	21.0	1931	810 / Big Quad, Eclipse Starter	40.0
1932	618 / Speeditwin	25.0	1931	811 / Big Quad, Eclipse, 5" Longer	40.0
1932	619 / Speeditwin 5" Longer	25.0	1931	812 / Big Four, Eclipse Starter	40.0
1932	620 / Speeditwin Electric	25.0	1931	813 / Big Four, Eclipse, 5" Longer	40.0
1932	621 / Speeditwin Electric 5" Longer	25.0	1932	814 / Big Four	40.0
1932	624 / Super 'C'	25.0	1932	815 / Big Four, 5" Longer	40.0
1932	625 / Super 'C' 5" Longer	25.0	1932	816 / Big Four Electric	40.0
1932	626 / Super 'C' Electric	25.0	1932	817 / Big Four Electric, 5" Longer	40.0
1932	627 / Super 'C' Electric 5" Longer	25.0	1932	818 / Big Four, Eclipse Starter	40.0
1932	630 / Speeditwin Racer	----	1932	819 / Big Four, Eclipse, 5" Longer	40.0
1932	631 / Super 'C' Racer	----	1932	820 / Big Quad	40.0
1933	634 / Speeditwin	21.1	1932	821 / Big Quad, 5" Longer	40.0
1933	635 / Speeditwin 5" Longer	21.1	1932	822 / Big Quad Electric	40.0
1933	636 / Speeditwin Electric	21.1	1932	823 / Big Quad Electric, 5" Longer	40.0
1933	637 / Speeditwin Electric 5" Longer	21.1	1932	824 / Big Quad, Eclipse Starter	40.0
1933	638 / Super 'C'	21.1	1932	825 / Big Quad, Eclipse, 5" Longer	40.0
1933	639 / Super 'C' 5" Longer	21.1	1932	826 / Four-Sixty Racer	----
1933	640 / Super 'C' Electric	21.1	1932	827 / Four-Sixty, Dual Ign.	----
1933	641 / Super 'C' Electric 5" Longer	21.1	1933	828 / Four-Sixty Racer	----
1933	642 / Super 'C' Racer	----	1933	829 / Four-Sixty, Dual Ign.	----
1933	643 / Speeditwin Racer	----	1931	900 / Junior Quad	18.0
1931	700 / Senior Quad	35.0	1931	901 / Junior Quad, 5" Longer	18.0
1931	701 / Senior Quad 5" Longer	35.0	1931	902 / Sportfour	18.0
1931	702 / Senior Quad Electric	35.0	1931	903 / Sportfour, 5" Longer	18.0
1931	703 / Senior Quad Electric 5" Longer	35.0	1933–36	904 / Centrifugal Pump, 2½"	8.5
1931	704 / Speedifour	35.0	1931–33	905 / Special Speedster	12.0
1931	705 / Speedifour 5" Longer	35.0	1931–33	906 / Special Speedster, 5" Longer	12.0
1931	706 / Speedifour Electric	35.0	1931–33	907 / Special Speedster, 10" Longer	12.0
1931	707 / Speedifour Electric 5" Longer	35.0	1933	909 / Hi Pressure Pump, 1½"	12.0
1931	708 / Senior Quad. Eclipse Starter	35.0	1931	910 / Hi Pressure Pump, 1½"	12.0
1931	709 / Senior Quad. Eclipse, 5" Longer	35.0	1933	911 / Hi Pressure Pump, 2"	12.0
1931	710 / Speedifour, Eclipse Starter	35.0	1932	912 / Sportfour	18.0
1931	711 / Speedifour, Eclipse, 5" Longer	35.0	1932	913 / Sportfour, 5" Longer	18.0
1932	715 / Speedifour	36.0	1932	914 / Junior Quad	18.0
1932	716 / Speedifour, 5" Longer	36.0	1932	915 / Junior Quad 5" Longer	18.0
1932	717 / Speedifour Electric	36.0	1932–36	916 / Speedibike	0.75
1932	718 / Speedifour Electric 5" Longer	36.0	1934	917 / Road King	0.5
1932	719 / Speedifour, Eclipse Starter	36.0	1932	918 / Lawn Boy Power Mower	0.75
1932	720 / Speedifour, Eclipse, 5" Longer	36.0	1933	920 / Sportfour	18.0
1932	721 / Senior Quad	36.0	1933	921 / Sportfour, 5" Longer	18.0
1932	722 / Senior Quad, 5" Longer	36.0	1933	922 / Sportfour Electric	18.0
1932	723 / Senior Quad Electric	36.0	1933	923 / Sportfour Electric, 5" Longer	18.0
1932	724 / Senior Quad Electric, 5" Longer	36.0	1933	924 / Junior Quad	18.0
1932	725 / Senior Quad, Eclipse Starter	36.0	1933	925 / Junior Quad, 5" Longer	18.0
1932	726 / Senior Quad, Eclipse, 5" Longer	36.0	1933	926 / Junior Quad Electric	18.0
1933	728 / Speedifour	31.2	1933	927 / Junior Quad Electric 5" Longer	18.0
1933	729 / Speedifour, 5" Longer	31.2	1933–35	928 / Lawn Boy Power Mower	0.75
1933	730 / Speedifour Electric	31.2	1934	929 / Lawn Boy Power Mower	0.75
1933	731 / Speedifour Electric, 5" Longer	31.2	1933–36	930 / Shop King	----
1933	732 / Senior Quad	31.2	1935–36	932 / Centrifugal H.P. Pump, 1½"	9.2
1933	733 / Senior Quad, 5" Longer	31.2	1935	933 / Centrifugal H.P. Pump, 1½"	9.2
1933	734 / Senior Quad Electric	31.2	1937–38	936 / Streamflow Bicycle, Standard	----
1933	735 / Senior Quad Electric, 5" Longer	31.2	1937–38	937 / Streamflow Bicycle, Imperial	----
1931	800 / Big Quad	40.0	1936	938 / Lawn Boy Power Mower	0.75
1931	801 / Big Quad, 5" Longer	40.0	1936	939 / Lawn Boy Power Mower	0.75
1931	802 / Big Four	40.0	1937–38	941 / Streamflow Bicycle, Standard	----
1931	803 / Big Four, 5" Longer	40.0	1937–38	942 / Streamflow Bicycle, Imperial	----
1931	804 / Four-Sixty Racer	----	1937–38	948 / Lawn Boy Power Mower	0.75

Year	Model	HP
1939-41	952 / Lawn Boy Power Mower	0.75
1938-42	958 / Lawn Boy Power Mower	0.75
1934	4000 / Single	2.2
1934	4001 / Single, 5" Longer	2.2
1934	4002 / Single	2.2
1934	4003 / Single, 5" Longer	2.2
1934	4004 / Single	2.2
1934	4005 / Single, 5" Longer	2.2
1934	4006 / Single	2.2
1934	4007 / Single, 5" Longer	2.2
1934	4008 / Single	2.2
1934	4009 / Single, 5" Longer	2.2
1934	4010 / Single	2.2
1934	4011 / Single, 5" Longer	2.2
1934	4012 / Single	2.2
1934	4013 / Single, 5" Longer	2.2
1934	4014 / Single	2.2
1934	4015 / Single, 5" Longer	2.2
1934	4016 / Fisherman	4.0
1934	4017 / Fisherman, 5" Longer	4.0
1934	4018 / Fisherman	4.0
1934	4019 / Fisherman, 5" Longer	4.0
1934	4020 / Lightwin	5.1
1934	4021 / Lightwin, 5" Longer	5.1
1934	4022 / Lightwin	5.1
1934	4023 / Lightwin, 5" Longer	5.1
1934	4024 / Lightwin	5.1
1934	4025 / Lightwin, 5" Longer	5.1
1934	4026 / Lightwin	5.1
1934	4027 / Lightwin, 5" Longer	5.1
1934	4028 / Midget Racer	----
1934-36	4029 / All Electric	----
1934	4030 / Lightwin Imperial	5.5
1934	4031 / Lightwin Imperial, 5" Longer	5.5
1934	4032 / Lightwin Imperial	5.5
1934	4033 / Lightwin Imperial, 5" Longer	5.5
1934	4034 / Fleetwin	8.5
1934	4035 / Fleetwin, 5" Longer	8.5
1934	4036 / Fleetwin Electric	8.5
1934	4037 / Fleetwin Electric, 5" Longer	8.5
1934	4038 / Fleetwin	8.5
1934	4039 / Fleetwin, 5" Longer	8.5
1934	4040 / Fleetwin Electric	8.5
1934	4041 / Fleetwin Electric, 5" Longer	8.5
1934-35	4042 / Lightfour Imperial	9.2
1934-35	4043 / Lightfour Imperial, 5" Longer	9.2
1934-35	4044 / Lightfour Imperial	9.2
1934-35	4045 / Lightfour Imperial, 5" Longer	9.2
1934-35	4046 / Lightfour Imperial	9.2
1934-35	4047 / Lightfour Imperial, 5" Longer	9.2
1934-35	4048 / Lightfour Imperial	9.2
1934-35	4049 / Lightfour Imperial, 5" Longer	9.2
1934	4050 / Lightwin Imperial	5.5
1934	4051 / Lightwin Imperial, 5" Longer	5.5
1934	4052 / Lightwin Imperial	5.5
1934	4053 / Lightwin Imperial, 5" Longer	5.5
1934	4054 / Lightwin Imperial	5.5
1934	4055 / Lightwin Imperial, 5" Longer	5.5
1934	4056 / Lightwin Imperial	5.5
1934	4057 / Lightwin Imperial, 5" Longer	5.5
1934	4058 / Single	2.2
1934	4059 / Single, 5" Longer	2.2
1934	4060 / Single	2.2
1934	4061 / Single, 5" Longer	2.2
1934	4062 / Single	2.2
1934	4063 / Single, 5" Longer	2.2
1934	4064 / Single	2.2
1934	4065 / Single, 5" Longer	2.2
1934	4066 / Fisherman	4.0
1934	4067 / Fisherman, 5" Longer	4.0
1934	4068 / Fisherman	4.0
1934	4069 / Fisherman 5" Longer	4.0
1934	4070 / Lightwin Imperial	5.5
1934	4071 / Lightwin Imperial, 5" Longer	5.5
1934	4072 / Lightwin Imperial	5.5
1934	4073 / Lightwin Imperial, 5" Longer	5.5
1934	4074 / Lightwin Imperial, 15" Longer	5.5
1934	4075 / Lightwin Imperial, 15" Longer	5.5
1934	4076 / Lightfour Imperial, 15" Longer	9.2
1934	4077 / Lightfour Imperial, 15" Longer	9.2
1934	4078 / Single	2.2
1934	4079 / Single, 5" Longer	2.2
1934	4080 / Single	2.2
1934	4081 / Single, 5" Longer	2.2
1934	4082 / Fisherman	4.0
1934	4083 / Fisherman, 5" Longer	4.0
1934	4084 / Fisherman	4.0
1934	4085 / Fisherman, 5" Longer	4.0
1934	4086 / Lightwin Imperial, 15" Longer	5.5
1934	4087 / Lightwin Imperial, 15" Longer	5.5
1934	4088 / Lightfour Imperial, 15" Longer	9.2
1934	4089 / Lightfour Imperial, 15" Longer	9.2
1935	4091 / Sportsman	1.5
1935	4092 / Fisherman, Weedless	4.0
1935	4093 / Fisherman	4.0
1935	4094 / Fisherman, 5" Longer	4.0
1935	4095 / Fisherman	4.0
1935	4096 / Fisherman, 5" Longer	4.0
1935	4097 / Lightwin	4.6
1935	4098 / Lightwin, 5" Longer	4.6
1935	4099 / Lightwin	4.6
1935	4101 / Lightwin, 5" Longer	4.6
1935	4102 / Lightwin Imperial	5.0
1935	4103 / Lightwin Imperial, 5" Longer	5.0
1935	4104 / Lightwin Imperial	5.0
1935	4105 / Lightwin Imperial, 5" Longer	5.0
1935	4106 / Lightwin Imperial	5.0
1935	4107 / Lightwin Imperial, 5" Longer	5.0
1935	4108 / Lightwin Imperial	5.0
1935	4109 / Lightwin Imperial, 5" Longer	5.0
1935	4111 / Lightfour Imperial	9.2
1935	4112 / Lightfour Imperial, 5" Longer	9.2
1935	4113 / Lightfour Imperial	9.2
1935	4114 / Lightfour Imperial, 5" Longer	9.2
1935	4115 / Lightfour Imperial	9.2
1935	4116 / Lightfour Imperial, 5" Longer	9.2
1935	4117 / Lightfour Imperial	9.2
1935	4118 / Lightfour Imperial, 5" Longer	9.2
1935	4119 / Midget Racer	----
1935	4121 / Weedless Fisherman	4.0
1935	4122 / Fisherman	4.0
1935	4123 / Fisherman	4.0
1935	4124 / Fisherman, 5" Longer	4.0
1935	4125 / Fisherman	4.0

Year	Model	HP		Year	Model	HP
1935	4126 / Fisherman, 5" Longer	4.0		1936	4193 / Service Twin	4.3
1935	4127 / Lightwin, 15" Longer	4.6		1936	4194 / Fisherman	4.4
1935	4128 / Lightwin, 15" Longer	4.6		1936	4195 / Ace, 5" Longer	1.4
1935	4129 / Lightwin Imperial, 15" Longer	5.0		1936	4196 / Lightwin Heavy Duty	4.7
1935	4131 / Lightwin Imperial, 15" Longer	5.0		1936	4197 / Lightwin H.D., 15" Longer	4.7
1935	4132 / Lightwin Imperial, 15" Longer	5.0		1936	4198 / Lightwin H.D., 5" Longer	4.7
1935	4133 / Lightwin Imperial, 15" Longer	5.0		1936	4199 / Lightfour H.D., 15" Longer	9.2
1935	4134 / Lightfour Imperial, 15" Longer	9.2		1936	4200 / Lightfour H.D., 5" Longer	9.2
1935	4135 / Lightfour Imperial, 15" Longer	9.2		1937	4201 / Scout	0.9
1935	4136 / Lightfour Imperial, 15" Longer	9.2		1937	4203 / Pal	0.9
1935	4137 / Lightfour Imperial, 15" Longer	9.2		1937	4205 / Ace	1.4
1935	4138 / Fisherman	4.0		1937	4206 / Ace, 5" Longer	1.4
1935	4139 / Sportsman, 5" Longer	1.5		1937	4207 / Sportsman	1.6
1935	4142 / Lightwin	4.6		1937	4208 / Sportsman, 5" Longer	1.6
1935	4143 / Fisherman	4.0		1937	4209 / Sportwin	2.5
1935	4144 / Yacht Fisherman	4.0		1937	4211 / Sportwin, 5" Longer	2.5
1936	4144 / Yacht Service Twin	4.3		1937	4212 / Handitwin	2.5
1936-37	4145 / Ace	1.4		1937	4213 / Handitwin, 5" Longer	2.5
1936	4146 / Sportsman	1.5		1937	4214 / Service Twin	4.3
1936	4147 / Sportsman, 5" Longer	1.5		1937	4215 / Service Twin, 5" Longer	4.3
1936	4148 / Fisherman	4.4		1937	4216 / Service Twin	4.3
1936	4149 / Fisherman, 5" Longer	4.4		1937	4217 / Service Twin, 5" Longer	4.3
1936	4151 / Service Twin	4.3		1937	4218 / Service Twin	4.3
1936	4152 / Weedless Fisherman	4.4		1937	4219 / Handifour	9.2
1936	4153 / Lightwin	4.7		1937	4221 / Lightwin	4.7
1936	4154 / Lightwin, 5" Longer	4.7		1937	4222 / Lightwin, 5" Longer	4.7
1936	4155 / Lightwin, 15" Longer	4.7		1937	4223 / Lightwin, 15" Longer	4.7
1936	4156 / Sportwin	2.5		1937	4224 / Lightwin Heavy Duty	4.7
1936	4157 / Sportwin, 5" Longer	2.5		1937	4225 / Lightwin H.D., 5" Longer	4.7
1936	4158 / Handitwin	2.5		1937	4226 / Lightwin H.D., 15" Longer	4.7
1936	4159 / Handitwin 5" Longer	2.5		1937	4227 / Fisherman	4.4
1936	4161 / Service Twin	4.3		1937	4228 / Fisherman, 5" Longer	4.4
1936	4162 / Service Twin, 5" Longer	4.3		1937	4229 / Weedless Service Twin	4.3
1936	4163 / Service Twin	4.3		1937	4231 / Lightfour	9.2
1936	4164 / Service Twin, 5" Longer	4.3		1937	4232 / Lightfour, 5" Longer	9.2
1936	4165 / Lightwin Imperial	5.0		1937	4233 / Lightfour, 15" Longer	9.2
1936	4166 / Lightwin Imperial, 5" Longer	5.0		1937	4234 / Lightfour Heavy Duty	9.2
1936	4167 / Lightwin Imperial, 15" Longer	5.0		1937	4235 / Lightfour H.D., 5" Longer	9.2
1936	4168 / Lightwin Imperial	5.0		1937	4236 / Lightfour H.D., 15" Longer	9.2
1936	4169 / Lightwin Imperial, 5" Longer	5.0		1937	4237 / Lightfour	9.2
1936	4171 / Lightwin Imperial, 15" Longer	5.0		1937	4238 / Lightfour, 5" Longer	9.2
1936	4172 / Lightwin Imperial	5.0		1937	4239 / Lightfour, 15" Longer	9.2
1936	4173 / Lightwin Imperial, 5" Longer	5.0		1937	4241 / Lightfour Heavy Duty	9.2
1936	4174 / Lightwin Imperial, 15" Longer	5.0		1937	4242 / Lightfour H.D., 5" Longer	9.2
1936	4175 / Lightwin Imperial	5.0		1937	4243 / Lightfour H.D., 15" Longer	9.2
1936	4176 / Lightwin Imperial, 5" Longer	5.0		1937	4244 / Midget Racer	----
1936	4177 / Lightwin Imperial, 15" Longer	5.0		1937	4245 / Handifour, 5" Longer	9.2
1936	4178 / Lightfour Imperial	9.2		1937	4246 / Handifour, 15" Longer	9.2
1936	4179 / Lightfour Imperial, 5" Longer	9.2		1937	4247 / Handifour Heavy Duty	9.2
1936	4180 / Lightfour Imperial, 15" Longer	9.2		1937	4248 / Handifour H.D., 5" Longer	9.2
1936	4181 / Lightfour Imperial	9.2		1937	4249 / Handifour H.D., 15" Longer	9.2
1936	4182 / Lightfour Imperial, 5" Longer	9.2		1937	4251 / Weedless Fisherman	4.4
1936	4183 / Lightfour Imperial, 15" Longer	9.2		1938	4252 / Ranger	1.1
1936	4184 / Midget Racer	----		1938	4253 / Pal	1.1
1936	4185 / Lightfour Imperial	9.2		1938	4254 / Sportsman	2.0
1936	4186 / Lightfour Imperial, 5" Longer	9.2		1938	4255 / Sportsman, 5" Longer	2.0
1936	4187 / Lightfour Imperial, 15" Longer	9.2		1938	4256 / Ace	1.8
1936	4188 / Lightfour Imperial	9.2		1938	4257 / Ace, 5" Longer	1.8
1936	4189 / Lightfour Imperial, 5" Longer	9.2		1938	4258 / Sportwin	3.0
1936	4190 / Lightfour Imperial, Heavy Duty	9.2		1938	4259 / Sportwin, 5" Longer	3.0
1936	4191 / Lightfour Imperial, 15" Longer	9.2		1938	4261 / Handitwin	2.8
1936-38	4192 / Yacht Fisherman	4.4		1938	4262 / Handitwin, 5" Longer	2.8

Year	Model	HP
1939-41	4263 / Mate	0.5
1939-41	4264 / Cub	0.5
1939	4265 / Ranger — to S/N 04000	1.1
1940	S/N 04001 to 05500	1.1
1941	S/N 05501 and up	1.1
1938	4266 / Pal — to S/N 02000	1.1
1939	S/N 02001 to 07000	1.1
1940	S/N 07001 to 12000	1.1
1941	S/N 12000 and up	1.1
1938	4267 / Fisherman	4.7
1938	4268 / Fisherman, 5" Longer	4.7
1938	4269 / Weedless Fisherman	4.7
1938	4271 / Lightfour	9.2
1938	4272 / Lightfour, 5" Longer	9.2
1938	4273 / Lightfour, 15" Longer	9.2
1938	4274 / Lightfour Heavy Duty	9.2
1938	4275 / Lightfour H.D., 5" Longer	9.2
1938	4276 / Lightfour H.D., 15" Longer	9.2
1938	4277 / Lightfour	9.2
1938	4278 / Lightfour, 5" Longer	9.2
1938	4279 / Lightfour, 15" Longer	9.2
1938	4281 / Lightfour Heavy Duty	9.2
1938	4282 / Lightfour H.D., 5" Longer	9.2
1938	4283 / Lightfour H.D., 15" Longer	9.2
1938	4284 / Midget Racer	----
1938	4285 / Sportsman	2.0
1938	4286 / Sportsman, 5" Longer	2.0
1938	4287 / Sportwin	3.0
1938	4288 / Sportwin, 5" Longer	3.0
1938	4289 / Lightwin	4.7
1938	4291 / Lightwin, 5" Longer	4.7
1938	4292 / Lightwin, 5" Longer	4.7
1938	4293 / Lightwin Heavy Duty	4.7
1938	4294 / Lightwin H.D., 5" Longer	4.7
1938	4295 / Lightwin H.D., 15" Longer	4.7
1939	4296 / Sportsman	2.0
1939	4297 / Sportsman, 5" Longer	2.0
1939	4298 / Sportsman	2.0
1939	4299 / Sportsman, 5" Longer	2.0
1939	4301 / Ace	1.8
1939	4302 / Ace, 5" Longer	1.8
1939	4303 / Sportwin	3.3
1939	4304 / Sportwin, 5" Longer	3.3
1939	4305 / Sportwin	3.3
1939	4306 / Sportwin, 5" Longer	3.3
1939	4307 / Handitwin	3.0
1939	4308 / Handitwin, 5" Longer	3.0
1939	4309 / Fisherman	5.4
1939	4311 / Fisherman, 5" Longer	5.4
1939	4312 / Weedless Fisherman	5.4
1939	4313 / Lightwin - to S/N 03000	5.0
1940	S/N 03001 to 04000	5.0
1941	S/N 04001 and up	5.0
	4314 / Lightwin, 5" Longer (S/N, year & HP same as model 4313)	
1939	4315 / Lightfour - to S/N 03000	9.7
1940	S/N 03001 to 04000	9.7
1941	S/N 04001 to 05000	9.7
1945	S/N 05001 to 90000	9.7
1941	S/N 90001 to 91000	9.7
1942	S/N 91001 and up	9.7
	4316 / Lightfour, 5" Longer (S/N, year & HP same as model 4315)	
	4317 / Lightfour, 15" Longer (S/N, year & HP same as model 4315)	
	4318 / Lightfour Heavy Duty (S/N, year & HP same as model 4315)	
	4319 / Lightfour H.D. 5" Longer (S/N, year & HP same as model 4315)	
	4321 / Lightfour H.D., 15" Longer (S/N, year & HP same as model 4315)	
1939	4322 / Lightfour - to S/N 03000	9.7
1940	S/N 03001 to 04000	9.7
1941	S/N 04001 to 05000	9.7
1945	S/N 05001 to 90000	9.7
1941	S/N 90001 to 91000	9.7
1942	S/N 91001 and up	9.7
	4323 / Lightfour, 5" Longer (S/N, year & HP same as model 4322)	
	4324 / Lightfour, 15" Longer (S/N, year & HP same as model 4322)	
	4325 / Lightfour Heavy Duty (S/N, year & HP same as model 4322)	
	4326 / Lightfour H.D., 5" Longer (S/N, year & HP same as model 4322)	
	4327 / Lightfour H.D., 15" Longer (S/N, year & HP same as model 4322)	
1939-41	4328 / Midget Racer	----
1939	4329 / Ace	1.8
1939	4331 / Ace, 5" Longer	1.8
1939	4332 / Handitwin	3.0
1939	4333 / Handitwin, 5" Longer	3.0
1939	4334 / Ranger - to S/N 04000	1.1
1940	S/N 04001 to 07000	1.1
1941	S/N 07001 and up	1.1
1939-41	4335 / Fleetwin	8.5
1939-41	4336 / Fleetwin, 5" Longer	8.5
	4337 / Lightwin Heavy Duty (S/N, year & HP same as model 4313)	
	4338 / Lightwin H.D., 5" Longer (S/N, year & HP same as model 4313)	
	4339 / Lightwin H.D., 15" Longer (S/N, year & HP same as model 4313)	
1940-41	4341 / Weedless Lightwin	5.0
1940	4346 / Sportsman	2.0
1940	4347 / Sportsman, 5" Longer	2.0
1940	4348 / Sportsman	2.0
1940	4349 / Sportsman, 5" Longer	2.0
1940	4351 / Ace - to S/N 03500	1.8

Year	Model / Description	HP
1941	S/N 03501 and up	1.8
	4352 / Ace, 5" Longer	
	(S/N, year & HP same as model 4351)	
1940	4353 / Sportwin	3.3
1940	4354 / Sportwin, 5" Longer	3.3
1940	4355 / Sportwin	3.3
1940	4356 / Sportwin, 5" Longer	3.3
1940	4357 / Handitwin – to S/N 04000	3.0
1940	S/N 04001 and up	3.0
	4358 / Handitwin, 5" Longer	
	(S/N, year & HP same as model 4357)	
1940–41	4359 / Zephyr	5.4
1940–41	4361 / Zephyr, 5" Longer	5.4
1940–41	4362 / Zephyr	5.4
1940–41	4363 / Zephyr, 5" Longer	5.4
1941	4364 / Sportsman – to S/N 10000	2.0
1942	S/N 10001 and up	2.0
	4365 / Sportsman, 5" Longer	
	(S/N, year & HP same as model 4364)	
	4366 / Sportsman	
	(S/N, year & HP same as model 4364)	
	4367 / Sportsman, 5" Longer	
	(S/N, year & HP same as model 4364)	
1941	4368 / Sportwin – to S/N 18000	3.3
1946	S/N 18001 and up	3.3
	4369 / Sportwin, 5" Longer	
	(S/N, year & HP same as model 4368)	
1941	4371 / Sportwin – to S/N 10000	3.3
1946	S/N 10001 to 30000	3.3
1947	S/N 30001 and up	3.3
	4372 / Sportwin, 5" Longer	
	(S/N, year & HP same as model 4371)	
1942	4373 / Lightfour Heavy Duty	9.7
1942	4374 / Lightfour H.D., 15" Longer	9.7
1943	4375 / Lightfour H.D., 15" Longer	9.7
1943	4376 / Lightfour H.D., 15" Longer	9.7
1943	4377 / Lightfour H.D., 15" Longer	9.7
1945–46	4378 / Zephyr	5.4
1945–46	4379 / Zephyr, 5" Longer	5.4
1945–46	4381 / Zephyr	5.4
1945–46	4382 / Zephyr, 5" Longer	5.4
1945	4383 / Lightfour – to S/N 04000	9.7
1946	S/N 04001 to 16000	9.7
1947	S/N 16001 to 25000	9.7
1948	S/N 25001 to 33000	9.7
1949	S/N 33001 and up	9.7
	4384 / Lightfour, 5" Longer	
	(S/N, year & HP same as model 4383)	
	4385 / Lightfour, 15" Longer	
	(S/N, year & HP same as model 4383)	
	4386 / Lightfour Heavy Duty	
	(S/N, year & HP same as model 4383)	
	4387 / Lightfour H.D., 5" Longer	
	(S/N, year & HP same as model 4383)	
	4388 / Lightfour H.D., 15" Longer	
	(S/N, year & HP same as model 4383)	
	4389 / Lightfour	
	(S/N, year & HP same as model 4383)	
	4391 / Lightfour, 5" Longer	
	(S/N, year & HP same as model 4383)	
	4392 / Lightfour, 15" Longer	
	(S/N, year & HP same as model 4383)	
	4393 / Lightfour Heavy Duty	
	(S/N, year & HP same as model 4383)	
	4394 / Lightfour H.D., 5" Longer	
	(S/N, year & HP same as model 4383)	
	4395 / Lightfour H.D., 15" Longer	
	(S/N, year & HP same as model 4383)	
1945	4398 / Lightfour Heavy Duty, 5" Longer	9.7
1946	4402 / Zephyr – to S/N 25000	5.4
1947	S/N 25001 to 40000	5.4
1948	S/N 40001 and up	5.4
	4403 / Zephyr, 5" Longer	
	(S/N, year & HP same as model 4402)	
	4404 / Zephyr	
	(S/N, year & HP same as model 4402)	
	4405 / Zephyr, 5" Longer	
	(S/N, year & HP same as model 4402)	
1946–47	4406 / Ranger	1.1
1946–47	4407 / Ranger	1.1
1946	4409 / Sportsman	2.0
1946	4411 / Sportsman, 5" Longer	2.0
1946	4412 / Sportsman	2.0
1946	4413 / Sportsman, 5" Longer	2.0
1947	4414 / Sportsman	2.0
1947	4415 / Sportsman, 5" Longer	2.0
1947	4416 / Sportsman	2.0
1947	4417 / Sportsman, 5" Longer	2.0
1947	4418 / Sportwin	3.3
1947	4419 / Sportwin, 5" Longer	3.3
1947	4421 / Sportwin	3.3
1947	4422 / Sportwin, 5" Longer	3.3
1948	4423 / Sportwin – to S/N 43000	3.3
1949	S/N 43001 to 80000	3.3
1951	S/N 80001 to 99999	3.3
1950–51	S/N with six digits	3.3
	4424 / Sportwin, 5" Longer	
	(S/N, year & HP same as model 4423)	
1948	4425 / Sportsman – to S/N 13000	1.5
1949	S/N 13001 and up	1.5
1950–51	S/N suffixed by 'C'	1.5
1949	4429 / Zephyr	5.4
1949	4431 / Zephyr, 5" Longer	5.4
1949	4432 / Sportster	5.0
1950	4434 / Fleetwin	7.5
1950	4435 / Fleetwin, 5" Longer	7.5
1950	4438 / Fastwin	14.0
1950	4439 / Fastwin, 5" Longer	14.0
1951	4441 / Fastwin – to S/N 20620	14.0
1952	S/N 20621 and up	14.0
	4442 / Fastwin, 5" Longer	
	(S/N, year & HP same as model 4441)	

Year	Model	HP
1951	4443 / Fleetwin – to S/N 43599	7.5
1952	S/N 43600 and up	7.5
	4444 / Fleetwin, 5" Longer (S/N, year & HP same as model 4443)	
1952	4447 / Fleetwin	7.5
1952	4448 / Fleetwin, 5" Longer	7.5
1949	5101 / Speedster	12.0
1949	5102 / Speedster, 5" Longer	12.0
1956	5512 / Fisherman	5.5
1956	5513 / Fisherman, 5" Longer	5.5
1957	5514 / Fisherman	5.5
1957	5515 / Fisherman, 5" Longer	5.5
1958	5516 / Fisherman	5.5
1958	5517 / Fisherman, 5" Longer	5.5
1959	5518 / Fisherman	5.5
1959	5519 / Fisherman, 5" Longer	5.5
1934	6000 / Speeditwin	21.1
1934	6001 / Speeditwin, 5" Longer	21.1
1934	6002 / Speeditwin Electric	21.1
1934	6003 / Speeditwin Electric, 5" Longer	21.1
1934	6004 Speeditwin	21.1
1934	6005 / Speeditwin, 5" Longer	21.1
1934	6006 / Speeditwin Electric	21.1
1934	6007 / Speeditwin Electric, 5" Longer	21.1
1934	6008 / Speeditwin Racer	----
1935	6011 / Speeditwin	21.1
1935	6012 / Speeditwin, 5" Longer	21.1
1935	6013 / Speeditwin Electric	21.1
1935	6014 / Speeditwin Electric, 5" Longer	21.1
1935	6015 / Speeditwin	21.1
1935	6016 / Speeditwin, 5" Longer	21.1
1935	6017 / Speeditwin Racer	----
1936	6018 / Speeditwin	21.1
1936	6019 / Speeditwin, 5" Longer	21.1
1936	6021 / Speeditwin Electric	21.1
1936	6022 / Speeditwin Electric, 5" Longer	21.1
1936	6023 / Speeditwin	21.1
1936	6024 / Speeditwin, 5" Longer	21.1
1936	6025 / Speeditwin Racer	----
1937	6026 / Speeditwin	22.5
1937	6027 / Speeditwin, 5" Longer	22.5
1937	6028 / Speeditwin Electric	22.5
1937	6029 / Speeditwin Electric, 5" Longer	22.5
1937	6031 / Speeditwin	22.5
1937	6032 / Speeditwin, 5" Longer	22.5
1937	6033 / Speeditwin Racer	----
1938	6034 / Speeditwin	22.5
1938	6035 / Speeditwin, 5" Longer	22.5
1938	6036 / Speeditwin Electric	22.5
1938	6037 / Speeditwin Electric, 5" Longer	22.5
1938	6038 / Speeditwin Racer	----
1939	6039 / Speeditwin – to S/N 01000	22.5
1940	S/N 01001 to 02200	22.5
1941	S/N 02201 to 05000	22.5
1946	S/N 05001 to 10000	22.5
1947	S/N 10001 to 11000	22.5
1948	S/N 11001 to 23100	22.5
1949	S/N 23101 to 26184	22.5
1950	S/N 26185 and up	22.5
	6041 / Speeditwin, 5" Longer (S/N, year & HP same as model 6039)	
1939-40	6042 / Speeditwin Racer	----
1941	6043 / Speeditwin Racer	----
1934	7000 / Speediquad	31.2
1934	7001 / Speediquad, 5" Longer	31.2
1934	7002 / Speediquad Electric	31.2
1934	7003 / Speediquad Electric, 5" Longer	31.2
1934	7004 / Speediquad	31.2
1934	7005 / Speediquad, 5" Longer	31.2
1934	7006 / Speediquad Electric	31.2
1934	7007 / Speediquad Electric, 5" Longer	31.2
1935	7008 / Speediquad	31.2
1935	7009 / Speediquad, 5" Longer	31.2
1935	7011 / Speediquad Electric	31.2
1935	7012 / Speediquad Electric, 5" Longer	31.2
1935	7013 / Speediquad	31.2
1935	7014 / Speediquad, 5" Longer	31.2
1936	7015 / Speediquad	31.2
1936	7016 / Speediquad, 5" Longer	31.2
1936	7017 / Speediquad Electric	31.2
1936	7018 / Speediquad Electric, 5" Longer	31.2
1936	7019 / Speediquad	31.2
1936	7021 / Speediquad, 5" Longer	31.2
1937	7022 / Speedifour	33.4
1937	7023 / Speedifour, 5" Longer	33.4
1937	7024 / Speedifour Electric	33.4
1937	7025 / Speedifour Electric, 5" Longer	33.4
1938	7026 / Speedifour	33.4
1938	7027 / Speedifour, 5" Longer	33.4
1938	7028 / Speedifour Electric	33.4
1938	7029 / Speedifour Electric, 5" Longer	33.4
1939	7031 / Speedifour – to S/N 01000	33.4
1940	S/N 01001 to 02000	33.4
1941	S/N 02001 to 03000	33.4
1946	S/N 03001 to 04000	33.4
1947	S/N 04001 to 07000	33.4
1948	S/N 07001 to 10000	33.4
1949	S/N 10001 to 12000	33.4
1950	S/N 12001 and up	33.4
	7032 / Speedifour, 5" Longer (S/N, year & HP same as model 7031)	
1939	7033 / Speedifour Electric – to S/N 01000	33.4
1940	S/N 01001 to 02000	33.4
1941	S/N 02001 and up	33.4
	7034 / Speedifour Electric, 5" Longer (S/N, year & HP same as model 7033)	
1942	7035 / Speedifour, 5" Longer	33.4
1953	7512 / Fleetwin	7.5
1953	7513 / Fleetwin, 5" Longer	7.5
1954	7514 / Fleetwin	7.5
1954	7515 / Fleetwin, 5" Longer	7.5

Year	Model	HP
1954	7516 / Fleetwin	7.5
1954	7517 / Fleetwin, 5" Longer	7.5
1955	7518 / Fleetwin	7.5
1955	7519 / Fleetwin, 5" Longer	7.5
1956	7520 / Fleetwin	7.5
1956	7521 / Fleetwin, 5" Longer	7.5
1957	7522 / Fleetwin	7.5
1957	7523 / Fleetwin, 5" Longer	7.5
1958	7524 / Fleetwin	7.5
1958	7525 / Fleetwin, 5" Longer	7.5
1934	8000 / Four-Sixty Racer	----
1934	8001 / Class 'X' Racer	----
1935	8002 / Four-Sixty Racer	----
1936	8003 / Four-Sixty Racer	----
1937	8004 / Four-Sixty Racer	----
1938	8005 / Four-Sixty Racer	----
1939-41	8006 / Four-Sixty Racer	----
1943	8008 / Storm Boat Motor	50.0
1946	8014 / Big Four	50.0
1949	8015 / Big Four	50.0
1934	9000 / Sportfour	16.2
1934	9001 / Sportfour, 5" Longer	16.2
1934	9002 / Sportfour Electric	16.2
1934	9003 / Sportfour Electric, 5" Longer	16.2
1934	9004 / Sportfour	16.2
1934	9005 / Sportfour, 5" Longer	16.2
1934	9006 / Sportfour Electric	16.2
1934	9007 / Sportfour Electric, 5" Longer	16.2
1935	9008 / Sportfour	16.2
1935	9009 / Sportfour, 5" Longer	16.2
1935	9011 / Sportfour Electric	16.2
1935	9012 / Sportfour Electric, 5" Longer	16.2
1935	9013 / Sportfour	16.2
1935	9014 / Sportfour, 5" Longer	16.2
1936	9015 / Sportfour	16.2
1936	9016 / Sportfour, 5" Longer	16.2
1936	9017 / Sportfour Electric	16.2
1936	9018 / Sportfour Electric, 5" Longer	16.2
1936	9019 / Sportfour	16.2
1936	9021 / Sportfour, 5" Longer	16.2
1937	9022 / Sportfour	16.2
1937	9023 / Sportfour, 5" Longer	16.2
1937	9024 / Sportfour Electric	16.2
1937	9025 / Sportfour Electric, 5" Longer	16.2
1938	9026 / Sportfour	16.2
1938	9027 / Sportfour, 5" Longer	16.2
1938	9028 / Sportfour Electric	16.2
1938	9029 / Sportfour Electric, 5" Longer	16.2
1939	9031 / Sportfour	16.2
1939	9032 / Sportfour, 5" Longer	16.2
1939	9033 / Sportfour Electric	16.2
1939	9034 / Sportfour Electric, 5" Longer	16.2
1940	9035 / Sportfour to S/N 01000	17.6
1941	S/N 01001 and up	17.6
	9036 / Sportfour, 5" Longer (S/N, year & HP same as model 9035)	
	9037 / Sportfour (S/N, year & HP same as model 9035)	
	9038 / Sportfour, 5" Longer (S/N, year & HP same as model 9035)	
1941	9039 / Heavy Duty Twin	15.0
1941	9041 / Sportfour	17.6
1956	10012 / Sportwin	10.0
1956	10013 / Sportwin, 5" Longer	10.0
1957	10014 / Sportwin	10.0
1957	10015 / Sportwin, 5" Longer	10.0
1958	10016 / Sportwin	10.0
1958	10017 / Sportwin, 5" Longer	10.0
1959	10018 / Sportwin	10.0
1959	10019 / Sportwin, 5" Longer	10.0
1953	15012 / Fastwin – to S/N 19000	15.0
1954	S/N 19001 and up	15.0
	15013 / Fastwin, 5" Longer (S/N, year & HP same as model 15012)	
1955	15014 / Fastwin	15.0
1955	15015 / Fastwin, 5" Longer	15.0
1956	15016 / Fastwin	15.0
1956	15017 / Fastwin, 5" Longer	15.0
1957	15020 / Fastwin	18.0
1957	15021 / Fastwin, 5" Longer	18.0
1958	15024 / Fastwin	18.0
1958	15025 / Fastwin, 5" Longer	18.0
1959	15028 / Fastwin	18.0
1959	15029 / Fastwin, 5" Longer	18.0
1956	15918 / Fastwin Electric	15.0
1956	15919 / Fastwin Electric, 5" Longer	15.0
1957	15922 / Fastwin Electric	18.0
1957	15923 / Fastwin Electric, 5" Longer	18.0
1958	15926 / Fastwin Electric	18.0
1958	15927 / Fastwin Electric, 5" Longer	18.0
1953	25012 / Big Twin – to S/N 70000	25.0
1954	S/N 70001 and up	25.0
	25013 / Big Twin, 5" Longer (S/N, year & HP same as model 25012)	
1954	25014 / Big Twin	25.0
1954	25015 / Big Twin, 5" Longer	25.0
1955	25018 / Big Twin	25.0
1955	25019 / Big Twin, 5" Longer	25.0
1956	25022 / Big Twin	30.0
1956	25023 / Big Twin, 5" Longer	30.0
1957	25028 / Big Twin	35.0
1957	25029 / Big Twin, 5" Longer	35.0
1958	25034 / Big Twin	35.0
1958	25035 / Big Twin, 5" Longer	35.0
1956	25526 / Lark	30.0
1956	25527 / Lark, 5" Longer	30.0
1957	25532 / Lark	35.0
1957	25533 / Lark, 5" Longer	35.0
1954	25916 / Big Twin Electric	25.0
1954	25917 / Big Twin Electric, 5" Longer	25.0
1955	25920 / Big Twin Electric	25.0
1955	25921 / Big Twin Electric, 5" Longer	25.0
1956	25924 / Big Twin Electric	30.0
1956	25925 / Big Twin Electric, 5" Longer	30.0
1957	25930 / Big Twin Electric	35.0
1957	25931 / Big Twin Electric, 5" Longer	35.0
1958	25936 / Big Twin Electric	35.0
1958	25937 / Big Twin Electric, 5" Longer	35.0
1959	35012 / Big Twin	35.0
1959	35013 / Big Twin, 5" Longer	35.0
1958	35514 / Lark	35.0
1958	35515 / Lark, 5" Longer	35.0

Year	Model	HP
1959	35516 / Lark	35.0
1959	35517 / Lark, 5" Longer	35.0
1958	50012 / Four-Fifty	50.0
1958	50013 / Four-Fifty, 5" Longer	50.0
1959	50016 / Four-Fifty	50.0
1959	50017 / Four-Fifty, 5" Longer	50.0
1958	50514 / Starflite	50.0
1958	50515 / Starflite, 5" Longer	50.0
1959	50518 / Starflite	50.0
1959	50519 / Starflite, 5" Longer	50.0
1959	50816 / Four-Fifty Electric	50.0
1959	50817 / Four-Fifty Electric, 5" Longer	50.0
1951	2001 / Big Twin – to S/N 11000	25.0
1952	S/N 11001 and up	25.0
	2002 / Big Twin, 5" Longer	
	(S/N, year & HP same as model 2001)	
1952	2003 / Big Twin	25.0
1952	2004 / Big Twin, 5" Longer	25.0
1952	3012 / Lightwin – to S/N 09000	3.0
1953	S/N 09001 to 34000	3.0
1954	S/N 34001 and up	3.0
	3013 / Lightwin, 5" Longer	
	(S/N, year & HP same as model 3012)	
1955	3014 / Lightwin	3.0
1955	3015 / Lightwin, 5" Longer	3.0
1955	3016 / Ducktwin	3.0
1956	3018 / Lightwin	3.0
1956	3019 / Lightwin, 5" Longer	3.0
1956	3020 / Ducktwin	3.0
1957	3022 / Lightwin	3.0
1957	3023 / Lightwin, 5" Longer	3.0
1957	3024 / Ducktwin	3.0
1958	3026 / Lightwin	3.0
1958	3027 / Lightwin, 5" Longer	3.0
1958	3028 / Ducktwin	3.0
1959	3030 / Lightwin	3.0
1959	3031 / Lightwin, 5" Longer	3.0
1959	3032 / Ducktwin	3.0
1960	3034 / Lightwin	3.0
1960	3035 / Lightwin 5" Longer	3.0
1960	3036 / Ducktwin	3.0
1961	3038 / Lightwin	3.0
1961	3039 / Lightwin 5" Longer	3.0
1961	3040 / Ducktwin	3.0
1962	3042 / Lightwin	3.0
1962	3043 / Lightwin 5" Longer	3.0
1962	3044 / Ducktwin	3.0
1963	3302 / Lightwin	3.0
1963	3303 / Lightwin 5" Longer	3.0
1963	3312 / Ducktwin	3.0
1964	3402 / Lightwin	3.0
1964	3403 / Lightwin 5" Longer	3.0
1964	3412 / Ducktwin	3.0
1964	3432 / Yachtwin	3.0
1964	3433 / Yachtwin 5" Longer	3.0
1965	3502 / Lightwin	3.0
1965	3503 / Lightwin 5" Longer	3.0
1965	3512 / Ducktwin	3.0
1965	3532 / Yachtwin	3.0
1965	3533 / Yachtwin 5" Longer	3.0
1966	3602 / Lightwin (Folding)	3.0
1966	3603 / Lightwin 5" Longer (Folding)	3.0
1966–67	3612 / Ducktwin (Folding)	3.0
1966	3632 / Yachtwin (Folding)	3.0
1966	3633 / Yachtwin 5" Longer (Folding)	3.0
1967	3702 / Lightwin (Folding)	3.0
1967	3703 / Lightwin 5" Longer (Folding)	3.0
1967	3706 / Lightwin (Rigid)	3.0
1967	3707 / Lightwin 5" Longer (Rigid)	3.0
1967	3712 / Ducktwin (Folding)	3.0
1967	3716 / Ducktwin (Rigid)	3.0
1967	3732 / Yachtwin (Folding)	3.0
1967	3733 / Yachtwin 5" Longer (Folding)	3.0
1967	3736 / Yachtwin (Rigid)	3.0
1967	3737 / Yachtwin 5" Longer (Rigid)	3.0
1968	3802 / Lightwin (Folding)	3.0
1968	3803 / Lightwin 5" Longer (Folding)	3.0
1968	3806 / Lightwin (Rigid)	3.0
1968	3807 / Lightwin 5" Longer (Rigid)	3.0
1968	3832 / Yachtwin (Folding)	3.0
1968	3833 / Yachtwin 5" Longer (Folding)	3.0
1968	3836 / Yachtwin (Rigid)	3.0
1968	3837 / Yachtwin 5" Longer (Rigid)	3.0
1970	4006 / Lightwin (Rigid)	4.0
1970	4036 / Yachtwin (Rigid)	4.0
1969	4902 / Lightwin (Folding)	4.0
1969	4906 / Lightwin (Rigid)	4.0
1969	4936 / Yachtwin (Rigid)	4.0
1963	5302 / Fisherman	5.5
1963	5303 / Fisherman 5" Longer	5.5
1964	5402 / Fisherman	5.5
1964	5403 / Fisherman 5" Longer	5.5
1965	5502 / Angler	5.0
1965	5503 / Angler 5" Longer	5.0
1960	5520 / Fisherman	5.5
1960	5521 / Fisherman 5" Longer	5.5
1961	5522 / Fisherman	5.5
1961	5523 / Fisherman 5" Longer	5.5
1962	5524 / Fisherman	5.5
1962	5525 / Fisherman 5" Longer	5.5
1966	5602 / Angler	5.0
1966	5603 / Angler 5" Longer	5.0
1967	5702 / Angler	5.0
1967	5703 / Angler 5" Longer	5.0
1968	5802 / Angler	5.0
1968	5803 / Angler 5" Longer	5.0
1970	6002 / Fisherman	6.0
1970	6003 / Fisherman 5" Longer	6.0
1965	6502 / Fisherman	6.0
1965	6503 / Fisherman 5" Longer	6.0
1966	6602 / Fisherman	6.0
1966	6603 / Fisherman 5" Longer	6.0
1967	6702 / Fisherman	6.0
1967	6703 / Fisherman 5" Longer	6.0
1968	6802 / Fisherman	6.0
1968	6803 / Fisherman 5" Longer	6.0
1969	6902 / Fisherman	6.0
1969	6903 / Fisherman 5" Longer	6.0
1970	9022 / Sportwin	9.5
1970	9023 / Sportwin 5" Longer	9.5
1964	9422 / Sportwin	9.5
1964	9423 / Sportwin 5" Longer	9.5
1965	9522 / Sportwin	9.5

Year	Model	HP		Year	Model	HP
1965	9523 / Sportwin 5" Longer	9.5		1967	33702 / Ski Twin	33.0
1966	9622 / Sportwin	9.5		1967	33703 / Ski Twin 5" Longer	33.0
1966	9623 / Sportwin 5" Longer	9.5		1967	33752 / Ski Twin Elec.	33.0
1967	9722 / Sportwin	9.5		1967	33753 / Ski Twin Elec. 5" Longer	33.0
1967	9723 / Sportwin 5" Longer	9.5		1968	33802 / Ski Twin	33.0
1968	9822 / Sportwin	9.5		1968	33803 / Ski Twin 5" Longer	33.0
1968	9823 / Sportwin 5" Longer	9.5		1968	33852 / Ski Twin Elec.	33.0
1969	9922 / Sportwin	9.5		1968	33853 / Ski Twin Elec. 5" Longer	33.0
1969	9923 / Sportwin 5" Longer	9.5		1969	33902 / Ski Twin	33.0
1960	10020 / Sportwin	10.0		1969	33903 / Ski Twin 5" Longer	33.0
1960	10021 / Sportwin 5" Longer	10.0		1969	33952 / Ski Twin Elec.	33.0
1961	10022 / Sportwin	10.0		1969	33953 / Ski Twin Elec. 5" Longer	33.0
1961	10023 / Sportwin 5" Longer	10.0		1960	35018 / Big Twin	40.0
1962	10024 / Sportwin	10.0		1960	35019 / Big Twin 5" Longer	40.0
1962	10025 / Sportwin 5" Longer	10.0		1961	35022 / Big Twin	40.0
1963	10302 / Sportwin	10.0		1961	35023 / Big Twin 5" Longer	40.0
1963	10303 / Sportwin 5" Longer	10.0		1962	35028 / Big Twin	40.0
1960	15032 / Fastwin	18.0		1962	35029 / Big Twin 5" Longer	40.0
1960	15033 / Fastwin 5" Longer	18.0		1960	35520 / Lark	40.0
1961	15034 / Fastwin	18.0		1960	35521 / Lark 5" Longer	40.0
1961	15035 / Fastwin 5" Longer	18.0		1961	35524 / Lark	40.0
1962	15036 / Fastwin	18.0		1961	35525 / Lark 5" Longer	40.0
1962	15037 / Fastwin 5" Longer	18.0		1962	35530 / Lark	40.0
1970	18002 / Fastwin	18.0		1962	35531 / Lark 5" Longer	40.0
1970	18003 / Fastwin 5" Longer	18.0		1962	35932 / Lark Sel.	40.0
1963	18302 / Fastwin	18.0		1962	35933 / Lark Sel. 5" Longer	40.0
1963	18303 / Fastwin 5" Longer	18.0		1970	37010 / Explorer 16' I/O	155.0
1964	18402 / Fastwin	18.0		1970	40002 / Big Twin	40.0
1964	18403 / Fastwin 5" Longer	18.0		1970	40003 / Big Twin 5" Longer	40.0
1965	18502 / Fastwin	18.0		1970	40052 / Big Twin Elec.	40.0
1965	18503 / Fastwin 5" Longer	18.0		1970	40053 / Big Twin Elec. 5" Longer	40.0
1966	18602 / Fastwin	18.0		1970	40072 / Lark Sel.	40.0
1966	18603 / Fastwin 5" Longer	18.0		1970	40073 / Lark Sel. 5" Longer	40.0
1967	18702 / Fastwin	18.0		1963	40302 / Big Twin	40.0
1967	18703 / Fastwin 5" Longer	18.0		1963	40303 / Big Twin 5" Longer	40.0
1968	18802 / Fastwin	18.0		1963	40352 / Big Twin Elec.	40.0
1968	18803 / Fastwin 5" Longer	18.0		1963	40353 / Big Twin Elec. 5" Longer	40.0
1969	18902 / Fastwin	18.0		1963	40362 / Lark Sel. (Bl.)	40.0
1969	18903 / Fastwin 5" Longer	18.0		1963	40363 / Lark Sel. (Bl.) 5" Longer	40.0
1970	25002 / Sportster	25.0		1963	40372 / Lark Sel. (Gr.)	40.0
1970	25003 / Sportster 5" Longer	25.0		1963	40373 / Lark Sel. (Gr.) 5" Longer	40.0
1969	25902 / Sportster	25.0		1964	40402 / Big Twin	40.0
1969	25903 / Sportster 5" Longer	25.0		1964	40403 / Big Twin 5" Longer	40.0
1970	27010 / Sportsman 16' I/O	155.0		1964	40452 / Big Twin Elec.	40.0
1962	28202 / Speeditwin	28.0		1964	40453 / Big Twin Elec. 5" Longer	40.0
1962	28203 / Speeditwin 5" Longer	28.0		1964	40462 / Lark Sel. (Bl.)	40.0
1963	28302 / Speeditwin	28.0		1964	40463 / Lark Sel. (Bl.) 5" Longer	40.0
1963	28303 / Speeditwin 5" Longer	28.0		1964	40472 / Lark Sel. (Gr.)	40.0
1964	28402 / Speeditwin	28.0		1964	40473 / Lark Sel. (Gr.) 5" Longer	40.0
1964	28403 / Speeditwin 5" Longer	28.0		1965	40502 / Big Twin	40.0
1970	33002 / Ski Twin	33.0		1965	40503 / Big Twin 5" Longer	40.0
1970	33003 / Ski Twin 5" Longer	33.0		1965	40552 / Big Twin Elec.	40.0
1970	33052 / Ski Twin Elec.	33.0		1965	40553 / Big Twin Elec. 5" Longer	40.0
1970	33053 / Ski Twin Elec. 5" Longer	33.0		1965	40562 / Lark Sel. (Bl.)	40.0
1965	33502 / Ski Twin	33.0		1965	40563 / Lark Sel. (Bl.) 5" Longer	40.0
1965	33503 / Ski Twin 5" Longer	33.0		1965	40572 / Lark Sel. (Gr.)	40.0
1965	33552 / Ski Twin Elec.	33.0		1965	40573 / Lark Sel. (Gr.) 5" Longer	40.0
1965	33553 / Ski Twin Elec. 5" Longer	33.0		1966	40602 / Big Twin	40.0
1966	33602 / Ski Twin	33.0		1966	40603 / Big Twin 5" Longer	40.0
1966	33603 / Ski Twin 5" Longer	33.0		1966	40652 / Big Twin Elec.	40.0
1966	33652 / Ski Twin Elec.	33.0		1966	40653 / Big Twin Elec. 5" Longer	40.0
1966	33653 / Ski Twin Elec. 5" Longer	33.0		1966	40662 / Lark Sel. (Bl.)	40.0

1966	40663 / Lark Sel. (Bl.) 5″ Longer	40.0		1963	75382 / Starflite (Bl.)	75.0
1966	40672 / Lark Sel. (Gr.)	40.0		1963	75383 / Starflite (Bl.) 5″ Longer	75.0
1966	40673 / Lark Sel. (Gr.) 5″ Longer	40.0		1963	75392 / Starflite (Gr.)	75.0
1967	40702 / Big Twin	40.0		1963	75393 / Starflite (Gr.) 5″ Longer	75.0
1967	40703 / Big Twin 5″ Longer	40.0		1964	75432 / Speedifour H.D.	75.0
1967	40752 / Big Twin Elec.	40.0		1964	75433 / Speedifour H.D. 5″ Longer	75.0
1967	40753 / Big Twin Elec. 5″ Longer	40.0		1964	75452 / Speedifour	75.0
1967	40772 / Lark Sel.	40.0		1964	75453 / Speedifour 5″ Longer	75.0
1967	40773 / Lark Sel. 5″ Longer	40.0		1964	75482 / Starflite (Bl.)	75.0
1968	40802 / Big Twin	40.0		1964	75483 / Starflite (Bl.) 5″ Longer	75.0
1968	40803 / Big Twin 5″ Longer	40.0		1964	75492 / Starflite (Gr.)	75.0
1968	40852 / Big Twin Elec.	40.0		1964	75493 / Starflite (Gr.) 5″ Longer	75.0
1968	40853 / Big Twin Elec. 5″ Longer	40.0		1965	75532 / Speedifour H.D.	75.0
1968	40872 / Lark Sel.	40.0		1965	75533 / Speedifour H.D. 5″ Longer	75.0
1968	40873 / Lark Sel. 5″ Longer	40.0		1965	75552 / Speedifour	75.0
1969	40902 / Big Twin	40.0		1965	75553 / Speedifour 5″ Longer	75.0
1969	40903 / Big Twin 5″ Longer	40.0		1965	75582 / Starflite (Bl.)	75.0
1969	40952 / Big Twin Elec.	40.0		1965	75583 / Starflite (Bl.) 5″ Longer	75.0
1969	40953 / Big Twin Elec. 5″ Longer	40.0		1965	75592 / Starflite (Gr.)	75.0
1969	40972 / Lark Sel.	40.0		1965	75593 / Starflite (Gr.) 5″ Longer	75.0
1969	40973 / Lark Sel. 5″ Longer	40.0		1966	80652 / Speedifour	80.0
1970	47010 / Sport Fisherman 19′ I/O	120.0		1966	80653 / Speedifour 5″ Longer	80.0
1960	50522 / Starflite	75.0		1966	80682 / Starflite (Bl.)	80.0
1960	50523 / Starflite 5″ Longer	75.0		1966	80683 / Starflite (Bl.) 5″ Longer	80.0
1961	50524 / Starflite	75.0		1966	80692 / Starflite (Gr.)	80.0
1961	50525 / Starflite 5″ Longer	75.0		1966	80693 / Starflite (Gr.) 5″ Longer	80.0
1962	50528 / Starflite	75.0		1967	80752 / Speedifour	80.0
1962	50529 / Starflite 5″ Longer	75.0		1967	80753 / Speedifour 5″ Longer	80.0
1961	50926 / Starflite U.C.	75.0		1967	80792 / Starflite	80.0
1961	50927 / Starflite U.C. 5″ Longer	75.0		1967	80793 / Starflite 5″ Longer	80.0
1962	50930 / Starflite Sel.	75.0		1970	85093 / Starflite 5″ Longer	85.0
1962	50931 / Starflite Sel. 5″ Longer	75.0		1968	85852 / Speedifour	85.0
1968	55872 / Triumph	55.0		1968	85853 / Speedifour 5″ Longer	85.0
1968	55873 / Triumph 5″ Longer	55.0		1968	85892 / Starflite	85.0
1969	55972 / Triumph	55.0		1968	85893 / Starflite 5″ Longer	85.0
1969	55973 / Triumph 5″ Longer	55.0		1969	85993 / Starflite 5″ Longer	85.0
1970	57010 / Dolphin 19′ I/O	210.0		1964	90482 / Starflite (Bl.)	90.0
1970	60072 / Triumph	60.0		1964	90483 / Starflite (Bl.) 5″ Longer	90.0
1970	60073 / Triumph 5″ Longer	60.0		1964	90492 / Starflite (Gr.)	90.0
1964	60432 / Sportfour H.D.	60.0		1964	90493 / Starflite (Gr.) 5″ Longer	90.0
1964	60433 / Sportfour H.D. 5″ Longer	60.0		1965	90582 / Starflite (Bl.)	90.0
1964	60452 / Sportfour	60.0		1965	90583 / Starflite (Bl.) 5″ Longer	90.0
1964	60453 / Sportfour 5″ Longer	60.0		1965	90592 / Starflite (Gr.)	90.0
1965	60532 / Sportfour H.D.	60.0		1965	90593 / Starflite (Gr.) 5″ Longer	90.0
1965	60533 / Sportfour H.D. 5″ Longer	60.0		1966	100683 / Starflite (Bl.) 5″ Longer	100.0
1965	60552 / Sportfour	60.0		1966	100693 / Starflite (Gr.) 5″ Longer	100.0
1965	60553 / Sportfour 5″ Longer	60.0		1967	100782 / Starflite	100.0
1966	60632 / Sportfour H.D.	60.0		1967	100783 / Starflite 5″ Longer	100.0
1966	60633 / Sportfour H.D. 5″ Longer	60.0		1968	100882 / Starflite	100.0
1966	60652 / Sportfour	60.0		1968	100883 / Starflite 5″ Longer	100.0
1966	60653 / Sportfour 5″ Longer	60.0		1970	107010 / 16′ Trailer W/O Brk.	----
1967	60732 / Sportfour H.D.	60.0		1970	115083 / Starflite 5″ Longer	115.0
1967	60733 / Sportfour H.D. 5″ Longer	60.0		1967-68	115742 / X-115 Racer	115.0
1967	60752 / Sportfour	60.0		1969	115983 / Starflite 5″ Longer	115.0
1967	60753 / Sportfour 5″ Longer	60.0				
1968	65832 / Sportfour H.D.	65.0				
1968	65833 / Sportfour H.D. 5″ Longer	65.0				
1968	65852 / Sportfour	65.0				
1968	65853 / Sportfour 5″ Longer	65.0				
1970	67010 / Rogue II 19′ I/O	210.0				
1963	75352 / Speedifour	75.0				
1963	75353 / Speedifour 5″ Longer	75.0				

Johnson. Like the lengthy Evinrude list, the Johnson guide was compiled to help dealers better identify customers' vintage motors. Although much of this document has been in circulation since the 1950s, the factory never updated it to include certain ''rare'' models from the 1920s-30s. Most of the missing motors are

variations of standard models identified on the Johnson chart. For example:

- Model C is an early-20s model A twin equipped with a canoe mounting bracket.
- Model B-35 is similar to K-35, except that its transom mount bolts to the boat's stern.
- PB motors have bronze lower units.
- "L" means long shaft.
- Electric-starting Johnsons from the early 30s built on the S and V model motors are called SE-50 and VE-50.
- Aquaflyer models from the early 1930s have electric starting but no integral fuel tank. These rigs were made specifically for custom Johnson boats and drink gas from onboard tanks. The Aquaflyer SA-50, PA-50, and VA-50s are among the rarest of Johnson outboard products.
- The 1931, limited-production, XR-55 racer doesn't show up on many Johnson lists. The idea of selling this 4-cylinder, high speed rig to depression-ravaged potential customers was a bit far-fetched.

The Johnson list does not identify certain carryover years of racing models. For example, the firm did make a 1933 PR-65 and a 1936 KR-80, but so few were produced that they were omitted from the list. Due to leftovers and economic considerations, some models were offered multiple years.

Other rather obscure Johnson products include the model AZ (as in AZ-50 and AZ-80). These opposed twins from the 1930s have above-water exhaust and may have been water pump powerheads (rated at 4 hp). The OB-60 (about 1932) was an opposed twin from Johnson's Canadian factory. This 4-hp kicker, equipped with a bronze lower unit, was probably built for export from North America. The 5-hp TS-20, an immediate post-World War II motor, wore rope (non-rewind) starting. TS-20 was an alternate-firing twin akin to the rewind-start TD-20.

Johnson

Year	Model	HP
1922–23	A	2
1922–23	BN	2
1924	A	2
1924	BN	2
1925	A-25	2
1925	AB-25	2
1925	J-25	1.5
1926	A-25	2
1926	AB-25	2
1926	J-25	1.5
1926	P-30	6
1928	A-35	2 ½
1927	J-25	1.5
1927	P-35	8
1927	K-35	6
1928	A-35	2 ½
1928	J-25	1.5
1928	K-40	7.15
1928	P-40	13.15
1928	TR-40	25.75
1929	A-45	3
1929	J-25	1.5
1929	K-45	7.15
1929	P-45	12
1929	S-45	13
1929	V-45	26
1929	SR-45	16
1929	VR-45	32
1929	TR-40	25.75
1930–32	J-25	1.5
1930–32	A-50	4
1930–32	K-50	8
1931–32	KR-55	12
1930–32	P-50	20
1930–32	PR-50	24
1931	PR-55	27
1932	PR-60	27
1930–32	S-45	13
1930–32	SR-50	16
1931	SR-55	18
1932	SR-60	
1930–32	V-45	26
1930	VR-50	32
1931–32	VR-55	36
1931–32	KR-55	12
1931–32	OA-55	3
1932	OA-60	3
1931–32	OK-55	8
1932	OK-60	7
1933	J-65*	*1.4
1933	OA-65	2.8
1933	A-65	4.1
1933	K-65	9.2
1933	S-65	13.3
1933	P-65	21.4
1933	V-65	26.1
1934	J-70	1.4
1934	F-70	3.3
1934	A-70	4.1
1934	K-70	9.2
1934	S-70	13.3
1934	P-70	21.4
1934	V-70	26.1
1935	J-75	1.4
1935	F-75	3.3
1935	300	3.7
1935	A-75	4.5
1935	K-75	9.3
1935	P-75	22
1935	OK-75	8.1
1936	A-80	4.5
1936	K-80	9.3
1936	J-80	1.7
1936	P-80	22
1936	100	1.7
1936	200	3.3
1936	300	3.7
1937	LS-37	2.1

1937	DS-37	2.1	1947	HD-25	2.5
1937	LT-37	4.2	1947	TD-20	5.0
1937	DT-37	4.2	1947	KD-15	9.8
1937	210	3.3	1947	SD-15	16.0
1937	110	1.7	1947	PO-15	22.0
1937	AA-37	4.5	1948	HD-25	2.5
1937	KA-37	9.3	1948	TD-20	5.0
1937	PO-37	22.0	1948	KD-15	9.8
1938	MS-38	1.1	1948	SD-15	16.0
1938	MD-38	1.1	1948	PO-15	22.0
1938	LS-38	2.1	1949	HD-25	2.5
1938	DS-38	2.1	1949	TD-20	5.0
1938	LT-38	4.2	1949	QD-10	10.0
1938	DT-38	4.2	1949	SD-20	16.0
1938	KA-38	9.3	1949	PO-15	22.0
1938	PO-38	22.0	1950	HD-25	2.5
1939	MS-39	1.1	1950	TN-25, 26	5.0
1939	MD-39	1.1	1950	QD-10, 11	10.0
1939	HS-39	2.5	1950	SD-20	16.0
1939	HA-39	2.5	1950	PO-15	22.0
1939	HD-39	2.5	1951	HD-26	2.5
1939	LT-39	5.0	1951	TN-27	5.0
1939	AT-39	5.0	1951	QD-12	10.0
1939	DT-39	5.0	1951	RD-10-11	25.0
1939	KA-39	9.8	1951	RD-12	25.0
1939	PO-39	22.0	1952	JW-10	3.0
1940	MS-15	1.5	1952	TN-28	5.0
1940	MD-15	1.5	1952	QD-13	10.0
1940	HS-10, 15	2.5	1952	RD-13	25.0
1940	HA-10, 15	2.5	1953	JW-10	3
1940	HD-10, 15	2.5	1953	TN-28	5
1940	LT-10	5.0	1953	QD-14	10
1940	AT-10	5.0	1953	QD-14A	10
1940	DT-10	5.0	1953	RD-14	25
1940	KA-10	9.8	1953	RD-15	25
1940	SD-10	16.0	1954	JW-10	3.0
1940	PO-10	22	1954	CD-10-11	5.5
1941	MS-20	1.5	1954	QD-15	10.0
1941	MD-20	1.5	1954	RD-16, 16A	25.0
1941	HS-20	2.5	1954	RDE-16, 16A	25.0
1941	HD-20	2.5	1955	JW-11	3.0
1941	TS-15	5.0	1955	CD-12	5.5
1941	TD-15	5.0	1955	QD-16	10.0
1941	KS-15	9.8	1955	RD-17	25.0
1941	KD-15	9.8	1955	RDE-17	25.0
1941	SD-10	16.0	1956	JW-12	3.0
1941	PO-15	22.0	1956	CD-13	5.5
1942	MS-20	1.5	1956	AD-10	7.5
1942	MD-20	1.5	1956	QD-17	10.0
1942	HS-20	2.5	1956	FD-10	15.0
1942	HD-20	2.5	1956	FDE-10	15.0
1942	TS-15	5.0	1956	RD-18	30.0
1942	TD-15	5.0	1956	RDE-18	30.0
1942	KS-15	9.8	1956	RJE-18	30.0
1942	KD-15	9.8	1957	JW-13	3.0
1942	SD-10	16.0	1957	CD-14	5.5
1942	PO-15	22.0	1957	AD-11	7.5
1946	HD-25	2.5	1957	QD-18	10.0
1946	TD-20	5.0	1957	FD-11	18.0
1946	KD-15	9.8	1957	FDE-11	18.0
1946	SD-15	16.0	1957	RD-19	35.0
1946	PO-15	22.0	1957	RDE-19	35.0

Year	Model	HP
1957	RJE-19	35.0
1958	JW-14	3.0
1958	CD-15	5.5
1958	AD-12	7.5
1958	QD-19	10.0
1958	FD-12	18.0
1958	FDE-12	18.0
1958	RD-19C	35.0
1958	RDE-19C	35.0
1958	RDS-20	35.0
1958	V4-10	50.0
1958	V4S-10	50.0
1959	JW-15	3
1959	CD-16	5.5
1959	QD-20	10
1959	FD-13	18
1959	RD-21	35
1959	RDS-21	35
1959	V4-11	50
1959	V4S-11	50
1960	JW-16	3
1960	CD-17	5.5
1960	QD-21	10
1960	FD-14	18
1960	RD-22	40
1960	RDS-22	40
1960	V4S-12	75
1961	JW-17	3
1961	CD-18	5.5
1961	QD-22	10
1961	FD-15	18
1961	RD-23	40
1961	RDS-23	40
1961	V4S-13	75
1961	V4A-13	75
1962	JW-17R	3
1962	CD-19	5.5
1962	QD-23	10
1962	FD-16	18
1962	RX-10C	28
1962	RD-24	40
1962	RDS-24	40
1962	RK-24	40
1962	V4S-14	75
1962	V4A-14	75
1963	JW-18	3
1963	CD-20	5.5
1963	QD-24	10
1963	FD-17	18
1963	RX-11	28
1963	RD-25	40
1963	RDS-25	40
1963	RK-25	40
1963	V4S-15	75
1963	V4A-15	75
1964	JW-19	3
1964	JH-19	3
1964	CD-21	5.5
1964	MQ-10	9.5
1964	FD-18	18
1964	RX-12	28
1964	RD-26	40
1964	RDS-26	40
1964	RK-26	40
1964	VX-10	60
1964	V4S-16	75
1964	V4A-16	75
1964	V4M-10	90

* J-65 1933 and all following motors are O.B.C. Certified Horsepower ratings.

Johnson Serial Numbers

PLEASE NOTE: Some of these serial numbers were actually stamped in motors produced very late in the year just previous to their true model year. For example, the 1953 Johnson, number 1,000,000, was built in November 1952.

Year	Numbers	
Very Late 1921	506 –	606
1922	606 –	3,930
1923	3,931 –	7,500
1924	7,501 –	20,000
1925	20,001 –	30,559
1926	30,560 –	44,977
1927	44,978 –	65,524
1928	65,525 –	96,408
1929	96,409 –	128,000
1930	128,001 –	152,777
1931	152,778 –	161,326
1932	161,327 –	167,430
1933	167,431 –	208,583
1934	208,584 –	219,371
1935	219,372 –	232,156
1936	232,157 –	252,675
1937	252,676 –	283,888
1938	283,889 –	315,166
1939	315,167 –	355,971
1940	355,972 –	397,900
1941	397,901 –	439,206
1942	439,207 –	460,782
1943–45*	460,783 –	491,736
1946	491,737 –	538,800
1947	538,801 –	614,514
1948	614,515 –	698,874
1949	698,875 –	787,023
1950	787,024 –	869,939 inclusive.
1951	869,940 –	920,479
1952	920,480 –	980,883
1953	980,884 –	1,079,711
1954	1,079,712 –	1,194,192
1955	1,194,193 –	1,328,372
1956	1,328,373 –	1,493,185
1957	1,493,186 –	1,660,474
1958	1,660,475 –	1,743,080
1959	1,743,081 –	1,995,465
1960	1,995,611 –	2,105,657**
1961	2,105,658 –	2,249,094

* Most of this production figure was assigned to military use.
** It is not certain why there are 146 missing serial numbers between 1959–60.

Mercury. The KG9-1 motor was the first Merc 4 cylinder to wear a re-wind starter. Previous KG9 and KF9 models had an exposed, chrome flywheel. While no official verification exists, some KF9/KG9/KG9-1 Mercs might have red (instead of the usual cedar green) paint. I have seen some red rigs that appear to be factory original. (Some Merc accessory catalogs list "Mercury Red" paint.) A few advertisements picture shiny, chromed (or buffed aluminum) early 4-cylinder Mercury powerhead cowling.

Some sources identify Mercs with long, Quicksilver lower units as "QS" motors. The KG4H and similar Quicksilver models were probably available on a limited basis through the late 1950s.

Mercury 1940–55 motors typically take ⅜ pint of oil per gallon of gasoline; racing versions use ¾ pint. The 1956–62 Mercs get 6 ounces of oil per gallon of gas, while racers take 12 ounces. By 1963, Mercury went to a 50 to 1 oil/gas mix (12 ounces per 5 gallons of gasoline). Merc said 6 ounces of regular oil per gallon was OK in a pinch. Check with a Mercury dealer for the best mixture.

Most Mercs with breaker points accepted a .018" setting. Spark plug gap generally was .025 on pre-1960 rigs.

An asterisk (*) after an HP rating indicates "horsepower varies with engine revolutions per minute." Most early Merc literature, however, carried no RPM rating for the high speed motors.

About 1958, Merc replaced the standard Mark 20H short Quicksilver racing lower unit drive-shaft housing with a chubby, "howler" tuned exhaust piece, sometimes called the "toilet-bowl" lower unit. The original Mark 20H Carter carburetor was switched to a Tillotson model.

The Mark 58 Super Thunderbolt also was available as: 58S, with electric start; 58E, with electric start and generator; and 58EL, with electric start and generator and long shaft.

Mercury's 1959 motors may also be tagged with the following designations: L (longshaft), M (manual start), S (electric start), E (electric start and generator). Top of the line models with chrome top and bottom cowl strips and chrome front shield and handle were available. "Dynafloat" suspension and a safety-tilt-up switch accessory were available on Mark 28A, 58A, and 78A.

Mercury

Year	Model	HP
1940	K1 / Special	2.5
1940	K2 / Standard	3
1940	K3 / Deluxe	3
1940	K4 / Alternate	6
1940	K5 / Alternate Deluxe	6
1941	KB1 / Comet	2.9
1941	KB1A / Comet Deluxe	3.1
1941	KB2 / Streamliner	3.2
1941–42	KB3 / Torpedo	3.2
1941–42	KB4 / Rocket	5.8
1941	KB-5 / Rocket Deluxe	6
1946	KB4-1 / Rocket	6
1946–47	KD3 / Comet	3.2
1946–47	KD4 / Rocket	6
1947	KD3S / Comet	3.2
1947	KD4S / Rocket	6
1947–48	KE3 / Comet Deluxe	3.6
1947–52	KE4 / Rocket Deluxe	7.5
1947	KE4A / Rocket Deluxe	6
1947–49	KE7 / Lightning Deluxe	10
1949–50	KF3 / Comet	3.5
1949–50	KF7 / Super 10	10
1949–50	KF7HD / Super 10 Heavy-Duty (racer)	10+
1949–50	KF7Q / Super 10 (w/long Quicksilver racing lower unit)	10+
1949–50	KF9 / Thunderbolt	25+*
1949–50	KF9Q / Thunderbolt (may also have been available in "HD" series)	25+*
1949–52	KF5 / Super 5	5
1950–52	KG4 / Rocket Hurricane	7.5+*
1950–52	KG4H / Rocket Hurricane (w/Quicksilver racing lower unit)	7.5+*
1950–52	KG7 / Super 10 Hurricane	10+*
1950–52	KG7H / Super 10 Hurricane (w/Quicksilver racing lower unit)	10+*
1950–52	KG7Q / Super 10 Hurricane (w/long Quicksilver racing lower unit)	10+*
1950–52	KG9 / Thunderbolt	25+*
1951	KG9-1 / Thunderbolt	25+*
1950–52	KG9Q / Thunderbolt (w/long Quicksilver racing lower unit) (Some sources call this motor the KG9QS.)	25+*
1952	KH7 / Cruiser (shift) (Also called Super 10 Hurricane Cruiser.)	10+*
1953–55	Mark 5 / (Also called Super 5.)	5
1953–55	Mark 7 / Rocket Deluxe	7.5
1953	Mark 15 / —	10
1953–55	Mark 20 / Hurricane	16
1953–54	Mark 40 / Thunderbolt	25+*
1953–55	Mark 40H / Thunderbolt (w/short Quicksilver racing lower unit)	25+*
1954–56	Mark 20H / Hurricane (w/short Quicksilver lower unit)	16+*
1954	Mark 50 / Thunderbolt	40
1954	Mark 50E / Thunderbolt MercElectric (electric start)	40
1955	Mark 6 / Comet (Silent Six)	5.9
1955	Mark 25 / Hurricane	18
1955	Mark 25E / Hurricane MercElectric (electric start)	18
1956–58	Mark 25 / Hurricane	20
1956–57	Mark 25E / Hurricane MercElectric	20
1955–58	Mark 55 / Thunderbolt	40
1955–58	Mark 55E / Thunderbolt MercElectric	40
1956–58	Mark 55H / Thunderbolt Hydro	40+*
1956–58	Mark 6 / Comet (Silent Six)	6
1956–58	Mark 30 / Turbo-Four	30
1956–58	Mark 30E / Turbo-Four MercElectric	30
1956–58	Mark 30H / Turbo-Four Hydro	30+*
1957–58	Mark 10 / Trol-Twin Rocket	10
1957–58	Mark 75 (E) / Marathon Six	60
1957–58	Mark 75H / Marathon Six Hydro	60+*
1958	Mark 28 / Super Hurricane	22
1958	Mark 58 / Super Thunderbolt	45

Year	Model	HP
1958	Mark 78E / Super Marathon Six (Also available w/longshaft and electric start as Mark 78EL)	70
1959	Mark 6A / Comet Silent Six	6
1959	Mark 10A / Trol-Twin Rocket	10
1959	Mark 15A / Rocket	15
1959	Mark 28A / Super Hurricane	22
1959	Mark 35A / Thunderbolt	35
1959	Mark 55A / Thunderbolt	40
1959	Mark 58A / Super Thunderbolt	45
1959	Mark 75A / Marathon Six	60
1959	Mark 78A / Super Marathon Six	70
1960	Merc 100 / (automatic transmission)	10
1960–61	Merc 150 / (automatic transmission)	15
1960–61	Merc 200 / (automatic transmission)	22
1960	Merc 300 / —	35
1960–61	Merc 400 / —	45
1960	Merc 600 / —	60
1960–61	Merc 700 / (direct-reverse)	70
1960–61	Merc 800 / (direct-reverse)	80
1961	Merc 800 / (gear shift)	80
1961–62	Merc 700 / (gear shift)	70
1961	Merc 500 / —	50
1961	Merc 350 / 4-Cylinder	40
1961–68	Merc 60 / —	6
1962–69	Merc 110 / —	9.8
1963–69	Merc 200 / (gear shift)	20
1962	Merc 250 / —	25
1963–65	Merc 350 / 2-Cylinder	35
1962	Merc 450 / —	45
1962–66	Merc 500 / "Jet-Prop"	50
1963–66	Merc 650 / —	65
1962	Merc 850 / (76 cubic inch version)	85
1963–64	Merc 850 / (90 cubic inch version)	85
1962–65	Merc 1000 / —	100
1964–68	Merc 39 / —	3.9
1968	Merc 60J / (w/small Quicksilver racing lower unit)	6
1965	Merc 900 / —	90
1966	Merc 950 / (also Merc 950SS in 66–67)	95
1966	Merc 1100 / (also Merc 1100SS in 1967)	110
1967	Merc 500S / (also 500M)	50
1967–69	Merc 500SS / —	50
1967	Merc 650S / —	65
1967–69	Merc 650SS / —	65
1968–69	Merc 1000SS / —	100
1666–69	Merc 350 / —	35
1968–69	Merc 1250SS / —	125
1968	Merc 1250BP / (w/racing lower unit equipped with shift)	125
1967–69	Merc 350 / —	35
1969	Merc 800 / (4-cylinder version)	80
1969	Merc 40 / —	4
1969	Merc 75 / —	7.5

Mercury Serial Numbers

PLEASE NOTE: Unlike Evinrude and Johnson, Mercury never offered consumers a serial number–oriented model/ year guide. The following list, compiled from a dealer's file, is our "best guess" for dating, by serial number, some classic green Mercs. Although the Mark 25 serial numbers seem to be out of sequence, they are correct. (It's possible that not every number in a given year's serial number allocation was used.)

Model	Numbers	Year
KE3	234324–238423	1947
KE3	238424–240823	1948
KE3	303054–334553	1948
KE4	214324–221341	1947
KE4	221342–247350	1948
KE4	247351–261720	1949
KE4	438834–450695	1950
KE4	465696 and up	1951–52
KE7	191001–210124	1947
KE7	210125–269765	1948
KE7	269766 and up	1949 (some late 1949 models were sold as 1950 motors)
KF3	358136–360135	1949
KF3	374545–375544	1949
KF3	414293 and up	1950
KF5	338136–358135	1949
KF5	372545–374544	1949
KF5	416793–425562	1950
KF5	425587–429080	1951
KF5	431834 and up	1952
KG4	under @450000	1950
KG4	above @450000	1951–52
KG7	402543–444870	1950
KG7	444871 and up	1951–52
Mark 5	574128–591627	1953
Mark 5	708000–711399	1954
Mark 5	762113–786612	1955
Mark 7	557618–564117	1953
Mark 7	756113–762112	1954
Mark 7	821413–825417	1955
Mark 20	700000–753906	1953
Mark 20	753907 and up	1954–55
Mark 25(25E)	860979–956419	1955
Mark 25(25E)	956420–1036986	1956
Mark 25	1042297–1047296	1957
Mark 25	1036987–1042296	1958
Mark 25	1047298 and up	1958

Gale Products Private Brands.

Gale Products produced many motors that were marketed under more than one marque. Where two model numbers appear in the charts, the first is the customer's number; the second (after the slash mark) is Gale's own designation. Otherwise, only one model number applies.

Gale Products

Year	Model	HP
	Western Auto "Western Flyer"	
1941–42	121W	2.5
1941–42	122W	2.5
1941–42	251W	5.0
1941–42	252W	5.0

Goodrich "Sea Flyer"

Year	Model	
1952	45-050 / 3D10	3
1951	64-180 / 5D10	5
1952	45-060 / 5D10	5
1952	45-070 / 12D10	12

Gamble Skogmo "Hiawatha"

Year	Model	
1948–49	840MI-25-7945A / 1H5	1.5
1941–42	25-S / 121	2.5
1941–42	25-DL / 122	2.5
1945–46	25-3258 / 131	3.0
1947	25-7955 / 1H1	3.0
1947	47-3S / 1H1	3.0
1947–48	25-7956 / 1H4	3.0
1948–49	840MI-25-7957A / 1H6	3.0
1949–50	050MI-25-7958A / 1H9	3.0
1941–42	50-S / 251	5.0
1941–42	50-DL / 252	5.0
1945–46	50-SA / 251A	5.0
1945–46	50-DLA / 252A	5.0
1947	47-5D / 2H2	5.0
1947	25-7970 / 2H2	5.0
1947–48	25-7971 / 2H3	5.0
1948	840MI-25-7972A / 2H7	5.0
1949–50	940MI-25-7972A / 2H7	5.0
1948	840MI-25-7980A / 2H8	12.0
1949–50	940MI-25-7980A / 2H8	12.0
1951	150MI-25-7959A / 3D10	3
1953	350MI-25-7959B / 3D10	3
1953	350MI-25-7959C / 3D11	3
1954	450MI-25-7959A / 3D11	3
1955	550MI-25-7959A / 3D11	3
1953	350MI-25-7972B / 5S10	5
1951	150MI-25-7973A / 5D10	5
1952	250MI-25-7973A / 5D10	5
1953	350MI-25-7973B / 5D10	5
1954	450MI-25-7973A / 5D10	5
1951	150MI-25-7981A / 12D10	12
1952	250MI-25-7981A / 12D10	12
1953	350MI-25-7981B / 12D10	12
1954	450MI-25-7982 / 12D11	12
1955	550MI-25-7982A / 12D11	12

Fedway "Saber"

Year	Model	
1953	3D10D / 3D10	3
1953	3D11D / 3D11	3
1953	5S10D / 5S10	5
1953	5D10D / 5D10	5
1953	12S10D / 12S10	12
1953	12D10D / 12D10	12

AMC "Saber"

Year	Model	
1955	3D12M / 3D12	3
1955	5S12M / 5S12	5
1955	5D11M / 5D11	5
1955	12D11M / 12D11	12
1955	22D10M / 22D10	22
1955	22DE10M / 22DE10	22
1956	3D13M / 3D13	3
1956	5S12M / 5S12	5
1956	5D12M / 5D12	5
1956	5D13M / 5D13	5
1956	12D13M / 12D13	12
1956	22D11M / 22D11	25
1956	22D13M / 22D13	25
1956	22DE11M / 22DE11	25

Atlas "Royal"

Year	Model	
1948–49	1A5	1.5
1950	1A9	3.0
1947–48	2A3	5.0
1949–50	2A7	5.0
1948–50	2A8	12.0
1952–53	3D10A / 3D10	3
1953–55	3D11A / 3D11	3
1955	3D12A / 3D12	3
1953–54	5S10A / 5S10	5
1955	5S11A / 5S11	5
1951–54	5D10A / 5D10	5
1955	5D11A / 5D11	5
1953	12S10A / 12S10	12
1951–53	12D10A / 12D10	12
1954–55	12D11A / 12D11	12
1955	22D10A / 22D10	22
1955	22DE10A / 22DE10	22
1955	22D12A / 22D12	22
1955	22DE12A / 22DE12	22
1956	3D13A / 3D13	3
1956	5D12A / 5D12	5
1956	5D13A / 5D13	5
1956	12D13A / 12D13	12
1956	25D11A / 22D11	25
1956	25D13A / 22D13	25
1956	25DE11A / 22DE11	25
1956	25DE13A / 22DE13	25

Gale Products "Buccaneer"

Year	Model	
1950	1B10	1.5
1950	1B9	3.0
1950	2B7	5.0
1950	2B8	12.0
1951–53	3D10B / 3D10	3
1953–55	3D11B / 3D11	3
1955	3D12B / 3D12	3
1951–54	5S10B / 5S10	5
1955	5S11B / 5S11	5
1951–54	5D10B / 5D10	5
1955	5D11B / 5D11	5
1951–53	12S10B / 12S10	12
1951–53	12D10B / 12D10	12
1954–55	12D11B / 12D11	12
1955	22D10B / 22D10	22
1955	22DE10B / 22DE10	22
1955	22D12B / 22D12	22
1955	22DE12B / 22DE12	22
1956	3D13B / 3D13	3
1956	5S12B / 5S12	5
1956	5D12B / 5D12	5
1956	5D13B / 5D13	5
1956	12S12B / 12S12	12
1956	12D13B / 12D13	12
1956	12D14B / 12D14	12
1956	12DE13B / 12DE13	12
1956	22D11B / 22D11	25
1956	22D13B / 22D13	25

1956	22DE11B / 22DE11	25
1956	22DE13B / 22DE13	25
1957	3D14B / 3D14	3
1957	5S13B / 5S13	5
1957	5D14B / 5D14	5
1957	12S13B / 12S13	12
1957	12D15B / 12D15	12
1957	12DE15B / 12DE15	12
1957	22D14B / 22D14	25
1957	22DE14B / 22DE14	25
1958	3D15B Deluxe	3
1958	5S14B Standard	5
1958	5D15B Deluxe	5
1958	12S15B Standard	12
1958	12D17B Deluxe	12
1958	22D15B Manual	25
1958	22DE15B Electric	25
1958	35DE10B Electric	35
1959	3D15B Deluxe	3
1959	5D16B Deluxe	5
1959	12D18B Deluxe	12
1959	22D16B Deluxe	25
1959	22DE16B Deluxe Electric	25
1959	35D11B Deluxe	35
1959	35D12B Deluxe	35
1959	35DE11B Deluxe Electric	35
1959	35DE12B Deluxe Electric	35
1960	3D16B Deluxe	3
1960	5D17B Deluxe	5
1960	15D10B Deluxe	15
1960	22D17B Deluxe	25
1960	22DE17B Deluxe Electric	25
1960	35D13B Deluxe	35
1960	35DE13B Deluxe Electric	35
1961	3D17B Deluxe	3
1961	5D18B, 5D19B, 5D21B Deluxe	5
1961	5DL18B, 5DL19B, 5DL21B	5
1961	15D11B, 15D12B Deluxe	15
1961	15DL11B, 15DL12B	15
1961	25D18B, 25D20B Deluxe	25
1961	25DL18B, 25DL20B	25
1961	25DE18B, 25DE20B Deluxe Electric	25
1961	25DEL18B, 25DEL20B	25
1961	40D14B Deluxe	40
1961	40DL14B	40
1961	40DE14B Deluxe Electric	40
1961	40DEL14B	40
1961	40DG14B	40
1961	40DGL14B	40
1962	3D18B Deluxe	3
1962	5D20B Deluxe	5
1962	5DL20B	5
1962	15D13B, 15D14B Deluxe	15
1962	15DL13B, 15DL14B	15
1962	25D19B Deluxe	25
1962	25DL19B	25
1962	25DE19B Deluxe Electric	25
1962	25DEL19B	25
1962	40D15B Deluxe	40
1962	40DL15B	40
1962	40DE15B Deluxe Electric	40
1962	40DEL15B	40
1962	40DG15B	40
1962	40DGL15B	40
1963	3D19B Deluxe	3
1963	5D22B Deluxe	5
1963	15D15B Deluxe	15
1963	15D15P	15
1963	15DL15B	15
1963	25D21B Deluxe	25
1963	25DL21B	25
1963	25DE21B Deluxe Electric	25
1963	25DEL21B	25
1963	40D17B Deluxe	40
1963	40DL17B	40
1963	40DE17B Deluxe Electric	40
1963	40DE17P	40
1963	40DEL17B	40
1963	40DG17B	40
1963	40DGL17B	40
1963	V-Sovereign	60

Spiegel "Brooklure"

1950	230-50-1 / 1S10	1.5
1950	230-50-3 / 1S9	3.0
1950	230-50-5 / 2S7	5.0
1950	230-50-12 / 2S8	12.0
1951–53	230-51-3D / 3D10	3
1953–55	230-51-3DA / 3D11	3
1955	230-51-3DB / 3D12	3
1951–54	230-51-5S / 5S10	5
1951–54	230-51-5D / 5D10	5
1955	230-55-5D / 5D11	5
1953	230-51-12S / 12S10	12
1951–53	230-51-12D / 12D10	12
1954	230-53-12D / 12D11	12
1955	230-55-22DS / 22D10	22
1955	230-55-22DE / 22DE10	22
1956	50T3341 / 3D13	3
1956	50T3342 / 5S12	5
1956	50T3343 / 5D12	5
1956	50T3343A / 5D13	5
1956	50T3344 / 12D13	12
1956	50T3345 / 22D11	25
1956	50T3346 / 22DE11	25
1957	50T3337 / 3D14	3
1957	50T3343B / 5D14	5
1957	50T3338 / 12D15	12
1957	50T3339 / 22D14	25
1957	50T3340 / 22DE14	25
1958	50Z3323 Deluxe	3
1958	50Z3324 Deluxe	5
1958	50Z3325 Deluxe	12
1958	50Z3326 Manual	25
1958	50Z3327 Electric	25

Goodyear "Sea Bee"

1948–49	025-3562 / 1G5	1.5
1949–50	025-3562A / 1G10	1.5
1945–46	025-3555 / 135A	3.0
1947	1G1	3.0
1947–48	1G4	3.0
1948–49	025-3563 / 1G6	3.0
1949–50	025-3566 / 1G9	3.0

Year	Model	Value
1945–46	025-3550 / 256A	5.0
1947	2G2	5.0
1947–48	2G3	5.0
1948	025-3564 / 2G7	5.0
1949–50	025-3564A / 2G7	5.0
1948	025-3565 / 2G8	12.0
1949–50	025-3565A / 2G8	12.0
1951–53	025-3567 (3D10G) / 3D10	3
1953	025-3567 (3D11G) / 3D11	3
1954–55	025-3574 (3D11G) / 3D11	3
1955	25-3574 (3D12G) / 3D12	3
1951–54	025-3568 (5S10G) / 5S10	5
1955	025-3602 (5S11G) / 5S11	5
1951–53	025-3569 (5D10G) / 5D10	5
1954	025-3573 (5D10G) / 5D10	5
1955	025-3603 (5D11G) / 5D11	5
1951–53	025-3570 (12S10G) / 12S10	12
1951–53	025-3571 (12D10G) / 12D10	12
1954–55	25-3572 (12D11G) / 12D11	12
1955	25-3604 (22D10G) / 22D10	22
1955	25-3605 (22DE10G) / 22DE10	22
1955	25-3604 (22D12G) / 22D12	22
1955	25-3605 (22DE12G) / 22DE12	22
1956	225-3606 (3D13G) / 3D13	3
1956	225-3607 (5S12G) / 5S12	5
1956	225-3608 (5D12G) / 5D12	5
1956	225-3608 (5D13G) / 5D13	5
1956	225-3609 (12D13G) / 12D13	12
1956	225-3609 (12D14G) / 12D14	12
1956	225-3610 (22D11G) / 22D11	25
1956	225-3610 (22D13G) / 22D13	25
1956	225-3611 (22DE11G) / 22DE11	25
1956	225-3611 (22DE11G) / 22DE13	25
1957	225-3612 (3D14G) / 3D14	3
1957	225-3613 (5D13G) / 5S13	5
1957	225-3614 (5D14G) / 5D14	5
1957	225-3615 (12D15G) / 12D15	12
1957	225-3616 (22D14G) / 22D14	25
1957	225-3617 (22DE14G) / 22DE14	25
1958	3D15 G Code 225-3619 Deluxe	3
1958	5S14G Code 225-3620 Standard	5
1958	5D15G Code 225-3621 Deluxe	5
1958	12D17G Code 225-3622 Deluxe	12
1958	22D15G Code 225-3623 Manual	25
1958	22DE15G Code 225-3624 Electric	25
1958	35DE10G Code 225-3625 Electric	35
1959	3D15G Code 225-3619 Deluxe	3
1959	5D16G Code 225-3450 Deluxe	5
1959	12D18G Code 225-3451 Deluxe	12
1959	22D16G Code 225-3452 Deluxe	25
1959	22DE16G Code 225-3453 Deluxe Electric	25
1959	35D11G Code 225-3454 Deluxe	35
1959	35D12G Code 225-3454A Deluxe	35
1959	35DE11G Code 225-3455 Deluxe Electric	35
1959	35DE12G Code 225-3455A Deluxe Electric	35

Montgomery Ward "Sea King"

Year	Model	Value
1948–49	84GG9003A / 1W5	1.5
1949–50	94GG9003B / 1W10	1.5
1941–42	24GG9351A / 125	2.5
1945–46	64GG9005 / 133	3.0
1947	74GG9005A / 1W1	3.0
1947–48	74GG9006 / 1W4	3.0
1948–49	84GG9007A / 1W6	3.0
1949–50	94GG9009A / 1W9	3.0
1941–42	14GG8826 / 253	5.0
1941–42	14GG8827 / 254	5.0
1945	54GG9010 / 253A	5.0
1945	54GG9011 / 254A	5.0
1946	64GG9010 / 253A	5.0
1946	64GG9011 / 254A	5.0
1947	74GG9011A / 2W2	5.0
1947–48	74GG9012 / 2W3	5.0
1948	84GG9014A / 2W7	5.0
1949–50	94GG9014A / 2W7	5.0
1948	84GG9017A / 2W8	12.0
1949–50	94GG9017A / 2W8	12.0
1951	15GG9004A / 3D10	3
1952	25GG9004A / 3D10	3
1953	35GG9004A / 3D10	3
1953	35GG9004B / 3D11	3
1954	45GG9004A / 3D11	3
1955	GG-9004A / 3D11	3
1955	GG-9004B / 3D12	3
1951	15GG9014A / 5S10	5
1953	35GG9014A / 5S10	5
1954	45GG9014A / 5S10	5
1955	GG-9001A / 5S11	5
1955	GG-9001B / 5S12	5
1951	15GG9015A / 5D10	5
1952	25GG9015A / 5D10	5
1953	35GG9015A / 5D10	5
1954	45GG9015A / 5D10	5
1955	GG-9013A / 5D11	5
1951	15GG9017A / 12S10	12
1953	35GG9017A / 12S10	12
1951	15GG9018A / 12D10	12
1952	25GG9018A / 12D10	12
1953	35GG9018A / 12D10	12
1954–55	GG-9016A / 12D11	12
1955	GG-9019A / 22D10	22
1955	GG-9020A / 22DE10	22
1955	GG-9019B / 22D12	22
1955	GG-9020B / 22DE12	22
1956	GG-9000A / 3D13	3
1956	GG-9001C / 5S12	5
1956	GG-9002A / 5D12	5
1956	GG-9002B / 5D13	5
1956	GG-9016B / 12S12	12
1956	GG-9021A / 12D13	12
1956	GG-9021B / 12D14	12
1956	GG-9024A / 12DE13	12
1956	GG-9022A / 22D11	25
1956	GG-9022B / 22D13	25
1956	GG-9023A / 22DE11	25
1956	GG-9023B / 22DE13	25
1957	GG-9006A / 3D14	3
1957	GG-9003A / 5S13	5
1957	GG-8960A / 5D14	5
1957	GG-9016C / 12S13	12
1957	GG-8971A / 12D15	12

Sears, Roebuck and Co. Pre-World War II Private Brands.

Sears' oldest outboards, the 1914–27 Motorgos, were one-lung rowboat motors built by Lockwood-Ash. Early models had rudder steering. Some had flywheel magneto ignition, while less expensive styles fired via battery. All were about 2 hp. Late-30s Sears literature noted that "positive identification of these motors has been lost with the passing of years," so the ID numbers usually found on top of the cylinder assembly may not be of much use today.

In 1925, Sears catalogs carried standard-issue Johnson model A (catalog number 835), and model C (canoe mount, number 836) twins. No Sears ID appeared on these motors. Consequently, unless one has the original sales slip, identification of a 1925 Sears-Johnson is difficult. An April 1937 Sears information booklet describes these models as "outboard motors manufactured by Jacobsen Manufacturing Company, formerly Johnson Motors." The manual goes on to say that parts for such kickers should be ordered "from an authorized Johnson dealer, or direct from the Jacobsen Manufacturing Company of Racine, Wisconsin." Sears then states that parts lists for the Johnson models A and C are not available, and suggests that "sample parts be sent to Jacobsen to be duplicated." Since new/old stock Johnson A parts occasionally pop-up today, and were never impossible to find, such statements are puzzling. Furthermore, the claim that no Johnson parts lists existed in 1937 is very odd. And the Sears reference to a Johnson–Jacobsen Manufacturing Company relationship is one I cannot explain.

From 1928–32, Sears Motorgo outboards originated at the Caille Motor Company factory. (The 1931 Muncie Gear Works Motorgo was an exception.) Most Caille Motorgo models wore ID/serial numbers on the transom clamp bracket.

As a result of Caille's financial difficulties during the depression, Sears decided to purchase outboard products from Muncie Gear Works. The Sears Motorgo marque was continued until about 1934, when its kicker line was renamed "Waterwitch."

In 1936, Kissel Industries offered Sears outboard motors at prices they couldn't refuse. The giant retailer bought and sold gangs of these tiny eggbeaters, beginning with the 1936 Waterwitch model MB-10 single and MB-20 twin cylinder motors.

Year	Model / Sears Catalog Number	HP
	Caille Motorgo	
1928	Junior Twin / 5771-890	2¾
1929	Senior Twin / 5770	10
1930	Junior / 8206	6
1930	Senior / 8214	14
1930	Big Boy / 8220	20
1931–32	Junior / 7206	6
1931–32	Senior / 7214	14
1931–32	Big Boy / 7220	20
	Muncie Gear Works	
1931	Motorgo OB-2CD / Special	3
1931–32	Motorgo OB-3 / 7203	3
1933	Motorgo OB-4 / Special	4
1933	Motorgo OB-5 / 5805	5
1933–35	Motorgo Waterwitch OB-1 / 5802	2
1933–34	Motorgo Waterwitch OB-15 / 5816	15
1934	Waterwitch OB-31 / 5804	4
1935	Waterwitch OB-61 / 5805	6

1935	Waterwitch OB-32C / 5804	4
1935	Waterwitch OB-63 / 5806	6
1935–36	Waterwitch OB-16 / 5816	16
1936	Waterwitch OB-11 / Special	2
1936	Waterwitch OB-34 / Special	4
1936	Waterwitch OB-64 / Special	6
	Waterwitch (Kissel)	
1936–37	MB-10	2.5
1936	MB-20	4
1937	571.20	4
1938	571.21	4
1938	571.10	2.5
1938	571.30	¾
1938–40	550.75 (Johnson Waterwitch)	8.5
1939	571.31 (571.32)	¾
1939	571.11	2.5
1939	571.22	4.75
1940	571.33 (571.34 & 34A)	¾
1940	571.40	2.75
1940	571.12	3.5
1940	571.23	5.75
1941	571.35	1
1941	571.41 (571.42 & 43)	3
1941	571.13 (571.14)	3.5
1941	571.24	5.75
1941	571.50 (alternate firing twin)	10
1942	571.36	1
1942–45	571.44	3
1942	571.15	3.5
1942	571.26	5.75
1945	571.44W**	3

** Assembled by West Bend from new/old stock Kissel parts.

Caille.

Some true "gadgeteer's motors" sported this marque. Caille's background in slot machine manufacturing led them to produce outboards with interesting features like variable pitch propellers, dual carburetors/linkage, and tractor lower unit. (Because Caille props and related linkage were so complex, hitting a rock or other underwater obstruction could be costly.) Many Caille cylinders were fitted with "priming cups" for easier starting. One could pour a few drops of gas into the cup, open the spigot, and introduce fuel directly into the firing chamber. Multiflex (or Multi-Flex) was Caille's "multi-flexible control" handle, which facilitated steering, throttle setting, and propeller pitch adjustment.

The settings in a 5-Speed-model Caille were: reverse; neutral; trolling; low-speed forward; and high-speed forward.

Caille's "Red Head" trademark was made memorable by its logo: A pretty young woman's head, red hair streaming back, rising from a Caille-powered boat. Appropriately, these gas tanks were usually painted red.

A good Caille had a solid feel not present in many other brands. (Caille is pronounced "Kale.")

Caille

Year	Model	HP
1913	Rudder steered single without skeg	2
1914	Rudder steered single with skeg	2
1915–25	Single cylinder 5-Speed (some had rewind start)	2
1916	Heavy single	3.5
1917–25	Neptune (Caille's bargain brand; regular & canoe versions)	2
1917–31	Liberty Single (direct drive prop shaft; slight variations during production run)	2
1924–28	Liberty Twin (direct drive prop shaft)	4
1925–27	Lightweight Twin 5-Speed (also called Pennant)	2¾
1927	Master Twin 5-Speed	4.5
1928	Junior Twin model 10 (also available in 5-Speed)	2¾
1928	Master Twin model 20	6
1928	Racer model 30	10
1929	5-Speed model 12	2¾
1929	5-Speed model 22 Master Twin	6
1929	Champion Racer model 34 (tractor lower unit)	14
1929	Commodore model 32	12
1929	Admiral model 42	18
1929	Flash Racer model 36 (tractor lower unit/dual carbs)	16.5
1929	Streak Racer model 46 (tractor lower unit/dual carbs)	22
1929	Monarch Racer model 44 (tractor lower unit)	20
1930	Master 14 Red Head (also "Companion" model 14*)	6
1930	Master Multiflex 15 (15A) Red Head	6
1930	Model 25 (Utility) Red Head	15
1930	Model 26 (Utility Multiflex) Red Head w/electric start	15
1930–32	Model 40 Racer (tractor lower unit/dual carbs)	17
1930	Model 45 (Utility) Red Head	21
1930	Model 47 (Utility Multiflex) Red Head w/electric start	21
1930–32	Model 50 Racer (tractor lower unit) Red Head	23
1930–35	Model 51 (Utility Multiflex) Red Head (also model 51A)	23
1931–35	Model 16 (Utility) Red Head	8
1931–35	Model 15 (Utility Multiflex) Red Head (1933 model 15A – 10HP)	8
1931–35	Model 27 (Utility) Red Head	15
1931–32	Model 28 (Utility) Red Head w/electric start	15
1931–35	Model 29 (Utility Multiflex) (also model 29A)	16
1931	Model 35 Racer (tractor lower unit/dual carbs)	12
1931–35	Model 48 (Utility) Red Head	21
1931–32	Model 49 (Utility) Red Head w/electric start	21
1932–35	Model 79 single ($79)	4
1934–35	Model 88 single	2¼
1934–35	Model 99 single	5½
1934–35	Model 109 single	2¼
1934–35	Model 119 single (also model 119A)	5½
1934–35	Model 129	10
1934–35	Model 144	10+
1934–35	Model 169 (also model 169A)	10+
1934–35	Model 197	16+

1934–35	Model 232 (also model 232A)	16+
1934–35	Model 249	23
1934–35	Model 296 (also model 296A)	23

* Companion Model 14 could be made more compact by removing two bolts on driveshaft housing, and separating lower unit from top of motor.

Champion.

The point gap setting for Champion motors is generally .018". Most models use ½ pint of oil per gallon of gasoline. Hot Rod models take ¾ to 1 pint, depending on application. "Hydro-Drive" models featured a hydraulic fluid drive style lower unit transmission. Its "Magic-Wand" control lever could be positioned for propeller slippage, facilitating very accurate trolling speeds.

Champion

Year	Model	HP
1946–47	1J Standard Single	4.2
1946–47	2J Deluxe Single	4.2
1948	1K Standard Single	4.2
1948	2K Deluxe Single	4.2
1948	4K Twin	7.9
1949	1K	4.2
1949	2K	4.2
1949	4K	7.9
1949	4KS Special Racer	7.9
1950	1L	4.2
1950	2K	4.2
1950	2L-HD (Hydro-Drive)	4.2
1950	4K	7.9
1950	4L-HD (Hydro-Drive)	7.9
1950	4LS Special Racer	7.9
1951–52	1L	4.2
1951–52	2K	4.2
1951–52	2L-HD	4.2
1951	4K	7.9
1951–52	4L	8.5
1951–52	4L-HD	8.5
1951–52	4L-S Hot Rod	8.5
1953	2M	3.5
1953	3M-GS (Gear Shift)	5
1953	4M-GS	7.5
1953	4M-HD (Hydro-Drive)	7.5
1953	6M-GS	15
1953	6M-HD	15
1953	4M-HR Class "J" Hot Rod	7.5
1953	5M-HR Class "A" Hot Rod	----
1953	6M-HR Class "B" Hot Rod	15
1954	2MM	3.5
1954	3M-GS	5
1954	4M-GS	7.5
1954	4M-HD	7.5
1954	6M-GS	14
1954	6M-HD	15
1954	4M-HR Class "J" Hot Rod	----
1954	4M-HR "J" Hot Rod Midget w/extra small lower unit	----
1954	5M-HR	----
1954	6M-HR	----
1955	2MM	3.5
1955	3MM-GS Power Shift	5.5
1955	4MM-GS Power Shift	7.5
1955	6MM-GS Power Shift	16.5
1955	6MS-GS (w/Mid-Ship controls)	16.5
1955	4MM-HR	----
1955	6MM-HR	----
1956	2N	4.2
1956	3N-S	6
1956	4N-D	7.8
1956	6N-D	16.5
1956	6N-MS (w/Mid-Ship controls)	16.5
1956	6N-HR Class "B" Hot Rod	----
1957–58	2N	4.2
1957–58	3N-S	6
1957–58	4N-D	7.8
1957–58	6N-D	16.5
1957–58	6N-MS	16.5
1957–58	T6N-MS Tandem 33 (this package consisted of twin 16.5-hp Champions)	33
1957–58	6N-HR Class "B" Hot Rod	----

Corsair.

Corsair outboards, built by Scott-Atwater, take ½ pint of oil per gallon of gasoline. Breaker point setting is .020".

Corsair

Year	Model	HP
1948	4820 (4821)	3.6
1948	4823	7.5
1949	4921	4
1949	4927	5
1949	4923	7.5
1950–51	5020 (5020–5120+ is 1951 version)	3.6
1950–51	5021 (5020–5121+ is 1951 version)	4
1950–52	5027 (5027–5127+ is 1951. 2725+ is 1952 motor)	5
1950–52	5023 (5023–5123+ is 1951. 2325+ is 1952 motor)	7.5
1950–52	5028 (5028–5128+ is 1951. 2825+ is 1952 motor)	10
1953	2735	5
1953	2335	7.5
1953	2835	10
1954	2745	5
1954	2345	7.5
1954	2845	10
1954	2945	16
1955	2755	5
1955	2355	7.5
1955	2855	10
1955	2955	16
1956	2765	5
1956	2365	7.5
1956	2965	16
1956	2665 (2665-3 if electric start)	30

Elgin (Sears, Roebuck and Co.).

The point gap setting for Elgin motors is .020". Most models use ½ pint of oil per gallon of gasoline; some pre-1952 models take ¾ pint.

Serial numbers are found immediately after the model numbers. A 1949–50 version of the 16-hp model

was designated 571.5882. Elgin's "571" models were built by West Bend; "574s" came from McCulloch Corp.

Elgin

Year	Model	HP
1946	571.58301	1 ¼
1946	571.58401	2 ½
1946	571.58501	3 ½
1946	571.58601	5 ½
1947	571.58521	3 ½
1947	571.58611	5 ½
1947	571.58621	5 ½
1948	571.58521	3 ½
1948	571.58621	5 ½
1948	571.58721	6
1949	571.58541	5
1949	571.58731	7 ½
1950	571.58531	5
1950	571.58551	5
1950	571.58701	6
1950	571.58741	7 ½
1951	571.58561	5
1951	571.58641	6
1951	571.58751	7 ½
1951	571.58821	16
1951	571.58841	16
1952	571.58201	2
1952	571.58561	5
1952	571.58751	7 ½
1952	571.58822	16
1952	571.58842	16
1953	571.58202	2
1953	571.58562	5
1953	571.58642	6
1953	571.58761	7 ½
1953	571.58823	16
1953	571.58824	16
1953	571.58843	16
1953	571.58844	16
1954	571.58211	2
1954	571.58571	5
1954	571.58651	6
1954	571.58652	6
1954	571.58771	7 ½
1954	571.58772	7 ½
1954	571.58851	16
1955	571.58211	2
1955	571.58571	5
1955	571.58711	7 ½
1955	571.58772	7 ½
1955	571.58901	12
1955	571.59401	25
1956	571.58211	2
1956	571.5950	5 ½
1956	571.5970	7 ½
1956	571.5890	12
1956	571.5940	25
1956	571.5960 (electric start)	25
1957	571.58221	2
1957	571.58781	7 ½
1957	571.59521	5 ½
1957	571.59721	7 ½
1957	571.58941	12
1957	571.58951 (longshaft)	12
1957	571.59421	30
1957	571.59431 (longshaft)	30
1957	571.59621 (electric start)	30
1957	571.59631 (electric start / longshaft)	30
1957	571.59801 (electric start / generator)	30
1957	571.59811 (electric start / generator / longshaft)	30
1958*	5823	2
1958	5953	5 ½
1958	5973	7 ½
1958	5978	7 ½
1958	5896	12
1958	5897 (longshaft)	12
1958	5893	12
1958	5944	35
1958	5945 (longshaft)	35
1958	5982 (electric start / 6 Amp generator)	35
1958	5983 (electric start / longshaft w/6 Amp generator)	35
1958	5990 (electric start w/20 Amp generator)	35
1958	5991 (electric start w/20 Amp generator and longshaft)	35
1959	571.5824	2
1959	571.5879 "Special Value Motor"	7 ½
1959	571.5954	5 ½
1959	571.5974	7 ½
1959	571.5898	12
1959	571.5899 (longshaft)	12
1959	571.5982 (electric start / generator)	35
1959	571.5983 (electric start / generator w/longshaft)	35
1959	571.5990 (electric start / generator)	35
1959	571.5991 (electric start / generator w/longshaft)	35
1959	574.6025	25
1959	574.6026 (longshaft)	25
1959	574.6027 (electric start / generator)	25
1959	574.6028 (longshaft)	25
1959	574.6040	40
1959	574.6041 (longshaft)	40
1959	574.6042 (electric start / generator)	40
1959	574.6043 (longshaft)	40
1959	574.6060 (electric start / generator)	60
1959	574.6061 (longshaft)	60

*1958 model numbers may be preceded by "571."

Firestone. Firestone's 1950s motors were made by Scott-Atwater. Some parts are interchangeable between the two marques.

All models generally use ½ pint oil per gallon of gasoline. Breaker point setting is .020".

Firestone

Year	Model	HP
1946	133-6-460 (also: -462, -463; -464 if rewind starter)	3.5
1947	133-7-476 (-477 if rewind starter)	3.5
1947	133-7-479	7.5
1948	133-8-486 (-487 if rewind starter)	3.5

Year	Model	HP
1948	133-8-489	7.5
1949	10-A-1 (-2 if rewind starter)	3.6
1949	10-A-51	4
1949	10-A-52	5
1949	10-A-53	7.5
1950–55	10-A-71	3.6
1950	10-A-72	4
1950–53	10-A-73	5
1950–52	10-A-74	7.5
1950–52	10-A-75	10
1953–55	10-A-103	7.5
1953–55	10-A-104	10
1954–55	10-A-102	5
1954–55	10-A-105	16
1956–57	10-A-111	3.6
1956–57	10-A-112	5
1956–57	10-A-113	10
1956–57	10-A-114	16
1956	10-A-115 (-116 if electric start)	30
1957	10-A-117	35
1957	10-A-118 (w/electric start; -119 if longshaft)	35
1958	1085	3.6
1958	1785	5
1958	1885	10
1958	1985	16
1958	1685	38
1958	1316 (w/electric start; 1416 if longshaft)	38
1959	10-A-111	3.6
1959	10-A-112	5
1959	10-A-120	10
1959	10-A-114	16
1959	10-A-122 (w/electric start; -123 if longshaft)	39.1

Flambeau.

Flambeau's odd appearance set it apart from mainstream motors and made it, at best, a novelty. One used-outboard price guide estimated the 1955 trade-in value for a 1947-48 Flambeau at about five bucks! By 1958, the firm was defunct.

Breaker point setting is .020". Oil/gas mix is ⅔ pint per gallon. Although spec sheets often indicate all 1950-56 models had rewind start, Flambeaus from that vintage have turned up without such a convenience. Rewind was an option (according to company literature) during 1946-49.

Flambeau

Year	Model	HP
1946–47	2.5-46-1	2.6
1946–47	5-46-1	5.1
No commercial production	10-46-1	10
1948–49	174520	2.5
1948–49	174050	5
1950	105030 (1950 onward has burgundy-red tops)	3
1950	105060	6
1951–52	174520 (1951 onward single and twin have flush-out fitting)	2.5
1951–57	174050 (1953–57 has cavitation plate)	5
1953–57	125520	2.5
1953–57	125050 (this # might not have been used)	5

Note: Very little Flambeau advertising exists past 1954. Boat show annuals do not list Flambeau in 1957 or afterward.

Hiawatha.

From 1946 to 1955, Hiawatha motors were built by Gale Products (see Gale Model/Year charts). By 1956, they were produced by Scott-Atwater.

Hiawathas have a .020" breaker point setting. The oil/gas mix is ½ pint per gallon.

Hiawatha

Year	Model	HP
1956	7960A / 4065+	3.6
1956	7970A / 4765+	5
1956	7985A / 4365+	7.5
1956	7995A / 4965+	16
1956	8005A / 4665+	30
1956	8006A / 4665-3+ (w/electric start)	30
1957	4075	3.6
1957	4775	5
1957	4375	7.5
1957	4975	16
1957	4675 (4675-3 if electric start)	35
1958	4085	3.6
1958	4785	5
1958	4385	7.5
1958	4885	10
1958	4985	16
1958	4685 (346+ if electric start)	38
1959	7960 / 140A+	3.6
1959	7987 / 4385+	7.5
1959	7992 / 4885+	10
1959	8001 / 145A+ (8002 / 345A+ if electric start)	25
1959	8015 / 4685+ (8016 / 346+ if electric start)	38
1959	8018 / 346A+	40

Lauson.

Lausons have a 4-cycle powerhead; don't mix oil and gas. Breaker point gap is generally .020".

Lauson

Year	Model	HP
1947	OB-410	2.5
1948–49	S-300	3
1948–49	T-600	6
1950	S-350	3
1950	T-650	6
1951–52	T-651 (R if reverse)	6
1952	S-351	3
1953–56	S-353	3
1953–56	T-653	6
1953–55	T-653R (reverse gear)	6
1955–56	T653N (Neutral clutch)	6

Majestic and Voyager. These outboards were built by Champion. Some parts are interchangeable with those of the "parent" motors. Champion offered these kickers through a "blind," Minneapolis, Minnesota post office box, as well as wholesaling them to numerous sporting goods and chain store outlets. Consequently some owners may refer to their Majestic/Voyagers as products of a specific retailer.

Breaker point settings are .018". 1949–53 models (except 1953 M-3L-GS/V-3L-GS) use ¾ pint of oil per gallon of gasoline. All others take ½ pint. GS models featured a gear shift.

Majestic/Voyager

Year	Model	HP
1949–50	1MB / 1VB (1950–51)	4.2
1949–52	2MB (rewind start)	4.2
1949–52	4MB	7.9
1950–51	1MBB	4.2
1953	M-2L / V-2L	3.5
1953	M-4L-GS / V-4L-GS	8.5
1953–54	M-3L-GS / V-3L-GS	5.5
1954–55	M-2LL / V-2LL	3.5
1954–55	M-3LL-GS / V-3LL-GS	5.5
1954–55	M-4LL-GS / V-4LL-GS	7.5
1954–55	M-6LL-GS / V-6LL-GS	15
1956–58	M-2N / V-2N	4.2
1956–58	M-3N-GS / V-3N-GS	6
1956–58	M-4N-GS / V-4N-GS	7.8
1956–58	M-6N-GS / V-6N-GS	15

Martin. In 1951, Martin literature unveiled a 17-hp model 200. I do not know if any of these, aside from a pre-production motor, were put into circulation. Any reference to a 17-hp Martin is a "false start" notation.

EHA indicates motors with factory installed fuel pump and auxiliary Cruise-More tank; EHO indicates motors without fuel pump and tank. Some 200 models simply begin identification with the EH designation. There are also EHO engines with dealer or owner installed fuel pumps. Some read EHD or EHO3.

The 200 Silver Liner was to be a full shift version of the standard, forward-only 200. Although there is evidence of one being demonstrated, none have surfaced since then. The 1953 shift 200 is also questionable.

The 200-M differed from the standard motor in that a section of its underwater exhaust outlet was cut off, eliminating some exhaust restriction. It also had a streamlined, racing gearcase cap. A full race version called the 200-S had an underwater exhaust section which was 3 inches shorter. It was equipped with a fuel pump, fitted for a racing throttle cable, and wore a very pointy, streamlined gearcase nose cap.

Because items like fuel pump, racing exhaust, gearcase cap, and racing throttle linkage could be purchased as accessories, it is difficult to identify "factory-equipped" Martin racers.

Martins typically have a breaker point setting of .020". Specs for the 200 models, as well as most of the 60s and 75s, call for ¾ pint of oil per gallon of gasoline;

others take ½ pint. Racers in the 200 series need 1¼ pints.

A few "leftover" Martin 60 Hi-Speed Racers were marketed in 1951.

Martin

Year	Model*	HP
1946	60 / 5,000	7.2
1947	40 / 5,000	4.5
1947	60 / 20,000	7.2
1948	20 / 5,000	2 ⅓
1948	40 / 19,665	4.5
1948	60 / 69,083	7.2
1949	40 / 37,924	4.5
1949	60 / 93,374	7.2
1949	60 Hi-Speed	7.2+
1950	20 / 11,635	2 ⅓
1950	40 / 44,987	4.5
1950	60 / C96,000	7.2
1950	60 Hi-Speed	7.2+
1950	66 / TC105,669	7.2
1950	100 / D5,000	10
1951	20 / 11,699	2 ⅓
1951	45 / BB50,638	4.5
1951	75 / CB108,003	7.5
1951	100 / DA17,171	10
1951	200 Twist-Shift	17
1951	200 Hi-Speed, model P-T	17
1952	45 / BB58,635	4.5
1952	75 Twist-Shift / CC116,949	7.5
1952	100 Twist-Shift / DB18,901	10
1953	20 / A15,846	2 ⅓
1953	45 / BB59,904	4.5
1953	75 Twist-Shift / CC152,469	7.5
1953	100 Twist-Shift / DB28,439	10
1953	200 Silver Streak / EHA-9,000	20
1953	200 Silver Streak / EHO-9,000	20
1953	200 (w/gear shift) (same as other 1953, 200)	20
1954	20	2 ⅓
1954	45	4.5
1954	75	7.5
1954	100	10
1954	200 Standard Silver Streak	20
1954	200 Silver Liner	20
1954	200-M	20
1954	200-S	20

*Number after slash is serial number for first motor that year.

Muncie/Neptune. The breaker point setting for these motors is .015" for pre-1947 models. Others had a .020" factory breaker point setting. Oil/gasoline mixtures are as follows: 9.5, 10, and 1949 10.5-horse motors take 1 pint per gallon. All other 1945–49 models use ⅔ pint. Model AA6 takes ¾ pint, as does AA2. Remaining 1950–56 motors accept ⅔ pint per gallon. The Mighty-Mite kickers run well on ½ pint.

Muncie/Neptune

Year	Model	HP
1945–46	15A1 (Neptune) / 15B1 (Muncie)	1.5

1945–46	15B2	2
1945–46	15A3 (also 15AA3 in Deluxe style)	3.5
1945–46	15B4 (Muncie)	4
1945–46	15A6 (also 15AA6 in Deluxe version)	6
1945–46	15A9 (also 15AA9)	9.5
1947	17A1	1.5
1947	17A2	2
1947	17A3	3.5
1948–51	A1 (Available in 1948 as B1 without motor cowling)	1.7
1948–49	A2	3.3
1948–51	AA2	3.3
1948–51	AA4	5
1948–51	AA6	7
1948–51	AA10 (10 HP rating in 1948)	10.5
1952–53	(no motors produced)	
1954–56	AA1 (Some A1 "leftovers" sold)	1.7
1956–59	AA1-A (Mighty-Mite)	1.7

Oliver.

All models have a breaker point setting of .018" except the 1957s which have a .020" setting. All 1955–56 motors use ½ pint oil per gallon of gas; others use ⅜ pint, except models J3, J-4, J5, and J-5L, which take ½ pint.

The 5.5-, 6-, 15-, and 16-HP models have similarities to the Chris-Craft outboards they replaced.

Oliver

Year	Model	HP
1955	J (Some designated 55-J)	5.5
1955	K (Some designated 55-K)	15
1956	J2	5.5
1956	K2 (K2E if electric start)	15
1957	J3	6
1957	K3 (K3E if electric start)	16
1957	B	35
1958	J-4	6
1958	K-4 (K-4E if electric start)	16
1958	B-2	35
1959	J-5 (J-5L if longshaft)	6
1959	K-5 (K-5E if electric start; K-5L if longshaft)	16
1959	B-3 (B-3L if longshaft)	35
1959	B-3CR (Two 35-hp motors sold as package; B-3CRL if motors are longshaft)	70*

* Combined HP rating. Twins factory equipped with counter rotating props.

B.F. Goodrich Sea Flyer.

Sea Flyers from 1951–52 were built by OMC's Gale Products; 1953–54 models came from Champion Outboard Company. Gale Sea Flyers use ½ pint oil per gallon. Their breaker point setting should be .020". Champion-made Sea Flyers have a .018" breaker point setting. The 1953, 3.5- and 8.5-horse motors use ¾ pint oil per gallon of gas; others take ½ pint.

B.F. Goodrich Sea Flyer

Year	Model	HP
1951–52	5D10	5
1952	3D10	3

1952	12D10	12
1953	G-2L	3.5
1953	G-3L-GS*	5.5
1953	G-4L-GS*	8.5
1954	G-3LL	5.5
1954	G-3LL-GS*	5.5
1954	G-4LL-GS*	7.5
1954	G-6LL-GS*	15

* Gear shift model.

Scott-Atwater.

On many Scott-Atwater motors, the serial number follows the model number.

Point setting is .020". Fuel mixture is generally ½ pint oil per gallon of gasoline; 1959 models use ⅜ pint.

Scott-Atwater

Year	Model	HP
1946	461	3.6
1946	467	3.6
1947	470	3.6
1947	471	3.6
1947	473	7.5
1948	480	3.6
1948	481	3.6
1948	483	7.5
1949	480*	3.6
1949	481*	3.6
1949	483*	7.5
1949	491 Shift	4
1949	497 Shift	5
1949	493 Shift	7.5
1950	500	3.6
1950	501	4
1950	507	5
1950	503	7.5
1950	509	16
1951	510 (non-shift) "1-12"	3.6
1951	511 "1-14"	4
1951	517 "1-16"	5
1951	513 "1-20"	7.5
1951	518 "1-25"	10
1951	519 "1-30"	16
1952	3025 "1-12" (non-shift)	3.6
1952	3725 "1-16"	5
1952	3325 "1-20"	7.5
1952	3825 "1-25"	10
1952	3925 "1-30"	16
1953	3035 (non-shift)	3.6
1953	3735	5
1953	3335 Gold Pennant Motor	7.5
1953	3835 Gold Pennant Motor	10
1953	3935	16
1954	3045	3.6
1954	3745 Bail-A-Matic	5
1954	3345 Bail-A-Matic	7.5
1954	3845 Bail-A-Matic	10
1954	3945 Bail-A-Matic	16
1955	3055	3.6
1955	3755	5
1955	3355	7.5

Year	Model	HP
1955	3855	10
1955	3955	16
1955	3655 (Also available w/electric start)	30
1956	3065 Sportster	3.6
1956	3765	5
1956	3365	7.5
1956	3865	10
1956	3965	16
1956	3965-3 (electric start)	16
1956	3665	33
1956	3665-3 (electric start)	33
1957	3075	3.6
1957	3775 ("-2" suffix if longshaft)	5
1957	3375 ("-2" suffix if longshaft)	7.5
1957	3875 ("-2" suffix if longshaft)	10
1957	3975 ("-2" suffix if longshaft)	16
1957	3975-3 (electric start; "-4" if longshaft)	16
1957	3675 ("-2" suffix if longshaft)	40
1957	3675-3 (electric start; "-4" if longshaft)	40
1957	3675-5 Royal Scott ("-6" if longshaft)	40
1958	3085 Scotty	3.6
1958	3785 (1237 if longshaft)	5
1958	3385 (1233 if longshaft)	7.5
1958	3855 (1238 if longshaft)	10
1958	3985 (1239 if longshaft)	16
1958	135 (235 if longshaft)	22
1958	335 (w/electric start/generator; 435 if longshaft)	22
1958	3685 (1236 if longshaft)	40
1958	1336 (w/electric start/generator; 1436 if longshaft)	40
1958	1536 (w/electric start/generator; 1636 if longshaft)	40
1958	332 (w/electric start/generator; 432 if longshaft)	60
1959	130A	3.6
1959	137A	5
1959	133A	7.5
1959	138A	10
1959	135A (235A if longshaft)	25
1959	335A (w/electric start/generator; 435A if longshaft)	25
1959	136A (236A if longshaft)	40
1959	336A (w/electric start/generator; 436A if longshaft)	40
1959	536A (w/electric start/generator; 636A if longshaft)	40
1959	332A (w/electric start/generator; 432A if longshaft)	60

*Leftover 1948 non-shift models.

West Bend.
Pre-1955 West Bend-labeled motors were built for the export market. The 2-hp model has an air-cooled powerhead. West Bend outboards typically use ½ pint oil per gallon of gasoline. Breaker point setting is .020". Some West Bend components are interchangeable with Sears Elgin motors.

West Bend

Year	Model	HP
1955–56	160211	2
1955	160571	5
1955	160772	7.5
1956	160501	5.5
1956	160701	7.5
1956	160902	12
1956	1609403	25
1957	160221	2
1957	160521 (160531 if longshaft)	6
1957	160721 (160731 if longshaft)	8
1957	160941 (160951 if longshaft)	12
1957	160421 (160431 if longshaft)	30
1957	160621 (w/electric start; 160631 if longshaft)	30
1957	160801 (electric start w/generator; 160811 if longshaft)	30
1958	280	2
1958	680 (681 if longshaft)	6
1958	880 (881 if longshaft)	8
1958	1280 (1281 if longshaft)	12
1958	3580 (3581 if longshaft)	35
1958	3582 (w/electric start; 3583 if longshaft)	35
1958	3584 (w/electric start/standard generator; 3585 if longshaft)	35
1958	3586 (w/electric start and Super Alternator/Generator; 3587 if longshaft)	35
1959	290	2
1959	690 (691 if longshaft)	6
1959	890 (891 if longshaft)	8
1959	1290 (1291 if longshaft)	12
1959	1690 (1691 if longshaft)	16
1959	3594 (3595 if longshaft)	35
1959	3598 (w/electric start/generator; 3599 if longshaft)	35
1959	4090 (4091 if longshaft)	40
1959	4096 (w/electric start/generator; 4097 if longshaft)	40

Wizard.
During the summer of 1963, the Kiekhaefer Corp. released a chart linking various Mercury outboards with the Wizard motors it built for Western Auto. Many Mercury dealers were unhappy that the less expensive, private-brand Wizard line shared so many Mercury characteristics. Kiekhaefer claimed that "Wizard outboards do not incorporate all the features of Mercury Outboard Motors, nor are all the parts interchangeable"; but there were enough similarities to warrant compilation of the following table.

Wizard	Mercury
WA2	K1
WA3	K2
WA6	K4 – K5
WB2	KB1
WB3	K2 – KB2 – KB3
WB4	KB4
WB6	KB5
WD3	KD3
WD3S	KD3S
WD4	KD4
WD4S	KD4S
WF4 – WG4	KD4
WF7	KE7 – KF7

WG7 – WG7A	KG7
WH7	KH7
WH6 – WH6A	Mark 6
WK7	Mark 20* – Mark 20**
WJ7 – WM7	Mark 20* – KG7**
WM7A	Mark 25* – KG7**
WN7 – WN7A	Mark 25*
WA25 – WA25E	Mark 30 – Mark 30E

* Type Powerhead
** Type Lower Unit

Breaker point setting for Wizard motors is .018", except .010" for the 1956–57, 25-hp motor, and .020" for 1959 models. The 1959 line requires ½ pint oil per gallon of gasoline. The 1955–58s (except the 1958, 5.5-horse outboard) take ⅜ pint per gallon. Wizards from 1947–54 like ¾ pint, while the oldest, 1946 Wizards use ½ pint oil to each gallon of gasoline. Any Mercury-built Wizard on a Quicksilver racing lower unit should get greater lubricating consideration.

Because many Western Auto stores were owned and operated independent of the Western Auto parent organization, some leftover Wizards may have been locally marketed a few years after their actual model year.

Wizard

Year	Model	HP
1946	WD-3	3.2
1946	WD-4	6
1947–48	WD-3S	3.2
1947–48	WD-4S	6
1949–50	WF-4	6
1950	WF-7	10
1951–54	WG-4	6
1951–53	WG-7	10
1952–53	WH-7	10
1953	WG-7A	10
1954	WJ-7	10
1954	WK-7	12
1955–56	WH-6	5
1955	WM-7	10
1955	WN-7	12
1956–57	WM-7A	10
1956–57	WN-7A	12
1956–57	WA-25 (WA-25E if electric start)	25
1957	WH-6A	5
1957	Powermatic 15 (OC-1575)	15
1958	OC-585	5.5
1958	OC-1585	15
1958	OC-3585 (OC-3585E if electric start)	35
1959	MLM-6903A	3.6
1959	MLM-6907A	7.5
1959	MLM-6910A	10
1959	MLM-6925A	25
1959	MLM-6940A (MLM-6941A if electric start)	40

British Seagull (1963 and Onward).

Those with these neat little English kickers dating back to the height of the James Bond era can date their motor via the following code (as quoted from a Seagull service bulletin).

"From 1963, a letter and number code is used at the end of the engine number to denote the month and year of manufacture. The letter indicates the month and the number the year of manufacture, i.e. A3 = January 1963, B3 = February 1963, M3 = December* 1963, etc. From 1973, two letters were used in the code to indicate the month, i.e. AA3 = January 1973, to MM3 for December* 1973. *The letter 'L' (typically employed to denote long shaft models) was not used in either sequence."

Canadian OMC Production.

Members of the Antique Outboard Motor Club's Maple Leaf Chapter were able to access factory documentation at the old OMC Peterborough, Ontario, facility. Before closing in the 1990s, what had been originally built as a Johnson plant turned out various Elto, Evinrude, and Johnson outboards unique to the Canadian assembly line.

Elto (Canadian Post–World War II).

When, as of 1950, the Elto marque was permanently retired in the U.S., it continued in Canada through 1958. Please note that not all of the numbers were used. Also be advised that some records show serial numbers assigned to model years as opposed to calendar years. That could mean that a 1956 motor was actually built in late 1955. It's best to treat serial number/year produced lists with a bit of leeway.

Year	Serial Number Range
1950	5001–7600
1951	7601–10,200
1952	10,201–12,800
1953	12,801–15,050
1954 (some are actually late 1953 motors)	15,051–18,150
1955	18,151–19,800
1956–57	19,801–28,055
1958	28,056–31,005

Evinrude (Canadian). The following 1945–59 Evinrude models were produced in Canada (as well as the U.S.). Typically, model numbers for both countries' output were the same (and may be checked via the regular Evinrude Model/Year Guide), but serial number banks differed. A check of the small metal tag on transom bracket or steering arm assembly should tell whether the motor came from Peterborough, Ontario, or Milwaukee, Wisconsin.

Year	Model
1945–59	Sportwin
1946–49	Zephyr
1946–49	Lightfour
1946–51	Speeditwin
1947	Ranger
1947–49	Speedifour
1947–51	Sportsman
1950–58	Fleetwin
1950–59	Fastwin
1951–59	Big Twin
1952–59	Lightwin
1957–59	Fisherman
1958–59	Four-Fifty

Johnson (Canadian). Johnson motors built in the firm's Peterborough, Ontario, plant were stamped with serial numbers unique to Canadian output. Some of these engines had sand-cast parts where the U.S. versions might have been die-cast. A few models, while variations on U.S.-built engines, were exclusively Canadian. The 8.1 hp Eskimo Motors OK-10 from 1940–45, OK-15 of 1946–48, and OK-20 from 1949–50 serve as examples. Note that there are some serial digits missing between 1932–33. Overlapping likely existed between 1945 and 1946 production, as the actual model/year break (to 1946) might have been at motor #48579. The 1954–55 enumeration gets a bit fuzzy with motor #172513 possibly being the first of 1955's run. Please note that the old records—from which many of these digits were gleaned—were not perfect. In fact, Outboard Marine and Manufacturing Company of Canada's *The Service Bench* (issue #261, "Serial Number Record of Johnson Motors . . . ") contained a misspelling of the Ontario community in which the OMC factory was located ("Peterboro" instead of "Peterborough")! Suffice it to say the following numbers should be used with some leeway. Some record keeping was done by model year, others by calendar year. So, for example, a motor serialized near the end the 1956 block in one list might actually be shown as a 1957 motor in another roster. Consider serial number listings to provide a general whereabouts. It should also be mentioned that not all of the numbers were utilized. And some figures, like #64409 and #64410, were 1947 Canadian Johnson model TD "cutaway" show motors that were never intended for public sale.

Year	Serial Number Range
1929	11,616–13,926
1930	13,927–15,782
1931	15,783–16,990
1932	16,991–17,889
1933	20,000–20,930
1934	20,931–22,534
1935	22,535–25,096
1936	25,097–29,174
1937	29,175–33,434
1938	33,435–39,155
1939	39,156–43,565
1940	43,566–47,252
1941–44	none
1945	47,253–48,748
1946	48,749–55,511
1947	55,512–68,210
1948	68,211–80,312
1949	80,313–95,877
1950	95,878–110,202
1951	110,203–119,367
1952	119,368–135,972
1953	135,973–153,937
1954	153,938–174,552
1955	174,553–199,013
1956	199,014–218,513
1957	218,514–244,739
1958	244,740–271,519
1959	271,520–282,137
1960	282,138–294,095

Caille (A Few Derivatives). Besides complex gadgets like multiplayer slot machines, Caille built small brass cannons that one could fire for "ornamental noise" from the front lawn or the deck of a yacht. Of course, our Caille focus is the firm's outboard production. And a few more nuanced models have surfaced since *The Old Outboard Book*'s first Caille list was printed. AOMCI's Caille special interest buff, Randy Kallevig, reminded me of their appearance in sundry Caille documents. They include the Master Twin in Racing Trim (streamlined, nonvariable pitch prop lower unit) for 1927, a 1928 Scout with 2 ¾ hp, the 1932–33 Models 27E and 29E (both fitted with electric starter), and 1934's Models 109 and 169 Gear Shift Control, which was a new name for what had been termed "Multi-Flex" variable pitch propeller operation. The 1917–25 Caille Neptune motors were the firm's low-price offering. These single-cylinder rowboat motors typically had fewer features than the regular Cailles. In most cases, though, they were identified with a Neptune decal on the side of their fuel tank and Caille on the back. At one time, it was speculated that Caille tried to hide their bargain motors' true identity. Finally, there may have been a small run of 1930–35 class B and C Cailles, factory fitted with the Bendix (crank-up and release) inertia starter. It is not known whether these motors were given a special model designation. If so, it would likely be a suffix letter (perhaps "I") after the regular model number.

Champion (Pre-1946).
These engines were actually produced by Scott-Atwater before it had its own label. Pre–World War II "Champs" typically sold through Firestone auto and tire stores. "M" series motors are Mariner brand.

Model	Year	HP
A	1935	3.2
1B	1936	3.2
2B	1936	4.4
3B	1936	7.6
S1C	1937	2.9
D1C	1937	3.2
		(also model R1C)
S2C	1937	3.4
D2C	1937	4.4
D3C	1937	6.6
S1D	1938	2.9
D1D	1938	3.2
S2D	1938	3.4
D2D	1938–39	4.4
D3D	1938–39	6.6
S1E	1939	2.9
D1E	1939	3.2
S1F	1940	3.2
		(also models D1F and B1F)
S2F	1940	3.4
D2F	1940	5.5
S1G	1941	3.0
		(also models M1G and D1G)
S4G	1941	3.6
		(also models M4G and D4G)
2G	1941	5.3
		(also model M2G)
3G	1941	6.1
1H	1942	3.9
2H	1942	5.8
3H	1942	7.0

Evinrude Mate/Elto Cub.
When the Evinrude Model/Year Guide was first published in 1959, it generalized the production years and serial number coding of some motors thought to be pretty much out of circulation by that time. Cubs and Mates were notorious for having been persnickety from the start, so probably figured into the "why bother?" rubric surrounding the Guide's compilation criteria for obscure models. But the popularity of these cute ½ hp egg-beaters with collectors sent buffs searching through pages of documents until pay dirt was struck in the seemingly arcane Evinrude-Elto Service Bulletin of 19 November 1951. There, statistics more precise than the Guide's 1939–41 Cub/Mate indication were discovered.

Elto Cub	Serial Numbers	Year Built
4264	00001–04062	1939
4264	04063–05164	1940
4264	05165 and up	1941

Evinrude Mate	Serial Numbers	Year Built
4263	00001–03474	1939
4263	03475–04055	1940
4263	04056 and up	1941

Some sources list the Mate as current from 1939–42, but Cub only from 1939–41. The Mate was cataloged in 1942. It is doubtful that any Mates were built much past a spring 1941 production run. Leftovers of both Mates and Cubs could probably be had into the war years and, at a remote dealer or two, maybe even through 1945–early 1946.

Flambeau (Be on the Lookout for F-N-R).
Leo T. Kincannon served as Mercury's first chief engineer, and reportedly was the guy responsible for much of the innovation in Merc's debut (1940) line. The story goes, though, that E. C. Kiekhaefer, the head of Mercury, fired Kincannon because he requested some time off to go bow hunting. After concocting a stealth steam outboard for the U.S. Navy during World War II, Kincannon was scouted by the new Flambeau outboard people and signed on to design the ultrastreamlined Flambeau motors. The Flambeau serial number system remains enigmatic with exact year pinpointing sometimes impossible. Kincannon probably didn't devise that system, but it may be that he planned a full F-N-R gearshift Flambeau. A 1954 listing has surfaced showing the 5 hp twin with shift. It may be that a few were built and are out there somewhere. No doubt the shift version would have required a whole new motor leg with a bigger gear case. Flambeau gear cases were cast as part of the assembly—in two halves—from just below the powerhead to the skeg. Whatever the F-N-R engine looked like, its manufacturer was pretty much out of the picture by 1955, and officially vanished circa 1957. By that time Kincannon had been snapped up by Evinrude to work with OMC engineering maven Finn Irgens.

Johnson (Nuances and Misstrikes).

In some listings, Johnson's limited production racers are omitted. Most notable are the 1928 opposed twins: KR-40 (11 hp), and PR-40 (16.5 hp). A piece of circa November 1922 Johnson literature mentions special racing Model "A" Waterbug/Lightwin outboards, but it is not known whether these were uniquely marked. Some 1920s Model "A" Johnson Lightwins were designated Model "AS" to indicate a shock absorber component in the driveshaft that provided some "give" when the propeller hits something. Midyear upgrades sometimes caused Johnson to code a motor with an extra letter designation. For example, the 1954 Sea Horse 25 model RD-15 also came in an RD-15A version. The latter simply meant that this engine was fitted with "a new [or different] shift rod lever clip and screw." Coincidentally, two Johnson model P-25 motors surfaced around 1999. While such engines have never been mentioned in Johnson literature (there was a renowned 1926 model P-30 of identical appearance and specifications), both P-25 engines appear to be legitimate—with matching serial numbers on the crankcase and rope sheave plate—and fall in the 1926 serialization range. Buffs wonder if this coding is a result of a careless or misinformed employee who simply picked up the wrong metal stamp? Or, perhaps these P-25 engines are "pre-production" P-30 Johnsons? There are a handful of motors bearing blatantly incorrect model stampings, such as the S-54 (from 1929) that should read S-45. Suffice it to say that a long-ago assembly line worker's bad day can sure drive collectors nuts now.

Mercury (Numbers KF-7, KF-9, and KG-9).

Missing from the earlier editions' Merc serial number roster are the following.

Model	Year	Serial Numbers
KF-7	1949–50	360,137–372,536, 387,686–390,185
KF-7	1950	393,943–402,542
KF-9	1949–50	377,150–379,008
KG-9	1950	405,293–408,292
KG-9	1952	495,755–495,761, 521,402

Some KG-9 motors have a KG-9-1 designation. Records show a batch of 1952 KG-9 engines from somewhere around numbers 498,—— to 499,261.

Muncie/Neptune (Pre-1945).

Prior to World War II, Muncie/Neptune offerings included the "standard" Muncie, and "deluxe" Neptune. In some cases the "A" indicated Neptune, while the secondary Muncie motors were identified with a "B." "Sears" (in parentheses) designates outboards marketed by the catalog store under their Motorgo name.

Model	Year	HP
OB2, OB2A	1930	2 ¾
OB2A, OB2CB	1931	2 ¾
OB2C (Sears)	1931	2 ¾
OB4A	1931	4
OB15A	1931–34	16
OB3, OB3U (Sears)	1932	4
OB3A, OB3AU	1932	4
OB3B, OB3BU	1932	4
OB4A	1932–33	6
OB4, OB4U (Sears)	1933	4
OB4B, OB4BU	1933	6
OB5, OB5U (Sears)	1934	4
OB15B	1934	16
OB51, OB61	1934	6
OB1	1935	2
OB63	1935	6
OB32	1935	4
OB16	1935–37	16
OB11	1936–37	2
OB34	1936	4
OB64	1936–37	6
OB14	1937	4
OB12A	1937	2
OB35A	1937	4
OB65A	1937	6
OB17A	1937	16
138A, B, or C	1938	1.2
238A, B, or C	1938	2
438A or B	1938	4
638A or B	1938	6
938A or B	1938	9
1638A or B	1938	16
——	1939	(same as 1938 coding, except with 39 instead of 38 in model number)
10A1, 10B1, 10C1	1940	1 ½
10A2, 10B2	1940	2
10A4, 10B4	1940	4
10A6, 10B6	1940	6
10A10, 10B10	1940	9 ½
10A16, 10B16	1940	16
11A1, 11B1	1941	1 ½
11A2, 11AA2, 11B2	1941	2
11A3, 11AA3, 11B3	1941	3 ½
11A4, 11B4	1941	4
11A6, 11AA6, 11B6	1941	6
11A9, 11AA9, 11B9	1941	9 ½ (also models in the 11A10, 11AA10 series)
11A16, 11B16	1941	16

Scott (An Odd One to Look For). When McCul-
loch bought Scott-Atwater in the late 1950s, it was known to
offer a few "specials" that didn't appear in the main catalogs.
This is noted via the Scott Model 535. The green two-cylinder
1958 outboard with 22 hp is very stripped down, having no
tiller, hood, or belly pan. Arcane rosters that do make mention of the 535 simply ID it as "manual/economy 22 hp."
While it has a standard lower unit, racing throttle linkage
suggests that the motor might have been concocted as some
kind of Outboard Pleasure Craft competition model, or simply
a plain-Jane version of Scott's colorful fiberglass-hooded 22
and targeted to informal cottage racers. It may have been
that Scott dealers were obliged to take a few of these uncata-
loged "specials" with their shipment of regular models. If so, it
would give Scott a quick way to generate a few extra bucks
and use up some surplus parts.

Milburn Cub (The Legacy). Late 1948 saw the
advent of a $69.50 "economy" kicker that morphed into a
remarkable abundance of brands before disappearing in the
late 1970s. The following list guesstimates this cheapo, air-
cooled outboard's lineage. All of its makers were based in
Southern California, except My-te of Indianapolis, which utilized what looked to be an old Milburn style lower unit, and
Minneapolis-based Sports-Jets. In any event, the Milburn Cub
represents one of outboarding's most "passed along" designs.
Actually, though, the original powerhead had been dropped
in favor of a Tecumseh mill by about 1964, with a redesigned
lower unit appearing on circa 1967. One could make a chal-
lenging hobby of trying to collect a motor (and nuanced vari-
ants) from each of these firms!

Model	Manufacturer	Year
Milburn Cub	H. B. Milburn Co.	1948–50
Budbilt Cub	Budbilt Mfg.	1949–5?
Wego Junior	Wego Motor Co.	1949–5?
Master Cub	Water Masters, Inc.	1949–5?
Milburn Cub	L. K. Products Co.	1951–52
Continental Sport	Continental Mfg. Corp.	1956–64 (also: The Kit for $59.95 and Comanco Sport)
My-te (electric)	City Engineering	1959–70
Husky	Ward Intl., Inc.	1963, 1966–67
Commando	McMar	1966–70s
Sea Lion	McMar	1968
Sports-Jet	Sports-Jets Industries	196?

Appendix B
Outboard Motor Spark Plug Chart

The Champion Spark Plug Company has been catering to outboard motor applications for decades. The following lists identify such plugs, and which engines they fit. Listings from 1954 through 1970 are included herein. They cover most every model. Brands on the chart, not otherwise handled in this book (such as Boatimpeller, Anzani-Pilot, etc.) are typically of foreign manufacture.

Champion Outboard Spark Plugs by Heat Range

THREAD SIZE	HEAT RANGE	OUTBOARD TYPES	THREAD SIZE	HEAT RANGE	OUTBOARD TYPES
14mm ⅜" Reach	HOT ▲ ↕ ▼ COLD	J-12J...... J-11J...... J-8J....... J-7J....... J-6J....... J-62R...... J-4J....... J-57R...... J-2J.......	14mm ½" Reach	HOT ◆ COLD	L-9J...... L-7J...... L-4J......
14mm Surface Gap			14mm ¾" Reach	HOT ▲ ▼ COLD	....
⅜" Reach	....	J-19V......			
½" Reach	....	L-20V......			
½" Reach	....	L-19V......			
¾" Reach	....	N-19V......	18mm ½" Reach	HOT ▲	D-16J.... K-15J....
14mm ⅜" Reach Bantam Type	HOT ▲ ▼ COLD	CJ-14...... CJ-11...... CJ-8...... CJ-6...... CJ-4......	**⅝" Reach	▼ COLD	D-9J.... ....
14mm ⅜" Reach Special*	HOT ◆ COLD	....	⅞"-18	HOT ▲ ▼ COLD	....

(1970)

MODEL	PLUG	GAP
AERO MARINE 4 h.p.	J-14Y	.035
5 h.p.	H-10J	.035
7½ h.p.	CJ-8	.035
AIRBOY (Air Propeller) Mdl. 20, 40	J-8J	.030
Model 50	J-6J	.030
ANZANI Pilot (British)	L-10	.020
APACHE J-5	TJ-8J	.030
J-9	J-12J	.030
BOATIMPELLER	D-9	.020
BRITISH SEAGULL All	D-21	.020
BROOKLURE All	J-6J	.030
BUCCANEER All mdls. thru '59	J-6J or J-4J	.030
For later models see Gale		
BUNDY 1961 models	J-6J	.025
All others	L-86	.025
CAILLE 35, 40, 45, 50	K-60R	.016
All other 18mm Heads	UD-16	.025
All ⅞" Heads	W-14	.025
CAL-JET Jetmaster	H-4	.030
Econojet, Ramjet	J-8J	.030
CHAMPION A, 1B, R1C, S1C, S1D	D-16	.025
2B, 3B, D1C, D1D, D3D, S2C, S2D	D-16	.025
D2C, D2D, D1E, S1E, 1J, 2J, 1K, 2K, 4K, 1L,		
4L, 2M, 2L-HD, 4L-HD, B1F, D1F, D2F,		
S1F, S2F, 2G, M2G, 2H, 2MM, 2N	D-16	.030
3G, 1H, 3H, M1G, D1G, S1G	H-10J	.025
D4G, M4G, S4G	H-10J	.025
4KS, 4LS, 4LS-1X (Normal)	D-6	.030
(Racing)	K-60R	.020
4KS (Normal)	D-9	.015
(Racing)	K-60R	.020
3M-GS, 4M-GS, 3MM-GS, 4MM-GS,		
3N-S, 4N-D	J-7J	.030
4M-HR, 6M-HR, 4MM-HR, 6MM-HR	J-62R	.020
6M-GS, 6MS-GS, 6MM-GS, 6M-D,		
6N-MS	J-8J	.030
6N-HR	K-60R	.020
CHIEF J-5	TJ-8J	.030
J-9	J-12J	.030
CHRIS-CRAFT All	J-8J	.028
CHRYSLER All 3½ h.p.	H-8J	.030
1967 6 h.p.	H-10J	.030
1967 Models 9.2, 20, 35, 45, 50, 75, 100	J-4J	.030
1968-'70 Models 4.4, 5, 6.6, 7, 9.9,		
20, 35, 45 h.p.	L-4J	.030
1968-'70 70, 75, 85, 105, 120, 135 h.p.		
w Magnapower Ign.	L-20V	—
55 h.p. w/Magnapower Ign	L-20V	—
All other 55 h.p. models	L-4J	.030
CLINTON J-7, J-8	H-10J	.030
J-9	J-12J	.030
J-5	TJ-8J	.030
BJ9, AJ9, J-200, J-350, J-500, J-700	CJ-8	.030
COMMANDO All models	J-11	.025
COMMODORE 2 h.p.	H-10J	.030
7½, 10 h.p.	H-8J	.030
18, 40 h.p.	J-4J	.030
CORSAIR All 3.6, 4, 5, 7½ h.p. mdls	H-10J	.035
1950-'52 10 h.p.	CJ-8	.035
1953-'56 10 h.p.	H-10J	.035
All 16 h.p. models	D-9J	.035
1956 (30 h.p.)	J-6J	.030
CROFTON	J-6J	.025
CROSS 563-S	D-9J	.020
582-R	K-57R	.015
Radial & All others	UD-16 or D-16	.025
ECLIPSE thru 1936	J-8J	.025
1937 thru 1942	J-8J	.025
ELGIN 58201, 58202 (2 h.p.), 58401 (2½ h.p.),		
58561, 58562, 58571, 58651 (5 h.p.),		
58641, 58642, 58652 (6 h.p.), 58851, 58821		
thru 58824, 58841, 58843,		
58844 (16 h.p.)	J-12J	.050
58231, 58250 (2 h.p.), 58501 thru 58551,		
58601 thru 58621, 58701 thru 58731,		
58741 (7½ h.p.), 58751, 58761, 58772		
(7½ h.p.), 58211, 58771 (7½ h.p.),		
58711, 58221, 5833 (2 h.p.), 58781		
(7½ h.p.)	J-11J	.050

MODEL	PLUG	GAP
ELGIN—Continued		
58321, 58331, 58241 & 59241 (2 h.p.); 6001,		
58563, 59501, 59521, 59541 (5.5 h.p.)		
6002, 6003 (3½ h.p.); 6006 (6 h.p.);		
6009, 6010 (7½ h.p.)	H-10J	.030
59701, 59721, 59731, 58741, 59741, 59751,		
58791, 58341, 59791 (7.5 h.p.); 59011		
(8 h.p.); 59891 (10 h.p.); 58902, 58912,		
58941, 58961, 58971, 58951, 58801, 58891,		
59561, 59881, 58991, (12 h.p.); 59601,		
59861, 59871, (25 h.p.); 59421, 59431,		
59621, 59631, 59801, 59811, (30 h.p.);		
59402, 59403, 59412, 59413, 59441,		
59451, 59831, 59821, 59901,		
59911, (35 h.p.)	H-8J	.030
6012 (12 h.p.); 6025, 6028, 6032 (25 h.p.);		
6040, 6043-6047 (40 h.p.); 6060-6063		
(60 h.p.); 6013, 6014, 6015, 6069 (14 h.p.);		
6033, 6035 (27.7 h.p.); 6034, 6036, 6037,		
6038 (28 h.p.)	J-6J	.035
59661, 59671 (18 h.p.); 594001, 594011,		
594021, 594031, 59461, 59471 (40 h.p.);		
6070 (28 h.p.)	J-4J	.030
6005 (5 h.p.); 6008 (7½ h.p.); 6068		
(6 h.p.); 6060, 6061 (7½ h.p.)	H-10J	.035
6052, 6053 (43.7 h.p.); 6072, 6073 (75.2 h.p.)		
6054, 6055, 6056, 6057 (45 h.p.);		
6074, 6075, 6076, 6077 (75 h.p.)	J-4J	.035
60900 (2 h.p.); 6092 (3½ h.p.)	TJ-8J*	.030
*Engs. without Spec. Connector use CJ-8		
6091 (3½ h.p.); 6066, 6067 (9 h.p.)	CJ-8	.030
6062, 6063 (45 h.p.)		
6064, 6065 (75 h.p.)	UJ-17V	—
ELGIN (Canada) 6 h.p.	H-10J	.030
3½, 7½, 12, 30 h.p.	H-8J	.030
9.2, 20, 45, 50, 80 h.p.	J-4J	.030
ELTO Foldlight (2¾ h.p.)	K-15J	.025
Fisherman, Lightwin, Imperial		
Service "A", Super "A"	K-15J	.025
Fleetwind (8.5 h.p.), Senior Speedster		
(13.7 h.p.)	K-15J	.025
Single, Super Single (2.2 h.p.)	K-15J	.025
Big Quad, Speeditwin, Super "C",		
Senior & Junior Quad	D-9J	.025
Handifour, Lightfour, Imperial	D-9J	.025
Spec. Speedster (9 h.p.)	UD-16 or D-16	.025
Speedster (Small 12 h.p.),		
Sportster (5 h.p.)	J-6J	.025
ELTO (Canada) after 1949 - Except		
C2E7 & C2E8	J-6J	.030
C2E7, O2E8	J-6J	.030
ESKA 300	J-11J	.030
400, 1703, 1713 (3.5 h.p.), 1183, 1185,		
1187, 1193, 1195, 1197	J-8J	.030
1705, 1715 (5 h.p.)	J-6J	.030
1707, 1717 (7 h.p.)	UJ-10Y	.030
500, 600	CJ-8	.035
Models using Clinton J-5 Eng.	TJ-8J*	.030
*Engs. without Spec. Connector use CJ-8		
EVINRUDE Big Four 1946-'50 (50 h.p.)	K-60R	.020
Big Twin '51-'55 (25 h.p.), Fleetwin 1950-'58		
(7½ h.p.), Fastwin '50-'52 (14 h.p.), '55-'57		
(15 h.p.), Super Fastwin '53-'54, Lightwin		
'52 (5.2 h.p.), Sportsman '48-'51 (1½ h.p.)		
Sportwin '48-'51 (3.3 h.p.)	J-6J	.030
Big Twin '56-'70 (30-40 h.p.),		
1969-'70 Sportster (25 h.p.), Speeditwin		
'62-'64 (28 h.p.), Lark '56-'70 (30-40 h.p.),		
Four-Fifty (50 h.p.), Starflite (75 h.p.),		
Speedifour '63-'67 (75 h.p.), Sportfour		
'64-'67 (60 h.p.), Ski Twin '66-'70		
(33 h.p.)	J-4J	.030
Starflite '64-'65 (90 h.p.)	J-4J	.030
Starflite '66-'67 (80-100 h.p.)	J-4J	.030
Models w. CD Ignition:		
Speedifour 85, Sportfour 65, Starflite 85,		
Starflite 100S, Starflite 115S,		
Triumph, X115 (55-115 h.p.)	L-19V	
Speeditwin '50-'52 (22½ h.p.)	D-9J	.030
Fastwin '58-'70 (18 h.p.), Ducktwin (3 h.p.),		
Lightwin '53-'70 (3-4 h.p.), Fisherman		
'56-'70 (5½-6 h.p.), Sportwin '56-'70		
(10 h.p.), Mate (1½ h.p.), Angler '65-'68		
(5 h.p.), Yachtwin '64-'70		
(3-4 h.p.)	J-6J or J-4J	.030

MODEL	PLUG	GAP
EVINRUDE—Continued		
Light Four (9.7 h.p.), Speedifour		
18mm Head	D-9J	.025
Ranger (1.1 h.p.)	H-10J	.025
Zephyr (5.5 h.p.)	J-6J	.025
Acquanaut (Diving Unit)	CJ-14	.025
FAGEOL 44	J-6 or J-6J	.025
FIRESTONE All 3.6, 4, 5, 7½ h.p. mdls	H-10J	.035
1950-'52 10 h.p.	CJ-8	.035
1953-'56 10 h.p.	H-10J	.035
All 16 h.p. models	D-9J	.035
1956 30 h.p.	J-6J	.035
1960-'62 Models (2 h.p.)	H-10J	.030
7½, 8, 12, 25, 30 h.p.	H-8J	.030
40 h.p.	J-4J	.030
1966 Featherweight 5	J-12J	.030
FISHER-PIERCE Bearcat 55	J-6	025
FLAMBEAU Single (2.5 h.p.),		
Twin (5 h.p.)	J-8J	.025
FOREMOST 3½ h.p.	H-8J	.030
6 h.p.	H-10J	.030
9.2 h.p.	J-4J	.030
GALE Buccaneer		
3, 5, 5.5, 12, 15, 25 h.p.	J-6J or J-4J	.030
Buccaneer 35, 40, 60 h.p., Sovereign 35,		
40, 60 h.p.	J-4J	.030
GULF QUEEN	J-12J	.030
GUPPY	J-8J	.030
HARTFORD All models	UD-16 or D-16	.020
HIAWATHA thru 1949	J-7J	.030
1950 thru 1955	J-6J	.030
1956-'62 3, 3.6, 5, 6, 7½ h.p.	H-10J	.035
1956-'60 16 h.p.	D-9J	.030
1956 30 h.p., 1957 35 h.p.	J-6J	.030
1958-'62 12, 25 h.p.	J-6J	.035
1958-'62 38, 40 & 60 h.p.	J-4J	.035
HOMELITE (4-cycle)	J-6	.025
INDIAN All models	UD-16 or D-16	.025
JOHNSON 1969-'70 Models:		
115, 85, 60, 55 h.p.	L-19V	—
40, 33, 25 h.p.	J-4J	.030
20, 9½, 6, 4, 1½ h.p.	J-6J or J-4J	.030
A & AA Series (2-4½ h.p.); BN;		
F70, F75 (3.3 h.p.); J25 to J75		
(1½ h.p.) OA55 to OA65 (3 h.p.);		
SD20 (16 h.p.); 200, 210 (3.3 h.p.);		
K50 to K70 (8-9 h.p.); K75, K80,		
KA37, KA38 (8-9 h.p.); KA10,		
KA39, KD15, KS15 (9-10 h.p.);		
SD10, SD15 (16 h.p.); SD5 (6 h.p.)	D-9J	.030
AD Series (7½ h.p.); CD Series		
(5½ -6 h.p.); FD, FDE, FDEL, FDL		
Series (15-20 h.p.); HD Series (2½ h.p.);		
JH & JW Series (3 h.p.); LD (5 h.p.);		
MD20, MS20 (1½ h.p.); MQ Series		
(9½ h.p.); QD, QDL Series (10 h.p.);		
SC (1½ h.p.); TD, TN, TS		
Series (5 h.p.)	J-6J or J-4J	.030
RD, RDE, RDEL, RDL, RDSL, RDS, RJ, RJE,		
RJEL, RK, RKL, RX Series (25-40 h.p.)		
V4, V4H, V4A, V4AL, V4S, VX, VXH,		
VXL Series (50-75 h.p.)	J-4J	.030
1964-'65 V4M (90 h.p.)	J-4J	.030
1966 V4ML Golden Meteor V-100	J-4J	.030
AT10 to AT39 (5 h.p.); DS37, DS38 (2 h.p.);		
DT10 to DT39 (5 h.p.); HA10 to HA39		
(2½ h.p.); HD, HS Series (2½ h.p.);		
J-80 (1.7 h.p.); LS37, LS38 (2 h.p.);		
LT10 to LT39 (5 h.p.); MD, MS Series		
(1½ h.p.); 100, 110 (1.7 h.p.);		
300 (3.7 h.p.)	J-8J	.030
K35 (6-7 h.p.); PO15 1949-'50 mdls.		
(22 h.p.); VE50 (26 h.p.)	K-60R	.020
K40, K45 (6-7 h.p.); OK55 to OK75,		
P35 (8 h.p.)	K-60R	.020
P40 (13 h.p.); P45 (12 h.p.); P50 (20 h.p.);		
P65, P70 (21.5 h.p.); P75, P80, PA50,		
PE50, PO10 to PO39 (22 h.p.); S45 to		
S70, SA50, SE50 (13 h.p.); TR40,		
V45 to V70, VA50	K-60R	.020

If desired, special spark plug types with Gold Palladium alloy electrodes may be substituted as follows:

UJ-11G	J-7J, J-8J, J-11J	UJ-7G	J-4J, J-6J

(1970)

MODEL	PLUG	GAP
JOHNSON—Continued		
Models w/CD Ignition: GT, TR, V4A, V4S, V4TL, VX, VXH (55-115 h.p.)	L-19V	—
Air-Buoy (Diving Unit)	CJ-14	.025
KONIG Racing	L-57R	.016
500 c.c. 75 h.p. model	L-54R	.016
LAUSON thru 1949	J-8 or J-8J	.025
After 1949	J-8 or J-8J	.030
MAJESTIC 1MB, 2MB, 4MB, 1MBB, M-2L, M-4L-GS, M-2LL, M-2N	UD-16 or D-16	.030
M-3L-GS, M-3N-GS, M-4N-GS, M-3LL-GS, M-4LL-GS	J-7J	.030
M-6LL-GS, M-6N-GS	J-8J	.030
MARINER (See Champion)		
MARTIN 20 (2⅓ h.p.), 100 (10 h.p.)	J-6J	.035
40 (4½ h.p.), 45 (4½ h.p.)	J-8J	.035
60 (7.2 h.p.), 66 (7.2 h.p.), 75 (7½ h.p.)	J-8J	.035
60 High Speed (7½ h.p.) (gasoline)	J-6J	.035
(alcohol mixture)	J-57R	.020
200 Silver Streak (17 h.p.)	J-62R	.023
McCULLOCH 1964-'69 Models		
3½, 7½ h.p., 4 h.p. w/Long shaft	H-10J	.035
4 h.p.	J-14Y	.035
9 h.p.	CJ-8	.035
9½ h.p.	J-7J	.035
14 h.p., OX140 (14 h.p.)	J-4J	.035
Manual: 28, 45 h.p., OX450 (45 h.p.)	J-4J	.035
Electric: 45 h.p., OX450 (45 h.p.)	UJ-17V	—
590/630	J-4J	.035
75 h.p.	UJ-17V	—
Diesel Engine	AG-10	—
MERCURY Mark 20H (16 h.p.); Mark 55H (40 h.p.)	J-62R or J-57R	.025
K1 (2.5 h.p.); K2, K3 (3 h.p.); K4, K5 (6 h.p.); KB1 (2.9 h.p.); KB1A (3.1 h.p.); KB2; KB3 (3.2 h.p.); KB4 (5.8 h.p.); KB5 (6 h.p.); KB4-1 (5.8 h.p.); KD3 (3.2 h.p.); KD3S (3.2 h.p.)	J-8J	.025
KD4, KD4S (6 h.p.); KE3 (3.6 h.p.); KE4 (7.5 h.p.); KE4A (6 h.p.); KE7 (10 h.p.); KF3 (3.5 h.p.); KF5 (5 h.p.); KF7 (10 h.p.); KF9 (25 h.p.); KG4 (7.5 h.p.); Mark Series 5 (5 h.p.); 6 (6 h.p.); 7 (7.5 h.p.); 10, 15 (10 h.p.); 15A (15 h.p.)	J-7J	.025
Merc 39 (3.9 h.p.) (Prior to 1967)	J-8J	.025
Merc 39 (3.9 h.p.) 1967-'68; Merc 40 (4 h.p.) 1969	L-9J	.030
Merc 60 (6 h.p.) 1967-'68; Merc 75 (7.5 h.p.) 1969	L-7J	.030
Merc Series 60 (6 h.p.); 100, 110 (10 h.p.); 150 (15 h.p.); (Prior to 1967)	J-7J	.025
Merc 110, 200, 500M, 500S 650S (65 h.p.) 1967-'68	L-4J	.030
Merc 110, 200	L-4J	.030
Merc 350 (35-40 h.p.)		
Thru 1965	J-6J	.025
1966	J-4J	.025
1967-'69	L-4J	.030
KG7, KH7, KG7H (10 h.p.); KG4H (7.5 h.p.); KG9, KG9H (25 h.p.)	J-6J	.025
Mark Series: 20 (16 h.p.); 25 (25 h.p.); 28 (22 h.p.); 58 (45 h.p.); 30, 30H (31 h.p.); 35A (35 h.p.); 50, 50H, 55 (40 h.p.); 75 (60 h.p.); 78 (70 h.p.)	J-6J	.025
Merc Series: 200 (20-22 h.p.); 250 (25 h.p.); 300 (35 h.p.); 400, 450 (45 h.p.); 600 (60 h.p.); 700 (70 h.p.)	J-6J	.025
500 (50 h.p.) '65-'66 models; 650 & 650S (65 h.p.); 850 (85 h.p.); 900 (90 h.p.); 1000 (100 h.p.)	J-4J	.025
Merc 800E (80 h.p.) Ser. No. 1403610 and below	J-2J	.025
Merc 800EL (80 h.p.) Ser. No. 1405606 and below	J-2J	.025
All other Merc 800E and 800EL mdls	J-4J	.025
Merc 950 (95 h.p.); 1100 (110 h.p.)	L-4J	.025
1966-'70 All models w/Thunderbolt (C.D.) Ignition	L-19V	—
MID-JET M-2, M-3	J-4J	.030
M-4	L-4J	.030
MILBURN Cub	J-11J	.018
MONARCH	J-11J	.032
MUNCIE 11B1, 15B1 (1½ h.p.)	J-11J	.025
11B4, 11B6, 11B10, 15B4, 17B1	J-6J	.025
11B2, 15B2 (2 h.p.); 11B16 (16 h.p.)	K-15J	.025
WC-1 (1.7 h.p.)	J-8J	.025
MY-TE-IV Power Products Engine	J-8J	.030
NEPTUNE OB1, 2, 2C, 3, 4, 5, 31, 32, 51, 63	UD-16 or D-16	.025
OB15, 16, 17 (16 h.p.)	K-57R	.015
OB11, 12, 34, 64, 65, 102, 112, 238, 239, 438, 439, 638, 639, 1016; 1638, 1639 (16 h.p.); 10A16, 11A16 (16 h.p.); 11A2 (2 h.p.); 16A39	K-15J	.025
101, 189, 139; 1A39, 10A1 (1½ h.p.)	J-8J	.025
111, 11A1, 15A1 (1½ h.p.)	J-11J	.025
104, 106, 113, 114, 116, 539, 938, 939, 1010, 1110, 4A39, 5A39, 9A39, 10A4, 10A6, 11A3, 11AA3, 11AA10; 10A10 (9½ h.p.); 11A6, 11AA6 (6 h.p.); 15A3, 15AA3 (3½ h.p.); 15A6, 15AA6 (6 h.p.); 15A9, 15AA9 (9½ h.p.); 17A1, 17A2, 17A3, A1, AA1, AA1A, A2, AA2, AA4, AA6, AA10 (10 h.p.)	J-6J	.025
OLIVER Challenger J, J-2 (5.5 h.p.); J-3, J-4, J-5, J-6 (6 h.p.)	J-8J	.030
Commander (15 h.p.); K, K-2 (15 h.p.); K-3, K-4, K-5, K-6 (16 h.p.)	H-8J	.030
B, B-2, B-3 (35 h.p.)	D-9J	.030
OUTBOARD JET J55, J55B (5.5 h.p.)	J-6J	.030
PEERLESS J-5	TJ-8J	.030
J-9	J-12J	.030
PERKINS		
1959-'61 6 h.p.	J-8J	.028
16 h.p.	H-8J	.028
40 h.p.	L-86*	.035
1959-'60 35 h.p. (18mm Hd.)	D-9J	.035
1961 35 h.p. (14mm Hd.)	L-86*	.035
1962-'65 4½ h.p., 6½ h.p.	J-8J	.028
18 h.p.	H-8J	.028
30 h.p., 40 h.p.	L-86*	.035
*Alternates—L-85 or H-8J		
RILEY 75 h.p. Four Cycle 5-Cyl. Radial	J-6	.025
ROYAL (Atlas) thru 1949	J-7J	.030
After 1949	J-6J	.030
SABER (Fedway) All models	J-6J	.030
SEA-DOO Jet-Powered Aqua Scooter w/Rotax Engine	K-9	.025
SCOTT (McCulloch)		
1959-'60 12, 25, 40 & 60 h.p.	J-6J	.035
3.6, 6, 7½ & 10 h.p.	H-10J	.035
1961 43.7, 75.2 h.p.	J-4J	.035
14.1, 27.7 h.p.	J-6J	.035
7.5 h.p.	H-10J	.035
1961 75.2 Custom	UJ-17V	—
1961-'62 Scotty (3.5 h.p.)	H-10J	.035
1962-'63 Flying Scott (75 h.p.)	UJ-17V	—
Royal Scott Elec. (45 h.p.)	UJ-17V	—
Royal Scott Manual (45 h.p.)	J-4J	.035
Sports Scott (28 h.p.)	J-6J	.035
Fleet Scott & Power Scott (14 h.p.)	J-6J	.035
Fishing Scott (7.5 h.p.)	H-10J	.035
Diesel Mdls. (glow plug)	AG-10	—
SCOTT-ATWATER All 3.6, 4, 5, 7½ h.p. 1953-'58 10 h.p.	H-10J	.035
1950-'52 10 h.p.	CJ-8	.035
All 16 h.p.	D-9J	.035
1955 30 h.p.	J-6J	.030
1956 33 h.p.	J-6J	.030
1958 22-25 h.p.; 40 h.p.; 60 h.p.	J-6J	.035
SEA-BEE (Goodyear) 1946 thru 1949	J-7J	.025
1950-'59	J-6J	.030
1960 models	J-6J or J-4J	.030
SEA-FLYER (Goodrich)	J-6J	.030
SEA-KING (Ward's) 371, 373	K-15J	.025
712	K-57R	.018
Others thru 1949	J-7J	.025
1950-'63 All 1½-25 h.p. mdls.	J-6J or J-4J	.030
All 35-60 h.p. mdls.	J-4J	.030
1964-'70 3½, 5.8 h.p.	H-8J	.030
1964-'65 9 h.p.	H-8J	.030
1966-'69 9.2 h.p.	J-4J	.030
1964-'67 20-80 h.p.	J-4J	.030
1967-'70 6 h.p.	H-10J	.030
1968-'70 9.6, 20, 35, 45, 55 h.p.	L-4J	.030
SEARS 1964-'65 6003 (3½ h.p.); 6004 (6 h.p.); 6010, 6012 (7½ h.p.)	H-10J	.035
6015 (14 h.p.); 6037, 6038 (28 h.p.)	J-6J	.035
6056, 6057, 6058 (45 h.p.); 6076, 6077, 6078 (75 h.p.)	J-4J	.035
6091 (3½ h.p.)	TJ-8J	.030
5927 (12 h.p.)	H-8J	.030
5941 (35 h.p.)	J-4J	.030
1966 6091, 6094	CJ-8	.030
SPRITE J-5	TJ-8J	.030
STARLING JET 5 h.p.	J-12J	.025
SWANSON-CHAMP		
Hot Rod 5NHR	J-57R	—
6NHR	K-57R	—
TERRY TROLLER (4-cycle) Mdl. T4T	J-8J	.025
Mdl. T5T	H-10	.025
VIKING thru 1949	J-8J	.025
1950-1965	J-6J	.025
1965-'70 Models:		
3½, 15 h.p.; 9 h.p. (1965)	H-8J	.030
6 h.p.	H-10J	.030
9.2 ('66-'70), 20, 35, 50 h.p. (thru '67)	J-4J	.030
1968-'70 9.6, 20, 35, 55 h.p.	L-4J	.030
VOLVO-PENTA		
Acquamatic BB70	J-6 or J-6J	.028
Sustained Hi-Speed	J-4J	.028
Acquamatic 100	L-5	.028
VOYAGER 1VA, 2VA, 1VB, V-2L, V-4L-GS, V-2LL, V-2N	UD-16 or D-16	.030
V-3L-GS, V-3N-GS, V-4N-GS, V-3LL-GS, V-4LL-GS	J-7J	.030
V-6LL-GS, V-6N-GS	J-8J	.030
WESTERN FLYER (Western Auto)	J-7J	.025
WEST BEND		
1955 5 h.p.	J-12J	.050
1955 7½ h.p.	J-11J	.050
1956-1958 2 h.p.	J-11J	.050
1956 5½ h.p.	H-10J	.035
1956-1957 12 h.p.	H-8J	.025
1956-1963 7½, 25, 30 h.p.	H-8J	.030
1957-1959 6 h.p.	H-10J	.030
1957 8 h.p.	H-8J	.035
1958-1960 8, 16, 35, 40 h.p.	H-8J	.030
1958-1963 12 h.p.	H-8J	.030
1959-1961 2 h.p.	H-10J	.030
1960-1962 18 h.p.	J-4J	.030
1961 6 h.p.	H-8J	.030
1961-1962 40 h.p.	J-4J	.030
1961-1965 20, 45, 80 h.p.	J-4J	.030
1962-1965 3½, 9, 10 h.p.	H-8J	.030
1963-1965 6 h.p.	H-10J	.030
1964-1965 35, 50 h.p.	J-4J	.030
WIZARD WD3, WD3S (3.2 h.p.); WF4, WG4 (6 h.p.); WF7, WG7, WH7, WG7A, WJ7 (10 h.p.)	J-8J	.025
WD4, WD4S (6 h.p.); WH6, WH6-1 (5 h.p.); WK7, WM7, WM7A (10 h.p.)	J-7J	.025
WN7, WN7A (12 h.p.); WH6A (5 h.p.); WA25, WA25E (25 h.p.)	J-6J	.025
OC575, OC585 (5.5 h.p.)	J-8J	.030
OC1575, OC1585 (15 h.p.)	H-8J	.030
OC3585 (35 h.p.)	D-9J	.030
1959-'64 3½, 6, 7½, 10 h.p.	H-10J	.035
12, 14, 25 h.p.	J-6J	.035
40, 60 h.p.	J-4J	.035
1965 thru '70 3½ h.p.; 9 h.p. (1965)	H-8J	.030
6 h.p.	H-10J	.030
20 h.p. (thru '67); 9.2 h.p. ('66-'70)	J-4J	.030
20 h.p. ('68-'70)	L-4J	.030
YAMAHA All models	L-86	.025

If desired, special spark plug types with Gold Palladium alloy electrodes may be substituted as follows:

UJ-11G .... J-7J, J-8J, J-11J   UJ-7G J-4J, J-6J

(1954)

OUTBOARD MOTORS

NOTE—Most manufacturers recommend use of non-detergent motor oils or special outboard oils. For breaking-in new or reconditioned motors it is generally advisable to use 50% more oil in the gasoline for the first 12 hours. Follow manufacturer's recommendations. The following oil-fuel mixes are listed as a convenient reference only. Always check Operators' Manuals.

MAKE AND MODEL	Spark Plug Type	Spark Plug Gap	Contact Point Gap	Oil Fuel Mix Per Gallon	
				Pints	SAE Grade
ANZANI Pilot (British)	L-10	.020	.018	½	30
BENDIX (See "Eclipse")					
BOATIMPELLER ☆	5 Com. or H-17-A*	.020	.020	⅜	40
BROOKLURE ☆ 1200	J-6J	.030	.020	1	30
All others	J-6J	.030	.020	½	30
BUCCANEER ☆ All models	J-6J	.030	.020	½	30
CAILLE 35, 40, 45, 50	R-1	.025	.020	½	30
All other 18mm Hds	7	.025	.020	½	30
All ⅞" Hds	1 Com.	.025	.020	½	30
CHAMPION ☆ A, 1B, R1C, S1C, S1D	9 or C-15*	.025	.018	½	30
2B, 3B, D1C, D1D, D3D, S2C, S2D	9 or C-15*	.025	.018	¾	30
D2C, D2D, D1E, S1E, 1J, 2J, 1K, 2K, 4K, 1L, 4L	7	.030	.018	¾	30
B1F, D1F, D2F, S1F, S2F, 2G, M2G, 2H	7	.030	.015	¾	30
1J, 2J, 1K, 2K, 2L-HD, 4L-HD	7	.030	.018	¾	30
3G, 1H, 3H, M1G, D1G, S1G	H-10	.025	.015	¾	30
D4G, M4G, S4G	H-9	.025	.015	¾	30
4KS, 4LS, 4LS-1X (Normal)	4 Com. or H-16-A*	.030	.018	2	30
(Racing)	R-7	.020	.018	2	30
4KS (Normal)	5 Com. or H-17-A*	.030	.018	2	30
(Racing)	R-7	.020	.018	2	30
3M-GS, 4M-GS, 4M-HD	J-7J	.035	.018	½	30
4M-HR, 6M-GS, 6M-HD, 6M-HR (Normal)	J-7J	.035	.018	¾	30
(Racing)	J-3	.025	.018	¾	30
CHRIS-CRAFT ☆ J (5.5 h.p.)	J-8J	.028	.018	½	30
Commander K (10 h.p.)	J-7J	.028	.018	½	30
CLARKE TROLLER ☆	V-1	.014	.018	½	30
CORSAIR ☆ 5028 (10 h.p.) thru '52	HT-10J	.035	.020	½	30
5020 (3.6 h.p.), 5021 (4 h.p.), 5023 (7.5 h.p.), 5027 (5 h.p.)	H-10J	.035	.020	½	30
1953 (10 h.p.)	H-10J	.035	.020	½	30
CROSS Radiut	C-7	.025	.020	½	30
563-S	5MJ	.020	.020	½	30
582-R	R-1	.015	.020	½	30
All others	7	.025	.020	½	30
ECLIPSE thru 1936	J-8J	.025	.020	½	30
1937 thru 1940	H-10J	.025	.020	¾	30
ELGIN ☆ 58201, 58202 (2 h.p.)	J-12J	.050	.020	½	30
58301 (1¼ h.p.)	J-12J	.040	.020	¾	30
58401 (2½ h.p.)	J-12J	.050	.020	½	40
85501 thru 58551	J-11J	.050	.020	¾	30–40
58561, 58562 (5 h.p.)	J-12J	.050	.020	½	30–40
58561 (5 h.p.), 58562	J-12J	.050	.020	½	30–40
58601 thru 58621	J-11J	.050	.020	¾	30
58641 (6 h.p.)	J-12J	.050	.020	¾	30
58642 (6 h.p.)	J-12J	.050	.020	½	30
58701 thru 58731	J-11J	.050	.020	¾	40
58741 (7½ h.p.)	J-11J	.050	.020	¾	30–40
58751, 58761 (7½ h.p.)	J-11J	.050	.020	½	30–40
58761	J-12J	.050	.020	½	30–40
58821 (16 h.p.)	J-12J	.050	.020	¾	30
58822	J-12J	.050	.015	½	30–40
58823	J-12J	.050	.020	½	30–40
58843, 58824 (16 h.p.)	J-12J	.050	.020	½	30
58841 (16 h.p.)	J-12J	.050	.015	¾	30
ELTO ☆					
Ace, Handitwin—1936	9 or C-15*	.025	.020	⅓	40
1937 thru 1941	C-7	.025	.020	⅓	40
Cub (½ h.p.) 1939	J-12J	.025	.020	⅓	40
1940 thru 1941	H-10J	.025	.020	⅓	40
Pal (1.1 h.p.) 1937 thru 1941	H-10J	.025	.020	⅓	40
Lightweight 1929-'30	7	.025	.020	⅓	40
1931 thru 1933	6M	.025	.020	⅓	40
Lightwin (5 h.p.) 1920-'27	7	.025	.020	⅓	40
1934 thru 1941 (4-5 h.p.)	6M	.025	.020	⅓	40
Service Twin 1928-'31 (3-4 h.p.)	7	.025	.020	½	40
1936 thru 1937 (4.3 h.p.)	6M	.025	.020	½	40
Quad 1928 thru 1929 (30 h.p.)	7	.025	.020	⅓	40
Fisherman, Lightwin, Imperial, Service "A" Super "A"	6M	.025	.020	½	40
Fleetwin (8.5 h.p.) Senior Speedster (13.7 h.p.)	6M	.025	.020	1	40
Foldlight (2¾ h.p.)	6M	.025	.020	¾	40
Single, Super Single (2.2 h.p.)	6M	.025	.020	⅔	40
Big Quad, Speeditwin Super "C", Senior Quad Junior Quad	5MJ	.025	.020	1½	40
Handifour, Lightfour, Imperial	5MJ	.025	.020	¾	40
Spec. Speedster (9 h.p.)	7	.025	.020	¾	40
Speedster 1928-'31 (7 h.p.)	7	.025	.020	¾	40
1949 (12 h.p.)	J-6J	.025	.020	1	40
Sportster (5 h.p.)	J-6J	.025	.020	½	40
ELTO RACING ☆					
Midget Racer	R-1	.015	.015	1½	60
Racing Speedtwin 1934	R-1	.015	.015	2	60
1935	R-11	.015	.015	2	60
Racing 460, 1933-'34	R-1	.015	.015	2	60
1935	R-11	.015	.015	2	60
Racing Super "C" 1930-'33	R-1	.015	.015	2	60
Model 460 1930-'32	R-1	.015	.015	2	60
EVINRUDE ☆ Big Four 1931-'32	5MJ	.025	.020	1½	40
1946 thru 1950 (50 h.p.)	R-7	.020	.020	¾	40
Big Twin 1931-'32 (4 h.p.)	0 Com.	.025	.020	½	40
1951-'54 (25 h.p.)	J-6J	.030	.020	½	*40
Single "A" (2 h.p.)	0 Com.	.025	.020	⅔	40
Fleetwin 1928-'29 (6-7 h.p.)	0 Com.	.025	.020	⅔	40
1930 thru 1934 (8-11 h.p.)	6M	.025	.020	1	40
1950 thru 1954 (7½ h.p.)	J-6J	.030	.020	½	30–40
Speeditwin 1927-'29 (16 h.p.)	0 Com.	.025	.020	2	40
1930 thru 1931 (22½ h.p.)	7	.025	.020	2	40
1950 thru 1952 (22½ h.p.)	5MJ	.030	.020	¾	40
Fastwin 1927-'29 (4-14 h.p.)	0 Com.	.025	.020	1½	40
1930 thru 1933 (14 h.p.)	6M	.025	.020	1½	40
1950 thru 1952 (14 h.p.)	J-6J	.030	.020	½	30–40
Super Fastwin '53-'54 (15 h.p.)	J-6J	.030	.020	½*	30–40
Lightwin 1931-'38 (4-5.6 h.p.)	6M	.025	.020	⅓	40
1952 (5.2 h.p.)	J-6J	.030	.020	½	30
1953-'54 (3 h.p.)	J-6J	.030	.020	½	30
Fisherman (5.4 h.p.)	6M	.025	.020	½	40
Sturditwin (8 h.p.)	6M	.025	.020	1	40
Foldlight (2¾ h.p.)	6M	.025	.020	¾	40
Sport Single (2.2 h.p.)	6M	.025	.020	⅔	40
Light Four (9.7 h.p.)	5MJ	.025	.020	¾	40
Speedifour, Speediquad, Speediquad Imperial	5MJ	.025	.020	1½	40
Sport Four, Sport Four Imperial	5MJ	.025	.020	1	40
Mate (½ h.p.), Ranger (1.1 h.p.)	H-10J	.025	.020	⅓	40
Scout	J-8J	.025	.020	⅓	40
Sportsman 1935-'38 (1½ h.p.)	9 or C-15*	.025	.020	⅓	40
1939 thru 1947 (2 h.p.)	H-10J	.025	.020	⅓	40
1948 thru 1951 (1½ h.p.)	J-6J	.003	.020	⅓	30–40
Sportwin '36-'38(2½-3 h.p.)	9 or C-15*	.025	.020	⅓	40
1939 thru 1947 (3 h.p.)	H-10J	.025	.020	⅓	40
1948 thru 1951 (3.3 h.p.)	J-6J	.030	.020	⅓	30–40
Zephyr (5½ h.p.)	J-6J	.025	.020	½	40
*1954 Models 1 qt. to 5 gallons					
EVINRUDE RACING ☆					
Racing Speeditwin 1931-'34	R-1	.015	.015	2	60
After 1934	R-11	.015	.015	2	60
Racing 460 1933-'34	R-1	.015	.015	2	60
After 1934	R-11	.015	.015	2	60
Model 460 1931	R-7	.015	.015	2	60
1932	R-1	.015	.015	2	60
FIRESTONE ☆ 10-A-75 (10 h.p.)	HT-10J	.035	.020	½	30
10 h.p. 1953, All others thru 1953	H-10J	.035	.020	½	30
FLAMBEAU Single (2.5 h.p.), Twin (5 h.p.)	J-7J	.025	.020	⅔	40
HARTFORD All models	8 Com.	.020	.018	½	30
HIAWATHA ☆ thru 1949	J-7J	.030	.020	½	30
1950 thru 1953	J-6J	.030	.020	½	30
INDIAN ☆ All models	7	.025	.020	½	30
JOHNSON ☆					
A; A25-A45 (2-3 h.p.); A50-A80; AA37 (4½ h.p.); BN; F70, F75 (3.3 h.p.); J25-J75 (1½ h.p.); J80 (1.7 h.p.); OA55, 60, 65 (3 h.p.); SD20 (16 h.p.); 200, 210	5MJ	.030	.020	½	40
AT10-AT39 (5 h.p.); DS37, DS38; DT10-DT39; HA10-HA39 (2½ h.p.); HD10-HD39; HS10, HS15, HS39 (2½ h.p.); LT10-LT39; LS37, LS38, MS & MD15, 38, 39; 100, 110, 300	J-8J	.030	.030	½	40
HS & HD 20, 25 (2½ h.p.), 26; MD & MS 20 (1½ h.p.); QD10-QD14 (10 h.p.); RD10, RD11; TN25-TN28; TS & TD15, 20 (5 h.p.)	J-6J	.030	.020	½	40
JW10 (3 h.p.); RD12-RD15 (25 h.p.)	J-6J	.030	.020	½	30
K35 (6-7 h.p.); PO15 1949 & 1950 models	R-7	.020	.020	½	40
K40, K45; OK55, OK60, OK75 (7.8 h.p.); P35	R-7	.020	.020	¾	40
K75, K80; KA10-KA39; KS15, KD15 (9.8 h.p.); SD10, SD15 (16 h.p.)	5MJ	.030	.020	1	40
K50, K65, K70; P30	5MJ	.030	.020	¾	40
P40-P80; PE & PA50; PO10-PO39 (22 h.p.); S45-S70 (13.3 h.p.); SE50, SA50; TR40; V45-V70 (26 h.p.); VE & VA50	R-7	.020	.020	1	40
LAUSON ☆ thru 1949	J-8	.025	.020	....	30†
1950 thru 1953	J-8	.030	.020	....	30†
†4-cycle engine. Crankcase oil only. Do not mix oil and gasoline.					
LOCKWOOD ☆	6M	.025	.020	½	30
MAJESTIC ☆ thru 1952, M-2-L, M-4-LGS	7	.030	.018	¾	30
M-3-LGS	J-7J	.035	.018	½	30
M-6-LGS	J-7J	.035	.018	¾	30

OUTBOARD MOTORS—Continued

NOTE—Most manufacturers recommend use of non-detergent motor oils or special outboard oils. For breaking-in new or reconditioned motors it is generally advisable to use 50% more oil in the gasoline for the first 12 hours. Follow manufacturer's recommendations. The following oil-fuel mixes are listed as a convenient reference only. Always check Operator's Manuals.

(1954)

MAKE AND MODEL	Spark Plug Type	Spark Plug Gap	Contact Point Gap	Oil Fuel Mix Per Gallon	
				Pints	SAE Grade
MARINER ☆ M1G, M4G	H-10	.025	.020	½	30
M2G	7	.025	.020	½	30
MARTIN ☆ 20 (2⅓ h.p.), 100 (10 h.p.)	J-6J	.035	.020	½	40
40 (4½ h.p.), 45 (4½ h.p.)	J-8J	.035	.020	½	40
60 (7.2 h.p.), 66 (7.2 h.p.), 75 (7½ h.p.)	J-8J	.035	.020	¾	40
60 High Speed (7½ h.p.) (gasoline)	J-6J	.035	.020	1	40
(alcohol mixture)	J-2	.035	.020	1	40
200 Silver Streak (17 h.p.)	J-3	.025	.020	¾	40
MERCURY ☆ For Racing all mdls.	K-3	.025	.018	¾	30
K1 (2.5 h.p.); K2, K3 (3 h.p.); K4, K5 (6 h.p.); KB1 (2.9 h.p.); KB1A (3.1 h.p.); KB2; KB3 (3.2 h.p.); KB4 (5.8 h.p.); KB5 (6 h.p.); KE41 (5.8 h.p.); KD3 (3.2 h.p.); KD3S (3.2 h.p.)	J-8J	.025	.018	Mfr. recommends mixing: ½ pint Aeromarine 2-cycle oil or ½ pint premium 100% non additive SAE 30 oil with one gallon auto type gas min. 72 octane.	
KD4, KD4S (6 h.p.); KE3 (3.6 h.p.); KE7, KF7 (10 h.p.); Mark 7 (7.5 h.p.)	J-7J	.025	.018		
KE4 (7.5 h.p.); KF5 (5 h.p.)	J-7J	.030	.018		
KF3 (3.5 h.p.) Phelon Magneto	J-7J	.035	.018		
Scintilla Magneto	J-7J	.025	.018		
KG4 (7.5 h.p.); KG4H (7.5 h.p.)	J-7J	.035	.018		
KG7 (10 h.p.) Phelon Magneto	J-6J	.035	.018		
Scintilla Magneto	J-6J	.030	.018		
KH7 (10 h.p.); KG7Q (10 h.p.)	J-6J	.030	.018		
KG4Q (7.5 h.p.)	J-6J	.035	.018		
Mark 5 (5 h.p.)	J-7J	.030	.018		
Mark 15 (10 h.p.)	J-7J	.040	.018		
Mark 20 (16 h.p.); KG7H (10 h.p.)	J-6J	.030	.018		
KF9 (25 h.p.)	J-7J	.030	.016	¾	30
KG9 (25 h.p.)	J-6J	.030	.016	¾	30
KG9Q (25 h.p.)	J-6J	.025	.018	¾	30
Mark 40 (25 h.p.)	J-6J	.030	.012	¾	30
Mark 40H (25 h.p.)	J-6J	.025	.012	¾	30
MILBURN ☆ Cub	J-11	.018	.018	1	40
MONARCH ☆	J-11J	.032	.020	½	30
MUNCIE ☆ 11B1, 15B1 (1½ h.p.)	J-11J	.025	.015	⅔	30
11B4, 11B6, 11B10, 15B4, 17B1	J-6	.025	.020	⅔	40
11B2, 15B2 (2 h.p.)	6M	.025	.015	⅔	30
11B16 (16 h.p.)	6M	.025	.020	1	40
NEPTUNE ☆ OB1, 2, 2C, 3, 4, 5, 31, 32, 51, 63	7	.025	.020	⅔	30
OB15, 16, 17 (16 h.p.)	R-1	.015	.020	1	40
OB11, 12, 34, 64, 65, 102, 112, 238, 239, 438, 439, 638, 639, 1016	6M	.025	.020	⅔	30
1638, 1639 (16 h.p.)	6M	.025	.020	1	30
10A16, 11A16 (16 h.p.)	6M	.025	.020	1	40
11A2 (2 h.p.), 16A39	6M	.025	.015	⅔	30
101, 189, 139	J-8J	.025	.020	⅔	30
1A39, 10A1 (1½ h.p.)	J-8J	.025	.020	1	40
111, 11A1, 15A1 (1½ h.p.)	J-11J	.025	.015	⅔	30
104, 106, 113, 114, 116, 539, 938, 939, 1010, 1110, 4A39, 5A39, 9A39, 10A4, 10A6, 11A3, 11AA3, 11AA10	J-6J	.025	.020	⅔	30
10A10 (9½ h.p.)	J-6J	.025	.020	1	40
11A6, 11AA6 (6 h.p.)	J-6J	.025	.020	⅔	40
15A3, 15AA3 (3½ h.p.)	J-6J	.025	.015	⅔	30
15A6, 15AA6 (6 h.p.)	J-6J	.025	.015	⅔	40
15A9, 15AA9 (9½ h.p.)	J-6J	.025	.015	1	40
17A1, 17A2, 17A3, A1, A2, AA2, AA4, AA6	J-6J	.025	.020	⅔	30
AA10 (10 h.p.)	J-6J	.025	.020	1	40
ROYAL ☆ (Atlas) thru 1949	J-7J	.030	.020	½	30
1950 thru 1953	J-6J	.030	.020	½	30
SABER (Fedway) All models	J-6J	.030	.020	½	30
SCOTT-ATWATER ☆ 461 thru 497	H-10J	.032	.020	½	30
500 thru 507	H-10J	.035	.020	½	30
509, 1-30 (16 h.p.)	5MJ	.035	.020	½	30
1-12 (3.6 h.p.), 1-14 (4 h.p.), 1-16 (5 h.p.), 1-20 (7.5 h.p.)	H-10J	.035	.020	½	30
1-25 (10 h.p.) thru 1952	HT-10J	.035	.020	½	30
(10 h.p.) 1953	H-10J	.035	.020	½	30
SEA-BEE ☆ (Goodyear) 1946 thru 1949	J-7J	.025	.020	½	30
1950 thru 1953	J-6J	.030	.020	½	30
SEA-FLYER ☆ (Goodrich)	J-6J	.030	.020	½	30
SEA-KING ☆ (Ward's) 371, 373	6M	.025	.020	½	30
712	R-1	.020	.020	½	30
Others thru 1949	J-7J	.025	.020	½	30
1950 thru 1953	J-6J	.030	.020	½	30
THOR ☆ 10mm Heads	Y-6	.025	.020	⅔	30
18mm Heads	6M	.020	.020	1	30
VIKING ☆ (Canada)	J-8	.025	.020	½	30
VOYAGER ☆ thru 1952, V-2-L, V-4-LGS	7	.030	.018	¾	30
V-3-LGS	J-7J	.035	.018	½	30
V-6-LGS	J-7J	.035	.018	¾	30
WATERWITCH ☆ (Sears) MB10, MB20, 10, 11, 20, 21, 22	C-7	.025	.020	¾	30
30, 40	J-11	.025	.020	¾	30
31 thru 34A, 41 thru 44W, 90	J-7	.030	.020	¾	30
35, 36, 50	H-10	.025	.020	¾	30
12 thru 15, 23, 24	C-7	.025	.020	¾	30
WESTERN FLYER ☆ (Western Auto)	J-7J	.025	.020	½	30
WEST BEND ☆ (Canada) 15030 (1½ h.p.)	J-12J	.040	.020	¾	30
15040 (2½ h.p.)	J-12J	.050	.020	½	40
15050-15055, 15074 (7½ h.p.)	J-11J	.050	.020	¾	30–40
15056 (5 h.p.), 150202 (2 h.p.), 150823 (16 h.p.)	J-12J	.050	.020	½	30–40
15064 (6 h.p.), 15082 (16 h.p.), 15084 (16 h.p.)	J-12J	.050	.020	¾	30
15060-15062	J-11J	.030	.020	¾	30
15075 (7½ h.p.), 150761 (7½ h.p.)	J-11J	.050	.020	½	30–40
WIZARD ☆ WD3 (3.2 h.p.)	J-8J	.025	.020	½	30
WD4 (6 h p.)	J-7J	.030	.020	½	30
WD4S (6 h.p.)	J-7J	.030	.020	¾	30
WD3S (3.2 h.p.)	J-8J	.025	.020	¾	30
WF4 (6 h.p.)	J-8J	.025	.020	¾	30
WF7 (10 h.p.)	J-8J	.025	.020	¾	30
WG4 (6 h.p.)	J-8J	.025	.020	¾	30
WG7 (10 h.p.)	J-8J	.025	.020	¾	30
WH7 (10 h.p.)	J-8J	.025	.020	¾	30
WG7A (10 h.p.)	J-8J	.025	.020	¾	30

Discont'd Plug Type	Replaced Plug Type
0-COM	W10
C0	W14
E0-COM	EW90
1	W14
C1	W18
1-COM	W14
ORD-1	XMJ14
QN1	N1
TAC-1	REL88B
2	W18
2-COM	W18
2-COM-L	W18
AG2	CH2
J2	J57R
J2J	UJ2J
L2G	L55G
N2	N2C
N2G	N2C
ORD-2	XMJ17
ON2	ON2C
ON2G	ON2C
RN2	RN2C
RN2G	RN2C
TAC-2	RML12
3	W16Y
3-COM	W18
AG3	CH3
BL3	V4C
L3G	L77JC
N3	N3C
N3G	N3C
ON3	ON3C
QN3	ON3C
RN3	RN3C
RN3G	RN3C
XN3	RN3C
4	W16Y
4-COM	D6
AG4	CH4
BL4	V4C
C4	W16Y
C4X	W16Y
J4	J4C
J4J	J4C
J4JM	J4C
L4G	L77JC
L4J	L82C
N4	N4C
N4G	N4C
RJ4	J4C
RJ4J	J4C
RL4J	RL82C
RN4	RN4C
RN4G	RN4C
TAC-4	XML12
UCJ4G	CJ4
UJ4J	UJ81C
UL4J	UL81C
X4-COM	D6
XJ4J	J4C
XN4	RN4C
Y4	UY6
Y4A	UY6
5	3X
5-COM	D9
5M	D9J
5MJ	D9J
AG5	CH3
BL5	V4C
C5	W14
E5-COM	ED9
J5	J8C
J5-COM	RJ81B
J5J	J6C
L5	L82C
L5J	L82C
N5	N5C
N5M	N5C
N5G	N5C
RN5	RN5C
X5-COM	RD9
XE5-COM	ED9
XEJ5	RJ8C
XJ5	RJ8C
XN5	RN5C
Y5	UY6
6	W18
6-COM	D14
6-COM-D	D14
6-COM-62	D14
6M	K15J
6MJ	K15J
A6	A6YC
A6Y	A6YC
AG6	CH6
BN6Y	S6YC
DJ6	DJ6J
E6-COM	XED14
EJ6	XEJ6
EJ6J	XEJ6
J6	J6C
J6JM	J6C
JT6	CJ6
KCJ6	CJ6
L6G	L82C
N6	N5C
N6Y	N6YC
N6YCX	N6YC
N6GY	N6YC
P6	P7
R6	A6YC
R6G	A6YC
RA6	RA6YC
RA6Y	RA6YC
RBN6Y	RS6YC
RCJ6	CJ6
RD6	D6
RN6	RN5C
RN6GY	RN6YC
RN6Y	RN6YC
UJ6	J6C
UJ6M	J6C
X6-COM	RD14
XD6	D6
XE6-COM	XED14
XEJ6J	XEJ6
XJ6	RJ6C
XJ6J	RJ6C
XN6	RN5C
Y6	UY6
XY6	UY6
7	D16
7-COM	D16
BL7Y	V9YC
BN7Y	S7YC
C7	D16
E7	XED16
F7Y	F7YC
J7	J8C
J7J	J8C
J7JM	J8C
L7	L82C
L7J	L82C
N7GY	N7YC
N7Y	N7YC
P7Y	P8Y
QL7J	RL82C
QL7J5	RL82C
R7B	D6
RBL7Y	RV9YC
RBN7Y	RS7YC
RJ7	RJ8C
RL7J	RL82C
RN7GY	RN7YC
RN7Y	RN7YC
UCJ7G	CJ8
UJ7G	UJ11G
RP7	P7
UK7	K7
XE7	XED16
XEJ7	XEJ8
XEL7A	REL88B
XJ7	RJ8C
XL7	RL82C
Z7G	Z8
8	D16
8-COM	D16
8-COM-C	D23
8-COM-D	D23
8-COM-K	D15Y
8-SPEC	D16
A8	A8YC
A8Y	A8YC
BL8	RV8C
D8	K97F
DJ8	DJ8J
DL8	K98F
DL8C	K98F
E8-COM	XED16
ED8	K97F
EDL8	K98F
EH8	XEH8
EJ8	XEJ8
EJ8J	XEJ8
H8JM	H8J
J8	J8C
J8J	J8C
J8JM	J8C
JT8	CJ8
K8G	K8
L8	L90
L88	L90
N88	N8
NA8	N5C
N8Y	N9YC
P8G	P7
R8	RA8YC
RA8	RA8YC
RA8Y	RA8YC
RBL8	RV8C
RBL8-6	RV8C6
RJ8	RJ8C
RJ8J	RJ8C
TJ8J	CJ8
UCJ8	CJ8
UJ8	J8C
X8-COM	RD16
XE8-COM	XED16
XEH8J	XEH8
XEJ8J	XEJ8
XH8	RH8
XH8J	RH8
XJ8	RJ8C
XJ8J	RJ8C
XN8	RN8
XN88	RN8
XNA8	RN5C
Y8	UY6
Z8	RZB
9	D21
9-COM	D23
AG9	CH9
BN9Y	S9YC
D9JM	D9J
E9	XEH8
EK9	ED9
F9Y	F9YC
H9	H8
H9-COM	H8
H9J	H8J
J9-LONG	H10
J9	J6C
J9J	J6C
J9Y	J12YC
K9	K8
L9G	L82C
L9J	L90C
N9Y	N9YC
O8L9Y	RV9YC
RBL9Y	RV9YC
RBN9Y	RS9YC
RF9Y	RF9YC
RF9Y5	RF9YC
RN9GY	RN9YC
RN9Y	RN9YC
UF9Y	F9YC
UN9Y	N9YC
XD9	RD9
XE9	XED16
XED9-COM	XED16
XEH9	XEH8
XEK9	ED9
XH9	RH8
XJ9Y	RJ12YC
XN9Y	RN9YC
10	D16
10-COM	D23
10-COM-64	D23
A10	A8YC
C10S	XEJ6
C10S	XEJ6
D10	D9
EC10	EW90
EH10	XEH8
F10	F10C
H10JM	H10J
HT10J	CJ8
J10	J62R
J10-COM	J6C
J10-COM-J	J6C
J10Y	J12YC
L10	L90C
L10S	L82C
N10PY	N11YC
N10Y	N11YC
N10Y4	N11YC4
NA10	N3C
P10	P8Y
R10	A8YC
RF10	RF10C
RJ10Y	RJ12YC
RN10GY	RN11YC
RN10Y	RN11YC
RN10Y4	RN11YC4
XEF10	EF10
XEH10	XEH8
XF10	RF10C
XH10	RH10
XH10J	RH10
XL10S	RL82C
XN10Y	RN11YC
Z10	Z9Y
Z10G	Z9Y
11	W10
BL11Y	V12YC
CJ11	CJ8
EH11	XEH8
EJ11	XEJ12
F11Y	F11YC
H11	H10
H11J	H10
J11JM	J11J
J11Y	J12YC
K11	UK10
L11S	L82C
N11Y	N11YC
OJ11Y	RJ12YC
ON11Y	RN11YC
RBL11Y	RV12YC
RBL11Y6	RV12YC6
RF11Y	RF11YC
RJ11Y	RJ12YC
RN11Y	RN11YC
UF11Y	F11YC
UJ11P	UJ11G
XEH11	XEH8
XEJ11	XEJ12
XF11Y	RF11YC
XH11	RH10
XJ11	RJ11
XJ11Y	RJ12YC
12	D16
12-6	D16
BN12Y	RS12YC
EJ12	XEJ12
H12J	H12
J12	UJ12
J12JM	J12J
J12Y	J12YC
L12Y	L87YC
N12Y	N12YC
NA12	N57R
ON12Y	RN12YC
P12Y	P10Y
RBL12	RV12C
RBL12-6	RV12C6
RBN12Y	RS12YC
RF12	RF10C
RF12-5	RF10C
RJ12Y	RJ12YC
RJ12Y6	RJ12YC6
RL12Y	RL87YC
RN12GY	RN12YC
RN12Y	RN12YC
RZN12Y	RS12YC
RZN12Y5	RS12YC6
UJ12Y	J12YC
UL12Y	L87YC
UN12Y	N12YC
XH12	RH10
XJ12	RJ12
XJ12J	RJ12
XJ12Y	RJ12YC
XL12Y	RL87YC
XN12Y	RN12YC
13	D16
A13	30
J13	30
J13-0	30
J13Y	J12YC
N13L	RN13LYC
N13Y	N12YC
OJ13Y	RJ12YC
RBL13Y	RV12YC
RBL13Y6	RV12YC6
RBN13Y	RS12YC
RJ13Y	RJ12YC
UBL13Y	V12YC
XJ13Y	RJ12YC
14	D16
A14	30
A14-0	30
C14	30
D14M	W10
EC14	EW90
EF14	EF10
EJ14	XEJ12
F14Y	RF14YC
HO14S	REB37E
J14	UJ12
J14C1	J99
J14-64CL	J99
J14J	CJ14
J14Y	J14YC
L14	L90C
MJ14	XMJ14
NA14	N54R
N14Y	RN14YC
RBL14Y	RS14YC
RBN14Y4	RS14YC
RF14Y	RF14YC
RF14Y4	RF14YC
RJ14Y	RJ14YC
RN14Y	RN14YC
RN14Y6	RN12YC6
UEJ14	XEJ12
UF14Y	RF14YC
XD14	RD14
XEJ14	XEJ12
XH14Y	H14Y
XJ14Y	RJ14YC
XN14Y	RN14YC
15	D16
15A	D16
15-SPEC	D16
A15	25
C15	D21
J15	K15J
L15Y	L95Y
RBL15Y	RV15YC
RBL15Y4	RV15YC4
RBL15Y6	RV15YC8
RBL15Y8	RV15YC8
UD15Y	D15Y
UL15Y	L95Y
XEC15	XED16
C16C	W16Y
D16M	D16
ED16	XED16
H16	D6
H16A	D6
N16Y	N16YC
RN16Y	N16YC
UED16	XED16
UK16V	K7
XD16	RD16
XD16J	RD16J
XN16Y	RN16YC
H17	D9
H17A	D9
RBL17Y	RV17YC
RBL17Y6	RV17YC6
UDJ17V	CJ4
UJ17V	UJ2J
UL17V	UL81C
18	K15J
J18Y	J18YC
N18	N16YC
RJ18Y	RJ18YC
RJ18Y6	RJ18YC6
RJ18Y8	RJ18YC8
XJ18Y	RJ18YC
XEN18	XEN14
XH18Y	RH18Y
J19V	UJ2J
L19V	L20V
UL19V	UL81C
XMJ19	XMJ20
20	W20
RJ20Y	RJ18YC
XJ20Y	RJ18YC
21	W10
XED21	XED16
22	W20
F22	F11YC
J23	25
A24	25
G24	34
A25	25
A26	D16
C26	M41E
C27	M41E
AG28	CH28
29	30
31	25
AG32	CH32
A34	32
35-COM	W18
36	C97B
C36	B86N
AG39	CH39
40	K96F

Index

A

accessories, 63–67
Acco outboards, 170
Admiral outboards, 72
Aeromarine. *See* Kiekhaefer Aeromarine Motors
Aero Marine outboards, 170–71
Aerothrust outboards, 72–73
Ailsa-Craig outboards, 202
Air-Boy outboards, 73, 243
Airdrive outboards, 73
Airex outboards, 114
Aldens outboards, 73, 181
Allen, Clarence, 74–75, 183
Allen Portable Electric Propeller, 157
All Sport outboards, 171
AMC Saber, 73
American Engine Co., 74
American Marc, Inc., 74
American Motor Co., 3–4
America's Best outboards, 171
Amphion outboards, 74–75
Anderson Engine Co., 75
Antique Outboard Motor Club (AOMC), 62, 68–70
antique outboards
    accessories, 63–67
    determining value, 57–61
    finding, 52–57
    obtaining parts, 61–62
    price guide, 233–45
    rarity guide, 245–59
Anzani outboards. *See* British Anzani outboards
Apache outboards, 88, 171. *See also* Clinton outboards
Apex outboards. *See* Coventry Apex outboards
Aquabug outboards, 171–72
Aqua-Jet Miner outboards, 152
Aquajet outboards (U.K.), 202
Aqua-Jet outboards (U.S.), 76
Aqua Scooter outboards, 172
Aqua-Sport Outboard Attachment, 151

Aqua-Vic outboards, 190
Armsco outboards, 172
Arrow Motor and Machine Co., 8, 76
Arrow outboards, 76–77
Ascoy outboards, 190
Ashbrook electric outboards, 158
Aspin outboards, 202
Atco Boatimpeller, 77
Atco outboards (U.K.), 202–4
Atco outboards (U.S.), 77
Atlas Royal outboards, 138
Australian outboards, 190–201

B

Bail-A-Matic water pumps, 142
Bantam (U.K.). *See* J.S.L. outboards
Bantam Products Co., 77
Bantam electric outboards, 158
Barracuda Outboard Co., 77–78
Barthel, Oliver, 6, 7
Basil Engineering outboards, 204, 221
Bearcat outboards, 101. *See also* Fageol outboards
Beaver outboards, 78, 172
Bendix outboards, 78–79
    Eclipse starters, 145
    electric, 158
    price guide, 235
    rarity rating, 245–46
Bermuda outboards, 204
Berning outboards, 204–5
Blakely outboards, 79
Blaxland outboards, 191
Blue Jet outboards, 79
Bourke-Cycle outboards, 79
BRD. *See* Bermuda outboards
Briggs, Stephen, 14, 31
Briggs and Stratton Corp., 14–16, 134, 172
Britannia outboards, 199, 205–7
Brit Engineering outboards, 207